The Collected Works of

Langston Hughes

Volume 6

Gospel Plays, Operas, and
Later Dramatic Works

Projected Volumes in the Collected Works

The Poems: 1921–1940

The Poems: 1941–1950

The Poems: 1951–1967

The Novels: *Not without Laughter*
   and *Tambourines to Glory*

The Plays to 1942: *Mulatto* to *The Sun Do Move*

Gospel Plays, Operas, and Later Dramatic Works

The Early Simple Stories

The Later Simple Stories

Essays on Art, Race, Politics, and World Affairs

Fight for Freedom and Other Writings on Civil Rights

Works for Children and Young Adults: Poetry,
   Fiction, and Other Writing

Works for Children and Young Adults: Biographies

Autobiography: *The Big Sea*

Autobiography: *I Wonder As I Wander*

The Short Stories

The Translations: Federico García Lorca,
   Nicolás Guillén, and Jacques Roumain

An Annotated Bibliography of the
   Works of Langston Hughes

Publication of

The Collected Works of Langston Hughes

has been generously assisted by

Landon and Sarah Rowland

and

Morton and Estelle Sosland

The Collected Works of

Langston Hughes

Volume 6

Gospel Plays, Operas, and
Later Dramatic Works

Edited with an Introduction
by Leslie Catherine Sanders

University of Missouri Press
Columbia and London

Copyright © 2004 by Ramona Bass and Arnold Rampersad,
Administrators of the Estate of Langston Hughes
Introduction copyright © 2004 by Leslie Catherine Sanders
Chronology copyright © 2001 by Arnold Rampersad
University of Missouri Press, Columbia, Missouri 65201
Printed and bound in the United States of America
All rights reserved
5 4 3 2 1   08 07 06 05 04

Library of Congress Cataloging-in-Publication Data

Hughes, Langston, 1902–1967
  [Works. 2001]
  The collected works of Langston Hughes / edited with an introduction
    by Leslie Catherine Sanders
    p.   cm.
  Includes bibliographical references and indexes.
  ISBN 0-8262-1477-0 (v. 6 : alk. paper)
    1. African Americans—Literary collections. I. Sanders, Leslie Catherine. II. Title.
PS3515 .U274 2001
818/.5209—dc21   00066601

⊗™This paper meets the requirements of the
American National Standard for Permanence of Paper
for Printed Library Materials, Z39.48, 1984.

Designer: Kristie Lee
Typesetter: Bookcomp, Inc.
Printer and binder: Thomson-Shore, Inc.
Typefaces: Galliard, Optima

Contents

Acknowledgments

This project was begun in collaboration with the late George Houston Bass. I hope he would be pleased by the results. Many people have helped bring this volume to fruition, and I thank them. For typing, checking, and text comparisons, Karen Bernard, Tess Chakkalakal, Susan Goldberg, Chandra Hodgson, Nancy Johnston, Evelyn Marrast, Peggy Pasternak, Peter Sinema, Rebecca Waese, Michael Wiebe, and most especially Christine Kim. For help and editing counsel, Lesley Higgins. For their endless helpfulness and courtesy, the staff at the Beinecke Library with whom I have worked over the years, especially Steve Jones and Timothy Young and, most recently, June Hadassah Bik. For help contacting estates, Darryl Taylor, and with permissions, the Kurt Weill Foundation. For her careful editing and cheerful patience, Jane Lago of University of Missouri Press. Special thanks are due to Elicia Clements for her meticulous research and her advice on issues related to Hughes's work in music, to James Dapogny for the text of *De Organizer* as performed in 2002, and to David Amram for the text of *Let Us Remember* and his recollections of Langston Hughes. Thanks are also due to Yale University, Beinecke Library, for a Visiting Fellowship and to the Social Science and Humanities Research Council of Canada for a major grant in support of this project.

The University of Missouri Press recognizes that the *Collected Works* would not have been possible without the support and assistance of Patricia Powell, Chris Byrne, Wendy Schmalz, Laura Bucko, and Phyllis Westberg of Harold Ober Associates, representing the estate of Langston Hughes, and of Arnold Rampersad and Ramona Bass, co-executors of the estate of Langston Hughes.

For permissions to reprint specific works, see 689.

Chronology
By Arnold Rampersad

1902 James Langston Hughes is born February 1 in Joplin, Missouri, to James Nathaniel Hughes, a stenographer for a mining company, and Carrie Mercer Langston Hughes, a former government clerk.

1903 After his father immigrates to Mexico, Langston's mother takes him to Lawrence, Kansas, the home of Mary Langston, her twice-widowed mother. Mary Langston's first husband, Lewis Sheridan Leary, died fighting alongside John Brown at Harpers Ferry. Her second, Hughes's grandfather, was Charles Langston, a former abolitionist, Republican politician, and businessman.

1907 After a failed attempt at a reconciliation in Mexico, Langston and his mother return to Lawrence.

1909 Langston starts school in Topeka, Kansas, where he lives for a while with his mother before returning to his grandmother's home in Lawrence.

1915 Following Mary Langston's death, Hughes leaves Lawrence for Lincoln, Illinois, where his mother lives with her second husband, Homer Clark, and Homer Clark's young son by another union, Gwyn "Kit" Clark.

1916 Langston, elected class poet, graduates from the eighth grade. Moves to Cleveland, Ohio, and starts at Central High School there.

1918 Publishes early poems and short stories in his school's monthly magazine.

1919 Spends the summer in Toluca, Mexico, with his father.

1920 Graduates from Central High as class poet and editor of the school annual. Returns to Mexico to live with his father.

1921 In June, Hughes publishes "The Negro Speaks of Rivers" in *Crisis* magazine. In September, sponsored by his father, he enrolls at Columbia University in New York. Meets W. E. B. Du Bois, Jessie Fauset, and Countee Cullen.

1922 Unhappy at Columbia, Hughes withdraws from school and breaks with his father.

1923 Sailing in June to western Africa on the crew of a freighter, he visits Senegal, the Gold Coast, Nigeria, the Congo, and other countries.

1924 Spends several months in Paris working in the kitchen of a nightclub.

1925 Lives in Washington for a year with his mother. His poem "The Weary Blues" wins first prize in a contest sponsored by *Opportunity* magazine, which leads to a book contract with Knopf through Carl Van Vechten. Becomes friends with several other young artists of the Harlem Renaissance, including Zora Neale Hurston, Wallace Thurman, and Arna Bontemps.

1926 In January his first book, *The Weary Blues,* appears. He enrolls at historically black Lincoln University, Pennsylvania. In June, the *Nation* weekly magazine publishes his landmark essay "The Negro Artist and the Racial Mountain."

1927 Knopf publishes his second book of verse, *Fine Clothes to the Jew,* which is condemned in the black press. Hughes meets his powerful patron Mrs. Charlotte Osgood Mason. Travels in the South with Hurston, who is also taken up by Mrs. Mason.

1929 Hughes graduates from Lincoln University.

1930 Publishes his first novel, *Not without Laughter* (Knopf). Visits Cuba and meets fellow poet Nicolás Guillén. Hughes is dismissed by Mrs. Mason in a painful break made worse by false charges of dishonesty leveled by Hurston over their play *Mule Bone.*

1931 Demoralized, he travels to Haiti. Publishes work in the communist magazine *New Masses.* Supported by the Rosenwald Foundation, he tours the South taking his poetry to the people. In Alabama, he visits some of the Scottsboro Boys in prison. His brief collection of poems *Dear Lovely Death* is privately printed in Amenia, New York. Hughes and the illustrator Prentiss Taylor publish a verse pamphlet, *The Negro Mother.*

1932 With Taylor, he publishes *Scottsboro Limited,* a short play and four poems. From Knopf comes *The Dream Keeper,* a book of previously published poems selected for young people. Later, Macmillan brings out *Popo and Fifina,* a children's story about Haiti written with Arna Bontemps, his closest friend. In June, Hughes sails to Russia in a band of twenty-two young African

Americans to make a film about race relations in the United States. After the project collapses, he lives for a year in the Soviet Union. Publishes his most radical verse, including "Good Morning Revolution" and "Goodbye Christ."

1933 Returns home at midyear via China and Japan. Supported by a patron, Noël Sullivan of San Francisco, Hughes spends a year in Carmel writing short stories.

1934 Knopf publishes his first short story collection, *The Ways of White Folks*. After labor unrest in California threatens his safety, he leaves for Mexico following news of his father's death.

1935 Spends several months in Mexico, mainly translating short stories by local leftist writers. Lives for some time with the photographer Henri Cartier-Bresson. Returning almost destitute to the United States, he joins his mother in Oberlin, Ohio. Visits New York for the Broadway production of his play *Mulatto* and clashes with its producer over changes in the script. Unhappy, he writes the poem "Let America Be America Again."

1936 Wins a Guggenheim Foundation fellowship for work on a novel but soon turns mainly to writing plays in association with the Karamu Theater in Cleveland. Karamu stages his farce *Little Ham* and his historical drama about Haiti, *Troubled Island*.

1937 Karamu stages *Joy to My Soul*, another comedy. In July, he visits Paris for the League of American Writers. He then travels to Spain, where he spends the rest of the year reporting on the civil war for the *Baltimore Afro-American*.

1938 In New York, Hughes founds the radical Harlem Suitcase Theater, which stages his agitprop play *Don't You Want to Be Free?* The leftist International Workers Order publishes *A New Song*, a pamphlet of radical verse. Karamu stages his play *Front Porch*. His mother dies.

1939 In Hollywood he writes the script for the movie *Way Down South*, which is criticized for stereotyping black life. Hughes goes for an extended stay in Carmel, California, again as the guest of Noël Sullivan.

1940 His autobiography *The Big Sea* appears (Knopf). He is picketed by a religious group for his poem "Goodbye Christ," which he publicly renounces.

1941 With a Rosenwald Fund fellowship for playwriting, he leaves California for Chicago, where he founds the Skyloft Players. Moves on to New York in December.

1942   Knopf publishes his book of verse *Shakespeare in Harlem*. The Skyloft Players stage his play *The Sun Do Move*. In the summer he resides at the Yaddo writers' and artists' colony, New York. Hughes also works as a writer in support of the war effort. In November he starts "Here to Yonder," a weekly column in the Chicago *Defender* newspaper.

1943   "Here to Yonder" introduces Jesse B. Semple, or Simple, a comic Harlem character who quickly becomes its most popular feature. Hughes publishes *Jim Crow's Last Stand* (Negro Publication Society of America), a pamphlet of verse about the struggle for civil rights.

1944   Comes under surveillance by the FBI because of his former radicalism.

1945   With Mercer Cook, translates and later publishes *Masters of the Dew* (Reynal and Hitchcock), a novel by Jacques Roumain of Haiti.

1947   His work as librettist with Kurt Weill and Elmer Rice on the Broadway musical play *Street Scene* brings Hughes a financial windfall. He vacations in Jamaica. Knopf publishes *Fields of Wonder*, his only book composed mainly of lyric poems on nonracial topics.

1948   Hughes is denounced (erroneously) as a communist in the U.S. Senate. He buys a townhouse in Harlem and moves in with his longtime friends Toy and Emerson Harper.

1949   Doubleday publishes *Poetry of the Negro, 1746–1949*, an anthology edited with Arna Bontemps. Also published are *One-Way Ticket* (Knopf), a book of poems, and *Cuba Libre: Poems of Nicolás Guillén* (Anderson and Ritchie), translated by Hughes and Ben Frederic Carruthers. Hughes teaches for three months at the University of Chicago Lab School for children. His opera about Haiti with William Grant Still, *Troubled Island*, is presented in New York.

1950   Another opera, *The Barrier*, with music by Jan Meyerowitz, is hailed in New York but later fails on Broadway. Simon and Schuster publishes *Simple Speaks His Mind*, the first of five books based on his newspaper columns.

1951   Hughes's book of poems about life in Harlem, *Montage of a Dream Deferred*, appears (Henry Holt).

1952   His second collection of short stories, *Laughing to Keep from Crying*, is published by Henry Holt. In its "First Book" series for children, Franklin Watts publishes Hughes's *The First Book of Negroes.*

1953 In March, forced to testify before Senator Joseph McCarthy's subcommittee on subversive activities, Hughes is exonerated after repudiating his past radicalism. *Simple Takes a Wife* appears.

1954 Mainly for young readers, he publishes *Famous American Negroes* (Dodd, Mead) and *The First Book of Rhythms.*

1955 Publishes *The First Book of Jazz* and finishes *Famous Negro Music Makers* (Dodd, Mead). In November, Simon and Schuster publishes *The Sweet Flypaper of Life,* a narrative of Harlem with photographs by Roy DeCarava.

1956 Hughes's second volume of autobiography, *I Wonder As I Wander* (Rinehart), appears, as well as *A Pictorial History of the Negro* (Crown), coedited with Milton Meltzer, and *The First Book of the West Indies.*

1957 *Esther,* an opera with composer Jan Meyerowitz, has its premiere in Illinois. Rinehart publishes *Simple Stakes a Claim* as a novel. Hughes's musical play *Simply Heavenly,* based on his Simple character, runs for several weeks off and then on Broadway. Hughes translates and publishes *Selected Poems of Gabriela Mistral* (Indiana University Press).

1958 *The Langston Hughes Reader* (George Braziller) appears, as well as *The Book of Negro Folklore* (Dodd, Mead), coedited with Arna Bontemps, and another juvenile, *Famous Negro Heroes of America* (Dodd, Mead). John Day publishes a short novel, *Tambourines to Glory,* based on a Hughes gospel musical play.

1959 Hughes's *Selected Poems* published (Knopf).

1960 *The First Book of Africa* appears, along with *An African Treasury: Articles, Essays, Stories, Poems by Black Africans,* edited by Hughes (Crown).

1961 Inducted into the National Institute of Arts and Letters. Knopf publishes his book-length poem *Ask Your Mama: 12 Moods for Jazz. The Best of Simple,* drawn from the columns, appears (Hill and Wang). Hughes writes his gospel musical plays *Black Nativity* and *The Prodigal Son.* He visits Africa again.

1962 Begins a weekly column for the *New York Post.* Attends a writers' conference in Uganda. Publishes *Fight for Freedom: The Story of the NAACP,* commissioned by the organization.

1963 His third collection of short stories, *Something in Common,* appears from Hill and Wang. Indiana University Press publishes

Five Plays by Langston Hughes, edited by Webster Smalley, as well as Hughes's anthology *Poems from Black Africa, Ethiopia, and Other Countries.*

1964 His musical play *Jericho–Jim Crow,* a tribute to the civil rights movement, is staged in Greenwich Village. Indiana University Press brings out his anthology *New Negro Poets: U.S.A.,* with a foreword by Gwendolyn Brooks.

1965 With novelists Paule Marshall and William Melvin Kelley, Hughes visits Europe for the U.S. State Department. His gospel play *The Prodigal Son* and his cantata with music by David Amram, *Let Us Remember,* are staged.

1966 After twenty-three years, Hughes ends his depiction of Simple in his Chicago *Defender* column. Publishes *The Book of Negro Humor* (Dodd, Mead). In a visit sponsored by the U.S. government, he is honored in Dakar, Senegal, at the First World Festival of Negro Arts.

1967 His *The Best Short Stories by Negro Writers: An Anthology from 1899 to the Present* (Little, Brown) includes the first published story by Alice Walker. On May 22, Hughes dies at New York Polyclinic Hospital in Manhattan from complications following prostate surgery. Later that year, two books appear: *The Panther and the Lash: Poems of Our Times* (Knopf) and, with Milton Meltzer, *Black Magic: A Pictorial History of the Negro in American Entertainment* (Prentice Hall).

The Collected Works of

Langston Hughes

Volume 6

Gospel Plays, Operas, and
Later Dramatic Works

Introduction

Langston Hughes's lifelong engagement in theater and other perfor-mance arts is the least known aspect of his rich and complex contribution to African American expressive culture. Yet, as this volume and the pre-vious, *The Plays to 1942: "Mulatto" to "The Sun Do Move,"* reveal, all the performing arts, and theater in particular, engaged his interest and imag-ination. His love of theater, fostered by his mother, began in childhood; one of his earliest publications was a play for children, *The Gold Piece,* and when he finally arrived in New York in 1921 to attend Columbia University, it was the gallery seats for the wildly popular black Broadway musical *Shuffle Along* rather than the classroom that claimed him.

Hughes's contribution to African American theater is foundational. In addition to his plays, his forays into a variety of other performance genres—opera and musicals, gospel and other religious lyrics, blues and popular songs, radio plays and ballet choreography—all bespeak his de-termination to inject an African American presence into a range of cul-tural forms. As well, by the 1940s, Hughes was the best known of African American poets, and his colloquial and honed eloquence attracted the interest of a variety of composers—classical, jazz, and popular—eager to create musical settings for his poems or to invite his collaboration. In addition to Hughes's five completed operas and several cantatas, there are hundreds of musical settings of his poems as well as several hundred of his own lyrics, some written for musicals and others composed singly.

Two Broadway productions frame Hughes's theatrical career. His first full-length dramatic work, *Mulatto,* premiered on Broadway in 1935, albeit with alterations not entirely of his choosing, ran for more than a year, and then toured for two seasons. His last full-length production, *Tambourines to Glory* (1963), also made it to Broadway, although for a short run. In the main, however, Hughes's more than thirty plays provided to community theaters and collegiate, church, and amateur groups aimed at instructing, delighting, and giving voice to his chosen audience, the "low-down" folks, as he called them in his 1925 manifesto "The Negro Artist and the Racial Mountain."

Yet Hughes had mainstream theater and white audiences in mind as well. For example, *Mulatto,* written in 1930, sought to revise serious and

I

sympathetic stage portrayals of African Americans by such white writers as Paul Green, Marc Connelly, and Eugene O'Neill. Not only *Mulatto*'s characters but also its plot boldly challenged their representations of the place of African Americans within the nation, especially through the hero's insistence on the legitimacy of his filial claims. Hughes's comedies of the 1930s eschewed all traces of minstrelsy and vaudeville, which inflected, however faintly, even the period's stage comedy by African Americans, as well as the skits that formed part of theatrical and club revues. Hughes's history plays provided uncompromising portraits of African American anguish and aspiration.

For Hughes, the 1930s were an intensely productive time in theater, in part because he had encouraging and readily accessible venues for his work. In Cleveland, Karamu House's Gilpin Players premiered three Hughes comedies, *Little Ham, When the Jack Hollers* (written with Arna Bontemps), and *Joy to My Soul,* and performed three dramas, *Troubled Island, Mulatto* (using Hughes's original text), and *Front Porch,* the latter also a premier. They also revived both *Little Ham* and *Joy to My Soul.* Beginning in 1938, Hughes started three theaters of his own, the Harlem Suitcase Theatre in New York, the Skyloft Players in Chicago, and the New Negro Theatre in Los Angeles. For the Skyloft Players, he completed *The Sun Do Move;* in New York and Los Angeles, his *Don't You Want to Be Free?* and satirical skits, written for the Harlem Suitcase Theatre, provided the theatrical fare. During this decade as well, he wrote, with Ella Winter, the full-length play *Harvest* (never performed) and, alone, the agit-prop piece *Scottsboro, Limited,* as well as several one-act plays, including his tragicomedy *Soul Gone Home.*

Hughes's work from this first decade of writing for the stage is, for the most part, formally conventional, although it is always radical in its representation of African American life and outlook. His comedies replace stereotype with black humor and black laughter. His dramas insist on the complexity of black life and history and depict racism as a form of human behavior for which people must be held accountable rather than as a context or inevitable condition of black existence. His formal conventionality is crucial to the project of change, of course: depicting black characters and concerns from a black perspective, using the very forms in which they had been so distorted, challenges those offensive representations and provides dramatic alternatives.

Hughes also experimented. His 1933 travels in the USSR, documented in his second autobiography, *I Wonder As I Wander,* introduced him to what he called "interesting ways of staging plays" and other new theatrical possibilities that influenced his later dramatic work in many ways. He himself credits his experience in the USSR with introducing him to a theatrical form that he first employed in *Don't You Want to Be Free?* (1938) and that would characterize many of his later plays. Episodic in structure, *Don't You Want to Be Free?* depicts what Hughes called the "emotional history" of African Americans. Each scene uses his own poetry, as well as blues and spirituals, to dramatize a particular, emblematic instance of black suffering and struggle, yet the rhythm of the play moves insistently toward self-assertion and the battle for rights. Characters are social types rather than individuals (for example, Boy, Girl, Young Man, Old Woman); not only do characters address the audience, but the distinction between actors and audience becomes blurred; finally, one of the play's overt purposes is to provide social commentary and to produce social change.[1]

As the plays in this volume reveal, Hughes returned to the form repeatedly. Important, although not published here, are several revisions of *Don't You Want to Be Free?* written between 1938 and the final "Centennial" version of 1963. In each version, the final parts of the play are altered to provide commentary and discussion of immediate issues in the struggle for freedom. For example, the 1944 version addresses the discrimination against Negro workers in defense plants, arguing that combating racism at home is critical to the war effort. In 1952, there is an argument against equating the fight for black freedom with communism; the Centennial version invokes the Freedom Rides and other fronts of the civil rights struggle. These revisions were needed because, as Hughes boasted to his friends Rowena and Russell Jelliffe in 1952, *Don't You Want to Be Free* "was the most performed play of our time," a favorite especially of theaters in the historically black colleges.[2]

Although Russian theater certainly influenced Hughes's vision of theatrical possibility, the form he used in *Don't You Want to Be Free?* resonates in other ways that more fully account for the play's popularity and

---

1. These are all characteristic of various dramatic practices that Hughes encountered both in the USSR and in radical theater in New York. See Leslie Sanders, " 'Interesting Ways of Staging Plays': Hughes and Russian Theatre," *Langston Hughes Review* 15.1 (spring 1997): 4–12; *The Collected Works of Langston Hughes, Volume 14, I Wonder As I Wander,* ed. Joseph McLaren (Columbia: University of Missouri Press, 2003), 208.

2. Langston Hughes to Rowena and Russell Jelliffe, January 12, 1952, Langston Hughes Papers, James Weldon Johnson Collection, Yale Collection of American Literature, Beinecke Rare Books and Manuscripts Library. Hereafter referred to as LHP.

the form's usefulness in Hughes's later endeavors. *Don't You Want to be Free?* shares characteristics with the pageant, an enduring American and African American folk form and a staple of community, school, and civic functions. Pageants typically illustrate and celebrate a historical narrative. Their purpose is both educational and inspirational; their meaning, the creation and affirmation of community. In the African American context, perhaps the most famous and celebrated venture into pageantry is W. E. B. Du Bois's three-hour extravaganza, *The Star of Ethiopia,* staged in 1913, 1915, and 1925; the largest of these productions had twelve hundred participants and an audience of six thousand. The pageant form, "too pictorial to be a parade, but not dramatic enough to be a play," in more modest dimensions and intimate settings, did incorporate speeches and dramatic scenes.[3] Du Bois saw pageantry as a way of teaching African American history to blacks and whites alike, and other African American dramatists provided pageant scripts for community and collegiate use.[4]

In addition to the styles of radical theater and the familiarity of secular pageantry, forms of the religious pageant, long a staple of black churches, also resonate in *Don't You Want to Be Free?* and were relied on by Hughes in a variety of later theatrical projects. In the oldest religious pageants, according to William H. Wiggins Jr., spirituals provided the plots and action. The first such pageant to move from church to professional stage, *Heaven Bound,* was performed in Atlanta in 1931 and repeated by the Federal Theatre there in 1937 and 1938. Later, in his *From Auction Block to Glory* (1942), William Brewster combined historical and religious pageant traditions and was the first to compose gospel music specifically for the production rather than to rely on traditional material.[5]

Hughes's most important dramatic works during this second phase of his involvement with the stage are, of course, the gospel plays, which he began writing in the 1960s. They include *Jericho–Jim Crow,* his theatrical

3. James V. Hatch and Ted Shine, *Black Theatre U.S.A.: Plays by African Americans: The Early Period: 1847–1938* (New York: Free Press, 1996), 86. For example, those Willis Richardson published in his 1930 anthology *Plays and Pageants of Negro Life* intended for use by schools, clubs, and other organizations, emphasize speech over spectacle.

4. David Levering Lewis, *W. E. B. Du Bois: Biography of a Race, 1868–1919* (New York: Henry Holt and Co., 1993), 459.

5. William H. Wiggins Jr., "William Herbert Brewster: Pioneer of the Sacred Pageant," in *We'll Understand It Better By and By: Pioneering African American Gospel Composers,* ed. Bernice Johnson Reagon (Washington, D.C.: Smithsonian Institution Press, 1992), 246–47.

contribution to the civil rights struggle, in the style of *Don't You Want to Be Free?* but animated by gospel music, and that staple of Christmas celebrations in countless African American churches, *Black Nativity*. There is no evidence that Hughes knew, or was influenced by, Brewster's work. An ability to meld folk and modern art forms characterized Hughes's genius in many genres; as theater congenial to Broadway audiences as well as to the smallest of church congregations, his gospel plays perfectly exemplify this gift.

Despite his avowal to his dear friend Arna Bontemps in 1941 that he had "retired from the show business" and would "devote the rest of my creative life to words on paper not on the stage," Hughes never kept away.[6] This volume presents Hughes's plays after 1942 as well as other works written for performance, including operas, musicals, radio plays, ballet librettos, and song lyrics. During the 1930s, Hughes began his collaboration with William Grant Still on the opera *Troubled Island* while at the same time writing song lyrics, revue material, and, with Clarence Muse, a stereotype-filled screenplay for the film *Way Down South* (1939), for which he was lambasted (his defense was that it paid many many bills, something his radical plays, no matter how popular, failed to do). With Arna Bontemps and composer Margaret Bonds, he wrote a musical revue, *Tropics after Dark*, for the 1940 American Negro Exposition. Like other writers, particularly those of any prominence, Hughes involved himself in the war effort, decrying racism in the United States, especially segregation in the Armed Forces and the marginalization of African American workers in the defense industries, while at the same time promoting African American support for the war. In this collection, *For This We Fight* (1943); his radio plays *Booker T. Washington in Atlanta* (1940), *Brothers* (1942), *Pvt. Jim Crow* (1943), and *In the Service of My Country* (1944); and several song lyrics represent his wartime writing.

By the end of World War II, Hughes had already become, as he called himself, a "literary sharecropper," constantly seeking projects, or agreeing to those offered him, in a continual struggle to stay ahead of his bills.[7] One of these projects in particular, besides being lucrative, added luster to his reputation in American theater: his lyrics for Kurt Weill's *Street Scene*, book by Elmer Rice (1947). Others, for example his collaboration with the Jewish-refugee composer Jan Meyerowitz,

6. Hughes to Bontemps, February 14, 1941, quoted in Arnold Rampersad, *The Life of Langston Hughes, Volume 2, 1941–1967: I Dream a World* (New York: Oxford University Press, 1988), 11.
7. Hughes to Bontemps, December 27, 1950, LHP.

produced little financial reward or acclaim, despite the frequent good reviews accorded his librettos and lyrics: for the operas *The Barrier* (1950), *Esther* (1956), and *Port Town* (1960) and the cantatas *The Five Foolish Virgins* (1953), *On a Pallet of Straw* (1954), *Godly Is the House of God* (1955), *The Glory around His Head* (1957), and, with David Amram, *Let Us Remember* (1965).

The extent of Hughes's engagement in opera may seem surprising, yet as early as the 1926 he and Zora Neale Hurston planned a Negro opera, hoping to collaborate with the well-known African American composer Clarence Cameron White. As well, Hughes's 1928 preliminary notes for a play on Haiti—which was to become *Emperor of Haiti* and eventually the opera *Troubled Island*—envisioned a "singing play," an idea that languished when White completed *Ouanga,* an opera on the same topic, the life of the Haitian leader Dessalines.[8] Hughes thus welcomed composer William Grant Still's 1935 invitation to collaborate, offering to turn his *Emperor of Haiti* into a libretto. As noted above, more invitations followed: in 1937, he was approached by jazz musician and composer James P. Johnson to collaborate on what became *The Organizer.* In 1946, he was invited by Kurt Weill to write the lyrics for *Street Scene;* the following year Jan Meyerowitz proposed an opera based on *Mulatto,* which became *The Barrier.* Two other Meyerowitz-Hughes operas would follow: *Esther* and *Port Town.*

Hughes and Hurston's, and a decade later Hughes and Still's, envisioning of African American stories as grand opera coincided with modern American opera's search for an indigenous musical idiom and voice. Overviews of American opera frequently cite George Gershwin's *Porgy and Bess* (1935) as the watershed production in this search. In book and music, its indebtedness to African American culture is patent, although only the performers were African American. A year earlier, Virgil Thompson and Gertrude Stein's *Four Saints in Three Acts,* performed with an all-black cast, had captivated New York. This was the first professional theatrical production to employ a black cast in roles written for whites, a decision made by Thompson, who thought they would do a better job with both words and music than would white performers. As they

8. White began work on the opera in the summer of 1928 when he and librettist John Matheus, White's colleague at West Virginia State College, visited Haiti to do research. *Ouanga* was first performed in concert in 1932 under the auspices of the American Opera Company of Chicago. "Clarence Cameron White: 1880–1960" (Biography Resources Center, Gale Group, 2001, http://www.africanpubs.com/Apps/bios/1100WhiteClarence.asp).

had a decade before, when black musicals such as *Shuffle Along* defined Broadway entertainment, African American talent and culture infused this critical moment in American expressive culture. In *Opera in America: A Cultural History,* John Dizikes includes early twentieth-century black musicals, indeed the entire tradition of the American musical, as an important aspect of America's operatic development. According to biographer Scott E. Brown, James P. Johnson saw himself as the black Gershwin, both in his songs and in his serious compositions.[9] Yet major opera houses rarely performed American opera of any kind, and operas by African American composers rarely obtained even concert productions.

Arnold Rampersad is puzzled by Hughes's continued willingness in the 1950s to collaborate on operas with Jan Meyerowitz, given Hughes's apparent lack of interest in the genre, and in art music generally. However, Hughes's earlier work with Still, Johnson, and, indeed, with Meyerowitz on *The Barrier,* might be understood as expressing his understanding, and that of his collaborators, that the tragedy and grandeur of the African American experience might be eloquently expressed through the majestic staging of emotions at which traditional opera is particularly adept. Moreover, as Michael Denning argues in *The Cultural Front,* the political Left, from the 1930s until its postwar repression, sought to unite jazz and opera. For example, John Houseman directed *Four Saints in Three Acts,* Duke Ellington began composing his never-completed opera *Boola,* and later Kurt Weill created *Street Scene.*[10] Neither Still nor Johnson was a part of this political milieu; however, Hughes's connections to it were deep, perhaps the deepest of any of the writers of the Harlem Renaissance.

Nonetheless, by the 1950s Hughes's attention was turning to a different kind of production. In 1943, he had brought into being what would become his most famous character, Jesse B. Semple, not for the stage but for a newspaper column he would write for the *Chicago Defender* for fifteen years and then for the *New York Post* until 1965. The acclaim was almost immediate; Simple rapidly became the talk of black communities. Inevitably, Simple moved to other venues: Hughes revised and

9. Ann Douglas, *Terrible Honesty: Mongrel Manhattan in the 1920s* (New York: Farrar, Strauss and Giroux, 1995), 117; John Dizikes, *Opera in America: A Cultural History* (New Haven: Yale University Press, 1993); Scott E. Brown, *James P. Johnson: A Case of Mistaken Identity* (Metuchen, N.J.: Scarecrow Press and Institute of Jazz Studies, Rutgers University, 1986), 112.

10. Rampersad, *Life,* 2:250; Michael Denning, *The Cultural Front: The Laboring of American Culture in the Twentieth Century* (London and New York: Verso, 1996), 319; Ellington's *Black, Brown, and Beige* was to be a part of his opera.

collected the stories into four books and following the success of his second collection, *Simple Takes a Wife* (1953), composed a play with the same name, which he later turned into the musical *Simply Heavenly* (1957) at the request of the play's sponsor.[11] Although Rampersad speculates that Alice Childress's highly praised *Just a Little Simple* (1950), a staged version of some Simple columns, inspired Hughes to do his own version, his staged Simple lacked the sly and incisive social commentary that endeared the Simple of Hughes's columns and books to his audience. He became the hero of "a Broadway musical," rather than the distinctive voice of the ordinary man of Harlem. *Simply Heavenly* had mixed reviews. The play was enjoyed by white critics but greeted with ambivalence or unease by some black members of his audience.

Staging Simple was, however, atypical of the trajectory of Hughes's theatrical interests in this postwar period. Rather, it was African American music that engaged him, particularly gospel music, which was, in the 1950s, acquiring significant crossover success. Gospel music had been a special love of Hughes's since childhood; however, in the 1930s when he first began incorporating music into his plays, it was to blues and spirituals that he turned. But gospel is most deeply the music of the Great Migration, the music through which newly urbanized black migrants worshiped and found strength. It is not surprising that Hughes's theatrical career would culminate in a mining of gospel music's possibilities, for it was the people of that migration who most deeply inspired his imaginative power.[12]

Rampersad suggests that it was the extraordinarily successful Newport Jazz Festival of 1956 that inspired Hughes to turn to black music and the black church in his search for a Broadway hit. Before *Simply Heavenly* had found a producer, Hughes began writing another musical: *Tambourines to Glory* was to be about gospel music, and he wrote it in a matter of days during the summer of 1956. To his good friend Arna Bontemps he crowed: "It's a singing, shouting, wailing drama of the old conflict between blatant Evil and quiet Good, with the Devil driving a Cadillac." So pleased was he with it that he immediately turned it into a novel by the same name. Yet it would be seven years before *Tambourines*

11. Rampersad, *Life*, 2:246; Donna Akiba Sullivan Harper, *Not So Simple: The "Simple" Stories by Langston Hughes* (Columbia: University of Missouri Press, 1995), provides a brilliant and comprehensive analysis of Hughes's achievement.

12. Bernice Johnson Reagon, "Pioneering African American Gospel Music Composers: A Smithsonian Institution Research Project," in *We'll Understand It Better By and By*, ed. Reagon, 3–18.

would arrive on Broadway, to mixed reviews. Loften Mitchell's comments to Arnold Rampersad that the audience didn't know what it was looking at in *Tambourines to Glory* speak to several of Hughes's ventures on the white Broadway stage; not only the audience but also the producers and directors did not understand, and so were unable to translate his distinctive vision. In response to Alice Childress's earlier discomfort with *Simply Heavenly,* Hughes had responded: "The only way to achieve even partially what one wishes in a show is not only to write it—but produce it, direct it, and ACT it all by one's self—also own the theatre."[13]

It is striking how much of Hughes's theatrical work involved music. Aside from the educational or occasional pieces, represented in this volume by *For This We Fight* (1943) and *The Ballot and Me* (1956), virtually all of Hughes's works for the stage after 1942 were operas, musicals, about music, or gospel plays. *The Organizer,* the first of his operas to be performed, with music by James P. Johnson, was presented at the 1940 ILGWU convention, held in Carnegie Hall. *Troubled Island,* written in the 1930s, was not performed until 1949, and the other operas, *The Barrier, Esther,* and *Port Town,* were performed within the next decade. His musicals include *Simply Heavenly* (1957), *Tambourines to Glory* (1963), and *Jericho–Jim Crow* (1963), while the gospel plays include *Black Nativity* (1961), *The Gospel Glow* (1962), *Master of Miracles* (1962), and *The Prodigal Son* (1965). In addition, Hughes wrote *Mister Jazz* (1960) as an opener for *Shakespeare in Harlem,* a dramatic piece fashioned out of Hughes's poetry by Robert Glenn.[14]

It was inevitable that Hughes, the most prolific of African American playwrights at that time, would seek to employ the musical genre that dominated Broadway during the 1940s and 1950s to tell stories of his own creation, and *Simply Heavenly* and *Tambourines to Glory* both work within the genre's conventions. But Hughes never abandoned the determination expressed in his "Note on Commercial Theatre" ("You've taken my blues and gone . . .") to resist white appropriation of African American expressive forms. The popularity of gospel was exploding when Hughes turned to writing his gospel plays. His earlier ventures into religious music had been with composers such as Margaret Bonds and Jan Meyerowitz; although these artistic collaborations were fruitful, the musical idioms with which Hughes was more at home were jazz, blues, and gospel.

13. Rampersad, *Life,* 2:254–55; Hughes to Bontemps, July 26, 1952, LHP; Rampersad, *Life,* 2:370; Hughes to Childress, June 8, 1957, LHP.
14. *Mister Jazz* and *Master of Miracles* may never have been performed.

In *Black Nativity,* Hughes set out to enact the drama of gospel songs.[15] In doing so, he both invented a new form and reinvented for the world stage the older tradition of religious pageants in which the spirituals were reenacted. This coincidence of tradition and invention in Hughes's final theatrical work is fitting. It is not in commercial theater that Hughes's dramatic legacy lives on most vividly, but rather in the gospel plays, which provide scripts for traditional African American forms of worship, shaping and celebrating practices at the heart of African American life. In this sense, his attainment in the theater resembles the achievement of his poetry, making art of African American voice.

In 1948, while attempting to pay some bills by writing lyrics for the musical *Just around the Corner* (music by Joe Sherman, book by Bernard Drew), Hughes wrote to Arna Bontemps: "I WARN YOU ONE MORE TIME ABOUT FOOLING AROUND WITH THE THEATRE. It does more than cripple your legs. It cripples your soul."[16] Yet Hughes's intense engagement with theater and other performance arts lasted more than thirty-five years. In every genre he attempted—tragedy and comedy, history play and musical, opera and gospel play, religious and popular song—Hughes left memorable and transformative work, giving rise to the range and richness of contemporary African American theatrical achievement.

15. Rampersad, *Life,* 2:345.
16. Hughes to Bontemps, December 17, 1948, quoted in Rampersad, *Life,* 2:157.

A Note on the Text

Wherever possible, I have used an already published edition of a text; otherwise the text comes from whatever coherent typescript was available. Song lyrics posed particular problems because there typically was a difference between Hughes's typescripts, as found in the Langston Hughes Papers, and the texts as set to music (where the score was available). For most lyrics, I have chosen to use Hughes's typescript, selecting the version most likely to be the final one. As in Volume 5, the source of each text is indicated in the notes prefacing the work.

Also as in Volume 5, the format for all of the plays has been standardized here. However, except as noted, the only alterations to the original texts themselves are silent corrections of typographical and spelling errors.

Operas

Troubled Island
An Opera in Three Acts

1937, 1949
Libretto by Langston Hughes
Music by William Grant Still

Approached by William Grant Still in 1935, Hughes completed the libretto for *Troubled Island,* based on his play *Emperor of Haiti,* in 1937 and then left for Spain. Unable to complete changes required during the course of musical composition, Hughes agreed that Still should turn to his wife, Verna Arvey, for assistance. The arias "In Childhood Together" and "This Land, This Dark Land" and the duet "Love Calls" are hers.[1] Still completed the opera in 1939; however, it would be ten years before he secured a production. Rejected by the Metropolitan Opera, his first choice, he received a positive response in 1944 from Leopold Stokowski, then director of the New York City Center of Music and Drama, where the New York City Opera was just being formed. Five more years of difficulty were to ensue, particularly around issues of funding, but finally, on March 31, 1949, the opera premiered, with Laszlo Halasz, then head of the New York City Opera, conducting. It was the first performance by a major opera company of an opera by an African American composer. The reviews, unfortunately, were very mixed. On the whole, critics found the music uneven; reception of the libretto ranged from praise to dismissal. *Troubled Island* closed on May 1, 1949, after only three performances.

At Still's insistence, *Troubled Island* had a mixed cast: although African American Larry Winters played Dessalines on the second night, other principals were in blackface. Still hoped thus to have the opera understood as an American, rather than a "Negro," opera of the ilk of *Porgy and Bess,* and he felt that conventional expectations had caused the music to be misunderstood.[2]

Despite the opera's critical reception, the April 10 performance of *Troubled Island* was recorded by the U.S. State Department for distribution abroad and broadcast in Paris and Brussels a year later, sparking interest in Paris for a touring production. However, the recordings were abruptly withdrawn by the State Department, confirming Still's suspicions that the opera's critical difficulties were caused by other than artistic failings. One source of its difficulties, he believed, was the leftist views and reputation of his librettist, from whom, by the opera's premiere, he was estranged. *Troubled Island* has not been mounted again, but the recording is available from William Grant Still Music.

In 1941, Hughes, Still, and Arvey gave Leeds Music Corporation rights to publish both the libretto and the music. That 1949 publication is reproduced here.[3]

The Cast

CELESTE
POPO
AZELIA
DESSALINES
MARTEL
VUVAL
STENIO
PAPALOI
MAMALOI
CLAIRE
1st SERVANT
2nd SERVANT
3rd SERVANT
CHAMBERLAIN
MESSENGER
STEWARD
FISHERMAN
MELON VENDOR
MANGO VENDOR

Overture

Night—a sea of vastness and of stars wherein there floats a troubled island, Haiti. The year is 1791. Napoleon's threat over Europe crushing dreams of freedom. Freedom is enchained in Haiti, too. But the dream stirs even in its chains. In the darkness men rise from their knees to their feet to lift gnarled hands against the forces of slavery. The night is ominous, throbbing with a power long suppressed, full of strange portent. Sea-waves lick at the Haitian shores. In a rumble of silence, the mountains lift jagged heads to the stars. Haiti, a troubled island in the night.

Act I

Moonrise. In the vast interior of an abandoned Sugarmill, the slaves are gathering, men, women, children, to strike for freedom. A door opens to the palm trees and the stars. Outside, POPO, a ragged slave on sentry duty, paces. Softly against the night, but suddenly like a shaft of light, a mother's voice rises calm and clear. Gently, tenderly, very sure with that surety of life and earth that women know, CELESTE sings to her baby in her arms.

CELESTE: Little dark slave child,
    No slave to me!
    You are my son, child,
    Who must be free.

    Barren this barn, child,
    No place to rest.
    Lay your dark head
    On mother's breast.

    Sleep now, my baby,
    Sleep now, my son.
    Mother will free you
    Ere night is done.

    Dream your sweet dreams, child,
    That have no name.
    Mother will dream now
    A dream of flame—

    Flame that will sweep
    Our slavery away!
    Sleep on, my little one,
    Till the new day.
        (POPO stops before the door.)
POPO: Not so loud, Celeste!
    The woods have ears tonight.

No sound to warn the whites—
Until the drums speak!
CELESTE: I know, no sound!
Until through the darkness
The slave people come
To await the beat
Of Legba's drum.
Oh, sleep now, my baby,
Sleep now, my son.
You will be free
Ere night is done.
> *(There is a noise in the underbrush. POPO stands alert, then cries out.)*
POPO: Halt! Who goes there?
AZELIA: Azelia!
POPO: Azelia? Friend, enter then!
AZELIA: Heavy this load I bear!
POPO: What is it you bring?
Melons or mangoes?
AZELIA: Neither melons nor mangoes, friend—
Weapons I bring!
Hidden here beneath this fruit
Are whips that sting!
Blades that cut! Cane knives bold!
Spanish pistols rusty and old.
Weapons I bring to free the slaves—
For my Jean Jacques.
CELESTE: And for our freedom!
AZELIA: Yes! For our freedom.
> *(Together they hide the weapons in a dark corner of the mill.)*
POPO: We'll need them all, Azelia.
Every whip, every cane-knife.
Every pistol, rusty or old.
But where is Jean Jacques?
AZELIA: Through the woods in the dark
Comes Jean Jacques.
Drawing near by no one seen
Steals Jean Jacques.
Lest our masters become wise

And learn too soon of our secret plan,
By hidden paths through the jungle
With a guard of slaves
Walks Jean Jacques.
POPO: Our leader, Jean Jacques!
CELESTE: Our guide, Jean Jacques!
AZELIA: My husband, Jean Jacques—
Through the woods in the dark,
Himself a spark
To light the flame that will spread
Terror and dread
To our masters!
The flame that will sweep
Our slavery away—
And bring to our people
A new day!
CELESTE: To me and my little one a new day!
VOICES: To the slaves in the darkness a new day!
    (JEAN JACQUES DESSALINES stands at the door, handsome,
    tall, powerful, black, surrounded by a crowd of slaves in rags.)
POPO: Dessalines!
AZELIA: Jean Jacques!
SLAVES: Our leader, Jean Jacques!
POPO: What's news without?
What's in the wind?
Do our masters suspect?
Do the Frenchmen know
How the straws blow?
DESSALINES: They do not know!
In their silken beds
Our masters sleep—
But the woods are alive
With slaves who creep
Through the darkness
To strike for freedom's sake.
Our masters do not know
What this night brings for them—
What woe! The end of time!
Our masters sleep!

(From the mouths of the slaves comes a whiplash of laughter that dies as CELESTE lifts her child in her arms.)

CELESTE: My son sleeps, too.

Little one,

Yesterday was for our masters.

Tomorrow is for you!

(The SLAVES lift their hands toward the child.)

SLAVES: Tomorrow for you!

For you! For you!

DESSALINES: Make haste! Move! We must prepare!

Enough of standing here!

Mount guard without, Popo!

You, Celeste, to the crossroads go!

You others, too, take up posts

By every path there be,

That not may pass

Except slaves sworn to revolt.

POPO: Jean Jacques, we go!

SLAVES: We go! We go. . . . .

(They depart in a rumbling murmur of fading voices. It is suddenly very quiet in the vast mill. AZELIA and DESSALINES are left alone. She puts her arms about him, but he draws back with a cry of pain.)

AZELIA: Jean Jacques!

DESSALINES: Don't touch me!

Too sore, too sore yet, Azelia!

My back where my master has beaten me

Is red with scars.

AZELIA: Jean Jacques!

DESSALINES: These scars

That make even love a trial!

Last night they beat me

Until even your soft hands hurt

When they touch my flesh.

I don't belong to you, Azelia,

Nor you to me—

We belong to our masters.

We are slaves

Who *must* be free!

AZELIA: We must be free, Jean Jacques!
    Yet I—I am afraid!
DESSALINES: Afraid? Afraid of what?
AZELIA: Afraid that freedom
    Will rob me of you.
DESSALINES: Don't make me laugh!
    A man must be free!
    Better death than these scars.
AZELIA: Not death! No! No!
    Not death for you—
    I could not live.
DESSALINES: A man must be free.
    None has the right
    To own you or me.
AZELIA: But you must not die!
    Jean Jacques, you must not die!
    You are my world to me—
    I love you!
    We worked together as children
    In cane-fields green in the sunlight.
    I loved you!
    Jean Jacques, I loved you!
    Together we felt the lash—
    Its pain brought us together.
    I loved you!
    Jean Jacques, I loved you!
    Together we watched
    The boiling cane in the night—
    Then one night in the firelight
    As the flames lept high,
    I was your wife, Jean Jacques—
    I who loved you!
DESSALINES: My wife? A word the French use, Azelia.
    No priest or wedding papers for a slave!
AZELIA: No priest or papers did we need.
    Love was our priest and love our creed.
DESSALINES: Priest or papers had we never.
AZELIA: Only love, Jean Jacques!
    Our love forever!

DESSALINES: Night in the slave huts,
    Woman of mine,
    Love we shared together.
AZELIA: Day in the cane fields,
    Husband of mine,
    Work we shared together.
DESSALINES: On rocky hills and country roads,
    In blazing sun our heavy loads
    All we shared together.
    Though come terror and turmoil,
    Sting of lash and sweet of toil,
    Death we'll share together.
AZELIA: Love we'll share together!
DESSALINES: Azelia!
AZELIA: Jean Jacques!
BOTH: Together!
        (*In the doorway a group of SLAVES appear, among them MAR-
        TEL, old and wise out of Africa.*)
MARTEL: Jean Jacques, my son!
    Dark as night
    Through the night
    The slaves are coming,
    You are their leader.
DESSALINES: Martel! Wise art thou!
    Old art thou! Africa art thou!
    Speak to us of Africa, Martel!
SLAVES: Speak to us now of Africa, Martel!
MARTEL: Africa!
    I remember Africa!
    A black man's land where,
    Tall and proud,
    Black kings and chiefs held sway!
    Well do I remember Africa!
    Well do I remember, too,
    That most unlucky day
    The slavers came,
    Stole me away.
SLAVES: Stole me away. . . . away. . . . .
MARTEL: In the dark hold of a slave ship

Over the Western Ocean in chains
To this island, Haiti, we came—
Where men are slaves.
SLAVES: In chains. . . . where men are slaves.
MARTEL: And now, like dew upon
This troubled island
Fall our tears—
For we are slaves,
And Africa is far away,
So long, so far away!
DESSALINES: Chains! . . . Beatings!
Pain!. . . . The whip!. . . . My scars!
SLAVES: Slaves in this world are we,
Children of misery!
Workers who get no pay,
Driven like beasts all day,
Knowing no light,
Living in night,
Children of misery!
Tillers of soil, burden bearers—
Makers of wealth but never sharers
Workers who get no pay,
Driven like beasts all day,
Children of misery—
Tomorrow we must be free!
DESSALINES: Tomorrow we WILL be free!
SLAVES: Free! Free! Free!
DESSALINES: Sons of Africa! Join with me!
Tomorrow we'll be free!
Come forth now, Senegalese,
Tall and proud like coconut trees!
You from the Coast of Calabar!
Men from the Congo, join, too!
The Congo drums will beat for you!
Ashanti men, be with us then!
Africa in Haiti now
Lifts high her head in Freedom's vow!
Sons of Africa, join me!
Tomorrow—we'll be free!

*(A sudden mist of discord steals across the spirit. VUVAL and
STENIO, two mulattoes, appear in the doorway. They are free men,
but insecure, caught between the master and the slave.)*

POPO: Jean Jacques, there are two
Mulattoes here who wish to join us.

SLAVES: Mulattoes?
No mulattoes can we trust!

CELESTE: Mulattoes? Half men, half free!
They don't belong with me!

MARTEL: Quiet here! Our friends
We need not fear!

DESSALINES: Let them in, Popo.

MARTEL: Their fathers were white, it is true.
But blood of Africa is theirs, too.
We need their help. Like us,
Oppression they have known—
In that we slaves are not alone.

DESSALINES: I say, let them in—
Vuval, and Stenio, his friend!
You'll join with us
And fight like men!

STENIO: We'll fight like men!

VUVAL: For liberty we'll fight like men!

MARTEL: You free mulattoes can read and write.
We slaves cannot. We need your help—
For not alone by swords do we fight.

DESSALINES: We need your help! Vuval,
As my aide, I charge you, come with me.
I with my word, you with your pen—
Together we will win!

VUVAL: Liberté!

STENIO: Equalité!

VUVAL: Fraternité!

STENIO: So the French cry!
So cry we—

ALL: Liberty!

(A drum throbs in the dark. Then another takes up the call.)

MARTEL: The drums!

AZELIA: The papaloi comes!

DESSALINES: The mamaloi comes!

CELESTE: The drums! The voodoo drums!

POPO: Papaloi! Mamaloi! Come!

CELESTE: One brings a cock—

POPO: That shall not crow twice!

AZELIA: One brings a goat
>   For the sacrifice!
>   Tonight in the hills. . . . .

MARTEL: Great Gods of Africa, be with us now—
>   To consecrate our freedom's vow!

MAMALOI: Legba!

PAPALOI: Legba! Legba! Alouba!
>   *(The SLAVES begin to dance as the priests of voodoo and their*
>   *attendants enter.)*

SLAVES: Damballa Wedo! Ogun Balandjo!
>   Ogun Sabaho! Nago Shango!
>   Kanga Joue! Papa Simba!
>   Osange Batagri! Congo Guinee!
>   Madame Claireme! Ibo Laylee!
>   Gods of Voodoo, earth and sea,
>   Gods of Rada, be with me!
>   Gods of Congo Land, hold my hand!
>   Damballa Wedo! Dahomey Preda!
>   Dahomey Sobo! Damballa Wedo!
>   Alouba! Legba!

PAPALOI: The hour has come!
>   The Gods say go!
>   Dessalines!
>   Bow low!

MAMALOI: Damballa Wedo! Dahomey Sobo!
>   *(The MAMALOI lifts high the sacred cock. Its throat is slit by*
>   *the gleaming knife of the PAPALOI. Its red blood drips on the*
>   *black head and scarred back of DESSALINES. There is a great*
>   *cry to Legba as the voodoo priests disappear into the darkness and*
>   *DESSALINES rises to lead the slaves to freedom.)*

DESSALINES: Our time has come!
>   Over all Haiti now the time has come
>   To give the signal, sound the great drum—
>   Send forth the word from Le Mol to Gonaives
>   That never again will a master own slaves.
>   Never again will a man say to me,
>   *You are my bondsman, dog! I am free!*
>   I have labored too long in the burning sun!

Too long cut their cane! All that is done!
I shall be free!
Too long have I bowed my weary back,
Suffered the whip, the chain, the wrack!
No more! I shall be free!
From early dawn till day was done,
I've worked their fields in the burning sun.
For pay—these scars!
Look what they gave me for my pay—
Behold my scars!
> (*He bares his back to the horrified cry of the SLAVES. The fresh welts there are red and raw. A drum begins to beat louder than ever.*)
Give out the weapons!
Men, away!
Slaves to the hills!
Arise! Follow me!
Strike to be free!
SLAVES: To the hills!
To the hills that rise
Against the skies!
To the hills!
To the hills where the brave
Must lead the slave!
To the hills!
Where sheltering caves give strength,
And weary backs all bent with pain
Shall rise to the heights of a man again—
To the hills:
Black men, to the hills—
Where the rocks are a-tremble
And the wide sky thrills
With the song of the free
In the hills!
To the hills!
Free men—
To the hills!
> (*A crescendo of song like sparks of sound bursts against the sky. Darkness. Great names, Christophe, Leclerc, Toussaint move across the minds of men.*)
CURTAIN

Act II, Scene 1

When light comes again it is a silken shiny light revealing a palace and a
throne whereon sits DESSALINES, now Emperor. He dictates letters to
VUVAL, his secretary.

DESSALINES: Twenty thousand francs
    I order Stenio to pay without delay.

VUVAL: Too much, my Lord!
    My cousin cannot pay.

DESSALINES: Why can't he?
    I made him head of a rich estate.
    Write him what I say—
    Tell him the Emperor has need
    Of labor and of money
    To build roads and schools
    To make our Haiti great.
    Tell Stenio to send
    His taxes here post haste—
    Or I'll send soldiers
    To remove him from his place!

VUVAL: Very well, my Lord,
    I'll write as you dictate.
    And now?

DESSALINES Read the next letter!

VUVAL: But, Sire! It grows late,
    And I am tired. Besides, you know,
    The Lords and Ladies are bidden here
    For a banquet of state.
    The hour draws near.

DESSALINES: Read, Vuval!

VUVAL: Very well, I'll read.
    It's from the barracks at Acul,
    Signed, *Major Longuet:*
    Send me ten burro loads of power,
    And one thousand purple uniforms today,
    Also a thousand scarlet plumes
    For my troops to wear on dress display.

DESSALINES: Tell him—
    Tell him to go to hell!
    I wish I could write!

I'll send the powder,
But no scarlet plumes!
What is this thing,
That every man in Haiti
Wants to dress like me—
And I'm the King?
VUVAL: Each man a king
Would be, it seems—
Slaves suffering from illusions
In their dreams!
DESSALINES: Speak not of slaves, Vuval!
Each man in Haiti now is free.
Read the next letter.
VUVAL: But, Sire, it is late!
DESSALINES: Speak not of slaves, Vuval!
Each man in Haiti now is free.
Read the next letter.
VUVAL: But, Sire, it is late!
DESSALINES: Read, Vuval!
VUVAL: This one is written in so poor a hand
It's hard for me to understand.
Some peasant, it seems,
Who scarce knows how to spell—
DESSALINES: Read it, Vuval!
I'll understand it well.
I was a peasant once.
VUVAL: It says:
Most high and mighty King of Haiti,
Liberator of the slaves,
We, the peasants of Gros Morne salute you!
And we beg of you an humble favor:
We want a school!
We want a school and books and a teacher
So that we might learn to read and write.
Please, Emperor of the Blacks,
Send us a teacher soon.
The peasants of Gros Morne
Beg of you this favor,
And send to you our love
Respectfully,
Blacksmith Henri.

Ha, ha, ha, ha, ha, ha!
The peasants want a teacher!
Ha, ha, ha, ha, ha!
DESSALINES: Why do you laugh, Vuval?
Why do you laugh?
Is it because you know
I sit here helpless, too,
Upon this throne?
I cannot read nor write myself—
And we have no teachers
To send the villages.

Why do you laugh, Vuval?
Is it because you see
How ignorance binds the hands
Of men who would be free?

Why do you laugh, Vuval?
I say why do you laugh
At them—and me?

Enough of you! Get out!
Go write your letters
In the alcove there!
Bring them for me to sign
Ere the moon rises!
Now, get out! Vuval, get out!
> (VUVAL *exits rapidly as* DESSALINES *sinks wearily on the arm of his throne. The aged* MARTEL *enters slowly.*)
MARTEL: My son, Jean Jacques,
You must be tired!
DESSALINES: Tired, Martel, tired!
Too heavy are the cares of state.
I do not understand them well,
Nor know I what to do.
The fields are all untilled,
The taxes are unpaid,
The cane uncut,
The roads unmade.
Does no one care about
This dream we dreamed, Martel?
This dream of Haiti

Where each black man
Can lift his head in pride!
MARTEL: Be patient, son!
The people yet will learn
Men have only
What men earn.
By work and trade alone
Can Haiti live.
We must invite the French boats
Here again.
For trade, the French are best.
DESSALINES: The French?
Our former masters? No!
Napoleon's people?
The very mention of those knaves
Brings back to me
The memory of bitter whips
On the backs of slaves.
No, no! The French
Must never cross our harbor bars.
Too deep and lasting, Martel,
Are my scars! . . . . My scars!
Keep them afar! Let Haiti be
A land where black men
Govern—free!
Our world—for you and me.
MARTEL: In my old age,
An even bigger dream than that,
I dream, Jean Jacques.
DESSALINES: What dream, Martel?
MARTEL: A land where all live well!
Listen, my son, I dream
A world where man
No other man will scorn,
Where love will bless the earth
And peace its paths adorn.
I dream a world where all
Will know sweet freedom's way,
Where greed no longer saps the soul
Nor avarice blights our day.

A world I dream where black or white,
Whatever race you be,
Will share the bounties of the earth
And every man is free,
Where wretchedness will hang its head
And joy, like a pearl,
Attends the needs of all mankind—
Of such I dream, my world!
DESSALINES: Too big a dream, alas!
MARTEL: But mark my words, Jean Jacques,
In time it will come to pass.
DESSALINES: But now I'll bend my will on Haiti!
Task enough at hand have I
To make *my* country great.
But that *I will*—
If not by words and pleading,
Then by force!
The whites called me the tiger once
When I turned my sword on them.
The blacks will know this sword, too,
Unless my work they do!
MARTEL: Son, take care!
It is not wise to be
A master over any man.
DESSALINES: I am the Emperor, Martel!
Let all respect me well!
MARTEL: These times are troublous!
My son, take care! Beware!
(*CLAIRE, pale and lovely quadroon mistress of the Emperor, comes
into the room.*)
CLAIRE: Jean Jacques!
DESSALINES: My Claire!
CLAIRE: Why do you linger here within?
'Tis sunset in the garden.
Flowers fair
Release their perfume
On the evening air.
Everywhere the earth
Is drenched in colors rare,
By light empearled.

MARTEL: Jean Jacques, beware!
CLAIRE: In amethyst and gold
   The sky's arrayed
   To bid the day goodbye,
   Now gentle night,
   With stardust in her hair,
   Steals o'er the world.
DESSALINES: My Claire!
CLAIRE: 'Tis sunset in the garden.
   Why linger here?
DESSALINES: Affairs of state—
CLAIRE: Let such cares be!
   Come out with me!
   Laugh! Be free!
DESSALINES: I love you so!
      (He embraces her but she withdraws.)
CLAIRE: Let go!
   You'll spoil my gown!
   You'll spoil my hair!
DESSALINES: Sweet Claire!
      (A knock and POPO enters.)
POPO: My Lord,
   Your robes of state
   And crown await you.
   Your ermine cape
   And scarlet cloak are ready.
   Will you come now,
   Jean Jacques, and dress?
DESSALINES: I'll come with you now.
   Await me here,
   My Empress, Claire.
CLAIRE: I'll await you,
   Emperor, here.
      (In her red lips his title is a slur. With POPO, DESSALINES
      withdraws.)
   Sunset in the garden—
   I am lonely here.
   I hate this court!
   I hate this savage land
   Where men were slaves.

That stupid king—
Who does not understand me—
Thinks me true!
If he but knew how much
I hate this savage land—
And that black king
Who keeps me lonely here
When I would rather be far away
Across the sea in Paris—
Where customs please me better
And no savage drums
Beat always on the ear.
    (VUVAL, sleek and handsome, enters with the letters.)
VUVAL: My Claire!
CLAIRE: Vuval!
VUVAL: Are you not glad to see me?
    Your face is drawn with anguish.
CLAIRE: I am lonely.
    Ill does this savage land
    Become me, sweet Vuval.
VUVAL: But this black land confines
    One pearl most rare—
    You, my Claire!
    Its drumbeats sounding,
    Its wild jungle cries
    Pall on your ears
    And spoil your dreaming.
    I know! I understand!
CLAIRE: My dear, what brings you here?
VUVAL: To leave these letters
    For your stupid husband.
    I have written them all wrong—
    Filled with vile insults
    And words he never dreamed
    To tell his subjects.
    If he but knew—
    The false for us is true,
    Eh, Claire?
CLAIRE: How go our plans, my sweet?
    When do we fly from here?

VUVAL: If all goes well, tonight
    We leave for the Coast.
CLAIRE: Tonight?
VUVAL: Tonight!
    Already in the South
    Stenio's soldiers
    All the forts have seized.
    The generals everywhere are ready to revolt—
    To end this dark rule of a tyrant,
    Dessalines—
    Who makes his soldiers work
    Like peasants in the field!
    Stenio, my cousin and my friend,
    Will no doubt be
    Haiti's future majesty.
CLAIRE: Good, Vuval!
    But we go to Paris!
    Well have you planned.
    Tonight, you say, we flee from here?
VUVAL: Tonight! When the banquet's over
    I'll have the horses ready.
    We'll fly through the dark.
    Tomorrow we'll be far away
    With Stenio on the coast—
    And in due time in Paris.
CLAIRE: Ah, sweet Paris!
VUVAL: Paris with you, my Claire,
    Will be like Paradise!
    Already I dream
    Of love's delights in store.
CLAIRE: Whisper in my ear, Vuval,
    And tell me more.
VUVAL: Love calls us
    To Paris where hearts are ardent.
    Love calls us
    Where beauty reigns and life is gay
    In Paris.
CLAIRE: Sometimes,
    Even there, I fear

I'll remember
These lonely hours here.
VUVAL: These hours will be forever dead.
CLAIRE: Their ghosts will rise
    To haunt my soul.
VUVAL: Their ghosts will disappear
    When you breathe the air of Paris—
    When you feel my arms about you!
CLAIRE: When your tender lips touch mine!
VUVAL: In one long embrace, my Claire!
BOTH: We'll dwell in joy at last—in Paris!
CLAIRE: Down the boulevards we'll wander—in Paris!
VUVAL: With *real* kings and counts—
    Not slave-marked ever—
    We will speak in Paris.
CLAIRE: At the splendid balls we'll revel!
VUVAL: In affairs of state we'll mingle!
BOTH: Paris and all its beauty—
    Where love calls us!
    Ah, my sweet! In Paris!
VUVAL: You and I!
CLAIRE: Vuval!
VUVAL: My Claire!
BOTH: In Paris!
    (The sunset flames to rose and gold as they embrace.)
CURTAIN

Act II, Scene 2

Two lanterns reveal the dim outline of a long banquet table set on an elevated terrace open to the sky and the fronds of tall palms. Female SERVANTS bustle about singing in a droll manner.
SERVANTS: To polish and shine,
    That fate is mine.
    To clean, clean, clean,
    Till we're old and lean.
    To cook and scrub
    Or wash in a tub—

Rub-a-dub-dub!
Rub-a-dub-dub!
Rub-a-dub-dub!

Up at dawn
And running all day.
Wash the dog,
Put out the cat!
Hurry do this!
Hurry do that!
Do this and that!
This and that!

Sweep the floors
And set the table!
Work as long
As we are able!
Oh, that's the life
Of a servant girl
Anywhere in this
Devilish world!
Ah, me! Ay! Uh!
Oh, my soul!

> (*AZELIA, DESSALINES' wife of his slave days, enters tired and worn as if she has come a long way.*)

MAID: Who's that?

COOK: She don't belong here, that's sure!

DUSTER: Some peasant's wandered into court, it seems.

MAID: Look at them clothes! Ha, ha!

COOK: She has no shoes!

DUSTER: Slaves are free—yet she has no shoes!

MAID: Ah, me! Who's she?

AZELIA: I'm Azelia!

COOK: Azelia who?

DUSTER: Yes, who are you?

> (*In her poor clothes, distraught and confused, AZELIA looks about bewildered, faced with a mocking group of SERVANTS.*)

AZELIA: Azelia! I am Azelia!

SERVANTS: Azelia?

COOK: What do you want here?

AZELIA: I'm looking for my Jean—

MAID: Your Jean?
DUSTER: What Jean?
AZELIA: My Jean Jacques.
SERVANTS: Ha, ha, ha, ha, ha!
COOK: You mean the Emperor?
MAID: Jean Jacques, the King?
DUSTER: You mean Jean Jacques, the Liberator?
AZELIA: I mean Jean Jacques, my husband.
COOK: Crazy she must be! Old fool!
AZELIA: Tell me, where is he?
MAID: You mean the King?
AZELIA: I mean the King! Where is he?
 There's something I must tell him soon—
 Ere the rising of the moon.
 Warnings I bring, the breath of woe!
 I've come from the Coast to tell him so.
 The King! My husband, the King.
 Where is he? Please! Where is he?
COOK: He's where you cannot go.
DUSTER: What could *you* tell the King
 He needs to know?
AZELIA: He's where such as you don't see!
COOK: In the throne room there below, maybe!
DUSTER: Or in his chamber, perchance!
MAID: Or he's in the garden
 with his lady fair.
COOK: You can't go there!
DUSTER: You can't go there!
MAID: Not there!
AZELIA: But I must see him!
 Tell me where is he?
  (To confuse AZELIA the SERVANTS playfully point in various
  directions at once.)
MAID: He's there!
COOK: No, there!
DUSTER: He must be in there!
MAID: That way!
COOK: No, there! Hey, hey!
SERVANTS: Ha, ha, ha!
 For this is the life

Of a servant girl
Anywhere in this
Devilish world—
Do this! Do that!
Ah, me! Uh!
Oh, my soul!

    (The SERVANTS bustle about their work again as AZELIA wan-
    ders away bearing her burden of grief and fear for DESSALINES.
    A trumpet sounds. The SERVANTS scurry faster than ever as the
    CHIEF STEWARD enters to inspect the tables. He is followed by
    CANDLE-BEARERS and FOOTMEN in livery. BOYS begin to
    fill the crystal glasses. Other SERVANTS enter with tapers. Soon
    the whole terrace is ablaze with light, the crystal and the silver on
    the banquet table gleam luxuriously. The CHAMBERLAIN en-
    ters followed by a HERALD who takes his place on the platform.
    The STEWARD shoos the SERVANTS away. The trumpet sounds
    again as the HERALD unfurls his scroll.)

STEWARD: Hurry! Scurry! Hurry!
    Servants, hurry!
CHAMBERLAIN: Call now the list of nobles!
    The banquet will commence!
THE HERALD: Hear ye! Hear ye!
    The guests of the Emperor—
    Bidden to a Banquet of State
    In honor of his Majesty!

    (The HERALD announces the guests. As each couple's name is
    called, they take their places on the lower terrace to await the ar-
    rival of the Emperor. Their costumes are gorgeously grotesque copies
    of various European court styles and periods, but giving in the en-
    semble an effect of tragi-comic splendor. Some of the guests enjoy
    themselves immensely, but others are obviously uncomfortable in
    their regal clothes, while many are gnarled old peasants too bent
    to ever appear at ease in ruffled Parisian finery.)

CHORUS: The Duke and Duchess of Dondon!
    Count and Countess Claudel de Zouba!
    Lord and Lady Toutemonde!
    General Abelard and Madame La Pompeuse!
    Duke of Marmelade and La Countess Louise!
    Baron Antoine and the Baroness!
    Madame the Duchess of Limonade!
    Madame Camille Nereide!

The Governor of Milot with Lady Fifi Beauregard!

Duchess Lulu Minette and her husband!

>*(Enter a very large duchess with a very small husband. There is a moment of giggling, nervous fanning, and late couples stealing in unannounced. On the upper terrace a lady in waiting to the Empress proceeds to arrange her Majesty's seat.)*

The court arrives!

His Majesty, the Emperor!

First Liberator of the blacks!

Chief ruler of Haiti—

Jean Jacques Dessalines!

>*(Preceded by pages, and followed by POPO, MARTEL, and numerous others of the retinue, DESSALINES enters with CLAIRE on his arm. All guests bow low. DESSALINES and CLAIRE take their seats. An attendant offers the Emperor his crown on a silken cushion. POPO presents the royal sceptre.)*

CHORUS: Dessalines! Hail!

Hail! Dessalines!

>*(Trumpet call! The guests sit down, a glittering row of velvet busts and dark, genial faces behind the crystal and silver.)*

DESSALINES: I am the great Dessalines!

I have covered my scars with diamonds!

I have covered my head with plumes!

I have made myself Emperor of Haiti!

I am the great Dessalines!

I have sent the French to their tombs.

Women of beauty surround me,

Rich foods and red wines are mine.

Greatest Emperor in the world am I,

King and ruler divine!

COURTIERS: Dessalines! Dessalines!

DESSALINES: I have covered my scars with diamonds.

I have covered my land with glory.

Emperor of all the Haitians am I,

Hero of song and story.

COURTIERS: Dessalines! Dessalines!

DESSALINES: I am the great Dessalines!

COURTIERS: Dessalines! Dessalines! Dessalines!

>*(Unnoticed by the guests, there is great commotion among the guards and servants at the door. At the door AZELIA attempts to break away from the guards onto the upper level of the terrace.)*

THE CHAMBERLAIN: No! Don't let her in!
> *(Screaming AZELIA struggles.)*
AZELIA: Jean Jacques!
> *(CLAIRE embraces DESSALINES and prevents him from seeing AZELIA.)*
CLAIRE: Dessalines! My sweet Emperor!
AZELIA: Jean Jacques! Jean Jacques! Jean Jacques!
> *(The guards drag AZELIA off, struggling. The HERALD approaches the center of the terrace.)*
HERALD: Your Majesties! Messieurs!
  Mesdames! The ballet!
> *(Mulatto dancing girls, trained in Paris, begin a dance of formal French pattern, similar to the minuet, that greatly pleases the Empress. But most of the court are bored. CLAIRE sits by DESSALINES, dazzlingly beautiful, but evil, too, like a silver serpent. As the dance progresses, onto the scene steal dark dancers, whose anklets are of beaten gold and whose bushy hair is adorned with the teeth of animals. For the moment they remain hidden behind the girls, then leap forward and begin a voodoo dance, as the mulatto dancing girls exit. A tall male dancer enters, feathered and painted like a voodoo god. Before him the group of dark dancers bow and retreat. Then, assuming postures of supplication, they approach him, and dance around him in movements suggesting worship not free of fear. Gradually the dance becomes fierce, provocative and terrible, reaching its climax. CLAIRE, in fright, covers her ears with jewelled hands, and calls aloud to DESSALINES.)*
CLAIRE: Oh! Stop the drums!
  Stop those drums!
DESSALINES: Stop! . . . . . Stop!
> *(The dancing ceases. The dancers steal off. DESSALINES rises commandingly.)*
  My Empress does not like drums.
> *(Another drum takes up the beat.)*
  Stop those drums!
  Stop them, Vuval!
VUVAL: But, Sire!
DESSALINES: Stop them, I say!
VUVAL: But, Sire, those drums are far away
  Off in the hills somewhere.

DESSALINES: I don't care where they are!
  Have them stopped!
VUVAL: I go, my Emperor! We go!
      (*Exeunt VUVAL and other mulattoes. DESSALINES in scorn-
      fully deliberate manner berates his guests.*)
DESSALINES: Drums in the court!
  Voodoo drums in the Emperor's court!
  When I would build a civilization here
  Equal to anywhere!
  And you will not help me!
  My Lords and Ladies,
  Our taxes are unpaid.
  Our lands untilled!
  You lazy Dukes and Counts
  Are all to blame!
  From this night on,
  Back to the soil return,
  With toil and sweat you'll learn
  That nothing makes a man
  Save what he earn!
CHORUS: What? Work again?
  Make slaves of us?
  Oh, no! No! No!
DESSALINES: Silence! Listen!
  I fought to make Haiti free.
  Now we must make it great.
  If you'll not help me willingly
  Then I'll *make* you help me!
  I am your Emperor!
  From canefields to this palace,
  From a slave hut to a throne I came—
  To this crown on my head
  And this ermine cape cov'ring my scars,
  To this jewelled sceptre in my hand
  I fought my way!
  I did it by the sword!
  The whites called me the tiger then.
  If I must be a tiger now—
  I will be!
  On your feet! Drink to me!

(MARTEL sounds an unheeded warning as the guests leap to their feet and raise trembling glasses in the air while the servants scurry about.)

MARTEL: Oh, son, take care!

    Glory is a passing thing!

    Beware!

        (MESSENGER dashes up the stairs to the terrace.)

MESSENGER: My Lord! My Lord!

    The garrisons in the South have revolted,

    The generals turn against you,

    The mulattoes rise against you.

DESSALINES: What? Where come you?

        (The guests begin to leave hastily stealing away.)

MESSENGER: From the Coast! Rebellion's everywhere!

DESSALINES: Then to the Coast I go!

    The rebels there

    Need but see my face

    To know I am their master.

    Boy, my horse!

    Popo, take my sceptre and my crown.

    Bring me my sword instead!

    Dessalines, the tiger fights again!

    Martel! Remain here, faithful friend.

    Attend the palace.

    Take care of my sweet Claire.

    Empress, good night!

CLAIRE: Goodbye, my Lord!

        (They embrace.)

DESSALINES: Not goodbye, good night!

    I shall return

    Ere dawn shall come to light.

CLAIRE: My Lord, good night!

POPO: Here's your sword and helmet, Sire!

    Your horse is ready, and mine.

    I ride with you.

        (As DESSALINES straps on his sword for the first time he notices that the terrace is empty save for POPO and MARTEL.)

DESSALINES: But where are all the others?

POPO: Without your leave, Sire,

    They are gone!

MARTEL: Yes, son, they are gone.
> *(Angrily DESSALINES draws his sword.)*

DESSALINES: I go, too! Unleash my horse!
 All traitors I will meet head-on!
 The tiger rides into the dawn.
> *(He strides from the terrace. Horses' hooves disappear in the distance. Silence. Then as the slow ominous beating of a drum is heard MARTEL blows out the candles on the banquet table. Darkness settles over Haiti. The drum is like a desperate heartbeat in the night.)*

CURTAIN

Act III

The quai of a fishing village. High noon. Beyond the sea-wall the sails of ships rock on water. Nets hang to dry. Market women spread their wares on the ground at the foot of the sea-wall before the custom's house. FISHERMEN and PEASANTS bargain and buy.

CROWD: A peasant folk are we!
 A fisher folk are we—
 Living from the earth
 And living from the sea.

 A barefoot folk are we!
 A water folk are we!
 Plowing, planting, reaping,
 Sailing on the sea.

 Lowering our nets
 In the singing spray,
 In the open air
 Beneath the bright sky,
 Our days go by.

 A peasant folk are we!
 A fisher folk are we—
 Born of the earth
 And the singing sea.
 Sons of Haiti!
 A peasant, a fisher
 Folk are we!

VENDORS: Fish! Coconuts! Sugar cane! Fish!
  Yams! Coconuts! Salt! Sea fish!
  Mangoes! Bananas! Thimbles! Fish!
  Pears! Sugar cane! Deep sea fish!
    (The fishermen strut flirtatiously,
    Teasing the market women.)
FISHERMAN: Hello, lady, dressed so fine!
  You've got a good man on your mind!
MANGO VENDOR: No good man do I need—
  One more mouth for me to feed!
FISHERMAN: Listen, woman, understand
  I'm an honest fisherman!
MANGO VENDOR: Out of my way and let me pass!
  All men's tongues are full of sass!
VENDORS: Out of her way and let her pass!
  All men's tongues are full of sass!
FISHERMAN: My good woman, can it be
  You turn up your nose at me?
MANGO VENDOR: I'd turn my nose up twice at you!
  I've got one man and I don't need two!
VENDORS: Out of her way and let her pass!
  All men's tongues are full of sass!
FISHERMAN: Ah, poor me! Alas, alas!
VENDORS: All men's tongues are full of sass!
FISHERMAN: Then, I'll go! Men, follow me!
  Come on, let these women be!
    (The MEN mount the sea-wall.)
FISHERMEN: Men, to the boats—
  The sea breeze is blowing.
VENDORS: Get along, you!
FISHERMEN: Nets to the deep
  It's time to be lowering.
VENDORS: Goodbye! Get along, you!
FISHERMEN: Out in the blue,
  Wild waves are dancing.
VENDORS: Get along, you!
FISHERMEN: Sun and wind
  Together romancing.
  Off to sea!
VENDORS: Get along, you!

FISHERMEN: Men, to the boats!
   Off to the sea!
   Sails in the breeze
   Like bright flags are blowing.
   Leaping the fish,
   All silvery glowing.
      (Not noticed, a band of RAGAMUFFINS enter, stealing the fruit
      of the WOMEN as they wave to the FISHERMEN.)
   Men, to the boats,
   For the sea breeze is blowing!
   Nets to the deep
   'Tis time to be lowering.
   Men, to the boats!
   Off to the sea!
   Off to the sea!
      (The MELON VENDOR turns, sees the RAGAMUFFINS, and
      utters a cry.)
MELON VENDOR: Look! Look! There's thieves!
      (The MARKET WOMEN chase the RAGAMUFFINS away. They
      drop yams, cocoanuts, mangoes as they scamper off.)
VENDORS: Away, you thieves!
   Get out! Get out!
   You thieves! Away!
      (Industriously the MARKET WOMEN rearrange their merchan-
      dise as into the square, with hair dishevelled and eyes dulled and
      mindless, comes AZELIA, on her head a wicker tray of fruit.)
MELON VENDOR: Look who comes here!
   That crazy old woman
   With a basket of dry bananas!
MANGO VENDOR: Move on!
VENDORS: Move on, move on!
MELON VENDOR: We pay taxes here to sell our wares!
MANGO VENDOR: What do you pay?
VENDORS: Move on, move on!
AZELIA: Always move on!
   For me—move on!
      (She puts her basket down on the wall.)
   I'm tired! So tired.
MELON VENDOR: Don't rest here, you crazy loon!
VENDORS: Move on!

AZELIA: Perhaps in there
Where the soldiers are
I can rest.
VENDORS: Move on, move on!
MANGO VENDOR: The soldiers are gone
Since early dawn,
Stupid!
MELON VENDOR: Since sun-up they've been away.
VENDORS: Move on!
MANGO VENDOR: Trouble's brewing on the Coast today.
VENDORS: Move on!
    (AZELIA attempts to lift her basket but fails.)
AZELIA: Ay! Heavy this load I bear!
MANGO VENDOR: You've only melons there!
AZELIA: Your mistake!
Weapons I bring!
    (AZELIA throws her head back proudly.)
Hidden beneath this fruit
Are whips that sting,
Knives that cut, cane knives bold,
Spanish pistols rusty and old—
For my Jean Jacques!
    (The MARKET WOMEN laugh in derision.)
MELON VENDOR: Jean Jacques!
MANGO VENDOR: This crazy old woman
Speaking of Jean Jacques!
AZELIA: Shhh! Weapons I bring!
MELON VENDOR: Mad words you speak!
MANGO VENDOR: Away with you!
VENDORS: Away, away!
AZELIA: Too heavy this load I bear
And none who care!
    (Slowly AZELIA lifts her basket and leaves.)
MANGO VENDOR: Listen!
The sound of marching feet!
Let's go see!
    (She mounts the steps of the sea-wall and gazes off in the distance.)
CHORUS: What can it be? Let's see!
MANGO VENDOR: A strange troop of soldiers coming—
Whose uniforms I do not know.

MELON VENDOR: Trouble! Trouble! Woe!

VENDORS: Trouble is brewing!

MELON VENDOR: Haiti pursuing!

MANGO VENDOR: They are drawing near.

MELON VENDOR: Cry out our wares!

    Perhaps we'll make a sale!

VENDORS: Sea fish! Deep sea fish! Melons!

    Sugar cane! Melons ripe! Melons sweet!

    Yams! Pears! Cocoanuts! Salt sea fish!

     (In charge of VUVAL and STENIO soldiers enter marching in formation.)

STENIO: Company halt! Right, face!

    Men, we remain here! Clear the square!

    Get all these old women out!

    Break ranks! Go ahead!

VENDORS: What does he mean?

    How can it be?

    He'll drive us away?

    Not me! Not me!

VUVAL: You market folk, clear out at once!

    Be quick, be quick!

STENIO: Or else my men'll show you

    How a bayonet can prick!

VENDORS: Oh, no! No! No!

OTHERS: We'll go!

     (The MARKET WOMEN are driven away by the soldiers. STENIO addresses his troops.)

STENIO: 'Tis here our noble Emperor will come

    Thinking to find his traitorous generals.

    Instead he'll find his end!

    Formation, men!

    A grave and patriotic duty has befallen us!

    To rid our land of one

    Who ill becomes free men—

    To put an end to Dessalines!

     (The SOLDIERS murmur in surprise.)

SOLDIERS: To Dessalines? The Emperor Dessalines?

STENIO: Silence! You have heard me speak.

    Soon will come the one we seek—

    That Dessalines who sets himself up

As a King!

He is no more than other men.

A slave in charge of Haiti! Bah!

VUVAL: You who once were slaves

About to be made slaves again

By your king!

STENIO: But that we will prevent.

Today we'll end his reign

And set up instead another government.

Perhaps myself, or Vuval as President.

Men, you're to take prisoner Dessalines!

(VUVAL has mounted the sea-wall to watch for DESSALINES.)

SOLDIERS: Take prisoner Dessalines? Take the Emperor?

STENIO: Silence! When he enters,

At my command lay hands on him.

If he resists, I'll draw my sword

And teach him who is lord at arms.

VUVAL: Nearer and nearer draws that dust cloud

The Emperor and his horsemen

Raise as they come!

Let's place our men!

STENIO: Break ranks!

You two take stations there in yonder doorway.

You others behind the sea-wall hide.

Vuval, you there.

I, near the road will stand

Ready to command you. So!

(VUVAL and the SOLDIERS hide as ordered. The quai is empty now. The dark clouds of fate conspire to trap the Emperor who rides into the square.)

DESSALINES: Halt! Tie the horses here, Popo,

In front of headquarters.

How quiet it is!

Where have the soldiers gone?

Where are the people?

The market women at their stalls?

POPO: This village deserted seems, my lord.

I like not the feel of things at all.

Be on your guard, Jean Jacques!

The barracks here are empty!

DESSALINES: What soldiers dare desert their posts?
   What generals dare defy the King?
   Popo, mount yonder wall and see
   Where are the boats, and where the fishermen?
   Where all the market folk
   Who once hailed me their Liberator?
POPO: None do I see, Jean Jacques, not one!
   (STENIO emerges from his hiding place.)
STENIO: Seize the prisoners!
   (The soldiers seize POPO, but those who approach DESSALINES
   fall back in awe and terror at his glance.)
   Seize him, I say!
   (But none dare touch the Emperor.)
DESSALINES: Thus it is, you repay me!
   Stenio!
   You traitorous dog!
STENIO: Black slave!
DESSALINES: I swear by ev'ry scar I've borne
   You'll pay for this!
   You never were a slave, it's true!
   Yet you dare command my men
   Whom I have freed,
   To lay their hands on me!
   They're afraid! Are you afraid, too?
   We'll see!
      (DESSALINES and STENIO draw their swords. They meet and
      parry fiercely. DESSALINES strikes STENIO's sword from his
      hand but VUVAL emerges from hiding, raises his pistol and fires.
      The shot strikes DESSALINES in the back. His royal sword clat-
      ters to earth. The Emperor turns, looks at the man who betrayed
      him and falls to the ground, dead. VUVAL stands rooted as if in
      a daze. STENIO walks over to the body.)
STENIO: Traitorous dog am I, heh? Ha, ha!
   Well, less than a dog are you now!
   Food for worms!
      (To the SOLDIERS.)
   Men, to the barracks!
   Take that prisoner, Popo, and lock him up!
   Vuval, why so woebegone?
   It's not *your* heart that's punctured!

You've done well, my friend.
They'll write your name in history
As the man who freed our Haiti.
Put your gun away. Come!
The lovely Claire is waiting.
Let's go and sip a glass of wine!
> *(He picks up DESSALINES' sword.)*
This little trinket here is mine.
VUVAL: The body?
STENIO: That's for the buzzards and the daws.
> *(STENIO and VUVAL leave DESSALINES alone on his back in the dust, dead. Peeping and peering from either side of the quai, come the RAGAMUFFINS who earlier plagued the market women. The RAGAMUFFINS steal in awe around the body, then silently creep up and touch it. When they find that the corpse does not move, they cry aloud in their unintelligible dialect, jabbering in wonder at the tassels of gold on his shoulders, the heavy gold cords at the cuffs, his shiny boots. One of the RAGAMUFFINS picks up the Emperor's hat with the purple plume and puts it on his head, breaking into laughter. Two of the boys turn the body over, unbutton the coat, and take it off. While they squabble over the coat, a third removes his silken shirt, the color of wine, and rubs it against his face, groaning voluptuously at the sleekness of the cloth. The body of the Emperor now lies face downward on the earth, his back bare to the sun. The old welts of his slave days stand out like cords across his shoulders. The boys begin to dance about the corpse, gibbering as they dance. . . . AZELIA enters, bearing her wicker tray of fruit. She puts the tray on the sea-wall and fiercely turns on the vagabonds, frightening them. Jabbering, they run off with their stolen finery.)*
AZELIA: Get away!
That poor man is sick, or maybe dead,
And you robbing him of his clothes! Away!
> *(She goes toward the body, unaware of its identity, kneels and lifts the dusty head of the corpse in her hands. Suddenly her face is frozen with the horror and pain of recognition.)*
Jean Jacques!
> *(Sobbing, she falls across his body, hiding the heavy scars on his back. Then she rises slowly to her knees and looks down at the man who was once her husband, remembering all that they have known together.)*

Jean Jacques, my lover,
My husband, mine!
In death you lie so still,
Broken your pride and broken your will.
Deserted now—by all save Azelia!
I will never desert you,
For I love you!
Jean Jacques, I love you!
Night in the slave huts,
Husband of mine,
Love we shared together.
Day in the canefields,
Husband of mine,
Work we shared together.
Then came fame—and you were King!
All the world your praise did sing—
But I was forgotten!
Emperor in golden crown,
Full of greatness and renown—
Forgotten, still I loved you!
Now lonely years like dark shadows,
Husband of mine,
I must face tomorrow—
But the memory of our love,
Husband of mine,
Lights my path of sorrow.

Your destiny is in the stars!

I live. . . . to kiss. . . . your scars.
    (The two are bathed in sunshine as the curtains close.)
THE END

The Organizer
A Blues Opera in One Act

1940
Libretto by Langston Hughes
Music by James P. Johnson

Approached by jazz musician and composer James P. Johnson in 1937 about collaborating on a opera, Hughes responded enthusiastically: "I think we could work out something really Negro, modern, and interesting. I hope so."[1] The one-act blues opera that emerged combines blues and gospel elements; its portrayal of the then well-known struggle to form a sharecroppers' union that united the concerns of poor southern blacks and whites is both ideological and topical. The Woman's song, "Ma man is like John Henry," may allude to the successful Seattle Federal Theatre production of Theodore Browne's *John Henry* (1937), which Johnson had been asked to turn into an opera. He had approached Hughes about turning Browne's script into blank verse, a project Hughes never undertook.[2] Plans to mount *De Organizer* for the second season of Hughes's Harlem Suitcase Theatre, as well as the possibility of a production at Café Society, did not come to fruition. However, on May 31, 1940, a concert version was performed at Carnegie Hall in New York City as part of the convention of the International Ladies Garment Workers Union, by the ILGWU Negro Chorus and the ILGWU Symphony Orchestra with Eva Jessye as choral director. Oddly, no reviews of the production exist, despite the prominence of both the composer and the librettist. Then the music was lost—for more than fifty years.

In 1997, James Dapogny of the University of Michigan, Ann Arbor, discovered among Jessye's papers, left to the university's African American Music Collection, a notebook containing melody and text. Among the Johnson papers in Riverside, California, he located sufficient sketches of the music to reconstruct the score. Two performances in December 2002, one in Ann Arbor and the other in Detroit, recuperated both the least-known aspect of Hughes's varied career and the famous jazz composer's classical aspirations.

This text is taken from the typescript in the James P. Johnson Papers in Los Angeles. It has copious notes and some textual changes and additions in James P. Johnson's hand, as well as a few in Hughes's. It reinserts an aria, "Glad to See You Again," which is missing from the versions of the libretto in the Langston Hughes Papers at the Beinecke Library and at the Schomburg Centre for Research in Black Culture. It is the text used for the reconstruction of the opera by Dapogny.

Characters

THE ORGANIZER — Baritone
THE WOMAN — Contralto
THE OLD MAN — Bass
THE OLD WOMAN — Soprano
BROTHER DOSHER — Tenor
BROTHER BATES — Tenor
THE OVERSEER — Bass

SCENE: *Interior of a cabin on a backward plantation in the South. Night. The room is full of ragged sharecroppers, men and women.*
WOMEN: Where is that man?
MEN: He ought to be here now!
CHORUS: De organizer! Organizer!
WOMEN: Where is that man?
MEN: He ought to be here now!
CHORUS: De organizer! Organizer!
    Where is that man? He ought to be here now!
OLD WOMAN: Brother Dosher, it's gettin' late.
DOSHER: Sit down, sister, you got to wait.
OLD WOMAN: Brother, I'm tired of o' waitin'.
    He ought to be here now.
DOSHER: You might be tired o' waitin',
    But we got to wait anyhow!
    You didn't get your freedom in one day.
    We can't get a union by hurryin' this way.
OLD WOMAN: Well, then, where is that man?
CHORUS: He ought to be here now.
BATES: Yes, where is that man?
CHORUS: He ought to be here now.

BATES: Organizing a union is all right,
   But damn if I can organize all night!
OLD WOMAN: Yes, where is that man?
CHORUS: He ought to be here now!
   The good Lawd knows,
   He ought to be here now.
BATES: Yes, he ought to be here now!
DOSHER: Don't worry! He'll be here.
   He's a sharecropper, too,
   Just like me and you.
OLD MAN: Sharecroppers!
OLD WOMAN: Sharecroppers! . . . . . Oh!
CHORUS: Plantin', plowin', hoein'!
   Gettin' up early in de mornin'.
   Plowin', plantin', hoein'!
   Out in de fields at dawnin'.
   Always watchin' cotton growin'.
   Plowin', plantin', hoein'!
   Wonder where that cotton's goin'?
   Plantin', plowin', hoein'!
   Wonder where my life is goin'?
   Plowin', plantin', hoein',
   Wonder where my life is goin'?
OLD MAN: Just poor sharecroppers,
   That's all we is:
CHORUS: Plantin', plowin', hoein'!
DOSHER: Just poor sharecroppers, yes!
   But we ain't gonna be always.
   We gonna get together
   And end these hongry days.
   Folks, I've got them hongry blues—
   And nothin' in this world to lose.
   People's tellin' me to choose
      'Tween dyin',
      And lyin',
      And keepin' on cryin'—
   But I's tired o' them hongry blues.
   Listen! Ain't you heard the news?
   There's another thing to choose:

A brand new world, clean and fine,
Where nobody's hongry and
There's no color line!
A thing like that's worth
Anybody's dyin'—
Cause I ain't got a thing to lose
But them dog-gone hongry blues!
CHORUS: We ain't got a thing to lose
But them dog-gone hongry blues!
Not a dog-gone thing to lose
But them dog-gone hongry blues!
OLD WOMAN: I done washed so many clothes
My hands is white as snow.
Done got to de place that I
Don't want to wash no more.
I'm goin' up to heaven,
Say, good Lawd, here am I!
BATES: But, Sister Mary, de Lawd's gonna say:
You can't come in here till you die.
CHORUS: Oh, Sister Mary de Lawd's gonna say
You can't come in here till you die!
OLD WOMAN: Well, I've got them hongry blues.
CHORUS: But nothin' in this world to lose!
DOSHER: Folks, ain't you heard de news.
There's another thing to choose:
A brand new world, clean and fine,
Where nobody's hongry and
There's no color line—
A thing like that's worth
Anybody's dyin'—
CHORUS: Cause we ain't got a thing to lose
But them dog-gone hongry blues!
OLD WOMAN: Where is that man? He ought to be here now.
OLD MAN: Yes, where is that man? Where is that man?
BATES: Where is that man? Where is that man?
OLD MAN: Maybe I better go and take a look once more.
DOSHER: Shade de light, brother, 'fore you open de door.
OLD WOMAN: Yes, shade that light, so's the boss won't see.
BATES: And when you hits de pike, walk quietly.

OLD MAN: I'll walk quietly.
 But that man, which way'll he come?
 From de East or from de West?
DOSHER: He's comin' from de West,
 Where de Union's best.
  (A WOMAN's voice giving the password outside)
WOMAN: Jerico! . . . . . Jerico!
CHORUS: Shsss-sss-ss-s! Who can that be?
WOMAN: Jerico!
DOSHER: One!
WOMAN: Jerico!
DOSHER: Two!
WOMAN: Jerico!
DOSHER: Three!
 Then she's due to be!
 Open de door, let's see.
  (The OLD MAN opens the door. The WOMAN enters, bringing
  leaflets.)
WOMAN: Folks, it's me!
DOSHER: Yes, she's due to be!
 She brings us news about that man.
 And something here for us in her hand.
CHORUS: Strange woman, where is that man?
OLD WOMAN: That organizing man?
CHORUS: Yes, where is that man?
WOMAN: That man is comin' by a secret way.
 That man is comin' all alone.
 That man is like de giant Goliath[3]
 What threw that mighty stone.
 Cause he's de organizer!
CHORUS: He's de organizer! He's de organizer!
WOMAN: That man, he travels on de wings of song.
 He travels on de air.
 He travels like a cloud by night.
 That man is everywhere
 Cause he's de organizer!
CHORUS: He's de organizer! Organizer!
WOMAN: He's gonna help us build a union,
 Build it of white and black,
 Cause de people that works in de fields all day

Is tired of de landlords on our back.

Yes. We people that works in de fields all day.

CHORUS: Yes, we's tired of de landlords on our backs.

WOMAN: Folks, I bring you leaflets!

Folks, you read 'em well.

This little bit of paper here's

Got a lot to tell.

It says:

Ten thousand bales of cotton to de landlord!

How much was ours?

Ten thousand acres of cane to de big boss!

How much was ours?

A million water melons to the de market!

How much was ours?

How can we get them things

That should be ours?

Here, take this little leaflet, folks,

And read it well.

This little bit of paper's got

A lot to tell.

OLD MAN: What does it say?

CHORUS: How can we get them things that should be ours?

OLD WOMAN: Which is de way?

BATES: Them things we plant and plow and hoe for

Underneath these southern skies?

DOSHER: How can we make a living?

WOMAN: Organize!

CHORUS: Organize! . . . . . Organize!

OLD WOMAN: This here little leaflet says, Organize!

CHORUS: Organize! . . . . . Organize!

O-R-G-A–N-I-Z-E!

O-R-G-A–N-I-Z-E!

OLD MAN: Who ever wrote this paper sure must be wise!

CHORUS: Cause this here little leaflet says ORGANIZE!

OLD WOMAN: But where is our man?

BATES: Yes, where is that man?

OLD MAN: Maybe something's happened to our man?

OLD WOMAN: Woman, now you tell us where is that man?

WOMAN: He'll be here soon.

He travels on de air.

DOSHER: He travels like a cloud by night.
    That man is everywhere.
WOMAN: He'll be here.
OLD WOMAN: He's your man?
WOMAN: Yes, he's my man. I love him, too.
OLD WOMAN: But ain't you scared for your man?
WOMAN: No, he'll be here soon. He's coming to you.
    He's helping us all. And I can't be selfish
    About him. Of course, sometimes I miss him because
    My man's an organizer.
    My man's an organizer.
    He moves from place to place.
    I guess I wouldn't be human—
    If I didn't miss his loving face.
    So I admit:
    Sometimes I'm lonely when he's gone away,
    But I keep thinking there will come a day
    When this man of mine will do
    All the things he's wanted to,
    And the better world he's dreamed of will come true.
    Then what will it matter all these
    Days we've spent apart,
    There'll be a future bright
    Blooming in my heart,
    All the poor folks in the world
    Will be poor no more,
    For my man's an organizer and
    That's what he's working for.
    And although I'm lonely when he's gone away from me,
    Tomorrow he'll be with me and tomorrow we'll be free,
    You and I, my man and me, we'll be free!
OLD WOMAN: I believes you. You sure do love him.
    But when's he comin' here.
OLD MAN: But we can't wait. It's gettin' late!
BATES: We got to go.
WOMAN: Listen!
        (A MAN's voice heard without giving the password)
ORGANIZER: Jerico! . . . . . Jerico!
DOSHER: Now, I reckon you'll stay.
BATES: Yes, I'll stay! Get out o' my way.

ORGANIZER: Jerico!

DOSHER: One!

ORGANIZER: Jerico!

DOSHER: Two!

ORGANIZER: Jerico!

DOSHER: Three!

    It's de organizer! Glory be!

CHORUS: It's de organizer! Yes, it's he!

    It's de organizer! Thank God a-Mighty!

    It's de organizer! It's him alrighty!

    Lawd! De organizer! Thank God a-Mighty!

    It's de organizer!

        (The door opens and the ORGANIZER enters.)

DOSHER: Jackson, where you been so long?

ORGANIZER: I been organizing.

DOSHER: Where you been organizing?

ORGANIZER: Been way cross Mississippi organizing.

DOSHER: Who you been organizing?

ORGANIZER: I been organizing black folks!

    And organizing white folks!

    And organizing peoples on de land!

    I been tellin' everybody

    In de cotton and de cane fields,

    Been tellin' everybody they's a man!

OLD MAN: And de white folks, what they sayin'?

ORGANIZER: De poor white folks is with us.

    De rich white folks is mad.

WOMAN: But, baby, how you feelin'?

ORGANIZER: Lawd, I'm feelin' mighty glad!

CHORUS: Mighty glad! Mighty glad!

ORGANIZER: Oh, I'm feelin' mighty glad!

        (As he mounts a box to speak.)

CHORUS: De organizer's here and

    We's feelin' mighty glad!

    Mighty glad! Mighty glad!

    Yes, de organizer's here and

    We feelin' mighty glad!

        (Mighty glad! Mighty glad! continues softly as the WOMAN lifts
        her voice in praise and love.)

WOMAN: Oh! Ma man is like John Henry.

My man is big and strong.
Nothin' in this world can scare him.
Nothin' makes my man do wrong.
Yes, ma man is like John Henry.
He's a hero in de land.
And folks deep in troubles
Comes a lookin' for ma man.
Yes, they comes a lookin' for ma man,
Cause ma man is like John Henry 'cept he's
Put his hammer down.
Now, just like John Henry, he
Goes from town to town.
Oh! Ma man is like John Henry, but he
Don't drive steel no more.
What ma man is doin' now is
Organizin' poor—
When he gets done organizin' we
Can take this world in hand.
Cause ma man is like John Henry and
John Henry was a man!
CHORUS: John Henry was a man, Lawd!
John Henry was a man!
ORGANIZER: Folks, you is hongry!
Folks, you need bread!
What you gonna do, folks?
CHORUS: Get mad! Get mad!
ORGANIZER: Folks, that ain't de way!
Folks, that ain't right.
The way we get what we all need's
Unite! . . . . . Unite!
You don't get mad at de rain, do you?
You don't get mad at de sun?
Ain't no use to get mad then
At a big boss with a gun!
De rain you stores in cisterns.
De sun gives de berries their juice.
De union can take any old boss
And turn him every way but loose!
When we get a big strong union, folks,
A union of black and white,

They'll be more difference in this old South
Then there is twixt day and night.
So to organize is right!
CHORUS: Yes, to organize is right!
Right! . . . . . Right! . . . . . Right! . . . . . Right!
Yes, to organize is right.
ORGANIZER: Sharecroppers all over Dixie,
Farmhands and tenants as well,
De union is de only way
To free ourselves from hell.
CHORUS: To free ourselves from hell!
Yes, to free ourselves from hell!
You don't get mad at de rain, do you?
You don't get mad at de sun?
Ain't no use to get mad then
At de big boss with a gun!
De rain you stores in cisterns.
De sun gives de berries their juice.
De union can take any old boss
And turn him every way but loose!
When we get a big strong union, folks,
A union of black and white,
They'll be more difference in this old South
Then there is twixt day and night.
So to organize is right!
Yes, to organize is right!
ORGANIZER: Then, Brother Dosher, take de chair,
And let's get de meetin' started here.
OLD WOMAN: Yes, let's get de meetin' started here.
> (*As the others begin to re-arrange their seats and assemble for the meeting, the WOMAN and the ORGANIZER draw near to each other and embrace for the first time.*)
ORGANIZER: You know I ain't much[4]
For talkin' about love,
But what I want to tell you now
Is true as the stars above:
Glad to see you again!
I been a long ways away.
Glad to see you again,
That's all I can say.

If I tried to tell you all that's in my heart,
Babe, there wouldn't be no way for me to start.
It would take all night
And all day tomorrow, too—
Just glad to see you again,
So I'll let that do.
Plenty of sweet words I could whisper in your ear,
But there ain't no sweet words sweet enough for you, dear.
So even if I said 'em,
I'd say 'em in vain.
Just lemme kiss you, baby,
Glad to see you again.

> *(This is repeated in a duet together, and by now the others are ready to start the meeting.)*

ORGANIZER: You know I ain't much for talkin' about love—
But what I want to tell you now is true as the stars above:
WOMAN: Glad to see you again!
I been a long ways away.
ORGANIZER: Glad to see you again—
That's all I can say.
WOMAN: If I tried to tell you
All that's in my heart,
ORGANIZER: Babe, there wouldn't be no
Way for you to start.
WOMAN: It would take all night
And all day tomorrow, too—
Just glad to see you again,
ORGANIZER: So I'll let that do.
WOMAN: Plenty of sweet words
I could whisper in your ear,
ORGANIZER: There ain't no sweet words
Sweet enough for you, my dear.
WOMAN: So even if I said 'em,
I'd say 'em in vain—
ORGANIZER: You'd say 'em in vain
WOMAN: Just lemme kiss you, baby,
TOGETHER: Glad to see you again!
We're together again!
OLD MAN: Brother Dosher, I wants de floor.
I have a word to say.

DOSHER: Wait a minute, Brother John,
   Till de meetin's underway.
OLD MAN: Well, when de meetin's underway,
   I has a word to say. And it is this:
   The sooner we on this plantation organizes,
   the better, because the way things is going now,
   if we don't organize, we is gwine to get put off,
   and if we get put off we's got no place to go,
   and no work, and to get relief is hell, and I
   don't want relief nohow! I likes to work, so let's
   get together and organize and protect ourselves
   and these here fields and this here state and our
   country, because. . . . .
      (*Loud shots are heard outside.*)
OLD WOMAN: Uh-oh! That's de overseer!
BATES: De overseer!
DOSHER: Put out that light!
ORGANIZER: Keep quiet! Don't run!
   Let him in if he knocks!
   We might as well face him now
   And tell him what we've made up our minds to.
CHORUS: Face him! Tell him! Yes, that's true!
      (*A commanding voice is heard outside.*)
OVERSEER: You John! . . . . . You Mary!
   You must think I can't see that light!
   You'll hold no meeting there tonight!
OLD WOMAN: That's de overseer!
OVERSEER: You-all croppers think you're wise
   Sneaking off to the woods to organize!
      (*Knocking loudly.*)
   Open up that door!
OLD MAN: Come in, if you want to come in!
OVERSEER: (*Kicking in door*)
   I'll come in all right!
   What's going on in here tonight?
ORGANIZER: We's organizing!
OVERSEER: What? . . . . . That's a damned disgrace!
   You'll have no union on this place!
   Don't you know the landlord don't allow no organizing here?
CHORUS: What?

OVERSEER: The landlord don't allow no organizing here![5]
  I've got my whip, got my gun—
  You'll get no organizing done!
  The landlord don't allow no organizing here!
CHORUS: But there's gonna be some organizing here!
  Yes, there is gonna be some organizing here!
  We don't care what de landlord 'lows
  We gonna organize anyhow.
  There is gonna be some organizing here!
OVERSEER: What? What's that? What's that I hear?
CHORUS: We said there's gonna be some organizing here.
  Yes, there's gonna be some organizing here.
ORGANIZER: In spite of your whip
  Spite of your gun,
  We gonna get some organizing done!
CHORUS: There'll be some organizing done right here!
  Yes, there'll be some organizing done right here now!
OVERSEER: Who are you dogs?
  Who's talking back to me?
CHORUS: Look in Alabama, man, and you will see!
  Look in Mississippi! Look in Tennessee!
  Take a look at Dixieland and you will see!
ORGANIZER: (*Lighting up his own face*)
  Take a look at me!
      (*Others light up their faces, too, until the OVERSEER is sur-
      rounded by a sea of faces glowing in the night.*)
OTHERS: And me!
  And me!
  And me!
OVERSEER: (*Cracking his whip angrily*)
  But I said there'd be no organizing here!
  I mean there'll be no organizing here!
CHORUS: You may crack your whip!
  Shoot your gun—
  But we's made up our minds
  To get some organizing done.
OVERSEER: I said NO!
      (*He shoots four times. Quickly, the SHARECROPPERS surround
      him and take his gun.*)

ORGANIZER: All the bullets in the world
    Can't shoot me!
OTHERS: Nor me!
    Nor me!
    Nor me!
CHORUS: We're four million croppers
    Determined to be free!
OLD MAN: Mary, take that gun and put it on de shelf.
    (To the OVERSEER)
    If you want to 'tend this meeting,
    You behave yourself!
ORGANIZER: We've got too much business here tonight
    To be interrupted by outsiders
    Who want to start a fight.
    Brother John, while you're over in that corner,
    Bring the flag along.
OLD MAN: I will.
    This here flag I carried at San Juan Hill.
    My son followed it in France when he was killed.
ORGANIZER: It's your flag, Mister OVERSEER.
    And my flag, too.
    So listen what us croppers have
    To say, to say to you:
VOICE: I've chopped de cotton all my life long, —Yes!
CHORUS: To want a little freedom now can't be wrong. —No!
VOICE: I've worked in de sun all day long, —True!
CHORUS: So to want a little freedom now can't be wrong. —True!
VOICE: I've plowed with old Jennie all my life long. —Yes!
CHORUS: To want a little freedom now can't be wrong. —No!
VOICE: I got up at sunrise all my life long. —True!
CHORUS: To want a little freedom now can't be wrong. —True!
VOICE: Plowing, planting, hoeing, all life long.
CHORUS: To want a little freedom now can't be wrong.
OVERSEER: You-all say *freedom?*
    Don't look at me.
    I work for the landlord, too.
    I ain't free!
WOMAN: Then take this here leaflet.
    Read it and be wise.

If you want to be free,
Organize!
CHORUS: Organize! Organize!
If you want to be free,
Organize!
OVERSEER: How many's in this union?
CHORUS: Everybody here!
OVERSEER: I'm going back and tell the landlord.
OLD WOMAN: Huh! We don't care!
ORGANIZER: All we want is, be sure to get it right!
Tell him we organized a UNION here tonight!
CHORUS: Yes, we organized a union here tonight!
OVERSEER: Lemme out of here!
(He rushes out)
CHORUS: We organized a union here tonight!
(EVERYBODY dances, joins hands, exultantly with joy. Happy movement. Large signs appear, SHARECROPPER'S UNION.)
MEN: Fight! . . . . . Fight!
WOMEN: Right! . . . . . Right!
CHORUS: We organized a union here tonight!
CURTAIN

The Barrier
An Opera

1950
Libretto by Langston Hughes
Music by Jan Meyerowitz

In a piece he prepared for the *New York Times,* Hughes recollected that when the Jewish-refugee composer Jan Meyerowitz, who had already set a number of his poems to music, asked him for a libretto, his play *Mulatto* "immediately came to mind. But I had sworn never to have anything more to do with the non-commercial theatre since lecturing and teaching, I had found, met the demands of the landlord so much better. But Meyerowitz began to work on the music even before I had made up my mind to transpose the play into musical words. So persuasive were his melodies that I succumbed . . . [M]y lawyer . . . said, 'What! Another opera!' And in his voice was not delight, but despair. I said, 'But this will be a very exciting one.' "[1]

First staged at Columbia University's Opera Workshop, opening on January 18, 1950, for ten performances, *The Barrier* was a "stunning success."[2] With two black leads, Muriel Rahn and Mattiwilda Dobbs as the mother and sister, Robert Goss as Robert, and Paul Elmer as Colonel Norwood, the opera seemed headed for Broadway. However, a Washington, D.C., production the following September met with critical hostility, generated more by the opera's story than by its musical or literary merits. The Broadway production, which opened on November 12, 1950, received mixed reviews and closed two days later. Yet over the next decade *The Barrier* would be revived several times in New York, successfully performed in Italy and Japan, and recorded by Radio VARA, Hilversum, in the Netherlands.

According to a note on the typescript in the Langston Hughes Papers, this text is as scored for the Columbia Workshop production.

Singers

WILLIAM (Baritone)
SALLY (Soprano)
LIVONIA (Soprano)
SAM (Tenor)
NORWOOD (Baritone)
CORA (Soprano)
HIGGINS (Tenor)
ROBERT (Baritone)
YOUNG CORA (Soprano)

Dancers

YOUNG CORA
YOUNG NORWOOD
THE BRIDE

Actors

TALBOT, Overseer at Albamar
STOREKEEPER, at Norwood's Commissary
UNDERTAKER, from a nearby town
UNDERTAKER'S HELPER
THE MOB: Off-Stage Voices

Characters

COLONEL THOMAS NORWOOD: Plantation owner, a still vigorous
  man of about sixty, nervous, refined, quick-tempered and command-
  ing; a widower who is the father of four living mulatto children by
  his Negro housekeeper.
CORA LEWIS: A brown woman in her forties who has kept the house
  and been the mistress of COLONEL NORWOOD for some thirty
  years.
SALLY LEWIS: The seventeen year old daughter.

FRED HIGGINS: A close friend of COLONEL NORWOOD's, a country politician; fat and elderly, conventionally Southern.

WILLIAM LEWIS: The eldest son of CORA LEWIS and the COLONEL; an easy-going, soft-spoken Mulatto of twenty-eight.

ROBERT LEWIS: Eighteen, the youngest boy, strong and well-built; a light Mulatto with ivory-yellow skin and proud thin features like his father; as tall as the COLONEL, with the same grey-blue eyes, but with curly black hair instead of brown; of a fiery, impetuous temper—proud, immature and willful—presenting the circumstances of his birth and the color line of the South.

SAM: An old Negro retainer, a personal servant of the COLONEL'S.

LIVONIA: A Negro servant girl.

TALBOT: A white overseer.

The action takes place on a single day in early September, Georgia, U.S.A., circa 1920.

Prologue: Noon.

Act I: Early Afternoon

Act II: Scene 1. Sunset.

Scene 2. Night.

Prologue

SETTING: *Only a juke box is seen, garish in the darkness, its harsh wavering green, red and yellow lights varying in intensity, marking its blatant outlines. A record is playing—a high weird blues-like female voice. As the lyric stops, the lights reveal that the juke box is a part of the interior of a small-town General Store with a shabby counter at one side for ice cream and soft drinks.*

ACTION: *Sitting on a stool, a young WHITE MAN is drinking a root beer. Other WHITE MEN loll about, including the STOREKEEPER of Albamar Plantation, and the local UNDERTAKER. It is a hot afternoon, so the UNDERTAKER is licking an ice cream cone, while the clerk, MISS GRAY, is wrapping some merchandise. But these details are seen after the juke box has ceased its song. At first in the dark only its vari-colored lights are visible as the record spins.*

JUKE BOX: Sometimes there's a wind in the Georgia dusk,
    That cries and cries and cries,

It's lonely pity through the Georgia dusk,
That veils what the darkness hides.

Sometimes there's blood in the Georgia dusk,
Blood from a streak of the sun.
A lonely trickle in the Georgia dusk.
Whose blood? . . . . Everyone's.

Sometimes a wind in the Georgia dusk,
Scatters words like seeds.
That sprout their bitter barriers,
Where the sunset slowly bleeds . . .
  (LIGHTS up full, revealing group in store)
STOREKEEPER: Out where we are, it sure is a little cooler than here in town.
UNDERTAKER: Yes, but the mosquitoes bother you at night.
STOREKEEPER: Rather have mosquitoes than this heat, Undertaker. Come on, gimme my stuff—till my order comes. I got to get back to my commissary. Them darkies'll be raising sand if I run out of tobacco.
UNDERTAKER: Looks like to me darkies are getting worse and worse since the war's been over—sassing white folks and trying to set their own wages.
STOREKEEPER: We don't have much trouble with 'em out at Albamar —I mean them that works under Talbot. Of course, them that works at the Big House—
  (He shrugs his shoulders. As the WHITE MEN talk, a ragged but clean young NEGRO enters and timidly stops a few feet from the counter.)
UNDERTAKER: Norwood's damn lucky he's got Talbot for an overseer. I hope he knows it.
STOREKEEPER: I been in charge of Norwood's commissary store for ten years, sir, and I know before he hired Talbot, his cotton crop wasn't half what it is now.
  (The NEGRO comes to the end of the counter and waits patiently)
He knows how to keep 'em working, all right. Like me, he's worked on mighty near every big plantation in Georgia.
  (Taking his package and preparing to leave)
Thank you, Miss Gray! I'll be seeing you-all, folks. Take it easy, "Mortician." We call 'em Undertakers out in the country.
UNDERTAKER: Well, whatever you call me, I'm at your service.

STOREKEEPER: "Burial with a smile," heh?

 (Laughter)

No offense, just kidding your type of service. I hope you keep busy—so long as you don't service me!

UNDERTAKER: I can't complain about business—somebody kicks the bucket every week.

 (General laughter)

STOREKEEPER: Well, goodbye!

OTHERS: So long!

 (As the STOREKEEPER leaves, MISS GRAY, without moving, calls to the NEGRO at the end of the counter)

MISS GRAY: What do you want, Eddie?

NEGRO: A box of White Mule Snuff, please, M'am, Miss Gray. It's for Granny Longshaw.

 (As she hands him the snuff)

MISS GRAY: Is your Granny still taking in washing?

NEGRO: Yes, M'am, Miss Gray! Yes, M'am, eighty-two years old and still washing.

MISS GRAY: Well, I know she's thankful she's got work to do.

NEGRO: Yes, M'am! Good evenin', M'am.

MISS GRAY: 'Bye, Eddie.

 (As the NEGRO reaches the door, the WHITE MAN at the soda fountain calls him)

MAN ON STOOL: Hey, come back here, boy! I hear tell you can sing the blues right good. Hit us up a tune, there!

NEGRO: Yas, sah, I sings but you know Mr. Higgins don't—

UNDERTAKER: Then tell us about rolling them lucky sevens, heh, boy?

NEGRO: Yes, sah! Sho can roll 'em, sah!

 (He demonstrates, snaps his fingers)

Baby needs new shoes! Yas, sah!

 (The WHITE MEN laugh as the NEGRO slyly ingratiatingly plays for them the part expected of him, even to the traditional "good natured" grin)

WHITE MEN: Ha! Ha! Ha! Ha! Ha!

 (Suddenly the laughter dies—BERT enters. The quietness ties itself into a knot. The last record on the juke box has run out. All eyes watch the young Mulatto as he approaches the soda fountain)

BERT: A root beer, please.

 (In a slow southern drawl, MISS GRAY replies)

MISS GRAY: You just wait until I get around to it.

(There is an awkward pause, then one of the MEN starts ribbing the NEGRO again)

UNDERTAKER: Boy, lemme hear that one about how you got your name. Who did you say your father is?

NEGRO: My daddy's name is stacks, sah!

UNDERTAKER: Stacks, who?

NEGRO: Stacks dollars, sah.

UNDERTAKER: What does that make your name?

NEGRO: Small change.

WHITE MEN: Ha! Ha! Ha! Ha! Ha! Ha!

(But the laughter trails off into unfriendly silence as BERT approaches the juke box and is about to put a coin in it. MISS GRAY sees him and says matter-of-factly)

MISS GRAY: Bert, you know you can't play that juke box.

(BERT turns)

BERT: No?

MISS GRAY: No, Mr. Higgins don't like for Negras to lounge around here. Just buy, and go on out. Negras don't play records. Just buy . . . and go . . . I'm fixin' your root beer now.

(MISS GRAY mixes a drink in a paper carton, puts a top on it, slips the container into a paper bag, and hands it to him. But while she is ringing up the change, BERT takes the carton from the bag and places it on the counter. As she gives him his change, she looks at him, puzzled)

Of co'se you're gonna take your root beer outside, Bert?

BERT: No, Miss Gray, I'm going to drink it here.

(More in astonishment than anger, MISS GRAY says)

MISS GRAY: Why, Bert, you know colored folks can't eat and drink in this store. This soda fountain's for white folks.

(But suddenly her tone changes as she remembers)

Have you been up north in school too long, boy? I do declare, I'm beginning to believe you're a little too smart for your own good.

UNDERTAKER: You see what I told you about 'em—since the war. Sassy! Forward!

(Timidly, the NEGRO cautions)

NEGRO: Bert, we colored folks takes ours out the side door in the alley when we wants a drink. Maybe you forgets?

MAN ON STOOL: He must of forgot!

BERT: No, I haven't forgotten—My money's as good as a white man's any day.

(BERT takes the top off the container)
MISS GRAY: I say take it outside, Bert.
BERT: No, Miss Gray.
  (He drinks. Bedlam breaks loose)
UNDERTAKER: Well, I'm be god-damned!
MISS GRAY: Mr. Higgins! Mr. Higgins!
MAN ON STOOL: That nigger sassed a white woman!
UNDERTAKER: I tell you about them smart sons of bitches.
MISS GRAY: Mr. Higgins! Mr. Higgins!
MAN ON STOOL: Won't say "Yes, M'am" to a white woman!
BYSTANDER: That boy don't know his place!
UNDERTAKER: Give 'em an inch and they'll take an ell.
  (During the hubbub, the store owner, HIGGINS, enters. To him
  MISS GRAY explains what happened. He turns on BERT, shaking
  with flustered indignation)
MISS GRAY: . . . . . and he sassed me!
HIGGINS: Just who in hell do you think you are, Bert?
BERT: You know who I am, Mr. Higgins.
HIGGINS: Yes, you're a forward sassy nigger!
BERT: I am not, sir.
UNDERTAKER: Listen to that, goddamn it!
BYSTANDER: You better watch out!
HIGGINS: You impudent black rascal!
BERT: You know I'm not all colored, Mr. Higgins.
HIGGINS: You're Cora Lewis' boy.
BERT: Yes, Cora Lewis is my mother—
  But Colonel Norwood is my father.
  I'm Colonel Norwood's son.
  (Pandemonium as the WHITE MEN, infuriated, turn on BERT.
  Blackout. But their fury is drowned by the music, which continues
  until the curtain rises on Act I)

Act I

SETTING: *The living room of the Big House at Albamar, a plantation in*
  Georgia. There are double doors leading to the porch and, at each side
  of the doors, tall windows with lace curtains. On one side of the room
  a broad flight of stairs leads to the second floor. Beneath the stairs, a
  doorway leading to the dining room and kitchen; at the foot of the steps,

a door to the library. The room is furnished with out-dated elegance, a crystal chandelier, a large old-fashioned rug, a marble-topped table and upholstered chairs. On the wall at the turn of the stairs there is a large painting of NORWOOD's wife of his youth. There is a decanter and glasses on a small cabinet. It is a very clean, still charming, but now somewhat shabby room. The windows are raised and the afternoon sunlight streams in.

ACTION: *As the curtain rises, SALLY, dressed for travelling, except for hat and jacket, stands near the door taking a last affectionate look at the landscape outside. Across the room, a servant girl, LIVONIA, is dusting. WILLIAM runs an old-fashioned carpet sweeper.*

QUARTET

WILLIAM: September sunlight!
 Warm and hazy in the sunlight.
 What's out yonder lazy growing?
 Cotton all white.
  (SALLY looks about her lovingly)
SALLY: There's something about home, Livonia,
 No place as lovely as home, Livonia—
 These fields, the cotton all white,
 This house, so pretty and bright—
 There's something about home, Livonia.
  (LIVONIA stops her work)
LIVONIA: That's what you say, Sally,
 But if I ever got away, Sally,
 If I ever got the nerve to dare,
 If I ever got away somewhere,
 Believe me, girl, Livonia would stay!
 I'd like to see them city lights,
 I'd like to hear the jazz bands play.
 I'd like to wear fine city clothes—
 If I only could get away!
SALLY: It's peaceful here and quiet, Livonia.
  (SAM enters, scolding LIVONIA)
SAM: Ah-ha-aa-a-a! I know you wish that you
 Was lazing in the sunlight—
 But that sure ain't right.
 Dust them chair legs, wipe that table,

Don't get lazy, hazy, crazy,
From the sunlight.
(SAM looks toward the door annoyed)
Aw, my lands! Always something to spoil the day—Here comes that
old Overseer field-boss! Now, what do he want? Livonia, make haste
and get out of here! And you, Sally, better stop posing in that door
like white folks and go on upstairs and help your mama, sweating
and packing to make you ready to leave on time.
*(TALBOT enters. The GIRLS exit, half contemptuous of the
OVERSEER's presence)*
TALBOT: Say, you-all, where's Colonel Norwood? Is he anywhere
   around?
(SAM sing-songs his answer)
SAM: He's walking yonder in the sunlight,
WILLIAM: Looking at the fields and flowers.
SAM: All that's his'n—sure ain't ours—
BOTH: In the sunlight.
TALBOT: The Colonel better stay out of that sunlight—as hot as it is
   today. Hey, you, William! I need you down in the South patch.
SAM: William's helping me here in the house, Mr. Talbot—according
   to the Colonel's orders.
(WILLIAM exits, silently)
TALBOT: That burly young darkie'd do better pushing a hoe.
SAM: Maybe so, but my mind tells me the Colonel's gonna keep William
   right here in the big house from now on—cause Cora depends on
   William whilst the rest of her children is off getting educated.
TALBOT: If the Colonel spent more time thinking about his crops than
   he does educating niggers, he'd make some money out of Albamar.
SAM: It never comes into my head to criticize the Colonel, Mr. Talbot.
TALBOT: Who cares what comes into your thick skull? I ain't asking
   you nothing. I didn't come here for no lip out of you—
(He looks toward the kitchen)
Nor none of the rest of you sassy darkies up here living on the fat of
the land. . . .
*(The library door opens and COLONEL NORWOOD enters. In-
stantly TALBOT quiets down. He wipes his brow)*
Good morning, Colonel Norwood.
NORWOOD: Good morning, Talbot.
TALBOT: Sir, I come to see you about getting William to help out down
   in the South patch. I can use him.

NORWOOD: No trouble with the boll weevils this year, heh?

TALBOT: No, sir, that's why the cotton's ready for all hands. Add William to them I've got and—

> *(NORWOOD continues to ignore his request)*

NORWOOD: Do you think you and your storekeeper've got your commissary accounts in order so I can see them this evening? We haven't checked up lately.

TALBOT: We try to keep 'em in order, sir. Now about—

NORWOOD: Then suppose you come back around sundown. I'm kind of busy right now.

> *(Exit TALBOT, frowning. NORWOOD addresses SAM)*

Sam, I wish you'd get your cleaning done earlier from now on. I'd like to have a little privacy before the mornings are over.

SAM: Yes, sah.

NORWOOD: Tell Cora to come down here, Sam.

SAM: Yes, sah.

> *(SAM goes upstairs for CORA as the COLONEL glances at his watch. CORA enters, looking down affectionately from the stairs)*

DUET

CORA: Colonel Tom,
> Now that the heat of noon is blazing,
> Why don't you lie down a spell
> And take a little nap
> And have a rest?

NORWOOD: I am not tired, Cora.

CORA: Than let me fix you a nice cool drink.

NORWOOD: I am not thirsty, Cora.
> *(Pause)*
> Does that child of yours
> Mean to leave here this afternoon?

CORA: Yes, sir, I'se getting her ready now,
> 'Course, she wants to tell you goodbye
> Before she leaves.

NORWOOD: Well, send her down here.
> Who is going to drive her to the railroad?

CORA: Her brother, Bert.
> He ought to be back here most
> Any minute now with the car.

NORWOOD: What? Ought to be back here?
    Who gave him permission
    To be driving off in the middle of the morning?
CORA: Nobody, sir. . . . but. . . .
NORWOOD: But, what? . . . . Cora,
    Don't you think we could have
    A little peace in this house again?
    That son of yours has given us
    Nothing but trouble since he's been back here.
    I'm telling you, he worries me!
    Just because I've been damn fool enough
    To send him off to school for five years,
    Does Bert think he can refuse to work
    And loaf around showing off his education. . . .
CORA: But, Colonel Tom—
NORWOOD: I know what you're going to say—
    I don't give a damn whose child he is!
    There's no darkie on this plantation
    Going to disobey me.
    I'll put Bert in that field to work.
    I'll tell the overseer. . . .
CORA: But, Colonel Tom,
    Don't be so angry with my child.
    He don't mean nothing—
    He's just young and smart.
    He's only kinda careless
    Like my mother said you used to be
    When you was eighteen.
    Don't be angry with my chile—
    Sir, he's forgotten what the South is like.
    It broke his heart—coming here—
    When his hand reached for yours
    And you refused to give him your hand,
    Colonel Tom!
NORWOOD: But don't you remember, my Cora,
    I've shared all my pleasures with you.
    But this world we're living in
    Is so far from paradise.
    And I did not make this world.
CORA: But we've been happy here

In this house all these years,
Days have passed on sparrows' wings
So full of happiness.
Now we're old, let us keep it as it was.
NORWOOD: It's true what you say, Cora,
But here things don't work that way.
My father sat in this chair,
My grandfather before him, in peace,
But now I sit here puzzled,
Worried—and alone.
CORA: Not alone. . . .
NORWOOD: Cora, get on upstairs.
CORA: Does you still be in the mind
To tell Sally goodbye?
NORWOOD: Of course, surely, send her down here.
*(CORA exits up the stairs, passing SAM as he enters and timidly
approaches the COLONEL)*
SAM: 'Scuse me, please sah!
(NORWOOD ignores him)
'Scuse me, please sah!
NORWOOD: Yes?
SAM: Sir, I wanted to ask you is it all right to bring that old big trunk
what you give to Sally down by the front steps? We ain't been able
to tote it down them narrow little back steps, sah. The trunk is that
wide and. . . .
NORWOOD: No other way?
(SAM shakes his head)
Then pack it on through to the back, quick! Don't let me catch you
going through that front door.
(Aside but slightly jovial)
Give a darkie an inch and he'll take an el.
Give the devil a finger and he'll bite off your arm.
(As the trunk goes down)
Do you hear me? Don't let them use that front door, heh? No one of
my colored folks ever dared to use that front door! And tell them to
watch out what would happen if I ever see them do it! You hear me?
SAM: Yes, sah!
NORWOOD: You hear me?
SAM: Yes, sah!
NORWOOD: *(Mocking SAM)* "Yes, sah! Yes, sah!"
You're mighty glib with them, "Yes, sah's."

SAM: Yes, sah!
>   (*The COLONEL smiles*)
NORWOOD: All right, Sam. You haven't changed.
>   (*SAM exits*)
>   But no Negro's going to come in my front door.
>   It would be myself I'd be afraid of
>   If I ever should see it.
>>   (*CORA comes to top of steps with SALLY, then returns to her room. SALLY comes shyly down the stairs and approaches her father. She is dressed in a little country-style coatsuit, ready for travelling. COLONEL NORWOOD gazes down at her without saying a word as she comes meekly toward him, half frightened*)
SALLY: I just wanted to tell you goodbye,
>   Colonel Tom,
>   And thank you for letting me
>   Go back to school another year,
>   And for letting me work
>   Here in the house all summer
>   Where mama was!
>>   (*NORWOOD does not say a word*)
>   You been mighty nice to your—
>   I mean, to us colored children,
>   Letting my sister and me go off to school.
>   Mama says
>   You are the best white man in Georgia.
NORWOOD: Stand upright
>   And let me see how you look.
>   Yeah! Kinda grown,
>   Kinda grown and already womanish,
>   Quite womanish.
>   Do they teach you in that colored school
>   To have good manners,
>   Not to be afraid of work
>   And to respect white folks?
SALLY: Yes, sir.
NORWOOD: Well, that's good.
>   I'm thinking about you going up North
>   With your sister in a year or two.
SALLY: But I want to live down here with mama.
NORWOOD: No! You are getting too old
>   To be around here and too womanish.

Anyhow, I'm glad you and Martha
Turned out right well, yes.
You know I tried to do something
For those brothers of yours—
They've had lots of advantages,
Schooling, plenty to eat—
Nothing to worry about!
But William's stupid as an ox.
He's good for work, though.
Whereas Robert—
Just an impudent hard-headed, yellow young fool!
If he gives me any trouble,
I'll put Talbot on him.

SALLY: Please, sir,
Don't put the Overseer on Bert!
He was always the first in school.
He's so smart—

NORWOOD: Smart! That's just the trouble with him—
That boy is much too smart for his own good!
So you just hush.
(CORA enters with bundles and umbrella)

CORA: Colonel Tom, Sally ain't got much time now.
Come on, chile, Bert is here.
Everybody's waiting at the back door
To say goodbye.

NORWOOD: While you are riding with him,
You better put some sense in his head,
And tell him that I want to see him
As soon as he gets back here.

SALLY: Yes, sir, I'll tell him.

NORWOOD: Sally, whose car is that coming up the drive?

SALLY: Mr. Higgins' car, Colonel Tom.
Reckon he's coming to see you.

NORWOOD: Hurry up out of this front room
While I open the door for Mr. Higgins.
(NORWOOD gives SALLY a cross)
Here's a little present for you.

SALLY: Oh, thank you, Colonel Tom!
Look, mama, it's gold!

CORA: It's beautiful!

NORWOOD: It's very old. . . .
 It's a holy cross to bless you
 On your journey.
SALLY: Mama, it's gold!
CORA: It's beautiful—and it's gold!
SALLY: I'll wear this chain around my neck—
 And at night I'll sleep with
 This cross right on my heart.
NORWOOD: Write your mother, little Sally.
CORA: And remember Colonel Tom.
SALLY: Oh, yes, I will remember!
 Goodbye, Colonel Tom!
NORWOOD: Yes, yes. Goodbye. Get on now.
  (SALLY and CORA exit)
 Well, well! Howdy do, Fred.
 Come in, come in!
  (HIGGINS enters)
 How's the rheumatiz today?
 Women or licker or heat must have made it worse,
 From the looks of your speed.
HIGGINS: I'm in no mood for fooling, Tom. Not now!
NORWOOD: What's the matter?
 But first, permit me to offer you a drink.
  *(Offstage FRIENDS bid SALLY farewell as NORWOOD mixes
  drinks)*

SONG

NEGROES: Little girl, goodbye!
 Happy trip to you!
 Goodbye, Sally girl, goodbye!
 Old train's gonna take,
 Gonna take you a-way!
 Have a good trip! So long!
HIGGINS: Tom, listen to that! What kind of crazy coons have you here?
 Sounds like a black baptist picnic to me.
NORWOOD: They're seeing Sally off to school, and I don't mind them
 enjoying themselves sometimes.
HIGGINS: You're too easy on them, Tom, and it's not going to do
 anybody any good. Why, your darkies are getting a better education

than most white children in this county. And you allow that young black buck of yours to drive your new car. It's unheard of! That's what I came to talk to you about. That boy's not gonna be around here long, not the way he's acting. The white folks in town'll see to that—and I don't know what good the jail would do him, once he got in there. I was thinking how *weak* the doors to that jail are—after what happened this morning.

NORWOOD: What the hell!

(*CORA enters to pass a tray of cookies*)

HIGGINS: You haven't heard? Why, it's all over town already. He came strutting into my store and told my clerk, Miss Gray, to give him a bottle of root beer. Do you think he took it outside to drink it like the rest of the niggers do when they're thirsty? No! Bert stood right there at the counter like a white man and drunk that soda. When Miss Gray told him to take his root beer out in the alley, Bert said, No, his money was as good as a white man's any day. He didn't see why a Negra couldn't drink a soda in a public place. Facts is, he sassed Miss Gray! And in front of all them folks in my store, he said he wasn't all colored nohow.

(*CORA exits worried*)

Said he was Colonel Norwood's son! Boasting to the white folks standing there—and they didn't like that! Besides insulting a white woman!

NORWOOD: Ah! That ape! I'll show him! I—I—

(*He rises angrily*)

ARIETTA

HIGGINS: Tom, you get excited too easy for warm weather.
  Don't show black folks they got you going.
  Keep calm—then you command.
  You should have married again.
  Tom, you should have married again.
  In this big old lonely house,
  Tom, you should have married again.

NORWOOD: Reckon you're right, Fred,
  But it's too late to marry again now.
    (*Changes the subject*)
  I'll ride down with you to the South field.
  Let's take a look at the crops.

HIGGINS: All right with me.

NORWOOD: Cora!
    (CORA enters)
CORA: Colonel Tom?
NORWOOD: I want to see that boy of yours when I get back.
CORA: Yes, sir, I'll have him waiting here.
    (HIGGINS and NORWOOD exit as CORA's anxiety grows)
    William! William!
    (WILLIAM enters)

DUET

WILLIAM: What's the matter, mama?
CORA: Oh, I'se scared to death!
    William! William!
    Scared to death for my boy!
    I tried, I tried to tell him.
    I'se scared to death!
WILLIAM: My brother is a damn fool!
    Don't seem like he knows nothing.
    Sho, he'll make it bad for all of us down here.
CORA: I tried and tried to tell him.
    I'se scared! I'se scared to death!
WILLIAM: Bert's always made trouble for us
    Even when he was little—
    Like that time when he was seven.
CORA: Oh, you remember!
WILLIAM: He run in the horse stables
    When the Colonel showed his horses
    To fine white folks from in town.
    Bert run in and called him, "Papa,"
    Called the Colonel, "Papa,"
    And the Colonel knocked him down
    Under the horses' feet—
    And since that day he loved him no more.
CORA: And afterwards he beat him merciless!
    I thought he was gonna kill my chile that time.
    And since that day he *hated* the boy.
    Oh, why did I bring him back here?
    I'm sorry, Lawd!
    (In despair CORA prays)

PRAYER

> Help me, Lawd! Help me, Lawd!
> Let nothing happen to my child.
> The bad dream, the bad dream
> That I had last night—
> I'm still trembling,
> Still trembling in my heart.
> And I seed the moon all red with blood,
> And the house overflowing with blood.
> Help me, Lawd!
> Help or something's gonna happen to my child.
> Help me, Lawd, and save my child!

WILLIAM: Help us, Lawd!
> Help or something's gonna happen to us all today.
> Help us, Lawd! Oh, be with us!

CORA: He's my baby boy.
> He don't know the way.
> But I'll tell him what to do.
> He sho will listen to me.
> He must have pity
> On his mama's sorrow and pain.

WILLIAM: Mercy! Mercy, Lawd!
> Humbly I pray to thee, have mercy!

CORA: Mercy on my child.
> *(A boy's whistle is heard without)*

WILLIAM: That sounds like Bert!

CORA: There's my boy, now.
> Let's go to the back and talk to him.

WILLIAM: I hope you will talk to him.
> Somebody needs to straighten him out once for all.

CORA: But, what's he doing?

BOTH: He's coming through the front door!
> *(WILLIAM rushes to bar the front door with outstretched arms.*
> *BERT enters, picks him up and spins him around playfully)*

WILLIAM: Bert, don't play around here in this room.

BERT: Rabbit! Why don't you act like your white half, not like your
> black half?
> *(BERT looks toward the door)*

ARIA

The sun is shining bright today,
And the sky is as blue as can be.
But something's wrong with the folks down here.
Or maybe—it could be me.
WILLIAM: It's you, all right! Why don't you come in the door you're
supposed to come in?
BERT: Supposed to come in?
WILLIAM: The back door.
BERT: Front doors are made for everyone.
Don't you think we're human, too?
Why should there be one door for some—
But another door for you?
WILLIAM: This ain't the North.
BERT: I know it's not the North—and things aren't perfect there,
either—but I was born here, and this is my home.
My old man lives in a fine big house,
My mother once lived in a shack.
I wonder where I'm supposed to live,
Being neither white nor black?
(Then suddenly gay again, BERT hugs CORA teasingly)
Hello, ma!
Your daughter got off and I've come back
To keep you company in the parlor.
Bring out the cookies and lemonade—
Mister Norwood is here!
(Suddenly serious)
But, mama, what's the matter?
Did I scare you? Your eyes are all wet.
CORA: Why don't you mind me, son?
Ain't I told you *and told you*
Not to come in that front door—never?
BERT: I knew the Colonel was not here.
I passed him on the South road.
(Half playfully)
Anyhow, isn't this my old man's house?
Ain't I his son and heir?
Am I not Mr. Norwood, Junior?
CORA: Hush, boy!

WILLIAM: I believe you're going crazy.
   I believe you wants to get us killed,
   Or run away,
   Or something like that!
   Boasting like a fool,
   Usin' the front door like the white folks,
   Getting everybody riled up against us here!
BERT: I'm gonna act like my white half,
   Not like my black half—
   Nobody's gonna keep me in my place.
   We're old man Norwood's sons.
   Don't I look like my father?
   Ain't I as light as he is?
   Ain't this our house?
CORA: Lawd, have mercy!
WILLIAM: You fool, you!
   You should have stayed where you was.
   Coming back here ruining everybody!
   I wish—I wish you never had come back!
     (WILLIAM exits, unable to bear it any longer. Quietly, CORA
     calls her son)
CORA: Come here, chile, right here a minute,
   And listen:
     (BERT sits in his father's favorite chair)

ARIA

   I have worked
   In this very place all my life,
   Here down South,
   And that's all I've knowed and done.
   When the Colonel's wife died childless,
   I come here and bore you children.
   My baby boy, you are my youngest son.
   Now all I want in life is to see you happy.
   Listen, chile, I know *hate* can twist the heart.
   Listen, chile, there're some things that just can't be.
   We have lived in peace down here,
   And we've known happy days,
   Before this time of trouble.

I'se scared to death for you, my boy,
Cause you don't seem to know where you is at.
You don't seem to know that here in Georgia
You are not your father's son.
BERT: Mama, I love you,
More than I love anyone in all this world.
But I can't understand now what you're saying.
All I know is, I am his son—
And not in Georgia, nor anywhere else,
Should a man deny his son.
(*NORWOOD enters and stares unbelievingly at BERT*)
NORWOOD: Get up—out of *my* chair!
BERT: Didn't you want to talk to me?
NORWOOD: Get out of here!
(*He points with his riding crop toward the back door. CORA attempts to guide BERT there*)
BERT: Not that way, ma.
(*NORWOOD raises his crop to strike BERT*)
NORWOOD: Get out of here!
(*BERT snatches the whip from his father and breaks it*)
BERT: Not that way!
(*ROBERT walks proudly past his father and out the front door. NORWOOD, in an impotent rage, crosses the room to a small cabinet, opens it nervously, takes out a pistol, and starts toward the door. A few feet from the door he stops, unable to fire at his son. Shaken, weak, confused, he turns back toward CORA. As NORWOOD reaches the table, the gun slips from his hand. He sinks into his chair as CORA comforts him, her arms about his shoulders*)
CORA: Tom. . . . . Tom. . . . .
CURTAIN

Act II, Scene 1

SETTING: *The same.*
ACTION: *As the curtain rises, NORWOOD is seated in a big chair alone. Through the French doors the late afternoon sun as it sets makes a bright path across the room.*

RECITATIVE AND ARIA

NORWOOD: He's a puzzle to me, that boy,
    A painful terrible puzzle to me.
    Flesh of my flesh and bone of my bone,
    The strength of my strength
    Thirty years ago,
    The steel of the Norwoods
    Now darkened by Africa.
    Old and lonesome as I am
    Why can't I love this child,
    This boy who's so much—
    Who's so *damn much* like me—
    As any father in the world might love his child?
    Good God! A foolish, foolish thought!
    How can a bastard ever be
    Thomas Norwood's son and heir?
    But, nevertheless,
    He's flesh of my flesh and bone of my bone.
    Painful terrible puzzle without answer.
      (CORA enters)
CORA: Colonel Tom,
    Why don't you sit out on the porch.
    It's nice and cool out in the air. . . .
NORWOOD: Send Bert in here.
    (CORA wants to say something, but NORWOOD intimidates her
    with a commanding look. Almost voiceless, she answers)
CORA: Yes, sir.
    (CORA motions to ROBERT to come in. He enters)

TRIO

For God's sake
Don't aggravate him anymore, honey.
Listen to me!
Please agree to whatever he will say.
I say that, child, 'cause I love you so.
Please don't rile him anymore.
You must not forget all the other
Colored folks on this place.

BERT: All right, mama—
    But the old man better dare not
    Start to beat me again.
    I'm a man now, quite grown up now,
    And he better dare not lay his hands on me again,
    Better not, better not.
NORWOOD: A sad thought makes my heart beat fast—
    There stands that boy so near to me,
    There stands my son—
    So near, yet further away than ever.
CORA: When you talk to him do not forget
    That you are colored.
BERT: Why shouldn't I forget it—
    If he can forget I am his son—
    And he is my father?
CORA: Do not forget yourself,
    Think of all the colored folks
    Here on this place.
        (CORA gives an anguished sign to ROBERT. NORWOOD suddenly turns around and CORA exits)

DUET

NORWOOD: Robert, I don't want to have to
    Raise my hand to you another time
    As I did when you defied me today.
    Next time it might be fatal.
    I might kill you if I touched you again.
    I've been running this plantation for thirty-five years
    And I never had any trouble with my colored folks.
    They do what I say and that is all there is to it!
    They work, they get paid, and they know their place.
    And to Cora's young ones, for her sake, I give all the chances
    Any colored folks ever had in these parts—
    And that is more than many white children get!
    Now, tell me what's wrong with you—
    Whether you are crazy or not.
    If you are not,
    You better change your ways a damn sight,
    Or it won't be safe for you here.

I'm warning you, boy! Goddamn it!

Now I want you to talk right.

BERT: What do you mean, "Talk right?"

NORWOOD: I mean talk like a nigger should to a white man.

BERT: Oh, but I'm not a nigger, Colonel Tom—

I'm your son.

NORWOOD: You are Cora's boy!

BERT: Fatherless?

NORWOOD: Bastard!

You. . . . black. . . . bastard!

> (*Silence. The wind blows the lace curtains at the windows and sweeps the shadows of leaves across the paths of sunlight on the floor*)

BERT: I've heard that before.

I' heard it from Negroes,

And I've heard it from white folks—

And now I hear it from you.

You are talking about my mother.

NORWOOD: Well, what can you do about it?

BERT: (*Almost voiceless, half a whisper, half a sob*)

I'd like to kill every hypocrite in the world like you.

NORWOOD: Madmen like you are hung to trees.

BERT: I'm not a madman.

Aren't you my father?

And a hell of a father you are—

Calling your son a bastard.

NORWOOD: I'll break your neck for you!

Don't talk to me like that.

BERT: You'll break my neck?

You just try! You just try it!

> (*Shaking with rage NORWOOD draws his pistol*)

NORWOOD: You leave this house at once—

Or you'll be regretting it

If I ever lay eyes on you again!

I'll fill you full of bullets

If you ever dare come back here.

And get the hell out of this county—

Now! Tonight! Go on!

> (*He indicates the rear door*)

BERT: *Not that way!*

I'm not your servant,

And I'm not scared.
You can't drive me out the back way like a dog,
Or like a field-hand you can't use any more.
Yes, I'll go out of here,
But proudly I'll walk out—
'Cause it's my own father's house.
> (NORWOOD, *pistol in hand, springs between his son and the front door, but BERT does not swerve*)

NORWOOD: Don't you dare put your hands on me!
> (BERT *comes toward him calmly, grasps his father's arm and twists it until the gun falls to the floor. The older man bends backward in startled fury and pain, then attacks his son, but is overpowered*)

BERT: Why don't you shoot, papa? . . . . Why?
> (As NORWOOD *struggles hysterically,* BERT *takes his father by the throat and chokes him until his body grows limp*)

Why don't you shoot, papa? . . . . Why?
> (*Hearing the struggle,* CORA *appears at the top of the stairs, sees what has happened and rushes down.* ROBERT *bends over the body of his father in a path of red from the setting sun*)

CORA: Oh, my God!
He's your father, boy!
BERT: He's dead!
The white man is dead!
My father is dead!
But me—I am living!
> (CORA *falls across the body*)

CORA: Tom! Tom! Tom!
> (*Picking up the pistol*)

BERT: This is what he wanted to kill me with.
I can use it now—
Because they'll be coming looking for me.

DUET

CORA: Quick, chile, out of here!
Make for de swamp, honey!
Cross de fields, go de creek way—
In running water, dogs can't smell no tracks.
BERT: Yes, mama,
But if they gonna get me

Before I reach the swamp,
I'll come back here
And let 'em take me out of my father's house—
If they can.

CORA: Run, chile! Hurry, chile!
Fo' God's sake, run, chile!

BERT: They are not going to string me up
To some roadside tree
For those damn crackers
To laugh at me.

CORA: Run, chile!

> (BERT *opens the door and the sunset streams in like a river of blood. He starts toward the swamp.* CORA *stands as if petrified. Suddenly* TALBOT *and the* STOREKEEPER *enter*)

TALBOT: Hello, Cora! What's the matter with you? Where's that damn fool boy of your'n goin? Comin' out the front way like he owns the house! What's the matter with you? Can't you talk? Where's Norwood? Let's have some light in this place!

> (He *turns on the lights*)

STOREKEEPER: Talbot, look at this!

> (The two WHITE MEN *stop in horror before the sight of* NOR-WOOD'S *body on the floor. One bends over to examine the body*)

TALBOT: He's blue in the face! He's dead!

STOREKEEPER: That black boy we saw runnin' out the front door!

TALBOT: That bastard! He's running toward the swamp now!

STOREKEEPER: We'll get him!

TALBOT: Telephone town! Telephone the sheriff! Get men, get dogs after that black boy!

> (STOREKEEPER *picks up the telephone as* CORA *listens and* TALBOT *rushes to the door to peer into the twilight*)

STOREKEEPER: Sheriff! Is this the sheriff? I'm calling from Norwood's plantation. That nigger, Bert, has just killed Norwood—and run, headed for the swamp. Notify the gas station at the crossroads! Tell the boys at the sawmill to head him off at the creek. Warn everybody to be on the lookout. Call your deputies! Spread a dragnet. Meanwhile, we'll start after him.

> (He *slams the phone down*)

TALBOT: Cora, where's Norwood's car? In the barn?

> (CORA *does not answer*)

Talk, you black bitch!

STOREKEEPER: Come on, let's go!
> *(The two men rush out. CORA is alone)*

ARIA

CORA: My poor boy can't get to the swamp no more.
    He'll come back home to his mother now—
    But they won't get him
    For I'll make a place for to hide him
    Upstairs in my room safe in my bed.
    In a minute my boy'll be running from the white folks
    With their hounds, and their ropes, and their guns,
    And everything they use to kill poor colored folks with.
> *(CORA stands over the COLONEL's body)*

    Why don't you get up and stop them,
    Colonel Tom?
    I calls you to help me now
    And you just lays there.
    Whenever you called me in the night to love you
    I woke up and always reached out my arms—
    And I loved you.
> *(Suddenly angry)*

    I been sleepin' with you too long,
    Colonel Tom,
    Not to know that it ain't you
    Layin' down there with your eyes shut
    On the floor.
    You can't fool me!
    You ain't never been so still
    Like this before.
    You's out with the mob—
    Runnin' my boy through the fields!
    Runnin' my poor little helpless Bert
    Through the fields in the dark
    To lynch him!
> *(CORA lifts her clenched fists above his body)*

    Damn you, Colonel Tom!
    Damn you, Thomas Norwood!
    God. . . . damn. . . . you!
VERY FAST CURTAIN

Orchestral Interlude

(*"Didn't My Lord Deliver Daniel?"*)

Act II, Scene 2

SETTING: *The same with night-lights on dimly.*

ACTION: *As the curtain rises the UNDERTAKER is talking to SAM. The UNDERTAKER'S HELPER stands near the front door. In the darkness outside the approach of the manhunt is felt.*

UNDERTAKER: Reckon there won't be no orders to bring his body back out here. They'll have the funeral in town. Ain't nothing but colored folks left out here now.

    (SAM is very frightened)

SAM: Yes, sah! You's right, sah!

    Nothing but us colored, sah!

UNDERTAKER: The Colonel didn't have no relatives far as you know, did he, Sam?

SAM: No, sah, you's right, sah!

    Ain't had none, sah!

UNDERTAKER: Well, you got everything of his locked up around here, I see. Too bad there ain't no white folks around to look after the Colonel's stuff. But every white man that's able to walk's out with the posse. They'll have that young bastard swinging before long.

    (SAM trembles in fright)

SAM: Yes, sah! I 'spects so! Yes, sah!

UNDERTAKER: Say, where's that woman the Colonel's been living with? Where's that black housekeeper, Cora—that murdering black boy's mother?

SAM: She's here, sah! She's up in her room.

UNDERTAKER: Get her down here! I'd like to see how she looks.

    (SAM hurries up the stairs)

    Bad business, a white man having sassy black children on his hands, and his black woman living in his own house.

HELPER: Damn right, Charlie!

UNDERTAKER: Norwood didn't have a gang o' yellow gals, though, like Higgins and some o' those big bugs. Just this one bitch far's I know—living with him damn near like a wife. Didn't even have much company out here. They tell me ain't been a white woman stayed here overnight since his wife died.

(SAM descends in fear, followed by CORA, who comes slowly and with great dignity down the stairs. She says nothing)

UNDERTAKER: Well, so you are the Cora that's got them educated black children, hum-mm-m? Well, I guess you'll see one of 'em swinging full of bullet-holes pretty soon. They'll probably hang him to that tree down there by the gate, or maybe they'll burn him. How'll you like him swinging there roasted in the morning when you wake up, girlie?

CORA: *(Calmly)* Is that all you wanted to say to me?

UNDERTAKER: Don't get smart! Maybe you think there's nobody to boss you now! We gonna have a little drink before we go. Get out a bottle of rye.

CORA: I take my orders from Colonel Norwood, sah.

UNDERTAKER: Well, you'll take no more orders from him. He's dead out there in my wagon, so get along and get the bottle!

CORA: He's out yonder with the mob, not in your wagon.

UNDERTAKER: Goddamn! I believe this woman's gone crazy! Get the keys out for that liquor and be quick about it.

HELPER: To hell with the liquor, Charlie. They should have found that murderer by now. Let's get out of here. We're missing all the fun.

UNDERTAKER: All right, Jim.

(To CORA and SAM)

Don't you all go to bed until you see that bonfire. We'll burn a few more of you if you don't be careful.

(UNDERTAKER and HELPER rush out)

ARIA

SAM: No, I don't want to die!
   I swear, no, I don't want to die!
   Cora, is you a fool?
   Is you a fool?
   Why didn't you give the man the liquor?
   Riled as these white folks is!
   Oh, Lord! Ma Lord!
   In my old age,
   Is I gonna be burned by the crackers?

(Suddenly schemingly calm)
I don't have to stay here tonight, does I?
William is gone, everybody is gone,
All the field hands is gone.
The Colonel can't be wanting nothing.
He's with Jesus—or with the devil.
    (Elatedly)
I's gwine on away from here.
Sam's gwine in town to his chillun's house.
I ain't gwine by no road neither—
I don't want to meet all that white mob neither.
Sam gwine in town to his chillun's house.
    (SAM exits. CORA, seated on the stairs alone, begins to speak as if
    remembering a dream)

ARIA

CORA: Colonel Thomas Norwood,
    I am just poor Cora Lewis—
    Little black Cora Lewis.
    I am just fifteen years old,
    You remember, Colonel Tom?
    Thirty years ago there by the gate in the dark
    You put your hands on me
    To feel my breasts in the dark
    And you say
    'You pretty little piece of flesh, so black and sweet!'
    And you pulled me near to you
    There by the gate in the dark
    And I left up my face
    And I see your grey eyes.
    I was proud and afraid
    'Cause you was tall and strong.
    And called me sweet
    And you called me pretty.
    My heart woke up when you talked to me.
    And that night we lay together
    Under the tree in the dark,
    And I feeled your loving eyes

Which looked at me in the dark.
I was happy and I liked you
'Cause you was so proud and tall,
Thirty years ago
The first time I was yours
In the dark. . . .
> *(As the room darkens and unseen voices are heard singing, CORA looks into the past, seeing in a dream her first tryst with COLONEL TOM)*

TRIO

YOUNG NORWOOD: That night that we always remember,
> That night when we first met for love,
> Flowers filled the ev'ning air,
> And from the earth a sweetness rose
> Much more than we could bear.

YOUNG CORA: The moon hung so high up in heaven,
> But we hid in shadows our love.
> Flowers filled the evening air,
> And from the earth a sweetness rose
> Much more than we could bear.
>> *(The rising moon reveals a forest of live oaks garlanded with mimosa and hanging moss. Beneath the trees against the moon a YOUNG MAN holds a dark girl in his arms as CORA's vision becomes visible in a dance)*

YOUNG NORWOOD: My young arms caressed you, my sweet one.
> The spell was unbroken for us.
> Flowers filled the evening air,
> And from the earth a sweetness rose
> Much more that we could bear.

YOUNG CORA: It was many years ago—
> I was proud of you,
> 'Cause you was tall and strong
> And I reached out my arms and I loved you.
> You remember, Tom?
> You remember?
>> *(Dance music rises brightly, bitter-sweet, heart-breaking)*

POLONAISE

YOUNG CORA: That night you brought your bride to Albamar,
    The night you held your new love in your arms,
    Your bride so pale and lovely fair,
    As white as snow, all dressed in white
    And with blossoms of verbena in her hair,
    And her eyes of blue were shining like the stars—
    But I—I—
    Was not there.
        (The dance music is loud again as CORA watches them in desper-
        ation)
    Dance, lovers, dance!
    Dance on my heart!
    Dance with my lover—
    But not with me!
    Dance, pale and lovely one,
    Tom! Tom! Tom!
    Your child I bear, Tom,
    While the white dancers dance.
    Your dreams I share—
    But I cannot dance!
    My love is there—
    But I cannot dance!
        (For a brief moment COLONEL NORWOOD and his BRIDE
        dance by)
    Oh, lover, please,
    May I dance with you?
    For my cup of love
    Is a bitter, bitter brew!
    I hear the music, too.

WALTZ

CORA: Cora danced for you
    She danced, too—
    Don't you remember? In the darkness alone
    With the wild music playing,
    Cora danced alone.
    In the darkness, lonely swaying—

All the night through
There alone, heart-broken. . . . .
>	(*Sudden scream. Pregnant and alone, a DARK GIRL dances among the trees*)

Don't you remember?
Don't you remember?
>	(*Gradually CORA's arms form a cradle as though she were rocking a child. Slowly the light dies. The music of the dance becomes the music of a lullaby, a mother's song, low and comforting*)

NORWOOD: Long ago I remember. . . . .
>	(*Lullaby music merges with the rhythm of the dance as CORA rocks her child to sleep*)

LULLABY

YOUNG CORA: Go to sleep, go to sleep,
>	Chile of the moon and of the night,
>	Sweetly, quietly, my baby, go to sleep.
>	In the trees, in the trees
>	The summer breeze whispers low.
>	Hush, my baby! Don't cry!
>	Moon baby, don't cry!
>	Once there was a night
>	When the moon in the sky
>	Was a big yellow paper-lantern on high.
>	Go to sleep, go to sleep.
>	Chile of the moon and of the night
>	Sweetly, quietly, my baby, go to sleep.
>	Sleep, sleep. . . . .

CORA: And the scent of flowers
>	Filled the summer evening air,
>	And from the earth a sweetness rose
>	Much more than we could bear.

YOUNG NORWOOD: Flesh of my flesh
>	And bone of my bone—
>	The fruit of that night, my son. . . . .
>>		(*The vision fades. Complete silence. The stage gradually lightens, revealing the living room again and CORA sitting on the stairs alone, her arms curved as though cradling her child. Suddenly the noise of the manhunt is heard roaring through the night—shouts,*

curses, cries, the horns of cars, full of malignant force and power.
CORA rises)
CORA: But what's that? Where's my son?
   Oh, my Lawd! Where am I?
   Ah, I know—Bert's coming back!
   Bert's coming back running from the mob!
      (Desperately she kneels)

STRETTA

   I lived right, Lawd!
   I tried to live right,
   Lawd! My Lawd!
   And this is what you give me!
   What is the matter, Lawd!
   Ain't you with me?
      (VOICES outside, and ever-louder sounds of the approaching mob
      as the headlights of cars flash across the room)
VOICES: He's somewhere on this lot. . . .
   Don't shoot, men, we want to get him alive. . . .
   The porch, there he is. . . .
   In the bushes by the house. . . . .
   Running to the door. . . . .
      (Suddenly shots are heard just outside the house. The door bursts
      open and BERT enters, his father's pistol in his hand. Flares, lights,
      voices, curses, shots, cries, then sudden quiet, as CORA closes the
      door after BERT's entrance)

DUET

CORA: I was waiting for you, honey.
   Your hiding place is all ready,
   Upstairs in my room there in my bed.
BERT: No time to hide, ma,
   And only one bullet left, ma—
   It's for me.
CORA: Yes, it's for you, save it.
   Go upstairs in mama's room,
   Lay on my bed and rest.
      (BERT goes slowly toward the steps)

BERT: Goodnight, mama!

    I'm awfully tired of running, mama.

        (They embrace)

    They've been chasing me for hours, mama. . . . .

CORA: Goodnight son.

        (CORA follows him to the foot of the steps as the roar of the MOB increases without. BERT, pistol in hand ascends the stairs. As he disappears above, the front door bursts open. A great crowd of WHITE MEN led by TALBOT pours into the room with guns, ropes, clubs, flashlights, and knives. CORA turns and faces them quietly. The MOB stops)

TALBOT: Where's that yellow bastard of yours? Upstairs?

        (CORA motions for silence)

CORA: Yes. . . . He is going to sleep.

    Be quiet, you all. . . . . wait. . . . .

TALBOT: Wait, hell! Come on, boys! Let's search the house.

        (A single shot is heard upstairs)

    What's that?

CORA: Ma boy. . . . . is gone. . . . .

    To sleep. . . . .

THE CURTAIN FALLS

Esther
Opera in Three Acts

1956
Libretto by Langston Hughes
Music by Jan Meyerowitz

Regarding the triumphant premiere of *Esther* at the Festival of Contemporary Arts at the University of Illinois, Urbana-Champaign, Hughes wrote his old friend Carl Van Vechten, "It came off right well—like a Sunday School card set to music."[1] This was Hughes's second Meyerowitz opera, again undertaken at the composer's request. His relationship with the composer was often vexed, yet, according to Hughes's secretary Raoul Abdul, Hughes was fond of him, in part because he was so difficult.[2] Nonetheless, their achievements together were considerable. This opera was commissioned by the Fromm Foundation, and composed for the feast of Purim. Hughes's libretto was especially praised: one review terming it "powerful," another both "intelligent and beautiful."[3] Hughes's interest in Jewish culture had begun in high school; his work with Meyerowitz and later with David Amram displayed the depth of his connection to it.[4] Yet he commented ironically to composer Elie Siegmeister, another collaborator, regarding *Esther:* "Jewish theme, Gentile cast, cullud lyrics! American! By a Hebrew Catholic."[5] Written at the same time that Hughes was exploring his preferred religious music, gospel, *Esther* displays the breadth of his vision and his deep respect for faith.

This version is from a typescript in the Langston Hughes papers, copyrighted 1956, but noting details of the premiere.

Characters
(According to Score)
(In order of appearance)

HEBREW SAGES:
DANIEL	Baritone
HISDA	Tenor

ELEAZAR	Bass
ESTHER	Soprano
SEVEN HANDMAIDENS	Chorus
SENTRIES:	
BIGHAN	Baritone
TERESH	Baritone
KING AHASVERUS	Bass-Baritone
CHAMBERLAIN	Bass
VASHTI, the Queen	Mezzo-Soprano
EXECUTIONER	(Silent)
PUBLIC CRIER	Baritone or Bass
MORDECAI	Tenor
HAMAN, the Grand Vizier	Baritone
ZARESH, Haman's Wife	Mezzo-Soprano
ARIDATHA, Haman's Son	Tenor
TWO ASTROLOGERS	Baritones

COURTIERS, SOLDIERS, SENTRIES, SERVANTS and PASSERS-BY.

Scenes

Act I
Scene 1: Room of the Hebrew Sages
Scene 2: Courtyard of the King
Scene 3: Spotlight on a Public Crier
Scene 4: Room in Mordecai's House

Act II
Scene 5: Esther's Room at the Palace
Scene 6: Spotlight on a Public Crier
Scene 7: An Outer Gate of the Palace
Scene 8: Esther's Royal Chamber

Act III
Scene 9: Room in Haman's House
Scene 10: The King's Chamber
Scene 11: Esther's Royal Chamber
Scene 12: The Throne Room
Scene 13: The Throne Room, later

Scene 14: The Gate of Esther's Apartment
Scene 15: Esther's Garden at Evening
Scene 16: Room of the Hebrew Sages

Act I, Scene 1

*A quiet room at the end of the Sabbath where three HEBREW SAGES and
    a SCRIBE conclude the ceremony of dipping candles into wine. (It is
    the first Sabbath after the events shown from Scenes 2 through 15.)*
DANIEL: Blessed art thou,
    Lord God of mine,
    King of all the Universe
    And maker of the wine.
        (He pours in the cup, which overflows)
HISDA: Blessed art thou,
    Lord God our Sire,
    King of all heavens
    And maker of light and fire.
        (He dips the Sabbath candle into the wine, which extinguishes it)

TERZETTINO

DANIEL: Now this Sabbath
    That is ending,
    Of oppression
    Marks the ending.
    Let us thank and praise our God then!
    Let us thank and joyfully praise him!
ALL THREE: After sorrow thanks are given
    After darkness light is with us—
    Now this Sabbath that is ending
    Marks the end of dark oppression.
        (While lights are seen approaching)
HISDA: After darkness light is with us.
    See our Queen, our great Queen cometh!
    Esther, who is our Hadassah,
    With her faithful maidens cometh,
    For the Sabbath is now over.

(With her retinue of SEVEN HANDMAIDENS, in a flow of light, radiant ESTHER enters as the SAGES bow before her. She addresses them with great enthusiasm)

ESTHER: Dear elders, dear sages,
Dear guardians of the wisdom of all ages,
Dear scribes whose Holy Scrolls contain
All the records of our sorrow and our pain,
Dear elders, dear sages,
Inscribe upon your parchments now
Another story
Telling how the Jews are saved
Through grace of God
To live.

MAIDENS: Inscribe, etc. . . . .

ESTHER: You tell the world
Of Haman's dark deceit,
Of Mordecai's great honor,
Of days of gloom and danger
Ere our foes' defeat.
(Most excitedly they sing)

ESTHER and MAIDENS: In joyous letters write
How out of darkness comes the light.
In joyous letters write
The light, the light!
(ESTHER sees that the SAGES are slightly bewildered by her excitement. She now pleads quietly)

ESTHER: Write our story down forever.
Write it in the Holy Books.
Write it here
Plain and clear—
Let our scrolls reveal
The glory of this happy year.

DANIEL: But Esther, our beloved Queen,
Other nations then might envy us
And seek our people to demean.

ESTHER: Such thoughts may well, dear sage, occur to some—
But to all persecuted such as we
Who have looked terror in the face,
Driven hither, yon, from place to place,

Who have twice known captivity,
Our story a source of strength will be!
MAIDENS: A source of strength unto posterity!
O, sages, write our story down,
Write it down. . . . .
ESTHER: For me!
(There is a pause as the SAGES ponder. Finally they reply)
SAGES: So shall it be, Queen Esther,
So shall it be!
(ESTHER is enraptured)
ESTHER: What you will[6] write tonight, dear sages,
Will illuminate the ages.
When centuries hence your Scrolls unfold,
To the world our story will be told.
SAGES: Our story, Esther, we will tell!
ESTHER: Thank you, dear sages,
And farewell!
(Simultaneously)
MAIDENS and SAGES: Farewell.
(ESTHER and MAIDENS exeunt joyously. The SAGES unroll an enormous scroll. On this scroll DANIEL begins to write)

SALMODIA

DANIEL: Now it came to pass in the days of Ahasverus who reigned from India even unto Ethiopia, King Ahasverus sat on the throne of his kingdom Shushan, and made for seven days a feast unto the people, unto the people of the court. . . . .
(Fanfare, as light fades)

Act I, Scene 2

The Royal Courtyard of the Oriental Palace of Shushan. At one side the facade of the women's quarters housing the Queen, VASHTI. Guests look at the terrace below where a feast is being held. BIGHAN and TERESH are sitting on stairs.
BIGHAN: The King is in his cups.
TERESH: The King is in his cups, you say?
I'm in my cups myself.

This feast is fine,
But after seven days
Of nothing but men and games and wine,
I wish I had a woman here
To hug me near.
BIGHAN: That's what the King seems now himself to think!
Here he comes—if you ask, he might
Bring forth concubines tonight.
(*AHASVERUS enters followed by the CHAMBERLAIN and a
few COURTIERS*)
AHASVERUS: Ungrateful swine,
Who swill my wine!
Why did you walk out on my feast?
Hast ever seen a better feast than this?
What do you miss?
BIGHAN and TERESH: Women, King, women!
AHASVERUS: Women 'tis you lack?
I'll show you one who takes the place of all.
Most shapely of hussies—
Hey, what say I?
Most lovely of the women of my kingdom, I mean!
Bring me my wife, my Queen—
For all to see.
Vashti, come Vashti out to me.
BIGHAN: Your Queen, my Lord, has thrice said she'll not come
Since you are. . . . .
AHASVERUS: Drunk? I am NOT drunk—
But seven days hilarious, that is all!
Vashti has her wine within—
Her wine, and women drinking with her there.
Does Vashti love these women more than me?
That she should wine and dine and dance with them alone—
When Ahasverus calls her to his throne?
I shall see . . . I say: Bring me my Queen!
And fill my goblet full again of wine
That I may drown her royal snub to me and mine.
TERESH: Sire—
AHASVERUS: If need be, drag her to my feet!
BIGHAN: Sire, we do not dare lay hands upon the Queen . . .
TERESH: And she herself has said she will not come. . . . .

BIGHAN: No matter how we try . . .
TERESH: No matter how we plead nor what we do.
BIGHAN: The Queen has locked her gate
    And ordered us to state
    She will have none of you!
AHASVERUS: She will have none of me.

ARIA

I loved that woman once,
I loved her so!
And she was lovely for a man to see,
With wine in her mouth
And sun in her eyes,
The melons of her breasts,
The pillars of her thighs
A tower of delight
For the mirror by day,
And for the King by night.

O, luscious, live, and lovely Queen,
So ripe, so mealy, and so mean!
My grape of a Queen!
My fig of a Queen!
My lily, my rose, my thorn of a Queen!

Take heed, go tell her
Who it is again that calls.
The King! 'Tis I, Ahasverus.
    (*The CHAMBERLAIN goes reluctantly to the Queen's courtyard.
    There he knocks*)
CHAMBERLAIN: Great Queen—
    Beloved Queen,
    I beg you to receive my message.
    In the name of the King I call.
        (*VASHTI appears at the window*)
VASHTI: The King!
    That stableboy of a King!
    And it's not the wine that is speaking:
    It's I, Vashti.
    Granddaughter of Nebuchadnezzar,

Daughter of Belsatzar
Who could drink a thousand toasts and not get drunk!
I pay no heed to such as he who kept our horses once.
Where would he be if it were not for me?
Tell Ahasverus I will not come.
Let him come here—a Queen to see. . . . .
> *(She disappears. . . . . . A pause)*

BIGHAN: Did you hear, King, did you hear?

AHASVERUS: I hear.

CHAMBERLAIN: What if this gets abroad to other women in the land?

TERESH: No one will obey her husband's own command . . .

AHASVERUS: I hear, I hear and stand no more!
Slut, harlot, wh . . .
> *(Fanfare, drowning out his words)*

Hakaman, killer, your sword. . . . .

ARIOSO

Go split her wide!
Split her white body—
Till, like her thighs, her trunk is two,
Her breasts divided,
Her heartless head one-sided
Lies on the ground in her own blood.
Unsheathe your sword, Hakaman, go!
Or I will fell YOU
With my own sword's blow!
> *(The EXECUTIONER strides towards the Queen's door, his sword
> drawn)*

BLACKOUT

Act I, Scene 3

Spotlight on a PUBLIC CRIER, reading from a scroll.

THE CRIER: Ahasverus, King of all the Medes and Persians, King
of Ethiopia and India, ruler of Shushan, hereby does this day decree that on the third quarter of the ninth moon unto his court in
Shushan shall be conveyed all virgins, untouched, in the Kingdom
who are young and of comely mien, that he, the King, might choose

from them a Queen. On pain of death, Ahasverus does command
that his decree be read, posted and obeyed throughout the land.
Hear ye, hear ye! In every city, town, village, house and state. . . . .
> *(Lights fade as the CRIER continues)*

I repeat, Ahasverus, King of all the Medes and Persians, King of
Ethiopia, ruler of Shushan, hereby does decree. . . . .
> *(His voice is lost in the distance)*

BLACKOUT

Act I, Scene 4

*MORDECAI rocks and wails in a room in his house as his friends HISDA
and DANIEL keep him company.*

MORDECAI: Woe, oh woe! In this house, woe, of woe!
> Esther, my ward, my child I have loved so—
> Now is the day that she must go.
> Orphan to whom I have given shelter,
> Protected, loved, and tended like a flower in our garden,
> Now to a king who loves not flowers
> But wars and beasts and wine and hunting,
> She must go my lovely Esther—
> And I promised her dying parents to keep her safe.

DANIEL: Suppose you kept her safely hidden, Mordecai,
> And did not give her to the eunuchs of the King?

HISDA: Suppose you answered not the door when they knock?

MORDECAI: Then Death might well descend upon our house!
> For myself I have no fear—
> But for the child, that Esther be maltreated.
> No! Risking death to stay—
> Or risking worse to go?
> Which way? Which way?

GRANDE QUARTETTO

> A bitter, terrible choice!
> A bitter and terrible decision!
> In danger is her life if I don't let her go.
> In danger is her soul where pagans live in sin
> And lust is king!

(ESTHER enters serenely)

ESTHER: I am not afraid to go.

    I am not afraid, dear uncle.

    You taught me that the Lord will hold me in his hand,

    You taught me that the Lord still lives in pagan land.

    The gates of Shushan hold for me no fear.

    (Simultaneously the THREE MEN sing)

MEN: The gates of Shushan hold for her no fear.

HISDA: Take comfort, Mordecai!

    The faith of our Fathers strong must be

    To give such strength to frail virginity.

MORDECAI: Faith of our fathers, help me bear

    The fate that taketh one so fair!

    (The MEN address ESTHER)

MEN: The faith of Moses lock you in your heart.

    And hide it as you hide your grief,

    Lest pagans seek to trample your belief.

    Where golden idols play God's part

    Keep Moses' laws engraved upon your heart.

ESTHER: I keep the laws within my heart.

    (ALL sing together)

ESTHER: I am not afraid, etc. . . . . .

MORDECAI: A bitter terrible choice, etc. . . . . .

HISDA and DANIEL: Take comfort, etc. . . . . .

    (A knock is heard. The CHAMBERLAIN's voice calls from outside)

CHAMBERLAIN: We come for the virgin sheltered in this house,

    The virgin who will come now to the King.

    Is she ready?

    (The door opens)

MORDECAI: Yes, she is ready for the King.

    (ESTHER embraces her uncle. Veiling her face, and bowing her head to hide her tears, ESTHER exits)

CURTAIN

Act II, Scene 5

Esther's room in the women's quarters at the palace of Shushan where her SEVEN MAIDS are assembled to prepare her for the King, a rich array of roses and veils about them.

MAIDENS: How long it takes to purify
 A virgin for the King!
 Strange customs here!
 To see each virgin first
 The King must wait a year
 While herbs and ointments, perfumes rare
 Anoint her skin and soak her hair
 And rest and sleep and milk and food
 Do her good.
2ND MAID: Esther, our Esther is so sweet and kind,
 She is like a sister.
1ST MAID: Do you think the King will find her fair?
MAIDENS: Unless he is blind.
1ST MAID: I do not mean her face alone,
 But the light that from her face is shone.
CHORUS: It's true, it's true:
 About her is a light,
 More than from her eyes or face,
 A woundrous kind of holy grace.
 Some inner things
 Seem almost to give her wings.
2ND MAID: That wild King!
 Who's known so many women!
 So many times before!
 From Princess Royal, to. . . .
CHORUS: Shhhhhhh. . . .
 Do not talk about the King, it is not wise—
 Doors may have ears, walls may have eyes.
  (ESTHER enters, fresh from the bath)
MAIDENS: Esther, Esther,
 Your very presence sweet perfumes the air.
 Your robe, my dear, your heavy robe—
 It's chilly here.
 You've never seen a King . . .
 Now your day has come . . .
 Are you afraid?
ESTHER: No, I am not afraid.
 But, I wonder . . .

ARIA

I only wonder
When I go in unto the King
With golden sandals on my feet,
With precious jewels in my hair,
I wonder, oh, I wonder,
Will the King find me fair?

When I go in unto the King,
A virgin still untouched by man
With only goodness as my crown
And purity the robe I wear,
I wonder, oh, I wonder
Will the King find me fair?

MAIDENS: How could he
Other than good be
To one so lovely and so sweet?
And we will dress thee
That you will seem
A vision in a wondrous dream.

He will see, he will see
Rainbow and starlight,
Sunrise and dawn white,
Beauty of morn he will see.

And when he lifts your veil
He will see,
In wonder he will see
Never such a one as thee!
(The light fades slowly)
He will see, he will see . . . . .

BLACKOUT
(Somber fanfare. Suddenly a CHORUS is heard backstage)
CHORUS: Hail, hail our lovely Queen!
Hail, our new and lovely Queen!

Act II, Scene 6

Spotlight on a CRIER.
CRIER: Hear ye! Hear ye!
   This day the King
   From among a thousand virgins he has seen,
   Has chosen for his throne a Queen.
      (Voices in distance)
CHORUS: A Queen, a Queen!
CRIER: The King has found a Queen,
   An orphan child named Esther,
   Of sweet and lovely mien.
CRIER and CHORUS: Hail, our new and lovely Queen!
BLACKOUT

Act II, Scene 7

The outer gate of the palace of Shushan, a sunny afternoon. TWO SEN-
   TRIES, BIGHAN and TERESH, keep guard, stopping to talk to each
   other as their paths cross while they pace before the palace wall.
TERESH: Did you hear, friend Bighan?
   The King departs tonight by chariot
   With his armies for the front.
BIGHAN: This war with Egypt bodes nobody good.
TERESH: It drains the land of young men.
   Saps the youth
   And burdens with taxes
   Even me who has so little,
   For Ahasverus' vanity and pride!
BIGHAN: The world is wide
   And he would conquer it all,
   Become a mightier Lord.
TERESH: Sometimes I think the King's possessed of madness.
   The way he alternates
   Up and down, excitement, boredom,
   Joy and sadness.
BIGHAN: He's always either doing too much
   Or doing nothing.
TERESH: True!

As now he plans to carry out a conquest,
   Driving his chariot himself before the soldiers.
   And other times he lies slothful for weeks . . .
BIGHAN: Drunk with wine and sorrow
   Pitying himself. . . . .
BOTH: And dangerous to approach.
TERESH: Who comes there?
BIGHAN: That sad old man who likes to sun himself outside the gate.
TERESH: He does not understand our dialect
   And we can talk before him without fear.
   Hearing, he cannot hear.
BIGHAN: I have a thought in mind to tell you later,
   And something in my pouch to show you.
TERESH: What?
BIGHAN: Wait.
    (The SENTRIES take their posts at the gate as MORDECAI and
    DANIEL enter)
MORDECAI: Each day, Daniel, this is where I rest
   Awaiting news from Esther who's within,
   Elevated by the Almighty to great station.
DANIEL: Esther, above all women in the nation!
MORDECAI: Dear Queen, whom now I seldom see,
   But not even walls can keep her love from me.
DANIEL: Esther's fared well with the King these many months.
   He has treated her as befits a Queen.
MORDECAI: But each absence of the King brings release,
   That she may worship our own God in peace.
   And I'm still mourning that I had to give
   The apple of my eyes to those who as pagans live.
DANIEL: Yes, Ahasverus holds despotic sway—
   But so are things in this, our world today.
MORDECAI: But in Shushan all could be worse—
   If Haman were the ruler, then our land is accursed!
   He wears his heathen idol on his breast.
   To our people who know only one God,
   He would give no peace, no rest.
DANIEL: Grand vizier now, may his power no greater grow!
MORDECAI: I, for one, no honor will show him!
DANIEL: You must be careful, Mordecai.
   He's dangerous, that Haman,

Dangerous and sly.
> *(Very tenderly)*

I go now friend, goodbye.

MORDECAI: May peace go with you, Daniel, goodbye.
> *(DANIEL exits as the SENTRIES huddle together)*

BIGHAN: Come here and see what I have got.
> *(He suddenly pulls out a glass jar and scares TERESH with it)*

I've got a snake!

TERESH: A snake!

BIGHAN: Yes, whose fangs are full of poison.

TERESH: Aye! take care!!

BIGHAN: It's in a jar, sealed, with holes for air.

TERESH: Why carry about a snake?

BIGHAN: For those I hate.

I drop the jar—
The jar will break.
The snake will bite.
My enemies, good night!

TERESH: Oh. . . . .

BIGHAN: With small snake, imagine—*Me*
Sending a man into eternity.

TERESH: A sly little silver snake. . . . .
Only its head is red.

BIGHAN: But it could sting
A king.

BOTH: Sting, sting a king!

TERESH: I wish I had one, too—
I'd kill a Jew.
I'm like Haman, I hate them.
But I've never seen a Jew,
Have you?

BIGHAN: One or two, long ago.
> *(Here MORDECAI smiles at them. They greet him casually)*

TERESH: But if a Jew were anywhere near
He'd better quake and shiver with fear—
I'd take my sword and run him through!
> *(A horrifying fanfare is heard from the palace. A general commo-*
> *tion starts people running in to observe)*

BIGHAN: Someone of state
Emerges from the Palace gate.

TERESH: So many people have to pass
    Each time a great man shows his face.
BIGHAN: Watch out for assassins!
TERESH: Fanatics!
BIGHAN: Jews!
    (The SENTRIES drive the crowd back from the gate. All retreat
    but MORDECAI who remains seated where he is as HAMAN and
    his retinue emerge and the CROWD grovels before him)
OLD MAN: Haaaaa-man, great Haaaaa-man!
CROWD: Great Haaaa-man!
    We respect you, Haaaman!
    We revere you, Haaaman!
    We bow down, Haaaman!
    If there was no King above you,
    We would worship you alone, Haaaman!
    We love you, Haaaman!
    And kiss your feet on the throne, Haaaman!
    (Almost dreamily HAMAN murmurs)
HAMAN: Someday I might have a throne.
CROWD 1ST HALF: Then we will double respect you, Haaaaman.
CROWD 2ND HALF: Triple respect you, Haaaman.
1ST HALF: *Twice* bow!
2ND HALF: Nay, *thrice* bow!
1ST HALF: Four. . . . .
2ND HALF: Five. . . . .
1ST HALF: *Six* times bow, Haaaman!
    Bow down to the ground. . . . .
2ND HALF: Lower, if I could . . .
1ST HALF: Lower than the ground.
ALL: Down, down, down, Haaa-man!
HAMAN: Down then, down, dogs—
    Down!
CROWD: Yes, Haaaman . . .
    (Importantly HAMAN proclaims)
HAMAN: I, Haman, set by the King above all the princes of Persia, do
    announce to the world that our King the great Ahasverus this day
    makes war on Egypt, and sets forth at the setting of the sun with all
    his legions.
    (Silence. No one moves. HAMAN notices MORDECAI sitting
    quietly in the sun)

And who are you that you do not bow before me?
And never bow each day when I come out this gate?
Who are you, I say?
MORDECAI: I am a man.
HAMAN: What man? What do you do here?
MORDECAI: I sit and contemplate.
HAMAN: Contemplate what?
MORDECAI: The laws of the Prophets.
HAMAN: You may contemplate only what the King permits.
MORDECAI: One higher than a King permits this.
HAMAN: Well, I permit it not!
Do you know me?
(Very quietly MORDECAI replies)
MORDECAI: I trust, sir, I do not.
(HAMAN is outraged)
HAMAN: You will, Jew!
(Excited he kicks one of the prostrate figures)
Get out of my way!
*(He is gone. The crowd disperses. Only BIGHAN, TERESH and
MORDECAI remain)*
TERESH: So he's a Jew, imagine that!
BIGHAN: No need to whisper,
He does not understand our tongue.
(Simultaneously)
MORDECAI: They think I do not understand—
But they don't know the sages of our people
Know all the tongues of all the lands.
BIGHAN: You see! One never knows whom one is greeting.
TERESH: Surely it's not a lucky day.
Tonight we go to war—
And I don't want to go
To break my neck for crazy Ahasverus.
BIGHAN: I'll tell you what we'll do—
If this snake were drowned in wine
A man who drinks of it would die.
I'll drop this snake in the King's wine.
(Unobtrusively MORDECAI rises and goes into the courtyard)
MORDECAI: They plot against the King
The King so kind to Esther
I must warn her
That she may warn him of his wine.

(MORDECAI exits as the TWO SENTRIES prance about gaily)

TERESH: Nor you, nor me, nor son of mine

Will go to war because of wine.

BIGHAN: No war we'll make!

No tax we'll pay—

And home we'll stay

Thanks to a snake.

BOTH: No war tonight, tonight no King!

Poor men like us may drink wine and sing.

(Their march becomes almost a dance step)

Poor men like us may drink. . . . . and. . . . .

(They pace proudly back and forth grinning before the gate. Suddenly the EXECUTIONER appears with TWO AIDES. The SENTRIES freeze in their tracks as they see him standing there resting his hands on his great sword pointed on the ground. His AIDES seize the SENTRIES. They are rapidly overpowered and searched. The glass jar falls to the ground)

BLACKOUT

Act II, Scene 8

Esther's royal chamber. ESTHER is just returning from the King's farewell embrace. She greets her MAIDENS with effusion.

ESTHER: Greetings, dear ones! Hebrew maidens,

How good to be among you all again!

How heavy seem these jewels in my hair.

With them I cast away

Vain glory and the pomp of court.

While I reign over half the world as Queen

And keep the secret of my exile and my faith,

The temple of my God is still in ruins,

And impure reptiles dwell where once the inner sanctum stood.

Oh, Jordan land, Oh, land so fair!

SONG AND CHORUS

ESTHER AND MAIDENS: I dream sometimes of a land so fair,

Of Jordan land and I wish I were there.

I dream David's harp on a willow tree.

I know Jordan land is the home for me.

By the hills of Zion I see a place
Where Abraham stood with his shining face.
Sweet Sarah lived to a hundred years
In Jordan land where there are no fears.

In Jordan land sweet myrtles sprout.
The temple walls are strong and stout.
The altar of God is holy and high,
His songs of praise rise to the sky.

Jordan land! Oh, Jordan land!
Sweet Jordan land!
      (*They cover their faces with black veils. The lights dim slowly*)
CURTAIN

Act III, Scene 9

A room in HAMAN's house. HAMAN's wife, ZARESH, and the eldest of
    their sons, ARIDATHA, converse as HAMAN enters.
HAMAN: The King defeated now at arms,
      Shadowed by disgrace,
      Does not wish to look upon any human face.
      He asks for no one but the bearer of his wine.
      The running of the Kingdom he leaves to me and staff of mine.
      I'll ask his seal upon a new decree
      Already written—see!
      This will humble *all* the Jews to me.
           (*HAMAN displays an official parchment*)
ZARESH: Humble?
HAMAN: Humble! In that none there'll be!
      (*With joyful astonishment*)
ARIDATHA: Extermination?
HAMAN: Extermination! All! . . .
      And legal, by decree.

TERZETTO

My wife, my son,
The time has come
To avenge Amalek, our nation
By Moses' evil magic once defeated,

And to avenge our ancestor, Agag,
    Callously slain by Samuel, the traitor.
ALL: Remember Amalek and show to them no pity!
HAMAN: And Mordecai
    Who sits without the gate and does not bow,
    His end I vow.
    But his end alone is nothing—
    They all must die.
    They all offended me!
       (With demented hate)
ALL: Now help me cast the lot,
    The day to set, the time to see,
    Know when the stars bode well or ill,
    Know when to stay my hand and when to kill.
       (ARIDATHA brings the dice, large cubes of wood, and they pre-
    pare to cast lots as ZARESH watches excitedly)
HAMAN: I'll roll first, you roll last.
    The figures that come twice will be
    The day and month we'll write in this decree
    That gives the fate of all the Jews to me.
       (With a great sweep HAMAN rolls several dice on the floor. When
    he wants to examine them, ARIDATHA stops him)
ARIDATHA: No, father, I would not seek a day.
    More favored of the Gods to seek a month.
    Soothsayers say
    God made some part of the world on each day
    And rested on the seventh—
    Thus no day of the week is favorable for their destruction.
    Let these purim find the fatal *month.*
       (HAMAN takes another set of dice)
HAMAN: Since other hands than mine control their numbers
    As they will, I'll let them roll.
       (He rolls and then stoops to examine the results)
    Scales!
       (They look at a large Hebrew calendar)
ARIDATHA: Tishri!
    This month is not good for their death:
    Tishri is the month of Atonement.
    Roll again.
       (HAMAN casts the dice again)
HAMAN: Goat!

ARIDATHA: Tebet!
Month of weddings
And month of wedding blessings.
Try again.
(*HAMAN does*)
HAMAN: Waterbearer!
(*And again*)
ARIDATHA: Shebat!
That's when the trees in their holy land were planted
And their prayers for rain are answered.
(*HAMAN furiously rolls another time*)
HAMAN: Archer!
ARIDATHA: Kislev!
Not bad enough, therefore no good—
Their God himself spoke in this month
To their prophet Zachariah.
(*This time ARIDATHA rolls*)
HAMAN: Fish!
(*ARIDATHA cries in delight*)
ARIDATHA: Adar!
In Adar Moses died!
And in despair he died!
God showed him Canaan,
But entrance he denied!!
HAMAN: Adar, Adar
Will be their fatal month.

TARANTELLA

We'll make them run,
Climb over walls,
And break through fences,
And disappear into holes,
And try to escape through cracks and fissures.
ZARESH and ARIDATHA: We'll make them run!
HAMAN: Stumble, fall, pant, choke,
Cry, rise and fall again!
ALL THREE: And roll in blood and dust and die!
The month is Adar!
ZARESH: But the Jew who sits without the palace gate—

HAMAN: Mordecai . . .

ZARESH: Don't let him live until Adar.
   Build a gallows!

ARIDATHA: Speed his hour!

ZARESH and ARIDATHA: Build a gallows for the man you hate!
   Let him swing at the city gate!

HAMAN: Let his eyes be eyes
   For the crows to pluck
   And his lips be lips
   For the wind to suck.
      (More and more enraged)

ALL: Let his blood drip down
   In the dust and muck
   And the world be rid
   Of such worthless truck!
   Build a gallows for the Jew to hang
   Like the clapper of a bell that will not clang!
      (Ferociously)
   Remember Amalek and show to them no pity!
      (They exit jubilantly)

BLACKOUT

Act III, Scene 10

The King's chamber, dark and gloomy. AHASVERUS sits on a golden chair on a raised dais with his back to the audience, only an arm showing, hanging from the sleeve of a silken gown. On his finger is a huge signet ring, his seal of state. Several feet behind the royal chair kneels HAMAN with a document in his hands.

HAMAN: Almighty King!

AHASVERUS: What Haman?
   Speak to me where you are
   For I would see no one.

HAMAN: Almighty King!
   Great ruler of all the provinces of Persia,
      India, even unto Ethiopia. . . . .

AHASVERUS: Speak, get about the business, that's all!

HAMAN: I have here a decree that I would have you seal, great Lord!

AHASVERUS: Decree, what decree?

HAMAN: Concerning the Jews.
AHASVERUS: Who cares about the Jews?
HAMAN: With that, sire, I agree.
AHASVERUS: Read then, read.
>   (*HAMAN reads in a hurried whisper*)
HAMAN: To all within the borders of my realm:
>   I, Ahasverus, the King, do hereby grant
>   To Haman, Grand Vizier of the realm,
>   The right to carry out this decree
>   Which all the governors in each province
>   Are instructed to obey.
>   For there are among us a certain malignant people
>   Following a life strange to our laws,
>   Worshipping only their only God,
>   Doing evil to our state and welfare—
>   *The Jews.*
>   I signify to you through Haman,
>   Have them, with all their wives and children,
>   On the 13th day of the month of Adar
>   *Utterly destroyed*—without mercy!
>   To this decree do I, Ahasverus,
>   Hereby affix the royal seal.
AHASVERUS: And these Jews, who are these Jews?
HAMAN: They are a stubborn and malicious people.
>   They are haughty and they curse the King.
>   If a fly falls into their wine,
>   The Jews remove the fly and drink.
>   Yet they would scorn to drink from yours,
>   The King's own cup of gold.
>   Not to you, nor to me, nor to our Gods will they kneel.
>   All this shall end with this decree
>   That now awaits your seal.
>   (*The King seems to have fallen into some sort of stupor*)
HAMAN: Sire. . . . .
AHASVERUS: Huh?
HAMAN: It awaits your seal. . . . .
>   (*As the King does not react, HAMAN takes AHASVERUS' hand
>   and affixes the ring to the decree*)
BLACKOUT

Act III, Scene 11

Violent orchestra interlude. The lights come up.
Esther's chamber where her HANDMAIDS light the evening candles.
> *MORDECAI enters, distraught in sackcloth and ashes, crying aloud:*
MORDECAI: Eli, Eli, Lama Asaphtani.
MAIDENS: Go, call Queen Esther!
> Call the Queen!
MORDECAI: Eli, Eli, Lama Asaphtani.
> *(ESTHER enters with great authority)*
ESTHER: What insolent intruder
> Dares to profane this peaceful dwelling?—
> Mordecai!
MORDECAI: My daughter!
ESTHER: Mordecai!
> An angel of the Lord
> Has kept your coming hidden.
> But why such grief and sorrow?
> These ashes on your head . . .
> These rags . . .
MORDECAI: Have you not heard of this decree?
ESTHER: I've heard of no decree, kinsman of mine.
MORDECAI: This decree that should strike the grape
> From the living vine!
> Haman is the one who signed—
> And beneath Haman's name
> Is the royal seal
> From which there can be no appeal.
> *(ESTHER collapses after looking at the decree)*
> Leave weeping to your maidens!
> Don't falter! Understand
> That terror and dark death
> Invade the land.
ESTHER: Ah, terror and death invade the land!
MORDECAI: Israel weeps,
> Death is before our eyes!
> You alone can save our people—
> Go to the King and tell him who you are!

ESTHER: No hope!
    You know the fearful law
    That shields the King from every mortal eye.
    Whoever goes unbidden to the King
    Is struck to death—
    Unless to him the King his scepter does extend.
    Before this cruel law we all are equal.
    He has not called me since he has returned.
    Three guardians are watching his threshold,
    Their swords drawn—ready to kill.
MORDECAI: Almighty is the holy one, our Lord,
    But he'll withdraw his hand if we are cowards!
    He raised you to this rank to prove your heart.
ESTHER: Oh, what for me the path ahead?
MORDECAI: He raised you to this rank to prove your heart.
    *(Pause, in which ESTHER gathers all her strength with an extreme
    effort)*
ESTHER: Tell all the faithful in this town
    To pray for me, to fast for me three days.
    Prepare my royal robe and bring my crown,
    For I shall go now, go now to the King.
    (MORDECAI is seized with sudden panic)
MORDECAI: Esther, Esther,
    My ward, my child!
    I urged you, now I tremble. . . . .
    (The HANDMAIDENS help ESTHER dress)
ESTHER: If the wine of my blood
    Flows swiftly away,
    And the sight of my eyes
    Be blinded to day,
    And the beat of my heart
    Be heartbeat no more,
    And death sucks the breath
    From my body's sweet store,
    I walk through the door
    Where the grim terrors start—
    For the sake of my people
    Who live in my heart.
ALL: For the sake of her people who live in
    her heart. . . . .

ESTHER: For the sake of my people
    Whose servant am I,
    If I perish, I perish.
    I die, I die.
        (The HANDMAIDENS place a crown on her head)
    I go now to the King,
    Mordecai.
        (Followed by THREE MAIDENS who hold her train, ESTHER
        exits)
        Frightful, mysterious fanfares from all sides.
BLACKOUT

Act III, Scene 12

A curtained corridor before the throne room. ESTHER, veiled, enters. She
    falters.
ESTHER: My Lord, why hast Thou forsaken me?
        (The curtains part revealing the KING on his throne, wine cup
        in hand, his crown glittering. Head down, he does not see ES-
        THER until THREE SOLDIERS rush forward and the KING
        cries out)
AHASVERUS: Who dares defy the threshold of the throne?
        (ESTHER faints)
    Esther! My Queen!
    I put my scepter on your shoulder
    That you may live.
    No other living in my kingdom
    Would dare to be so brave.
        (Descending from the throne, he extends his scepter, then lifts her in
        his arms. The SOLDIERS retire)

DUETTO

    I grant you life
    Although you came unbidden.
    I grant you grace
    Who vanquished your king by your grace.
    Do not fear,
    Do not fear a law for you not intended.

I grant you life,
My Queen, my lovely wife.
ESTHER: Voice of salvation,
I hear in a dream your boon.
From descent to Death
Back comes my spirit
At your bidding.
Your call of love
Brings life anew.
AHASVERUS: Greater in might
Than the King's own edict of Death
Is the might of virtue.
I surrender, I surrender.
Innocent sweet virtue
Lifts from my heart despair.
Loveliest Queen,
You are welcome here.
    (Together)
ESTHER: Like an angel your glory appeared to me!
Like an angel of the Lord,
Like the angel of Death
Did you appear, oh beloved King!
AHASVERUS: Calm all your fears—
I'm your guardian, your friend
I'm your love, I'm your friend.
Do not fear.

Look into my eyes and speak
For all that you desire.
Even unto half of my kingdom shall be thine.
    (Completely herself again, very simply, ESTHER sings)
ESTHER: I will tell you, my King—
But if it seem good to you
Come dine with me in the coolness of my garden
That I may tell you there.
And with you bring your friend, the Vizier,
Haman,
If it seem good to you.
AHASVERUS: Your invitation puzzles me,

But I will come with Haman,
And in your garden find out why
These tears stand in your eye.
>   *(While the orchestra intones the "Astitit Regina a Dextris Tuis,*
>   *Domine")*
Come sit with me beside the throne, at my right hand.
I'll call the princes of the land,
I will hold court again—
You brought me back to life and joy.
Thank you, my Queen.
>   *(At the sign of the KING, his COURTIERS enter, marvelling at*
>   *the KING's transfiguration)*
BLACKOUT

Act III, Scene 13

Lights on same setting, but dark and intimate. AHASVERUS and TWO
>   *ASTROLOGERS confer.*
AHASVERUS: And no reward did I bestow on him?
ASTROLOGERS: My Lord and master,
>   Our chronicles don't mention it. . . . .
AHASVERUS: Your charts, your stars, your maps of Heaven,
>   What say they of tonight?
ASTROLOGERS: For all things good the stars are right.
AHASVERUS: So thought I,
>   And thought well,
>   Oh, wondrous sky!
ASTROLOGERS: The stars are as they were that day
>   When Mordecai warned Esther of the danger to your life—
>   That day we hanged two villains in the court.
AHASVERUS: You do well recalling me that day,
>   For after all the months gone by
>   I will honor Mordecai.
ASTROLOGERS: It would be well, so your stars say.
AHASVERUS: Call Haman!
>   And you, wise men, on your way!
>   *(The ASTROLOGERS exeunt. HAMAN enters)*
HAMAN: Almighty King, most mighty Lord. . . . .

AHASVERUS: Haman, I have a plan:—
    I wish to honor a most honorable man
    With all the honor that I can bestow,
       And publicly so all may know.
      (Aside HAMAN exults)
HAMAN: He must mean me!
AHASVERUS: Advise me now what I should do.
HAMAN: The finest of the King's own robes you let him wear,
    The King's own crown may grace his hair.
    And on the whitest of steeds through the streets he will ride
    And a worthy prince may walk by his side
    Proclaiming the merits of this excellent man.
AHASVERUS: This pleases me!
    And you, my vizier, will go
    And inform that man whom I will honor so.
HAMAN: Inform. . . . .What man?
AHASVERUS: Mordecai, the Jew.
HAMAN: Sire! Sire! What say you?
    (The KING repeats a little louder, but very simply)
AHASVERUS: Mordecai, Mordecai, the Jew.
    (A slight pause, as HAMAN gathers his wits)
HAMAN: There are many Jews called Mordecai in town.
AHASVERUS: I mean that man who always sits at the palace gate.
    (HAMAN is stunned)
HAMAN: There are many gates to the palace.
AHASVERUS: The gate of the Women's Palace.
HAMAN: Sire, could you not give this man money, gold?
    Not honor?
AHASVERUS: I wish to give him honor.
HAMAN: Sire, I have ten sons—
    Let them be his slaves. . . . .
AHASVERUS: Slaves, no!
    I would give him honor!
    Above all—honor!
HAMAN: Make him ruler of a province—
    Give him land—
    My land—
    (The KING raises his voice)
AHASVERUS: No, honor!
    I said: HONOR!

Be quick for you are bidden with me to dine
In her garden, with my Queen tonight.
Go! First honor Mordecai throughout the town,
Then come back here, before the sun goes down.
    (HAMAN exits abjectly. Discordant fanfare in distance)
BLACKOUT

Act III, Scene 14

*The entrance to Esther's apartment as the sunset softens into twilight. At the
gate, ESTHER and her HANDMAIDENS are gathered to welcome
the KING who enters. They sing in chorus, repeating the words.*

MADRIGALETTO I

MAIDENS: In our sweet refreshing leafy garden,
    Come, oh King, and rest from all your work and care.
    Breezes sweet cool the evening air.
    Leave behind you the weight of work and care.
ESTHER: I am grateful, Lord, that you come to me,
    And that Esther is so dear to you.
    I am grateful that you find me fair,
    Oh, so grateful!
AHASVERUS: Your words fall gracefully on my heart.
    I must tell you what your tender love means to me.
        *(They all exit happily within the gate. HAMAN and ZARESH
        enter)*
HAMAN: No, no! Oh no!
    I did not think that I would suffer so!
    I did not think that I would love to stride
    On foot beside a Jew while that Jew ride.
    I built a gallows on the edge of town
    To string him up and cut him down.
    It's empty, empty! When can I use it? When?
    Now that this Jew is honored above all other men?
ZARESH: And Adar is still a while away. . . . .
HAMAN: Yes, their month of doom!
    Death is on the way!
ZARESH: Death? Oh Haman, I fear!

Unlucky stars have crossed our paths this year!
HAMAN: Unlucky stars? Don't fear, don't cry!
I'll get my due from Mordecai!

ARIA

ZARESH: Haman, listen before it is too late:
Little hope now,
Little hope for you and me!
Dreams will die here—
Troubled is this country—
People hate us, I know!
I can see it in their eyes
When through the streets I go.
I wish I could return to the land
Where I was born,
That far-away Thracian land
Beside the Hellespont
Where your ancestors knew,
Long ago, refuge from the vengeance of the Jew
When they were driven out of Idumea!
Oh, that no such fate should overtake you here!
Haman, let not yourself be now undone!
Go in unto the King before the setting of the sun.
HAMAN: Mordecai—honored in the town!
ZARESH: Go in unto the King and Queen
Before the sun goes down!
(*At these prophetic words of ZARESH the light goes out*)

Act III, Scene 15

*Beneath a sky spangled with stars, the QUEEN serves supper in the garden
of the women's quarters of the palace of Shushan. There are hanging
lights of brass, tall palms and flowering bushes scent the air. SLAVES
pass golden platters and WINEBEARERS bring goblets of gold—and
all for just three people, the KING, HAMAN, and ESTHER as the
HANDMAIDENS sing.*

MADRIGALETTO II

MAIDENS: In our sweet and leafy garden,
    Stay, oh King, and rest from worries.
    Here the soft refreshing breezes
    Cool the air with perfumed flurries. . . . .
AHASVERUS: Sweet I find this perfumed garden.
    'Neath the gently shaded bowers,
    In the presence of my loved one
    I will spend my evening hours. . . . .
ESTHER: Just for us has the new moon risen.
    Just for us the stars are alighted.
    Bright is the sky with a golden glow above us.
BOTH: For us all this splendor
    The sky has alighted.
AHASVERUS: Your words are rich with true grace!
    What great good fortune brought you to this place?
    What woman gave you birth?
    What sire fathered you of what great race?
ESTHER: My King, but by your grace I live.
AHASVERUS: What you would tell me, Esther, tell me now.
    What you ask, I give.
    Even unto the half of my Kingdom,
    If you should ask, I give.
    (ESTHER shakes her head, no)
AHASVERUS: Then were I king of the heavens,
    Heaven would be yours,
    For you I love.
    (Gravely ESTHER looks at the ring)
ESTHER: Yet you would have me die.
AHASVERUS: Die? You? Die?
    What do you mean, die?
    (Solemnly and slowly)
ESTHER: You have commanded by decree
    The death of all my people—and of me.
AHASVERUS: What?
    (ESTHER rises in great emotion from her seat)
ESTHER: We are sold to be destroyed,
    To be slain and to perish!

You have given unto Haman's hand
The fate of all those in this land
Whom men call Jews!
I'm kin to Mordecai!
I am a Jew.

> *(The KING rises in rage. First he wants to do violence to HAMAN,*
> *but then as if suffocating, he rushes from the garden. Terrified,*
> *HAMAN throws himself at ESTHER's feet)*

HAMAN: Great Queen, great Queen,
My life, I beg you, save!
I'm stunned! I did not know the truth.
Some enemy of the Jews has filled my mind with evil.
But now I shall protect your people.
Tell me: whose blood must flow?
I will be servant to you and your people,
    Forever.

ESTHER: My God, protector of the innocent,
Has judged you!
Tremble! Tremble!
Your power is done!

HAMAN: Great Queen,
I beg you to save me.
Save me from the King.

> *(As he reaches out to embrace ESTHER's feet, AHASVERUS re-*
> *turns with SOLDIERS and COURTIERS)*

AHASVERUS: He dares touch you!
To lay hands on my Queen?

> *(He pushes HAMAN away with his foot)*

Dog! Dog!

CHAMBERLAIN: It was he who ordered a gallows built
For Mordecai at the edge of town.

AHASVERUS: Hang Haman on that gallows!
Take him away! Away!

> *(HAMAN is covered with a black cloth. The SOLDIERS drag*
> *him out. He has fainted, there is no sound. THE KING looks at*
> *ESTHER, seated with her head bowed)*

Esther, by this ring
That my dark decree did seal,
By this royal ring I swear you
Its repeal!

In Adar no slaughter will there be:
Your people live—
And you will live—for me.
>   *(They embrace as the lights fade)*

Act III, Scene 16

Room of the sages again, as in Scene 1, where DANIEL, HISDA and
>   *ELEAZAR are gathered as DANIEL writes upon the scroll.*
DANIEL: And Mordecai went out from the presence of the King, in-
>   vested with all the power that once was Haman's. And the Jews had
>   joy and gladness in the month of Adar.
ELEAZAR: The stars had deceived Haman:
>   Adar is the month of Moses' death—
>   But also the month of his birth.
>   *(The door burst open and light pours in as ESTHER, MORDE-*
>   *CAI and MAIDENS enter with lighted candles, food, wine and*
>   *fruit, happy and dancing)*

FINALE

MAIDENS: Let there be joy
>   Let laughter be reborn!
ESTHER: Let there be joy, joy!
>   *(MORDECAI addresses the SAGES)*
MORDECAI: Let your scrolls say
>   This be feast day!
>   Ages hence, on this day,
>   Israel's happy songs fill the air—
>   For on this day
>   Will answered be our prayer!
>   And God's own *will* prevaileth everywhere.
ALL: Light and love illuminates the happy air
>   And God's own will prevaileth everywhere!
>   *(DANIEL presents the scroll to ESTHER)*
ESTHER: The story that you wrote, dear sages,
>   Will illuminate the ages.
>   *(MORDECAI gives thanks to Heaven)*
MORDECAI: Jubilation

Overflowing,
Like an ocean
Overflowing!
ALL: After sorrow
    Thanks are given!
    After darkness
    Light is with us!
    Let us thank and praise our God!
        (Suddenly all turn to ESTHER and solute her in her radiance)
    And his handmaid, lovely Esther!
CURTAIN
The End

Port Town
An Opera In One Act

1960
Libretto by Langston Hughes
Music by Jan Meyerowitz

Written for Jan Meyerowitz at his request because he had always loved Hughes's 1926 poem of the same name, *Port Town* premiered at Tanglewood, Massachusetts, on August 4, 1960. The opera was not well received, and Hughes did not enjoy the event, vowing to his friend Carl Van Vechten to take "no more parts of operas or rural life ever!" Particularly galling was a complaint he had made frequently to Meyerowitz before: that his libretto was inaudible. "As operas are done in America, the words might had just as well be nonsense syllables. I see no point in spending long hours of thought, and weeks of writing seeking poetic phrases and just the right word—and then not enough of the librettist's lines are heard for anybody to know what is being sung," he retorted when Meyerowitz invited him to collaborate on yet another opera. *Port Town* was to be his last effort in the genre.[1]

This text is taken from a typescript in the Langston Hughes Papers.

Characters
(In order of appearance)

MRS. WINKELBAUM, a shopkeeper	Mezzo Soprano
MR. SWARTZ, a barkeeper	Bass
MAGGIE, a come-on girl	Contralto
FIRST SAILOR	Tenor
SECOND SAILOR	Baritone
THIRD SAILOR	Tenor
BOSUN	Baritone
FOURTH SAILOR	Tenor
FIFTH SAILOR	Bass
SIXTH SAILOR	Tenor

crewmen (*S.S. Sea Horse*)

COP	Baritone
MISS HELGSTRUM, a teacher	Dramatic Soprano
MISS GARY, a teacher	Mezzo Soprano
JEANNETTE, a girl of sixteen	Soprano
SMITTY, a young sailor	Baritone
GAY GIRL	Mezzo Soprano

CHORUS (townspeople, sailors, Seminary girls)

TIME: *1919 or 1946 following a major World War*

SETTING: *It is a port town on a foreign shore, quaintly attractive as many port towns are* not—*but as* some *port towns are. It is Port Street, ugly—but roughly charming as sometimes port streets are. It is a corner facing the quay. At the very corner is the* SWARTZ BAR AND GRILL *with a catty-cornered entrance with a post at the sidewalk point of the triangle of the entrance. Next door, on the side of the street we see most, is* WINKELBAUM'S NOVELTY AND TOBACCO SHOP. *Over this shop is a window from which a woman named* MAGGIE *sometimes calls to sailors. Port Street faces a pier and, newly moored there today, is the* Sea Horse, *a dirty old merchant steamer whose gangplank juts down into the street. The bar has old-fashioned swinging doors, but over its entrance is a modern neon sign.*

TIME: *Late afternoon.*

I. INTRODUCTION: PASSACAGLIETTA

As the curtain rises, two or three MERCHANT SEAMAN *are painting or swabbing the railings and deck of the visible portion of the* Sea Horse. *On the quay,* MR. SWARTZ *is sweeping the sidewalk in front of his bar.* MRS. WINKELBAUM *is just emerging from her shop also with a broom.* MRS. WINKELBAUM *and* MR. SWARTZ *are urging* MAGGIE, *painted and powdered, off the street.*

II. TRIO

MRS. WINKELBAUM: Get away, get away, please!
   Get upstairs, Maggie, out of sight!
   Get on upstairs—
   And don't come down until tonight.
MR. SWARTZ: Get away, get away, please!

Get upstairs, Maggie, out of sight!
Get on upstairs—
And don't come down until tonight.
MRS. WINKELBAUM: The young ladies from the Seminary
Conducted by Miss Helgstrum
And protected by Miss Gary,
On their annual tour of the port . . .
MR. SWARTZ: *(Mysteriously)* To study the *front* of the waterfront—
Not what's behind the waterfront . . .
MRS. WINKELBAUM: This group of fine young ladies
Is heading this way,
So you, dear Maggie,
Get upstairs—
And stay!
MAGGIE: Well, I'll be—!
Tonight, Mister Swartz, you'll want me to steer
The sailors to buy your wine and your beer—
Into your lousy old grog shop,
Into your filthy old joint,
To fill your coffers, drinking your slop,
While coins are clinking, making you rich.
But, maybe I won't!
Maybe I'll take them down
To the Golden Eagle instead—
Before I take them
To bed.
MRS. WINKELBAUM and MR. SWARTZ: You're all right, Maggie,
Now don't get insulted.
You're O.K.—
But
Just for an hour,
Respect the Chamber of Commerce,
Maggie, please!
Stay away!
MRS. WINKELBAUM: *(Grandly)* Innocence is coming!
Virgins!
Stay away!
MAGGIE: O.K.
Young innocence is coming—

So *me,*
I'll go upstairs.
Upstairs—
And
Stay!
> *(Exit MAGGIE in anger up to her room)*

III. *RECITATIVE*

MRS. WINKELBAUM: Innocence, young innocence!
    Ah, Mister Swartz, I remember when I
    Was also young and sweet and shy.
MR. SWARTZ: Missus Winkelbaum, don't lie.
MRS. WINKELBAUM: No lie, Mr. Swartz,
    I once *was* young and shy.
    And innocent was I.
    In the days before I met my Harry
    I was just like them ladies from the Seminary.
    (She weeps politely)
MR. SWARTZ: Missus Winkelbaum, don't cry!
    Sweep your sidewalk and let your eyes dry.
    Over spilt milk there is no use to cry.
MRS. WINKELBAUM: Spilt beer, you mean,
    And the rum he drank!
    I hate drunken sailors in spite of the fact
    That their trade keeps a roof over my head
    In this shack.
    (Angrily she points to his bar)
    Cover up that nude on the window sign there,
    Young ladies mustn't see grown women bare.
MR. SWARTZ: You're right, Missus Winkelbaum.
    Damn right you are!
    But remove from your window those brass knucks
    And rubber can-can dancers, and such sailor's truck!
MRS. WINKELBAUM: Huh! You take down from your wall
    Those "Artistic Poses"
    And that low degrading muck!
    It's a disgrace!
MR. SWARTZ: Ah! But then those nice young ladies
    Won't enter my place.

MRS. WINKELBAUM: How will we keep them fresh young sailors out
   of the way—
   And them navy-boys that are just as bad?
MR. SWARTZ: That's for the police,
   Not for us to say.
MRS. WINKELBAUM: Too bad, too bad.
   That bad ship there,
   The *Sea Horse*.
   Is paying off today!
MR. SWARTZ: Them sailors are bad on that freighter.
MRS. WINKELBAUM: Too long away . . .
MR. SWARTZ: Been to Africa, Turkey, the Red Sea,
   The Orient.
MRS. WINKELBAUM: And no telling where else that nasty old tub
   went
MR. SWARTZ: I hope those young ruffians don't get fly
   With those nice visiting young ladies
   From that nice private school.
        (*Eight sharp bell strokes sound*)

IV. *SCENA CON CORO*

MRS. WINKELBAUM: Eight bells on the *Sea Horse*!
   Soon that crew'll be ashore! Ashore!
        (*MAGGIE appears in her window*)
MAGGIE: In port! In port!
MRS. WINKELBAUM: Just when them school-girls are visiting the
   port,
   Just now must that crew come into port!
MR. SWARTZ: In port!
MAGGIE:) In port!
MR. SWARTZ:)
MRS. WINKELBAUM:)
   Dirty old port!
   Sinful old port!
        (*CROWD enters*)
CHORUS: But we love it,
   We love our old port!
        (*With a loud whoop a SAILOR slides down a rope from the ship as
        OTHERS come down the gangplank*).

FIRST SAILOR: Yee-ee-ee-ee!
   Here's me!
   First ashore!
   But there'll be more!
      (Sliding down the rope another SAILOR appears)
SECOND SAILOR: Yee-ee-ee-ee!
MAGGIE:)
MR. SWARTZ:)   Skipper, who are you?
MRS. WINKELBAUM:)
SECOND SAILOR: I'm Buddy Mc Coy!
   Get out of my way!
   I'm some boy!
      (Other SAILORS slide to the deck)
THIRD SAILOR: Yee-ee-ee-ee!
CHORUS: Hey there! Hey there!
   Hey there, Sailor, let's get going!
THIRD SAILOR: I been in every port,
   In every no-good land—
   And the women everywhere,
   Yes, they swear
   I'm a good man!
ALL: In port, in port!
   Dirty old port!
   Sinful old port!
   But we love it,
   Our port!
      (The BOSUN enters down the gangplank walking bowlegged)
BOSUN: What are you drinking, chum?
   Whiskey, wine, beer or rum?
CHORUS: All of it! All of it!
   And then some!
FIRST SAILOR: Gimme Scotch 'cause it creeps on you—
THIRD SAILOR: Gimme wine 'cause it makes me dreamy.
SECOND SAILOR: I'll take brandy—
   It has a kick.
FOURTH SAILOR: Gimme ale that's nice and creamy.
FIFTH SAILOR: Gin and bitters will turn the trick!
SIXTH SAILOR: But there's nothing like beer
   Any old time,
   And a glass of beer
   Costs only a dime.

SONG

SAILORS, TOWNSPEOPLE, ALL PRESENT SOLOISTS:
 What is money for?
  To spend, says the sailor!
 What is red wine for?
  To drink, says the sailor!
 And women?
  To love!
 And "right now"?
  For joy!
 "To-morrow?"
  For joy!
 What's a man's life for, say?
  "Live it up!"
 And the green sea?
  For sailing!
 And the brown land?
  For laughter?
 For love and laughter!

 What's the wide world for?
  To roam, says the sailor!
 What's a new land for?
  For fun, says the sailor!
 And girlies!
  To love!
 And Women!
  To love!
 And Madams!
  For Love!
 What are two arms for, say?
  "Hug 'em tight"!
 And their red lips?
  For kissing!
 And their bright eyes?
  For winking!
 For right-now, without thinking!
CHORUS: But, now it's time for licker . . .
 So put it down the hatch
 And let's get really sky-high . . .

All of it is licker!
All of it is good!
Down the hatch with that fiery old licker!
Down the hatch with that stuff!
  (The COP enters and there is sudden quiet)
COP: Gentlemen, gentlemen!

ARIOSO

The young ladies from the Seminary
Will shortly be along—
And I don't want no cussing
No shouting, and no drunken song.
Once a year and only for an hour
Or two that day,
Do such gentle, such lovely
And such—*young* girls
Come this way.
So get inside,
Off the street, now,
Get out of the way, boys—
Please!
SAILORS: Aw, eat your hat! . . .
  Aw, copper, at ease! . . .
  Just take it slow! . . .
  Just cool off, old man! . . .
  We're heading in the bar anyway,
  But we're gonna come out rolling some!
    (Very subdued)
  All of it is licker,
  All of it is good!
    (Still more subdued)
  Down the hatch with that fiery old licker,
    (Suddenly howling as they head for the bar)
  Down with that stuff!
    (Exit ALL except COP. Loud laughter inside the bar, then silence.
    The GIRLS from the Seminary and TEACHERS enter)

V. SCENA E CANZONE DEL CORO

MRS. WINKELBAUM: Good afternoon, Miss Helgstrum!
  Good afternoon, Miss Gary!

And good afternoon to you
Young ladies from the Seminary!

MISS HELGSTRUM:	)	Good afternoon,
MISS GARY:	)	Good afternoon,
THE GIRLS:	)	Good afternoon,

ARIOSO

MRS. WINKELBAUM: I'm still doing business at the same old shop
　　Where every time you're invited to stop,
　　For young ladies, of course, I don't have very much.
MISS GARY: Thank you, Madam,
　　But we'll not come in.
　　Our young ladies are interested
　　In import and export
　　The general business of the port.
　　Being in the upper form,
　　Economically
　　And sociologically speaking
　　Statistics on shipping is what they are seeking.
　　Are we not, girls?
THE GIRLS: *(Eagerly)* Yes, Miss Gary!
MISS GARY: *(Emphatically)* Are we not, girls?
THE GIRLS: *(Deflatingly)* Yes, Miss Gary!
MISS HELGSTRUM: Of course, the colorful background
　　That shipping gives our town
　　Is of interest, too.
　　But our time is limited,
　　Missus Winkelbaum,
　　We have so much to do!
　　We regret we cannot stop.
　　To shop
　　With you!
　　Don't we, girls?
THE GIRLS: *(As before)* Yes, Miss Helgstrum!

MISS HELGSTRUM:	)	
MISS GARY:	)	Don't we, girls?

THE GIRLS: Yes, Miss Gary!
MISS HELGSTRUM: So we won't tarry.
　　We have still to cover,
　　The waterfront—

Along the waterfront—
     (Quasi refrain)
To the Custom's Office
And the Harbor Master!
To the Ship's Chandler's,
And the Anchor Caster,
The Import-Export office as well,
     (Expressively)
Then we're to have supper
With the Captain
Of the *Mary Belle.*
     (The Seminary party starts to move along)
MISS HELGSTRUM:)
MISS GARY:)   To the Custom's office. . . . etc.
THE GIRLS:)
     (A SAILOR comes out of the bar, drunk, overhears the end of their talk, and puts himself in their way)
FIRST SAILOR: Aw, I wouldn't eat on that old tub,
    That transatlantic ferry!
    You oughta put some real seafaring grub
    In the craws of your Seminary.
    To hell with that passenger's slop on the *Mary Belle!*
     (The COP interferes and the SAILOR withdraws)
MISS GARY: Girls, let's continue our trip
    This corner, as you can see,
    Is hardly one of pure commerce and industry.
     (In canon)
MISS HELGSTRUM:)   Goodbye, Missus Winkelbaum,
MISS GARY:)
THE GIRLS:)   See you next year!
MISS HELGSTRUM: Girls, come along!
    We've got to get along the waterfront,
    Along the waterfront
    To:
MISS HELGSTRUM:)   The Custom's Office,
MISS GARY:)
THE GIRLS:)   And the Harbor Master's,
    To the Ship Chandler's,
    And the Anchor Caster's
    The Import-Export office as well—

Then we're to have supper
With the Captain
Of the *Mary Belle.*
> (*ALL exit except MRS. WINKELBAUM and the lovely JEAN-
> NETTE, who turns back furtively*)

VI. *RECITATIVE*

JEANNETTE: Missus Winkelbaum,
> I heard my grandfather mention you.
> He was a seafaring man.
MRS. WINKELBAUM: I've been here for many a year,
> So I probably knew your grandfather,
> My dear.
> > (*MAGGIE appears on the balcony*)
MAGGIE: If he was a man, you did!
> > (*MAGGIE disappears again*)
JEANNETTE: I love the sea myself,
> Missus Winkelbaum.
> But my folks will hardly ever
> Let me come down to the port,
> Or even look at the sea.
> My parents owned a lot of ships once,
> But they are dead now.
> All they left me is money.
MRS. WINKELBAUM: Money! What a shame, honey!
JEANNETTE: Missus Winkelbaum, I envy you,
> With your wonderful view of the harbor and sea.
MRS. WINKELBAUM: Sweet child, I'm so glad somebody envies me.
> But go now; catch up with your mates.
> Go darling, they will be worried.
JEANNETTE: Yes, I know.
> Goodbye, I'll go.
> > (*MRS. WINKELBAUM disappears inside her shop. JEAN-
> > NETTE stops, turns, and comes back to the corner. She stands alone
> > on the quay, looking at the sea, as dusk deepens into sunset*)

VII. *RECITATIVO ED ARIA*

JEANNETTE: The sea, the sea,
> My grandfather loved the sea!

I love it, too.
Grandfather didn't just *own* ships—
He sailed them.
I wish I could sail away . . .
Somewhere . . .
On a ship . . .

ARIA

Over the white foam
Over the sea—
Over the endless billows
I would follow thee.

I'm a lonely girl—
On the shelf my dolls—
But dolls are lifeless—
Answering not at all.

I'm a lonely girl,
With an empty heart,
My dreams alone to cherish,
All I have is my dreaming.

Over the white foam,
The billowing waters,
Over the endless ocean,
I'd seek
After
Thee.

> (*As the sun, blood red, sinks into the sea, she stands forlornly at the edge of the quay, her shadow a long shadow on the dock. Suddenly at the top of the gangplank, just as the neon sign over the bar comes gaily on, a young sailor appears—SMITTY, who is like every girl's dream of a sailor—handsome, impudent, blonde, and as clean as the sea is clean*)

VIII. SCENETTA

SMITTY: You're lonely, kid?
JEANNETTE: Lonely, very lonely.
SMITTY: I'm lonely, too—
    Lonely, very lonely.

JEANNETTE: I've been lonely all my life.
SMITTY: So have I.
　　Let's stop being lonely.
JEANNETTE: Oh, that I could!
SMITTY: Little girl, I might show you how.
JEANNETTE: What's your name?
SMITTY: Smitty.
JEANNETTE: Mine's Jeannette.
SMITTY: Jeannette . . . Jeannette . . .
　　　　(*In wonder he holds out his arms to JEANNETTE. Slowly, as in a dream, she comes toward him. But the dream is broken by a harsh, seductive voice calling from the window over the tobacco shop*)

IX. *SCENE E CANZONE*

MAGGIE: Hey, there! Sailor! What's your story?
　　Drop that kid, too young!
　　She's a morning glory
　　Who will wilt on your wine!
　　Anyhow, she's taking my trade—
　　You're due to be mine.
　　Besides, you know the law—
　　You'd better be wary,
　　And leave that youngster to the Seminary!
　　Are you blind? Can't you see?
　　She's under-age . . .
　　　　(*MAGGIE comes down to the street as JEANNETTE, frightened, withdraws to one side*)
SMITTY: Gee—I guess she's right.
　　What am I thinking of?
　　And I haven't had a drink tonight!
　　　　(*But SMITTY continues to gaze at JEANNETTE as MAGGIE sings*)

SONG

MAGGIE: Hey, there
　　Sailorboy,
　　In from the sea.
　　Listen,
　　Sailor,
　　Come with me.

Come on,
Drink Cognac!
Rather than wine?
Come here,
Come and be mine.

Come on,
Sailorboy,
Out of the sea—
Let's go,
Sweetie,
Come with me!

X. SCENA, ARIOSO CON CORO

> *(A police whistle is heard in the distance)*
MAGGIE: The police!
> *(MAGGIE disappears)*
SMITTY: The police!
JEANNETTE: The police!
> *(Another whistle, very near. Voices are heard inside)*
PEOPLE: The police!
JEANNETTE: The police!
>   Miss Helgstrum, Miss Gary!
SMITTY: What?
JEANNETTE: The teachers from the Seminary.
SMITTY: Your teachers?
JEANNETTE: Yes, I'll have to go!
>   Smitty, hide me, please!
>   I don't want to go back
>   To the Seminary!
>   I hate Miss Helgstrum—
>   I hate Miss Gary!
>   Hide, oh hide me, please!
>> *(Again the police whistle. This time very near. JEANNETTE is frightened, as is the young SAILOR, sensing danger. She seeks the shelter of his arms. Then as voices are heard, SMITTY runs pulling JEANNETTE after him toward a huge barrel. He lifts up the barrel and hides JEANNETTE underneath it. The sailor takes a seat nonchalantly upon the barrel and lights a cigarette as the*

crowd pours from the bar. People appear in doors, windows, and at the rail of the ship)

CHORUS: The police! The police!
   A police whistle in this neighborhood
   Does not indicate anything too good!
   Things must be getting pretty rough
   If the cops on our beat are getting tough!
      (Excitedly, various POLICEMEN and MISS HELGSTRUM en-
      ter looking for the girl)

COP: Has anyone of you seen
   A young lady from the Seminary?

CHORUS: No!

COP: No?!

CHORUS: No!

COP: No??

CHORUS: No!!

MISS HELGSTRUM: We missed her at the Captain's table
   At the supper on the *Mary Belle.*

COP: That girl is from the Seminary!

MEN: What would we do
   With a young chick from the Seminary? . . . .
      (Simultaneously, the WOMEN cry out)

WOMEN: Ridiculous, ridiculous!

MEN: With men like us,
   Such girls don't tarry.

FIRST SAILOR: But we might make some time with *you* . . .

MISS HELGSTRUM: Ooooh! . . .

COP: Stand back! None of your sass!
   Get out of the way
   And let this lady pass.

CHORUS: Let her pass, let her pass!

MAGGIE: Let the old witch pass.

COP: Say there, Mister Gunner's mate,
   Have you seen a young lady out so late
   In this rough neighborhood
   Which, for a nice girl, ain't no good.

SMITTY: No, sir, I have not.
   Just now, I've set my foot ashore.
   These "ladies" I have seen—
   These "ladies", but no more.

MISS HELGSTRUM: Officer! Officer! We must find that child!
  Her guardians with grief will be wild!
  As for our school, what scandal!
CHORUS: For the school, what a flop!
MISS HELGSTRUM: I, twenty years a teacher, might lose my job.
CHORUS: For the school, what a flop!
MISS HELGSTRUM: Men! Women!
  I'm so upset!
  Help me to find Jeannette!
GAY GIRL: Lady,
  My name's Jeannette!
    (*COP and MISS HELGSTRUM exit frantically as the crowd teases the street girl*)
CHORUS: Ha-ha! It isn't you, I bet!
  It isn't you, you're not Jeannette.
  Let's go to the bar and forget Jeannette!
  Forget
  Jeannette!
    (*ALL exit except SMITTY. By now it is late evening. The street is empty*)

XI. *RECITATIVO E DUETTO*

SMITTY: Jeannette—
    (*He lifts the barrel and the girl comes out of hiding*)
JEANNETTE: Smitty—
    (*He takes her in his arms*)
SMITTY: Would you consider
  Being a sailor's wife?
JEANNETTE: Myself, I've fancied
  Being a sailor's wife.
SMITTY: But I—I'd maybe have to go away a lot.
JEANNETTE: I'd be with you.
  I'd follow you everywhere,
  Everywhere you go.
    (*He takes her to the edge of the quay*)
SMITTY: Would you?
  Would you follow me
  Even to Zanzibar?
JEANNETTE: Even to Zanzibar.
  But is there really a place called Zanzibar?

SMITTY: Certainly there is, Jeannette.
> *(They look in wonder toward the far horizon as night begins to fall over the port)*

JEANNETTE: Where? Where?

SMITTY: Just right over there—
A dream beyond a star—
Yet not so far away
Is Zanzibar.

Dreams are mountain high,
But when you climb that far,
Beneath a velvet sky
Is Zanzibar.

JEANNETTE: Just a heartbeat away,
And just the touch of a hand,
Just a rainbow's flight
To a wonderland.

BOTH: See it over there—
A dream beyond a star—
Yet not so very far—
Zanzibar.

XII. *FINALE*

> *(A searchlight, unnoticed by the lovers, scans the scene from side to side)*

SMITTY: Let's marry!

JEANNETTE: Oh, yes!

SMITTY: But is it true—
You're underage?

JEANNETTE: I'm sixteen!
> *(A second searchlight sweeps the docks)*

SMITTY: In some countries
Folks marry at sixteen!

JEANNETTE: Where—in Zanzibar?

SMITTY: Yes—in Zanzibar!
> *(JEANNETTE's cry becomes a plea)*

JEANNETTE: Smitty!
Take me to Zanzibar!
> *(The two searchlights simultaneously merge on the couple. Sirens, whistles, auto horns sound as the CROWD inside cry out)*

CHORUS: Again? What's up now?

(They pour from the bar)
There's hell to pay!
   *(MISS HELGSTRUM, MISS GARY, COP and OTHER COPS
   enter)*
MISS HELGSTRUM: There she is!
MISS GARY: And with a sailor!
MISS HELGSTRUM: Jeannette!
MISS GARY: You naughty girl!
   (The TEACHERS call angrily as the COP strides forward)
BOTH: Jeannette!!!
COP: Ah-ha! Young lady,
   I figured we'd find you yet!
   *(The TEACHERS pull JEANNETTE from SMITTY's grasp and
   haul her away toward the left while the COPS pull SMITTY
   toward the right. Just as they are about to lose sight of each other,
   each breaks away for a hurried moment. But, seeing they cannot
   meet, JEANNETTE takes a golden locket from her throat and
   tosses it to SMITTY. In turn, SMITTY takes his jaunty cap from
   his head and throws it to JEANNETTE. As MISS HELGSTRUM
   and MISS GARY reach the girl, she stuffs the cap into her bosom
   and, looking back longingly, she is carried off by the irate TEACH-
   ERS. The POLICEMEN release SMITTY, and exit left. The crowd
   laughs)*
CHORUS: So that's the girl from the Seminary!
   Underage! Shouldn't be out so late!
   Poor li'l thing, too young to marry—
   Yet running around with a gunner's mate!
   *(Wild hilarity, dancing and general excitement which gradually
   subsides as MRS. WINKELBAUM comes forward)*
MRS. WINKELBAUM: There is nothing like a port town—
   What sights you see
   Every day . . .

MRS. WINKELBAUM:	)	On a port street
MR. SWARTZ:	)	
FIRST SAILOR:	)	In a port town, heh,
GAY GIRL:	)	

   Wouldn't you say?
   *(All exit, except SMITTY, who slowly mounts the gangplank with
   Jeannette's locket in his hand. MAGGIE approaches him, repeat-
   ing her invitation of the early evening)*

MAGGIE: Hey, there! Sailor boy!
  Salty as the sea.
  Listen, sailor,
  Come with me!
  Come on, sailor,
  Out of the sea—
  Let's go sweetie,
  Come
  With
  Me.
    *(The young sailor does not answer. Slowly he puts the locket into
    a pocket over his heart. Then SMITTY turns and walks up the
    gangplank, back to his ship)*
CURTAIN
CADE IL SIPARTO

Musicals

Tropics after Dark

1940
By Langston Hughes and Arna Bontemps
Music by Margaret Bonds
Additional Music by Zilner Randolph

In 1940, Hughes was contracted to write two pieces for the Chicago American Negro Exposition celebrating the Diamond Jubilee of Emancipation. One was a compendium of scenes from black musicals, to be called *Jubilee: A Cavalcade of the Negro Theatre;* the other was the revue *Tropics after Dark.* Neither work was actually mounted, although Hughes's dialogue was stripped from *Tropics after Dark,* and the songs mounted as a beer hall revue. Ten days after the exposition's opening, Hughes wrote to Margaret Bonds: "I have only three songs left in the show, two of Randolph's and your PRETTY FLOWER. . . . The Expo is (confidentially) in a very bad way finally, so I guess we're lucky to get what little we did get out of the show. Doubt if we'll get another penny, except what we might be able to do with the book and music on our own."[1]

A period piece replete with stereotypes, *Tropics after Dark* moves indiscriminately between popular song and the shadows of the blues, contrasting masculinities and banal sentimentality. It represents Hughes's frequent engagement with popular forms of entertainment, all in the interest of paying the rent—in this case, unsuccessfully.

The text is taken from the typescript in the Langston Hughes Papers at the Beinecke Library.

TIME: *The Present*
PLACE: *Caribbean Islands*
SET: *A plaza by the sea:*
　　ACT I: Late Afternoon
　　ACT II: Carnival Night

Cast

BILLY, a sailor from Chicago
BUDDY, a tourist from Harlem
COLOMA, a girl from Trinidad
CHORUS: LOLA
    LUPE
    PAQUITA
    CARMENCITA

Act I

Market day in the plaza. Sea wall with steps upstage leading down to beach.
Palm trees. Top of a sail. Fishing nets hanging up to dry. Edge of
building with sign CAFE at left. Runway leading into audience.
CURTAIN: *At rise the ladies of the ensemble dressed as MARKET*
WOMEN in the Martinique costume with wide skirts of gay colors,
polka dots, and bright head-cloths, bearing wicker trays of fruit and
flowers, sing MARKET DAY IN MARTINIQUE. Each girl takes a
verse, selling her wares to the audience from the runway.

MARKET DAY IN MARTINIQUE

CHORUS: We are the market ladies
    Down in Martinique.
    We have lots of things to sell
    Just tell us what you seek:
        Mangoes! Mangoes!
    Don't you want to buy some mangoes?
        I got mangoes taste like wine.
        Finest mangoes you can find.
    Mangoes! Mangoes!
    Don't you want to buy some mangoes?
    Magnolias! Magnolias!
    Don't you want to buy some magnolias?
    They're white as the foam of the sea.
    Perfumed with tropic mystery.
    Magnolias! Magnolias!
    Don't you want to buy some magnolias?

Bananas! Bananas!
Don't you want to buy some bananas?
I got 'em red! I got 'em sweet!
I got 'em yellow with sugar meat!
Bananas! Bananas!
Don't you want to buy some bananas?

Yams! Yams!
Don't you want to buy some yams?
I got yams taste like hams,
Great big good old juicy yams.
Yams! Yams!
Don't you want to buy some yams?

Coconuts! Coconuts!
Don't you want to buy some coconuts?
My coconuts are full of juice.
Just the thing to make your joints get loose.
Coconuts! Coconuts!
Don't you want to buy some coconuts?
We are the market ladies
Down in Martinique.
We have lots of things to sell
Just tell us what you seek:
> (*As they finish singing, BILLY enters in a very tight white sailor suit, cap on side of his head. He carries a red cage with a parrot inside. The GIRLS rush toward him crying their wares.*)

GIRLS: Mangoes! Mangoes!
Magnolias! Magnolias!
Yams! Yams!
Coconuts! Coconuts!

BILLY: (*Struggling to get away from the GIRLS and dropping his parrot cage.*) Here! Here! Here! I don't want no yams nor coconuts neither. Ain't none o' you-all got no cherries?

GIRLS: No savvy! No savvy!

LUPE: Magnolias! Magnolias!

BILLY: What I want with a flower? Come here, lemme see *you.*

GIRLS: (*Holding out wares*) Buy! Buy! Buy!

BILLY: Huh! You-all know one English word, anyhow. Buy! How much them coconuts? I'm liable to need one for a weapon 'fore the day's over.

GIRL: *(Holding up five fingers)* Cinco centavos!

BILLY: What lingo's that? French or Spanish?

GIRL: Yo, espanola!

BILLY: You don't say! Well, where you live at? I want to know.
    (As GIRL doesn't answer)
    Where's your domicile?

GIRL: No savvy.

BILLY: You one o' them no-savvy's too?
    (To another GIRL)
    Say baby, what's your name?

GIRL: No savvy.

BILLY: I ask you what's your name. You know *name*, NAME! What your papa give you.

GIRL: No savvy.

BILLY: You know, Mary? Jennie? Maggie-Lou? Johnson? Jenkins? What?

GIRLS: No savvy! No savvy!

BILLY: You with the bananas! What's ——

GIRL: *(Pushing tray toward him)* Bananas! Bananas! Buy? Buy?

BILLY: Huh! You can sure savvy buy, can't you? *(Trying to make out their names)* You—Cuba Libre?

GIRL: No! Carmencita.

BILLY: Uh-huh! Now, I'm getting somewhere. You, fat one there, Dolores?

GIRL: No, senor, Paquita.

BILLY: Paquita? Now that's a juicy name. Hey, you—Maria?

GIRL: No, Lola! You—who you?

BILLY: Me? You want to know who I am? Womens, I'm sweet Billy Mitchell from Chicago, Listen:

BOULEVARD COWBOY

I

I'm a boulevard cowboy, a jitney man—
That's my pedigree.
And I live in the Carrie, 47th and Prairie.
Everybody in Chicago knows me.
You can dig me at Ernie's old Chicken Shack—
    Pickin' bones, you know,
        Take my gal to the Regal when *I'm* holding plenty jack
            Make her stay home when *her* funds are low.

2

Now, I wear a drape model, the latest style,
Striped red and gray.
And I put all my numbers in the Black Gold every day
But they come out in some book I don't play.
Once at Kelley's big Keno I won the pot—
Mean Jack pot and all.
And the next day I lost back every single dime and dollar,
Left me muggin' way behind the 8 ball.

3

But I'm a boulevard cowboy, a jitney man—Bad luck can't down me.
Cause I got a sweet baby, Jack, I really don't mean maybe
And she gives me more than her sympathy.
When I tell my chick, honey, I'm down and out
Here is what she'll say—
Jitney man, don't you worry, don't you scuffle, neither scurry—
You're my lovin cowboy from South Parkway—I'm just a cowboy from
    Oatmeal Boulevard.
But my baby said, Billy, don't mind when skies are gray—
          (I'LL TAKE CARE OF YOU)
Cause you're my sweet lovin' cowboy from South Parkway.
          (THAT'S WHAT I AM)
Just a cowboy from South Parkway.
GIRLS: Que chico! Que hombre tan chistosa! How fun-nee!
BILLY: I knew yo-all would like that.
          (To LOLA)
    Now, come here.
LOLA: No savvy.
BILLY: I mean you with the bananas—come here.
LOLA: Bananas! Oh, quiere bananas? Buy? Buy? Buy?
BILLY: Looks like you can really savvy buy. How come you can't savvy
    nothing else? Come here!
          (LOLA approaches)
    Gimme a kiss.
GIRLS: *(ALL)* No savvy! No savvy! No savvy!
          (They back away)
BILLY: Dog-gone my soul! I'm gonna pitch a fog in a minute—if you-all
    don't understand something.
          (Approaches GIRLS who back away. But LOLA stands her ground.)

You-all must think I'm Hitler the way you running. I done told you
who I am. I'm sweet Billy Mitchell from Chicago.

LOLA: *(Angrily)* No le hace quien tu eres! Caramba! No me importa
nada Chicago! Bah! Chicago!

BILLY: Say you know I like you! You ought to sell pepper instead of
bananas. Come here, sweets.

LOLA: No savvy, "Come here, sheets."

BILLY: You just come here and I'll make you savvy.

LOLA: No "come here."

BILLY: *(Grabs her)* Yes, you is, too.

LOLA: *(Screams)* Oh!

> *(BILLY pulls her to him roughly. Other GIRLS run away chattering)*

BILLY: I ain't gonna hurt you, baby. I'm just gonna put you in a
kitchenette.

LOLA: *(Struggling)* No! No! Dejame! No!

> *(Enter BUDDY, handsome young tourist in sport clothes.)*

BUDDY: Hey, sailor, what's going on here?

BILLY: Man, you better dust your broom and keep your nose out of my
business.

BUDDY: Is that any way for a deck hand to talk to a passenger?

BILLY: You might be a passenger on my ship, Jack, but you ain't nothing
to me ashore.

BUDDY: I'll report you to the captain—out here molesting women.

BILLY: Molesting, nothing! If you know what's good for you Jim,
you'll—

> *(LOLA breaks away and runs. Exits)*

Now look what you done done! Just when I was about to make that
woman understand, too. You know you just ain't got no mercy.

BUDDY: I merely wanted to keep you from getting in trouble Billy.
You're down here in a foreign land where you don't speak the
language.—

BILLY: Do you speak it?

BUDDY: No, I don't speak it either, but I have tact, finesse.

BILLY: Um-hum! Well, finesse right on after me, then, cause I'm going
after that gal.

> *(Starts away)*

She's gonna savvy something today before she gets through with me.

BUDDY: Boy, don't be foolish! Come on, let's go up to the bar and
have a cool drink.

BILLY: Cool drink, my eye! I want something without ice!
>*(Both exit after LOLA. Enter COLOMA with big straw hat on arm. She wears slacks and a long beach cape. She sings)*

LONELY LITTLE MAIDEN BY THE SEA

COLOMA: I've got two weeks vacation—
>But please broadcast to the nation
>That I'm NOT having any fun.
>All the other girls seem happy
>With boy friends that are snappy—
>But I haven't got a one:
>>I'm just a lonely little maiden by the sea.
>Nobody to even play with me.
>>>All this pretty sand
>>>And no one to hold my hand,
>>I'm bored all the time! Poor me!
>>If this lonely little maiden were to send
>>A letter to some all alone boy friend.
>>Would he pack his things and hurry
>>Here to help me stop my worry
>>And set my heart a-flurry at the end?
>>>For if it's any interest to you,
>>>And my poor love will do you,
>>I just want to tell you that my heart is free,
>>>Cause I'm feeling all alone
>>>For someone to call my own—
>>I'm just a lonely little maiden by the sea.
>*(As SHE sings she undresses and puts her clothes into the big hat she carries. At the end of the song she disappears down onto beach, removing last stitch of clothing as she exits. LOLA enters followed by BILLY)*

BILLY: *(Pleading)* Lola, look like if you didn't understand a word of English, you could tell what I mean by now. Ain't you got no feelings?

LOLA: No savvy!

BILLY: Ain't you got no heart?

LOLA: No savvy!

BILLY: *(On knees)* Ain't you got no mercy?

LOLA: No savvy!

BILLY: Well, ain't you got no—Shaw, ain't no use! I would give up—if
    I wasn't a jive man from way back. But I got more than jive, too.
    Now, sister, you listen:
    (*He grabs her and sings*)

I'LL MAKE YOU SAVVY

All this jive about "I don't understand"
Gets on a man's nerves, even in a foreign land.
I'm getting tired of this "no savvy" stuff,
So from now on I'm gonna be rough:
    If you no savvy, I'll make you savvy somehow,
    Cause when I want something I always want it now.
    I don't understand your language and don't know your style,
    But just gimme service, baby, and you'll always see me smile.
    But if you get stubborn and can't see your way clear
    To give me what I want, I'll raise a ruckus here.
        I'm meek and mild up to a point—
        But when that point is reached
    I'll wreck the joint.
    Cause I don't care nothing 'bout what no law don't allow—
    If you no savvy, I'll make you savvy somehow.
PATTER:
    You know I'm a sailor and I get around the world,
    And I got a way of meeting every situation, girl.
    If I get to Cuba and I want to eat,
    I just pinch the waitress and holler "Meat!"

    If I get to Haiti and need a drink,
    I point to my empty glass and wink.
    If I get to Martinique and desire a bed
    I just nod my sleepy head.

    And if I get to the Virgin Islands and want a gal—
    My Chicago jive will solve that, pal!
    Cause when I want something, I always want it now.
    But if you no savvy, I'll make you savvy somehow.

        I told you that I loved you, but you didn't understand.
        You gave me your foot when I reached for your hand.
        You started to holler when I grabbed you tight
        You acted like I was a varmint last night.

Now, when I say, Baby Doll, come here—
You pretend just like you can't even hear.
Now I ain't the type of cat to start no row—
But if you no savvy, I'll make you savvy somehow.

I mean that, mama! I'll make you savvy somehow.
> (*He drags her off as she struggles. Enter BUDDY left, COLOMA right in summery white dress, parasol*)

BUDDY: Coloma, you here?

COLOMA: Buddy!

BUDDY: I just came in today on the Calamares.
> (*The GIRL speaks with an accent*)

COLOMA: And I come yesterday on big white boat.

BUDDY: A whole week since I saw you in Trinidad! Gee, how I've missed you.

COLOMA: I miss you, too.

PRETTY FLOWER OF THE TROPICS

BUDDY: How did I know when I took that cruise
That I'd lose my heart in Trinidad?
In a tropic bower, I found a flower
And this is what I said:
Pretty flower of the tropics,
I love you.
Golden hour in the tropics
When I found you—
Your eyes are like the sunrise
Your lips are soft as dew.
Your arms are warm and tender,
Filled with tropic splendor.
Just to see you means surrender.
Pretty flower of the tropics,
Hold my hand.
You're the topic in the tropics
That makes me feel so grand.
There's something so sweet about you
That no one in this world could doubt you.
Dear, I can't do without you,
Pretty flower of the tropics.

COLOMA: I go now Buddy.

BUDDY: Go, Coloma?

COLOMA: Go dress. Carnival tonight. Beeg Carnival. Rumba. Everything.

BUDDY: That's right. Carnival tonight. We'll meet there.

COLOMA: Adios!

(COLOMA exits. Enter BILLY alone)

BUDDY: Where is she, boy? Where's your girl?

BILLY: Man, she got away. Just when I thought I had her, too.

BUDDY: Billy, you haven't got the right stuff with you. Now, we gentlemen from Harlem don't use that rough stuff you Chicago men pull off. We're suave, nonchalant. Not rough.

BILLY: No, you cats in Harlem can't be rough cause you don't get enough to eat. You ain't got the strength to be rough, Jack.

BUDDY: What do you mean, we folks in Harlem don't get enough to eat?

BILLY: Man, when I come through Harlem, a girl invited me out to dinner and you know what she serve?

BUDDY: No, what did she serve?

BILLY: Shadow soup and air waffles.

BUDDY: Shadow soup and air waffles?

BILLY: That's all. And you know when you was over in Chicago we fed you corn bread, dumplings, chine bones, sweet potatoes, cabbage, cold slaw, watermelon pickles, plum preserves, hot biscuits, and strawberry short cake.

BUDDY: You sure did. But you folks in Chicago haven't got any elevators in your apartment houses. You have to walk up 90–11 flights of stairs.

BILLY: Um-hum! But we got back porches and alleys. You-all ain't even got a alley in Harlem.

BUDDY: That's right! Sure haven't! But we got buildings up there so tall we can reach out and touch the moon.

BILLY: You mean so close together you reach out and touch your neighbors' hips.

BUDDY: No, you're wrong. Why in Harlem, we've got all modern convenience. Take our Eighth Avenue subway. It runs 90 miles an hour.

BILLY: That's nothing. Our cowboys out here run 110 with no meter.

BUDDY: And our cops in Harlem, man, they're big, bad, and terrific.

BILLY: Ain't got a thing on Two-gun Pete, though.

BUDDY: And the girls in Harlem! Man! All kinds! Short and tall! Slim and fat! Ebony and pink!

BILLY: But they got skeeter legs.

BUDDY: What?

BILLY: Yes, they got skeeter legs! But the Chicago girls, man! Built like a brick venus!

BUDDY: No wonder! They have to walk so far to get to a car line. But in Harlem, we have transportation on every street.

BILLY: You do?

BUDDY: Yes. And furthermore, we have street lights that make the night like day.

BILLY: Who in the hell wants the night like day?

BUDDY: And we don't park our cars in the streets at night, either. We put them in a garage.

BILLY: You mean you does all your necking in a garage?

BUDDY: Don't be facetious! I'm speaking about the municipal advantages.

BILLY: You-all has multiplicational advances?

BUDDY: Of course. There's no place like Harlem.

BILLY: But you ain't got no Joe Louis.

BUDDY: What?

BILLY: You heard me. You-all ain't got no Joe Louis.

BUDDY: No.

BILLY: And you-all ain't got no Tiny Parham.

BUDDY: No. No.

BILLY: And you-all ain't got no Rev. Cobbs.

BUDDY: But we've got Father Divine.

BILLY: Shaw! He can't holler nothing like Sister Lucy Smith.

    (BILLY gets happy in a sanctified manner)

BUDDY: Let's talk about something else. Where did the Lindy Hop come from? Right out of the Savoy in New York.

BILLY: Where did the boogie woogie come from?

BUDDY: Where?

BILLY: Right out in the South Side.

BUDDY: But we originated the jitterbug in New York.

BILLY: You did? I don't see how you could on a empty stomach, but let's see how you dance it.

BUDDY: Just like this, man.

    (BUDDY does a polite version of the jitterbug)

BILLY: Pshaw! That ain't a thing. You dance like you gonna get arrested if you cut loose. Man, listen:

THE WAY WE DANCE IN CHICAGO

Ain't you heard about that music, Chicago style?
The kind of music that drives you wild?
Ain't you heard about the way we dance it out?
Then lemme tell you what it's all about:
    First you grab your gal like a hep cat, Jack,
    And jitterbug her lightly then you throw her back.
    ⌐et your hips swing loose when you're moving—
    wing most any way long's you groovin'.
ʻou take it slow while she gets way down.
You're feelin' acrobatic, then you throw her round.
Then you separate, take a solo—
    Jump back and go boogie!
    Aw! Boogie woogie!
    Peck a little! Truck a little!
Now if anyone here is still in doubt
As to what this jitterbuggin' is all about,
I'll expostulate all that I know
'Bout the way we dance in Chicago—
BUDDY: Expostulate, Jack!
    Expostulate!
        (As he sings the GIRLS enter and BILLY teaches them the Chicago style Jitterbug. COLOMA pulls away from BUDDY when he gets too violent. She slaps him)
COLOMA: I no like it. You hurt me. What you think I am—a bag of meal? You nasty boy! I go away! Now!
    (COLOMA exits as BUDDY pleads)
BUDDY: Don't go! I'm sorry, darling! Please don't go!
BILLY: Aw, let the chick go, man! Grab another one. Let's dance.
    (The song and dance goes on)
CHORUS: Jump back and boogie!
    Aw! Boogie woogie!
    Peck a little! Truck a little!
Now if anyone here is still in doubt
As to what this jitterbuggin' is all about,

I'll expostulate all that I know
'Bout the way we dance in Chicago.
    (CHORUS exits jitterbugging)

BUDDY: Gee, I feel bad, you see, my girl's left me. You saw how she got mad and slapped me.

BILLY: I saw her slap you. And you didn't hit her back?

BUDDY: I don't believe in chastising women.

BILLY: You New York men is really something! Ain't you got no backbone?

BUDDY: Sure I've got a backbone.

BILLY: Then why don't you haul off and hit her with it?

BUDDY: Why, I wouldn't think of hitting that girl. I want to marry her.

BILLY: Marry her? You Harlem men is really weak.

BUDDY: I'm a gentleman. I don't want to take advantage of her otherwise.

BILLY: Her *otherwise*?

BUDDY: Of *her,* otherwise.

BILLY: Oh! So you gonna marry. Well, have you heard the one about the old man who had three sons?

BUDDY: No.

BILLY: And they married three sisters on the same day?

BUDDY: No. How does it go?

BILLY: Well, the old man was very rich.

BUDDY: Very rich?

BILLY: Yes. But he was also very old. And he knowed he couldn't live long to enjoy all that money he had, so he made up his mind to give some of it away before he died.

BUDDY: I see.

BILLY: So he told his three sons he wanted to have a little wedding supper for them on the night of their wedding.

BUDDY: On the night of their wedding.

BILLY: Yes, but beings as he was very old, and didn't like crowds, he couldn't stand no other people around but his three sons and their brides—three beautiful girls. So the supper was arranged. And after the ceremony, when they were all at the table, the old man at the head and the three boys on one side and the three brides on the other side, the old man said, "Children, just before I say grace, I have a little announcement I want to make. You all know I'm very rich. And I'm very old. And I won't live to spend all my money.

But no telling, I might live a *long* time yet, anyhow. So I want to give some of my money away now. To the first couple here at this table that brings me a grandchild—I say, to the first couple here that brings into this world a baby—I'm gonna give a Million Dollar.

BUDDY: A Million Dollar?

BILLY: Yes, a Million Dollars. Now, children, let us bow our heads and I'll say grace. The old man bowed his head to say grace—and when he lifted his head—there wasn't a soul at the table. All gone!

BUDDY: A marathon.

BILLY: Gone!

> *(Enter CARMENCITA)*

BUDDY: Just look at that beautiful brownskin! These girls in the tropics have got my head in a whirl!

BILLY: Her name's Carmencita. Call her, boy.

BUDDY: No, you call her.

BILLY: Let's both call her. Carmencita!

BUDDY: Carmencita!

> *(CARMENCITA looks back)*

BILLY: Tell her something, man, tell her something.

> *(BUDDY sings)*

CHOCOLATE CARMENCITA

BUDDY: Listen, dusky charmer, draw a little near.
  There's something I want to whisper in your ear.
  If you don't like flirting, I'm sorry as can be.
  I have to do it cause my heart is hurting me:
    Dusky Rio Rita!
    Chocolate Carmencita!
    How I'd like to meet ya,
    You cute little baby!
    Where the maracas are shaking
    How I would like to be taking
    Time out for a little love making.
    It's for you I'm craving.
    Got me misbehaving, Cuban Rio Rita.
    Got me at your feet, yet I'm up a tree.
    I'm up a tree till you belong to me,
    My Chocolate Carmencita.

(Entire COMPANY enters to take part in a CONGA finale. All are dressed in gay Spanish colors.)
CURTAIN

Act II

A night of carnival. Over the sea the moon has risen and stars shine. Lanterns gleam. The town is in fiesta. Balloons. Torches. Confetti. Masked dancers pass to and fro. Some carry musical instruments. Pranks are played. Rope skipping. Somersaults. Flirting.
Curtain: *Entire COMPANY in masks—one a DOG, another a BEAR, another a CLOWN, etc. TWO GIRLS in half masks. BILLY is handsomely dressed in a flowing red cape, satin suit, and cap of gold braid. He is masked as a romantic-looking BULLFIGHTER. As the curtain rises the entire cast is engaged in a*
    DANCE OF THE MASKS
to the music of LA CUCARACHA or a similarly familiar melody of Latin America. As they dance, the BULLFIGHTER takes the beautiful girl, LOLA, in his arms and makes gentle love to her. She melts into his embrace. He wraps her in his cloak. As the dance ends, ALL exit except LOLA and the BULLFIGHTER. LOLA pulls at his mask, anxious to see his handsome face.
LOLA: Take off! *Quiteselo!* Take off!
    (The BULLFIGHTER removes his handsome mask—and turns out to be BILLY.)
BILLY: Baby, here I am!
    (LOLA screams in fright and astonishment. She runs away. Heartbroken, BILLY pleads.)
Come back! Lola, please come back! I ain't gonna hurt you. You know I'm just bluffing when I act tough. Sure enough, baby, I love you. I want to marry you. Lola! . . . . . . Lola!
    (But she disappears in the distance.)
Poor me! All by myself way down here in Cuba or Martinique or somewhere or 'nother. Can't speak Spanish. Can't make no headway a-tall. Looks like my luck's done run down. What am I gonna do?
    (Enter a WITCH DOCTOR who squats at left of stage, spreads his wares on the ground before him, bones, black candles, and incense which he lights. BILLY addresses the WITCH DOCTOR)

Mister, tell me, what am I gonna do? I love that woman. I really love
that woman. She done put the hammer on my heart.
   (It grows dark as he sings)

VOODOO MAN

I wish I was a Johnny Barrymore—
Then maybe I could hold my paramour.
But she has gone away,
So far away from me.
Please listen to my plea:
   Voodoo man! Voodoo man!
   Make me a toby if you can.
   A toby that will bring my sweet gal back to me.
   Voodoo man! Voodoo man!
   Please make your hoodoo understand
I want to hold my sugar close again to me,
   If your hoodoo spell don't bring my baby back,
   John De Conq'or Root, I'll have a heart attack!
   Go get a black cat's bone and sprinkle goofer dust,
   Cause I've got to have my baby! Good Lawd, I must!
   Voodoo man! Voodoo man!
   Say you can help me! I know you can—
   Cause love has got me worried, Mister Voodoo Man!
         *(As BILLY stops singing there is a flash of fire and a DEVIL is
         revealed at the back of the stage. The WITCH DOCTOR croons as
         the DEVIL begins to dance.)*

DEVIL DANCE

         *(BILLY trembles with fright, but the DEVIL has him hypnotized,
         and as the dance ends, BILLY follows the DEVIL down toward the
         sea. . . . . BUDDY and COLOMA enter, holding hands. They sit
         on the sea wall together against the stars.)*
BUDDY: Darling, I was afraid you'd gone forever. You scared me.
COLOMA: Me no get mad with you. I——I——Oh! I can't tell you with
   English! I speak my own language. *Yo te amo!*
BUDDY: No savvy honey.
COLOMA: *Yo te amo! Te quiero mucho, mucho!*
         (She kisses him passionately)

BUDDY: Now! I understand that.

> (*BUDDY sings. On the second chorus he is joined by COLOMA in a duet.*)

SWEET NOTHING IN SPANISH

Down in Rumba land
It's hard to understand
If you don't know the lingo.
But when you speak to me
I'm lucky as can be—
I always seem to comprendo.
This game must never end though:
  My heart is burning
  And we've let the moon vanish
  While I've been learning
  Your sweet nothings in Spanish.
Don't know what the words mean,
But I know what your eyes mean.
I don't know your customs
But I know how my heart hums.
It's beating in a way that's so very Americanish
While I listen to your sweet
Little nothings in Spanish.
You say, *Yo te amo*—
And though I don't know Spanish
Your lips tell me, *I love you so,*
And all my fears vanish.
When you say, *si, si,*
And when you look at me
The way you do,
Then I could listen forever
To your sweet nothings in Spanish—
To your sweet little nothings in Spanish.

> (*As they sing, TWO GIRLS dressed in old Spanish lace with mantillas on their high combs, enter. They carry large lace fans. TWO OTHERS are dressed as MEN, caballeros, and the three couples join in a Spanish waltz. As the last chorus of the song and the waltz end, the couples drift away in the moonlight. Exit ALL. . . . Enter*

*BILLY very dejected. One of the men returns with a roulette wheel
which he sets up on the sea-wall. BILLY is attracted by it.)*

MAN: Roulette.

(He spins the wheel)

BILLY: Huh?

MAN: Roulette—win mon-nee.

BILLY: Win money? Then lemme play.

MAN: Red, me win. Black, you loose.

BILLY: Um-hum! Much as I been at Kelly's Keno, I know how to play
anything. Here, try this dollar.

(BILLY tries several dollars and loses each time.)

MAN: You loose.

BILLY: Say listen here! Let's play something else. Let's play black jack.

MAN: No savvy.

BILLY: Now there you go, no savvy. Let's play poker.

MAN: No savvy.

BILLY: Skin?

MAN: No savvy.

BILLY: Then just plain old craps. I tried to be high brow. Now let's
shoot some dice.

MAN: No savvy.

(BILLY starts to sing)

BILLY: Well, if you no savvy, I'll make you savvy somehow.
You shake your head and say you don't speak my lingo.
You don't play poker and you don't play bingo.
You act like you don't even recognize Georgia skin—
So let's see what you do when a dice game begin.
I'm gonna get your money out of your pocket today.
So you might as well give it to me some kind of way.
You know I don't care nothing 'bout what no law don't allow—
If you no savvy, Jack, I'll make you savvy somehow.
Shoot a rough!

*(The MAN fades BILLY for a dollar and the game is on. But
BILLY loses each pass. The MAN wins all his money. Then BILLY
gets mad. The MAN prepares to leave.)*

MAN: Me win—you loose!

BILLY: You stop that jive! You might of won, but you ain't gonna leave
here with it. Dog-gone your soul! Gimme my money back, you slick-
headed Spanish rascal, you! Hand it here! Now!

MAN: Me go!

BILLY: Hold it! Hold it right there! You ain't goin' no place. Gimme
me my money.

MAN: No savvy.

BILLY: I said, gimme my money.

MAN: No savvy.

(*BILLY starts to sing and reaches for his knife*)

BILLY: If you no savvy, I'll make you savvy somehow.
I'm getting tired of you no savvying now.
To tell you the truth if you don't gimme back
Every last red penny of my jack
I'll make you savvy so fast your head will crack.
I got Indian blood so don't let me start no pow-pow,
Cause if you no savvy, you sure better learn how.
You may be deaf and you may be Spanish and dumb—
But I'm gonna start you to talking some.
Hep cat or not, you sure better meow—
Cause if you no savvy, I'll make you savvy now.

(*BILLY draws his switch-blade and starts after the MAN who
drops money, roulette wheel, and all and flees. Exits*)

Pshaw! I knowed I'd make him savvy. Now if I can just make Lola
understand. (*Puts knife back*) But I'm gonna be gentle with her.
She's too sweet to rile.

(*Distant drum beats are heard, then nearer. Cries and laughter.*)

Listen! Must be the carnival coming! I always heard about this fiesta
in rumba land. I'm gonna see.

(*BILLY exits. There is a burst of light as the RUMBA
DANCERS with their DRUMMERS leap into the plaza. Confetti. Noise. Gaiety.*)

ORELIA AND PETE
Rumba Festival

(*Gradually the whole COMPANY gather to watch the dancers and
cheer them on clapping hands and throwing colored streamers. As
they finish BILLY and LOLA enter in close embrace. BUDDY and
COLOMA welcome them*)

BILLY: Man! Lola's beginning to savvy now. Buddy, I just asked this
woman to marry me, and she said *si, si*.

BUDDY: Solid Jack! Coloma's going to marry me, too. So let's have a
double wedding.

BILLY: Won't them chicks in Chicago be mad when they hear about this! Done lost sweet Billy Mitchell—down in Rumba Land. 47th Street gonna weep. Mourning in the Palm Tavern.

BUDDY: Billy, I feel so happy I could sing.

>*(BUDDY sings the verse to COLOMA and is joined by entire COMPANY on the chorus in a grand finale of dancing, confetti, drums)*

Come a little closer let me whisper in your ear
A message from a sunny tropic clime.
We work hard all day but when night's drawing near
Every body knows that's dancing time:
>   When the sun goes down in Rumba Land
>   And the one you love has you by the hand—
>   That is something only angels understand
>   When the sun goes down in Rumba Land
>   When the moon come up in Rumba Land
>   By those beaches where the white waves kiss the sand
>   And the maidens all are fair
>   With sweet flowers in their hair—
>   Well, a man ain't nothing there if he ain't a man—
>   So you find your partner and you say,
>   Don't you hear those drums a-playin' soft and gay?
>   Don't you hear that music's lovin' call
>   By that tropic water-fall
>   When the sun goes down in Rumba Land!

CURTAIN[2]

Simply Heavenly
A Comedy

1957
Music by David Martin

Simply Heavenly is based on Langston Hughes's brilliant and immensely popular Simple stories, published first in the *Chicago Defender* and later in the *New York Post* and collected by Hughes into five volumes. Turned into a musical at the request of a sponsor, *Simply Heavenly* was plagued by difficulties. It premiered on May 21, 1957, at the 85th Street Playhouse and ran for much of the summer, until it was closed by the Fire Department. Producer Stella Holt then moved the production to Broadway's 48th Street Playhouse, where it lasted another sixty-two performances, whereupon Holt moved it again, to 144 Bleeker Street, for a brief run. A spring production in London followed.

Despite many enthusiastic reviews, particularly of the initial production, *Simply Heavenly* was controversial. Many black members of the audience felt compromised by its play with stereotype; besides, the decade of increasingly tense civil rights struggles could not countenance its apparent lack of political awareness and its lightheartedness. In London, it failed utterly. Certainly the stage Jesse B. Semple, while comic, is a far cry from the deeply humorous and brilliantly satirical denizen of Hughes's columns. Moreover, Hughes felt neither the actors nor the director understood how to convey a "dignified comedy of black life," falling into farce rather than understanding the nature of the simplicity that defined his characters.[1]

Yet African American playwright Owen Dodson expressed interest in presenting *Simply Heavenly* at Howard University, and Randolph Edmonds, a major figure in the development of drama at the historically black colleges, mounted a hugely successful version in Jacksonville and Tampa, Florida, as well as staging it for the USO. In the latter venue, it did not fare well. Edmonds wrote to Hughes that small stages in the service clubs were not the only problem: "The main thing, however, is that some soldiers, both white and colored, saw things they did not like. The white soldiers did not like the Mississippi scene. The colored soldiers looked upon the characters as stereotypes. Mamie says truthfully that a Negro cannot do anything without some other Negro calling him a stereotype. . . . So we gave, for the most part, our variety show, 'Showtime.' We changed it, however, and included the production number of 'Did You Ever Hear the Blues.' It always received an ovation."[2] The reception of *Simply Heavenly* certainly bears out Hughes's complaint: "It's the old story—and the problem I've been wrestling with for years—how to get everything to suit everybody into one piece. When it comes to plays, it is a miracle to end up with anything at all one wishes left in the play."[3]

This text is that printed in *Five Plays by Langston Hughes,* edited by Webster Smalley (Bloomington: Indiana University Press, 1963), which is, according to Hughes, the version published by Dramatists Play Service.[4] There are other versions. Hughes wrote Owen Dodson,

> What script are you using, the off-Broadway version, the Broadway one, or the London one? Each has (progressively) more songs. The version which the Dramatists Play Service is publishing in January has the least songs. Otherwise, they are about the same as to dialogue.
>
> The SIMPLE TAKES A WIFE script I sent you is simply SIMPLY HEAVENLY without songs—a version prepared really for Europe where they can't translate the lyrics or cope with the blues. So please return this script back to me. I can use it for groups who might wish to do the play without music.[5]

Dodson replied that he wanted the one with the "most songs." There is a typescript of *Simple Takes a Wife* in the Langston Hughes Papers, with notes that other libraries have been supplied with copies.

Characters

JESSE B. SEMPLE	*Harlemite*
MADAM BUTLER	*Simple's landlady*
ANANIAS BOYD	*Simple's neighbor*
MRS. CADDY	*Joyce's landlady*
JOYCE LANE	*Simple's girl*
HOPKINS	*A genial bartender*
PIANIST	*A barfly*
MISS MAMIE	*A plump domestic*
BODIDDLY	*A dock worker*

CHARACTER	*A snob*
MELON	*A fruit vendor*
GITFIDDLE	*A guitar player*
ZARITA	*A glamorous goodtimer*
ARCIE	*Bodiddly's wife*
JOHN JASPER	*Her son*
ALI BABA	*A root doctor*
A POLICEMAN	
A NURSE	

TIME: *The present*
PLACE: *Harlem, U.S.A.*
MOOD: *Of the moment*

Scenes

Character Notes

GENERAL: The characters in "Simply Heavenly" are, on the whole, ordinary, hard-working lower-income bracket Harlemites. Paddy's Bar is like a neighborhood club, and most of its patrons are not drunkards or bums. Their small kitchenette rooms or overcrowded apartments cause them to seek the space and company of the bar. Just as others seek the church as a social center, or the poolhall, or dancehall, these talkative ones seek the bar.

SIMPLE: Simple is a Chaplinesque character, slight of build, awkwardly graceful, given to flights of fancy, and positive statements of opinion —stemming from a not so positive soul. He is dark with a likable smile, ordinarily dressed, except for rather flamboyant summer sport shirts. Simple tries hard to succeed, but the chips seldom fall just right. Yet he bounces like a rubber ball. He may go down, but he always bounds back up.

JOYCE: Joyce is a quiet girl more inclined toward club work than bars, toward "culture" rather than good-timing. But she is not snobbish or cold. She is tall, brownskin, given to longish ear-rings, beads, scarfs, and dangling things, very feminine, and cries easily. Her charm is her sincerity.

BOYD: Boyd has probably been half-way through college before his army service in Europe. Serious-minded, pleasant-looking, trying to be a writer, perhaps taking English courses at New York University on the last of his G. I. money. Almost every Harlem bar has such a fellow among its regular customers, who acts sometimes as a kind of arbiter when "intellectual" discussions come up.

ZARITA: Zarita is a lively bar-stool girl wearing life like a loose garment, but she is *not* a prostitute. Brassy-voiced, good-hearted, good-looking, playing the field for fun and drinks, she lives a come-day-go-day existence, generous in accepting or giving love, money, or drinks. A good dancer.

MISS MAMIE: Mamie is a hard-working domestic, using biting words to protect a soft heart and a need for love too often betrayed.

GITFIDDLE: Gitfiddle is a folk artist going to seed, unable to compete with the juke box, TV, and the radio, having only his guitar and his undisciplined talents. He furnishes all the music, with the Barfly pianist, for the songs and interludes.

MADAM BUTLER: Madam Butler has a bark that is worse than her bite—but her bark is bad enough. Large, fat, comical and terrible, she runs her rooming house as Hitler ran Germany.

Musical Numbers
(Music by David Martin)

Act I

Scene 2: Simply Heavenly	Joyce and Simple
Scene 5: Did You Ever Hear the Blues?	Mamie and Melon
Scene 6: Deep in Love With You	Simple
Scene 7: I'm Gonna Be John Henry	Simple

Act II

Scene 1: When I'm in a Quiet Mood	Mamie and Melon
Look for the Morning Star	Pianist and Zarita
Scene 2: Look for the Morning Star	Joyce and Simple
I Want Somebody To Come Home To	Joyce
Scene 3: Let's Ball Awhile	Zarita and Guests
Scene 9: A Good Old Girl	Mamie
Scene 11: Look for the Morning Star	Ensemble

[The following information is provided in the 1959 Dramatists Play Service Acting Edition of the text]

GUITAR MUSIC: The guitar music is all live, provided for interludes between scenes by Gitfiddle offstage in wings, with amplifier if needed on guitar. This music may be variations on "Did You Ever Hear the Blues?" or improvised blues chords. The interlude music is not published. If guitarist is a good folk musician, he can easily improvise it. If not, use sufficient portions of "Did You Ever Hear the Blues?" to cover the stage waits between scenes; or any traditional folk blues.

The set is divided into three sections: D.R., Simple's room; D.L., Joyce's room; and U.C., Paddy's Bar. A traveler, or a scrim of Lenox Avenue shops and bars, can be used to block off the bar during the scenes in Joyce's and Simple's rooms. Scenes on the street are played D.C., in front of Paddy's Bar. The traveler can be closed during these scenes also. The entrance to Simple's room is downstage in the R. wall. There is a bed against the U.C. wall of the room, and a dresser marks

the L. wall of his room. The entrance to Joyce's room is downstage
in the L. wall, with the bed against the upstage wall of the room and
the dresser marking the R. wall. Joyce's room also has a screen or a
closet U.L. A chair in each bedroom.

In Paddy's Bar, the entrance is upstage in the R. wall. The bar runs
parallel to the rear wall. The piano is against the R. wall, below the
entrance door. A stool L. of the piano and another stool just below
it. Three tables with chairs are scattered around the bar. All furniture
in the bar section is located upstage of the traveler.

Act I, Scene 1

A lonely guitar is playing in the darkness—it's the Blues . . .

*SIMPLE's room. Early spring evening. SIMPLE, just coming home from
work, removes his jacket as he enters, but before he can hang it up,
the voice of MADAM BUTLER, his landlady, is heard calling up the
stairs, through the half-open door.*

LANDLADY: Mr. Semple! Oh, Mr. Semple!

SIMPLE: Yes'm?

LANDLADY: I heard you come in! Mr. Semple, would you mind taking
Trixie out for a walk? My arthritis is bothering me.

SIMPLE: Madam Butler, please! I've got no time to walk no dog tonight. Joyce is waiting for me.

LANDLADY: From all I've heard, that girl's been waiting for you to
marry her for years! A few minutes of waiting for you to show up
tonight won't hurt.

SIMPLE: Madam, my private affairs ain't none of your business.

LANDLADY: Um-hum! Well, you don't need to take Trixie to no tree—
just the nearest fireplug. *(BOYD, a fellow-roomer, peers in)*

SIMPLE: Aw, I ain't hardly got home from work good, yet . . . Hello,
Boyd. Come on in. Landladies is a bodiddling! How come she never
make none of the other roomers—or you—to walk her dog?

BOYD: She knows I won't do it, that's why.

SIMPLE: Don't you ever get behind in your rent?

BOYD: Not to the point of walking dogs. But you seem to walk Trixie
pretty often.

SIMPLE: Mostly always.

LANDLADY: Did you say you would take the dog?

SIMPLE: Oh, hell, lemme go walk the bitch.

LANDLADY: No profanity in my house.

SIMPLE: Madam, that's a perfectly good word meaning a fine girl dog—bitch—for female dog.

LANDLADY: There'll be no bitches in my house—and that goes for your girl friend, Zarita, too.

SIMPLE: I'll thank you to leave my friends out of this.

LANDLADY: I'll thank you to keep your profanity to yourself. This is a decent house. Now, come on and walk my dog—else pay me my rent.

SIMPLE: I'll walk your dog—because I love Trixie, though, that's what! If I had a dog, I wouldn't keep it penned up in the house all day neither. Poor old thing, airless as she is.

LANDLADY: She's not hairless.

SIMPLE: I said *airless*, Madam! Shut up airtight, wonder Trixie don't get arthritis, too. Dog and womens, dogs and womens! Damn! What am I gonna do?

BOYD: Good luck, pal. *(SIMPLE and BOYD exit. BLACKOUT. In the darkness, Trixie's bark is heard. Auto horns, street noises. SIMPLE's voice addresses the barking dog)*

SIMPLE: Now, Trixie, come on now. Come on, Trixie, do your duty. Leave that other dog alone, Trixie! Hound, get away from here! O.K., O.K., let's head on in the house. *(Bark)* Now, go on to your madam. I guess you love her. Well, I love somebody, too! My choice, Joyce! She's the one I found—and that's where I'm bound. Trixie, that's where I am bound. *(The music of "Simply Heavenly" rises happily as the LIGHTS COME UP to reveal JOYCE's room)*

Act I, Scene 2

JOYCE's room a bit later. JOYCE is singing as, in a frilly dressing gown, she is putting her clothes away.

JOYCE: Love is simply heavenly!
What else could it be?
When love is made in heaven
And you are made for me.
Love is simply heavenly!
What else can I say?
When love sends me an angel

To hold me close this way.
I know love is like a dream
That's too good to be true,
But when your lips kiss mine
The dream turns into you.
Yes, it's simply heavenly!
Our love's just divine—
For love is made I heaven
And you, my love, are mine!

Love is simply heavenly—
(Voice of her LANDLADY calls from below stairs)
MRS. CADDY: Oo-oo-oo-oo! Miss Lane!
JOYCE: Yes?
MRS. CADDY: I'm letting Mr. Semple come up. O.K.?
JOYCE: Yes, indeed, Mrs. Caddy, I'm expecting him. *(SIMPLE knocks lightly and enters grinning)*
SIMPLE: Hey, Baby! *(He closes the door, to which JOYCE objects)*
JOYCE: Jess! No! Just a crack. . . .
SIMPLE: Aw, your old landlady's worse than mine. At least I can shut my door when I got company.
JOYCE: You're a man. I'm a— *(SIMPLE hugs JOYCE)*
SIMPLE: Lady! Which is what I like about you. Joyce, morals is your middle name. But you can still be a lady behind closed doors.
JOYCE: I know, Jess, those are the landlady's rules. Besides, I respect Mrs. Caddy.
SIMPLE: She don't respect you if she thinks soon as the door is shut . . .
JOYCE: Sshhss! Come on, rest your jacket, honey. It's warm.
SIMPLE: I knowed there was something! I forgot to bring your ice cream! I passed right by the place, too!
JOYCE: We can walk out for a soda.
SIMPLE: Or a beer?
JOYCE: Tomorrow's communion Sunday, and I do not drink beer before communion.
SIMPLE: You just don't drink beer, period! Gimme a little sugar and we'll skip the beer.
JOYCE: Don't think I'll skip the ice cream.
SIMPLE: Let's set on the— *(He dances toward the studio bed)*
JOYCE: There's a chair.
SIMPLE: Baby, what's the matter? Don't you trust me yet?

JOYCE: I don't mind you being close to me. But when you get close to a bed, too—

SIMPLE: Then you don't trust yourself.

JOYCE: Have you ever known me to—

SIMPLE: That's the trouble . . .

JOYCE: That goes with marriage, not courtship. And if you don't move on from courtship to engagement soon, Jess Semple, and do something about that woman in Baltimore.

SIMPLE: My wife! Isabel—she run me out—but she could claim I left her. She could find some grounds to get a divorce.

JOYCE: Since you're not together, why don't you get one?

SIMPLE: Joyce, I don't want to pay for no woman's divorce I don't love. And I do not love Isabel. Also, I ain't got the money.

JOYCE: I would help you pay for it.

SIMPLE: One thing I would not let you do, Joyce, is pay for no other woman's divorce. No!

JOYCE: Well, if you and I just paid for half of it, you'd only be paying for your part of the divorce.

SIMPLE: That woman wants me to pay for it all! And, Joyce, I don't love her. I love you. Joyce, do you want me to commit bigamy?

JOYCE: Five years you've been away from your wife—three years since you met me! In all that time you haven't reached a point yet where you can ask for my hand without committing bigamy. I don't know how my love holds out so long on promises. But now my friends are all asking when I'm going to get married. Even my landlady's saying it's a mighty long time for a man to just be "coming around calling," just sitting doing nothing.

SIMPLE: I agree, baby—when there ain't no action, I get kinder drowsy.

JOYCE: Well, to me, a nice conversation is action.

SIMPLE: Conversationing makes me sleepy.

JOYCE: Then you ought to go to bed early instead of hanging over Paddy's Bar until all hours. You have got to go to work just like I do.

SIMPLE: When I sleep, I sleep fast. Anyhow, I can't got to bed early just because you do, Joyce, until—unless—

JOYCE: Until what?

SIMPLE: Until we're married.

JOYCE: Simple!

SIMPLE: But, listen! It's Saturday night, fine outside. Spring in Harlem! Come on, let's us get some ice cream.

JOYCE: O.K., but, Jess, are you coming to church in the morning to see me take communion?

SIMPLE: You know I'll be there. We'll just take a little stroll down Seventh Avenue now and catch some air, heh?

JOYCE: And you'll bring me home early, so we can both get our rest.

SIMPLE: In a jiffy, then I'll turn in, too.

JOYCE: You don't mean into a bar?

SIMPLE: Baby, one thing I *bar* is bars.

JOYCE: Turn your back so I can dress.

SIMPLE: Don't stand over there. Anybody could be looking in.

JOYCE: There are no peeping-toms in this house. *(SIMPLE turns his back as she dresses, but drops his pack of cigarettes on the floor, bends down to get it, then remains that way, looking at JOYCE from between his legs)* Baby, is your back turned?

SIMPLE: Yes'm. *(JOYCE glances his way, clutches her dress to her bosom and screams)*

JOYCE: Oh, Simple!

SIMPLE: I love it when you call me Simple. *(Head still down, he proceeds to turn a somersault, coming up seated on the floor with his back toward her)* Now say my back ain't turned.

JOYCE: I didn't mean you had to turn inside out.

SIMPLE: That's the way you've got my heart—turned in . . . *(He turns his eyes to look at her)*

JOYCE: Then turn your head so I can dress.

SIMPLE: O.K., Joyce. Now, is everything all right?

JOYCE: Everything is all right.

SIMPLE: So you feel O.K.?

JOYCE: Simply heavenly! Oh, Jess, it's wonderful to be in love.

SIMPLE: Just wonderful—wonderful—wonderful— *(As JOYCE dresses, they sing)*

BOTH: Love is simply heavenly!
    What else could it be?
    When love is made in heaven
    And you are made for me.
    Love is simply heavenly!
    What else can I say?
    When love sends me an angel
    To hold me close this way.
    I know love is like a dream
    That's too good to be true,
    But when your lips kiss mine

The dream turns into you.
Yes, it's simply heavenly!
Our love's just divine—
For love is made in heaven
And you, my love, are mine!
SIMPLE: Love is simply heavenly!
What else could it be?
When love is made in heaven
And you are made for me.
JOYCE: Love is simply heavenly!
What else can I say?
When love sends me an angel
To hold me close this way.
SIMPLE: Love is like a dream
That's too good to be true,
(Dressed now, JOYCE emerges and SIMPLE rises to embrace her)
JOYCE: But when your lips kiss mine
The dream turns into you.
BOTH: Yes, it's simply heavenly!
Our love's just divine—
For love is made in heaven
And you, my love, are mine!
BLACKOUT

Act I, Scene 3

Paddy's Bar. Midnight.
At a battered old piano in the corner a roustabout PIANIST is playing a
syncopated melody while HOPKINS, the bartender, beats lightly on the
bar with a couple of stirrers as if playing drums. The music ceases as
MISS MAMIE, a large but shapely domestic servant, enters and sits at
her usual table.
HOPKINS: Good evening, Miss Mamie. How's tricks?
MAMIE: Hopkins, them white folks over in Long Island done like to
worked me to death. I'm just getting back to town.
PIANIST: You ought to have a good man to take care of you, Miss
Mamie—like me.
MAMIE: Huh! Bill, from what I see of you, you can hardly take care of
yourself. I got a mighty lot of flesh here to nourish.
PIANIST: Big woman, big appetite.

MAMIE: Right—which is why I like to work for rich folks. Poor folks ain't got enough to feed me.

PIANIST: I never eat much. But I sure am thirsty.

MAMIE: Stay that way! Hopkins, gimme a gin. *(BODIDDLY, a dock worker, leaps in shouting)*

BODIDDLY: Hey, now, anyhow!

MAMIE: Anyhow, what?

BODIDDLY: Anyhow, we's here! Who's setting up tonight? *(Dead silence. No one answers)* Well, Hop, I'll take a short beer.

MAMIE: It ain't nobody's payday in the middle of the week, Bodiddly. And the only man in this bar who manages to keep a little change in his pocket is Mr. Boyd here, drawing his G. I. pension.

BODIDDLY: *(Points at BOYD proudly)* My boy!

BOYD: Hi, Bo!

MAMIE: Huh! There's as much difference between you and Ananias Boyd as between night and day.

BODIDDLY: Yeah, I know! His predilect's toward intellect—and mine's toward womens.

HOPKINS: And beer.

BODIDDLY: Boyd's the only man around here who's colleged.

BOYD: For all the good it does me. You dockworkers make more a week than I ever see writing these stories.

BODIDDLY: But none of us gets pensions.

MAMIE: None of you all in the war and got wounded neither. But if I was a man, I would have gone to war so I could get me a pension.

PIANIST: They had lady soldiers.

BODIDDLY: Whacks and Wavers.

MAMIE: By that time I were too big. *(A LITTLE MAN in nose glasses, carrying an umbrella, enters with an armful of highbrow papers and magazines. Noticing no one, he takes a table and begins to remove his gloves)* There comes that characters trying to make people think he's educated. One thing I like about Boyd here, even if he is a writer, he ain't always trying to impress folks. Also he speaks when he comes in a public place. *(The LITTLE MAN sits at an empty table)*

CHARACTER: A thimble of Scotch, please.

BODIDDLY: A thimble of Scawtch! *(All laugh but BOYD)*

CHARACTER: And a tumbler of plain water, no ice.

HOPKINS: Right, sir! Like the English. *(As if to show her derision MAMIE orders loudly)*

MAMIE: Hopkins, gimme some more gin.

HOPKINS: Coming up, Miss Mamie! *(A Vendor's cry is heard outside. Carrying a watermelon, a jovial fellow, WATERMELON JOE, enters)*

MELON: Watermelons! Juicy sweet!
Watermelons! Good to eat!
Ripe and red—
That's what I said—
Watermelons!

MAMIE: Joe, you better shut up all that catterwalling! You ain't working this time o' night?

MELON: Yes I is. I done sold all but one watermelon. Who wants it? Sweet as pie! No lie! My, my, my!

MAMIE: *(Inspects the melon)* Hmmm! It do look good. Thumps good, too. Leave it for me behind the bar. I'll take it.

MELON: Thank you, Miss Mamie.

BODIDDLY: Better tie your pushcart to the curb 'fore somebody steals it.

MELON: I'm ahead of you, Diddly—got it locked to the lamp post. Boy, when I cry "Watermelons!" do you all know what happens to womens?

BODIDDLY: What?

MELON: Their blood turns to water and their knees start to shake— 'cause they know I'm a man, and no mistake! Why, I sold a woman a watermelon one day and moved in and stayed three years.

BODIDDLY: That's nothing. I just spoke to a strange lady once setting on a stoop—and went upstairs and ain't come down yet. That was in 1936.

MELON: Diddly, you lying. Your wife done run you out twice with a kitchen knife.

BODIDDLY: I mean, excusing temporary exits.

MAMIE: Well, I been buying watermelons, Joe, for two summers, and I finds your fruits sweeter than you.

MELON: That's because you don't know me well, baby. Besides, I do not use my professional voice in your personal presence:
Wa-ter—melons!
Melons! Melons! Melons!
Sweet as they can be!
Sweet, good Lord!
But they ain't as sweet as me!
Watermelon Joe has got your
Wa-ter—melons!

(He eases up to her cheek)
Me-lawns! . . . Me-loans! . . . Me-loons!

MAMIE: Man, you better get away from me! You know I got a husband, Watermelon Joe.

MELON: Where's he at?

MAMIE: I don't know where he's at, but I got one. And if I ain't, I don't want you.

MELON: *(Croons in here ear)* Watermelons. Wa-ter-mel-ons. . . .

MAMIE: I sure do like your watermelons, though.

MELON: Nice red melons . . .

CHARACTER: *(Rises indignantly)* Stereotypes! That's all both of you are. Disgraceful stereotypes!

MAMIE: *(Turns on him furiously)* Mister, you better remove yourself from my presence before I stereo your type! I like watermelons, and I don't care who knows it. That's nothing to be ashamed of, like some other colored folks are. Why, I knowed a woman once was so ashamed of liking watermelons that she'd make the clerk wrap the melon up before she'd carry it out of the store. I ain't no pretender, myself, neither no passer.

BODIDDLY: What do you mean, passer?

MAMIE: Chitterling passer—passing up chitterlings and pretending I don't like 'em when I do. I like watermelon and chitterlings both, and I don't care who knows it.

CHARACTER: Just stereotypes, that's all. *(He shakes his head)*

MAMIE: Man, get out of my face!

CHARACTER: Stereotypes . . . stereotypes . . . stereo . . . *(He retreats muttering)*

MAMIE: Why, its getting so colored folks can't do nothing no more without some other Negro calling you a stereotype. Stereotype, hah! If you like a little gin, you're a stereotype. You got to drink Scotch. If you wear a red dress, you're a stereotype. You got to wear beige or chartreuse. Lord have mercy, honey, do-don't like no blackeyed peas and rice! Then you're a down-home Negro for true—which I is—and proud of it! *(MAMIE glares around as if daring somebody to dispute her. Nobody does)* I didn't come here to Harlem to get away from my people. I come here because there's more of 'em. I loves my race. I loves my people. Stereotype!

CHARACTER: That's what I said, stereotypes!

MAMIE: You better remove yourself from my presence, calling me a stereotype.

CHARACTER: Tch-tch-tch! *(Clicking his tongue in disgust, the LITTLE MAN leaves the bar as MAMIE rises and threatens him with her purse. The PIANIST rushes over to congratulate her)*

PIANIST: Gimme five, Miss Mamie, gimme five! *(They shake hands)*

MAMIE: Solid!

PIANIST: You and me agreed! I could drink on that.

MAMIE: You go right back where you was and set down.

BODIDDLY: Who agrees is me! Bartender, set up the bar—this far—from Mamie to me. What'll you have, Cleopatra, a beer?

MAMIE: You know I drinks gin, Bodiddly. And I needs another one. That character done got me all upset. Where's all the decent peoples tonight? Where's Jess Simple?

BODIDDLY: I seen old Simp a couple of hours ago walking down Lenox Avenue with his girl. But Joyce turns in early. And when she turns in, she turns him out.

MAMIE: That's what I call a decent woman.

MELON: Damn if I do.

MAMIE: And that Simple is a good man. He needs himself a decent woman—instead of gallivanting around with chippies like Zarita that keeps a bar door flapping all night long. I never seen a woman could run in and out of a bar so much and so fast.

BODIDDLY: Ah, but that Zarita, she's sure a fine looking chick.

MAMIE: She wears her morals like a loose garment. Ain't no woman's man safe with her around.

MELON: She sure will drink a body up. Zarita damn near drunk me out of a whole car load of melons one night.

MAMIE: You sure is weak for young womens.

MELON: Miss Mamie, I could be weak for you.

MAMIE: Melon, scat! I done told you, get from over me! Scat!
(The door flies open and a seedy looking fellow rushes in calling to the bartender)

GITFIDDLE: Hey, Hop! Hey, Hop! Lend me my guitar from behind the bar there, please. Hurry up, man! I'll bring it back.

HOPKINS: What's the hurry?

GITFIDDLE: There's a big party of folks in the Wonder Bar down the street spending money like water.

HOPKINS: Here you are, Git.

GITFIDDLE: Thank you, man! *(He takes guitar and exits)*

HOPKINS: I sure hope he can play up a few dollars—that man has been broke so long, it just ain't fair.

MAMIE: A good musicianer—doing nothing but playing for quarters folks throw him!

MELON: They say a woman brought old Gitfiddle low.

MAMIE: Getting high brought him low! Womens helps more mens than they don't.

MELON: I sure wish you'd help me.

MAMIE: Wish again, honey, because I ain't coming. I likes a man who works in one place, with one job, not all up and down the streets where he's subject to temptation. And as for me, I don't need nobody to help me.

MELON: *(Shrugs)* Well, so that's that!

SIMPLE: *(Entering)* Good evening!

MAMIE: We been missing you. Excusing Boyd there, this bar's full of nothing but characters.

BOYD: Thank you, Miss Mamie.

MAMIE: Where you been, Simple?

SIMPLE: Eating ice cream.

CROWD: What?

SIMPLE: And I had my picture took.

BODIDDLY: With your lady fair.

SIMPLE: For my lady fair. All posed like this. *(He assumes an attitude)*

HOPKINS: She must've fell out laughing at that pose.

SIMPLE: She did not. That's one thing about Joyce. She never laughs at nothing about me, never does, which is why I loves that girl.

BOYD: You can find more reasons for liking a woman, Jess. Every time, a different woman, it's a different reason.

HOPKINS: Pay him no mind, Mr. Boyd. Zarita laughs with him and at him.

SIMPLE: Zarita's different. I do not, never will, can't—won't, and don't love no jumping jack of a Zarita. A man can't hardly keep Zarita in his arms, let alone in his heart.

HOPKINS: So we know, Jess Simple!

SIMPLE: But I have kept Joyce in my heart ever since I met her—and she is there to stay. Dog-gone it, I wish I had my divorce from Isabel. But at last, it looks like I am making some headway. They say a man's life changes every seven years. I sure hope I am going through the change.

HOPKINS: Mr. Change, what are you drinking?

SIMPLE: *(Takes an envelope from his pocket)* Give me and Boyd a couple of beers. Then I want you to read something. Didn't even show it to Joyce yet—not to get her hopes up too high. It's from my wife.

BOYD: I don't want to read your personal letters, Jess.

SIMPLE: Here, pal, read it—because I can't believe my eyes.

BOYD: Um-mmmm! Well, here goes: "Dear Mr. Semple: Jess, at last I have found a man who loves me enough to pay for my divorce. This new man is a mail clerk, his first wife being dead, so he wants me for his second."

SIMPLE: Thank you, Father!

BOYD: "He knows I been married and am still married in name only to you, as you have not been willing to pay for the legal paper which grants freedom from our entanglement. This man is willing to pay for it. He says he will get a lawyer to furnish me grounds unless you want to contest. I do not want no contest, you hear me! All I want is my divorce. I am writing to find out if you will please not make no contest out of this. Let me hear from you tonight as my husband-to-be has already passed the point where he could wait. Once sincerely yours, but not now, Isabel."

SIMPLE: Sounds just like my wife!

HOPKINS: I suppose you've no intention of cross-filing.

SIMPLE: I would not cross that wife of mine no kind of way. My last contest with that woman was such that the police had to protect me. So that man can have her. I do not even want a copy of the diploma. I told Isabel when we busted up that she had shared my bed, my board, my licker, and my hair oil, but that I did not want to share another thing with her from that day to this, not even a divorce. Let that other man pay for it—they can share it together. Me, I'll be married again before the gold seal's hardly out from under the stamper.

HOPKINS: Good! Perhaps you'll settle down, stop running around, and stay home nights with Joyce.

SIMPLE: Married, I'll get somewhere in the world, too. Let's drink to it. And that man in Baltimore better pay for my wife's divorce! If he don't, I'll fix him. Here's my toast. *(He lifts his glass of beer)*
> In a horserace, Daddy-o,
> One thing you will find—
> There ain't NO way to be out in front.
> Without showing your tail
> To the horse behind . . .
> *(ZARITA enters glittering)*

ZARITA: Hey now! Hi, all and sundry!

SIMPLE: Zarita!

ZARITA: Excuse me, folks, for being in a hurry.

MAMIE: I told you so!

ZARITA: Jess, I'm going to Jersey! Come on! Coleman and his girl've got their car outside.

SIMPLE: The one with the top down?

ZARITA: That's the chariot—and I got nobody to ride back there with me.

MAMIE: Don't that child just bring you to tears?

SIMPLE: Is Coleman sober?

ZARITA: Just feeling a little groovy that's all! Come on!

BODIDDLY: Woman, shut that outside door! It's chilly. You know it ain't official summer yet.

ZARITA: Your blood's thin. My, it's hot in here! Come on, Jess. The motor's running.

SIMPLE: The motor might be running, but I ain't. Come here, girl. I got somethings to say to you. Zarita, you know I'm almost engaged to be married. I can't be running around with you.

ZARITA: You really got yourself tangled up. Well, anyhow, we'll just ride over the bridge to a little after-hours spot in Jersey for a few drinks, and come right back. There's no harm in that.

SIMPLE: You sure you coming right back? And Coleman is gonna drive me right to my door?

ZARITA: Or mine! Your room is kinder little and small and cold. Sugar, is you is, or is you ain't? *(She moves toward the door)*

SIMPLE: Zarita, it's chilly out there and I ain't got my top coat.

ZARITA: Oh, Knuckle-Nose, we got a fifth of licker in the car to keep us warm. And there's some fine bars just across the George Washington bridge. You does or you don't?

SIMPLE: Aw, Zarita!

ZARITA: Old Simple Square, do I have to beg and plead with you? Listen! I've got my own money. I'll even treat you to a couple of drinks. Come on! Aw, come on! *(She entices him with a caress and they exit)*

MAMIE; There goes a lamb to slaughter again. Ain't it a shame the kind of a deal a good woman gets when she goes to bed early!

BODIDDLY: Huh?

MAMIE: I ain't talking about a man like you with 17 children. I'm talking about Joyce.

BODIDDLY: Oh!

MAMIE: She goes to bed early, leaving Simple to yield to temptation.

MELON: I'd never yield, Miss Mamie. But if I did, I'd yield with you.

MAMIE: Melon, I say, get out of my face. It's mighty near midnight.
Lemme go home.

MELON: If I didn't have my pushcart to wheel, I would 'scort you,
Miss Mamie.

MAMIE: Watermelon Joe, with you at the handle, I might have to
jump out and walk—or roll out, one—wild as you is with womens.
Hopkins, hand me my watermelon and let me go to my virtuous
couch. Good night, all, good night! *(She exits with her watermelon
under her arm)*

MELON: Huh, so she don't trust me to 'scort her home. Anyhow, I
think I'll truck along after her and see can't I tote her melon to a
taxi. Watermelons! Nice red one! *(He exits)*

BODIDDLY: Gimme a sherry, man. What'll you have, Boyd?

BOYD: Nothing, thanks.

(ARCIE enters bustling)

BODIDDLY: Arcie, my love, what you doing out this time of night?

ARCIE: I come out looking for you—and done looked in seven bars.

(HOPKINS automatically pours ARCIE some sherry.)

BODIDDLY: And had a drink in each and every one!

ARCIE: Naturally! A lady don't go in a bar and not buy nothing. Diddly,
lover, listen, there ain't but five of our children home—which means
an even dozen is still out in the streets.

BODIDDLY: The children's big enough to take care of themselves.

ARCIE: If you was any kind of a father—If you was any kind of . . .

BODIDDLY: Woman, hush! And put that sherry wine down—before
you be walking sidewise to keep from flying. Let's be getting upstairs
—before some more of our children don't get home. Be seeing you,
folks!

ARCIE: That man! *(ARCIE and BODIDDLY go out. The bar is empty
except for BOYD who rises to leave)*

HOPKINS: Say, Boyd, as a writer, would you say them folks are stereotypes?

BOYD: In the book I'm writing they're just folks. Good night, Hop.

GITFIDDLE: *(Comes reeling into the bar as BOYD exits)* Got-dog it! I
done broke another string!

HOPKINS: Well, did you make any money?

GITFIDDLE: They paid me off in drinks. I had nothing to eat all day.

Here, Hop, lend me another half for a sandwich—and keep this for security. *(He offers his guitar to HOPKINS)*

HOPKINS: You must think Paddy's Bar is a bank. I lent you two dollars and a quarter already this week. Here's fifty cents more.

GITFIDDLE: Thanks, Hop! But wait a minute, Hop—lemme play you just one more blues. *(The woebegone GITFIDDLE strums a lonesome blues on his guitar as the lights fade to darkness)*

BLACKOUT

Act I, Scene 4

Hospital room. Next day. During BLACKOUT a bed backed by a white screen already attached is wheeled D. S. C. with SIMPLE already propped up in bed, very quiet. Both his legs are up in traction. Near the head of his bed is a single white chair. A NURSE all in white tip-toes in and calls softly. He answers with a groan.

NURSE: Mr. Semple.

SIMPLE: Aw-um-mmm-mm-m!

NURSE: Such groaning! You aren't that bad off.

SIMPLE: When I suffers, Nurse, I like to suffer loud.

NURSE: There's a gentleman to see you. *(She beckons the caller)* Here he is, sir.

MELON: Thank you, Nurse. *(MELON enters. NURSE exits)* Oh, man! You're all packed for shipping!

SIMPLE: Strung, hung, and slung's what I am. Melon, this is the most! Um-mmm-mm-m!

MELON: All I heard was, you was in an accident.

SIMPLE: It were an accident, all right. Got-dog that Zarita! My mind told me—

MELON: Never mind what your mind told you, Daddy-o, just gimme the details. Here.

SIMPLE: What's that?

MELON: I brought you some books.

SIMPLE: I wish you'd of brought me a quart of beer and some pigs feet. I ain't much on books.

MELON: Comic books, man.

SIMPLE: Oh, *Horror in Hackensack. Terror in Trenton.*

MELON: Man, that's the crazy history of New Jersey.

SIMPLE: This makes me feel better already. Thanks, Melon.

MELON: Now, tell me what happened.

SIMPLE: The car tried to climb the George Washington Bridge, instead of going *across* it—turned half over—Coleman, his girl, and Zarita and me. But I was the *only* one that got throwed out, and on my—bohunkus. Melon, I'm all bruised up on my sit-downer.

MELON: I told you, you should stop balling, and take care of yourself.

SIMPLE: If I had took care of myself, I would not have these pretty nurses taking care of me now.

MELON: But look at the big hospital bill when you get out.

SIMPLE: Lemme hit one number, I'll settle it. But what worries me is when I'm going to get out.

MELON: You will never get out if you don't observe the rules and stop telling folks to bring you beer and pigs feet and things you are not supposed to have.

SIMPLE: But alcohol had nothing to do with it.

MELON: Oh, no?

SIMPLE: Women aggravate a man, drunk or sober. Melon, I hope Joyce knows Zarita ain't nothing to me, even if I do accidentally go riding with her. But I don't want to discuss how come I'm in this hospital. You know, no matter what a man does, sick or well, something is always liable to happen—especially if he's colored. In this world, Melon, it's hard for a man to live until he dies.

    (NURSE enters)

MELON: I think you'll make it.

NURSE: There's a Miss Joyce Lane to see you. *(A look of great helplessness comes over SIMPLE. He appeals to his friend)*

SIMPLE: Melon . . .

MELON: It's Joyce.

SIMPLE: Just like a man has to face his Maker alone, the same goes for facing a woman.

MELON: You want to see her, don't you?

SIMPLE: Worse than anything, I want to see Joyce, Melon. Also, I—I—I—

MELON: Also, you don't want to see her. I know. Good luck, old man.

    (The NURSE shows MELON out. As they exit, JOYCE enters)

JOYCE: Jess! *(Tears come, and she takes out her handkerchief)*

SIMPLE: Baby, please don't cry. I'm all right.

JOYCE: But your legs! Are they broken?

SIMPLE: Doc says they ain't. But they sure are bent.

JOYCE: Then why are they all trussed up that way?

SIMPLE: Because I can't lay on my hine, that's why.

JOYCE: Your what?

SIMPLE: My hindparts is all skint up, Joyce. I hope that's a polite word for saying it.

JOYCE: But aren't you hurt badly?

SIMPLE: No.

JOYCE: I am.

SIMPLE: Baby, don't you want to set down? Here on the bed. Then pull your chair up close, please.

JOYCE: Oh, Jess!

SIMPLE: I know, Joyce, I know. I hadn't ought to done it.

JOYCE: With a drunken driver, too—and Zarita.

SIMPLE: You know I love you.

JOYCE: And that's the way you show it? With your legs tied up in the air—on account of a—

SIMPLE: Auto wreck—

JOYCE: Woman.

SIMPLE: Just a little old innocent joy ride.

JOYCE: Oh, stop it!

SIMPLE: Baby, did you taken communion this morning?

JOYCE: Yes, Jess, I did. I was almost late. I waited for you to go with me.

SIMPLE: Did they sing, "Jesus Knows Just How Much I Can Bear"?

JOYCE: Not today.

SIMPLE: I used to like that song. You know how I feel now? Just like I felt the last time Aunt Lucy whipped me. Did I ever tell you about that, Joyce?

JOYCE: No.

SIMPLE: It were a girl caused that whipping.

JOYCE: I'm not surprised, Jess.

SIMPLE: Aunt Lucy is dead and gone to glory, Joyce. But it were Aunt Lucy taught me right from wrong. When I were a little young child, I didn't have much raising. I knocked around every-which-where, pillar to post. But when Aunt Lucy took me, she did her best to whip me and *raise* me, too—'cause Aunt Lucy really believed in her Bible. "Spare the rod and spoil the child." I were *not* spoiled. But the last whipping is what did it—made me the man I am today. . . . I could see that whipping coming, Joyce, when I sneaked out of the henhouse one of Aunt Lucy's best hens and give it to that girl to roast for her Sunday School picnic, because that old girl said she was aiming to picnic *me*—except that she didn't have nothing much to put in her basket. I was trying to jive that girl, you know. Anyhow, Aunt Lucy found out about it and woke me up the next morning with a switch in her hand. . . . But I got all mannish that morning, Joyce. I said, "Aunt Lucy, you ain't gonna whip me no more, I'se a man now—and you ain't gonna whip me." Aunt Lucy said, "You know you had no business snatching my best laying hen right off her nest." Aunt Lucy was angry. And big as I was, I was scared. . . . Yet I was meaning not to let her whip me, Joyce. But, just when I was aiming to snatch that switch out of her hand, I seed Aunt Lucy was crying. I said, "What you crying for?" She said, "I'm crying 'cause here you is a man and don't know how to act right *yet,* and I done did my best to raise you so you'll grow up to be a good man. I wore out so many switches on your back—still you tries my soul. But it *ain't* my soul I'm thinking of, son, it's you. Jess, I wants you to carry yourself right. You understand me? I'm getting too old to be using my strength up like this. Here!" Aunt Lucy hollered, "Bend over and lemme whip you one more time!" . . . Big as I was, Joyce, you know I bended. When I seen her crying, I would have let Aunt Lucy kill me before I raised a hand. When she got through, I said, "Aunt Lucy, you ain't gonna have to whip me no more—I'm going to do my best to do right from now on, and not try your soul. And I am sorry about that hen. . . ." Joyce, from that day to this, I have tried to behave myself. Aunt Lucy is gone to Glory, now, but if she's looking down, she knows that's true. That was my last whipping. But it wasn't the whipping that taught me what I needed to know. It was because she cried and cried. When peoples care for you and cry for you—and *love* you—Joyce, they can straighten out your soul. *(SIMPLE, lost in his story, had not been looking at JOYCE. Instead, as he finishes, he is looking at the ceiling. Suddenly, JOYCE turns to bury her head on the back of her chair, sobbing aloud. SIMPLE, forgetting that his legs are tied and that he cannot get out of bed, tries to rise)* Joyce! . . . Joyce! . . . Joyce! *(If he could, he would go to her and take her in his arms)* Joyce you're crying for me!

JOYCE: I'm not! I'm crying for your grandmother.

SIMPLE: It wasn't my grandmother I was telling you about, Joyce, it were my Aunt Lucy.

JOYCE: Well, whoever it was, she had her hands full with you.

SIMPLE: She loved me, Joyce, just like I love you. . . . Come here, feel my heart—it's beating just for you. . . . Joyce, please come here.

(He reaches out his hand and JOYCE comes. She takes it, and he pulls her toward him) Feel my heart. *(He puts her hand on his heart. But suddenly JOYCE buries her head on his chest and sobs violently. SIMPLE puts an arm about her and smiles, quietly happy)*
BLACKOUT

Act I, Scene 5

Paddy's bar. Saturday night. The joint is jumping. GITFIDDLE is plunking his guitar. BODIDDLY is at the bar, HOPKINS behind it. MAMIE and MELON sit at a table. ARCIE is in the middle of the floor, cutting up as if she were a young woman. JOHN JASPER, one of her teen-age jitterbug sons, comes in, hits a few steps himself, whirls around, then taps on her shoulder.

JOHN JASPER: Mama! Hey, Mama!

ARCIE: *(Stops dancing)* Get away from me, son! Can't you see your mama is having a good time and don't want to be bothered with no children? Stop that dancing! Where's all my children? Arcilee and Melinda and Mabel and Johnny and Little Bits and Cora? Also Lilac? Huh?

JOHN JASPER: They all in the street, gone to Saturday night parties and things. Mama, lend me a quarter. I want to take the bus down to 96th Street to the Swords and Sabres dance.

ARCIE: Ask your daddy. He ain't paid me off yet. *(She again continues dancing as the boy approaches BODIDDLY at the bar)*

JOHN JASPER: Hey, Daddy, gimme a quarter.

BODIDDLY: Scram! You too young to be in this bar, John Jasper. Here take this quarter, boy, and scram! Children all under a man's feet!

JOHN JASPER: Thanks, Dad! *(He skips off. MISS MAMIE and MELON do a slow Lindy hop to the music)*

BODIDDLY: Woman, you better stop spending my money before you get it. Is you done your Saturday night shopping yet?

ARCIE: Can I do it on credit? Hand it over, Diddly, lover!

BODIDDLY: Many mouths as you got to feed, you better get to the stores before they close.

ARCIE: Them's your children, too. Ain't you gonna help me carry the grits?

BODIDDLY: Woman, you know I'm tired. Go do your shopping.

ARCIE: Treat me first.

BODIDDLY: Hop, give this woman a glass of Domesticated Sherry. (*HOPKINS laughs and pours her another glass of sherry before she exits. ZARITA enters. MELON and MAMIE stop dancing*)

ZARITA: Simple hasn't been in yet tonight, has he, Hop?

HOPKINS: Not yet.

BODIDDLY: But if he's able to walk, he'll be here before it's over.

ZARITA: He's been back at work three or four days, and I haven't seen him. You know, Hop, when I went by Harlem Hospital, he acted like he was mad at me.

HOPKINS: No wonder—you took him riding and got him all banged up.

ZARITA: He didn't have to go. Nobody forced him. I just said, "Come on." Say, Hop, what you doing this morning when you get off from work?

HOPKINS: I'm going home, Zarita.

ZARITA: There's a nice new after-hours spot opened down on Seventh Avenue.

HOPKINS: I said, I am going home.

ZARITA: You didn't always go home so early after work, Mr. Hopkins.

HOPKINS: Do you call three o'clock in the morning early?

ZARITA: Real early! Don't you remember that night you drove me over to Newark?

HOPKINS: I remember.

ZARITA: And we didn't get back early either.

HOPKINS: Zarita, this is one morning I'm turning in. Maybe Simple'll take you to this new Bottle Club.

ZARITA: Maybe he will—if he ain't still mad. Anyhow, if you see him, tell him I'll be back. I will be back.

HOPKINS: Cool, Zarita, cool. (*ZARITA exits in rhythm to GITFID-DLE's guitar*)

MELON: Hey, Git, you sounds mighty good plunking over there in the corner. C'mon, Miss Mamie, let's dance some more.

MAMIE: Yes, you ought to be on the juke box.

GITFIDDLE: Juke boxes is the trouble now, Miss Mamie. Used to be, folks liked to hear a sure-enough live guitar player. Now, I start playing, somebody puts a nickel in the piccolo, drowns me out. No good for musicianers any more, but I got to make the rounds, try to hustle. See you later, Miss Mamie.

MAMIE: Git, I'd rather hear you than records any day. When you come back, I'm gonna throw you a dollar just to pick a blues for me.

GITFIDDLE: I won't be long, Miss Mamie, won't be long. (*He exits as JOHN JASPER runs in. At the piano the BARFLY continues to jazz*)

JOHN JASPER: Papa!

BODIDDLY: John Jasper, now what you want? A man can't . . .

JOHN JASPER: Ronnie Belle . . .

BODIDDLY: A man can't enjoy his self . . .

JOHN JASPER: Ronnie Belle . . .

BODIDDLY: . . . without some child stuck up in his face.

JOHN JASPER: (*Dances as he talks*) Ronnie Belle says she won't stay home and mind the babies, and it's my turn to go out this Saturday night. She says if I go, she's going.

BODIDDLY: You tell Ronnie Belle I'll come up there and fan her good, if she don't do what she's supposed to. I declare to goodness, these young folks nowadays! You get upstairs, John Jasper, and tell your sister what I said.

JOHN JASPER: Yes, sir, Papa! (*He exits*)

MAMIE: Diddly, you sure got some fine children.

BODIDDLY: And every one of them born in New York City, Harlem. When I left the South, I never did go back. (*JOHN JASPER returns, dancing to the piano*)

BODIDDLY: Lord, that boy's back again. John Jasper, now what do you want?

JOHN JASPER: Mama says for you to come on upstairs and bring her a pint of cooking sherry.

BODIDDLY: You know your mama ain't gonna do no cooking this time of the night! Tell Arcie to come down here and get her own wine. Scat, boy, scat! (*JOHN JASPER dances out*)

MAMIE: Diddly, that's the cutest one of your children. I'll give him a dime myself.

BODIDDLY: Lemme get way back in the corner so's no more of my kin folks can find me—not even my wife. (*He goes into a corner as SIMPLE enters*)

MAMIE: Look who's coming there!

PIANIST: Hy, Jess!

MELON: Jess Semple!

HOPKINS: (*Lifting a bottle of beer*) It's on the house!

MAMIE: Welcome home!

BODIDDLY: To the land of the living!

MAMIE: Amen! Bless Jess!

HOPKINS: Zarita was just looking for you. (*Happily the customers retire to tables with the drinks as SIMPLE remains leaning stiffly on the bar*)

SIMPLE: Don't mention Zarita, please, Hop! She's near about ruint me. Joyce is treating me cool, cool, cool, since I come out the hospital and I explained to her over and over I was just out riding. Hop, oh, Hop! Oh, man, have I got a worried mind! You know when I reached home my old landlady come handing me a Special Delivery from my wife which stated that the Negro in Baltimore has only made one payment on our divorce, leaving two payments to go. Hop, you're educated! How much is one payment on $400, leaving two payments to go?

HOPKINS: $133.33 and one-third cents.

SIMPLE: Now I could just about pay one-third cents.

HOPKINS: I thought you said that man in Baltimore loved your wife so much he was willing to pay for the whole divorce.

SIMPLE: Inflation's got him—so he just made one down payment. Isabel writ that if I would make one payment now, she would make one, then everybody could marry right away. But I cannot meet a payment now—with the hospital bill, rent up, food up, phones up, cigarettes up—everything up—but my salary. Divorces are liable to go up, too, if I don't hurry up and pay up. Lord! Women, women, women! *(He paces the floor)*

MELON: Don't let women get you excited, man! Set down and take it easy.

(Offered a seat, SIMPLE protects his haunches with his palms)

SIMPLE: The last thing I want to do is set down!

MAMIE: Then stand up to it like a man! You made your own bed hard. What you drinking?

SIMPLE: Whiskey.

VOICES: Whiskey?

MELON: And you're usually a beer man!

SIMPLE: Tonight I want whiskey. Hop, I said, whiskey! I'm broke, busted, and disgusted. And just spent might near my last nickel for a paper—and there ain't no news in it about colored folks. Unless we commit murder, robbery or rape, or are being chased by a mob, do we get on the front page, or hardly on the back. Take flying saucers. For instance according to the *Daily News,* everybody has seen flying saucers in the sky. Everybody but a Negro. They probably won't even let flying saucers fly over Harlem, just to keep us from seeing one. Not long ago, I read where some Karl Krubelowski had seen a flying saucer, also Giovanni Battini saw one. And way out in Pennsylvania mountains some Dutchman named Heinrich Armpriester seen one. But did you read about Roosevelt Johnson or Ralph Butler or Henry Washington or anybody that sounded like a Negro seeing one? I did not. Has a flying saucer ever passed over Lenox Avenue yet? Nary one! Not even Daddy Grace has glimpsed one, nor Ralph Bunche. Negroes can't even get into the front page news no kind of way. I can't even see a flying saucer. When I do, that will be a great day.

HOPKINS: It would probably scare you to death—so you wouldn't live to see your name in the papers.

SIMPLE: Well, then—I could read about it in the other world then—and be just as proud—me, Jess Semple, kilt by a flying saucer.

ARCIE: *(Enters yelling tipsily)* Bodiddly! Bodiddly! Why don't you come on upstairs?

BODIDDLY: Aw, woman, hush! Every time I turn around there's families under my feet. Set down and leave me be.

ARCIE: I did not come to set down. It's past midnight. I come to get you to go to bed.

BODIDDLY: I know when to go to bed my own self.

ARCIE: Then come on, you great big no-good old bull-necked son-of-a-biscuit eater!

BODIDDLY: Sit down, I'll buy you a sherry wine. Hop!

> *(ZARITA enters with ALI BABA, an enormous well-dressed fellow in a turban)*

ZARITA: Hello, you all! Hey, Jess Semple! Folks, dig this champion roots-herbs—and numbers-seller from south of the border. I just come by to show you my new man I met at the Baby Grand. Don't he look like a sultan? But we got business. Come on! We're gonna do the town, ain't we, Ali Baba?

MAMIE: Ali Baba?

ZARITA: Sugar Hill, Smalls, and every place! Come on, Texas Tarzan, come on! Jess, I'm glad you came out of that little accident O.K. 'Bye, all!

> *(ZARITA kisses ALI BABA. He sneezes. MELON ducks. As ZARITA and her new man exit, SIMPLE looks sheepish)*

BODIDDLY: She don't need us tonight.

HOPKINS: She's got her a two-ton Sugar Daddy.

MELON: She's got her a human shower.

MAMIE: Paddy's Bar is small-time to Zarita this evening. She'll be in here Monday all beat out, though—and looking for Jess Semple.

SIMPLE: Or somebody else simple—but it won't be me.

MELON: Where have I heard that before?

SIMPLE: Where have I heard that before? *(They glare at each other)*
MELON: Where have I heard that before? *(SIMPLE's feelings are hurt)*
SIMPLE: I'm going and see Joyce. I need to see somebody that loves me.

> *(A Policeman's Voice is heard in the street)*

POLICEMAN: Hey, you! Stay off the street with that noise box. Don't you know it's against the law, out here hustling for dimes? Next time I hear that racket, I'll run you in.
GITFIDDLE: Yes, sir, Officer! *(GITFIDDLE enters crestfallen)* A man can't play music nowhere no more. Juke box drowns him out in the bars, cops run him off the streets, landlady won't let you play in your own room. I might as well break this damn box up!
MAMIE: Gitfiddle, I told you, you can play for me.
BODIDDLY: Me too.
ARCIE: Sure, Git.
MELON: And me, Git.
MAMIE: Come on, now! Let's have some music like you feels it, Git-fiddle.
MELON: Did you ever hear the Blues?
On a battered old guitar:
Did you ever hear the Blues
Over yonder, Lord, how far?
Did you ever hear the Blues
On a Saturday night?
Did you ever hear the Blues
About some chick ain't done you right?
Baby, did you ever hear the Blues?
MAMIE:Did you ever hear the Blues
On an old house-rent piano?
Did you ever hear the Blues
Like they play 'em in Savannah?
Did you ever hear the Blues
In the early, early morn?
Wondering, wondering, wondering
Why you was ever born?
Folks, did you ever hear the Blues?
MELON: When the bar is quiet
And the night is almost done,
Them old Blues overtake you
At the bottom of your fun.

Oh, Lord, them Blues!
Echo . . . echo . . . echo . . . of the Blues!
MAMIE: Good morning, Blues! Good morning!
Good morning, Blues, I say!
Good morning, Blues, good morning!
You done come back to stay?
You come back to bug me
Like you drug me yesterday?
MELON: I heard you knock last night,
But I would not let you in.
Knock, knock, knock, last night
But I would not let you in.
I tried to make believe
It weren't nothing but the wind.
ALL: Blues, Blues, Blues!
It were the Blues!
Maybe to some people
What the Blueses say is news
But to me it's an old, old story.
MAMIE: Did you ever hear the Blues
On a battered old guitar?
Did you ever hear the Blues
Over yonder, Lord, how far?
Did you ever hear the Blues
On a Saturday night?
BOTH: Did you ever hear the Blues
About some chick ain't done you right?
ALL: Baby, did you ever hear the Blues?
BLACKOUT

Act I, Scene 6

JOYCE's room. Sunday evening.
JOYCE is sewing. The bell rings seven times. The Landlady calls from
offstage.
MRS. CADDY: I'll answer it, Miss Lane. I'm right here in the hall.
JOYCE: Oh, thank you, Mrs. Caddy. You're about the nicest landlady I
know.

MRS. CADDY: Are you decent? Do you want to see Mr. Semple? He's
kinda cripple—so down here or up there?

JOYCE: I'm sewing, so let him come up here, please—if he can make it.

SIMPLE: *(Enters and closes the door)* I've made it. Well, I'm back on my
feet, up, out, and almost at it.

JOYCE: I see. You may come in. Remember the door—Mrs. Caddy's
rules.

SIMPLE: *(Opens the door a crack)* Dog-gone old landlady! Joyce, I know
I'm a black sheep. But I explained it all to you the last time you come
by the hospital.

JOYCE: I accepted your explanation.

SIMPLE: But you don't seem like you're glad to see me, now I'm out—
the way you didn't say almost nothing when I come by Friday.

JOYCE: I'm glad to see you.

SIMPLE: Then lemme kiss you. Ouch! My back! *(He yells in pain as he
bends over)*

JOYCE: Oh!

SIMPLE: I think my veterbrays is disconnected.

JOYCE: What did the X-rays show?

SIMPLE: Nothing but a black mark. The doctor says I'm O.K. Just can't
set down too suddenly for a while.

JOYCE: Then have a slow seat.

SIMPLE: Joyce, is you my enemy? You sound so cool. Am I intruding?

JOYCE: Oh, no. I'm just having a nice peaceful Sunday evening at
home—which I must say, I haven't had too often since I've been
knowing you.

SIMPLE: Baby darling, I'm sorry if I'm disturbing you, but I hope
you're glad to see me. What you making?

JOYCE: Just lingerie for a girl friend who's getting married.

SIMPLE: Step-ins or step-outs?

JOYCE: Slips, Jess, slips. Jess Semple, stop breathing down my neck.
The way you say things sometimes, you think I'm going to melt
again, don't you! Well, instead you might get stuck with this needle.
Listen, hand me that pattern book over there. Let me see how I
should insert this lace.

SIMPLE: What're you doing with all those timetables and travel books,
baby?

JOYCE: Just in case we ever should get married, maybe I'm picking out
a place to spend our honeymoon—Niagara Falls, the Grand Canyon,
Plymouth Rock . . .

SIMPLE: I don't want to spend no honeymoon on no rock. These books is pretty, but, baby, we ain't ready to travel yet.

JOYCE: We can dream, can't we?

SIMPLE: Niagara Falls makes a mighty lot of noise falling down. I likes to sleep on holidays.

JOYCE: Oh, Jess! Then how about the far West? Were you ever at the Grand Canyon?

SIMPLE: I were. Fact is, I was also at Niagara Falls, after I were at Grand Canyon.

JOYCE: I do not wish to criticize your grammar, Mr. Semple, but as long as you have been around New York, I wonder why you continue to say, I were, and at other times, I was?

SIMPLE: Because sometimes I were, and sometimes I was, baby. I was at Niagara Falls and I were at the Grand Canyon—since that were in the far distant past when I were a coachboy on the Santa Fe. I was more recently at Niagara Falls.

JOYCE: I see. But you never were "I were"! There is no "I were." In the past tense, there is only "I was." The verb *to be* is declined, "I am, I was, I have been."

SIMPLE: Joyce, baby, don't be so touchous about it. Do you want me to talk like Edward R. Murrow?

JOYCE: No! But when we go to formals I hate to hear you saying, for example, "I taken" instead of "I took." Why do colored people say, "I taken," so much?

SIMPLE: Because we are taken—taken until we are undertaken, and, Joyce, baby, funerals is high!

JOYCE: Funerals are high.

SIMPLE: Joyce, what difference do it make?

JOYCE: Jess! What difference does it make? Does is correct English.

SIMPLE: And do ain't?

JOYCE: Isn't—not ain't.

SIMPLE: Woman, don't tell me *ain't* ain't in the dictionary.

JOYCE: But it ain't—I mean—it isn't correct.

SIMPLE: Joyce, I gives less than a small damn! What if it aren't? (*In his excitement he attempts to sit down, but leaps up as soon as his seat touches the chair*)

JOYCE: You say what if things aren't. You give less than a damn. Well, I'm tired of a man who gives less than a damn about "What if things aren't." I'm tired! Tired! You hear me? Tired! I have never known any one man so long without having some kind of action out of

him. You have not even formally proposed to me, let alone writing
my father for my hand.
SIMPLE: I did not know I had to write your old man for your hand.
JOYCE: My father, Jess, not my old man. And don't let it be too long.
After all, I might meet some other man.
SIMPLE: You better not meet no other man. You better not! Do and I
will marry you right now this June in spite of my first wife, bigamy,
your old man—I mean your father. Joyce, don't you know I am not
to be trifled with? I am Jesse B. Semple.
JOYCE: I know who you are. Now, just sit down and let's spend a nice
Sunday evening conversing, heh?
SIMPLE: *(Sits down, but it hurts him)* Ouch!
JOYCE: Oh, Sweety! Let me make you a nice cool drink. Lemonade?
SIMPLE: Yes, Joyce, lemonade. *(JOYCE exits. Suddenly SIMPLE realizes
what he has agreed to drink and cries in despair)* Lemonade! *(He sits
dejected until JOYCE returns)* Baby, you ain't mad with me, is you?
(JOYCE smiles and shakes her head, no) Because I know you know
what I mean when I say, "I is"—or "I are" or "was" or whatever it
be. Listen, Joyce, honey, please. *(He sings)*
When I say "I were" believe me.
When I say "I was" believe me, too—
Because I were, and was, and I *am*
Deep in love with you.

If I say "You took" or "taken"
Just believe I have been taken, too,
Because I were, and am, and I *is*
Taken in by you.

If it *is* or it *ain't* well stated,
And it *ain't* or it *aren't* said right,
My love still must be rated
A love that don't fade over night.

When I say "I am" believe me.
When I say "I is" believe me, too—
Because I were, and was, and I *is*
Deep in love with you.

Damn if I ain't!
JOYCE: A small damn? *(He grabs her. JOYCE screams)*
BLACKOUT

ACT I, Scene 7

SIMPLE's room. A month later.
MR. BOYD comes down the hall and sees SIMPLE's door ajar. He looks in.
BOYD: Hey, fellow, what you doing home on Saturday night?
SIMPLE: Boyd, man, come on in. Joyce is gone to some gal's wedding shower—and damn if I'm going out to any bar. Still and yet, Boyd, I'm in a good mind to take that money I been saving and blow it all in, every damn penny, because man, it looks hopeless. Push done come to shove on that divorce, I got to pay for my part of it. So last month I started saving. But, damn, I got so far to go!
BOYD: How much do you have to save in all?
SIMPLE: One hundred thirty-three dollars and thirty-three cents. I'm as far as Leviticus.
BOYD: What do you mean, Leviticus?
SIMPLE: Aunt Lucy always said, "The Bible is the Rock: Put your trust therein." So that's where I'm putting my money. I got to save $133.33. If I put a ten dollar bill in each chapter every week from Genesis on, in eighteen and a half weeks I will have it—and I'll only have to go as far as Nahum.
BOYD: Nahum?
SIMPLE: That's a book in the Bible, somewhere down behind Ezekiel. If I ever get to Nahum that's it. I done put ten in Genesis, ten in Exodus, and five in Levi.
BOYD: I thought you said *ten* every week.
SIMPLE: I were a little short this past week. Anyhow, I got twenty-five.
BOYD: Come on, let's go around to Paddy's.
SIMPLE: Thanks, Daddy-o! I will not yield to temptation! No! Not especially since I done got another letter from that used-to-be wife of mine, Isabel. Sit down, Boyd. Listen. "Jesse B. Semple, you are less than a man. You marry a girl, neglect her, ignore her, and won't help her divorce herself, not even when your part ain't only but one-third of the payment. You can go to hell! You do not deserve no gold seal on your decree, because you have not put a cent into it. Therefore, since I am going to pay for this divorce myself, your paper may not be legal. From now on, you kiss my foot! Isabel Estherlee Jones. P.S. I have taken back my maiden name, as I wants no parts of you attached to me any longer. MISS JONES."
BOYD: She's angry.

SIMPLE: Seems like it. Boyd, I will not let Isabel get the last word on me. I'll send that lawyer my part of the money next week, even if I have to put my whole paycheck in to do it. Right now I got twenty-five in the Bible. When I add my old check, that won't leave but about ah—er—a sixty to go. I can pawn a suit, one overcoat, and my radio—which might still leave about fifty. Boyd, can you lend me fifty?

BOYD: Fellow, are you out of your mind?

SIMPLE: This is an emergency. I need a gold seal on my divorce, too— so I got to pay for it. I got to have that gold seal, Boyd! I got to have it! It's got to be legal for Joyce. But then it's up to me to get that money, ain't it, Boyd? It ain't up to you nor nobody else—it's just up to me.

BOYD: Yes, Simple, I'm afraid it is. Get hold of yourself, make a man of yourself. You got to live up to your obligations.

SIMPLE: You done said a big word, Boyd.

BOYD: And it's a big thing you've got to do, fellow, facing up to yourself. You're not the first man in the world to have problems. You've got to learn how to swim, Jess, in this great big ocean called the world.

SIMPLE: This great big old white ocean—and me a colored swimmer.

BOYD: Aw, stop feeling sorry for yourself just because you're colored. You can't use race as an excuse forever. All men have problems. And even if you are colored, you've got to swim beyond color, and get to that island that is you—the human you, the man you. You've got to face your obligations, and stand up on that island of *you,* and be a man.

SIMPLE: Obligations! That's a word for you, Boyd! Seems like to me obligations is just a big old rock standing in a man's way.

BOYD: Then you've got to break that rock, fellow. Or, maybe I should say rocks.

SIMPLE: I know what you mean—like the beer rock, huh, Boyd?

BOYD: Um-hum!

SIMPLE: And the licker-rock—only I don't drink much whiskey.

BOYD: Well, say the bar-rock in general.

SIMPLE: That night-owl rock.

BOYD: Out until four A.M.

SIMPLE: Yes, the chick-chasing rock.

BOYD: Zarita!

SIMPLE: Not mentioning no names! But, man, I done shook that chick. But then there's always that old trying-to-save-money rock.

BOYD: You mean putting-it-off-until tomorrow rock.

SIMPLE: Which has really been my stumbling rock.

BOYD: You got to bust it, man. You know about John Henry, don't you?

SIMPLE: Sure I do.

BOYD: He was the champion rock-buster of them all.

SIMPLE: My Uncle Tige used to sing about him. Boyd, I been making up my mind to break through my rocks, too. *(BOYD smiles)* Yes, I is, Boyd, I is.

BOYD: You just got to bust 'em, fellow, that's all. *(BOYD exits)*

SIMPLE: *(Takes off his shirt and changes into a ragged pajama top)* Bust 'em! I got to bust 'em. Like that song of Uncle Tige's. That old man sure could sing—made up songs, too. *(SIMPLE sits on bed to take off his shoes)* Made his own about John Henry which went—lemme see. *(He tries to remember)* How did it go? Something about—

> They say John Henry was a man.
> And they say he took a hammer in his hand—
> *(He uses one shoe as a hammer)*

That's it!

> And busted a rock
> So hard he gave the world a shock!
> Yes, they say John Henry was a man.
> *(SIMPLE rises)*
> They say John Henry won a prize,
> And they say he gave his life to win that prize.
> *(He comes forward)*
> Yes, they say he hammered on
> Until his breath was gone!
> *(As if speaking to himself)*
> They say John Henry won a prize.
> *(He reaches toward his back pocket)*
> Well, there's a prize I'm gonna win,
> And the time's long gone I should begin.
> *(From his wallet he shakes his last five dollar bill, opens the Bible, and puts it in between the pages)*
> But it's better late than never,
> And no time ain't forever.
> *(He clasps the Bible to his chest)*
> So right now, I'm gonna start to win.

(He turns forward resolutely, putting Bible down)
It takes a long haul to get there, so they say,
And there's great big mountains in the way.
But I'm gonna make it through
If it's the last damn thing I do.
(He bangs his hand on the Bible)
I'm gonna be John Henry, be John Henry,
I'm gonna be John Henry, too.
CURTAIN

ACT II, Scene 1

The music of the Blues on the guitar, slow, haunting, syncopated, precedes the rise of the curtain.
Paddy's Bar. A week later. Evening.
ARCIE is sitting alone at a table drinking sherry wine and working a cross-word puzzle in the paper. BOYD is writing in a notebook at another table. The PIANIST lazily runs his fingers over the keys as HOPKINS, behind the bar, stifles a yawn.

HOPKINS: Blue Monday night, no money, and I feel like hell. What you writing, Boyd?

BOYD: Just making some notes for a story I might write—after observing life in Harlem over the weekend.

HOPKINS: You didn't go to Philly Sunday to see that young lady?

BOYD: She's vacationing in Paris, which is O.K. by me, because when we get ready to honeymoon, I won't have to take her to Europe.

HOPKINS: Far as I could take a chick on a honeymoon would be the Theresa Hotel.

BOYD: That's about as far as I could take one, unless I sell some of this stuff I've been writing.

(MAMIE enters, panting)

HOPKINS: Hey, Mamie! What's the matter?

MAMIE: I'm seeking escape—that Melon—*(MELON enters with a hangdog air)* Man, if you would just stop following me! Now that you're so bold as to call at my house every night, at least let me have a little peace when I take a walk, without you at my heels.

MELON: Aw, Miss Mamie, you know I'm drawn to you.

MAMIE: When I get home from work, man, *I am tired*. I just want to

set down, and rest, and read my paper. But Tang-a-lang-lang! You
ring the bell! It looks like here lately, at home, in the bar, anywhere,
every time—

> When I'm in quiet mood, here you come.
> When I'm deep in solitude, here you come.
> When I feel like settling down—

MELON: There I are!

MAMIE: When I'm gazing at the moon—

MELON: In falls your star!

MAMIE: My dial is set, the tone is low,

> There's nice sweet music on my radio.
> I take a book, the story's fun—
> But when you ring my bell, I never get my reading done.
> When I'm in a quiet mood, up you pop.
> When I'm playing solitaire, in you drop.

MELON: The way you upset me makes my heartstrings hum—

MAMIE: When I'm in a quiet mood

BOTH: Here you (I) come!

MAMIE: It's raining outside. It's nice in the house.

> Everything is cool—quiet as a mouse.
> The doorbell rings. Who can it be?
> My solitude is ended, Lord, you're looking for me!
> Slippers on my feet, in my rocking chair,
> F-M on the dial, "The Londonderry Air."
> The telephone rings, you say you're coming by.
> When you get to my door—

BOTH: My, Oh, my!

(MAMIE walks away, MELON follows)

MELON: Oh, you act so cute and you switch so coy—

> Mamie, I was meant to be your playboy.
> I dial your phone, hear you yell, "Damn Sam!"
> Which means that you know I'm your honey lamb.
> With hankering heart, I just follow you.
> Your kisses are as sweet as sweet mountain dew.
> I ring your bell, it's just old me.—
> I come around to try to keep you company.
> I've sampled lots of melons whose flavor's fine,
> But you are the sweetest melon on my vine.
> I know that you love me by the look in your eye.
> When I knock at your door—

BOTH: My! Oh, my!

MAMIE: When I'm in a quiet mood, up you pop.
          When I'm playing solitaire, in you drop.

MELON: They way you upset me makes my heartstrings hum.

MAMIE: When I'm in a quiet mood—

BOTH: Here you (I) come!

MAMIE: When the night is free to get my beauty sleep,
          I cannot sleep, so I'm counting sheep.
          The doorbell rings—I shoot the sheep—Bam! Bam!
          'Cause there in the door stands my honey lamb.
          I could scream! It ain't no dream—
          Here you come—to upset me! . . . And, honey, I'm leaving.
          Here I go! . . . And I mean it!

MELON: Well, I guess this time she really means it.

MAMIE: Well, if you're coming, come on!

MELON: I'm going to follow—here I come!

          (MAMIE and MELON exeunt. SIMPLE bursts in exuberantly)

SIMPLE: Hey, now, moo-cow! Gimme a little milk. Barman, untap your
          key. Suds us up! Let's drink to it, even if it is my last dollar.

HOPKINS: Your last dollar, didn't you get paid this week?

SIMPLE: I did, but I took that money—all of it—and added it to what
          was in the Bible and sent it off to Baltimore—$133.34. Being last on
          payments, I had to pay that extra penny to change Divorce Pending
          to Divorce Ending!

HOPKINS: Congratulations!

SIMPLE: Joyce knows I love her. But to get a woman to make his bed
          down, a man has to make his mind up. Joyce is sweet, I mean! My
          queen—my desire, my fire, my honey—the only woman who ever
          made me save my money!

ARCIE: Simple.

SIMPLE: Yes, ma'am?

ARCIE: What's a four-letter word for damn?

SIMPLE: Arcie, do you see that sign? *(He points to: "NO PROFANITY
          IN HERE")* Well, I do not repeat no four-letter words in public.

ARCIE: Damn! *(ZARITA enters briskly switching)*

ZARITA: Hi, folks! I thought I'd stop by and have a quick one. Mr.
          Semple, how do you do? Set me up, Hop. *(She approaches SIMPLE)*
          How are you, Sugar?

SIMPLE: Zarita, could I have a word with you, private?

ZARITA: Of course! It won't be the first time.

ARCIE: Hummmmm-mm-m! I thought so. That girl is like a magnet to that man.

> (*HOPKINS pours ARCIE a drink as SIMPLE and ZARITA go aside*)

HOPKINS: Stay out of other people's business, Arcie.

ARCIE: O.K! O.K!

ZARITA: So you're not even going to speak to me again?

SIMPLE: What I do say is, I ain't gonna talk to you. Good evening—and Good-bye! Excuse me.

ZARITA: Aw, not like that, Jess, listen . . . (*ZARITA puts an arm around SIMPLE*)

ARCIE: Hey there, you writer, Boyd. What is the path in the field which a plow makes called?

BOYD: Furrow.

ARCIE: Six letters, just right. Now, wait a minute. Tell me, what is a hole with just one opening?

BOYD: How many letters?

ARCIE: Six, starts with D.

HOPKINS: Dugout?

ARCIE: Just fits. A dead general. A God-damn dead general!

> (*SIMPLE pulls away from ZARITA*)

ZARITA: But, Jess, you know you and me together always has fun.

SIMPLE: Zarita, I'm the same as about to get married. I got responsibilities.

ZARITA: I am a lady, Jess Semple. Don't worry, I'll stay out of your life. I'm tired of paying you a sometime call when I'm feeling lonely. Anyhow, I always did bring my own licker. You never had none.

SIMPLE: But I always treat you when I meet you—when I can. Zarita, you know I'd give you the shirt off my back.

ZARITA: And I'd gladly give you mine. Go on and get your rest, Jess. You never turned in this early before.

SIMPLE: I still got to make a week's work before that lay-off comes.

ZARITA: I guess you'll say good night, even if you wouldn't say hello.

SIMPLE: Good night.

ZARITA: Good night.

> (*SIMPLE expects ZARITA to leave. Instead she stands there and smiles at him her sweetest smile. SIMPLE looks at the bar as if he wants to sit down on the stool again, then looks at ZARITA. Finally he decides to leave*)

SIMPLE: Going my way, Boyd?

BOYD: I might as well, it's getting late. So long, folks.

ARCIE: And I ain't finished this puzzle.

BOYD: Hop'll help you. Good night. *(SIMPLE and BOYD exeunt, as the PIANIST ripples the keys)*

ARCIE: It ain't but a quarter to twelve. What's happening to Simple?

ZARITA: He's getting domesticated. You know, Arcie, I wish someone would feel about me the way Simple feels about Joyce, and she about him, even if they do have their ups and downs. I guess a little trouble now and then just helps to draw people together. But you got to have somebody to come together with. *(The notes on the piano rise hauntingly)* Gee, Bill, you play pretty sometimes.

PIANIST: I studied to be a concert pianist, but the concert never did come off.

ZARITA: What's that you're playing now? Sounds familiar. *(She leans on the piano)*

PIANIST: Some new piece a colored boy wrote, I heard it on the radio. Let me croon it to you:
Just a little shade and shadow
Mixed in with the light
Helps to make the sunshine brighter
When things turn out right.

ZARITA: Just a little pain and trouble
Mixed in with the fair
Helps to make your joys seem double
When clouds are not there.

Look for the morning star
Shining in the dawn!
Look for the rainbow's arch
When the rain is gone!

Don't forget there're bluebirds
Somewhere in the blue.
Love will send a little bluebird
Flying straight to you.
(The light fades as JOYCE is heard singing)
Look for the morning star
Shine, shine, shining in the dawn!
Rainbow, rainbow, rainbow's arch
When the rain is gone.

Don't forget you'll find bluebirds
Somewhere in the blue.
Love will send a little bluebird
Flying straight to you. . . .
(BLACKOUT as the melody continues into the next scene)

Act II, Scene 2

JOYCE's room. Two weeks later.
JOYCE is serving SIMPLE some sandwiches as she continues to sing.
    SIMPLE looks very serious.
JOYCE: . . . Love will send a little bluebird
    Flying straight to you . . .
    Just a little shade and shadow . . .
SIMPLE: . . . Shades and shadows, just like the song says. Listen, Joyce,
    you know when I first met you on that boatride, I said to myself,
    "That girl's too good for me. I can't make no headway with that
    kind of woman." Yes, I did! To tell the truth, Joyce, you gave me a
    kinder hard road to go—you know, with your morals and—
JOYCE: And you already married.
SIMPLE: Yes, but not wedlocked. . . .
JOYCE: Still and yet there was a shadow between us. . . .
SIMPLE: Of bigamy,
JOYCE: And gossip,
SIMPLE: Old landladies,
JOYCE: Friends,
SIMPLE: And I run around a lot in them days, too. . . .
JOYCE: In shady places—speakeasies, and things, so you said . . .
SIMPLE: Shady nothing! Them places was really dark—after-hours
    spots, Joyce. Now I know better. I'm older! And when I look at
    you, oh, I can see the sun, Joyce! It was dark, but now the clouds
    are rolling by.
JOYCE: Just a little shade and shadow
    Mixed in with the light
    Helps to make the sunshine brighter
    When things turn out right.
SIMPLE: True, so true!
JOYCE: Just a little pain and trouble
    Mixed in with the fair

Helps to make your joys double
When clouds are not there.
SIMPLE: Wonderful the morning star
Shining in the dawn!
JOYCE: Wonderful the rainbow's arch
BOTH: When the rain is gone!
JOYCE: Don't forget you'll find bluebirds
Somewhere in the blue.
Love will send a little bluebird
Flying straight to you.
SIMPLE: Sing about the morning star
Shine-shine-shining in the dawn!
Rainbow, rainbow, rainbow's arch
BOTH: When the rain is gone.
JOYCE: I am sure we'll find bluebirds
Right here in the blue.
BOTH: Love has sent a singing bluebird
Straight to me and you.
(They kiss as the music rises lyrically)
JOYCE: Oh, Jess! Life is really wonderful!
SIMPLE: I wouldn't be caught dead without it. But—er—a—
JOYCE: But what, Jess?
SIMPLE: It's wonderful. But, Joyce, baby, something is always hap-
pening to a Negro—just when everything is going right. Listen—
I'm sorry, but there's something I got to tell you, much as I don't
want to.
JOYCE: About your divorce?
SIMPLE: No, sugar, that's all filed, paid for, ought to be ready for the
seal soon. Something else has come up. It's that—it's that—well, the
notice come last week that it was coming. I just didn't tell you—I'm
being laid off my job.
JOYCE: Oh, Jess! Not fired?
SIMPLE: No, not fired, just temporary, three or four months till after
New Year's while they converts. Converting! And us planning to get
married. Every time a Negro plans something—
JOYCE: Aw, come now! We'll get married, Jess.
SIMPLE: I can't even get my laundry out—let alone put my dirty shirts
in.
JOYCE: Jess, I'll do your laundry. Bring me a bundle tomorrow and I'll
bring them back to you—rub-a-dub-dub—white as snow.

SIMPLE: You're a doll, Joyce, you almost never come to my room.

JOYCE: Well, this'll give me a chance to see the curtains I made for you.

SIMPLE: Come see.

JOYCE: I will—when I bring this laundry, and if you need it, Jess, I can let you have a little money.

SIMPLE: I couldn't take no money from you.

JOYCE: But you can have it.

SIMPLE: I'd be embarrassed.

JOYCE: Have you got enough to eat?

SIMPLE: Oh, sure, I'll make out.

JOYCE: Well, on the weekend, Mr. Semple, you're going to dine with me. Make up your mind to that. And don't say one word about being embarrassed. Everything is going to be all right, I know. I talk to the Lord every night on my knees and I know.

SIMPLE: How long exactly it'll be before that job opens up again, to tell the truth, I don't know. Joyce, what are we going to do? We wants to get married, and all these years I have not saved a thing. Baby, have you figured up how much our wedding is going to cost?

JOYCE: There's no need to worry about that now. You've got enough on your mind tonight, darling. I just want you to know that I'm behind you.

SIMPLE: But, Joyce, baby, look! I ain't got nothing put away. I don't know if our plans are gonna go through or not.

JOYCE: Look, Jess, don't worry. If you ain't got the money to buy no license, well, when we get ready to get married we gonna get that license.

SIMPLE: But, Joyce, honey, I don't want you to be building no castles in the sand.

JOYCE: Jess, I have built my castles in my heart. They're not in no sand. No waves is gonna beat them down. No wind is gonna blow them apart. Nothing can scatter my castles. I tell you, nothing! Their bricks are made out of love and their foundations are strong. And you, Jess Semple, you are the gate-keeper of my castle—which is in my heart. You are the gate-keeper of my castle. *(JOYCE sits on the floor at SIMPLE's feet and lays her head in his lap)* Oh, Jess, we'll have our own little place, our own little house, and at night we'll both be there after jobs are done. Oh, Jess, baby, you don't know how much—

I want somebody to come home to

When I come home at night.

I want someone to depend upon
I know will do right.

I want somebody to come home to
I'm sure will be at home.
I want someone who is sweet and kind
I know will not roam.

I'm a homebody—and this homebody
Wants somebody to share my share
For each homebody needs somebody
Who will always be right there.

I want somebody to come home to
Who'll make my dreams come true
A nice someone who'll be the one
I know will be you.
(Repeating from release closing with this)
A nice homebody who's just somebody
Lovely to come home to.
BLACKOUT

Act II, Scene 3

SIMPLE's room. Early evening.
SIMPLE is lying on his bed, shoes off and shirt tail out, dozing. A doorbell is heard ringing madly. Commotion downstairs and in the hallway. ZARITA bursts in on a startled SIMPLE. A large red pocketbook swings from one of her arms.
ZARITA: It's my birthday, Jess! And I brought my friends around to celebrate—since you're broke these days and don't come out no more.
> *(SIMPLE leaps up and begins to tuck his shirt in and put on a shoe. Voices are heard on the stairs)*
BODIDDLY: What floor is it on?
HOPKINS: You're sure he's expecting us?
MAMIE: We rung the bell.
MELON: I been here before.
ARCIE: I'm having trouble with these steps.
> *(BOYD is seen outside SIMPLE's door)*

BOYD: Shssss-ss-sss! Be quiet. What the hell is going on? You want to get us in trouble with the landlady? *(By now the crowd—which includes all the bar customers and as many strangers as desired to make the staging lively—has pushed BOYD into the room)*

ZARITA: I tell you, it's my birthday, Jess! Come on in, everybody.

MELON: Happy birthday!

PIANIST: Happy birthday, Zarita!

(GITFIDDLE begins to play)

SIMPLE: Zarita, your birthday ain't mine. And I don't want—

ZARITA: But I want to share it with you, Daddy! We brought our own liquor. When it runs out, we'll send and get some more. Won't we, Melon?

MELON: Liquor's about gone now, Whoopee-ee-ee!

ARCIE: Have some o' my sherry, Simple. I got my own bottle.

ZARITA: Jess, honey, I forgot to tell you I'd be twenty-some odd years old today. We started celebrating this morning and we're still going strong.

BODIDDLY: The ball is on!

ZARITA: Let the good times roll!

BODIDDLY: Let the good times roll in "D"!

MELON: Whoopee!

(ZARITA begins to sing)

ZARITA: If you ain't got nothing
    And there's nothing to get,
    Who cares long as you're doing it?
    If you ain't got nothing
    Better to do,
    Why not do what's good to do?

MELON: What's that?

ZARITA: Ball, ball, let's ball awhile!
    Ball, ball, honey chile!
    Sing! Shout! Beat it out!

ALL: Dance! Prance! Take a chance!
    Grab the blues and get them told—
    When you're happy in your soul.

ZARITA: Start the music playing
    Let the good times roll.

ALL: Whail! Sail! Let it fly!

ZARITA: Cool fool: we're riding high!

ALL: Ball, ball, let's ball awhile!

*(Everybody dances wildly with a dazed SIMPLE in their midst, one
shoe still off)*

ZARITA: Ball, ball, let's ball awhile!
  Ball, ball, honey chile!
  Sing! Shout! Beat it out!
  Dance! Prance! Take a chance!
  Grab the blues and get them told—
  When you're happy in your soul.

  Start the music playing.
  Let the good times roll.
  Whail! Sail! Let it fly!
  Cool fool: We're riding high!
  Ball, ball, let's ball awhile!
  (ZARITA forces SIMPLE to dance)

ALL: Ball, ball, let's ball awhile!
  Ball, ball, honey chile!
  Sing! Shout! Beat it out!
  Dance! Prance! Take a chance!
  Grab the blues and get them told—
  When you're happy in your soul.

ZARITA: Start the music playing
  Let the good times roll!
  (The whole room starts rocking)

ALL: Whail! Sail! Let it fly!
  Cool fool! We're riding high!
  Ball! Ball! Let's ball awhile!

BODIDDLY: Hey, now!

ZARITA: Ow! It's my birthday! We're balling!

HOPKINS: Happy birthday, Zarita!

MELON: Dog-gone it! This bottle is empty.

ARCIE: Mine, too. Diddly, go get some more.

BODIDDLY: Send Melon. Here's fifty cents. *(He tosses MELON a coin)*

ZARITA: Play that again, Git, "Let's Ball Awhile."

MAMIE: Ball! Ball! Honey chile!
  Ball! Ball! Let's ball awhile!

ARCIE: Yippeee-ee-ee-e! Diddly, shake yourself! *(ZARITA's big red
  pocketbook is swinging wildly on her arms as the crowd stops dancing
  and moves back to let her and SIMPLE cavort madly together in a
  fast and furious jitterbug, each trying to outdo the other in cutting*

capers) Aw, do it, Zarita! *(ZARITA spins around and around with her purse in her hand swirling high above her head. Suddenly the clasp comes open—the innumerable and varied contents of her enormous pocketbook fly all over the room, cascading everywhere: compact, lipstick, handkerchief, pocket mirror, key ring with seven keys, scattered deck of cards, black lace gloves, bottle opener, cigarette case, chewing gum, bromo quinine box, small change, fountain pen, sunglasses, address books, fingernail file, blue poker chips, matches, flask and a shoe horn)*

ZARITA: Oh, ooo-oo-o! My bag! Stop the music! Stop, Git, stop!

ARCIE: Girl, your perfume done broke!

ZARITA: My *Night in Egypt*!

BODIDDLY: If you broke your mirror, it's seven years bad luck.

PIANIST: Help her pick her things up, man.

BODIDDLY: I'm helping. But what's this! *(Holding up a red brassiere)*

BOYD: Lord, women sure can have a lot of stuff in their pocketbooks!

MAMIE: She's even got poker chips!

ZARITA: Jess, you help me, baby. The rest of you all stay where you are. I don't know some of you folks, and I don't want to lose nothing valuable.

ARCIE: You ain't got nothing I want, child.

ZARITA: Where's my *China Girl* lipstick in the jade-studded holder? I don't want to lose that lipstick! Jess, you reckon it rolled outside?

SIMPLE: Might could be. Lemme look. *(Just then the doorbell rings nine times)* My ring!

ZARITA: My lipstick! Where's my lipstick? Help me, sugar. *(ZARITA pulls SIMPLE down with her on the floor to search for the lipstick in the doorway as the bell continues to ring)*

ARCIE: Somebody let Melon in with that licker.

BODIDDLY: Let that man in.

HOPKINS: The door's still open. He ought to have sense enough to come in.

BODIDDLY: I say to hell with the bell, and help Zarita find her stuff. Whee! Smell that "Night in Egypt"!

(SIMPLE finds the lipstick and ZARITA kisses him)

SIMPLE: Here it is!

ZARITA: Aw, goody! *(GITFIDDLE starts the music again and all dance)* Aw, Simple, just because we're dancing, you don't have to keep on kissing me.

SIMPLE: Who's kissing who, Zarita? *You're* kissing me.

BODIDDLY: Come up for air, you two! Come up for air! Aw, play it, Git.

> (*The music soars. But suddenly the room becomes dead silent as everyone stops still, except SIMPLE and ZARITA who are embracing. JOYCE is standing in the doorway. Drunkenly ARCIE speaks*)

ARCIE: Come on in, girl, and join the fun!

PIANIST: Slappy Slirthday!

JOYCE: (*Hardly believing her eyes*) This *is* Mr. Semple's room, isn't it?

PIANIST: Sure is. We're having a ball.

ZARITA: (*Back to the door, hollers*) Play it again, Git! Come on—"Let's Ball a While!" Where's Melon with the licker? . . . Oh! (*Suddenly both she and SIMPLE see JOYCE. SIMPLE is astounded*)

SIMPLE: Joyce!

JOYCE: Jess, I brought your laundry I washed for you. I thought you might want to wear one of the shirts Sunday.

ZARITA: Tip on in, Joyce, and enjoin my birthday. We don't mind. I'm Zarita. Just excuse my stuff all over the place. We been having a ball, Simp and me and—

JOYCE: I did not know you had company, Jess.

> (*WATERMELON JOE arrives with his arms full of bottles and pushes past JOYCE*)

MELON: Gangway! The stuff is here and it's mellowed! Get out of the door, woman! Make room for Watermelon Joe—and the juice with the flow.

JOYCE: (*Hands SIMPLE his bundle as MELON distributes bottles*) Excuse me for being in your guests' way. Here, please take your laundry.

> (*The loud voice of SIMPLE's landlady is heard calling angrily as she enters in kimono and curlers*)

LANDLADY: Wait a minute! I'm the landlady here, and what I want to know is, who is this strange man walking in my house with his arms full of bottles! And *who* left my front door open? Who? I want to know who? Did you, Jess Semple? This is a respectable house. What's going on here? Do you hear me, Mr. Semple?

SIMPLE: (*Meekly*) Yes'm. These is just some guests, that's all.

LANDLADY: Well, get 'em out of here—raising sand in my house! Get 'em out I say! (*She exits in a huff*)

JOYCE: I'm going—as quick as I can. (*She starts to pass SIMPLE*)

SIMPLE: Joyce! . . . Joyce! You know she don't mean you. I wants a word with you, Joyce.

JOYCE: *(Turns on him furiously, fighting back her tears)* With me? You don't need to explain to me, Jess Semple. Now I have seen that Zarita woman with my own eyes in your bedroom. No wonder you're giving a birthday party to which I am not invited. I won't be in your way tonight, Jess—nor ever—any more. *(She looks back into the room as she leaves)* Enjoy yourselves. Good night! *(JOYCE rushes down the hall and out of the house)*

SIMPLE: Joyce! . . . Joyce! . . . Joyce! . . .

ZARITA: Huh! Who does that old landlady think she is? You pay your rent, don't you, Simple? Come on, folks, let's ball awhile.

PIANIST: Happy slirthday!

SIMPLE: *(Stands holding his parcel of laundry)* I'm sorry, Miss Arcie, Boyd, Diddly! . . . *To hell with your birthday,* Zarita! . . . Folks, I'm sorry. Will you all go?

> *(ARCIE scurries out. The others follow. MELON retrieves several of the bottles and takes them with him. ZARITA picks up her red bag and swaggers out with MAMIE behind her)*

ZARITA: I know where we can ball, folks—at my house! Come on!

MAMIE: I been throwed out of better places than this.

> *(GITFIDDLE turns at the door and looks at SIMPLE as if to say he's sorry, but SIMPLE does not look up. BOYD, the last to go, closes the door. All exit down the stairs leaving SIMPLE in the middle of the floor. He feels his check, looks in the mirror, then takes his handkerchief and violently tries to wipe ZARITA's lipstick from his jaw. He throws the handkerchief on the dresser and sinks down on the bed, his head in his hands)*

SIMPLE: Oh, my God! *(GITFIDDLE's guitar is heard going down the stairs)* Oh, my God! . . . My God! . . . Oh, God! *(THE LIGHTS DIM TO A SINGLE SPOT on the forlorn figure. There is the snapping of a broken string on the distant guitar)*

BLACKOUT

Act II, Scene 4

Paddy's Bar. A quiet Sunday evening.
SIMPLE enters and gloomily begins taking articles from his pockets and putting them on the bar.

SIMPLE: Hop, is you seen Zarita?

HOPKINS: Nope. Guess she's still recovering from her birthday.

SIMPLE: If you do see her, give her this junk.

HOPKINS: Looks like to me you've snatched her purse.

SIMPLE: I'd snatch her head if I could! That woman has ruint me now—Joyce is out of my life.

HOPKINS: Have a drink, fellow, on me.

SIMPLE: This is one time I do not want a drink, Hop. I feel too bad. I have phoned her seventeen times, and Joyce will not answer the phone. I run her bell four nights straight. Nobody would let me in. I sent Joyce eight telegrams, which she do not answer.

HOPKINS: And Zarita?

SIMPLE: I don't never want to see Zarita no more. The smell of that "Night in Egypt" is still in my room.

HOPKINS: A man should not fool around with a bad woman when he's got a good woman to love.

SIMPLE: Don't I know that now!

HOPKINS: Have you tried to see Joyce today? Sunday, she might be home.

SIMPLE: Tried? Are you kidding? That's all I've done. These is my bitter days! Hop, what shall I do?

HOPKINS: I don't know, Jess.

SIMPLE: Negroes never know anything important when they need to. I'm going to walk by her house again now. I just want to know if Joyce got home safe from church.

HOPKINS: She's been getting home safe all these years.

SIMPLE: Hop, I'm nearly out of my head. I got to talk to her. I'll stand in front of her house all night if I have to.

(ZARITA enters, cool, frisky, and pretty as ever)

HOPKINS: Uh-oh!

ZARITA: Hel-lo! Jess, I'm glad I caught you. I was a little shy about coming around to your place for my things.

SIMPLE: I brought your things here, Zarita. *(HOPKINS puts them on the bar)*

ZARITA: I thought you might, you're so sweet, sugar. Lemme treat you to a drink, and you, too, Hop.

SIMPLE: No, thank you.

ZARITA: Don't be that way. Set us up, here, Hopkins.

SIMPLE: I'm not drinking no more myself.

ZARITA: What? Just because you're out of work, you don't have to put down all the pleasures. Say, listen, Jess, if you're broke, I can let you have a little money.

HOPKINS: Zarita!

ZARITA: But no jive, Jess. Because you're wifeless and workless, a nice little old guy like you don't have to go hungry, never. I cook stringbeans and ham almost every day.

SIMPLE: I don't like stringbeans.

ZARITA: I'll fry you some chicken, then.

SIMPLE: Forget it, please!

ZARITA: O.K. If you're that proud. *(She opens her purse)* Anyhow, here honey-boy, take this ten—in case you need it.

SIMPLE: Um-um! NO! Thanks, Zarita, no! *(He backs away)*

ZARITA: I meant no harm. I'm just trying to cheer you up. Like that party which I brought around to your house. Knowing you wasn't working, thinking maybe you'd be kinder embarrassed to come to my place for my birthday and not bring a present, I brought the party to you. Meant no harm—just to cheer you up.

SIMPLE: Please don't try to cheer me up no more, Zarita. Hop, I'm cutting out. I'm going by—you know where I told you, one more time. *(SIMPLE starts out)*

HOPKINS: Don't try to break her door down.

SIMPLE: I'm just gonna stand on the sidewalk and look up at her window.

HOPKINS: I hope you see a light, pal.

> *(SIMPLE exists as the PIANIST begins to play softly, "Look for the Morning Star." He sings, starting with the release)*

PIANIST: Look for the morning star
Shining in the dawn.
Look for the rainbow's arch
When the rain is gone.

> *(The remainder of the song he hums. ZARITA, lonely, looks around at the quiet bar, then cries in desperation)*

ZARITA: I'm lonesome, Hop! I'm lonesome! I'm lonesome! *(She buries her head on the bar and weeps as the piano continues)* I'm lonesome. . . .

BLACKOUT

Act II, Scene 5

SIMPLE's room. Late evening.

SIMPLE is lighting a cone of incense in a saucer on his dresser as BOYD pokes his head in the door, sniffs, and enters.

BOYD: Hy, fellow! What's that burning on the dresser?

SIMPLE: Incense. I lit it to keep warm. I really hates winter.

BOYD: Oh, man, cold weather makes you get up and go, gives you vim, vigor, vitality!

SIMPLE: It does not give me anything but a cold—and all that snow outside!

BOYD: Perhaps you are just not the right color for winter, being dark. In nature you know, animals have protective coloration to go with their environment. Desert toads are sand-colored. Tree lizards are green. Ermine, for example, is the color of the snow country in which it originates.

SIMPLE: Which accounts for me not having no business wading around in snow, then. It and my color do not match. But, please, let's stop talking about snow, Boyd.

BOYD: Agreed—as cold as it is in this icebox!

SIMPLE: Landladies has no respect for roomers a-tall, Boyd. In fact, ours cares less for her roomers than she does for her dog. She will put a roomer out—dead out in the street—when he does not pay his rent, but she does not put out that dog. Trixie is her heart! She keeps Trixie warm. But me, I has nothing to keep warm by, but incense. I'm sick of this kind of living, Boyd. Maybe if I just had a little something, a place to live, some money, I could win Joyce back. If I don't get her back, Boyd, I don't know! I just don't know!

BOYD: I can lend you a small amount, Jess, if you need it—you know, five or ten.

SIMPLE: But I borrows only when I *hope* I can pay back, Boyd. (*A creaking sound is heard on the steps. The LANDLADY's voice is heard outside*)

LANDLADY: I do believes somebody's smoking marijuana in my house.

SIMPLE: Listen! Don't I hear a elephant walking? (*She knocks loudly on SIMPLE's door*) Come in!

LANDLADY: Mr. Semple, I am forced to inform you that I allows no reefer smoking in my home.

SIMPLE: I allows none in my room, neither.

LANDLADY: Then what do I smell?

SIMPLE: Chinese incense from Japan.

LANDLADY: Is you running a fast house?

SIMPLE: Madam, you have give me a idea!

LANDLADY: I am not joking, Jess Semple. Tell me, how come you burning that stuff in my house? Is it for bad luck or good?

SIMPLE: I don't believe in no lucky scents. I am just burning this for fun. It also gives out heat. Here, I will give you a stick to perfume up your part of the house.

LANDLADY: Thank you, I'll take it, even if it do smell like a good-time house to me. And that nude naked calendar you got hanging on your wall ain't exactly what I'd call decent. Don't your licker store give out no respectable girls on their calendars?

SIMPLE: They do, but they got clothes on.

LANDLADY: Naturally! Never would I pose in a meadow without my clothes on.

SIMPLE: I hope not, Madam.

LANDLADY: Meaning by that . . . ?

SIMPLE: Meaning you have such a beautiful character you do not have to show your figure. There is sweetness in your face.

LANDLADY: I appreciates that, Mr. Semple. *(She shivers)* Whee! It *is right* chilly up here.

SIMPLE: It's a deep freeze.

LANDLADY: If you roomers would go to bed on time—and your guests would go home—including Mr. Boyd—I would not have to keep heat up until all hours of the night.

SIMPLE: Has the heat been up tonight?

LANDLADY: You know it were warm as toast in this house at seven P.M. Funny where *your* heat disappears to. Downstairs I fails to notice any change myself.

SIMPLE: Madam, science states that heat is tied in with fat.

LANDLADY: Meaning . . . ?

SIMPLE: You're protected.

LANDLADY: I don't study ways of insulting roomers, Jess Semple, and that is the second sly remark you made about me tonight. I'll thank you to regret it.

SIMPLE: Madam, I does regret it!

LANDLADY: To my face—fat! Huh! You heard him, Mr. Boyd. *(She exits muttering)* Elephant, huh? Behind in your rent, huh!

BOYD: Now our landlady's angry.

SIMPLE: I tell you, something's always happening to a colored man! Stormy weather! Boyd, I been caught in some kind of riffle ever since I been black. All my life, if it ain't raining, its blowing. If it ain't sleeting, it's snowing. Man, you try to be good, and what happens? You just don't be good. You try to live right. What happens? You look back and find out you didn't live right. Even when you're working, and you try to save money, what happens? Can't do it. Your shoes is wore out. Or the dentist has got you. You try to save again. What happens? You drunk it up. Try to save another time. Some relative gets sick and needs it. What happens to money, Boyd? What happens?

BOYD: Come on, man, snap out of it! Let's go down to Paddy's and have a drink. At least we can sit up in the bar and get warm—and not think about what happens.

SIMPLE: You go, Boyd. What happens has done already happened to me.

> (*Slowly BOYD leaves. Half through the door suddenly a bright thought comes to him. He smiles and snaps his fingers, then exits closing the door, leaving SIMPLE alone as the LIGHT FADES SLOWLY TO DARKNESS*)

BLACKOUT

Act II, Scene 6

Sidewalk on Lenox Avenue, D. S. apron, with a sign LENOX AVENUE, a let-down flap at L. Early evening. BOYD walks briskly down the street as if on a mission, entering R. Exits L. Following him, JOHN JASPER comes dancing along the sidewalk R. selling papers and stopping to hit a step now and then.

JOHN JASPER: Paper! . . . Amsterdam News! . . . Read all about it! Get your paper! (*He dances off L. BODIDDLY enters R. followed by ARCIE hobbling along behind him. BODIDDLY turns, stops*)

BODIDDLY: Woman, you better stop tagging *behind* me on the street, and walk *beside* me, like a wife should—before I lose my impatience.

ARCIE: Diddly, these new shoes hurt my feet.

BODIDDLY: I paid $20 for them shoes for you! Arcie, ain't you read in the Bible where Moses walked for forty years in the wilderness *barefooted*? Now, here you can't walk a block without complaining!

ARCIE: But Diddly, lover, I ain't Moses.

BODIDDLY: Aw, come on, woman! (*Exeunt. Enter MAMIE, trailed by MELON R.*)

MAMIE: Melon, you got more nerve that Liberace's got sequins. You ain't gonna get nowhere, so there's no need of you trailing me through the streets like this.

MELON: I can't help it, Miss Mamie. I'm marked by a liking for you!

(He addresses her in rhymed jive, spoken)
You're my sugar,
You're my spice,
You're my everything
That's nice.
MAMIE: Melon, I done told you—
You *ain't* my sugar
You *ain't* my spice.
If you was a piece of cheese
I'd throw you to the mice.
(She moves on with MELON in pursuit)
MELON: Miss Mamie—
Your words are bitter
But your lips are sweet.
Lemme kiss you, baby—
And give you a treat.
MAMIE: Melon—
When cows start playing numbers
And canary birds sing bass,
That is when you'll stick your
Big mouth in my face.
(MAMIE exits indignantly with MELON pleading as he follows)
MELON: Aw, Miss Mamie, listen!
Wait a minute now!
I ain't no canary bird,
And you *sure* ain't no cow.
But . . .
(Exit MELON)
BLACKOUT

Act II, Scene 7

JOYCE's room. Same evening.
BOYD stands at the door as JOYCE opens it.
BOYD: I hope you'll pardon me, Miss Lane—and maybe it's none of my business at all—but I was just walking down Lenox Avenue when the idea came to me and I felt like I ought to come and talk to you. *(He stands awkwardly)*
JOYCE: You may sit, Mr. Boyd. *(She takes his hat)*

BOYD: Thank you. I—I—

JOYCE: Yes?

BOYD: Well, it's about Simple. You know, I mean Jess Semple. He didn't ask me to come to see you. In fact, he doesn't know I'm here at all. But he's been rooming right next to me quite a while now, and I—well—well, I never saw him like he is before.

JOYCE: *(Begins to freeze)* You know him well?

BOYD: Very well.

JOYCE: Are you one of his drinking buddies of the Paddy's Bar set?

BOYD: I'm not much of a drinking man, Miss Lane. I'm a writer.

JOYCE: A writer! What do you write?

BOYD: Books.

JOYCE: Books!

BOYD: About Harlem.

JOYCE: Harlem! I wish I could get away from Harlem.

BOYD: Miss Lane, I'm worried about Simple.

JOYCE: You're worried about Simple. He never seems to worry about himself.

BOYD: I think maybe you really don't know about that birthday party.

JOYCE: There's really nothing I want to learn.

BOYD: Except that it wasn't Simple's party. He didn't plan it, and didn't know anything about it until it descended on him.

JOYCE: Huh! Just like that—from above.

BOYD: They came to surprise us.

JOYCE: You too? You don't look like the type of man to attract that conglomeration of assorted humans. If you're going to tell me something, Mr. Boyd, tell me the truth.

BOYD: Well, everybody just likes Simple. That's his trouble. He likes people, so they like him. But he's not going with all those women. He wasn't even going with Zarita.

JOYCE: *(Does not believe him)* You can have your hat, Mr. Boyd, if you will.

BOYD: *(Takes his hat and continues talking)* I mean, not lately, not for two or three years, since he's met you—why, he doesn't talk about anybody but you, hasn't for along time.—Joyce, Joyce, Joyce! Now, he's even talking to himself in the night, trying to explain to you. I room next door, and sometimes I can hear him crying late in the night. Nobody likes to hear a grown man crying, Miss Lane.

JOYCE: *(Sternly dismissing him)* Thank you very much, Mr. Boyd.

BOYD: Miss Lane!

(She closes the door as he backs out. JOYCE comes toward the center of the room, stops, thinks, then rushes to the closet and begins to put on her coat)
BLACKOUT

Act II, Scene 8

SIMPLE's room. Same evening.
SIMPLE is alone, standing beside his dresser turning the pages of the Bible.
SIMPLE: My old Aunt Lucy always said, "The Bible is the Rock, and the Rock is the Truth, and the Truth is the Light." Lemme see. *(He reads from Job)* It says here, "Let thy day be darkness. Let no God regard it from above, neither let the light shine upon it. . . . Man is born unto trouble." Lemme turn over! *(He tries the next page)* Uh-huh! This is just as bad. "They meet with darkness in the daytime and grope in the noonday like as in the night." Great Gordon Gin! What part of the Bible am I reading out of? *Job!* No wonder! He's the one what suffered everything from boils to blindness. But it says here the Lord answered Job. Looks like don't nobody answer me. Nobody! *(He shuts the Bible and goes to the window. JOYCE comes up the stairs and down the hall. Outside his door she calls)*
JOYCE: Jess! *(His body stiffens)*
SIMPLE: Am I hearing things?
JOYCE: Jess!
SIMPLE: I must be going crazy! Can't be that voice.
JOYCE: *(Knocks softly and enters)* Jess!
SIMPLE: Joyce! Why are you here?
JOYCE: To see you, Jess. There's something maybe I ought to tell you.
SIMPLE: There's nothing for you to tell me, Joyce.
JOYCE: But, Jess— *(After a long silence he speaks)*
SIMPLE: You've come to *me,* Joyce.
JOYCE: Yes, Jess.
SIMPLE: Every time something's happened between us, in the end you come to me. It's my turn to come to you now.
JOYCE: You tried. I wouldn't let you in. I got those messages. I heard you ringing my bell. It's my fault, Jess.
SIMPLE: It's not your fault, Joyce. I had no business trying to see you *then*. But I wasn't man enough not to try.
JOYCE: Jess, you were at my door and I wouldn't let you in.

SIMPLE: All my life I been looking for a door that will be just mine—and the one I love. Joyce, I been looking for *your* door. But sometimes you let the wrong *me* in, not the me I want to be. This time, when I come through your door again, it's gonna be the *me* I ought to be.

JOYCE: I know, Jess—we've had problems to solve. But—

SIMPLE: The problem to solve is me, Joyce—and can't no one solve that problem but me. Until I get out of this mud and muck and mire I been dancing in half my life, don't you open your door to the *wrong* me no more. *Don't open your door.* And don't say nothing good to me, Joyce. Don't tell me nothing a-tall. *(He has already risen. Now she rises, embracing him, but he pushes her away)* Joyce, baby, darling, no. . . . *(He wants to call her all the sweet names he knows, to take her in his arms, to keep her then and there and always. But instead he speaks almost harshly)* No! Don't say nothing—to me—Joyce. *(He opens the door. As JOYCE turns to go, she looks at JESS, lifts her head, and smiles the most beautiful smile a man has ever seen—a smile serene and calm and full of faith. THE LIGHTS DIM TO A SPOT on her face as she turns and leaves without a word. Suddenly there is a great burst of music, wild, triumphant, wonderful, and happy)*

BLACKOUT

Act II, Scene 9

Paddy's Bar on a winter night.

BODIDDLY, BOYD, GITFIDDLE and the PIANIST are scattered about. MELON leans over MISS MAMIE's table and emits a playful howl.

MELON: Ow-ooo-oo-o! Miss Mamie, you're a killer, that you is! Sweet my lands! You-oo-O!

MAMIE: Melon, I don't want no wolf-howling compliments. I just come here to set in peace. I don't want to be bothered with you drunken Negroes.

MELON: Who is drunk?

MAMIE: You!

BODIDDLY: She's right, you is.

MELON: Listen here! Diddly and Mamie, both you all belong to my church—the Upstairs Baptist—yet you go around talking about me like a dirty dog.

MAMIE: Well, you do drink—guzzle, guzzle, guzzle!

MELON: I don't get drunk!

MAMIE: I say you do!

MELON: Woman, listen! Miss Mamie, I respects you too much to dispute your word. If you say I do, I does.

MAMIE: Now that that's settled, come and have a drink on me. A little eye-opener in the morning, a bracer at noon, and a nightcap at night, never hurt nobody.

MELON: Mamie, you got money?

MAMIE: I always got me some money, been had money, and always will have money. And one reason I do is, I'm a lone wolf, I runs with no pack.

MELON: I would pack you on my back if you would let me.

MAMIE: I don't intend to let you. To tell the truth, I doubt your intentions. And, Melon, I wants you to know: *(She sings)*
I been making my way for a long, long time.
I been making my way through this world.
I keep on trying to be good
'Cause I'm a good old girl.
I been making my way with a boot and a shoe.
In no oyster have I found a pearl.
I trust myself—so I've got luck
'Cause I'm a good old girl.
Sometimes the devil beckons
I look at the devil and say, *(MELON touches her hand)*
Stop that!
Devil, devil, devil—
I been making my way through thick and thin
'Spite o' devilish men in this world.
There ain't no man can get me down
Not even Harry Belafonte,
'Cause I'm a good old girl.
(MAMIE rises and addresses the entire bar)
I make five or ten dollars, sometimes more a day.
You men what ain't working know that that ain't hay.
Don't let no strange man get his hand on you—
There's no telling, baby, what a strange man will do.
It takes all kinds of folks to spin this globe around,
But *one* bad actor tears your playhouse down.
Don't ever let no bad actor come around—
There's no telling, baby, what he's putting down!

Sometimes the devil beckons.
I look at the devil and say, *(MELON approaches)*
Devil, devil, devil—
Ain't you got enough trouble?
Devil, be on your way!
I been making my way through thick and thin
'Spite o' devilish men in this world.
There's no man can get me down
'Cause I'm a good old girl.
My name is Mamie—
I'm a good old girl!
Like Mamie Eisenhower,
I'm a good old gal!
(To shouts of approval from the bar crowd, she continues)
I been making my way for a long, long time!
Now listen, Punchy: I've been making my way:
I've been making my very own way for a long, long time.
I don't need you, Melon.
I've been making my way through this world.
Who needs that face?
I keep on trying to be good.
You think I'm a doll?
I'm a good old girl—
Might be a human doll! Anyhow—
I been making my way through thick and thin
'Spite o' devilish men in this world, *(MELON grins)*
You always been this ugly, Melon?
There ain't no man can get me down—
'Cause I'm a good old girl!
I keep repeating—I'm a good old girl!
Now, what's the sense of going on with this?

BODIDDLY: Melon, I guess you realize there's nothing more independent than an independent woman. You's better stop worrying Miss
Mamie or she'll floor you and stomp on your carcass.

MELON: Diddly, if you don't have some respect for my personal conversation, I'm going to bust a watermelon over your head.

BODIDDLY: Take it easy, man. See you later. Hi, Simp! *(SIMPLE enters
shivering, passing BODIDDLY as he exits)*

SIMPLE: Hi, Bo! Hop! Man, this bar is the warmest place I know in
winter. At least you keep steam up here.

HOPKINS: Cold as it is, do you mean to tell me you haven't got any steam in your room?

SIMPLE: I done beated on my radiator pipe six times today to let my old landlady know I was home—freezing.

HOPKINS: And what happened?

SIMPLE: Nothing—she just beat back on the pipes at me. Which is why I come down here, to get warm, just like Boyd.

HOPKINS: Want a drink?

SIMPLE: I sure could use one.

HOPKINS: Coming up.

SIMPLE: Hey Boyd! I got something to tell you. I'm working part-time, back down at the plant as a helper—helping reconvert.

BOYD: That's wonderful!

SIMPLE: With a good job and a good wife, man, it'll be like Joyce used to say when I kissed her—"Simply Heavenly." And when we get married, Boyd, you're gonna be standing there beside me at my wedding. You're gonna hand me the ring. Ain't that what the best man does?

MAMIE: Yeah, that's right. *(MELON approaches)* Melon, ain't you got no home?

BOYD: Hey, this is the first time you've sprung this on me, about being your best man. After all we've only known each other for a few years. A best man is usually somebody you grew up with, or something.

SIMPLE: I didn't grow up with nobody, Boyd. So I don't know anybody very well. So, will you please be my best man?

BOYD: Best man, eh? Then I'll have to start buying me a brand new suit. And a best man is due to give a bachelor's party for the groom a night or two before the ceremony. Your wedding's going to cost me a lot of dough, Jess.

SIMPLE: Just a keg of beer. I mean a private one—with my name on it.

BOYD: You got it, lad. I live to see the day! *(He rises)*

SIMPLE: Where you going, Boyd?

BOYD: Listen, Jess! Hot or cold. I've got to bust that book-writing rock and I've got to get home to my typewriter. Good night, all.

SIMPLE: Well, that's settled. Thank God, I don't have to worry about Zarita. I ain't seen her for months.

HOPKINS: Zarita's getting ready to fly to Arizona for Christmas. That Big Boy, Ali Baba, sent her a ticket. She's all set to go. I think they're going to get married.

SIMPLE: I wishes her all the luck in the world. But I sure wish I could understand a woman.

HOPKINS: Socrates tried, he couldn't. What makes you hold such hopes?

SIMPLE: Long as I live, Hop, I lives in hopes. *(Loud weeping is heard outside)* Damn, there's some woman hollering now.

HOPKINS: I wonder what's wrong. *(ARCIE enters crying and sinks at a table)* What's wrong, Arcie?

ARCIE: Gimme a sherry, Hopkins, quick! Gimme a sherry.

HOPKINS: What's the matter, Arcie?

ARCIE: Abe Lincoln is going to the army.

SIMPLE: The army?

ARCIE: My oldest son, Abraham Lincoln Jones.

SIMPLE: Well, why didn't you say so?

ARCIE: I'm trying to! Abe got his draft call.

SIMPLE: Don't cry, Arcie. The army'll do the boy no harm. He'll get to travel, see the world.

ARCIE: The first one of my children to leave home!

SIMPLE: As many as you got, you shouldn't mind *one* going somewhere.

ARCIE: I does mind. Abe is my oldest, and I does mind. Fill it up again, Hop.

SIMPLE: That boy Abe is smart, Arcie. You'll be proud of him. He's liable to get to be an officer.

HOPKINS: At least a sergeant—and come back here with stripes on his sleeve.

SIMPLE: Else medals on his chest. Now, me, if I was to go in the army today—now that we's integrated—I would come back a general.

HOPKINS: Quit your kidding.

SIMPLE: I would rise right to the top today and be a general—and be in charge of white troops.

MELON: Colored generals never command white troops.

SIMPLE: The next war will be integrated. In fact, I'd like to command a regiment from Mississippi.

HOPKINS: Are you drunk?

SIMPLE: No, sir.

MELON: Then why on earth would you want to be in charge of a white regiment from Mississippi?

SIMPLE: In the last war, they had white officers in charge of Negroes. So why shouldn't I be in charge of whites? Huh? General Simple! I would really make 'em toe the line. I know some of them Dixiecrats would rather die than left face for a colored man, but they would left face for me.

MELON: Man, you got a great imagination.

SIMPLE: I can see myself now, in World War III, leading white Mississippi troops into action. Hop, I would do like all the other generals do, and stand way back on a hill somewhere and look through my spy-glasses and say, "Charge on! Mens, charge on!" Then I would watch them Dixiecrats boys go—like true sons of the Old South, mowing down the enemy. When my young white lieutenants from Vicksburg jeeped back to headquarters to deliver their reports in person to me, they would say, "Captain General, sir, we have taken two more enemy positions." I would say, "Mens, return to your companies—and tell 'em to keep on charging on!" Next day, when I caught up to 'em, I would pin medals on their chest for bravery. Then I would have my picture taken in front of all my fine white troops—me—the first *black* American general to pin medals on white soldiers from Mississippi. Then, Hop—man, oh, man— then when the war be's over, I would line my companies up for the last time and I would say, "Mens, at ease. Gentlemen of the Old South, relax. Put down your fighting arms and lend me your ears—because I am one of you, too, borned and bred in Dixie. *(GIT-FIDDLE begins to play a syncopated march—a blend of "Dixie," "Swanee River," and "Yankee Doodle")* And I'm willing to let bygones by bygones, and forget how you failed to obey my orders in the old days and right faced-ted when I said, "Left," because you though I was colored. Well, I is colored. I'll forget that. You are me—and I am you—and we are one. And now that our fighting is done, let's be Americans for once, for fun. Colonels, captains, majors, lieutenants, sergeants, and, Hopkins, open up a keg of nails for the men—let's all drink to you, brave sons of the South! Drink, mens, drink! And when we all stagger back to peace together, let there be peace—between you, Mississippi, and me! Company—'tention! Right shoulder arms! . . . Forward, march! . . . Come on, boys, I'm leading you! Come on! By the left flank march!" *(SIMPLE proudly inspects his troops as they pass in review. Others in the bar, except MISS MAMIE, applaud and cheer)*

HOPKINS: March, fellows, march!

SIMPLE: By the right flank, march!

HOPKINS: March, fellows, march!

ARCIE: Ain't that fine!

HOPKINS: March, march, march!

SIMPLE: Forward! March!

HOPKINS: March! March! March! *(SIMPLE exits as if leading an army with banners. The music rises to a climax, then suddenly ends. In the silence MISS MAMIE speaks)*
MAMIE: You know something—that boy is sick!
BLACKOUT

Act II, Scene 10

A phone booth. Christmas Eve.
Chimes are softly tolling "Jingle Bells" as SIMPLE speaks excitedly into the phone.
SIMPLE: Joyce? . . . Joyce? . . . Is this Joyce? . . . Yes, it's Jesse B. . . . It's Simple, honey! . . . What? You say I sound like a new man? I *am* a new man! And I got something for you, Joyce. It's Christmas Eve and, you know, well—like it says in the Bible, "Wise men came bringing gifts." . . . Joyce, I got a few little gifts for you on my Christmas tree. . . . Sure, I got a tree! What's on it for you? . . . I don't want to tell you, Joyce. I want to show you. You say you're coming right over? . . . Oh, baby! *(With the receiver still in his hand, he rises excitedly and starts out, but is jerked back by the cord. Quickly he hangs up and leaves as the music of "Jingle Bells" fills the air)*
BLACKOUT

Act II, Scene 11

SCENE: SIMPLE's room.
TIME: Christmas Eve.
AT RISE: A star shines in the darkness. The lights come up revealing SIMPLE and JOYCE standing before a tiny Christmas tree. The star glows atop this tree hung with tinsel and little balls of colored glass. On the tree there are four gifts tied with ribbons: one is a letter, one a roll of paper, one a long parchment, and one is a tiny box. JOYCE has just entered the room.
JOYCE: Jess!
SIMPLE: Look. *(He shows her the tree)*
JOYCE: Oh! It's beautiful!
SIMPLE: May I take your coat? Won't you sit down? *(He hands her the parchment as JOYCE perches on the edge of a chair)*

JOYCE: Jess, what is it? A picture of some kind? Maybe a map? Why, it's all in Roman letters. It's a divorce!

SIMPLE: With a gold seal on it, too.

JOYCE: Free! Jess, you're free! Like in *Uncle Tom's Cabin*!

SIMPLE: Yes, baby, I'm free. That's the paper.

JOYCE: It's dated a whole month ago. Jess, why didn't you tell me you had your divorce?

SIMPLE: I was waiting for something else to go with it. Here, this is for you, too. *(He hands her an envelope)*

JOYCE: My father's writing!

SIMPLE: Read it. You see, your ole—your father—gimme your hand. *(While she reads the letter, SIMPLE opens the little box on the tree and polishes a ring on his coat lapel.)* Now, can I take your hand? *(He slips the ring on her finger)* For you—if you'll wear it?

JOYCE: Forever! *(She starts to rise, but gently he pushes her down and returns to the tree)*

SIMPLE: This is something only married people can have. And it's not ready, yet, either. They just about now digging the first hole in the ground—busting that first rock. We both got to sign our names—if you're willing.

JOYCE: An apartment! Oh, Jess! A place to live! An apartment!

SIMPLE: Can we both sign our names, Joyce?

JOYCE: Yes, Jess *(JOYCE rises, scattering papers, and flings her arms about him)*

SIMPLE: Now we can get ready for that wedding in June.

JOYCE: Oh, Jess! Jess, baby! Jess! *(Singing, they embrace)*

SIMPLE: Just for you these Christmas tokens
On our Christmas tree—

JOYCE: Help to make me know that you are
Santa Claus to me.

SIMPLE: Just a little pain and trouble
Mixed in with the past

BOTH: Help to make our joys double
When we're sure they'll last.

JOYCE: Wonderful the morning star
Shining in the dawn!

BOTH: Wonderful the rainbow's arch
When the rain is gone.

(The bar is revealed as the entire company enters singing and form tableaux, some around the piano, MAMIE at her table with MELON,

*BODIDDLY, ARCIE, and JOHN JASPER making a family group
at another table. The entire chorus of "Look for the Morning Star" is
repeated as all come forward for bows)*
ALL: Don't forget there's bluebirds
  Somewhere in the blue.
  Love will send a little bluebird
  Flying straight to you.
  (Repeat chorus on bows)
CURTAIN

Mister Jazz
A Panorama in Music and Motion
of the History of Negro Dancing

1960

Hughes wrote *Mister Jazz* as an opener for the Broadway production of *Shakespeare in Harlem*, a one-act play derived from his poetry by a young white playwright, Robert Glenn. So successful was the August 1959 production of *Shakespeare in Harlem* in Lucille Lortel's White Barn Theater in Westport, Connecticut, that she brought it to her Theatre de Lys in Greenwich Village for one night, October 27, 1959, pairing it with Hughes's *Soul Gone Home*. The Broadway production, at the 41st Street Theatre, was paired with a dramatic rendition of James Weldon Johnson's *God's Trombones*. It lasted only thirty-two performances despite good reviews. It seems that *Mister Jazz* has never been performed, although Alvin Ailey expressed interest in it as a ballet libretto.

The text reproduced here is in the Langston Hughes typescripts deposited at Harold Ober Associates. In the Langston Hughes Papers and included here among Hughes's lyrics is the song "The Blues," which Hughes wrote with Sammy Price for *Mister Jazz*.

JAZZ DANCES in Historical Sequence for MISTER JAZZ by Langston
    Hughes utilizing adaptations of the popular music of each period

Pre–Civil War:	AFRICAN DANCES
	JUBA DANCE
	BUCK-AND-WING
	JIG (JUMP JIM CROW)
	STRUT
	CAKE WALK
	SAND
	SOFT SHOE
Post–Civil War:	MARCH (NEW ORLEANS)
	TAG ALONG (SECOND LINERS)
	SLOW DRAG (RAG TIME)
	EAGLE ROCK

	SHIMMY
	CAMEL WALK
	TEXAS TOMMY
Roaring Twenties:	SUZY-Q
	SNAKE HIPS
	BALLING-THE-JACK
	CHARLESTON
	BLACK BOTTOM
	SHIM SHAM
	LINDY HOP
Depression:	JITTERBUG
	TRUCKIN'
	PECKING
	SHAG
	BIG APPLE
Latin:	RUMBA—CONGA
	MAMBO—CHA CHA
Contemporary:	BOP
	SLOP
	ROCK AND ROLL
	COOL

MUSIC: *African drums—a long rumbling roll gradually developing into syncopation as the house lights dim.*

SETTING: *A cyclorama or scrim before which dancing shadows are seen as stage light comes up.*

ACTION: *In silhouette the figures of AFRICAN DANCERS in feathered headdresses move slowly to tribal rhythms.*

MR. JAZZ: Africa! . . . . Long ago Africa! . . . . Then across the Western Ocean came drums—and dancers.

> *(As the African shadows fade to merge into the figures of SLAVES in Congo Square in New Orleans dancing much the same move-ments, only faster, the drums grow loud in fervid syncopation)*

Congo Square in New Orleans. . . . . Sunday—the slaves' one day for fun and dancing—the juba dance in Congo Square. In those feet, those hands, those drums—the roots of jazz.

> *(Drum beats merge into hand clapping)*

Where there were no drums, in the slave quarters of the cities, or on remote plantations, hands took over—just the clapping of hands.

> *(The CONGO DANCERS disappear and a single jiggling figure is seen)*

The Juba Dance became a jig. . . . the jig the buck-and-wing . . .
And sometimes after work in worn-out finery and hand-me-downs,
the slaves would get together for their walk arounds.

*(The DANCER dons a wide hat, picks up a cane and leads a
procession of shadow figures across the screen, dancing and clapping
hands)*

And maybe on holidays when they didn't have to walk the chalk,
they might celebrate with a big cake walk.

*(The scrim rises and lights come up to reveal MR. JAZZ leading
TIPPER and the DANCING SINGER in the cake walk as he calls
out gaily)*

Oh, walk your lady! . . . . . Walk for the cake! . . . . . Dance! Prance!
. . . . Step to the music!. . . .

*(As the DANCERS exit stepping lively, MR. JAZZ comes forward
to sing)*

That's how jazz was born—a long time ago. And the principal is still
the same. You just:

SYNCOPATE THE RHYTHM
WITH A STEADY BEAT,
LET THAT RHYTHM TINGLE
RIGHT FROM HEAD TO FEET—
THAT'S JAZZ!
MIX IT WITH A BLUE NOTE
LIKE A LONESOME MOAN,
ADD A LOT OF LAUGHTER
PLUS A JIVING TONE—
THAT'S JAZZ!
PLENTY ROOM FOR SWINGING,
PLENTY ROOM FOR PLAY,
ROOM FOR EVERYBODY
TO JAZZ IN HIS OWN WAY—
KEEP IT FREE AND EASY
SO YOUR HEART WON'T BREAK
THAT'S THE WAY TO JAZZ
THE JAZZING JAZZ MEN MAKE—
THAT'S JAZZ!

(He dances, then puts his hand to his ear)

Cock your ear a little. Listen to the past. New Orleans again! Oh,
my lands! Serenade wagons, marching bands! Famous for funerals—

(A typical old New Orleans marching band dirge is heard in slow tempo as Mr. Jazz continues to talk and TIPPER with bowed down head, as if following a casket, crosses to stage)

The living's got to live and the dying's got to die. Mourners got to mourn and criers got to cry—but when the dying is done and the last prayers have been said, I'm sorry—the living's got to live—though the dead is dead. On the way to the cemetery, sad and mournful is the beat—but it's a different story headed back to Rampart Street.

(Drum roll into syncopated tempo as both MR. JAZZ and the MOURNING FIGURE fall into rhythm and begin to dance in line behind the band as TAG ALONG enters to join them in rhythm)

MR. JAZZ: The Second Liners—jazzing with their feet!

TIPPER: Mr. Tipper!

TAG ALONG: Mr. Tag Along!

MR. JAZZ: Mister Jazz!

(Their half-prance half-dance gradually develops into a series of old jazz steps of former years as the music becomes a medley merging from the syncopated march into ragtime then into Dixieland and later jazz)

Where did these steps come from? Where were they born?

TAG ALONG: New Orleans marching bands, Buddy Bolden's horn.

MR. JAZZ: Jelly Roll's piano, Scott Joplin's ragtime beat.

TAG ALONG: That same old steady rhythm —

MR. JAZZ: Runs from head to feet.

ALL: That's jazz!

(As THEY dance, the GIRL SINGER enters to sing)

SINGER: TELL ME, BABY, WHERE DID
  ALL THIS SYNCOPATION START?

MR. JAZZ: IT MUST HAVE STARTED, BABY,
  IN THE HUMAN HEART.

TAG ALONG: ADAM'S JAZZ!

SINGER: EVE'S JAZZ!

MR. JAZZ: JUST JAZZ!

SINGER: TELL ME, TELL ME, DADDY,
  WHAT'S THAT NOTE I HEAR?

MR. JAZZ: BESSIE SMITH AND BILLIE
  WHISPERING IN MY EAR,

OLD JOE TURNER
WHO'S COME AND GONE.
SINGER: MA RAINEY, MAMA YANCEY—
HOW LONG? HOW LONG?
MR. JAZZ: C. C. RIDER,
SKINNY, TALL, AND BLACK—
SINGER: UP ON THE MOUNTAIN
TRYING TO CALL HIS BABY BACK.
ALL: WHEN YOU LAUGH TO KEEP FROM CRYING
'CAUSE THERE'S A SCREAM IN YOUR THROAT
AND YOU CAN'T BREAK LOOSE AND HOLLER—
IT'S A BLUE, BLUE NOTE—
THAT'S THE BLUES! THAT'S THE BLUES!
THE BLUES. . . . . .
> (MR. JAZZ steps aside, TAG ALONG and the SINGER dance to-
> gether a Slow Drag followed by each dance in succession as named,
> the SINGER changing partners as required, sometimes the men
> dancing alone)

MR. JAZZ: The Slow Drag.
The Camel Walk.
The Texas Tommy.
The Shimmy-Sha-Wobble.
The Eagle Rock.
And when the lights are low—
> (A sudden wail of sirens. Cymbals crash. The music changes to the
> blatant blare of the twenties)

The Roaring Twenties! Bootleg days!
Snake Hips.
Balling-The-Jack.
Suzy-Q.
Black Bottom.
Shim Sham.
And later came the Shag.
The Big Apple.
Trucking.
Pecking.
> (Suddenly the music stops and only clapping hands are heard)

And what do you know?
The Charleston, Joe!

(MR. JAZZ begins to Charleston as OTHERS take up the beat)
Not long after the Charleston, a great even took place. A man all by
himself went winging through space—and if you want the exact year
to be given, it was when Lindbergh flew the ocean in 1927 that the
Lindy Hop was born in joy at a dance hall in Harlem called the Savoy!
*(A COUPLE burst onto stage in a mad Lindy Hop. When dance
is over, as DANCERS take their bows, MR. JAZZ shoos them off
stage)*
Move on! I say, move on! I'm making like a cop.
(As DANCERS exit, he turns to audience)
Did anybody ever tell you to "Move on," when you want to stop?
TIPPER: What's that got to do with jazz?
MR. JAZZ: Did you ever get beat all over your head by a cop?
TIPPER: What's it got to do with jazz?
MR. JAZZ: Be-bop Mop! Mop! Mop! That's Be-bop.
TIPPER: What?
MR. JAZZ: Mop! Mop!
TIPPER: Be-bop Mop!
MR. JAZZ: Be-bop! Were you ever born dark with a very dark skin, and
walked up to some café and couldn't get in?
TIPPER: All the tables are gone.
MR. JAZZ: But that's just what I want—a *gone* table.
BOTH: Be-bop Mop! Mop! Mop! Ooool-ya-koo! Bop!
*(TIPPER and TAG ALONG do a brief bop dance as MR. JAZZ
leans against side of stage. When DANCERS finish, he speaks)*
MR. JAZZ: From my looks, you might not know that I'm old John
Henry, I'm Stackolee. And I could be John Lewis—if John Lewis
was me.
(Music a la Modern Jazz Quartet is heard)
TAG ALONG: Cool, fool, cool!
MR. JAZZ: I'm also Chico Hamilton. I'm Buddy Collette. I'm the bee
in the bop of the Modern Jazz Quartet. Mister Jazz!
TAG ALONG: Cool, fool, cool!
MR. JAZZ: I'm Casey Jones. I'm a folk song lane. I'm the motorman
on Duke's "A" train.
TAG ALONG: Cool, cat, cool!
(SINGER enters)
SINGER: I'm the Countess Fontessa—and I'll have you know, I'll be
cool when you're hot—down below.

TAG ALONG: Cool, girl, cool!

SINGER: I grew up at Juilliard, raised on ballet.

TAG ALONG: I got a beard on my—

MR. JAZZ: Come on, now, let's not play!

TAG ALONG: Cool, you-all, cool!

MR. JAZZ: I was beat before the beatniks.

TAG ALONG: Bopped before the bop.

SINGER: Progressed before progressive.

MR. JAZZ: And I don't intend to stop.

TAG ALONG: Cool, fools, cool!

MR. JAZZ: Jazz! Going to go right on!

ALL: Got to go right on!

MR. JAZZ: Yes! Just—

> *(He sings and ALL join in as a cool couple dances, followed by a burlesque of cool couples by TIPPER and TAG ALONG)*

MR. JAZZ: From marching bands to Dixieland to blues to bop—from hot to cool—put it all together and it's jazz!

> *(He sings)*

SYNCOPATE THE RHYTHM
WITH A STEADY BEAT.
LET THAT RHYTHM TINGLE
RIGHT FROM HEAD TO FEET.

ALL: THAT'S JAZZ.

MR. JAZZ: MIX IT WITH A BLUE NOTE
LIKE A LONESOME MOAN.

TAG ALONG: ADD A LOT OF LAUGHTER
PLUS A JIVING TONE.

ALL: THAT'S JAZZ.

MR. JAZZ: PLENTY ROOM FOR SWINGING

SINGER: PLENTY ROOM FOR PLAY

ALL: ROOM FOR EVERYBODY
TO JAZZ IN HIS OWN WAY

MR. JAZZ: KEEP IT FREE AND EASY—

SINGER: SO YOUR HEART WON'T BREAK

MR. JAZZ: THAT'S THE WAY TO JAZZ THE JAZZING
THAT JAZZ MEN MAKE.

ALL: THAT'S JAZZ.

TAG ALONG: YEAH, MAN! THAT'S JAZZ!

MR. JAZZ: OLD JAZZ! NEW JAZZ!

TAG ALONG: HOT JAZZ! COOL JAZZ!

SINGER: SWEET JAZZ! GOOD JAZZ!
MR. JAZZ: J—A—Z—Z—
ALL: JAZZ!
     (ALL dance as the curtain falls)
END

Jericho–Jim Crow
A Song Play

1963

Jericho–Jim Crow, Langston Hughes's stirring tribute to the Civil Rights Movement, opened on January 12, 1964, at the Sanctuary in New York City. Directed by Alvin Ailey and William Hairston, it was the most extravagantly praised of Hughes's works in theater. Lead Gilbert Price was hailed as the new Paul Robeson, and the song "Freedom Land," lyrics and music by Hughes, was applauded as a new classic of black music.[1]

In form, *Jericho–Jim Crow* draws on Hughes's most successful theatrical works. In his 1938 *Don't You Want to Be Free?*—an "emotional history"[2] of African Americans' struggle for freedom—the main characters, too, are named generically, and one white actor, trickster-like in his transformations, plays all the white roles. But it also reflects his gospel plays. Fresh from the resounding success of *Black Nativity* (1961), and having quickly composed two other gospel plays, *Gospel Glow* (alternately titled *Gospel Glory*) and *Man of Miracles,* Hughes had perfected the dramatic use of the music that so quintessentially embodies African American faith, hope, and courage and that animated the freedom struggle.

Jericho–Jim Crow also offered a response to those who deplored *Tambourines to Glory,* which had just closed on Broadway. While Hughes termed *Tambourines* a comedy, its critique of storefront churches raised hackles as, at best, inappropriate, during a time when the struggle for rights riveted the nation, and its failure to address the civil rights struggle was, to many, incomprehensible. Hughes dedicated *Jericho–Jim Crow* to "the young people of all racial and religious backgrounds who are meeting, working, canvassing, petitioning, marching, picketing, sitting-in, singing and praying today to help make a better America for all, and especially for citizens of color." The play received the imprimatur of the Congress of Racial Equality, the Student Non-Violent Coordinating Committee, and the NAACP. The proceeds from a benefit performance were split among the three groups, and Hughes waived royalty payments by nonprofit groups "whose ticket sales, collections, or donations received go to the freedom movement."[3] This gospel play for the freedom movement reprises Hughes's continual preoccupation with the faith and drama of the African American struggle, both embodied and celebrated in such plays as *Scottsboro, Limited* (1931), *Don't You Want to Be Free?* (1938), *The Sun Do Move* (1942), *For This We Fight* (1943), and *The Ballot and Me* (1956), as well as in his lyrics.

The text for *Jericho-Jim Crow* is identified as the final revised acting script and is in the Langston Hughes Papers.

TIME: *The present—with flashbacks of the past.*
SETTING: *Any church rostrum, platform or stage with chairs or choir loft for the SINGERS—or they may sit in the front row of the auditorium.*

Characters

BOY
GIRL
WOMAN
OLD MAN
OLD WOMAN
JIM CROW

The character JIM CROW is also:
KLANSMAN
AUCTIONEER
PLANTER
MINISTER
GOVERNOR
POLICEMAN
JAILER

STAGING: *There is no curtain. One or two spotlights may be used if available. If not, simply lower the house lights at opening, but keep stage brightly lighted, except where dimness or darkness is indicated. This production should be kept as simple as possible so that amateur groups, schools, or churches may present it. Costume changes may be suggested by hats, ties, aprons, jackets, etc., rather than entire changes. JIM CROW, as a symbol of oppression, plays various roles, changing clothing to suit the character. The CHOIR SINGERS wear vari-colored robes which are discarded for the final scene and left on chairs. The production should move swiftly, with nothing to cause halts or waits between scenes,*

one scene blending into another in full view of the audience. What props
are required, the actors bring onstage with them when they enter. Piano
and organ, or both, may be utilized as well as guitar, drums, tam-
bourines and other instruments if available. The songs may be sung in
the gospel manner or as traditional spirituals. Audience participation
is invited on familiar songs, particularly at the end of the play. On
stage are four chairs, two stools.

Musical Numbers

1.	A MEETING HERE TONIGHT	Chorus
2.	I'M ON MY WAY	Chorus
3.	I BEEN 'BUKED AND I BEEN SCORNED	Old Woman
4.	SUCH A LITTLE KING	Girl
5.	IS MASSA GWINE TO SELL US TOMORROW?	Boy and Chorus
6.	HOW MUCH DO YOU WANT ME TO BEAR?	Woman
7.	WHERE WILL I LIE DOWN?	Boy and Girl
8.	FOLLOW THE DRINKING GOURD	Woman and Chorus
9.	JOHN BROWN'S BODY	Male Singers
10.	BATTLE HYMN OF THE REPUBLIC	Chorus
11.	SLAVERY CHAIN DONE BROKE AT LAST	Old Woman and Chorus
12.	OH, FREEDOM!	Girl and Chorus
13.	GO DOWN, MOSES	Woman
14.	EZEKIEL SAW THE WHEEL	Old Man and Chorus
15.	STAY IN THE FIELD	Old Man and Chorus
16.	FREEDOM LAND	Boy
17.	GOD'S GONNA CUT YOU DOWN	Chorus
18.	BETTER LEAVE SEGREGATION ALONE	Chorus
19.	MY MIND ON FREEDOM	Chorus
20.	WE SHALL OVERCOME	Chorus
21.	THE BATTLE OF OLD JIM CROW	Chorus
22.	COME AND GO WITH ME	Chorus

OPENING—*A single powerful voice, unaccompanied, sings in the darkness.*

VOICE: MY LORD, HE CALLS ME!
HE CALLS ME BY THE THUNDER!
THE TRUMPET SOUNDS
WITHIN-A-MY SOUL. . . . .

WOMEN: THERE'S A MEETING,
THERE'S A MEETING.

VOICE: THE TRUMPET SOUNDS. . . . . .

WOMEN: THERE'S A MEETING HERE TONIGHT.

VOICE: WITHIN-A MY SOUL. . . . . . .

(The lights gradually come on as CAST enter down the aisles informally as if going to a meeting—robes and jackets in their hands)

SINGERS: THERE'S A MEETING HERE TONIGHT!
THERE'S A MEETING HERE TONIGHT! . . . . .
I KNOW YOU'LL WANT TO PRAY AND SHOUT.
THERE'S A MEETING HERE TONIGHT.
CAMP MEETING DOWN IN THE WILDERNESS,
THERE'S A MEETING HERE TONIGHT.
I KNOW ALL ITS AIMS THE LORD WILL BLESS.
THERE'S A MEETING HERE TONIGHT.
WE KNOW WE'RE AIMING FOR THE SKIES.
THERE'S A MEETING HERE TONIGHT.
FOLKS, WHAT WE'RE SAYING AIN'T NO LIES.
THERE'S A MEETING HERE TONIGHT.

(The BOY and GIRL sing with them)

GET YOU READY, THERE'S A MEETING HERE TONIGHT.
JOIN US NOW, THERE'S A MEETING HERE TONIGHT.
I KNOW YOU'LL WANT TO PRAY AND SHOUT.
THERE'S A MEETING HERE TONIGHT.

(The SINGERS take their seats. The BOY pantomimes the pulling of a light chain lowering the house lights, then turns a switch bringing up the stage lights. Then he addresses the AUDIENCE speaking rapidly, running his names all together)

BOY: My name is Nat Turner Frederick Douglass DuBois Garvey Adam Powell Martin Luther King Shuttlesworth James Lewis Farmer Meredith Moses Holmes Jones—that's me. And I got a hundred thousand more names, too—they're you. But for short, you can just call me Jones. And I'm on my way.

(GIRL enters to stand beside BOY)

GIRL: My name is Harriet Tubman Sojourner Truth Mary Church Ter-
rell Ida Wells Barnett Mary McLeod Bethune Autherine Lucy Rosa
Parks Daisy Bates Dianne Nash Charlayne Hunter Juanita Malone
Anniebelle Smith—that's me. But you can call me Anniebelle. And,
folks, I'm on my way.

VOICE: Where?

GIRL: To freedom!

OLD WOMAN: Me, too!

> *(An OLD MAN and OLD WOMAN stand together between the
> BOY and GIRL)*

OLD MAN: And me! Children, *you're* today. We was yesterday. We was
your grandparents and your great-great-grandparents before that
and on back through slavery to Africa. Here we is now—here—but
too old maybe to march.

OLD WOMAN: No such a thing! I ain't too old to march.

OLD MAN: We're sure ain't too old to want to vote.

OLD WOMAN: Which I ain't never did in Mississippi.

OLD MAN: But I want to vote. Yes, I do.

OLD WOMAN: And I wants to eat a dish of ice cream at that downtown store.

OLD MAN: And we want our grandchildren to go to the nearest school.

OLD WOMAN: And to whatever university they desires—Mississippi or
anywhere else.

OLD MAN: We want our children and our grandchildren—

OLD WOMAN: And ourselves—

BOTH: To be free!

> *(BOY and GIRL lead song)*

SINGERS: I'M ON MY WAY AND I WON'T TURN BACK.
I'M ON MY WAY AND I WON'T TURN BACK.
I'M ON MY WAY AND I WON'T TURN BACK.
I'M ON MY WAY, THANK GOD, I'M ON MY WAY.

> *(BOY and GIRL exit singing)*

OLD MAN: I'M GONNA TELL MY CAPTAIN BETTER LET ME
GO . . . etc . . .
IF HE SAYS NO, NO, NO, NO, NO, GONNA GO ANYHOW . . .
etc . . .

SINGERS: I'M ON MY WAY, THANK GOD, I'M ON MY WAY. . . .
etc. . . .

OLD WOMAN: Yes, indeed, no turning back! We gonna be here a
while! They forced us to come. Now America's got us—we gonna
be here.

OLD MAN: Seems like we got a mission to save America from herself.

OLD WOMAN: I got to save myself—for myself. The world knows what happened to us in slavery time and a long time since then. Fact is—
I BEEN 'BUKED AND I BEEN SCORNED. . . . etc. . . .
Like Sojourner Truth said, standing at night in the door of her slave cabin, "My children was sold down the river away from me, sold down the Mississippi River. I didn't know where they be, and they didn't know where I be. But in them days, we looked at the stars, my scattered children and me—we seed the same stars—and that's all we had in common in them days." Black mothers, black children—and stars—and all the cotton lands and rivers and marshes in between. I did not know where they be. My children did not know where I be. Oh, I remember when I were mighty nigh nothing but a child myself—a young girl—

GIRL: And I was bearing my first child—

OLD WOMAN: And it were Christmas—

GIRL: The time of that other Child in Bethlehem—

OLD WOMAN: And I knowed up at the Big House master and mistress was celebrating their plantation Christmas with lights and trees, oranges and presents. But none for my children.

GIRL: I knew, I knew there were no presents for me up there. Anyhow, I snuck out of my cabin one night, and I went up to the Big House to look though their windows at their lights and their tree and at the little cradle they had made beside the tree for that other Child that that other Mother had borne so long a time ago in Judea.

OLD WOMAN: That Holy Child who became the light of the world!

GIRL: I said, "Maybe my child will become a light, too." So I sang a song for my child—to that other Child:
(The GIRL cradles a baby in her arms)
HE'S SUCH A LITTLE KING, THIS LITTLE CHILD . . . etc . . .

OLD WOMAN: It said in the Bible that Mary and Joseph fled into Egypt—

GIRL: With their Son. But I didn't know no Egypt where I could flee.

OLD WOMAN: They sold my children away from me. When my first-born was just a little stripling boy, hardly big enough to work yet, they took my child and sold him away from me. They took my child.

GIRL: They sold my child! They sold my child!
(The GIRL drops her arms and exits with a scream)

OLD WOMAN: Every time the slave traders came and Old Massa needed money, he would sell somebody's child.

BOY: MAMA, IS MASSA GONNA SELL ME TOMORROW?

WOMEN: YES! . . . . . YES! . . . . . YES!
BOY: MAMA, IS MASSA GWINE TO SELL ME TOMORROW? . . .
  etc . . .
  (As the SINGERS hum, JIM CROW enters as a SLAVE
  TRADER to conduct an auction. He pulls the BOY to the slave
  block)
TRADER: Come on now—but up on the block! . . . . . How much am
  I bid? . . . A fine buck Negra here—pick more cotton in one day, I
  bet you, than any slave you ever owned! . . . . . How much? . . . One
  hundred? . . . Aw, no! You all get down to serious bidding now!
  (The song rises again)
WOMEN: GWINE TO SELL US DOWN IN GEORGIA?
SINGERS: YES, YES, YES! OH, WATCH AND PRAY!
TRADERS: How much? . . . Two! . . . Three! . . . That's more like it!
  What do I hear? Who'll make it Four! . . . Four? Going once, go-
  ing twice! Five Hundred Dollars! All right! . . . Do I hear Six? . . .
  Going, going, gone—for Five Hundred Dollars!
BOY: FAREWELL, MOTHER, I MUST LEAVE YOU.
WOMEN: YES, YES, YES! . . . . . etc. . . . .
  (Hum under)
OLD WOMAN: Watch and pray—that was all that we could do in
  slavery time about our children, watch and pray, hope and pray they
  wouldn't be snatched from us. No protection, nothing, just slaves,
  we black women. And they did us like they chosed. Treated us like
  dogs. That's why I had to cry out. I'm tired! Oh, Lord. . . . .
  (A VOICE rises in comment)
HOW MUCH MORE OF LIFE'S BURDEN CAN I BEAR?
HOW MUCH MORE OF LIFE'S SORROW MUST I SHARE?
THIS OLD WORLD IS CHANGING SO
UNTIL IT DON'T SEEM LIKE MY HOME ANY MORE.
I WANT TO KNOW JUST HOW MUCH BURDEN
DO YOU WANT ME TO BEAR?
HOW MUCH MORE? HOW MUCH MORE?
YES, HOW MUCH MORE? TELL ME, HOW MUCH MORE?
I WANT TO KNOW ALL ABOUT MY BURDENS,
YES, MY PAIN AND CARE.
DON'T YOU KNOW I PRAYED, AND I PRAYED AGAIN!
OH, SEEMS LIKE MY PRAYERS ARE ALL IN VAIN.
JUST HOW MUCH MORE, HOW MUCH MORE
OF THIS BURDEN DO YOU WANT ME TO BEAR?

WELL, HOW MUCH MORE? HOW MUCH MORE?
YES, HOW MUCH MORE? TELL ME, HOW MUCH MORE?
HOW MUCH MORE OF LIFE'S BURDEN
DO YOU WANT ME TO BEAR?
OH, DON'T YOU KNOW I PRAYED? LORD, I PRAYED AGAIN!
SEEMS LIKE MY PRAYERS, LORD, ARE ALL IN VAIN.
I WANT TO KNOW JUST HOW MUCH
DO YOU WANT ME TO BEAR.

(The OLD MAN and the BOY sit on the ground on opposite sides of the stage, miles apart in space and time)

OLD MAN: He was my son, too, that boy they sold—but I never saw him. I was sold off to another plantation even before he were born. They didn't let a black man and wife stay together in them days, if they wanted to sell them. I was sold away from the woman I loved before my son was borned. Sold from plantation to plantation. Sometimes I didn't know where I might lay my troubled head. My children, I reckon they did not know, either. I imagined sometimes I could hear them singing.

GIRL: *(Softly, as if far away, sings)*
WONDER WHERE MY BROTHER'S GONE?
WONDER WHERE MY BROTHER'S GONE?
TO SOME LONESOME PLACE, LORD,
FAR AWAY FROM HOME.

BOY: WONDER WHERE CAN I LIE DOWN, OH,
WONDER WHERE CAN'T I LIE DOWN?
IN SOME LONESOME PLACE, LORD,
DOWN UPON THE GROUND.

BOTH: WONDER WHERE CAN I LIE DOWN, OH,
WONDER WHERE CAN I LIE DOWN?
IN SOME LONESOME PLACE, LORD,
FAR AWAY FROM HOME.

(Hum continues under)

OLD MAN: Sometimes I can still hear their voices. Oh, God, I can still hear my children's voices singing. You know, somehow, I heared about freedom. In my old age, I heard about how Denmark Vesey riz up in Charleston, and Nat Turner started a rebellion against slavery in Virginny—and they both died fighting to be free. They killed them because they wanted freedom. But they spread the word to me and all the other slaves in the South that some day the walls of Jerico would come down. Yes, bless God! And that the evils of slavery couldn't last. I heard how some slaves climbed over the walls of Jerico and runned away, and got to the North, and worked with Abolitionists up there to break down the walls of slavery—like Frederick Douglass did. And then, do you know what I did? I made up my mind to run away, escape if I could—because I never did like to be cooped up. Yes, I made up my mind to do like Harriet Tubman said do. In fact, like she did when she hit the Underground Railroad and led many a slave to the North.

> *(The SINGERS pantomime the march toward freedom as they back the WOMAN in her song)*

WOMAN: FOLLOW THE DRINKING GOURD,
> FOLLOW THE DRINKING GOURD,
> FOR THE OLD MAN IS A-WAITING,
> FOR TO CARRY YOU TO FREEDOM,
> FOLLOW THE DRINKING GOURD.

SINGERS: WHEN THE SUN COMES UP
> AND THE FIRST QUAIL CALLS,
> FOLLOW THE DRINKING GOURD.
> FOR THE OLD MAN IS A-WAITING,
> FOR TO CARRY YOU TO FREEDOM,
> FOLLOW THE DRINKING GOURD.
> THE RIVER BANK'LL MAKE
> A MIGHTY GOOD ROAD,
> FOLLOW THE DRINKING GOURD.
> LEFT FOOT, PEG FOOT,
> TRAVELING ON,
> FOLLOW THE DRINKING GOURD.
> THE RIVER ENDS
> BETWEEN TWO HILLS,
> FOLLOW THE DRINKING GOURD.
> THERE'S ANOTHER RIVER
> ON THE OTHER SIDE,
> FOLLOW THE DRINKING GOURD.

OLD MAN: Barefooted—we made it. Made it through the swamps. There was snakes and 'gators there. Made it cross the fields through stubble and rubble. Made it down high roads thick with patterollers and polices on the lookout for me—through Carolina, Virginia, Maryland till, thank God, I got to the North.

> *(He looks around warily, then rapidly circles, seeking escape. He exits)*

OLD WOMAN: John followed the North Star to Freedom. My husband runned away, got to freedom, but I never saw him again. I died in slavery. I were never free myself. But for my children, old white John Brown fought for freedom at Harper's Ferry, and colored men died with him there. Oh, but they battled at Harper's Ferry.
   (A TRUMPET sounds. The OLD WOMAN rises)
Then the Civil War came. The Union Armies marched for freedom— and black men marched with them. Us colored folks in the slave cabins in the South, we heard their songs.
   (Softly, but gradually growing in volume:)
CHORUS: JOHN BROWN'S BODY LIES A-MOULDERING IN THE GRAVE,
   BUT HIS SOUL IS MARCHING ON.
   GLORY, GLORY, HALLELUJAH!
   HIS SOUL IS MARCHING ON . . . etc . . .
OLD WOMAN: And then in our cabins, in the night, way far off yonder where the union armies was, we heard that other song, almost just like John Brown's:
   (The song, in march tempo, rises in great volume)
CHORUS: MINE EYES HAVE SEEN THE GLORY
   OF THE COMING OF THE LORD.
   HE IS TRAMPLING OUT THE VINTAGE
   WHERE THE GRAPES OF WRATH ARE STORED.
   HE HAS LOOSED THE FATEFUL LIGHTNING
   OF HIS TERRIBLE SWIFT SWORD,
   HIS TRUTH IS MARCHING ON.
   GLORY, GLORY, HALLELUJAH! . . . . . etc. . . . .
OLD WOMAN: Abraham Lincoln signed the Emancipation Proclamation. Yes, he did! And it declared—
   (BOY unfurls a scroll)
BOY: " . . . all persons held as slaves within any State, or designated part of a State, shall be then, thenceforward, and forever free . . ."
SINGERS: SLAVERY CHAIN DONE BROKE AT LAST,
   BROKE AT LAST,
   SLAVERY CHAIN DONE BROKE AT LAST!
   GONG TO PRAISE GOD TILL I DIE.
   WAY DOWN IN-A THAT VALLEY
   PRAYING ON MY KNEES,
   TELLING GOD ABOUT MY TROUBLES,
   ASKING, HELP ME IF-A YOU PLEASE,

I DID KNOW MY JESUS HEARD ME
'CAUSE THE SPIRIT SPOKE TO ME
AND SAID, "RISE, MY CHILD,
YOUR CHILDREN AND YOU TOO SHALL BE FREE!"
SLAVERY CHAIN DONE BROKE AT LAST,
BROKE AT LAST,
SLAVERY CHAIN DONE BROKE AT LAST!
GONG TO PRAISE GOD TILL I DIE!
> *(Wild jubilation. Then, JIM CROW enters to place signs of segregation and discrimination amidst the jubilant shouters; WHITE ONLY; COLORED ENTRANCE; KEEP THE RACE PURE; WHITE WATER—COLORED WATER; and others)*

GIRL: The Civil War came too late to free my great-grandmother—but I was born under the blanket of freedom. But after the War, in Reconstruction times, life wasn't easy. Most of us didn't know how to read and write then. We had no schools, no work, no homes. They told us on the plantations either to work for nothing, or to get on away. Old Master, old Mistress said, "You don't belong to us no more. You're free now. We don't have to feed you. Get on away! Them Yankees made your bed hard, so let them take care of you!" . . . . . Reconstruction? It didn't happen. Nobody took care of us. But we're still here.

OH, FREEDOM! OH, FREEDOM!
OH, FREEDOM OVER ME!
AND BEFORE I'D BE A SLAVE
I'D BE BURIED IN MY GRAVE
AND GO HOME TO MY LORD AND BE FREE.

SINGERS: NO MORE MOANING, NO MORE MOANING,
NO MORE MOANING OVER ME!
AND BEFORE I'D BE A SLAVE
I'D BE BURIED IN MY GRAVE
AND GO HOME TO MY LORD AND BE FREE. . . . etc . . .
> *(At the back of the auditorium, there enters a KLANSMAN in white hood and robe. His name is JIM CROW. He carries a whip. He shouts)*

KLANSMAN: Who's talking about freedom? I say, who? What's going on here? What's this meeting all about? You-all know you ain't got no right to have no meeting talking about no equal rights—because you ain't gonna get 'em.

(The KLANSMAN strides up the aisle toward the platform. At that moment, the BOY faces him as he approaches the platform)
I say you Negras. . . . .

BOY: What do you say?

KLANSMAN: I say you ain't. . . . .

BOY: We ain't what?

KLANSMAN: You ain't gonna get no equal rights.

BOY: Says you!

KLANSMAN: Yes, me!

GIRL: Says you! And who are you?

KLANSMAN: My name is James R. Crow—but you can call me Mr. Jim. Now, take a taste of this! Freedom! Huh! You'll be dead before you're free—if I have my way—dead!

> *(KLANSMAN mounts the platform and begins slashing at the BOY, then the GIRL, and the SINGERS with his whip. HE drives the BOY and GIRL off stage. THEY exit, defeated but defiant. The SINGERS draw back, some cover their faces. The KLANS-MAN swaggers center stage and laughs. But suddenly a WOMAN emerges singing so loudly she startles JIM CROW out of his wits)*

WOMAN: GO DOWN, MOSES
WAY DOWN IN EGYPT'S LAND,
I SAID GO DOWN NOW, MOSES,
WAY DOWN IN EGYPT'S LAND,
GO DOWN, MOSES,
AND LET MY PEOPLE GO.
I SAID, LET MY PEOPLE GO!
I MEAN, LET MY PEOPLE GO!
I DON'T MEAN MAYBE—
LET MY PEOPLE GO!
OH, MOSES, YOU HEAR MY BEGGING—
PHARAOH, LET MY PEOPLE GO!
YOU HEAR ME PLEADING,
PHARAOH, LET MY PEOPLE GO!
I DONE BEEN PRAYING,
PHARAOH, LET MY PEOPLE GO!
IF YOU DON'T LET 'EM,
LISTEN, PHARAOH, I SAY
NO MORE MOANING.
NO MORE BEGGING, PHARAOH.

NO MORE PLEADING, PHARAOH
I'M TIRED OF THE WAY YOU BEEN TREATING ME.
I'M TIRED OF THIS STUFF, PHARAOH!
I'M TELLING YOU NOW
THAT YOU BETTER LET MY PEOPLE GO!
YES, LORD, GO!

OLD MAN: Help came to the newly freed men of the South. The Quakers sent teachers. The Home Mission Board founded colleges like Fisk. The Fisk Jubilee Singers carried the spirituals around the world and sent back to Fisk the money they earned to help us get an education. Hampton, Tuskegee, Talladega, Tougaloo came into being. Yes!

OLD WOMAN: Thank God for the help that came our way. But it warn't enough. And they kept on being so prejudiced.

OLD MAN: Why didn't somebody say to old Jim Crow, then, get out! Get along! Get going! Look at him coming yonder, still lord of the land.

> (*Faintly the music of* DIXIE *is heard—hummed by the* SINGERS *—as* JIM CROW *enters in the guise of a* SOUTHERN PLANTER *with wide-brimmed hat, flowing tie, white moustache. He leers at the* WOMAN *as he pushes the* BOY *away*)

PLANTER: Jezebel, old gal, you look right good when you got your cotton picking done and get all cleaned up. But what you hanging around with young no-account Mose there for? Ignore that upstart black buck, Jezebel, and come along with me. I'll give you a nice bed, board, and a few pennies. You won't have to sleep on your pallet on the floor no more.

GIRL: I prefers my pallet, sir.

BOY: You heard what she said!

PLANTER: You there, boy! You better stop talking so big, if you know what's good for you. You ain't Booker T. Washington. And I'll be damned if I'm going to invite you to eat with me in the White House like Teddy Roosevelt—that traitor to his race—did. You ain't never gonna eat with me, on matter how educated you get to be. And you'd best get that equality stuff out of your head and just learn to stay, you and your children, in your place.

OLD MAN: Do you know your Scripture, sir?

PLANTER: My scriptures?

OLD MAN: If you do, maybe you remember wherein the Bible says:

EZEKIEL SAW THE WHEEL
WAY UP IN THE MIDDLE OF THE AIR.
EZEKIEL SAW THE WHEEL
WAY IN THE MIDDLE OF THE AIR.
SINGERS: THE LITTLE WHEEL RUN BY FAITH
AND THE BIG WHEEL RUN BY THE GRACE OF GOD—
A WHEEL IN A WHEEL
WAY IN THE MIDDLE OF THE AIR.

>*(The OLD MAN, OLD WOMAN, and SINGERS begin to make their hands go flop around each other like wheels. JIM CROW looks from one to another, flabbergasted)*

ONE OF THESE DAYS ABOUT TWELVE O'CLOCK—
WAY IN THE MIDDLE OF THE AIR!
THIS OLD WORLD GWINE TO REEL AND ROCK.
WAY IN THE MIDDLE OF THE AIR.

>*(ALL repeat refrain. The OLD MAN bounces in rhythm toward JIM CROW, his hands revolving about each other. The OLD WOMAN does likewise. JIM CROW thinks they have gone mad, and backs away to exit frightened)*

JIM CROW: You Negras done gone crazy! You must have gone crazy!

>*(As JIM CROW exits, the song rises lustily)*

SINGERS: WHEEL IN A WHEEL
WAY IN THE MIDDLE OF THE AIR!
EZEKIEL SAW THE WHEEL
WAY UP IN THE MIDDLE OF THE AIR! . . . . etc . . .

>*(ALL laugh at JIM CROW's ridiculousness)*

OLD WOMAN: Seems like sometimes white folks don't have no sense of humor a-tall. But to tell the truth, things warn't funny in our youthhood. No, not a bit.

OLD MAN: Not a bit! A black man couldn't hardly work no place. Nothing but the hardest of hard labor. Unions wouldn't let us in if he knowed a trade. And schools wouldn't let us in to learn one.

OLD WOMAN: Just a vicious circle, that's what it were.

OLD MAN: That's what it were. Seems like sometimes we had to fight the Civil War all over again. But I had to stay in the field.

OLD WOMAN: Yes, we did, children. And you-all have got to do the same today.

OLD MAN: We stayed in the field. But it were terrible in them Reconstruction times.

OLD WOMAN: Poor and hungry!

OLD MAN: We was so poor we would cut a hard-boiled egg in two—eat half of it for lunch and the other half for dinner.

OLD WOMAN: I got so thin I had to stand up twice to cast a shadow.

OLD MAN: Oh, but them was hard times! But we kept wagging at the hill. And us ragged Negroes kept having meetings and conventions and things to try to better our condition. We talked up a breeze! But some members talked so much and did so little until I had to get up in meeting one night and speak my mind. I said, listen! I hear you-all bearing me up when I speak. But some of you-all don't mean what you says. I know it and you know it. Just Sunday soldiers, fair-weather shouters. Now, I ain't gonna point no finger, and I ain't gonna call no names, but—

Sister Sunday, don't forget on Monday,
You got to keep the spirit *all* week long.
If you give your Sunday dollar,
Then the next day you holler,
How you gonna sing a Freedom song?
Great hand-clapper, never do working,
You can't build freedom's kingdom
Whilst you're shirking.
You there, Brother Sunday, don't let it slip on Monday—
Keep your hand on the plow all week long—
Else, how do you look singing a freedom song?
When a famous speaker comes from out of town,
I see you settin' in the very first row,
But when your own committee meets
To get some hard work done,
Sister, you ain't got time to go.
Brother, at a fund raising dance,
Dress your best, you bet—
Come to the dance and dance on every set.
But when it's just committee meeting
And your advice is required,
You can't make it that night—because you're too tired.
Looks like you'd know the way is hard and long.
It takes more than singing to make a freedom song.
I'm talking to you-all
What's got your health and strength,

Look at me, ageable, all broke and bent—just look—old,
   sick, bended—
But I say my eyes is turned to the freedom gate—
Until this war is ended! And I'm gonna—
SINGERS: STAY IN THE FIELD, STAY IN THE FIELD
   OH, WARRIOR, STAY IN THE FIELD
   TILL THE WAR IS ENDED.
   MINE EYES ARE TURNED TO THE FREEDOM GATE
   UNTIL THE WAR IS ENDED.
   I'LL KEEP ON MY WAY OR I'LL BE TOO LATE,
   UNTIL THE WAR IS ENDED.
   THE TALLEST TREE IN PARADISE
   UNTIL THE WAR IS ENDED
   THE CHRISTIANS CALL THE TREE OF LIFE,
   UNTIL THE WAR IS ENDED.
   GREEN TREES BURNING! WHY NOT THE DRY?
   UNTIL THE WAR IS ENDED.
   MY SAVIOR DIED! WHY NOT I?
   UNTIL THE WAR IS ENDED.
   OH, STAY IN THE FIELD, STAY IN THE FIELD,
   OH, WARRIOR, STAY IN THE FIELD
   UNTIL THE WAR IS ENDED.
      (As SINGERS hum the refrain, the OLD FOLK speak)
OLD MAN: Stay in the field! Stay! Yet sometimes when you's all stove-
   up with rheumatiz—
OLD WOMAN: And feeling kinder broke down—
OLD MAN: Cataracts, eyes going back on you—sometimes maybe we
   can't all (lemme tell the truth now)—maybe we can't all march in
   the field like we want to.
OLD WOMAN: But we can back up the young folks with our songs and
   prayers—
OLD MAN: And nickels and dimes and quarters.
OLD WOMAN: Also with the faith we built on God's rock—and we're
   still building on it now. You know, God didn't mean for this world
   to be all unequaled-up like it is.
OLD MAN: No, He didn't! That I know.
SINGERS: Sure didn't! He didn't!
OLD MAN: Just look at the world—all chopped up into boundaries and
   binderies and things, into cold wars and hot wars, great powers and

no powers, into summits and valleys, black lands and white lands—
no! It ought to all be all one land—Freedom Land! Ain't that right,
son?

> *(BOY stands alone at center to sing)*

BOY: FREEDOM LAND, OH FREEDOM LAND,
I WONDER ON WHICH MAP YOU CAN BE FOUND?
I'M YOUNG! I'M GONNA LOOK AROUND
AND FIND YOU, FREEDOM LAND!
FREEDOM LAND, MY FREEDOM LAND,
UPON YOUR SOIL I WANT TO STAND AND SHOUT
YOUR NAME, GREAT FREEDOM ALL ABOUT.
WE'RE BUILDING FREEDOM LAND.
THE SKY IS HIGH—THE EARTH IS GREAT—
I KNOW THE SEEDS OF FREEDOM WAIT.
THEY'LL BURST IN BLOOM BENEATH THE SUN
WHERE FREEDOM LIVES FOR EVERYONE.
FREEDOM LAND, OUR FREEDOM LAND!
WE'LL SING YOUR NAME—WE ARE TOMORROW'S BAND—
AND FRIENDS WILL CLASP EACH OTHER'S HAND
IN FREEDOM, FREEDOM LAND!

OLD WOMAN: Oh, my friends, when we try to straighten out this
world and make it Freedom Land, we are just carrying out God's
will, that's all.

OLD MAN: Yes, we are! And our text is freedom!

> *(JIM CROW enters in the guise of a MINISTER)*

MINISTER: So your text is freedom? Well, I got another one. You all
in my congregation know Rev. Jim Crow don't take no stock in
the way black folks sing them old songs these days—trying to give
'em new meanings and such. Cullud folks better stop singing about
freedom and equality and such, and sing about their immortal soul.
Down in the gutter of sin where they are, they better be thinking
about salvation, not equality. Salvation—that is, if a black man has a
soul to save. In the old days, we did not believe a Negra had a soul.
But maybe he has. Rev. Jim Crow will grant him that much. But he
don't have no sense, a Negra don't. How can he have—expecting
and hoping and wanting to be the equal of a white man? God did not
mean it to be that way. When He made Ham, and Ham's sons, God
made 'em black! Why, look at 'em today in our white America! Look
at 'em! Ignorant, trifling, dumb, diseased, impudent, dangerous!
That's what they are—they're dangerous to you and me and our

way of life and the Free World. Why they even want to vote in Dixie. We got to curb them Negras. I say—

BOY: You ought to be ashamed of yourself—and a minister of the Gospel, too. You a faker, Rev. Jim Crow. I say God's gonna cut you down.

YOU MAY RUN ON FOR A LONG TIME,
RUN ON FOR A LONG TIME,
YOU MAY RUN ON FOR A LONG TIME,
BUT GOD A-MIGHTY'S GONNA CUT YOU DOWN.
GO TELL YOUR LONG-TONGUED LIARS,
GO TELL YOUR MIDNIGHT RIDERS,
TELL YOUR BOMBING RAMBLING DYNAMITERS,
TELL 'EM GOD A-MIGHTY'S GONNA CUT 'EM DOWN.

SINGERS: GREAT GOD A-MIGHTY, LEMME TELL YOU THE NEWS—
MY HEAD BEEN WET WITH THE MIDNIGHT DEWS.
I BEEN DOWN ON MY BENDED KNEE
TALKING TO THE MAN FROM GALILEE.
MY GOD SPOKE, HE SPOKE SO SWEET
I THOUGHT I HEARD THE SHUFFLE OF ANGELS' FEET.
HE PUT ONE HAND ON MY HEAD.
GREAT GOD A-MIGHTY, LEMME TELL YOU WHAT
   HE SAID—
YOU MAY RUN ON FOR A LONG TIME, RUN ON FOR A
   LONG TIME.
BUT GOD A-MIGHTY GONNA CUT YOU DOWN. . . . .
   etc. . . . .

   (REV. JIM CROW flees in fear)

GIRL: Lots of folks have been against us—ministers, politicians, editors, police, mayors, even governors. Our ways been cloudy, sometimes so cloudy it looks like I just don't know. I just don't know what to do.

BOY: When I volunteered in World War II, they wouldn't let me in the Navy. They told me the quota was filled or something. I got put in a labor battalion.

GIRL: And, remember when I tried to give my blood to the Red Cross for the soldiers, they wouldn't accept it—no black blood. But Jim Crow's over now in the armed forces.

   (As the BOY speaks JIM CROW sneaks in)

BOY: Yes, I can be a sailor now, or an airman—even a paratrooper. But I'd hate to be making jumps in Mississippi some day and come parachuting down on Eastland's plantation. Anyhow, things are not quite as rough as they used to be in some ways—and in some parts of our U.S.A. But it's still too rough to be decent, Anniebelle. There's still many a registration place won't register me. Many a ballot box is still closed to my ballot. They know we'd vote segregation out, if we had the chance. That's why that old registrar is standing there in the Court House telling us Negroes:

JIM CROW: YOU-ALL BETTER LEAVE SEGREGATION ALONE.
   WE LOVE SEGREGATION LIKE A HOUND DOG LOVES A
      BONE.
BOY: THEY TOLD ME EDUCATION
   OUR PROBLEMS ALL WILL SOLVE—
   JUST STUDY FOR TWO THOUSAND YEARS
   AND, BOY, HOW YOU'LL EVOLVE!
JIM CROW: MEANWHILE, JUST LEAVE SEGREGATION ALONE.
   WE LOVE SEGREGATION LIKE A HOUND DOG LOVES A
      BONE.
OLD WOMAN: You know, I been hearing them things all my life. Ever since slavery they been telling me:
JIM CROW: WHY DON'T YOU ALL BE PATIENT?
   STOP RAISING SO MUCH FUSS.
   YOU KNOW WE LOVES YOU NEGRAS,
   SO LEAVE EVERYTHING TO US—
   AND JUST YOU LEAVE SEGREGATION ALONE.
   WE LOVE SEGREGATION LIKE A HOUND DOG LOVES A
      BONE.
OLD MAN: GREAT BIG AD, *HELP WANTED*.
   I SAY, I'LL GIVE THAT JOB A TRY.
   BOSS MAN LOOKS AT ME AND YELLS,
   NO COLORED NEED APPLY.
JIM CROW: YOU BETTER LEAVE SEGREGATION ALONE.
   WE LOVE SEGREGATION LIKE A HOUND DOG LOVES A
      BONE.
GIRL: MY CITY OWNS THE SWIMMING POOL.
   WITH WHITE TILE IT IS LINED.
   WHEN I WANT TO TAKE A SWIM, THEY SAID,
   YOU MUST HAVE LOST YOUR MIND.
JIM CROW: YOU BETTER LEAVE OUR WHITE POOL ALONE.
   WE LOVE SEGREGATED WATER LIKE A HOUND DOG
      LOVES A BONE.

BOY: I WENT TO GET A HAIRCUT
  AT THE CAMPUS BARBER SHOP.
  WHITE BARBER SAW ME COMING
  AND HE RAN TO CALL A COP.
JIM CROW: YOU BETTER LEAVE SEGREGATION ALONE.
  WE LOVE SEGREGATION LIKE A HOUND DOG LOVES A
    BONE.
ALL FOUR: WE SAT DOWN IN THE DIME STORE
  TO GET OURSELVES A BITE TO EAT.
  THEY PUT ME IN THE JAIL HOUSE,
  SAID I TOOK A WHITE MAN'S SEAT.
JIM CROW: YOU ALL BETTER LEAVE SEGREGATED HOT
    DOGS ALONE.
  YOU ALL BETTER LEAVE SEGREGATED COFFEE ALONE.
  YOU ALL BETTER LEAVE SEGREGATED SUGAR,
  SEGREGATED SALT, SEGREGATED COKES AND SEGRE-
    GATED MALT ALONE—
  WE LOVE OUR SEGREGATION LIKE A HOUND DOG
    LOVES A BONE.
  LIKE A HOUND (Howl-ooo-oo-o!) DOG LOVES A BONE.
    *(JIM CROW, in the guise of a GOVERNOR puts on horn-rim
    glasses and stands on the steps with his back facing the audience
    as the BOY and GIRL face him carrying textbooks. The GOVER-
    NOR speaks with an exaggerated Southern accent)*
GOVERNOR: You-all are right. Ah do like the customs of ma city and
  county and ma state like a hound dog loves a bone. And ah am
  Governor here—the governor of this sovereign state—and no Negra
  children are going to enter this school. By the power invested in me
  by the voters of this state in the name of law and order and the
  sanctity of white womanhood, ah say the portals of this institution
  are closed to all but whites. And ah shall not be moved.
BOY: But, sir, the Supreme Court ruled that the schools of our country
  be open to all alike.
GOVERNOR: The Supreme Court has ruled contrary to the laws of my
  state. And ah hereby inform you—
GIRL: Sir, I hereby inform you that—
  I WOKE UP THIS MORNING WITH
  MY MIND ON FREEDOM.
BOY: I WOKE UP THIS MORNING WITH
  MY MIND ON FREEDOM.

FOUR: WE WOKE UP THIS MORNING WITH
    OUR MINDS ON FREEDOM.
SINGERS: HALLELOO! HALLELOO! HALLELUJAH! . . . . etc. . . .
    *(As the SINGERS surround the GOVERNOR he retreats, leaving
    the BOY standing in his place addressing a mass of people standing
    before him, the humming of the song continues under BOY's speech)*
BOY: I know I may be a little young to be up here on this box addressing
    many of you older people today, but young or not, somehow I got
    elected leader of this demonstration, and I welcome you here, all
    of you like me with your minds on freedom. Today we are going
    to move through the streets of our city that belongs as much to us
    as it does to anybody else. We are going to move down the main
    streets, too, not just through the old dark ugly alleys and bystreets
    and sidestreets of segregation. No, we are going to walk through the
    main streets—right is on our side, governor or no governor, sheriffs
    or no sheriffs, police dogs or no dogs, Ku Klux Klan or no Klan, we
    are going to march! March! Walk and sing; and now that Civil Rights
    Bill's been passed, we'll keep marching until it works—everywhere.
    March and sing!
SINGERS: WALKING AND TALKING WITH
    MY MIND ON FREEDOM! . . . . .
    HALLELOO! HALLELOO! . . . . etc. . . .
    *(The SINGERS become marching PICKETS carrying signs of
    various sorts: THE SCHOOLS BELONG TO ALL . . . WE ARE
    CITIZENS, TOO . . . YOU TAKE OUR TAXES—GIVE US
    OUR RIGHTS . . . AMERICANS ALL—WHITE OR BLACK
    . . . TAKE THE CROW OUT OF JIM CROW . . . DON'T BUY
    WHERE YOU CAN'T WORK . . . DON'T TRADE WHERE
    YOU CAN'T EAT . . . SEGREGATION IPSO FACTO, DE
    FACTO, AND EVERY OTHER KIND OF FACTO MUST GO)*
ALBANY, GEORGIA'S GOT
ITS MIND ON FREEDOM . . .
MISSISSIPPI'S GOT
ITS MIND ON FREEDOM . . .
WALK-A-WALK! WALK! WALK! WALK!
WALK WITH MY MIND ON FREEDOM. . . .
HALLELOO! HALLELOO! HALLELUJAH!
    *(As the demonstration ends and the SINGERS return to their
    places, ALL exit except the BOY and GIRL. They are seated on
    two stools at an imaginary counter. Soda fountain signs read:*

ICE CREAM SODAS 25¢ . . . BANANA SPLIT 30¢ . . . LIME
RICKEY 10¢ . . . HOT DOG 15¢ . . . etc.)

GIRL: Service, please.

BOY: She doesn't answer.

GIRL: Maybe she didn't hear me.

BOY: Miss! Miss, I'd like a strawberry soda, please.

GIRL: No answer.

BOY: I guess they are not going to serve us. Might as well open my book
and study.

GIRL: Me, too. . . . Except that they won't let us study—all these angry looking folks around us. "Get away from here! Get off that
chair," they're yelling. "You, boy, get away from that counter." They
push us.

BOY: Shove us!

GIRL: Knock our books out of our hands. They scream, "Get out of
here! And you, too, girl!" But we just sit there and sing.
WE SHALL OVERCOME. . . . .

BOY: WE SHALL OVERCOME. . . . .

(The SINGERS carry on the song as the BOY and GIRL tell of the
attack on them at the counter and act it out in pantomime)

SINGERS: WE SHALL OVERCOME, WE SHALL OVERCOME. . . . .
DEEP IN OUR HEARTS WE DO BELIEVE
WE SHALL OVERCOME SOME DAY.
TRUTH WILL MAKE US FREE,
TRUTH WILL MAKE US FREE,
THE TRUTH WILL MAKE US FREE SOME DAY.
DEEP IN MY HEART I DO BELIEVE
WE SHALL OVERCOME SOME DAY.
WE'LL WALK HAND IN HAND,
WE'LL WALK HAND IN HAND,
WE'LL WALK HAND IN HAND EACH DAY.
DEEP IN MY HEART I DO BELIEVE,
WE SHALL OVERCOME SOME DAY.

BOY: They yell, "Oh, so you won't be moved, heh?" And they jerk the
stool out from under me.

GIRL: They spit in my face.

BOY: They knock me down. They kick me.

(The BOY falls sprawling to the floor, books flying)

GIRL: They call me all kinds of dirty names, but we still try to sing.
DEEP IN MY HEART I REALLY DO BE. . . . .

Somebody threw a sugar bowl at me! . . . A woman pushed me! . . .
And then . . .
(JIM CROW enters in a POLICEMAN's uniform, club uplifted)
POLICEMAN: Get up from there!
(He jerks the GIRL off the stool and flings her around in front of him and pushes her)
Get out of here! You know this is a white place. Get out!
(As police sirens wail and the GIRL continues to sing, the PO-LICEMAN grabs the BOY's foot, snatches the GIRL by the arm, and drags them BOTH off to jail as the song rises. The stools on which they have been sitting, they raise upside down before their faces to simulate jail bars)
SINGERS: DEEP IN MY HEART I DO BELIEVE
WE SHALL OVERCOME SOME DAY. . . . .
(Spotlights now reveal the BOY and the GIRL behind bars)
BOY: So I'm in jail.
GIRL: So we're in jail.
BOY: Wonder what Ma'll say?
GIRL: Wonder what Dad'll say?
(The voices of the OLD WOMAN and the OLD MAN are heard, then they appear dimly apart from the cells)
OLD MAN: We'll say, God bless you!
OLD WOMAN: God love you, son. God help you.
OLD MAN: And we'll help you. What I never did, you've done.
OLD WOMAN: God bless you!
OLD MAN: And love you!
BOTH: And we'll help you.
OLD WOMAN: And I'll bring you the sweet potato pie to whatever jail you're in.
OLD MAN: We're together, son.
OLD WOMAN: Together.
BOY: Together, Mama—
GIRL: Together, Papa—
ALL: Together, we shall overcome. . . . .
(As the OLD MAN and OLD WOMAN disappear, SINGERS are heard softly humming until the end of scene)
SINGERS: DEEP IN MY HEART I DO BELIEVE
WE SHALL OVERCOME SOME DAY. . . . .
BOY: Nothing else to do, I believe I'll write a letter to Jim Crow.
GIRL: I believe I'll write a letter to Freedom.

(Each in a cell at opposite sides of the stage, THEY begin to dictate to each other as the melody of WE SHALL OVERCOME continues behind their words)

BOY: Please take my letter down, Anniebelle. . . . .

Dear Jim Crow, sir: I address you most respectfully because I do not want to get your temperature up any higher than it is now, also because I want you to understand that I can see your point of view. Raised wrong from the cradle, sir, you cannot see things straight. Taught a distorted view of history in your schools, you do not even know what made you what you are. Because you are ignorant, Jim Crow, I forgive you. I will try to teach you right from wrong myself, Jim, because I know in the end you will become my brother, and we'll walk hand in hand some day. Yes, deep in my heart I do believe, we'll walk hand in hand some day. Signed: *Moses Holmes Jones.*

(The melody of WE SHALL OVERCOME rises as the GIRL dictates her letter)

GIRL: Take this down, Jones. . . . .

Dear Freedom: I address you as if I have known you all my life. I have not. I have only known about you. But I know that you are waiting to take my hand as soon as I can get by the barriers some of my fellowmen have put between us. I mean to get by them, Freedom. I mean to open the gate that leads to your presence. I mean to let in the sunshine and the radiance of your beauty—because I know, Freedom, that you are my sister, and we'll walk hand in hand some day. Yes, deep in my heart I do believe, we'll walk hand in hand some day. Signed: *Anniebelle Smith.*

BOY: I know you don't believe us now, Jim, but you'll understand it better by and by. Now, you are not free yourself, chained in your hate and misunderstanding. But freedom is a mighty word, and you can't help but pay attention to its name.

GIRL: Freedom! So many great people I studied in my classroom have defined you—Freedom—Moses told us what freedom meant, and Christ, and Jefferson, and Lincoln, and Franklin Delano Roosevelt, and Martin Luther King, and the late President Kennedy. So I don't have to define freedom again. I'll just sing my song of what it means to me.

BOY: Just sing our song. And when we get out of here and go back to the people . . .

GIRL: When we get outside again. . . . . .

BOY: Out of this jail. . . .

GIRL: This cell here. . . .

BOY: We'll take up our songs again. . . .

GIRL: And sing them with you.

BOY: FREEDOM LAND, OH, FREEDOM LAND!

GIRL: I WONDER ON WHICH MAP YOU CAN BE FOUND?

BOY: I'M YOUNG! I'M GONNA LOOK AROUND.

BOTH: AND FIND YOU FREEDOM LAND!

GIRL: I DREAM A LAND CALLED FREEDOM LAND,
UPON YOUR SOIL I WANT TO STAND AND SHOUT
YOUR NAME, GREAT FREEDOM ALL ABOUT.
WE'LL BUILD OUR FREEDOM LAND.

BOTH: OUR SKY IS HIGH! OUR EARTH IS GREAT!
WE KNOW THE SEEDS OF FREEDOM WAIT
TO BURST IN BLOOM BENEATH THE SUN
WHERE FREEDOM LIVES FOR EVERYONE.

(JIM CROW enters in the form of a JAILOR)

JAILOR: Cut out that singing in here! Shut up, I say!

BOY: Mister, would you mind mailing a letter for me?

GIRL: And for me, too?

JAILOR: I might. Gimme them here!

(He takes the letters, looks at them, and tears them to bits)

Well, now! They ain't got no stamps on 'em. So I'm mailing them—
like this.

(He exits flinging bits of paper about him)

BOY: Funny—he thinks the world won't get our message—but it will,
in spite of what he's doing. He can't hold back history.

GIRL: Jim Crow trying to defend his Jerico. Trying to hold back freedom by putting you and me in jail, tearing up our letters, stopping
us from singing. To him, freedom's just a scrap of paper, in spite of
Civil Rights Bills.

BOY: He'll learn how precious it is some day.

GIRL: Even to him—and to America. America!

BOY: But there are still so many walls to break down, Anniebelle.

GIRL: But you are Joshua, aren't you?

(The BOY laughs)

BOY: Well, if you say that I am Joshua! I am! If you believe I am Joshua,
I'll be! Fact is, I *am* Joshua! Come on, kid, let's go fight this battle
modern style!

(THEY sing)

BOY: WE'LL FIGHT THE BATTLE OF OLD JIM CROW.

BOTH: OLD JIM CROW! OLD JIM CROW!

GIRL: WE'LL FIGHT THE BATTLE OF OLD JIM CROW—

BOTH: AND THE WALLS COME TUMBLIN' DOWN.

    (As the BOY calls out the names of various leaders in the Freedom Movement, ALL sing)

ALL: WE'LL FIGHT THE BATTLE OF OLD JIM CROW . . . etc . . .

BOY: *Dr. Du Bois* fit the battle of Old Jim Crow.

    Dr. King fit the battle of Old Jim Crow.

    Daisy Bates fit the battle of Old Jim Crow.

SINGERS: AND THE WALLS COME TUMBLING DOWN.

BOY: *James Meredith* fit the battle of Old Jim Crow.

    Jim Peck fit the battle of Old Jim Crow.

    Randolph fit the battle of Old Jim Crow.

SINGERS: AND THE WALLS COME TUMBLING DOWN.

BOY: *John Lewis* fit the battle of Old Jim Crow.

    James Farmer fit the battle of Old Jim Crow.

    Roy Wilkins fit the battle of Old Jim Crow.

    Kennedy fit the battle of Old Jim Crow.

SINGERS: AND THE WALLS COME TUMBLING DOWN.

BOY: The Promised Land's in sight—the America of our dreams! Come with me! Come on! Come!

    (THEY sing as ALL march toward exit)

SINGERS: COME AND GO WITH ME TO THAT LAND,

    COME AND GO WITH ME TO THAT LAND,

    COME WITH ME TO THAT LAND WHERE I'M BOUND,

    THERE'S NO HATRED IN THAT LAND . . . etc . . .

    I'M ON MY WAY AND I WON'T TURN BACK . . .

    GONNA ASK MY CAPTAIN, WON'T YOU LET ME GO . . . etc . . .

    IF HE SAYS NO, GONNA GO ANYHOW . . . etc . . .

    I'M ON MY WAY, THANK GOD, I'M ON MY WAY.

BLACKOUT

THE END

Tambourines to Glory
A Comedy

1963
Music by Jobe Huntley

Hughes wrote his first draft of *Tambourines to Glory* in 1956 in only ten days and then asked Harlem composer and singer Jobe Huntley to compose the music. About the play he enthused to Arna Bontemps: "It's a singing, shouting, wailing drama of the old conflict between blatant Evil and quiet Good, with the Devil driving a Cadillac." Almost immediately he turned it into a well-received novel by the same name, and nearly a decade later called it "my favorite since first I conceived it. . . . an entertaining slice of dramatic Negro life in Harlem that makes for great theater."[1] Despite some positive reviews of the 1960 Westport, Connecticut, tryout sponsored by the Theatre Guild, the play was roundly criticized, especially for its portrait of the black church. Its Broadway run, November 2–23, 1963, received cool reviews and more criticism.

Tambourines to Glory is a gospel-musical and, as such, represents Hughes's desire to preempt the kind of appropriation of black cultural expression of which he complained in his 1940 poem "Note on Commercial Theatre": "They've taken my blues and gone." By the midfifties, gospel music had become "a spectacle on the music scene"; on Broadway, the musical reigned. "An urban-folk-Harlem-*genre*-melodrama," Hughes called his play focused on black storefront churches.[2] *Tambourines to Glory* is simultaneously comical, satirical, and critical of certain religious practices, yet it affirms the power of black religious musical expression and the faith it supports. White critics were, at best, puzzled; black critics deplored the play's negative portrait of black churches, saw stereotype where Hughes saw "simplicity," and decried its avoidance of the struggle outside the theater doors, especially striking in the year that saw dogs and hoses used to rout black protesters and four little black girls killed in a church bombing, both in Birmingham, Alabama, as well as the murder of Medgar Evers in Mississippi.

Yet others blamed the production: Hughes's secretary George Bass reflected that director Nikos Psacharopolulos did not understand the play; Loften Mitchell told Arnold Rampersad that the critique of the black storefront churches was justified, and the play's engagement with religion "far from superficial" but of little interest to white patrons. Whatever its merits, the play was out of step with the demands of the historical moment, yet it also birthed what many consider Hughes's finest theatrical contribution: the gospel play.

By the 1960 Westport tryout, Hughes complained that he had rewritten *Tambourines to Glory* ten times, and given the state of the various drafts in the Langston Hughes Papers, many more would follow. There is no coherent text reflecting the 1963 production. This text is taken from *Five Plays by Langston Hughes,* edited by Webster Smalley. In a letter to Smalley, Hughes indicated the script supplied to him was that of the revised Theatre Guild production—that is, a version that incorporates revisions made following the 1960 Westport tryout, but something short of the Broadway text.[3]

Author's Note

Tambourines to Glory is, in play form, a dramatization of a very old problem—that of good versus evil, God slightly plagued by the Devil, but with God—as He always intends—winning in the end.

Tambourines to Glory is a fable, a folk ballad in stage form, told in broad and very simple terms—if you will, a comic strip, a cartoon—about problems which can only convincingly be reduced to a comic strip if presented very cleanly, clearly, sharply, precisely, and with humor.

Tambourines to Glory is, on the surface, a simple play about very simple people. Therefore, all of its performers should be sensitive enough to appreciate the complexities of simplicity. All of them should be lovable, except BUDDY—whom one should love, too, in spite of one's better self.

The role of LAURA should be performed by a compelling personality, one not merely pretty, but capable of projecting sunlight, laughter, easygoing summer, and careless love. In contrast, the role of ESSIE is that of the good old earth, solid, *always* there come sun or rain, laughter or tears, the eternal mother image.

Much of the meaning of *Tambourines to Glory* lies in its songs, so both LAURA and ESSIE should be actresses who can sing. As if it were a rhythmic ballad, the overall conception of *Tambourines* must have rhythm—as "John Henry," "Casey Jones," "Stackolee," "Lord Randall," and "Mack the Knife" have rhythm. This the staging must achieve. When the curtain falls, the final effect must be that of having heard a song—a melodic, likable, dramatic song.

At certain points in the show audience participation might be encouraged—singing, foot-patting, hand-clapping, and in the program the lyrics of some of the songs might be printed with an invitation to sing the refrains along with the chorus of Tambourine Temple.

Characters

LAURA WRIGHT REED	*A home relief client*
ESSIE BELLE JOHNSON	*An evicted tenant*
MARIETTA JOHNSON	*Essie's daughter*
BIG-EYED BUDDY LOMAX	*A handsome hustler*
GLORIA DAWN	*A glamour girl*
C.J. MOORE	*A young saint*
BIRDIE LEE	*A lady drummer*
CHICKEN-CROW-FOR-DAY	*A sinner saved*
MATTIE MORNINGSIDE	*Mistress of the robes*
LUCY MAE HOBBS	*Head deaconess*
BROTHER BUD	*A poor old man*
CHARLIE WINDUS	*Laura's chauffeur*
JOE GREEN	*A chump*
MINISTERS OF MUSIC	*Temple pianist*
	Temple organist

DEACONS
BARTENDER
WAITER
PRISON WARDEN
POLICEMEN
THE GLORIETTAS
TAMBOURINE CHOIR
CABARET PATRONS
PASSERS-BY

Scenes

Prologue: Shadows of a street
Act I
Scene 1: Sidewalk before tenement
Scene 2: A street corner

Prologue

As lights dim half-way the leading man enters, spotlighted, and smiles before a scrim of Harlem.

BUDDY: You think I'm who you see, don't you? Well, I'm not. I'm the Devil. . . . In this play, according to the program, you might think I'm Big-Eyed Buddy Lomax—if I didn't tell you in front, no, I'm not. Big-Eyed Buddy is just *one* of my million and one names. I've got plenty of names, had plenty—some pretty big ones—Hitler, for example. *Yes, Hitler was me!* Mack-the-Knife, Gyp-the-Blood, Don Juan among the covers. Oh, yes! Henry the Eighth. Katherine the Great—I put on drag sometimes. Iago. Brutus—*et tu, Brute*—right on back to Cain. Little names, big names—I'm liable to have *your name* . . . The Devil comes in various guises—and disguises. I'm disguised now. I am not the *me* you see here—tall, handsome, brownskin. I am not always dark—sometimes I'm white. Sometimes yellow, sometimes Khrushchev. I speak all tongues—*tovarish, mon cher, kamerad, baby, daddy-o, amada, dulcissima*—all languages are mine. *Mais, oui! Si, señor!* In Harlem I'm cool, in Spain I'm hot. In Katanga I'm Tshombe. Sure, I have my troubles, get shot up once in a while, ambushed, assassinated. But, quiet as it's kept, I love being the Devil because I raise so much hell! Watch me this evening. I'll find work for idle hands—stage hands—to do. Unemployed actors, too. The Theatre Guild put me up to this. On with the show . . . Laura, are you in the wings?

LAURA: *(Answering offstage)* I'm here, Buddy.

BUDDY: Essie, you old character actress, are you setting where you ought to be, in place?

ESSIE: I'm setting.

BUDDY: Choir Director, you've got your pitch pipe?

CHOIR DIRECTOR: I got my pitch pipe.

BUDDY: Choir, are you ready to sing?

CHOIR: We're ready to sing!

BUDDY: Then, ladies and gentlemen—good folks and devils—the play will begin. On this stage you'll see sin and salvation, me and God, Beelzebub and Jehovah wrestling one more time. The old struggle between sanctity and Satan, the Christians and the damned! The damned, that's me. I never win—but I have a hell of a good time trying. And I'm generous. I'll even let the good church folks have a head start. Let's go! Come on! Sing, you Christians, sing!

>   *(Lights come up behind scrim to reveal the massed choir in a burst of song as they advance)*

CHOIR: If you've got a tambourine,
>   Shake it to the Glory of God.
>   Glory! Glory! Glory!
>   Shake it to the Glory of God! . . . (etc.)

>   *(As the song ends and CHOIR exits, Act I begins)*

Act I, Scene 1

A Harlem street on a night in spring. ESSIE has been evicted from her tenement room and her few belongings are piled on the curb. She is sitting on one of her suitcases as PASSERS-BY turn around to look at her plight. A TEENAGER stops.

YOUTH: Lady, what happened to you?

ESSIE: Evicted, that's all.

YOUTH: Damn! Ain't that enough?

ESSIE: No need to use profanity, son.

YOUTH: Excuse me, ma'am. *(As he exits he turns)* But I still say, damn!

WOMAN: *(Stops and speaks kindly)* Poor soul! Even though it is May, it's not warm yet. I hope you don't have to sit out here all night.

ESSIE: I reckon God'll provide for me. My credit's run out.

WOMAN: Don't you have any relatives?

ESSIE: Not a soul in New York.

WOMAN: Not even a husband?

ESSIE: When I had one he warn't much good.

WOMAN: You can say that again! Neither was mine.

> *(She exits. Suddenly ESSIE's face brightens as LAURA and JOE, a middle-aged man, enter slightly tipsy, with a wine bottle in a paper bag)*

ESSIE: Laura!

LAURA: What in God's name has happened to you?

ESSIE: Landlord finally put me out. But I warn't but three months behind on my rent.

LAURA: I'll move you back in.

ESSIE: You can't. The marshals put a padlock on my door.

LAURA: Bastards!

ESSIE: Laura!

LAURA: That's what they are. Joe Green, start lugging her things upstairs. Essie's my favorite neighbor. Treats me like a mother.

JOE: I didn't walk you all the way from Lenox Avenue to become a moving man, baby.

LAURA: Then be on your way, daddy! Thank you for the drinks you bought. Skeedaddle!

JOE: What? I thought we was gonna finish that bottle upstairs.

LAURA: You heard me! Beat it! And don't come back till pay day.

JOE: So that's the way you feel?

LAURA: That's the way I feel, chump. If you don't believe it—Essie, lend me that old knife you always keep in your pocket. *(LAURA reaches in ESSIE's coat pocket herself and comes out with a pearl-handled switchblade)*

JOE: *(Steps back)* Woman, I ain't for no playing.

LAURA: Neither am I! Goodnight.

JOE: Don't look for another drink on me soon. *(He exits)*

LAURA: Aw, you'll be back. Cheapskate! Just because he buys me a bottle of wine—

ESSIE: Laura, are you high again?

LAURA: Not high, just a little groovy, that's all. Essie, you can move in with me for the night. But, you know, I got too many boy friends to be having a permanent guest. I told you, you ought to get on Relief—like me. Else get yourself a man.

ESSIE: A man—to beat me all over the head? I'm old. I'm cranky. Besides, I'm disgusted with 'em. Lowdown no good men!

LAURA: *(Takes her bottle from the bag)* Here, take a taste of wine and get your spirits up.

ESSIE: No, thanks! I hate the stuff. Makes me sick at the stomach.

LAURA: You never do nothing but just set, like you're setting now—throwed out of your place, yet setting looking peaceful. Me, I'd be raising hell.

ESSIE: About all I can do, Laura, is ask the Lord to take my hand.

LAURA: Why don't you do that then? Get holy, sanctify yourself—since we're setting out here on the curb discussing ways and means. The Lord is no respecter of persons—if He takes the pimp's hand and makes a bishop out of him. You know Bishop Longjohn right over there on Lenox Avenue? That saint had three whores on the block ten years ago. He's got a better racket now—the gospel! And a rock and roll band in front of the pulpit.

ESSIE: Religion don't have to be a racket, Laura. Do it? Maybe he's converted.

LAURA: All the money he takes in every Sunday would convert me. Say, I got an idea! Why don't you and me start a church?

ESSIE: What denomination?

LAURA: Our *own*—then we won't be beholding to nobody else. You know my grandpa was a jackleg preacher, so I can rock a church as good as anybody.

ESSIE: Did you ever preach?

LAURA: No, but I've got the nerve to try. Let's start a church. Huh?

ESSIE: Where?

LAURA: On the street where the Bishop started his—outdoors—rent free—on the corner.

ESSIE: You mean down here in the gutter where I am.

LAURA: On the curb—*above* the gutter. We'll save them lower down than us.

ESSIE: Who could that be?

LAURA: The ones that do what you can't do—drink without getting sick. Gamble away their rent. Cheat the Welfare Department—more'n I do. Lay with each other without getting disgusted—no matter how many unwanted kids they produce. Blow gauge, support the dope trade. Hustle. Them's the ones we'll set out to convert.

ESSIE: With what?

LAURA: The Lord Jesus—He comes free. Just look up at the Lord above and the squares will think God is staring you dead in the face. Dig? We'll make money's mammy!

ESSIE: It ain't that easy to make money. Lord knows, I tried all last year to get enough money to send for my daughter. Marietta's sixteen and ain't been with me—her mama—not two years hand-running

since she was born. I always wanted that child with me. Never had
her. Laura, I were born to bad luck.

LAURA: Essie, raise your fat disgusted self up off that suitcase you're
setting on and let's go make our fortune saving souls. Remember
that white woman, that Aimee Semple McPherson what put herself
on some wings, opened up a temple, and made a million dollars?
Girl, we'll call ourselves sisters—use my name—the Reed Sisters—
even if we ain't no relation—sisters in God. I preach and you sing.
We'll let the sinners in the gutter come to us. Listen to my spiel.
I can whoop and holler real good. *(She mounts a pile of furniture
imagining herself a preacher)* I'll tell them Lenox Avenue sinners:
You all better come to Jesus! The atom bomb's about to destroy
this world and you ain't ready. Get ready! Get ready!
Lord above, I am lost
I have strayed from the cross
And I cry, Yes, I cry, save me now!

ESSIE: Lord above, hear my plea
And from sin set me free.
Fill my heart with righteousness right now!

BOTH: Lord above, you I seek
And I pray, humble, meek,
That you'll help me on my way.
Lord above, let your light
Be my guide through the night.
Hear, oh, hear me, Lord, as I pray.

LAURA: Step right up, join us, all you hellions of sin! Join our gospel
band and live in grace. *(Descends from pile of furniture)* Essie, broke
as we are, we *better* start a church.

ESSIE: But with what, Laura?

LAURA: Whilst taking my afternoon nap, today, I dreampt about fish.
I'm gonna look *fish* up in my Dream Book. I think it's 782 and that's
a good number. Lend me fifty cents so I can put it in early tomorrow
morning.

ESSIE: Girl, you need to be thinking about praying, not playing. Here,
I ain't got but a quarter.

LAURA: If 782 comes out, I'll put half of what I win down on a Bible.

ESSIE: We'll buy no Bibles with ill-gotten gains.

LAURA: Well, then, they got Bibles in the credit store for $18.50, $2
down. With a Bible you can read God's word—and with God's word
you can save souls. Let's get a Bible on credit.

ESSIE: I'm kinder lacking in credit, honey.

LAURA: Then you tell me, with what are we gonna found our church?

ESSIE: *(Suddenly rises, looking upward)* With faith! And I mean that! Right now, tonight! Laura, I just got a vision. A voice tells me to take you up on this—and try to save *you,* too.

LAURA: What? . . . Essie . . .

(As LAURA stares in amazement, ESSIE, her face flooded with radiance, mounts her pile of furniture and sings)

ESSIE: Upon this rock I build my church.
   The gates of hell shall not prevail.
   Upon this rock I build my church.
   With strength from God I shall not fail.

(ESSIE snatches LAURA's wine bottle and throws it away. LAURA, falling into the spirit of the thing, cries out dramatically)

LAURA: The call has come and I have heard!

BOTH: The Gates of hell shall not prevail!

ESSIE: I shall not doubt His holy word.

BOTH: With strength from God I shall not fail.

(Gradually as they sing, windows open and heads pop out. Two or three PASSERS-BY stop to watch and listen. Then a few more gather on the street)

BOTH: I say, oh yes, I build my church.
   The gates of hell shall not prevail.
   Upon this rock I build my church.
   In God's own grace, I shall not fail.

LAURA: Upon this rock I build my church.
   I shall not walk the devil's way.

ESSIE: Upon this rock I build my church.
   God's blessed hand will guide my way.

(The PASSERS-BY cry approval and join in their song. The street is filled with music)

CROWD: Amen! Hallelujah! Bless God! Yes! Amen! Amen!
   I say, oh, yes! I build my church!
   The gates of hell shall not prevail.
   Upon this rock I build my church!
   In God's own grace, I shall not fail!

(The light fades to pinpoint ESSIE alone upon her pile of furniture ecstatic)

   In God's own grace, I shall not fail!
   In God's own grace, I shall . . . not . . . fail!

BLACKOUT

MUSICAL BRIDGE: *Continuation of CROWD singing "Upon This Rock" into next scene.*

Act I, Scene 2

A Lenox Avenue Corner. Evening in late summer. There is a grocery store, and next to it a cleaners with a sign:

> WE SPECIALIZE IN REMOVING STAINS: GREASE, PAINT, INK, BLOOD, NAIL POLISH. ONE DAY SERVICE.

Auto horns honk and sirens scream. STROLLERS pass. Before the lights come up, we hear the shaking of a tambourine and a guitar playing softly as the song, "Upon This Rock," continues. A young man, C.J., sits on a camp stool with his guitar. On a second stool rests an enormous gilt-edged Bible. Some FOLKS stand talking at one side as ESSIE finishes her prayer which LAURA punctuates with loud Amens as the CROWD hums "Upon This Rock."

CROWD: Upon this rock . . . umm-umm-umm . . . (etc.)

ESSIE: . . . Grant us your grace, Jesus! Fill us with Thy word, Lord, and bless this corner on which we, Your humble servants, stand tonight. Hear us, Lord, I pray Thee! Amen!

LAURA: We got to get an audience, Essie. Ain't nobody paying you no attention. *(She shakes her tambourine violently)* Hallelujah! Bless God! Amen! Hey, you talking over there, come here! I say, come here! I got something to say to you.

YOUTH: Well, if you say so, ma'am—but after all, our conversation was private.

LAURA: Son, mine is for the world. Come here and hear me. *(A TEENAGE BOY blowing a mouth organ dances by)* Hey, you, boy! Stop rocking and rolling and listen to me.

BOY: Aw, lady, hush!

LAURA: *(Points at a LOITERER against a post)* And you, too. *(And at still ANOTHER)* You're a sinner, too! We're all sinners out here on this corner this evening.

ESSIE: Sinners! Sinners! Sinners!

LAURA: Yes, you sinners, I say, *Stop!* Stop in your tracks now and listen to my words. *(As she speaks gradually a CROWD gathers)* Lemme tell you how I got the call. It was one night last spring with Sister Essie here, right on the street, I saw a flash, I heard a roll of thunder, I felt a breeze and I seen a light and a voice exploding out of heaven cried, "Laura Wright Reed," it said, "Take up the Cross and follow Me!" Oh, yes, that voice said, told me to come out on this corner tonight and save you! You young man laughing and about to pass on by. Stop! Stop and listen to my word. "Take up the Cross," it said, "and follow Me. Go out into the highways and byways and save souls. Go to the curbstones and gutters," it said, "rescue the lost. Approach," I was told, "approach the river of sin and pull out the drowning." Oh, I were drowning, brothers and sisters, just like you, until I got saved. I were down there too, in sin's gutter, lower than a snake's belly—now look at me up here on the curbstone of life reaching out to you to come and be saved.

ESSIE: Come and accept His salvation. Come, come!

LAURA: Yes, because time is a candle—and everybody's burning time. Don't let your candle burn down before your soul gets right. Time is your electric light bill. Everybody is burning lights. Pay your bill before your lights is turned off and your soul left in darkness.

ESSIE: Pay your bill! Pay your bill!

LAURA: Sinner, don't let your lights go out before your soul gets right. I'm gonna pay my bill tomorrow, yes! And you pay yours—take care of Con Edison. But let your soul get right tonight . . . Listen to Sister and me, folks, listen. We're the Reed Sisters, friends. Our Church is this corner—our roof is God's sky—there is no doors. No place in our church not open to you, because there is no doors. Everybody's welcome, black, green, grizzly, and gray, because there is no doors. Speak Spanish, speak English, speak Pig-Latin, join with us because there is no doors. So come, be one with Sister Essie and me, one with God, and be saved. Babes and boys, draw nigh! Men and women, come! Approach! Children, stand near! Young and old, everybody, drop a nickel, dime, quarter in this tambourine as we sing:

> Lord above, look you down
> On this poor soul who's found
> No help, no friends on the way.

Sing, Sister Essie, while I pass this tambourine.

CROWD: Lord above, let your light
Be a guide through the night.
Hear me, hear me, Lord, as I pray.

LAURA: Everybody! Sing with us as you put your contributions in our tambourine. Better than in some juke box for the devil to get.

CROWD: Lord above, I was lost

I have strayed from the cross.

And I cry, yes, I cry, save me now.

Lord above, hear my plea.

And from sin set me free.

Fill my heart with righteousness right now.

> (*As CROWD hums a verse, LAURA shakes her tambourine before a MAN who does not seem inclined to put his hand in his pocket*)

LAURA: Brother you can't get saved for nothing.

> (*Embarrassed, the MAN drops a coin in as the CROWD continues singing*)

ESSIE: The Lord thanks you.

LAURA: And I do, too. Everybody help me stay on the right road. Put your money here. Help in the Lord's work. (*Almost EVERYONE in the Crowd contributes as LAURA moves among them*) That's right, Sister! . . . Thank you, folks! . . . Thanks, honey! . . . Thank you, sir! Good child, good, give your pennies for Jesus! "Suffer little children to come unto me."

ESSIE: Amen! Amen!

> (*C.J. leads the CROWD in a verse of the song sung softly as LAURA speaks*)

LAURA: Hear that beautiful guitar, folks, to warm our hearts this evening! The Lord sent C.J. to us! Last week this young man stepped right out of the crowd on this corner and began playing the gospels, making up his own songs, not rocking and rolling in sin!

ESSIE: Amen! Thank God! Folks, lemme tell you—

Upon this rock I build my church.

CROWD: The gates of hell shall not prevail.

Upon this rock I build my church.

With strength of God, I shall not fail . . .

> (*Singing continues softly under dialogue as a POLICEMAN saunters up to LAURA swinging his billy*)

COP: Say, listen, you women . . .

LAURA: I'll see you later, Mister Law. Let us sing God's songs. (*Aside, LAURA whispers*) Don't worry, man, just be cool. Be cool.

> (*The COP stands aside until the verse ends. ESSIE and the CROWD continue to hum chorus after chorus as LAURA comes over to the POLICEMAN away from the CROWD*)

COP: How about it?

LAURA: As long as you let us get ours, baby, you'll get yours. (*LAURA slips a greenback to the COP*)

COP: You gals really ought to get a license to sing on the street every night.

LAURA: We're getting money. Don't that do you?

COP: That does me. But the big brass downtown—

LAURA: Aw, they can be had, too, can't they?

COP: Not for ten bucks. So, divvy.

> *(The COP puts out his hand again but from the edge of the CROWD a solidly built, good-looking YOUNG MAN appears casually at his side)*

BUDDY: Say, Copper, let's take this thing step by step. The big brass—

COP: *(Growling at the intruder)* What? Who in the hell are you?

BUDDY: *(Jerks his head toward the next corner, as if someone of importance is standing there. He lowers his voice)* I work for Marty. *(Immediately the COP calms down)*

COP: Oh, I see. Well, let's keep this thing friendly—between the three of us. Go ahead with your singing, Sister.

CROWD: Upon this rock I build my church.

I shall not walk the devil's way.

Upon this rock I build my church.

His blessed hand will guide my way.

> *(The POLICEMAN walks away to exit. LAURA looks at the strange young man in astonishment)*

LAURA: Won't you come and join our meeting?

BUDDY: Don't worry about me. I'll be around when the fun is done.

LAURA: I beg your pardon?

BUDDY: I mean when the services are over. You go ahead back to your chores.

LAURA: Excuse me, then—for the moment. *(LAURA returns to the CROWD as BUDDY backs away into the shadows)* Ah, folks, miracles do happen! It's God's doing, so help me stay in His footsteps. When I pass this tambourine again, put a dime, a quarter, a dollar in.

> *(A wrinkled little OLD WOMAN in the crowd speaks up)*

BIRDIE: I done put a dollar in once tonight. Now, I wants to testify.

ESSIE: Speak, Sister, speak!

BIRDIE: I done put a dollar in once tonight. Now, I wants to testify. Backslid, backslid, backslid! Well, tonight I'm coming home—for which, Sister Essie I thank you! Sister Laura, I thank you, too! And this evening I'll tell the world, I makes my determination to stay on God's side from here on in—I mean to the Kingdom. *I've got a hold of God, and I'm gonna hold my holt.* Sister Laura, lend me your tambourine. Lemme shake it a mite to His glory—because I'm a sinner determined to be a saint. I'm gonna join up with you all in your holy work—now—and sing and shout out here on God's corner till winter comes, and nobody's gonna stop me, because I intends to be in that number when the saints go marching in. *(She lifts her tambourine and her voice)*

Oh, when the saints go marching in!
When the saints go marching in.
I want to be in that number
When the saints go marching in . . . (etc.)

> *(BIRDIE LEE and ESSIE shake their tambourines to LAURA's exasperation and jealousy. As a wave of song sweeps over the CROWD, she withdraws frowning from the circle and finds herself standing beside the handsome, brownskin, solidly built YOUNG MAN. CROWD hums "Saints" as they talk)*

BUDDY: Don't worry about that little old dried-up singing lady, baby.

LAURA: What?

BUDDY: She can't steal your thunder. You're still the *most* on this corner. You send me, Sister.

LAURA: And who might you be?

BUDDY: Buddy—Buddy Lomax—Big-Eyed Buddy. *(The music rises again to drown the conversation between LAURA and BUDDY but it is obvious he is making a play for her, and she is enjoying it)*

LAURA: Big-Eyed Buddy, I thank you for your favor. Have I observed you at services before?

BUDDY: I've observed *you.* How about a little refreshments when you get through tonight?

LAURA: A drink?

BUDDY: You're my kind of woman. I'll be leaning on the mailbox yonder when your work is done.

CROWD: Oh, when the saints go marching in! . . . (etc.)

> *(LAURA prances ecstatically back into the circle, snatches the tambourine from BIRDIE LEE and joins loudly in singing herself, soon bringing the song to a close)*

LAURA: And now, friends, that is all for this evening. Goodnight! God bless everyone.

> *(LAURA looks toward the corner to see if BUDDY is still there. He is coolly smoking a cigarette, his elbow resting on the mailbox. The CROWD begins to break up)*

ESSIE: Laura, you ended mighty short this evening. Are we through?

LAURA: Girl, I got business to attend to. Collection is took. Let's go.

ESSIE: I hates to just run off in a hurry. Sometimes peoples like to talk to me—they think I can help them.

LAURA: Maybe you *can* help them, but why bother tonight? We've helped ourselves.

ESSIE: Laura!

LAURA: Don't look so shocked. You're out here hustling just like I am—in God's name. *(LAURA transfers the greenbacks from the tambourine to her bosom, pours the coins into a bag and calls to the GUITARIST who is putting his instrument in its case)* C.J., help Sister Essie carry her Bible home.

C.J.: I will, Sister Laura. *(C.J. folds the camp stools and picks up Bible)*

LAURA: Essie, you carry the rest of the money home, except for these few bills I might need. Don't let nobody rob you on the way upstairs.

ESSIE: I got the same knife in my pocket I been had for twenty years, so I don't worry about being robbed, Laura. I worry about what we're doing, taking so much of these poor souls' money.

LAURA: As soon as we start doing right by us, you start worrying about doing wrong. Essie, is your wig gone?

ESSIE: Laura, I'm going home and pray.

> *(LAURA shrugs as ESSIE and C.J. exit. LAURA turns. BUDDY is coming halfway to meet her. Together they exit arm in arm as BUDDY gives his devil's cackle. There is a blare of night club music as the light fades)*

BUDDY: Ha! Ha! . . . Ha! . . .

BLACKOUT

MUSICAL BRIDGE: *A jazz piano plays "Scat, Cat!" very loud and lively. Before the curtain JITTERBUG DANCERS cavort, merging as the curtain rises into the next scene.*

Act I, Scene 3

The Roamer Club whose motto on the wall is:
> WHEN YOU ROAM AWAY FROM HOME, ROAMER'S IS THE PLACE TO ROAM.

There is a small bar, a piano, booths, and a cozy atmosphere. It is midnight and a TRIO of GIRLS about the piano are finishing a scat song as BUDDY and LAURA enter and head for a booth.

TRIO: Skee-daddle-dee-dee-dee!

Skee-daddle-dee-dow!
Ha-ha-ha—ha-ha!
Let's scat it now!
Skee-daddle-dee—da-da!
Lee-lee-lee-lee—lee!
Hey-hey-hey-hey—hey-hey!
Aw, scat with me!
GLORIA: Oooo-ooo-oo-o——ya-koo!
Bee-ba-ba-bee—be-be—Boo!
Scat, cat! Scat, cat! Scat!
Skee-daddle-dee-dee-dee!
Lay—lay-lay-lay—lay!
La—la-la—la-la!
Oh, scat today! Today! Today!
      (Applause as GLORIA rushes up to BUDDY effusively)
GLORIA: Buddy! Welcome! Haven't seen you for a week, Kid Big-Eyes.
BUDDY: I been around.
GLORIA: At Sugar Ray's maybe, the Shalimar, but not here.
BUDDY: I can't spend my life with you chicks. Laura, meet Gloria.
GLORIA: Hello, Laura.
LAURA: I'm Laura Reed.
BUDDY: Sister Laura. She can sing, too, believe you me.
LAURA: I'm a gospel singer.
GLORIA: Oh, I just love gospel songs. I grew up in the church.
LAURA: So did we all—but sometimes we stray.
BUDDY: Gloria's a stray—but we'll get her back. Heh, Laura? Come
    on, let's sit down. What are you drinking?
      *(GLORIA joins some of the other GIRLS and FELLOWS as the
      BARMAN comes to serve BUDDY)*
LAURA: Vat 69.
BUDDY: *(Puts one hand on LAURA's across the table)* What chaser?
LAURA: Ginger ale.
BUDDY: Only squares drink ginger ale with scotch, sugar.
LAURA: Oh! I just lately turned to whisky.
BUDDY: Two scotch and sodas, waiter.
BARMAN: Okey dokey, Big Eye.
LAURA: Everybody seems to know your name.
BUDDY: I get around—like I make the scene. Everybody's gonna know
    your name in a little while, too. You've got something on the ball—
    what I'd call personality.

LAURA: Aw, Buddy! *(This time LAURA puts her hand on his)*

BUDDY: You're forty!

LAURA: What? *(For a moment LAURA looks startled)*

BUDDY: You know, forty means fine, O.K., great. And you're great with me.

> *(They kiss. The music starts and among those rising is GLORIA, who addresses BUDDY as she dances by)*

GLORIA: You all are not dancing?

BUDDY: *(Frowns and answers abruptly)* No, but I see you are.

LAURA: Why do you look at Gloria that way?

BUDDY: Oh, I just like to look at a good-looking chick. But you're the most.

LAURA: Guess I'll have to get me a spangled gown to put on, too.

BUDDY: Baby, you'll have everything in due time—spangled gowns, diamonds, ermine coats. We gonna get there.

LAURA: We—?

BUDDY: Sure! I'm gonna help you. Listen. You want to know how to make some money out of this religious jive?

LAURA: I'm making money.

BUDDY: I mean a lot, baby, not peanuts.

LAURA: How?

BUDDY: I guess you know with cold weather coming, you have to get off the street or freeze your knees. Your crowd's getting too big anyhow. You got to get a church.

LAURA: A church?

BUDDY: A store front, or something, to start with.

LAURA: You know how hard it is to rent anything in Harlem.

BUDDY: Marty can fix that.

LAURA: Who's Marty?

BUDDY: Shss-ss-s! Once you got your own place, you can do anything —sell Holy Water from the Jordan, for instance.

LAURA: The Jordan? That's across the ocean, ain't it? How much does imported water cost?

BUDDY: Imported? Turn on the tap, that's all. For little or nothing I can get you a hundred gross of empty bottles with labels on them— HOLY WATER—a green river and some palms, you know, about the size of a dime store Listerine. Just take them to the sink.

LAURA: You mean the water ain't really holy?

BUDDY: It's holy if you bless it, Sister Laura.

LAURA: *(Laughs)* Holy if *I* bless it—ha-ha! Ain't that a gas! How much would I sell it for?

BUDDY: A dollar a bottle. The bottle and the label cost about two cents. The water's free. Figure the profit? See a Cadillac by Christmas? Humm-mm-m! *(BUDDY takes a long look at LAURA)* Baby, you're built—no false brassieres.

LAURA: Thank the Lord, He made me a high-breasted woman.

BUDDY: I'll say He did! A good-looking chick like you should be riding on rubber. You don't have to go to bed early, do you?

LAURA: What I really want is an apartment, Buddy.

BUDDY: I'll call up Marty.

LAURA: Just who *is* Marty?

BUDDY: The fixer—the man behind the men behind the men. He can get you anything.

LAURA: Is he colored?

BUDDY: You know he *can't* be colored.

GLORIA: Ladies and Gentlemen, this number is especially for Big-Eyed Buddy and the lady he is escorting this evening who is, I understand, an old gospel songstress.

> Oh, hand me down, hand me down,
> Hand me down my silver trumpet, Gabriel,
> Hand it down, throw it down,
> Any old way to get it down
> Hand me down my silver trumpet, Lord!
> I haven't been to heaven but I've been told
> Hand me down my silver trumpet, Gabriel,
> That the gates are pearl and the streets are gold.
> Hand me down my silver trumpet, Lord.
> Oh, hand me down, hand me down.
> Hand me down my walking cane, Gabriel,
> Hand it down, throw it down,
> Any old way to get it down
> Hand me down my walking cane, Lord.
>
> *("Walking Cane" refrain repeated by the TRIO as GLORIA does a dancing strut. Applause. Bows. Then the PIANIST begins to play the "New York Blues" for general dancing)*

BUDDY: Baby, are we together?

LAURA: Daddy, we *are* together!

BUDDY: Then let's demonstrate.

(BUDDY rises, pulls LAURA up, and the two dance slowly)
LAURA: You're holding me so tight, you're hurting me.
BUDDY: But it hurts so good, don't it, kid?
LAURA: You're strong! . . . Buddy, something's happening to me.
BUDDY: Something's happening to me, too, baby.
LAURA: Do you think it could be the same thing?
BUDDY: Could be! But you've got to tell me what's on your mind.
LAURA: Couldn't we sit down?
BUDDY: Sure. *(Music dies as they go to their table)* What's happening?
LAURA: Listen, I don't want you to think it's my likker talking, Buddy,
    but—let's get out of here. I want to sing just to you.
        When you hold me in your arms
        All other arms I ever knew I just forget.
BUDDY: Give her a little backing there, piano man, to waft us on our
    way.
        *(The PIANIST picks up the melody as the lights fade, the scrim
        falls, and a spot picks up BUDDY and LAURA in the street)*

Act I, Scene 4

*Shadows of a Harlem Street. Very close to BUDDY, LAURA looks up into
    his eyes as she sings.*
LAURA: I say, when you hold me in your arms,
    All other arms I ever knew, I just forget.
    When I look into your eyes
    Somehow I know, I just know that's it.
    I know yesterday is gone
    And tomorrow is a brand new day
    Put those mean old blues in pawn
    Lover, love is on the way!
    Oh, what blessings to receive!
    Oh, what joy I know is mine!
    Forever and always I'll believe
    Love is waiting down the line.
    So glad stormy weather's gone.
    We'll make tomorrow bright and gay.
    My heart sings to a new dawn.
    Lover, love is on the way!
    All my loneliness is gone

And happiness has come to stay,
Put those mean old blues in pawn—
Lover, love is on the way.
> *(They dance down the street together as the melody continues in up tempo. BUDDY turns his head to whisper an aside to the world as they exit)*

BUDDY: She don't know she's with the devil. Ha! Ha! . . .
BLACKOUT
MUSICAL BRIDGE: *Two VOICES are heard humming "Upon This Rock" behind the scrim.*

Act I, Scene 5

The interior of a store-front church with, behind the rostrum, a large mural of the Garden of Eden in which a brownskin Adam strongly resembles Joe Louis and Eve looks just like a chocolate Sarah Vaughn. Only the Devil is white. At a small table in front of the rostrum on which rests the collection tambourines, sits ESSIE in her ministerial robe of black, a ledger before her. A gray-haired man, BROTHER BUD, is putting the front row of folding chairs away as he sings and ESSIE hums behind him.

BUD: Upon this rock we build our church.
The gates of hell shall not prevail.
Upon this rock we build our church
With strength from God we shall not fail
Upon this rock we build our church.
The devil's wrath shall not avail.
On solid rock we build our church.
In God's sweet grace, I shall not fail.
Um-ummm-um-um! Um-ummmm-ummm-umm-um! . . .

ESSIE: Our little church is certainly growing, Brother Bud. All these extra chairs tonight.
BUD: Busting out at the seams—and it ain't been a month since we come with our mops and pails to clean and fix-up this old place.
ESSIE: Birdie Lee sure was a help. That little woman can scrub!
BUD: That soul's got spirit—when it comes to slinging water.
ESSIE: A willing worker!
> *(BROTHER BUD continues to sing until LAURA enters and shoos him out)*

LAURA: Listen, we're trying to have a meeting of the Board of Trustees, Brother Bud. This is it. I'm Secretary, Essie's Treasurer.
ESSIE: And God is President.
LAURA: Now, what's your mission?
BUD: I kind of stuck around to see if you can help me. My wife is sick, I'm out of work, and my grandchildren is hungry.
     (ESSIE immediately puts her hand in her tote-bag)
LAURA: Essie! . . . Brother Bud, Jesus will help you.
BUD: He don't come to earth very often.
ESSIE: Meanwhile, here, brother, here!
     (ESSIE hands him some money. LAURA shrugs)
BUD: Thank you, Sister Essie! Thank God! And bless you both! *(He exits)*
LAURA: Let's go on with the meeting. Now, as you were saying— *(LAURA flings one shapely leg over the arm of her chair and we see that she is wearing toreador pants beneath her churchly robe. As she turns, she glances at the mural behind her)* Just look at Joe Louis peeing out from behind that bush—Adam. That artist sure painted us a pretty Garden of Eden. I told him to make Eve look just like Sarah Vaughn—and he did.
ESSIE: Who told him to make the Devil white?
LAURA: Me—also to put a real diamond in the snake's head.
ESSIE: That snake should've been named Buddy.
LAURA: All right, Essie! Come on, let's hear the Treasurer's report.
ESSIE: I got two thousand dollars in my spice jar in the cupboard at home which I think we better take to the bank. Who'd ever thought you and me would be banking money?
LAURA: I've made another payment on my mink coat—gonna get it out for Christmas.
ESSIE: You deserves a nice Christmas present, Laura. But I wonder will I have my daughter with me by then?
LAURA: You said you wanted a nice place to bring Marietta to. Essie, suppose we take this two thousand dollars and move, instead of putting it in the bank?
ESSIE: No. Laura. The church needs a nest egg. We'll put it away.
LAURA: O.K., as you say. I'm happy—I got my man to keep me warm. Let's get down with this business so— *(There is a sound of a door slamming and a WOMAN'S VOICE is heard. BIRDIE LEE enters)* Uh-oh! Another worriation!
BIRDIE: My goodness! It sure is snowing. Sisters, I just can't walk

another step without going to the bathroom. I was passing by and seed the lights still on. You know, I drunk so much beer when I was a sinner I'm still going to the bathroom, now that I'm a saint.

(*LAURA frowns, ESSIE smiles, as BIRDIE LEE rushes to a sign pointing to Rest Rooms*)

LAURA: Can we finish our Treasurer's report?

ESSIE: To printer, $22.55, for new Sunday School cards, with black angels.

LAURA: I second everything black.

ESSIE: New tambourines—the old ones wore out—$17.50.

LAURA: We really work them tambourines.

ESSIE: To ward boss, $50, to keep from putting in fire extinguishers.

LAURA: That bald-headed politicianer!

ESSIE: And to C.J. for guitar strings, $1.00. Loan also to C.J. $44.00 for his schooling.

LAURA: All right, bleeding heart! What else? I wish you'd get yourself some new clothes.

(*BIRDIE LEE re-enters to cross toward exit*)

BIRDIE: Bless God! I guess I'll try and make it home now. Services sure were fine this evening. See you tomorrow. Hold your holt! (*BIRDIE exits*)

ESSIE: Good night, Birdie! Oh, but there's so much our church can do in Harlem—make a playground for the neighborhood kids, establish an employment office, set up a day nursery for children of mothers what works. I'll get me some new clothes in due time. But first I wants to make our church a *good* church, Laura. The needs is so big up here in Harlem, we have to do all we can, me and you—and you're God's handmaiden, even if you don't always act like a holy maiden do.

LAURA: Just how does a holy maiden act?

ESSIE: They be's not so bold with their sinning.

LAURA: There you go! Buddy again: (*LAURA rises and removes her robe*) I might convert that stud yet, who knows?

ESSIE: Looks like he's converting you—to sin—selling Holy Water from the sink.

LAURA: *I am*—as soon as the bottles come.

ESSIE: You'll never fill them from my faucet.

LAURA: I got a sink in my room. And I sure hope Buddy's there when I get home tonight.

ESSIE: You gave him a key?

LAURA: Of course! That locksmith around the corner's made so many keys to my keyhole he ought to know the shape of it by heart.

ESSIE: That's no way for a lady minister to do. And I don't like that holy water neither.

LAURA: Well, if you don't like it, just walk off the rostrum, go pray in the anteroom, but leave me be. I'm gonna live fine, and look fine.

ESSIE: Laura, one of these days the Spirit is going to strike vanity from your heart, lust from your body, and—

LAURA: And make me as stupid as you are, heh? Without an idea in your head until I put one there! Without me you'd still be on relief. Yet you want to cramp my style. Well, you won't. I'll tell you now, Essie, I'm getting a fur coat, a Cadillac, and buying a hi-fi set—for Buddy.

ESSIE: Do Jesus! All of that out of this poor little church!

LAURA: Poor? Running five nights a week and taking in two hundred dollars a night? Overflowing! We gonna have to move soon. All these old theatres in Harlem they're turning into churches. Maybe Marty can rent us one.

ESSIE: Marty? Who's Marty?

LAURA: Whoever he is, you'd think he was the devil—and Buddy his shadow in the form of a snake. Well, I'm not afraid of devils my-self. I've wrestled with them all my life—and some devils have got diamonds in their heads. Look ! My idea! *(LAURA switches out the lights. In the mural of the Garden of Eden the diamond in the snake's head glows brilliantly)* It was my idea to buy that light bulb in the wall behind that snake. My idea to paint black saints. Everything people are talking about around here was my idea. But what do you do? Criticize, criticize, criticize! Come on, Trustees' meeting is over, let's get the hell out of here. *(But ESSIE, head in hands, begins to cry. LAURA pauses, turns, regrets her anger, then comes back)* Essie, I'm sorry I blew my top. Look! Give away as much of that money as you want, lend it out, put that two thousand in the bank for the church, like you said. We'll take up more collections next week, and week after. If they're as big as they were this week, you take next week's money and send for your daughter. *(LAURA puts her arm about ESSIE's shoulders)* Essie, I want you to have something, too, out of this deal.

> *(ESSIE's sobs are like a prayer as the diamond in the serpent's head glitters in the darkness)*

ESSIE: My God! . . . Oh, my God, Laura! My God!
   (*Raucous jazz is heard on a hi-fi set far away*)
BLACKOUT
MUSICAL BRIDGE: *Modern jazz.*

Act I, Scene 6

Living room of an expensively furnished apartment, rather on the showy side, but ESSIE's large old-fashioned motto: GOD BLESS OUR HOME on the wall. There is a glowing electric cross in the panel between the two windows. BUDDY reclines on a long silken lounge reading "Playboy" and listening to jazz on the hi-fi. LAURA enters in a stylish negligee, trailing perfume. From behind, she puts her arms around BUDDY and caresses him.

BUDDY: Relax, woman, and let me listen to these fine sounds.
LAURA: Big-eyed Buddy! You sweet old joker, you!
BUDDY: Stop calling me them cute names—I'm no poodle puppy. Grrr-rr-r! (*Growling, he pulls her toward him and bites her sharply on the neck*)
LAURA: Oh, Don't bite so hard, Buddy!
BUDDY: Tastes good, baby.
LAURA: Tom cat! Billy goat! You big brown bar stud!
BUDDY: All right now, Laura! Don't get me roused up *again* this early in the evening.
LAURA: Chocolate daddy with coconut eyes! Want a little Scotch?
BUDDY: (*Shaking his head*) No.
LAURA: I do. Say, I love that old theatre we moved into! No more store fronts, thanks to you—and Marty.
BUDDY: Um-hum!
LAURA: I love my name up on the canopy—THE REED SISTERS TAMBOURINE TEMPLE—in lights where it used to say: *Lana Turner.*
BUDDY: You look good up on the stage, baby—
LAURA: Rostrum, honey.
   (*LAURA laughs, pours herself a drink and returns to BUDDY on the sofa as the record on the hi-fi runs out*)
BUDDY: This church racket's got show business beat to hell. But some churches don't have sense enough to be crooked. They really try to

be holy—and holiness don't make money. By the way, baby, I could do with a little change myself tonight. I might take a hand of stud at Shoofly's. How about table stakes?

LAURA: Table stakes?

BUDDY: Say, fifty simoleons.

LAURA: Aw, honey! That's a lot to gamble away.

BUDDY: I can't sleep here tonight, so Essie informs me, with that young girl coming. Something tells me that kid's going to be in our way, Laura.

LAURA: Essie's daughter is no kid, Buddy. She's sixteen.

BUDDY: Sweet sixteen—but I expect she's *been* kissed.

LAURA: Wonder if the girl'll get off the bus hungry?

BUDDY: I don't know about that girl, but me, I could give a steak hell right now—I like them rare, with the blood oozing out.

LAURA: They ought to be here soon, then me and Essie'll fix dinner. I told her to bring in some groceries. Meanwhile, I better get decent and put on a dress, heh? Also put this likker away *(LAURA takes glass from BUDDY)* That child might think something. After all, I'm gonna be her "Aunt Laura" so no bad examples the first day.

BUDDY: Do I look like a bad example?

(BUDDY slaps LAURA resoundingly on the fanny as he pulls her down on the couch)

LAURA: Ouch!

BUDDY: The hot half of the Reed Sisters!

LAURA: If I'm the body, Essie's the soul.

BUDDY: And I'm your stick man—with the extra dice up my sleeve. Holy Water from the Jordan at a buck a bottle! How simple can people get. Always looking for some kind of lucky stuff. I depend on myself, myself.

LAURA: Me too, Buddy.

BUDDY: Marty gave me a new idea the other day for you.

LAURA: What?

BUDDY: Numbers.

LAURA: Numbers? We can't play no numbers in the church.

BUDDY: Not play 'em, baby. No gambling. Just pronounce 'em.

LAURA: Pronounce them?

BUDDY: Give 'em out in service. You know, you all got a mighty big theatre now—

LAURA: Church.

BUDDY: Church there to fill. Let the word get around that you give out lucky numbers every Sunday—and it will be packed and jammed—Holy hymns from the pulpit of Bible texts with three numbers, that's all, and let people write them numbers down.
LAURA: Buddy, you got an idea!
(She kisses him square on the mouth then offers him a puff from her cigarette)
BUDDY: Marty's idea. His syndicate backs the biggest numbers bank in Manhattan.
LAURA: Lucky Texts! Each time I give out a text, I'll pass the tambourines for a quarter.
BUDDY: We'll add a few more hundreds to the bank account every week. And the government can't tax that church money.
LAURA: Amen!
BUDDY: Amen is right, baby. I want you to get me a red Cadillac—sport model—convertible.
LAURA: Ain't one Cadillac in the family enough?
BUDDY: You know I got a birthday next month.
LAURA: Well, maybe—but there's one little thing you could do for me, too.
BUDDY: What's that?
LAURA: Join the church.
BUDDY: Aw, there you go *again*!
LAURA: But, honey, you're in and out of the temple so much, lots of the saints are wondering how come you don't belong—why you're not converted.
BUDDY: Well, since nothing exciting happens in the middle of the week, I'll get converted next Wednesday.
LAURA: That might cool Essie down a little, she still thinks you're Satan. But listen, Daddy, after you get converted, don't go getting *too* holy. Just keep on being nice to me.
BUDDY: Don't give me no *do's* and *don'ts*! I know how far to go, up, down, right, left, or in between.
(VOICES are heard in the hall. LAURA runs to hide glasses and whiskey in the cabinet)
LAURA: Oh, here comes Essie. I'm gonna run and change.
(LAURA hurries off to exit, leaving BUDDY on the couch as ESSIE enters with a valise and a very pretty GIRL)
ESSIE: Why, good evening! I didn't know you'd still be here, Buddy. Marietta, this is Mr. Lomax.

BUDDY: Pleased to know you, Marietta. Essie, you've got a be-*ooo*-ti-ful daughter!

ESSIE: I'm blessed, Buddy.

(BUDDY holds MARIETTA's hand longer than necessary, squeezing it tightly until she jerks away)

MARIETTA: Oh, that hurts!

BUDDY: Just my way of welcoming you to Harlem. Hope you like it.

MARIETTA: Mama, it's so pretty in here! Oh, Mama, what a nice place, so modernistic. And a lighted cross on the wall!

ESSIE: We're all blessed, honey! But just wait till you see our new church. All of this is the Lord's own miracle, Marietta. Laura, where are you?

LAURA: I'm coming, Essie, coming. *(LAURA enters freshly dressed)* Child, I'm your Aunt Laura.

ESSIE: Marietta, this is my old friend, who's stuck by me through thick and thin.

LAURA: I'm so glad you're here, Marietta, so glad! This is your home.

(LAURA embraces MARIETTA)

ESSIE: Thank God! I just thank God for all.

BUDDY: God—and your tambourines! Marietta, can you play a tambourine?

MARIETTA: I used to try sometimes in church down home.

BUDDY: Then you'll fit.

MARIETTA: Are you in the choir?

BUDDY: No, baby, I'm just a backstage man.

LAURA: Buddy, her name's Marietta, not *baby.*

BUDDY: She's a baby to me. And I'm sure glad you got here, kid, so we can eat.

ESSIE: Oh, Laura! Meeting Marietta, I got so excited, I clean forgot to bring the chops. Ain't that awful?

BUDDY: My mouth's set on steaks, anyhow, so I'll go get 'em. Come on, Marietta, lemme show you where the butcher shops are in this neighborhood, since you'll be living here. We'll get some sirloin, ice cream, and beer. What else you need, Laura?

LAURA: Potatoes.

ESSIE: Marietta, ain't you kind of tired?

MARIETTA: Not really, Mama.

BUDDY: Oh, let the girl see what our block looks like—take a squint at Harlem. Come on, kid.

MARIETTA: *(Looking at her mother)* All right, Mama?

ESSIE: You all come directly back, then. Meanwhile, we'll set the table—soon's I catch my breath.

(BUDDY and MARIETTA exit)

LAURA: She's a mighty pretty girl, Essie—for this city of sin. Don't you think maybe Marietta should stay for a *little* visit, then go on back to her grandma down in the simple South? *(LAURA goes to the cabinet and pours a drink)*

ESSIE: After all these years, I just got my child with me. I want to keep her with me now, Laura, keep her here with her Mama.

LAURA: She's at the age, you know—

ESSIE: There's some mighty nice young mens in Harlem—in our church, in fact. I told C.J. my daughter was coming, and to drop around tonight.

LAURA: I hope C.J. don't bring that guitar of his, because the *last* thing I want is gospel music on my night off. Saturday night, I feel like letting my hair down.

ESSIE: Laura, I hope you don't drink so much no more, now that my daughter is here.

LAURA: Essie, I'll do my damnedest to respect your child. But you know, I ain't no saint. You just naturally got goodness in you. Me, I have to wrestle with temptation. You just take whatever comes.

ESSIE: I wrestle with temptation, too, Laura, in my heart. But somehow or other, I always did want to *try* to be good. Once I thought being good was doing nothing, like you said, I guess, so I done nothing for half my life. Now I'm trying to do *something*—and be good, too. It's harder.

LAURA: Um-hum!

ESSIE: What I'm trying to do, now that I got the time—

LAURA: And *money*—

ESSIE: —to set down and meditate, is to try to unscramble the good from the bad—in myself and others. If I can just separate the good, maybe I can hold on to it. I found a verse in the Bible I been studying over and over, says: "Canst thou by searching find out God?" *(ESSIE repeats it slowly)* "Canst thou by searching find out God?"

LAURA: What verse is that? Where is it?

ESSIE: Job 11:7.

LAURA: What a number! 11-7—wow! Rolled up in luck. That's gonna be one of my texts, too.

ESSIE: Laura, you thinking about numbers, and I'm thinking about God, finding out what *is* God in terms of what *we* is—us—on this earth. I'm just discovering there's so many ways to do good and be good I ain't found yet.

LAURA: Listen, you've been good ever since I've known you, Essie. But how good do you want to be—so good you ain't got a dime? I'm trying to figure how we can make *plenty* of money. You got a daughter up here in New York to educate—and that takes cash.

ESSIE: I want other people's daughters to get through school, too. There ain't no being good and keeping it to yourself. Is there, Laura?

LAURA: It's good to me when it's just *all* mine, Essie—like love—like Buddy. I don't want to share Buddy with nobody.

ESSIE: You talking about flesh-kind of love, not spirit.

LAURA: The spirit can't do a woman like me no good in bed.

ESSIE: Laura!

LAURA: Eat, drink, and love, that's what I live for!

(The buzzer sounds)

ESSIE: Laura, I want you to find a good man and get married.

LAURA: Good men are usually poor—and I never did like to be poor, Essie. Did you? But I always was poor until I hit on shaking a tambourine—and met Buddy. He'll do for me.

(ESSIE exits to answer door as buzzer sounds again)

ESSIE: Lemme see who's ringing.

LAURA: I want a man who knows all the angles! To get along in this world—*all the angles!*

(VOICES are heard in the hall)

ESSIE: Hello, C.J. Come in.

C.J.: Howdy, Miss Essie! Did your daughter come?

ESSIE: Yes, son, thank God, safely! Come in. *(ESSIE returns with the YOUNG MAN)* Marietta'll be here in a minute. I see you brought your guitar.

LAURA: Dear God!

C.J.: How are you, Sister Reed? I've been practicing all evening on that new song I made up for our church. Want to hear it?

LAURA: Some saints can over-do, C.J. Serenade the young lady when she comes. *(Buzzer sounds)* Must be them.

(LAURA exits into hall and VOICES are heard as BUDDY and MARIETTA enter with groceries)

BUDDY: We are loaded down.

LAURA: Looks like you tried to buy out the store.

BUDDY: Well, since I had such a swinging little helper . . .

LAURA: Come on to the kitchen with the stuff, Buddy. Marietta, you've got company already.

> *(LAURA takes bags from MARIETTA and exits to kitchen as BUDDY sits down to remove his shoes)*

BUDDY: Let me cool my feet here! Holy mackerel, Sapphire!

LAURA: Buddy!

BUDDY: I'm coming! *(He exits in his stocking feet with groceries)*

ESSIE: Daughter here's one of the young men of our church, C.J. meet Miss Johnson, Mr. Moore—Marietta, C.J. Now excuse me, children. I'm gonna help Laura get a quick dinner. I'll drop your bag in your room, Marietta. *(ESSIE exits)*

MARIETTA: Thank you, Mama! Mr. Moore, I—

C.J.: You can call me C.J.

MARIETTA: What does C.J. stand for?

C.J.: Just C.J., that's all. I only got initials for a first name—C.J.

BUDDY: *(Enters with three cans of beer and interrupts)* Certified jerk, consecrated jackass—that's what C.J. stands for—one of them holy and sanctified boys, baby. Probably won't even take a chick to the movies on Sundays.

C.J.: Sure I will.

BUDDY: Never see you around the pool halls.

C.J.: Well, with school work and all—

BUDDY: Square! Here, have a snizzle.

> *(He hands C.J. a can of beer. The BOY takes it with hesitation. BUDDY gets a glass for MARIETTA)*

Marietta, would you like a cool one?

MARIETTA: Not beer, sir. I don't . . .

BUDDY: Sir? I'm not your father, baby.

MARIETTA: I don't drink, Mr. Buddy.

BUD: Just *Buddy*. Well, I'll drink yours, Marietta. Drink up, C.J., and get ready for the weekend. Let's see your guitar, boy. I used to beat out a mean blues before I left Savannah. *(BUDDY picks up the guitar)*

C.J.: A blues? Sure, if the Sisters don't mind.

BUDDY: A little blues won't hurt the Reed Sisters. Hum-mmm, you got a pretty gitfiddle, boy,

C.J.: I play in the college orchestra sometimes.

> *(As BUDDY strums a soft slow blues, the two YOUNG PEOPLE talk as C.J.—afraid not to be a man—drinks his beer)*

MARIETTA: You go to college?

C.J.: Um-hum! I'm working my way.

MARIETTA: What are you taking?

C.J.: Chemistry. I can analyze that Holy Water they're gonna sell in church. I wish Sister Laura would give me a bottle tonight so I can tell what makes Jordan water different from what we have in New York City.

BUDDY: That water costs a dollar a bottle, boy, so they are not giving none away.

C.J.: Well, maybe I'll buy a bottle tomorrow.

BUDDY: I would advise you to leave that water alone.

C.J.: Why?

BUDDY: Just advice, that's all.

> *(There is a puzzled silence on C.J.'s part as BUDDY strikes a series of loud chords)*

C.J.: Marietta, where are you in school—still high school, or what?

MARIETTA: High school, but you know, down South, the schools aren't very good, especially for colored, and I'm afraid— *(BUDDY plays louder and louder as if trying to drown out their conversation. MARIETTA shouts)*—afraid I won't match up to the girls up North here.

C.J.: Oh, yes you will. You look real smart to me, Marietta. Besides, you're so pretty you scare me.

MARIETTA: C.J.!

C.J.: Like I'm trying to tell you!

> *(BUDDY turns on radio, "New York Blues" is playing)*

BUDDY: Hey, Marietta, listen to this! Did you ever dig the "New York Blues"? I guess not, down in the sticks where you've been. But after you're in Harlem for a couple of weeks, you'll understand. *(BUDDY sings)*

> When you hear the motors purring
> On the avenue
> And you see the hep cats tipping
> Through the evening dew,
> You think about that dot-on-the-map
> That once you knew—
> And you love New York!
> Baby, you love New York!
> You've got the New York Blues!
>
> When you're in a little jazz club
> Where the cool cats strum,

Stashed in a cozy nook
Where all the cute chicks come,
You think about old squareville
Where you hail from—
And you love New York!
Baby, you love New York!
You've got the New York Blues!

When you hear a blues that's got
A Charlie Mingus chord
And it reaches down inside you,
Makes you holler, Lord!
You know down home you'd never hear no
Such cool chord—
Then you love New York!
Baby, you love New York!
Baby, you love New York!
You've got those New York Blues!

Oh, if I was the devil and didn't have hell for my base, I'd choose
New York. It's an ace-town—so many beautiful women in it for a
devil to tempt.

When you get the blues-for-going
And you get the blues-to-stay
You've got the blues-for-leaving
But you cannot get away—
You think about that sleepy town
That you left flat one day
And you love New York!
Baby, you love New York!
You've got those New York Blues!
Those real c-ooo-oo-l New York Blues!

> *(During the song, C.J. holds MARIETTA's hand. As BUDDY
> ends the song, ESSIE enters with a kitchen apron on)*

ESSIE: Buddy! Cut this thing off. The neighbors'll hear all them blues
coming out of our apartment and think we forgot the gospel.

BUDDY: *(Throwing the guitar to C.J.)* Here, kid! You can play that
gospel stuff the Sisters like. But it all sounds like blues to me.

ESSIE: At least our words is different. But we don't need no music
now—we're about to put the steaks on the stove. Anybody want
to wash up for dinner?

C.J.: *(His hand is on his stomach as if slightly nauseated)* I do, Miss Essie. I'm not used to drinking beer.

ESSIE: Come on, I'll show you the place.

(C.J. and ESSIE exit. BUDDY approaches MARIETTA)

BUDDY: And I'd like to show *you* something. I believe it's up to me to school you.

MARIETTA: School me?

BUDDY: That's right. That gospel boy of a C.J. ain't dry behind the ears yet. Men don't start asking a sharp little chick like you what school you're in.

MARIETTA: Sharp?

BUDDY: Stacked, solid—neat, all-reet—boss, baby! That means—attractive.

MARIETTA: Thank you, Mr. Buddy.

BUDDY: Don't *Mister* me. Just Buddy, that's all—Big-Eyed Buddy—with eyes for you.

MARIETTA: Mama told me you're Miss Laura's friend.

BUDDY: Sure I'm her friend. But, Marietta, I'm gonna show you something. I'm gonna show you how fast a Harlem stud moves in.

MARIETTA: Moves in?

BUDDY: On a chick. *(MARIETTA tries to pass BUDDY as he approaches)* We start like this. *(Quick as a panther, BUDDY grabs MARIETTA and kisses her)*

MARIETTA: Oh!

(Before she can draw back, LAURA appears in the doorway, a dainty apron on. She catches them embracing, and speaks in slow anger)

LAURA: You said you liked your steaks rare, Buddy—with the blood oozing out.

BUDDY: *(Releasing the GIRL)* I do.

LAURA: And your women tender?

BUDDY: Could be.

LAURA: Huh! Miss Marietta, I reckon you ain't as innocent as you look.

MARIETTA: I tried to get past him, Aunt Laura, but he—

LAURA: Then get past, honey, *get past!* *(MARIETTA exits frightened toward the kitchen)* As for you, Buddy Boy—

BUDDY: Aw, old chick, don't get blood in your eyes.

LAURA: Nor on my hands? *(She stares at BUDDY silently)* I never knowed a man yet that didn't bleed—if cut.

ESSIE: *(Calling from the kitchen)* Let's go, everybody—dinner's on the table!

LAURA: Come on, Buddy, get your steak.

> (*LAURA walks indignantly toward the door. Suddenly like a panther, BUDDY grabs her, and swings her around into his arms*)

BUDDY: Listen, Laura! You know damn well you're my woman. Can't no young girl lay a candle to you! You've got something I want, something I love. (*As he embraces her roughly LAURA's struggles cease*) I said something I want, baby! . . . Come one, give me a little sugar—right now!

LAURA: Buddy! . . . We've got to go eat.

BUDDY: Kiss now—eat later! Kiss . . . *right* . . . *now!*

> (*Long and passionately their lips meet*)

BLACKOUT

MUSICAL BRIDGE: *The gospel music of "As I Go" rises in the darkness and carries over into the next scene.*

Act I, Scene 7

The glowing rostrum of Tambourine Temple in a newly converted theatre. It is a bright and joyous church. Besides an electric organ, there is a trio of piano, guitar, and drums—BIRDIE LEE is the drummer—with a colorfully robed CHOIR on tiers in the background, some SINGERS holding tambourines. DEACONESS HOBBS stands before the rostrum, an imposing woman with a big voice. On either side of her sway two tall DEACONS, and also DEACON CROW and BUD. The four men hum "As I Go" softly to end of refrain. As the curtain rises, the DEACONESS sings.

DEACONESS: I cannot find my way alone.

The sins that I bear I must atone

And so I pray thy light be shone

To guide me as I go through this world.

DEACONS: As I go, as I go,

Oh, Jesus, walk by my side as I go.

As I go, as I go,

Be my guide as I go through this world.

> (*Refrain repeats softly under talk*)

DEACONESS: Now, dear friends, as the preliminaries of this meeting draws to a close, we proceed to the main body of our ceremonies. I thank God for these long tall deacons, these basses of Jehovah—the Matthew, Mark, Luke, and John of this church—and your humble deaconess and servant, myself, Lucy Mae Hobbs, who prays—

As I go, as I go,

Oh, Jesus, walk by my side as I go.

As I go, as I go,

Be my guide as I go through this world.

BIRDIE: Sing the song, Sister, sing the song!

(DEACONESS HOBBS' voice soars in song as the FOUR DEA-CONS support her. On the final verse ESSIE enters singing)

ESSIE: I need some rock on which to stand,

Some ground that is not shifting sand,

And so I seek my Savior's hand

To guide me as I go through this world.

BIRDIE: Keep your hand on the plow, Sister Essie. Hold your holt on God!

(The refrain continues as the DEACONESS and the DEACONS retire to the choir stalls and ESSIE takes over at the rostrum)

ESSIE: Brothers and sisters, I am humble, humble tonight, humble in His presence. Pray for me, all of you, as I go! He has been so good to me! I thank God for His name this evening, for Sister Laura, for our fine Minister of Music there at the piano, for all of you congregation, for Deacon Crow, Sister Birdie Lee, young C.J., and for my daughter, Marietta, God has sent to me. Marietta, daughter, rise and state your determination.

(MARIETTA speaks as the CHOIR continues to hum "As I Go" to end of chorus)

MARIETTA: Dear friends, Jesus brought me out of the deep dark Southland up here to the light of New York City, up here to my mother, Essie. Jesus brought me to her, and to you, and to this church. I want to be worthy of your love, and of all my mother has done and is doing for me. And most of all, dear friends, I want to be worthy of the love of God. Friends—

I want to be a flower in God's garden,

To know each day the beauty of his love,

Take from the sun its warmth and splendor,

From gentle dews the kiss of heaven above.

I want to share each beam of holy sunshine,

Help make the world a radiant happy place,

A place of joy and love and laughter,

A howdy-do on everybody's face.

If God will give me understanding,

Lead me down the path his feet have trod,

If God will help me grow in wisdom,
Let my life be rooted in his sod.
Oh, just to be a flower in God's garden!
Oh, just to be a flower in his sight—
A tiny little flower in God's garden,
A flower in his garden of delight.
(The song becomes a prayer as the CHORUS joins MARIETTA)
Dear God, just give me understanding.
Lead me down the path your feet have trod.
Dear God, just help me grow in wisdom,
Yes, let my life be rooted in your sod.
I want to be a flower in your garden.
I want to be a flower in your sight.
A tiny little flower in God's garden,
A flower in your garden of delight.
(The song ends softly to subdued amens. There is a roll of drums. The spotlight falls on LAURA, regal at one side of the stage. Tambourines shimmer as she marches toward the rostrum to the melody of "Home to God")

LAURA: Oh, saints of this church, blooming tonight in God's garden! My heart is full of joy! See what Tambourine Temple has done— united mother and daughter, brought this young lamb to the fold, filled Essie's heart with joy for her child! Blessed me, blessed you! What other hearts here are filled with joy tonight? Who else wants to speak for Jesus as Marietta has done? Who else?

(A tall, scrawny old man, CHICKEN-CROW-FOR-DAY, emerges from the CHOIR)

CROW: Great God, I do! I has a determination to make.

LAURA: Make it, brother, make it! Deacon Crow-For-Day! Our friend converted to Jesus! Testify, brother!

ESSIE: Testify! Testify!

(CROW-FOR-DAY takes the center)

CROW: Oh, I am here to tell you tonight, since I started to live right, it is my determination to keep on—on the path to glory. In my sinful days, before I found this church, I were a dyed-in-the-wool sinner, yes, dyed-in-the-wool, sniffing after women, tailing after sin, gambling on green tables. Saratoga, Trenton, New Orleans—let 'em roll! Santa Anita, Tanforan, Belmont, Miami, I never read nothing but the racing forms. In New York, the numbers columns in the *Daily News,* and crime in the comic books. Now I've seen the light!

316 Gospel Plays, Operas, and Later Dramatic Works

Sister Essie and Sister Laura brought me to the faith. They done snatched me off the ship of iniquity on which I rid down the river of sin through the awfullest of storms, through gales of evil, hurricanes of passion purple as devil's ink, green as gall.

BIRDIE: Green, green, green as gall!

CROW: I shot dices. Now I've stopped. I lived off women. Uh-huh! No more! I make my own living now. I carried a pistol, called it *Dog*— because when it shot, it barked just like a dog. Don't carry no pistol no more. Carried a knife. Knives got me in trouble. Don't carry a knife no more. I drank likker.

BIRDIE: Me, too! Me, too!

CROW: It made me fool-headed. Thank God, I stopped.

BIRDIE: Stopped, stopped, stopped!

CROW: I witnessed the chain gang, the jail, the bread line, the charity house—but look at me now!

BIRDIE: Look, look, look!

CROW: I lived to see the chicken crow for day, the sun of grace to rise, the rivers of life to flow, thanks be to God! Lemme tell you, I've come to the fold! I've come—

> *(He sings and the whole church bears him up)*
> Back to the fold—
> How safe, how warm I feel
> Yes, back to the fold!
> His love alone is real . . .

BIRDIE: In the fold! The fold! Yes, in the fold!

CROW: Back to the fold
> How precious are my God's ways!

BIRDIE: Where the streets are streets of gold!

CROW: Back to the fold!
> So bright are all my days.

> *(BIRDIE LEE begins to bang her drums then leaps and dances in ecstasy as the CHORUS hums)*

BIRDIE: Hold your holt, Crow! Hold your holt on God! Hold your holt!

LAURA: Birdie Lee, why don't you set down?

BIRDIE: Set down? I can't set down—too happy to set down—got to stand—got to talk for Jesus—testify this evening in His name. I got to tell you where I come from—*underneath* the gutter. On the street, I heard Sister Laura preaching, Sister Essie praying, I said I got to take up the Cross and come back to the fold. Yes, they preached and prayed and sung me into the hands of God! I said goodbye to sin—and I wove my hand. *(She waves her hand)* Yes, I wove my hand to the devil—and said goodbye. That's why tonight, brothers and sisters, *I'm* gonna testify!

> *(Gradually her speaking rhythm merges into song as she returns to her drums and begins to play and sing)*

CROW: Testify, Sister, testify!

ESSIE: Tell the world about it, Miss Lee, tell the world!

BIRDIE: I'm gonna testify!

> I'm gonna testify!
> I'm gonna testify!
> Till the day I die.
> I'm gonna tell the truth
> For the truth don't lie.
> Yes, I'm gonna testify!
>
> Sin has walked this world with me.
> Thank God a-mighty, from sin I'm free!
> Evil laid across my way.
> Thank God a-mighty, it's a brand new day!
>
> I'm gonna testify!
> I'm gonna testify!
> I'm gonna testify!
> Till the day I die.
> I'm gonna tell the truth
> For the truth don't lie.
> Yes, I'm gonna testify!
>
> I didn't know the strength I'd find
> Thank God a-mighty, I'm a gospel lion.
> Things I've seen I cannot keep.
> Thank God a-mighty, God does not sleep!
>
> I'm gonna testify!
> I'm gonna testify!
> I'm gonna testify!
> Till the day I die.
> I'm gonna tell the truth
> For the truth don't lie.
> Yes, I'm gonna testify!

LAURA: No, the truth don't lie! How happy are the lambs of God!

Friends, I got a surprise for you, something new. I am going to give you texts for the week—Lucky Texts—picked out with prayer and meditation on my part from the Holy Book. And for each Lucky Text, I want you to drop a quarter in the tambourine. Ushers out there with your tambourines, pass among the congregation for their free-will gifts. Now write the numbers of these Lucky Texts, and study them during the week. That goes for you of the radio audience too. Just call Atwater 7-4352 any time and let me know how your blessings fall. Get your quarters and your pencils ready. Now write! *(LAURA turns the pages of the Bible)* Psalm 9 and 20. Got that? 9 and 20. Drop a quarter in the tambourines. For each text a quarter. Give God His and you'll get yours! Take all three numbers 9-2-0. Twenty-five cents. You'll have no luck if you don't give God His'n. Aw, let 'em clink! Let the holy coins clink! . . . Now ready? Next text. What a great text—Sister Essie's favorite—Job 11:7. 7-11 or 11-7, either way. Yes, bless God, children! 1-1-7, that's right. Job 11:7.

(On the rostrum a white telephone rings)

VOICES: Thank you! Thanks, Sister Laura! Thanks! Thanks! Amen!

LAURA: Hello . . . What's that, sister? . . . You say you know you're gonna be blessed. Well, I thank you for your faith in *me*—and God . . . Now, as I sing, I invite those of you who are sinners tonight to come into this church. Who wants to touch His garment this evening?

ESSIE: Who wants the Lord to claim him for His own?

(BOTH come forward)

LAURA: Who will come into the fold—the church that has no doors? Who wants to join Tambourine Temple?

ESSIE: And know the blessings of Christ!

LAURA: Who? Who? Who?

ESSIE: Who will come? Who?

LAURA: I know there is a lost lamb out there in this congregation somewhere.

ESSIE: Lost, lost, lost!

LAURA: Why don't you join us in this temple of the saved?

ESSIE: Yes, come into the fold.

(The piano begins to play very softly)

LAURA: There were ninety and nine that safely lay
    In the shelter of the fold,
    But one lamb was out in the hills away
    Far from the gates of gold,

Away on the mountain wild and bare,
Away from the tender shepherd's care.
CHORUS: Away from the tender shepherd's care.
  (A cry in heard in the CONGREGATION)
BUDDY: Save me, Lord, save me! I want to be saved.
LAURA: Oh, come, brother, come!
BUDDY: Help me, Lord!
  (BUDDY stumbles up the steps to kneel on the threshold of the rostrum as LAURA's voice rises loud and strong)
LAURA: All through the mountains thunder-riven
  And up from the rocky steep
  There arose a glad cry to the gates of heaven!
  Rejoice! I have found my sheep!
  (As LAURA reaches out her hands to BUDDY the CHORUS booms thunderously)
CHORUS: Rejoice! God has found his sheep!
  Rejoice! God has found his sheep!
  (ESSIE rises, glaring at BUDDY doubting his conversion)
BUDDY: I'm saved! Saved! Saved!
  (As "Amens" and "Hallelujahs" rend the air, ESSIE, her head down in shame, walks off the rostrum and exits, but LAURA and GLORIA are ecstatic)
LAURA: Converted! Converted! Brother Buddy Lomax converted!
CROW: Another sinner saved! Thank God! Thank God!
VOICES: Amen! Hallelujah! Praise God! Amen!
GLORIA: Buddy, I'm so glad you're saved. Glad you're saved.
LAURA: Stop interrupting the service!
GLORIA: Can't I say I'm glad he's saved?
LAURA: Gloria, your job is to sing. Sister Mattie, bring the church book.
  Let Brother Lomax sign his name.
MATTIE: *(Bringing the roster to BUDDY to sign)* Now you're on God's
  roll.
GLORIA: So glad! . . . So glad!
  (LAURA gives GLORIA a pointed look)
BIRDIE: God's roll! God's roll! God's roll!
LAURA: Oh, yes! Oh, yes! Yes! Let Brother Buddy speak his determi-
  nation. Tell 'em Buddy, tell 'em!
BIRDIE: Testify! Testify! Testify!
BUDDY: *(Rises from his knees to sing, glancing at GLORIA as he turns toward the congregation)* Church, what can I say? Except that—

The devil had a playground
In my heart one day.
He set up his tents of sin
And invited me to play.
It was so nice, so calm and cool
That I played just like a fool.
I almost lost my immortal soul—
Now I've got that devil told.

CHOIR: Devil, Devil, take yourself away!
Yesterday I played with you
But I ain't gonna play today.
I've changed my playground,
Changed my ways,
I've changed my habits
And I've changed my days.
My feet are anchored on the gospel shore
And I ain't gonna play no more.
(GLORIA *shouts ecstatically , approaching* BUDDY *as she does,*
LAURA *motions her angrily to her seat*)

BUDDY: I turn and look behind me,
This is what I see:
A world full of sinners
Just like I used to be
My heart is filled with pity, Lord,
And I feel the need to cry,
Com pitch your tents on the gospel shore
And let the world go by.
(BIRDIE, CROW-FOR-DAY, THE GLORIETTAS, *and*
LAURA, *join* BUDDY *in the song while* BIRDIE *quickens the*
tempo on her drums and the entire CHORUS *swings into the re-*
frain, as all point their fingers at sin in a big finale)

ALL: Devil, Devil, Devil,
Take yourself away!
Yesterday I played with you
But I ain't gonna play today
I've changed my playground,
I've changed my ways,
I've changed my habits
And I've changed my days—

My feet are anchored on the gospel shore
And I ain't gonna play no more!
CURTAIN

Act II, Prologue

Scrim of a Harlem street again.
BUDDY enters and jauntily takes center stage, flashing on his index finger
a diamond ring.
BUDDY: Folks, you see this ring? Don't let it blind you. It's the Devil's
ring—I'm wearing it. God is good to the Devil sometimes. He lets
him have a few little old things like diamonds, and Cadillac cars, or
Thunderbirds. And yachts if I want them. Country houses, villas,
chateaux in France. Of course, He makes me suffer for them—by
never letting me be anything but a Devil . . . Like the comedians
who always want to play Hamlet, sometimes I would like to play
God. Or at least J.B.—but since I can't, I'll have fun anyhow—my
damned self. I play with people. Let me tell you one of my secrets.
The way to get any good man—I mean he-man—on the Devil's
side is to put your hand in his pocket with something in it—money.
The root of all evil! . . . The way to get a woman is to put your arm
around her waist with your hand *empty*—and let your sense of touch
do the rest. Don't waste money on a woman. Any woman you can
buy is already on the Devil's side . . . Now, let me give you folks
out there a few tips on how to be an honest-to-God devil. Just be
yourself. Don't pretend to be good. If you pretend you're good,
and put too good a pretense at it, you'll fool nobody. Then folks will
certainly think you are a devil—and not only a devil, but a hypocrite.
Your devilishness will defeat itself if you behave too well. Be a devil
right out—like me. Then folks will think you are dashing, daring,
dangerous, darling, cute—especially the women. They will find it
hard to believe you've got a tail. (It's here, but you don't see it) . . .
Another tip on being a devil, friends—don't take yourself seriously.
Smile! You can't help being a devil, so don't worry about it. Just
pick your *fleurs de mal,* and enjoy their perfume. Ha-ha! You didn't
know I read Baudelaire, did you? Beelzebub reads everybody . . .
Ha-ha! M. B. Devil, that's me: Mephistopheles Beelzebub Devil,
alias Satan—nickname, Old Nick . . . I read Henry Miller, too. And

I *wrote The Carpetbaggers.* I gave Peyton those ideas for *Peyton Place.* I rigged the radio quizzes. I'm of the intelligentsia. Big business, too. The stock market, I fix it. Silos—I've built more out of thin air than Billie Sol Estes ever dreamed of. Pornography? I don't even own a pornograph. I *am* pornography—the gargoyle of sex—the original international playboy deluxe, and a millionaire. Money's no problem. I'm not needy—just greedy. I admit greed's a fault. Oh, well, even a devil has faults. Too bad I can't be perfect . . . but I am bad and know it. That's why I am disturbed by innocence. Innocence bugs me—especially young innocence. Just like I walked into the Garden of Eden and upset Adam and Eve in their purity, tonight I am going to—but why anticipate? Just wait a minute, you'll see—old Devil me! Ha-ha! On with the show, stage manager! *(Behind the scrim, the young voices of MARIETTA and C.J. are heard. The DEVIL laughs. The lights dim as he exits still laughing)* Ha! Ha! . . .

Act II, Scene 1

Living room of LAURA and ESSIE's apartment. A summer night. The lights are dim, but the cross glows softly. Through the open windows, the moon and stars are seen. On the sofa, C.J. holds MARIETTA in his arms, just releasing her from a kiss, but not from his embrace, as she begins to sing an old Southern play-song. She pushes C.J. away, but he keeps edging toward her, as she rises to act out the song.

MARIETTA: C.J., no! Be cool—as you all say in Harlem. Let's pretend we're kids again and play that little old game about being farmers.

C.J.: I know that game, but—

MARIETTA: Little boy, little boy!

C.J.: Yes, ma'am!

MARIETTA: Did you do your chores?

C.J.: Yes, ma'am!

MARIETTA: Did you milk my cow?

C.J.: Yes, ma'am!

MARIETTA:Did you feed my sheep?

C.J.:Yes, ma'am!

MARIETTA: Did you count my lambs?

C.J.:Yes, ma'am! Yes, ma'am! Yes, ma'am!

MARIETTA: Um-m-hun-n-n-n!

*(As the duet continues, it is obvious C.J. is more interested in the
girl than in the game)*

MARIETTA and C.J:

> Well, little boy, little boy!
> Yes, ma'am!
> Did you feed my hens?
> Yes, ma'am!
> Did you throw them corn?
> Yes, ma'am!
> Did the hens lay eggs?
> Yes, ma'am!
> Did you count them eggs?
> Yes, ma'am!
> Yes, ma'am!
> Yes, ma'am!

> Um-hum-m-m-!
> Well, little boy, little boy!
> Yes, ma'am!
> Did you take them to the cook?
> Yes, ma'am!
> Did she bake corn bread?
> Yes, ma'am!
> Was that corn bread hot?
> Yes, ma'am!
> Was that corn bread good?
> Yes, ma'am!
> Yes, ma'am!
> Yes, ma'am!

> Um-hum-m-!
> Say, little boy, little boy!
> Yes, ma'am!
> Do you love me true?
> Yes, ma'am!
> Will you feed my hens?
> Yes, ma'am!
> Will you count my eggs?
> Yes, ma'am!
> Shall I make corn bread?
> Oh, yes, yes!

Yes, yes, yes!

Yes, ma'am!

(As the song ends, C.J. takes MARIETTA in his arms, and smothers her last "Um-hun-n-n!" He kisses her passionately as he pulls her toward the sofa)

C.J.: Let me love you, Marietta, love you now! Love you like a man loves a girl!

MARIETTA: No! No, C.J., you don't mean this.

C.J.: Yes, I do!

MARIETTA: *(As C.J. tries to kiss her, she holds him off, speaking very gently, very softly)* C.J., if you was to make love to me now—the way you want to, then you wouldn't want me when we got married.

C.J.: Yes, I would, Marietta. I want you now—and I'd want you any time, all the time.

MARIETTA: You would disrespect me, C.J., if I gave in to you quickly like this; I love you, C.J., but I want you to love me, too, not just—be with me.

C.J.: I got to be with you, Marietta, I got to! I got to! . . . Oh, honey! sweetheart! . . . I got to!

MARIETTA: You will, sweetest boy in the world, you will—but not tonight!

C.J.: *(Frustrated and angry, jumps up)* Aw-www-ww-w! You're not all *that* pure.

MARIETTA: C.J., I'm not pretending to anything. I love you!

C.J.: I love you, too, Marietta, but I'll be damned if—pardon me, I'll be dogged if I don't want you—want you closer than you've ever been to me. If you loved me, you'd trust me. *(C.J. turns his back on her and looks out the window)*

MARIETTA: There are more ways to trust a boy than going to bed with him.

C.J.: Then you don't trust me. Look down there at the park—I'll bet it's full of kids making love. And look up there at the moon—it's happy about it. Aw, gee, Marietta, you make me feel like hell! Feel bad, like I do when I make up songs. Right now I could make up a hell of a song.

MARIETTA: *(Shrugs)* Then make up a song then.

C.J.: No! I'll sing you one I already made up. But it's not about you. And I won't be singing to you, either. I'll be singing to the moon. *(He sits in the window with his guitar and looks out as he sings)*

Moon outside my window,

Don't peep in on me.
I don't want you to see
How lonely I can be.

MARIETTA: *(Comes to stand behind him, an arm over his shoulder)* Oh, C.J., that's beautiful!

C.J.: *(Ignoring her, sings louder than ever)*
Moon outside my window,
Sail right on away.
I don't want you to know
My heart is sad today.

Moon so round and golden,
Moon up in the sky,
So many lonely lovers
Watched you fade and die.

Right outside my window,
Moon so bright above,
Moon outside my window,
Please, whisper to my love.

(Relenting, MARIETTA put both arms around C.J. as the song ends. He looks up—and they kiss. C.J. puts guitar down and takes her in his arms. At that moment BUDDY enters, startling them before they can release each other)

BUDDY: Ha-ha! What's that they say? When the cat's away, the mice *will* play. *(As C.J. puts his guitar back in is case, BUDDY walks up to MARIETTA and chucks her under the chin)* How are you tonight, Miss Innocence?

MARIETTA: Please, Mr. Buddy!

C.J.: Why do you say *please* to him? Just keep your hands off of her, Brother Lomax.

BUDDY: Keep your diaper on, Junior!

C.J.: I guess it's not enough you're doing, turning the Temple into a gambling den! Chasing all the young girls in the church! And don't think I don't know you've got a bunch of runners writing numbers for you in the block. Guys like you are no good for Harlem.

BUDDY: You talk like *I'm* not Harlem.

C.J.: You are not Harlem. Harlem is a dream—the dream black folks dream way down in the deep South. And then they come here and sometimes find it's a nightmare, because men like you trick and betray them. You're related to the devil, Buddy, that's what.

BUDDY: Ha-ha! How did you guess? Smart one, heh?

C.J.: Harlem is full of good people, and people trying to be good, trying to get somewhere. Some are already there, up in the world—in the City Council, in Albany and in Washington. We've got wonderful doctors now, and lawyers and writers like Ralph Ellison, and composers like Margaret Bonds, and ministers like Rev. Dempsey, and young people—like Marietta and me, even. I'm going to amount to something, Buddy, in spite of all.

BUDDY: *All* meaning me, huh? You bore me, kid. Marietta, where's your Aunt Laura? I'm hungry.

MARIETTA: Tambourines Chorus has a TV rehearsal today.

BUDDY: Oh, no wonder I didn't see Gloria in the bar. Did you eat yet?

MARIETTA: C.J. just came to take me out to dinner.

BUDDY: Hell of a way to be eating with his tongue down your throat.

C.J.: *(Rushes toward BUDDY)* You dirty low-down dog, you!

BUDDY: Oh, so you want to try me once? *(BUDDY pick C.J. up and throws him across the room)* Now gather yourself together, Samson.
>   *(C.J. slowly gets up off the floor, crouches, then rushes like a tiger at BUDDY. Blows are exchanged, but BUDDY get the best of the youngster, shortly knocking him out cold with an uppercut to the chin)*

MARIETTA: Oh—ooo-oo-o! How could you!

BUDDY: Cut the jive, baby, let's you and me get together. Remember the first kiss you got in New York? *(BUDDY stalks MARIETTA as she tries to pass him)*

MARIETTA: Let me go get some cold water and throw on C.J.

BUDDY: Don't worry about C.J., he will come to. I'm the one that needs cooling off right now.

MARIETTA: Buddy! *(Frightened, MARIETTA darts about the living room, trying to avoid him. Finally he corners her. MARIETTA screams, grabs BUDDY's shirt and rips it open as he holds her)* Oh-ooo-oo-o! C.J., somebody, help! Help!
>   *(As she struggles against BUDDY's caresses, WOMEN'S VOICES are heard. LAURA enters followed by ESSIE, who switches on the ceiling lights)*

LAURA: Say, what's going on here?
>   *(They hear MARIETTA's sobs, see the disheveled BUDDY, and C.J. lying on the floor)*

ESSIE: Marietta, what's wrong?

MARIETTA: Mama! Mama! Mr. Buddy, he—oh-ooo-oo-o!—I tried—

(*MARIETTA is weeping incoherently as ESSIE tries to comfort her. LAURA picks up an overturned chair*)

LAURA: All right, Buddy, what's your story?

BUDDY: These kids tried to gang me. You got a couple of juvenile delinquents on your hands.

MARIETTA: Buddy wouldn't let me go! He—he—kissed me . . .

BUDDY: Aw, you've been kissed before.

MARIETTA: But you—but you—Oh, Mama! He—

ESSIE: Come on, baby, we'll go in our part of the house and set down, and you tell Mama about it.

(*ESSIE leads MARIETTA out. They exit. LAURA glares at C.J. as he slowly sits up, head in his hands on the floor*)

LAURA: What have you been doing, C.J., taking a nap?

BUDDY: I put him to sleep . . . Laura, pour me a drink.

LAURA: What do you think I am, a barmaid? What's been happening here?

BUDDY: When I got in, it looked to me like C.J. was trying to rape Marietta. And I always take a virgin's side.

C.J.: (*Jumping up from the floor*) Marietta's my girl, Sister Laura, and he—

LAURA: C.J., take your guitar and get on over to the Temple to prayer meeting. Tell them I'll be along in time to wind up the services.

C.J.: God will take care of you, Buddy. If He don't *I will*.

BUDDY: That'll be the day you'll go ice skating in hell.

(*C.J. exits as BUDDY laughs contemptuously*)

LAURA: Can't you leave Marietta alone, Buddy? Right here in my own house! Can't you leave Essie's daughter alone? You know, I'm gonna get sick of you one of these days—damn sick and tired of you. Gloria, Marietta, God knows who else. You're nothing but a bastard with women.

BUDDY: Yeah? How could you get along without *me*? Where would you get your ideas from? How would you keep the inspectors off of that old fire trap of a theatre you're operating in? How would you ever get on TV? Who's got recording connections like me—and Gloria—have ? So stop talking jive. Come on, let's catch a little fresh air. Want a ride in my red Caddy? Want me to drop you off at prayer meeting?

LAURA: I've got a car—and I'm thinking about getting a chauffeur. I can get where I'm going.

BUDDY: All right, keep your hips on your shoulders, old chick. I've had enough yap-yapping. I'll dig you later, maybe in the wee small hours.

> (*BUDDY exits slamming the door. LAURA starts after him, stops, then sinks down on the sofa, in silence. After a moment, she calls*)

LAURA: Essie! Essie!

ESSIE: Yes, Laura? (*ESSIE comes to the entrance*)

LAURA: Don't you think you and me could skip going to prayer meeting tonight? They can get along for once without us at the Temple. Set down, let's talk. You always did have a calm mind. Essie, what's happening to me?

ESSIE: One thing I've decided, Laura—me and Marietta's got to move. I been thinking about buying that little house in Mount Vernon a right smart while now. Tomorrow I'm gonna make a payment on it. You was right when you said I ought to get my daughter out of here.

LAURA: I think so, Essie—since I can't get Buddy out of my life. I guess I don't want to. I love that man.

ESSIE: Marietta loves C.J., too, and he loves her. Oh, why can't Buddy let them young people alone.

LAURA: Why can't he let that Gloria alone?

ESSIE: Laura, if you don't mind my saying it, when you're trying to keep your hand on God's plow, you can't afford to let the Devil get a holt—he'll plow a crooked furrow every time and plant a bad seed.

LAURA: Looks like the more I do for him, the less he cares—and I need *somebody* to care for me.

ESSIE: Stray cats, stray dogs! You know, when I were a young woman down in Richmond, I took in a stray dog once, so frisky and friendly in the street, smart and clean-looking. After I had him two or three days around the house, I found out that dog had just about everything a hound could have. He was so frisky and leaped and jumped so much because he had fleas. He scooted and slid across the floor so funny because he had the itching piles. He sneezed so cute because he had distemper. He also had a pinch of ringworm behind his ear, which is catching to children and humans. I had to get rid of that dog I had taken into my home.

LAURA: I get your point, Essie. (*LAURA pours a big drink as they talk*)

ESSIE: Stray dogs, stray cats, stray people, you can never tell about 'em. Never tell.

LAURA: We got a church full of stray people.

ESSIE: True, but when folks is under the spell of Christ, they generally behave themselves. Yet even religion do not touch every heart in time to save it from hell. You better pray over Buddy.

LAURA: Love, loot, and likker, that's his speed. Unholy trinity! *(LAURA lifts her glass)*

ESSIE: Uh! Uh! Uh!

LAURA: But you know, Essie, Buddy's got ways of making money I never knew existed—also of making love. I wish I knew how to handle a man like Buddy. I wish I was like mama was. She wasn't soft and good like you. But mama really could handle a man, Essie, did I ever tell you about my mama?

ESSIE: Not much. But so much excitement today's tired me out. Since we ain't going to the Temple, I think I'll go to bed.

LAURA: Oh, Essie, please stick with me. Set right there and relax yourself a little if you want to. Loosen your girdle and lemme tell you about Mama.

ESSIE: *(Yawns as she stretches out on the couch)* Excuse me if I happen to sneeze.

(By now LAURA, more than a little tipsy, returns often to the bottle)

LAURA: Mama was the hell-raisingest woman in Charlotte society. She's dead now, but North Carolina ain't forgot about Mama yet. From a good family, too, but they put her out when I was born—I'm illegitimate, you know. The principal of the school was my father— married and a father twice before he fathered me. He never would graduate my mama from school after she became pregnant, which he did not consider respectable for a student to do. But do you think Mama cared? Never! She just said, "Who gives a damn?" and stayed right on there until the day she died having her thirteenth baby at the age of forty-four. Mama should have known better, but she kept on producing black, yellow, and brownskin children for thirty years. She had so many marriage licenses around the house that one overlapped the other! Every time Mama got drunk she wanted to get married. As for men, Mama could jive a man back, make him run and butt his head against the wall, lay down his month's salary at her feet, and then beg her for a nickel. But don't let a man do her wrong! Mama knew how to protect herself. Fight back like a wildcat! I *admired* my mother. I wish I had her gumption with men. If you think I got energy, you should've seen Mama. Ball all night, play all day, drink a bootlegger dry—and still looked like a glamor chick when she died. This whisky I'm downing tonight would be a soft drink to my mama. And that Big-Eyed Buddy I'm so weak about, that I'm worried as to where he's at right now—to Mama, Buddy would be nothing but a play toy. Take a man like Buddy seriously? Not Mama! She would bust his conk wide open. They made women in them days! I take after her, too. The rest of Mama's children turned out to be nothing—wasted—all fell by the wayside except me, Sister Laura Reed. *(ESSIE is sound asleep now, so LAURA's eyes turn to the past. She speaks to her mother)* I made it, mama! Look at this place, Mama! Look at this fine silk sofa. Look at these chairs—French, Mama. Look them drapes, the best money can buy. And what am I drinking? Ten dollar Scotch! *(LAURA fills her glass again, staggers proudly to the mirror, and lifts it to her own reflection)* Mama, you hear me, don't you? I'm gonna make a toast. A toast to your daughter, Laura. A toast—to Miss Bitch.

BLACKOUT

MUSICAL BRIDGE: *Choral singing of "What He's Done for Me" gradually growing in volume and intensity as the tambourines shimmer. The song continues into next scene under dialogue.*

Act II, Scene 2

Robing room under the stage of Tambourine Temple. Music and the beat of BIRDIE LEE's drums drift from above. MATTIE MORNINGSIDE, stout mistress of the robes, sits on the lap of Laura's chauffeur, CHAR-LIE WINDUS, a tiny little man in livery, completely hidden by her enormous girth.

MATTIE: Windus, where you left Sister Laura?

WINDUS: Setting by herself in the back seat of the car outside and she didn't look too happy—waiting to see—

MATTIE: *(Rises)* You don't have to tell me! Buddy comes driving up nowadays in that red sports car just as brazen, with Gloria setting beside him as if she were his wife. Sister Laura's going to crack-up and all over Buddy Lomax—who everybody knows is a mother-fouler.

WINDUS: "As the eagle fouleth his nest," the text goes.

MATTIE: Sister Essie's got plenty of sense, buying herself a home in the suburbs. She and her daughter seems so happy with it—a porch, a swing, a nice yard, grass—better'n being all crowded up here in Harlem with you devilish men. The ruination of *any* young girl.

(But LAURA has already appeared in the doorway. She enters)

LAURA: You needn't hurry now, Windus. Just hold the car at the door till services are over.

WINDUS: Yes, ma'am, Miss Laura. I'll be right outside. Right there!
  (The chauffeur exits)

LAURA: Is Sister Essie here yet?

MATTIE: No, ma'am. It takes a right smart time to get down from Mount Vernon.

LAURA: Seems so. I guess everybody else has come in.

MATTIE: Two of the Gloriettas are here, but not Miss Gloria. But the chorus is all upstairs singing beautiful. Hear Sister Birdie Lee now?

BIRDIE: What He's done for me!
  What He's done for me!
  I never shall forget
  What He's done for me!

MATTIE: That Birdie Lee! Ha-ha! Chipper as a cricket!

LAURA: I hear her attracting attention to herself. Hang my coat up carefully. On a hanger!

MATTIE: On a hanger!

LAURA: Minks don't grow on trees, Sister Mattie.

MATTIE: Sure don't, and you got a *fine* piece of skin for a lady minister.

LAURA: Prostitutes dress well, call girls and madams. I don't see why saints shouldn't.

MATTIE: No, ma'am! Saints should look the best. I'll bring your robes.
  (As MATTIE exits, laughter is heard from the hall. BUDDY, very well groomed, enters with a case of Holy Water. He is drunk)

BUDDY: Holy Water from the River Jordan! Ha! Ha! Ha!
  (GLORIA in dark glasses, sporty cap, and tight-fitting gown beneath a smart leather jacket, rushes in behind BUDDY)

LAURA: It's about time you're getting here. Gloria, you're late. I want everybody on that platform—including you—when I make my entrance.

GLORIA: I told Buddy to hurry.

LAURA: *You* told Buddy to hurry?

BUDDY: We just stopped for a little nip.

LAURA: Well, nip yourself on up the steps with some cases of that Holy Water.
  (As LAURA turns away, BUDDY pinches GLORIA playfully on the thigh. GLORIA giggles and prances tipsily toward the robe closet)

GLORIA: Sister Mattie, help me with my robe. It looks like I'm late.
  (GLORIA exits)
BUDDY: Aw, Laura, let your chauffeur lug that damn Holy Water around.
LAURA: He's paid to drive. This is your job.
BUDDY: Aw, well then, I might as will take off all my coats if I have to work. *(BUDDY tosses his camel's hair coat across the table, and removes his jacket as well, revealing a rich canary-yellow shirt)*
LAURA: How come Gloria can't make it here under her own steam?
BUDDY: All good-looking women like to ride on rubber—and Gloria *is* good looking.
  (GLORIA returns in a Chinese sequin outfit, more like a night-club costume than a robe. Her cap is still on her head)
GLORIA: I'm set to ascend the rostrum!
LAURA: About your sports cap, baby, ain't you gonna take it off?
GLORIA: Oh, that open car of Buddy's, the wind ruffles my hair!
  (GLORIA tosses her hat to BUDDY and exits laughing)
BUDDY: Cute kid!
LAURA: She can stay out of my car.
BUDDY: *(Looks at her nonchalantly)* You're bugging me, woman!
LAURA: What?
BUDDY: *(Playfully staggering toward her)* Do you want me to break one of these bottles of Holy Water over your head? Then you'd really be baptized.
LAURA: I'm not playing. Sometimes you try my soul, Buddy Lomax.
BUDDY: Jesus had a cross to bear, didn't He? Well, so has everyone. Let's put up with each other's crosses. Say, if you sell ten cases of this Holy Water tonight, we can get that color TV tomorrow.
LAURA: And who wants a color TV?
BUDDY: I do. Hey, did you see Gloria's picture in *Cue* this week? Marty's got a thousand juke boxes lined up for her record. And Laura, old kid, everybody in the syndicate's grinning like chess-cats the way the Harlem numbers bankers picked up business since you've been giving out texts. What luck, huh? The third week straight one of your numbers hit. That's got everybody talking—
LAURA: Don't try to change the subject, Buddy, sometimes I'm dis-gusted with you. Especially when you're high.
BUDDY: Aw, cut the yak-yak, Laura. I'm gonna pack this case of Jordan Water upstairs and listen to the rock and roll. Are you coming?

LAURA: In due time. I've got to robe myself pretty tonight—to compete with the Gloriettas.

BUDDY: Gild your lily, baby! Drape your frame!

(*BUDDY exits with a case of water. MATTIE returns with two robes, one green, one scarlet*)

LAURA: I'll take the red robe tonight.

(*MATTIE helps LAURA dress as ESSIE, MARIETTA, and C.J. enter, and hang their coats on the wall. Upstairs the CHORUS is singing with a rousing beat, "What He's Done for Me"*)

ESSIE: Good evening! Music sounds great upstairs.

LAURA: Long as I don't hear Birdie croaking! I believe I'm gonna have to get rid of that old woman.

ESSIE: Why? The way she hits them drums, the congregation loves her.

LAURA: That's just it, I want them to love *me*—and you—without competition.

ESSIE: They do, Laura.

MARIETTA: Mama, we're going on upstairs.

LAURA: C.J. should have been up there at eight o'clock like the others.

MARIETTA: It's my fault, Aunt Laura. He came up to Mount Vernon to spend the afternoon, and I made him a cake that was late getting out of the oven.

C.J.: It was good though—um-mm-m!

LAURA: Cooking for him already, and you're not married yet!

MARIETTA: We will be, soon's I graduate. Come on, C.J.

(*They exit. MATTIE exits also to return the green robe to the closet*)

ESSIE: C.J.'s a nice boy, Laura. I'm so glad for my child.

LAURA: Me, too. And I'm glad you've got Marietta in the country. Essie, powder your face a little, won't you, before you go upstairs? That spotlight on the rostrum shows up your liver spots. And tell them musicians I want plenty of drum rolls, tambourines, and hallelujahs tonight when I appear on the rostrum.

ESSIE: The spirit don't need all that theatre kind of ballyhoo, Laura.

LAURA: No, baby, but I do.

(*Meanwhile, LAURA has dumped the contents of her purse on the dressing table, as if searching for something*)

ESSIE: Laura, why are you dumping everything out on the table?

LAURA: Why don't you just go on upstairs, Essie, and make your presence known? . . . Sister Mattie, come here!

(*Puzzled, ESSIE exits, shaking her head. MATTIE bustles in*)

MATTIE: I'm coming.

LAURA: Mattie, go upstairs and tell Brother Buddy I said to come down here a minute—*now!* And suppose you sit in with the chorus and sing a little. I want to speak to him *private*.

> (*MATTIE exits singing "What He's Done for Me." Shortly BUDDY enters with mock piety*)

BUDDY: What wantest thou, Sister Laura?

LAURA: Did you take a one hundred dollar bill out of my purse?

BUDDY: Sure did.

LAURA: Ain't the cut you're getting from this church a plenty for you?

BUDDY: *(Answers impudently)* No.

LAURA: *(Rises angrily)* You still don't have enough of *my* money to spend on the bitch?

BUDDY: Watch your language, Sister! What bitch?

LAURA: Huh! The chick you and Marty like so much. Who's she sleeping with? Or does she rotate between you?

BUDDY: *(Moves toward LAURA threateningly)* I ought to knock your teeth down your throat—and don't think I won't. Lay off Gloria!

LAURA: That slut can't even sing in tune—a cheap little rock-and roller.

BUDDY: She's no rock-and roller. She's got a contract at the Vanguard, moving on up to the Blue Angel. Next thing you know she can say goodbye to this hallelujah house and open at the Copa because Marty's underwriting her.

LAURA: If she don't stay out of my car, somebody'll be undertaking her.

BUDDY: *(Cool again, grins as he takes out a cigarette)* Your car? *(He lights up nonchalantly)*

LAURA: Yes, I said *my* car. Who meets the notes? It's still not paid for. My car! Bold as that slut is, it's a wonder it's not all written up in *Jet* or some other gossip columns. Gloria Dawn—even her name sounds phoney. A little strumpet!

BUDDY: *(Takes a deep draw on his cigarette, obviously enjoying LAURA's jealousy)* She's young, baby. But you, pshaw, you been a good old wagon, but you done broke down.

> (*BUDDY blows the smoke of his cigarette into her face. Hurt, LAURA bites her lip in silence. Suddenly tears come against her will. Upstairs the CHORUS is singing loudly "When I Touch His Garment."*)

CHORUS: When I touch His garment . . . (etc.)

LAURA: Buddy, you don't have to go out of your way to hurt me. I just wondered who took my money, that's all.

BUDDY: You know who took it. I can have it, can't I?

LAURA: Yes, Buddy, I guess you can—anything I got. Buddy, tell me, why is it, looks like men can't never act right? You try to treat a man nice, and he turns around and drops the boom on you. Ain't a woman supposed to be nothing but dirt under a man's feet?

BUDDY: That's all, in my opinion—and you feel good under *my* feet. *(BUDDY grinds his cigarette butt beneath his foot)*

LAURA: You don't try to hide *your* way with women, do you?

BUDDY: Why try? You can't hide nothing from God, can you? Nor the police. So why try to hide it from anybody else? The police I can *pay* off. God you *pray* off.

LAURA: How about me?

BUDDY: *(Leaps forward savagely)* You? I'll slap the hell out of you if you fool with me—and make you like it. *(LAURA does not move)* Maybe you think I won't, heh? *(BUDDY slaps her full in the face. Her purse drops to the floor as she takes a step back to avoid a second blow)* And I'll do it again . . . I'll slug you right into your grave.

    (BUDDY glares at LAURA, then wheels to cross to a chair. LAURA, obviously frightened for her life, picks up her purse as BUDDY sits down. As BUDDY talks, she puts her purse into ESSIE's coat pocket where her hand lingers for a moment)

LAURA: What do you want to hit me like this for?

BUDDY: For kicks maybe, baby—to see you cry—so I can drink your tears.

LAURA: I'm not the type to cry, Buddy Lomax.

BUDDY: I'll make you! I guess you know, a used-up bitch like you is supposed to put out some money to keep a man like me around. And believe me, baby, now that you've got me, you're gonna *keep* me. I ain't gonna let you give me up. Two old saints like you and Essie might pull into the Temple wrecks out of the gutter like Crow-For-Day and Birdie Lee—but me, I bring in the young chicks. There's something about me that women go for. You admit I'm a man, don't you, kid? Heh, baby? I love you. Come here, lemme taste your lipstick.

LAURA: What?

BUDDY: Come here, I said! I want to kiss you.

LAURA: Kiss me? After the way you treat me?

BUDDY: Beat a woman till she cries, then kiss her till she laughs—is my recipe. Are you coming?

LAURA: No!

(As LAURA backs away, BUDDY lunges toward her like a monstrous ape)

BUDDY: God damn you, I'll kiss you! Or kill you, one! *(His arm is raised as if to strike her. But instead, he grabs her, one hand behind her head, and forces her to lift her lips to his. With savage ferocity he moans)* You sweet rascal of God! You . . . rascal . . . of God!

(With what appears to be a passionate embrace, they kiss. But as the wide sleeves of LAURA's scarlet robe sweep upward and her arms go about BUDDY's shoulders, there is the gleam of a switch-blade knife in her hand, raised in fear and self-defense. At that moment BIRDIE LEE enters on her way to the LADIES ROOM)

BBIRDIE: Oh! Excuse me—but I got to go!

(LAURA jerks loose from BUDDY. ESSIE's knife falls from her hand. A strange look comes over BUDDY's face—as he realizes the knife was buried in his back. He cries out, puts one hand to his mouth, and finds he is belching blood)

BUDDY: What did you—? Aw-aa-a! I'll kill you! You dirty—Ah-aaa-aa-a! I'll—I'll—I'll—kill you!

(BIRDIE sees BUDDY lunge at LAURA as she backs away. BUDDY falls to the floor flat on his face, the back of his canary yellow shirt red with blood. LAURA screams threateningly at the astonished BIRDIE LEE)

BIRDIE: Oh, my God! My God! Aw-aaa-aa-a—

LAURA: *(Covers BIRDIE's mouth)* Birdie Lee, don't call on God—or nobody else. Just shut up! Be speechless! If you so much as open your mouth, with my own hands I'll— *(The threatening claws of LAURA's fingers sweep upwards, ready to strangle. BIRDIE trembles)* Get back upstairs to your drums, Birdie Lee! And give me a great *big* drum roll when I ascend the pulpit. You hear me! A great . . . big . . . drum . . . roll!

(BIRDIE rushes off in a frightened exit. LAURA looks down for a moment at BUDDY's body. Then as the drums roll above and the tambourine's shake ecstatically, she throws one end of her golden stole about her throat and exits to join the services)

BLACKOUT

MUSICAL BRIDGE: *LAURA's entrance theme—shimmer of tambourines into mounting drum roll, crash of cymbals, then "Home to God."*

Act II, Scene 3

Rostrum of Tambourine Temple with full CHORUS, the GLORIETTAS,
 CROW-FOR-DAY, BIRDIE LEE and ESSIE present. ESSIE, at the
 center of the rostrum, sings as the CHOIR supports her.
ESSIE: I'm going to lay down my soul
      At the foot of the cross.
      I'm going to tell my Jesus
      Just what sin has cost.
      I'm going to find my Savior,
      Whisper in His ear,
      I'm going to tell Him, Savior,
      My salvation's near.
CHOIR: Oh, this world has been my dressing room,
      But now at last, dear Lord, I'm going home.
      Down, down in the mire
      Too long my feet have trod.
      Now, at last, I'm going home to God!
      (As the refrain nears its end, LAURA enters walking regally in
      rhythm from the wings, her scarlet robe swaying. ESSIE retires to
      her seat, leaving the pulpit to LAURA. The CHOIR continues to
      hum as she speaks)
LAURA: Move on up a little higher! Thank God! Casting off shackles,
    getting rid of devils, thank God! Wrestling with evil, and downing
    Satan! Oh, yes, this world is nothing but a dressing room where we
    put on our robes and prepare for Jordan, heavenly Jordan!
CHORUS: Amen! Amen!
LAURA: And now, directly from the Jordan River, I bring you again that
    precious water, that Holy Water that only Sister Laura has, imported
    just for you from the River of Life. Blessed water to purify your
    home. *(ESSIE rises with bowed head and exits as LAURA lifts a bottle)*
    While Sister Essie goes for her meditation, ushers, pass amongst the
    people. One dollar a bottle, children, just one dollar! Get a bottle
    tonight while there is yet time. Ushers, if you run out, there's more
    on the rostrum—just like the bottle I hold in my hand. *(A muffled*
    scream is heard off stage. Heads turn curiously as the humming stops.
    LAURA suddenly drops the bottle with a crash, but quickly recovers
    her poise) Oh, my friends, the power of this water—it almost makes
    me faint with glory! Buy a bottle! Buy a bottle tonight. But don't
    drop yours as I dropped mine. Now, whilst the ushers pass with

the bottles, let's have a few testimonials. Let one and all declare his determination. *(LAURA sings)*

Who will be a witness for my Lord?
Who will be a witness for my Lord
On the day of jubilee!
(BIRDIE LEE sings loudly)

BIRDIE: I will be a witness for my Lord!
I will be a witness for my Lord
On the day of jubilee!
Yes, I'll stand up and be a witness!

LAURA: *(Stares threateningly at BIRDIE, then walks over to MARI-ETTA)* Well, since Sister Birdie Lee seems to want to take over—Marietta, go tell your mother she can return from her meditations—and be a witness, too.

(MARIETTA exits. BIRDIE projects defiance as she leaves her drums)

BIRDIE: My testimony this evening is that I want to tell you all what it means to be a witness—I mean a witness for God, and a witness for men and women, too. Lord, lemme hold my holt! I were in a trial once, a court trial—and I lied. I let an innocent man go to jail for something he didn't do—to protect my man I thought I loved. Another man served time, innocent as a lamb. Whereas the one I lied for lived to cut up, and shoot up two or three more people. In fact, that man did not appreciate what I did for him. He lived to kick my—excuse me—I meant to say—to beat and mistreat me, too. And he were so mean he wouldn't let me do a damn—excuse me—I mean not a blessed thing. I'm just excited tonight, folks. But I tries always to keep bad words out of my mouth, now that I's a Christian woman. And what I's trying to say to everybody this evening is, that when the time comes, in God's name, I know I got a determination—and my determination is— *(Her speech blends into song)*

I'm gonna testify! I'm gonna testify!
I'm gonna testify till the day I die.
I'm gonna tell the truth
For the truth don't lie.
Folks, I'm gonna testify! . . .
(LAURA sits staring angrily into the audience)
I'm gonna tell the truth
For the truth don't lie!
Yes, I'm gonna testify!
(As BIRDIE finishes, LAURA rises defiantly)

LAURA: Lemme tell you one thing, church, I say—
> We all shall be free!
> Children, we all shall be free!
> Children, we all shall be free
> When the Lord shall appear.
> *(LAURA turns and looks at BIRDIE to intimidate her)*
> We want no cowards in this band
> That from their colors fly.
> We call for valiant hearted souls
> That are not afraid to die.
> I mean—
> Children, we all shall be free!

CHORUS: Children, we all shall be free!
> Children, we all shall be free!
> When the Lord shall appear.
> *(MARIETTA runs from the wings to whisper frantically to LAURA)*

MARIETTA: Sister Laura! Sister Laura! Oh, Sister Laura!

LAURA: Excuse me, saints, let me go to see what little sister Marietta wants that's so urgent. Until Sister Essie and me resume our seats on the rostrum, I'll turn the services over to our beloved deacon here, known in love to all of us as Brother Crow-For-Day. Deacon, come forward!
> *(LAURA follows MARIETTA. Both exit as BIRDIE gives a drum roll, then a contemptuous thump. CROW advances singing)*

CROW: Leaning, leaning,
> Leaning on the everlasting arms!
> Leaning, leaning,
> Leaning on the everlasting arms . . .
> *(As the CHORUS joins in, the song rises. Gradually lights dim to darkness, pinpointing DEACON CROW)*

BLACKOUT

MUSICAL BRIDGE: *Choral singing continuing "Leaning on the Everlasting Arms."*

Act II, Scene 4

Robing room. Having tried to minister to BUDDY, ESSIE is aghast over his body, with blood on her white robe. SISTER MATTIE MORNING-SIDE enters, stops at the doorway and begins to tremble at the sight.

MATTIE: Oh-ooo-oo-o, my God! Somebody's killed Buddy! Buddy! Buddy! Police! Somebody get the police! *(MATTIE runs to the door calling the chauffeur)* Windus! Windus! Get the police quick! The police. *(MATTIE returns to stare at the body. MARIETTA enters)* Lord have mercy! Sister Essie's knife right there on the floor.

MARIETTA: Mama didn't do it!

ESSIE: Mattie, you know I didn't do it.

MATTIE: Sister Laura were in the pulpit—it's your knife on the floor and there's blood on your robe.

ESSIE: Buddy were dead when I first touched him, stone cold dead. I tried to see if I could help him, but he were gone.

MATTIE: You didn't try to help him when he was living, did you? Folks know you couldn't abide him. Now look! *(MATTIE shudders)*

ESSIE: Somebody took my knife out of my pocket. I left it where it always was, in my coat. *(ESSIE goes to her coat hanging on the wall. She feels in her pocket and surprised, pulls out LAURA's purse)* Laura's pocketbook!

MATTIE: Sister Essie, you was the last one here.

MARIETTA: My mother couldn't do anything like that. She wouldn't! You know she wouldn't. She just couldn't. Oh, why don't Sister Laura come here?

ESSIE: *(Comforts MARIETTA)* God will straighten things out, Marietta.

> *(The music of "Leaning on the Everlasting Arms" comes drifting down as TWO POLICEMEN hurry in followed by the CHAUFFEUR)*

MATTIE: It's her knife on the floor. See the blood on her robe! Lord, how in a minute a saint can change into a sinner! Officer, who'd of thought it of Sister Essie?

COP: Don't nobody touch the body. We'll send for the coroner. Officer, put that woman in the squad car while I go phone.

> *(The COP exits. As the second OFFICER leads ESSIE out, MARIETTA follows weeping with ESSIE's coat)*

MATTIE: Poor Brother Buddy, God rest his soul!

> *(MATTIE exits. LAURA enters, takes off her scarlet robe, and with it covers BUDDY's body. Suddenly she buries her face in her hands)*

LAURA: Oh, my God! . . . Oh, God! . . . My God!

BLACKOUT

MUSICAL BRIDGE: *CHOIR humming "Bible" with high soprano obbligato between phrases.*

Act II, Scene 5

A jail cell. Alone in the darkness, the light gradually reveals the anguish in ESSIE's face as she sings, clasping a Bible.

ESSIE:Thank God, I've got the Bible in my hand . . . (etc.)

(MALE VOICES are heard approaching)

WARDEN: You're the first visitor she's had since your daughter came down with her last night.

CROW: I certainly thank you, sir, for escorting me in.

(WARDEN enters with CROW-FOR-DAY)

WARDEN: Mrs. Johnson, your husband to see you.

ESSIE: My husband?

CROW: *(Nervously motioning her to be silent)* Shsss-sss-ss-s!

ESSIE: Deacon Crow, I'm glad to see you.

WARDEN: I'll give you folks ten minutes together.

CROW: I thank you, sir. *(The WARDEN exits as ESSIE looks condemn-ingly at CROW who begins to explain)* Sister Essie, they said *nobody* but relatives. I had to tell some kind of little white lie to get in here.

ESSIE: Deacon Crow, you know we ain't—

CROW: I know it. We's related only in spirit. But to tell the truth, Sister Essie, I been kind of looking at you a right smart lately with a manly eye. Sometimes I says to myself, "Big Mama, you look good to me." Meaning no harm, of course.

ESSIE: Crow, this is no time for foolishness. I'm troubled in mind.

CROW: Put your mind at rest, Sister Essie. The Lord has already this morning give us glad tidings. You gonna get out of this mess. The church has got you and Sister Laura both the best lawyers in town. But the big news is, Sister Laura confessed—

ESSIE: Confessed?

CROW: That she killed Buddy Lomax. She prayed all night and con-fessed all morning—and nobody made her.

ESSIE: Poor Laura! Now she'll be behind bars.

CROW: I been behind bars fifty times. It ain't so bad.

ESSIE: This is my first time, and I sweated blood. But I guess if Jesus could stand what was done to Him, I can stand this mite of punish-ment visited on me. Deacon Crow, I deserve this punishment. When I seen what was happening in our church—all that unholy water sell-ing, numbers and stuff—I should have riz in my wrath and cleaned house. But no! Instead I just set and sung. That's what's been the matter with me all these years—setting, just setting—accepting what comes, receiving the Lord's blessings whilst the eagle foulest his nest—until he gets struck in the back with my own knife.

CROW: Sister Essie!

ESSIE: Lemme speak, Crow! It don't do to just set. Me, I let Buddy fill the house of God with sin, let vanities of vanities take over, let Laura parade her fur coats before them poor peoples what brought us their hard-earned money for God's work. Me, I let our church become the devil's playground. Religion's got no business being made into a gyp game. That part of God that is in anybody *is not to be played with*—and everybody has got a part of God in them. I let Laura play with God. Me, Essie Belle Johnson. Deacon Crow, if I get out of here—

CROW: You're gonna be cleared! Hallelujah!

WARDEN: Cut the noise! We keep a quiet jail.

ESSIE: Sh-sss-ss.

CROW: You're going to be cleared. You'll be out today, just as soon as your lawyer gets down here with the papers.

ESSIE: Then, Crow, lemme tell you one thing—from here on I, Essie Belle Johnson, am gonna run my church. And I'm gonna make it what I visioned—a Rock of Goodness in the heart of Harlem. We's a wealthy church now, Crow. I'm gonna buy that old building next door for a clubhouse for our anniversaries and teas and such. Oh, joyful Rock! That empty vacant lot, we're gonna turn into a playground so our teenagers can play basketball in summer and skate in winter.

CROW: Happy Rock!

ESSIE: And my daughter, Marietta, I'm gonna send to be a nurse—like she wants to be—so she can help me take care of the sick in our church. Whilst I pray with them, Marietta can relieve their pain. Oh, how great Tambourine Temple can be!

CROW: Amen! Amen! Amen!

WARDEN: I say, cut that noise. Your time's up anyhow.

CROW: See you at services this evening, Sister Essie.

(*CROW exits singing "Leaning" as WARDEN escorts LAURA handcuffed, dressed in black*)

ESSIE: Laura!

LAURA: I can't look at you, Essie.

ESSIE: You got to look at me, Laura.

(*WARDEN permits LAURA to pause*)

LAURA: Forgive me—after what I did to you.

ESSIE: I forgive you, Laura.

LAURA: Oh, pray for me, Essie, please. I couldn't let you go on trial for me. I told the police. I had to tell them. I confessed. Essie, I love you. Pray for me.

ESSIE: I pray for you, Laura. In my heart, I pray.

> (*The WARDEN leads LAURA away. Tears flow down ESSIE's face as she clutches the bars. The light fades. Suddenly there is a great burst of music as the CHOIR sings "God's Got a Way."*)

BLACKOUT

MUSICAL BRIDGE: *"God's Got a Way" as immediately revealed in the following scene.*

Act II, Scene 6

Tambourine Temple in a blaze of light. The CHORUS is newly and more beautifully robed than ever. For this gala night a trumpet, and perhaps other instruments have been added to the band. On one side of the banked platform is C.J. with his guitar, MARIETTA on the other. BIRDIE LEE is at the drums. Only GLORIA is missing as CROW stands singing proudly at the rostrum, backed by the CHOIR.

CHOIR: God's got a way!
> God's got a way!
> God's got a way!
> His wonders to perform.

CROW: Just trust in Him,
> Just trust in Him,
> Just trust in Him,
> He'll keep you from all harm.

BIRDIE: Hold your holt, Crow! Yes! Hold your holt on God!

CHOIR: God's love can save,
> God's love can save,
> God's love can save,
> Oh, yes, I know it can!

BIRDIE: It can! It can! It can! Yes, it can!

CHOIR: God's got a way,
> God's got a way,
> God's got a way,
> That's unbeknownst to man.

CROW: God's way—unbeknownst to man! What I wants to say tonight is, church, let him who is *without* sin cast the first stone—if he dares! Let him who is without sin put his feet in a saint's shoes— and see if he don't tread on thorns. Thorns! See if you ain't tried by the fire. And when you have been tried, you can never be the same again. What was we all once but wrecks on the shoals of life? *(CROW mounts the drum stand)* What was we all but flotsam and jetsam in the gutters of this world? But look up here tonight on this rostrum and see if you see flotsam. See if you see jetsam. See if you see anything up here but light—light and happiness and whole-sam and health-sam. No wrecks! No flots, no jets, no rolling stones tossed on the tides of sin. Tambourine Temple has saved many a soul.

BIRDIE: It saved me! Saved me! Saved me!

VOICES: Me, too! Me, too!

CROW: And when a soul is saved in this church, it is really saved.

BIRDIE: Yes, 'tis! Yes, 'tis! 'Tis! 'Tis! *'Tis!*

CROW: And who ought to know, better than you and me, Birdie Lee, because we was down there!

BIRDIE: Down there, Crow!

CROW: Down there!

BIRDIE: Yes, we was!

CROW: Down there! Now we got to save others. Ain't that right, Birdie Lee?

BIRDIE: Right! Right! Right, I say!

CROW: Then tell 'em about it, Sister Birdie, tell 'em!

> *(BIRDIE begins to testify in song as CROW takes over on the drums)*

BIRDIE: When you see some sinner leave
Iniquity's dark den
And turn his feet toward Canaan,
Just help him to begin.
Christians, take his hand
And show him God's his friend.
Just lead him on and say amen!
> *(BIRDIE descends from drum stand as CHOIR joins in)*
Let the church say amen!
Let the church say amen!
When a sinner comes to Jesus,
Let the church say amen!

Licker drinking brother
Drowned in alcohol,

Leave your empty glasses
And hear the Savior's call.
Christians, take his hand
And show him God's his friend.
Just lead him on and say amen!

CHOIR: Let the church say amen!
Let the church say amen!
When a sinner comes to Jesus,
Let the church say amen!

BIRDIE: *(Invites AUDIENCE to participate)* When I say *Amen,* let everybody say *Amen!* Come on, sing! Sing with me!
(The Refrain is repeated)

MATTIE: Listen, wayward sister,
Though you have sunk so low,
Ask—and He will wash your
Sins as white as snow.
Christians, take her hand
And show her God's her friend
Just lead her on and say amen!
(MATTIE shakes her tambourine)

CHOIR: Let the church say amen!
Let the church say amen!
When a sinner comes to Jesus,
Let the church say amen!
(Chorus is repeated as BROTHER BUD and MATTIE prance across the rostrum shaking tambourines in competition with each other)

ALL: Oh, let the church say amen!
Let the church say amen!
When a sinner comes to Jesus,
Let the church say amen!
(BIRDIE shouts. ESSIE rushes in with a newspaper in her hand)

ESSIE: God works in mysterious ways His wonders to perform. Church, Sister Laura's lawyers have got the detrimentation—the charge is not murder, not manslaughter—just self-defense. So she won't go to the electric chair—just the pen. See! *(ESSIE holds up the front page of the* Daily News *with a full page photo of LAURA. She reads its caption)* "SEPIA SONGSTRESS OF SALVATION SHEDS HER SHACKLES. Laura Wright Reed, darling of the District Attorney's Office since her sensational expose of Harlem rackets, is free on bail." Newspapers tonight just full of how the end of Buddy Lomax

unearthed a cesspool of crime in New York City and the Nation—
a syndicate with pay-offs from the corner candy store that writes
numbers, right on up to the cornerstone of government that protects
the Martys of the underworld. Behold! Let your eyes believe what
you see! Repentant—and with head bowed down—ready to serve
years up the river—Sister Laura comes back to the fold.

CROW: Back to the fold . . .

BUD: God's got a way! Oh, yes! He's got a way!

CROW: Back to the fold—

God's got a way! Oh, yes!

*(As the CHOIR sings, with head down LAURA enters clad in
black as she was in prison)*

CHOIR: God's got a way!

God's got a way!

God's got a way

His wonders to perform . . . hum . . .

(The CHOIR continues humming as LAURA kneels)

LAURA: Church, I know my punishment is coming, got to come. I
know it will. But help me to bear up, children, help me to bear up.
Tonight I'm out on bail, that's all. I still got to face the jury, stand
trial, and take my punishment. But thank God, for a little while, I'm
free, and back again with you, my friends, with you. And I have come
to confess to God, before this church and before the world tonight,
that I have sinned, I have sinned, sinned, sinned . . . *(Her anguish
turns into song)*

I have sinned,
Now I bow my head in shame,
Not for what sin did to me—
But to my Savior's name.
I have sinned,
Now I must atone
For others I have led astray,
Not for myself alone.
I could bear my agony
If all the hurt were mine,
But I have used the dust of sin
Others' eyes to blind.
I confess—confessing
That all the time I knew
When I was sinning, God,

I was sinning against you—
Against the one who loved me most—
Lord, God, against you.
   (She speaks against the music)
Mine was a sumptuous kind of sin
Wrapped in diamonds and fur,
Scattering money to the wind
Like frankincense and myrrh.
Mine was a giddy kind of sin,
Laughing without care
While others in this world I knew
Found no happiness anywhere.
Mine was a lustful kind of sin
Close, close in lustful arms.
Mine was a hungry kind of sin,
Hungry for a body's charms—
Not stopping, no, not thinking
Of another's harms—
The harms I brought to one who prayed
That I might know God's way.
The very ones who trusted me
Oh, God, I did betray. Ooooo-ooo-oo-o!
   (Sings)
I have sinned, sinned, sinned,
Now I bow my head in shame,
Confessing that I know I've sinned
Against my Savior's name,
Confessing all the time, I knew
That I was sinning against you—
Against the one who loves me most,
Lord, God, against you.
   Oh, pray for me, Church! Sister Essie, all of you, I beg sincerely,
      pray.
CROWD: We'll pray! Got to pray! Must pray! Amen!
LAURA: Church, can I pray with you?
CROWD: Pray with us! Pray! Sister Laura, pray!
LAURA: Can I sing, too, with you?
CROWD: Sing with us! Sing! Sister Laura, sing!
LAURA: Can I try to find my way back to salvation with you?
ESSIE: Laura, you can. Church, in the name of His charity and His

forgiveness, I request Sister Mattie now to place upon this come-home-again-lamb, her robe. Help her, Sisters, that she might be robed in the love of this Church.

(SISTERS of the church surround LAURA as she is robed)

CHOIR: God's love can save,

> God's love can save,
>
> God's love can save,
>
> Oh, yes, I know it can.

CROWD: So glad! Amen! So glad about God! Glad! . . . Glad! . . . Glad!

ESSIE: My heart is so full tonight—and for more reasons than one. Sister Laura back with us, and all you out there to witness her confession.

CROW: With that confession she'll be out in a year.

ESSIE: Now, another thing, you all don't know it, but you gonna have a matrimony here tonight. A surprise! Deacon Crow-For-Day come forward. *(A whisper of excited talk runs through the CHOIR at the expected marriage of CROW and ESSIE)* Deacon Crow, are you prepared for your function?

CROW: I is . . . And you, Essie Belle Johnson?

ESSIE: I am.

CROW: Then may I escort into your presence and the presence of Tambourine Temple our Rose of Sharon——

> *(MARIETTA rises and casts off her robe to reveal a wedding gown of white as a CHOIR MEMBER places on her head a veil of orange blossoms to the surprise of the church)*

And the Little David of our Church—

> *(C.J. doffs his robe to come forward in a summer tux with bou-tonniere. DEACON CROW takes his arm, while ESSIE leads her daughter by the hand to the altar)*

—that they might be united by the sweet honey of love.

CROWD: Thank God! Amen! Hallelujah!

LAURA: The marrying mother, Reverend Essie Bell Johnson! I am so glad I am here to witness this occasion.

CROW: Sister Essie, before you unite these children in holy wedlock, have you got a word to speak?

ESSIE: Deacon Crow, Sister Laura, church, everybody—my heart is too full to speak. Just gimme my tambourine. Let the music say it for me. Children, gather around and—

ALL: *(Sing)*

> If you've got a tambourine
>
> Shake it to the glory of God!

Glory! Glory! Glory!
Shake it to the glory of God!
    Tambourines!
Tambourines! Tambourines!
Tambourines to Glory!
WOMEN: If you've got a piano
    Play it to the glory of God!
Glory! Glory! Glory!
Play it to the glory of God!
    Piano
    Tambourines
Tambourines! Tambourines!
Tambourines to Glory!
LAURA: If you've got a song to sing
Sing it to the glory of God!
Glory! Glory! Glory!
Sing it to the glory of God!
    Song to sing
        Hallelujah!
        Hallelujah!
    Piano
    Tambourines
Tambourines! Tambourines!
Tambourines to Glory!
MEN: If you've got a drum to beat,
Beat it to the glory of God!
Glory! Glory! Glory!
Beat it to the glory of God!
    Drum to beat
    Song to sing
        Hallelujah!
        Hallelujah!
    Piano
    Tambourines
Tambourines! Tambourines!
Tambourines to Glory!
    *(There is a joyous singing, beating of drums, blowing of trumpets,
    and great shaking of tambourines as the curtain falls)*[4]

Gospel Plays

In 1963 Hughes wrote:

> The traditional Negro ministers—those who do not read their sermons but intone or shout them—are at their best when backed by swinging gospel choirs. The singers have a sense of drama equal to that of the ministers. Intuitively they know just when to sneak in a hum or moan a song behind the minister's words to heighten a sermon's dramatic values or embellish a Bible tale he may be telling. In the days when unwritten words made vivid the religious mysteries, the first plays grew out of the churches. Today in the American Negro churches of the gospel faiths, one can sometimes hear what amounts to highly effective religious drama, spontaneous and different at every service.
>
> In preparing my gospel song-play, *Black Nativity*, that is currently touring Europe, I visited a number of gospel temples in Harlem, usually arriving about ten at night when services were in full swing. I was never bored. Song and a sense of drama swirled around me. A mingling of ancient scripture and contemporary problems were projected with melodic intensity and rhythmic insistence. Every night I was drawn into the circle of oneness generated by the basic beat of the gospel tempo.[1]

Without a doubt, Hughes's gospel plays are his most enduring contribution to American theater, acclaimed by theater audiences and loved by church congregations who may know nothing of his other theatrical endeavors. *Black Nativity*, in fact, has become a Christmas staple of black churches all over the United States. Hughes originally called his first gospel play "Wasn't That a Mighty Day," but he changed the name to *Black Nativity* to honor what Arnold Rampersad describes as his "faith in the importance of a black racial sense," a decision made some years before *black* acquired general acceptance and one that caused some integration-minded actors originally cast for the production to leave. Finally, director Vinette Carroll assembled a company "almost entirely of true believers": Marion Williams and her all-woman "Stars of Faith" quartet, Rev. Alex Bradford to both sing and preach, and Princess Stewart as soloist.[2]

An immediate hit, *Black Nativity* opened on December 11, 1961, at the 41st Street Theatre on Broadway, moved to the York Theatre on First Avenue at Sixty-fourth Street, and closed at the end of January only for lack of a theater. Gian Carlo Menotti, the main force behind the Festival of Two Worlds at Spoleto, Italy, immediately arranged to bring it to his summer festival, and an extended European tour followed, the company returning to a sold-out week in Philharmonic Hall in Lincoln Center. An American tour followed that engagement, and European and American performances were frequent over the next three years, including ones in London and Chicago in 1963 and in Berlin in 1965. ABC televised the play on Christmas Eve 1962.[3]

Delighted with *Black Nativity*'s success, Hughes also recognized the delicate balance required to retain its integrity. He insisted, for example, that "the cast (in Act 2) must not be allowed to take bows after each number, as they did in London. They are portraying a revival or church meeting, NOT giving a concert. After reading the reviews of the return London engagement, he scolded the producers: "You will remember that I called to your attention something of this rather 'cute' quality in the narration at the Lincoln Center performances which seemed to me to give not quite the proper framework to the production, therefore throwing it a bit out of key and adding to its presentation a more 'childish' quality than is necessary." The role required, he reminded them, "an actor of dignity and presence who can give the narration the simple, straightforward, yet poetic feeling of reverence and wonder which its performance should have."[4]

Yet, in the gospel plays, Hughes recognized that he had found his form. According to Rampersad, he rapidly completed drafts of "Wasn't That a Mighty Day!" and *The Prodigal Son* in 1961, wrote *The Gospel Glow: A Passion Play* (alternately titled *Gospel Glory*) in 1962, and proposed *Master of Miracles: The Life of Christ* as the title for an evening incorporating all three plays.[5] A separate play named *Master of Miracles,* dated 1962, has since surfaced. *The Gospel Glow,* which Hughes described as the "first Negro passion play," premiered at Washington Temple, Church of God in Christ, in Bedford-Stuyvesant, New York, on October 26, 1962. *The Prodigal Son,* paired with Bertolt Brecht's *The Exception and the Rule,* opened at the Greenwich Mews Theatre on September 3, 1965, to enthusiastic reviews, drawing well after more than one hundred performances.[6] Producer Stella Holt closed the show to take *The Prodigal Son* on tour to Europe.

In a script of *The Prodigal Son* marked "Author's copy" and dated October 2, 1965, and which Hughes indicated was sent to the London production and to *Players Magazine,* the play continues on past the conclusion as published by the magazine. In this version, Jezebel takes center stage as the rest of the cast marches through the auditorium, and the Prodigal Son "breaks away to run smiling off with his Jezebel."[7] This graceful and humorous acknowledgment of human frailty and temptation's continual attraction is typical of much of Hughes's work. Why the editor chose not to publish Hughes' conclusion is unknown.

Hughes's gospel plays are, indeed, glorious. In them, Hughes accomplished a quintessential aspect of his artistic ambition: to enact and to celebrate his understanding of what W. E. B. Du Bois had so poignantly termed "The Souls of Black Folk" and the ways in which the language of faith expressed their sufferings, their aspirations, and their triumphs.

There is no coherent typescript for *Black Nativity* in the Langston Hughes Papers, and, in any event, there seem to be several versions of the play, using different songs in different sequences. The version reproduced here is that published in 1992 by the Dramatic Publishing Company, clearly in response to the demand for a readily accessible version of the often produced play. The typescripts for *The Gospel Glow* (there is a handwritten correction on the top page, which is marked "Revised Rehearsal Script," but a subsequent cover sheet uses "The Gospel Glory") and *Man of Miracles* were in a box at Harold Ober Associates; there is no evidence of the latter in the Langston Hughes Papers. The text of *The Prodigal Son* was published in *Players Magazine*, 43.1 (October/November 1967): 16–21.

Black Nativity
A Gospel Song-Play for a Variable Cast

1961, 1992[1]

Characters
(In order of appearance)

WOMAN
MAN
SINGERS (Townsfolk)
NARRATOR
OLD WOMAN
FOUR SHEPHERDS (Ned, Zed, Ted, Jed)
ELDER

Non-speaking roles

JOSEPH
MARY
THREE WISE MEN (Balthazar, Melchior, Caspar)

TIME: *When Christ was born.*
SETS: *None—only a platform of various levels and a star, a single glowing star high over a place that might be a manger.*
MOODS: *Reverence, awe, joy and jubilation.*
SONGS:

Act One: The Child Is Born

Joy To The World
My Way Is Cloudy
No Room At The Inn
Most Done Travelling
Oh, Jerusalem In The Morning

Poor Little Jesus
What You Gonna Name Your Baby
Wasn't That A Mighty Day!
Joy To The World—Reprise
Christ Is Born
No-Good Shepherd Boy
Go Tell It On The Mountain
Rise Up, Shepherd, And Follow!
What Month Was Jesus Born In?
Sweet Little Jesus Boy
Oh, Come All Ye Faithful

Act Two: The Word Is Spread

Meetin' Here Tonight
Holy Ghost, Don't Leave Me
We Shall Be Changed
The Blood Saved Me
Leak In The Building
Nobody Like The Lord
His Will Be Done
Said I Wasn't Gonna Tell Nobody
Get Away Jordan
Packin' Up
God Be With You

Act I

(*Prelude: Organ Music. Voices are heard offstage as MAN and WOMAN enter.*)
(*SONG: "JOY TO THE WORLD"*)
WOMAN: JOY TO THE WORLD!
   THE LORD HAS COME—
   LET EARTH RECEIVE HER KING.
   LET EVERY HEART PREPARE HIS ROOM.
MAN: LET HEAVEN AND NATURE SING.
   (*PILGRIMS enter down aisles to join WOMAN and MAN on stage.*)

SINGERS: JOY TO THE WORLD!
    THE LORD HAS COME—
    LET EARTH RECEIVE HER KING . . .
    (Light spots NARRATOR at side of stage.)
NARRATOR: IT CAME TO PASS IN THOSE DAYS, that there went
    out a decree from Caesar Augustus that all the world should be
    taxed. And this taxing was first made when Cyrenius was governor
    of Syria. And all went to be taxed, everyone into his own city.
    (The sunset lights left stage as MARY and JOSEPH enter.)
    And Joseph also went up from Galilee to be taxed—out of the
    city of Nazareth into Judea, unto the city of David which is called
    Bethlehem—with his wife, Mary, being great with child . . . "I think
    —oh, Joseph—I think my time's most come."
    (SONG: "MY WAY'S CLOUDY")
SINGERS: OH BRETHREN, MY WAY'S CLOUDY
    SEND ONE ANGEL DOWN!
WOMAN: THERE'S FIRE IN THE EAST,
    THERE'S FIRE IN THE WEST,
    THERE'S FIRE AMONG
    THE METHODISTS.
    SATAN'S MAD AND I'M SO GLAD
    HE MISSED THE SOUL HE THOUGHT HE HAD
    THIS IS THE YEAR OF THE JUBILEE,
    THE LORD HATH COME TO SET US FREE.
SINGERS: OH BRETHREN, MY WAY'S CLOUDY,
    SEND ONE ANGEL DOWN!
    (Almost, but not quite beneath the star, JOSEPH knocks repeatedly
    at the door. MARY, too tired to stand any longer, sinks to the
    roadway. An irate INNKEEPER's words are heard.)
NARRATOR: "I have no room! Didn't I tell you *no*, before? Why do
    you come back? What do you keep knocking for? My inn's full. I've
    got no room for you and that woman there. This is no hospital. I
    keep no midwives about. I'm sorry, but there's no place here. No
    room! No, I say, no!"
SINGERS: OH BRETHREN, MY WAY'S CLOUDY.
    SEND ONE ANGEL DOWN!
NARRATOR: No room! No room at the inn! No room at the rich fine
    hotel. No room!
    (JOSEPH lifts MARY to her feet. They struggle on, wandering
    through street after street searching for a place to stay.)

OLD WOMAN: Did you hear about it—a woman named Mary, they won't let her in the hotel?

WOMAN: Ain't that a shame?

OLD WOMAN: Did you hear about it? Big, rich, fine place—and no room for a poor woman to have her child! Did you-all hear?

WOMAN: Ain't it a shame?

(SONG: "NO ROOM AT THE INN")

WOMAN: IT WAS ACCORDING TO THE WORD,
THERE WAS A VIRGIN GIRL.
YOU KNOW THE MOTHER OF JESUS,
SHE WAS WANDERING AROUND AT NIGHT.
SHE WAS TRYING TO FIND A HOME
FOR THE SAVIOUR TO BE BORN,
BUT THERE WAS NO ROOM AT THE HOTEL.

SINGERS: NO ROOM, THERE WAS NO ROOM
AT THE HOTEL! NO ROOM!
OH, LORD, NO ROOM!
IT WAS THE TIME FOR THE SAVIOUR TO BE BORN
BUT THERE WAS NO ROOM AT THE HOTEL.

NARRATOR: No room. No room for Mary anywhere! No room for Joseph. No room. In all the great city of Bethlehem, no room. The night is late. The air is cold. The doors are locked. The lights are out. Good folks have gone to bed. The streets are deserted. "I can't! Oh, Joseph, I can't go on."

(SONG: "MOST DONE TRAVELLING")

SINGERS: POOR MARY'S ON THE ROAD—
MOST DONE TRAVELLING!
I'M BOUND TO CARRY
MY SOUL TO THE LORD!

NARRATOR: They are strangers here. Her time has almost come. Joseph does not know what to do, and in this place he has no friends. "Joseph! Joseph, I must lie down now. I must! Oh, I . . . Oh, no! I can't go farther! No! No . . . I can't." Joseph begs, "Wait! Wait here, I'll find a place."

SINGERS: POOR JOSEPH'S ON THE ROAD—
MOST DONE TRAVELLING!
I'M BOUND TO CARRY
MY SOUL TO THE LORD!

(MARY sits alone on the curb as the song dies and a new song begins.)

(SONG: OH, JERUSALEM IN THE MORNING!)
SINGERS: MARY, MARY, WHAT IS THE MATTER?
    OH, JERUSALEM IN THE MORNING!
    OH, POOR JOSEPH, WHAT IS THE MATTER?
    OH, JERUSALEM IN THE MORNING!
    NIGHT IS CHILLY, WHAT IS THE MATTER?
    OH, JERUSALEM IN THE MORNING!
    OH, POOR MARY, WHAT IS THE MATTER?
    OH, JERUSALEM IN THE MORNING!
    COWS A-LOWING, WHAT IS THE MATTER?
    OH, JERUSALEM IN THE MORNING!
    SHEEP A-BAAING! WHAT IS THE MATTER?
    OH, JERUSALEM IN THE MORNING!
    OXEN A-BAWLING! WHAT IS THE MATTER?
    OH, JERUSALEM IN THE MORNING!

    OH, POOR MARY, WHAT IS THE MATTER?
    OH, JERUSALEM IN THE MORNING!
NARRATOR: And so it was that her days were accomplished that she
    should be delivered. And she brought forth her first born son,
    wrapped him in swaddling clothes, and laid him in a manger—for
    there was no room for them in the inn.
        *(The WOMEN among the SINGERS appear in the shadows
        lamenting.)*
        (SONG: "POOR LITTLE JESUS")
WOMEN: POOR LITTLE JESUS,
    BORN ON CHRISTMAS
    AND LAID IN A MANGER
    WASN'T THAT A PITY AND A SHAME?
    POOR LITTLE JESUS, SON OF MARY,
    DIDN'T HAVE NO CRADLE.
    WASN'T THAT A PITY AND A SHAME?
    LORD, WASN'T THAT A PITY AND A SHAME?
NARRATOR: For unto us a Child is born, unto us a Son is given and
    the government shall be upon His shoulders, and His name shall
    be called Wonderful, Counselor, All Mighty God, The Everlasting
    Father, The Prince of Peace.
        (SONG: "WHAT YOU GONNA NAME YOUR BABY?")
WOMAN: MARY, MARY WHAT YOU GONNA NAME
    THAT PRETTY LITTLE BABY?
    GLORY BE TO THE NEW BORN KING!

NARRATOR: Some call Him one thing—she's gonna call Him Jesus.
WOMAN: SOME CALL HIM ONE THING.
　SHE'S GONNA CALL HIM JESUS.
SINGERS: GLORY BE TO THE NEW BORN KING!
NARRATOR: Some call Him Jesus—she's gonna call Him Emanuel.
WOMAN: SOME CALL HIM JESUS.
　SHE'S GONNA CALL HIM EMANUEL.
SINGERS: GLORY BE TO THE NEW BORN KING!
NARRATOR: Some call Him Emanuel—she's gonna call Him Wonderful.
WOMAN: SOME CALL HIM EMANUEL.
　SHE'S GONNA CALL HIM WONDERFUL.
SINGERS: GLORY BE TO THE NEW BORN KING!
NARRATOR: Some call Him Wonderful—she's gonna call Him the Prince of Peace.
WOMAN: SOME CALL HIM WONDERFUL.
　SHE'S GONNA CALL HIM PRINCE OF PEACE.
SINGERS: GLORY BE TO THE NEW BORN KING!
NARRATOR: Some call Him Prince of Peace—she's gonna call Him Jesus.
WOMAN: SOME CALL HIM PRINCE OF PEACE.
　SHE'S GONNA CALL HIM JESUS.
SINGERS: GLORY BE TO THE NEW BORN KING!
NARRATOR: And his name shall be called Jesus.
　(Enter a group of PILGRIMS)
　(SONG: "WASN'T THAT A MIGHTY DAY!")
SINGERS: WASN'T THAT A MIGHTY DAY,
　WHEN JESUS CHRIST WAS BORN!
　STAR SHONE IN THE EAST,
　WHEN JESUS CHRIST WAS BORN!
　THE ANGEL CAME FROM ABOVE,
　WHEN JESUS CHRIST WAS BORN.
NARRATOR: Yes, His name shall be called Jesus.
　(SONG: "JOY TO THE WORLD" REPRISE)
SINGERS: JOY TO THE WORLD,
　SO GLAD THE LORD IS COME!
　LET EARTH RECEIVE HER KING.
　LET EVERY HEART PREPARE HIS ROOM,
　AND HEAVEN AND NATURE SING.
　JOY TO THE WORLD,
　HALLELUJAH, THE SAVIOUR REIGNS!

LET WE THEIR SONGS EMPLOY,
WHILE FIELDS AND FLOODS,
ROCKS, HILLS, AND PLAINS,
REPEAT THE SOUNDING JOY.
JOY TO THE WORLD,
THE LORD IS COME.
NARRATOR: Rejoice! Rejoice, for the Lord is come!
    (SONG: "CHRIST IS BORN")
SINGERS: CHRIST IS BORN IN THE LAND OF JUDEA
    CHRIST IS BORN! CHRIST IS BORN!
    BORN OF THE HOLY VIRGIN MARY!
    CHRIST IS BORN! CHRIST IS BORN!
    PRETTY LITTLE HOLY BABY!
    CHRIST IS BORN! CHRIST IS BORN!
    WHY DON'T YOU COME ON TO THE MANGER?
    COME AND ADORE THE LITTLE STRANGER
    BABY WHO NEVER HAD NO CRADLE,
    AND HIS ONLY BED A MANGER
    SEE THE WISE MEN FROM AFAR,
    ALL WERE GUIDED BY A STAR.
    HERALD ANGELS LEFT FROM GLORY
    AND CAME TO EARTH TO TELL THE STORY.
    TELL THE STORY OF HIS GLORY—
    CHRIST IS BORN! CHRIST IS BORN!
        (A roadside leading to the pastures. Four SHEPHERDS enter,
        their talk leads into song.)
NED: My wife wonders why I have to tend sheep at night.
JED: So does mine. The old shepherds always get the best shifts—the
    day shift.
ZED: It's cold, dag-nab it! And I've got no coat.
JED: You're ragged as a goat herd without a goat.
        (Song-speech into song.)
NED: I've got a coat—
        (SONG: "NO-GOOD SHEPHERD BOY!")
NED: BUT YOU WON'T GET MINE—
    WASTING ALL YOUR MONEY
    ON WOMEN AND WINE.
    NO-GOOD SHEPHERD!
JED: NO-GOOD SHEPHERD!
TRIO: NO-GOOD SHEPHERD BOY!

ZED: Aw, get off of it! Are you not your brother's keeper?
NED: No, not when my brother—
 AIN'T NOTHING BUT A SLEEPER
 YOU RUN AROUND ALL DAY,
 SLEEP ON YOUR JOB ALL NIGHT.
JED: IF YOU GONNA BE A SHEPHERD,
 BE A SHEPHERD RIGHT.
TED: I hear tell you lost a ewe and a lamb?
ZED: I LOST MORE THAN THAT—
 I LOST A RAM.
TED: What you gonna do when Master counts his sheep?
ZED: JUST GET UNDER A TREE
 AND GO TO SLEEP.
TED: WHAT GOOD IS A SHEPHERD
 THAT GOES TO SLEEP?
 SUPPOSE A WOLF WOULD COME,
 AND STEAL YOUR LAMBS AWAY,
 WHAT YOU GONNA TELL
 YOUR MASTER NEXT DAY?
NED: IF YOU TELL A LIE
 YOUR TONGUE MIGHT SLIP.
JED: IF YOU TELL THE TRUTH,
 HE MIGHT BUST YOU IN THE LIP.
TRIO: NO-GOOD SHEPHERD!
NED: SLEEPY-HEADED SHEPHERD!
TRIO: NO-GOOD SHEPHERD BOY!
NED: YOU CAN'T PREACH ONE THING
 THEN UP AND DO ANOTHER,
TRIO: LOOK OUT FOR YOURSELF
 BUT TRY TO CON YOUR BROTHER.
 NO-GOOD SHEPHERD!
 NO-GOOD SHEPHERD!
ZED: I'm a—
ALL: NO NO-GOOD SHEPHERD BOY!
TRIO: WHAT GOOD IS A SHEPHERD
 THAT CAN'T HERD SHEEP?
TED: FOR IF YOU LOSE A EWE
 THEN YOU CAN LOSE A LAMB.
NED: IF YOU CAN LOSE A LAMB
 YOU CAN LOSE A RAM.

JED: IF YOU DO NOT GET
   YOUR LOST SHEEP BACK,
   THEN YOUR MASTER MIGHT
   GET MAD AND GIVE YOU THE SACK.
TRIO: NO-GOOD SHEPHERD!
   LAZY OLD SHEPHERD!
   NO-GOOD SHEPHERD BOY!
   YOU CAN'T SIT AROUND
   AND NEVER DO YOUR WORK WELL,
   SAY YOU'RE HEAVEN BOUND
   WHEN YOU KNOW YOU'RE BOUND FOR HELL!
   NO-GOOD SHEPHERD!
   NO-GOOD SHEPHERD!
   NO-GOOD SHEPHERD BOY!
ZED: JUST A NO-GOOD SHEPHERD BOY!
     (ZED shrugs his shoulders, sits down and pulls a flute from the
     folds of his ragged clothing. But his melody is a series of screeches.
     The other SHEPHERDS put their hands over their ears in protest
     and cry aloud.)
NED: WHAT GOOD IS A SHEPHERD
   WHO CAN'T PLAY A FLUTE?
JED: AND HOW IN THE WORLD
   CAN YOU ATTRACT A GIRL
   WHEN YOU SMELL LIKE SHEEP
   AND YOUR FLUTE, IT WON'T BEEP?
NED: AND WHAT GOOD'S THE MOON
   OR NIGHTS IN JUNE
   WHEN YOU'RE OUT OF KEY
   AND YOUR FLUTE'S OUT OF TUNE?
TRIO: NO-GOOD SHEPHERD!
   RAGGEDY SHEPHERD!
   NO-GOOD SHEPHERD BOY!
   YOU CAN'T SWEET-TALK GIRLS,
   PULL TRICKS YOU KNOW AIN'T NICE
   BE A SNAKE IN THE GRASS,
   UNLESS YOU PAY THE PRICE.
   NO-GOOD SHEPHERD!
   NO-GOOD SHEPHERD!
   NO-GOOD SHEPHERD BOY!
ZED: Oh, poor me!

(*ZED rises to sing dolefully.*)
WHAT GOOD IS A SHEPHERD
THAT'S GOT NO GIRL?
MARY AND HER LAMB
HAD FLEECE AS WHITE AS SNOW.
I SAID, *LOVE ME BABE.*
BUT SHE SAID, *NO! NO! NO!*
SAID, YOU'LL HOLD MY HAND,
YOU'LL KISS MY EAR—
BUT WHEN I'M IN NEED
I CAN'T FIND YOU NOWHERE NEAR!
NO-GOOD SHEPHERD!
JIVE-TALKING SHEPHERD!
TRIO: NO-GOOD SHEPHERD BOY!
ZED: She said—
YOU MEN SWEET-TALK GIRLS,
DO THINGS YOU KNOW AIN'T NICE—
DIRTY SNAKES IN THE GRASS,
YOU MAKE A GIRL THINK TWICE!
NO-GOOD SHEPHERD!
she said—
TRIO: HEART-BREAKING SHEPHERD!
ZED: NO! NO-GOOD SHEPHERD BOY!
Oh, she gave me down-the-country—that woman did!
TED: It's a sin to betray a girl, Zed.
NED: And you are nothing but a sinner! Zed, you're a sinner!
(*ZED hangs his head in shame as TED becomes more serious.*)
TED: WHAT GOOD IS A SHEPHERD
THAT DON'T KNOW GOD?
TRIO: WHEN OLD DEATH WILL COME
TO TAKE YOUR SOUL AWAY,
HOW YOU GONNA FACE
SAINT PETER THAT DAY?
TED: IF YOU LIVE IN SIN,
WHEN LIFE DOTH END,
THEN WHO WILL YOU HAVE BUT
THE DEVIL FOR YOUR FRIEND?
TRIO: NO-GOOD SHEPHERD!
SIN-LOVING SHEPHERD!
NO-GOOD SHEPHERD BOY!

YOU CAN'T DANCE AND BALL
AND HOLLER, *HUH! COME SEVEN!*
THEN WHEN DEATH COMES BY,
EXPECT TO GO TO HEAVEN,
NO-GOOD SHEPHERD!
NO-GOOD SHEPHERD!
NO-GOOD SHEPHERD BOY!

> *(There is sudden thunder, a flash of light. Then a distant trum-*
> *pet sounds. The SHEPHERDS are astounded. ZED backs away*
> *in fright and ALL flee. BLACKOUT. The spotlight centers on the*
> *NARRATOR as the scene changes. Lights fade, only NARRA-*
> *TOR is visible.)*

NARRATOR: Hear again the Christmas story—
Christ is born in all His glory.
Baby laid in manger dark,
Lighting ages with the spark
Of innocence that is the Child,
Trusting all within His smile.
Tell again the Christmas story
With the halo of His glory;
Halo born of humbleness
By the breath of cattle blest,
By the poverty of stall
Where a bed of straw is all,
By a door closed at the Inn
Where only men of means get in,
By a door closed to the poor.
Christ is born on earthen floor
In a stable with no lock—
Yet kingdoms tremble at the shock
Of a King in swaddling clothes
At an address no one knows
Because there is no hotel sign—
Nothing but a star divine,
Nothing but a halo bright
About His young head in the night.
Mary's Son in manger born!
Music of the Angel's horn!
Mary's Son in straw and glory!
Wonder of the Christmas story!

(Now the Star shines very brightly.)
(SONG: "GO TELL IT ON THE MOUNTAIN")
WOMAN: GO TELL IT ON THE MOUNTAIN,
   OVER THE HILLS AND EVERYWHERE!
   GO TELL IT ON THE MOUNTAIN
   THAT JESUS CHRIST IS BORN!
      *(The WOMAN carries the news to the whole city and everyone joins
      in the jubilation.)*
SINGERS: GO TELL IT ON THE MOUNTAIN,
   OVER THE HILLS AND EVERYWHERE!
   GO TELL IT ON THE MOUNTAIN
   THAT JESUS CHRIST IS BORN!
WOMAN: AN ANGEL CAME FROM GLORY
   TO HAIL THE SAVIOUR'S BIRTH,
   AND THEN A LIGHT FROM HEAVEN
   SHONE ON THE HEAVENLY PLACE.
SINGERS: GO TELL IT ON THE MOUNTAIN,
   OVER THE HILLS AND EVERYWHERE!
   GO TELL IT ON THE MOUNTAIN
   THAT JESUS CHRIST IS BORN!
      (The light fades to a spot on a SHEPHERD alone on a hilltop.)
NARRATOR: And there were in the same country shepherds abiding
   in the field, keeping watch over their flocks by night. And lo, the
   angel of the Lord came upon them, and the glory of the Lord shown
   round about them, and they were sore afraid. And the angel said
   unto them, "Fear not for behold, I bring you good tidings of your
   great joy which shall be to all people. For unto you is born this day
   in the city of David, a Saviour which is Christ the Lord."
SINGERS: WHILE SHEPHERDS KEEP THEIR WATCH
   O'ER SILENT FLOCKS BY NIGHT,
   BEHOLD THROUGHOUT THE HEAVENS
   THERE SHONE A HOLY LIGHT.
   GO TELL IT ON THE MOUNTAIN
   OVER THE HILLS AND EVERYWHERE
   GO TELL IT ON THE MOUNTAIN
   THAT JESUS CHRIST IS BORN.
WOMAN: THE SHEPHERDS FEARED AND TREMBLED
   WHEN, LO, ABOVE THE EARTH
   RANG OUT THE ANGELS' CHORUS
   THAT HAILED THE SAVIOUR'S BIRTH.

SINGERS: GO TELL IT ON THE MOUNTAIN
OVER THE HILLS AND EVERYWHERE
GO TELL IT ON THE MOUNTAIN
THAT JESUS CHRIST IS BORN.
NARRATOR: And this shall be a sign unto you: Ye shall find the Babe
wrapped in swaddling clothes, lying in a manger. And suddenly there
was with the angel a multitude of heavenly hosts praising God, and
saying: "Glory be to God in the highest, and on earth, peace, good
will toward men!"
(SONG: "RISE UP, SHEPHERD, AND FOLLOW!")
SINGERS: THERE'S A STAR IN THE EAST
ON CHRISTMAS MORN.
RISE UP, SHEPHERD, AND FOLLOW!
IT WILL LEAD TO THE PLACE
WHERE THE SAVIOUR'S BORN.
RISE UP, SHEPHERD, AND FOLLOW!
IF YOU TAKE GOOD HEED
TO THE ANGEL'S WORDS AND
RISE UP, SHEPHERD, AND FOLLOW
YOU'LL FORGET YOUR FLOCKS,
YOU'LL FORGET YOUR HERDS.
RISE UP, SHEPHERD, AND FOLLOW!
LEAVE YOUR SHEEP, LEAVE YOUR LAMBS.
LEAVE YOUR EWES, AND LEAVE YOUR RAMS
RISE UP, SHEPHERD, AND FOLLOW—
FOLLOW THE STAR OF BETHLEHEM.
RISE UP, SHEPHERD, AND FOLLOW!
NARRATOR: Look! Look there at the star!
I—I, just a poor shepherd—
I, among the least,
I will arise and take
A journey to the East.
But what shall I bring
As a gift for the King?
Shall I bring a song,
A song that I will sing?
A song for the King,
In the manger?
Watch out for my flocks!
Do not let them stray.

I am gong on a journey
Far, far away.
But what shall I bring
As a gift for the Child?
What shall I bring to the Manger?
Shall I bring a lamb,
Gentle, meek and mild,
A lamb for the Child
In the manger?
Very poor I am
But I know there is
A King in Bethlehem.
What shall I bring
As a gift just for Him?
What shall I bring
To the manger?
Shall I bring my heart—
And give my heart to Him?
I will bring my heart
To the manger.

    (Light fades as the SHEPHERD begins his journey toward the star.
    The SINGERS continue joyously in darkness.)
    (SONG: "WHAT MONTH WAS JESUS BORN IN?")

SINGERS: JUST TELL ME WHEN WAS JESUS BORN?
THE LAST MONTH OF THE YEAR.
WAS IT JANUARY, FEBRUARY, MARCH, APRIL, MAY
JUNE, JULY, AUGUST, SEPTEMBER, OCTOBER, NOVEMBER,
THE TWENTY-FIFTH DAY OF DECEMBER—
THE LAST MONTH OF THE YEAR.
HE WAS BORN OF THE VIRGIN MARY,
WRAPPED IN SWADDLING CLOTHES
AND LAIN IN A HOLY MANGER
ON THE TWENTY-FIFTH DAY OF DECEMBER—
THE LAST MONTH OF THE YEAR.

    (The VIRGIN enters with the CHILD.)

NARRATOR: And so the news spread, and the people heard, and the
people came to see Him—sweet little Jesus Boy, sleeping in a stable
among the swine.

    (A WOMAN stands above the seated MOTHER and CHILD.)
    (SONG: "SWEET LITTLE JESUS BOY")

WOMAN: SWEET LITTLE JESUS BOY,
    THEY MADE YOU BE BORN IN A MANGER,
    SWEET LITTLE HOLY CHILD,
    DIDN'T KNOW WHO YOU WAS
    DIDN'T KNOW YOU COME TO SAVE US, LORD,
    TO TAKE OUR SINS AWAY.
    OUR EYES WERE BLIND,
    WE COULDN'T SEE—
    WE DIDN'T KNOW WHO YOU WAS.
    LONG TIME AGO YOU WAS BORN,
    BORN IN A MANGER LOW.
    SWEET LITTLE HOLY CHILD!
    THE WORLD TREATS YOU MEAN, LORD,
    TREATS ME MEAN, TOO—
    BUT THAT'S HOW THINGS IS DOWN HERE
    WHERE WE DON'T KNOW WHO YOU IS.
    YOU DONE TOLD US HOW,
    AND WE BEEN TRYING.
    MASTER, YOU DONE SHOWED US HOW
    EVEN WHEN YOU WAS DYING.
    JUST SEEMS LIKE WE CAN'T DO RIGHT.
    LOOK HOW WE DONE TREATED YOU.
    WELL, PLEASE, FORGIVE US, LORD.
    WE DIDN'T KNOW IT WAS YOU.
    SWEET LITTLE JESUS BOY,
    BORN LONG TIME AGO.
    SWEET LITTLE HOLY CHILD,
    WE DIDN'T KNOW WHO YOU WAS.
NARRATOR: They shall call His name Jesus, for he shall save His people
    from their sins. They shall call His name Emanuel which being
    interpreted is, God is with us, Jesus, Lord, Emanuel! Now when
    Jesus was born in Bethlehem of Judea in the days of Herod the King,
    behold, there came Wise Men from the East saying, "Where is He
    that is Born King of the Jews? For we have seen His star in the East
    and have come to worship Him."
        (The THREE KINGS enter down the aisle as the SINGERS burst
        into song and there is a glare of light.)
        (SONG: "OH, COME ALL YE FAITHFUL")
WOMAN: OH, COME ALL YE FAITHFUL,
    JOYFUL AND TRIUMPHANT!
    OH, COME YE, OH, COME YE, TO BETHLEHEM.

COME AND BEHOLD HIM,
BORN THE KING OF ANGELS.
(*The WISE MEN, presenting their gifts, bow down before the CHILD as song fills the night and the SINGERS surround the manger.*)
SINGERS: OH, COME LET US ADORE HIM!
OH, COME LET US ADORE HIM!
OH, COME LET US ADORE HIM—
CHRIST THE LORD!
NARRATOR: It all began that first Christmas in Bethlehem when the star shone over the manger and there was born in the city of David, a Saviour whose name was Christ the Lord.
SINGERS: AMEN! . . . AMEN! . . . AMEN!
CURTAIN—END ACT I

Act II

(*The lights come up on two bands of CHRISTIANS entering from either side, marching in time to the music, as the NARRATOR sits to one side.*)
(*SONG: "MEETIN' HERE TONIGHT"*)
SINGERS: THERE'S A MEETIN' HERE TONIGHT,
MEETIN' HERE TONIGHT,
MEETIN' ON THE OLD CAMPGROUND.
NARRATOR: And so the star of Bethlehem became a symbol. The manger became a church. The three kings became Princes of the Church. Wise men became its ministers. The heavenly hosts became the singers of God's praises all over the world—for almost two thousand years ago now in the Bethlehem of Judea, Christ was born— born to preach to the elders in the temple—to pass the miracle of the loaves and fishes—to turn the water into wine—to heal the sick and raise the dead—to cause the lame to walk and the blind to see. He was crucified, dead, and was buried, and on the third day arose from the dead, ascended into heaven and sitteth at the right hand of God, the Father—who gave His only begotten Son that man might have eternal life. Now, today, here in this place, nineteen centuries removed from Bethlehem—in a land far across the sea from Judea— we sing His songs and glorify His name. This church where you see us gathered—this gospel church where His word is spread—is but an extension of His manger. Those gathered here are His worshippers

who have come tonight to make—as the Bible says—a joyful noise unto the Lord.

(Exit NARRATOR as the ELDER comes to center.)

SINGERS: THIS IS THE WAY WE SING ON THE OLD CAMP-GROUND.

THIS IS THE WAY WE SING ON THE OLD CAMPGROUND. . .

ELDER: Praise God! Bless His name! There's a meeting here tonight, oh, yes! We've come to spread His word and glorify His name. And what shall we tell the world? Tell the world that Jesus was born in Bethlehem! Tell the world that Christ was born to save this earth from sin. Tell the world that this sweet little Jesus-Boy was born to save you—and to save me—to show us how to find the path of salvation, earn a right to the tree of life—to show us how to turn our eyes to God—to show the nations how to beat their swords into plow-shares. Yes! That's why He came! He came to make the lion lie down with the lamb, the mighty to be meek, and the meet to be lifted up! Oh yes! Jesus came to ride me on the wings of His glory, to take me up in the chariot of His love, to wrap me in His glorious glory.

(SONG: "HOLY GHOST, DON'T LEAVE ME")

SINGERS: OH, HOLY GHOST, PLEASE DON'T LEAVE ME, GUIDE ME ON MY WAY.

OH, HOLY GHOST, DON'T LEAVE ME—
JUST GUIDE ME ON MY WAY.

WOMAN: We're going to sing for you now, "We Shall Be Changed—In The Twinkling Of An Eye!" Changed from mortal to immortality.

(SONG: "WE SHALL BE CHANGED")

SINGERS: WE SHALL BE CHANGED! WE SHALL BE CHANGED!
CHANGED FROM MORTALS TO IMMORTALITY
IN THE TWINKLING OF AN EYE.
I'LL SHOW YOU A MYSTERY—
WE SHALL NOT ALL SLEEP,
BUT BE CHANGED IMMEDIATELY—
IN THE TWINKLING OF AN EYE.
WHEN THAT FIRST TRUMPET SOUNDS,
ALL THE DEAD IN CHRIST SHALL RISE.
WE'LL MEET JESUS IN THE SKIES—
IN THE TWINKLING OF AN EYE.
WE'LL SHAKE OFF MORTAL,
PUT ON IMMORTALITY.

DEATH WILL BE SWALLOWED UP IN VICTORY—
IN THE TWINKLING OF AN EYE.
IF A MAN DIES
AND HE DIES SERVING THE LORD
HE SHALL LIVE AGAIN—
IN THE TWINKLING OF AN EYE
I TELL YOU, WE SHALL BE CHANGED!
WE SHALL BE CHANGED!
CHANGED FROM MORTALS TO IMMORTALITY
IN THE TWINKLING OF AN EYE!

WOMAN: One day when I was lost Jesus bled and died upon the cross.
That's why I know it was His blood—yes, it was—that saved me.
(SONG: "THE BLOOD SAVED ME")

SINGERS: I KNOW IT WAS THE BLOOD,
I KNOW IT WAS THE BLOOD SAVED ME.
ONE DAY WHEN I WAS LOST,
JESUS DIED UPON THE CROSS.
I KNOW IT WAS THE BLOOD SAVED ME.
HE SET THE SINNER FREE FROM SIN.
JESUS CAME AND TOOK US IN.
I KNOW IT WAS THE BLOOD SAVED ME.
WHEN THEY WHIPPED HIM UP THE HILL,
HE NEVER SAID A WORD.
THE DAY THE WORLD STOOD STILL,
HE NEVER SAID A WORD.
WHEN THEY HUNG HIM WAY UP HIGH,
JESUS NEVER SAID A WORD.
THEN THEY PIERCED HIM IN THE SIDE.
OH, HE NEVER SAID A WORD.
CAN'T YOU SEE HIM HANGING THERE?
HE WAS IN PAIN AND IN DESPAIR.
I KNOW IT WAS THE BLOOD,
I KNOW IT WAS THE BLOOD SAVED ME.

ELDER: Jesus died upon the cross that I might have life, and have it
more abundantly. Yes, he did! But we ought to try harder to deserve
God's love and goodness. We ought to look inside ourselves and see
if we need fixing, need any personal repair work done. I examined
myself one day, myself and my surrounding, and—
(SONG: "LEAK IN THE BUILDING")

SINGERS: I FOUND A LEAK IN MY BUILDING

AND MY SOUL HAS GOT TO MOVE—
BUT I THANK GOD I HAVE ANOTHER BUILDING
NOT MADE BY HANDS.
ELDER: ONE DAY AS I WAS WALKING ALL ALONE
I HEARD A VOICE SPEAK TO ME,
LOOKED ALL AROUND BUT I SAW NO ONE
THEN HE TOLD ME, "BEFORE I'M THROUGH
I'M GOING TO TELL YOU WHAT TO DO."
SINGERS: OH, I THANK GOD I HAVE ANOTHER BUILDING
NOT MADE BY HANDS.
ELDER: I FIXED MY LEAK IN THE BUILDING.
I WENT ON MY KNEES IN PRAYER.
I LAID MY FOUNDATION WHILE I WAS THERE.
OH, YES! OH, YES! OH, YES! OH, YES!
AND I BUILT MY WALLS WITH GRACE,
I COVERED MY ROOF WITH FAITH,
AND I BUILT MY DOORS WITH LOVE,
AND I PLACED GOD'S NAME ABOVE,
AND ABOUT THAT TIME MY LANDLORD CAME.
YOU OUGHT TO KNOW WHO I MEAN—
MY GOD AND YOUR GOD!
MY LORD AND YOUR LORD!
HE SAID, "I'M PLEASED WITH WHAT YOU'VE DONE.
AND YOUR RACE HAS BEEN WON.
I'M HERE WITH YOUR KEY,
AND I'VE GOT YOUR DEEDS WITH ME."
SINGERS: OH, I THANK GOD I HAVE ANOTHER BUILDING
NOT MADE BY HANDS, NOT MADE BY HANDS!
ELDER: Oh, yes, my soul had to move—but I moved with my hand in
the hand of the Lord. I moved knowing that I may search the whole
world over, but there's nobody like Him.
(SONG: "NOBODY LIKE THE LORD")
SINGERS: THERE'S NOBODY LIKE THE LORD—
NOBODY LIKE THE LORD!
YOU MAY SEARCH THIS WIDE WORLD
OVER AND OVER AGAIN,
BUT YOU WON'T FIND NOBODY LIKE HIM.
MOTHER'S MY FRIEND, FATHER'S MY FRIEND,
SISTER AND BROTHER, THEY ARE MY FRIENDS
BUT THEY CAN'T GO WITH ME EACH DAY

PROTECTING ME UNTIL THE END.
YES, YOU MAY SEARCH THE WIDE WORLD
OVER AND OVER AGAIN,
BUT YOU WON'T FIND NOBODY LIKE HIM.
NOBODY, NOBODY, LIKE THE LORD!

ELDER: There's nobody like the Lord! No matter what we try to do, God is God all by himself. Sometimes we think he don't come when he ought to, but He's God, and he knows what we need, so he's always there on time. We tried him a long time ago and we know him. He supplied our every need. There's so many of us that are too busy complaining about things we already have that we should be thanking God for. We are so busy complaining that we overlook his goodness. There's so much to thank Him for—for the blood still running warm in our bodies when we get up each morning, for our loved ones, for the joy and beauty of living. If I were you, I'd thank Him while I have a chance. There was a man who complained about his shoes until he saw a man who had no feet. There was a woman who complained about her clothes until she saw someone on a bed of affliction and she thanked God for what she had. No matter what you think about things, God knows all, and His will must done. Tell it in song, sister, tell it in song!

(SONG: "HIS WILL BE DONE")

WOMAN: IT MATTERS NOT TO ME
IF AGAIN I NEVER SEE.
HIS WILL MUST BE DONE.
HE IS MY STAFF, HE IS MY ROD
WHEREVER MY FOOTSTEPS TROD,
HIS WILL MUST BE DONE.
IN THIS ETERNAL DARKNESS
THAT COVERS ME TODAY,
I LIVE FOR MY SAVIOUR
AND I'LL LET HIM HAVE HIS WAY.
MY LIFE IS IN GOD'S HANDS
AND I'LL MOVE AT HIS COMMAND.
HIS WILL MUST BE DONE.
IF AGAIN I NEVER SEE
GOD KNOWS WHAT'S BEST FOR ME.
HIS WILL MUST BE DONE.
LORD, WHEN I HAVE DONE ALL I CAN
I'LL BE STANDING RIGHT HERE

WAITING FOR YOU—
YOUR WILL MUST DONE.
ELDER: Let everything that has breath praise the Lord! Put your trust in
    Him. Talking about religion may kill your faith. People who really
    believe don't worry about it—because the Lord is going to make
    a way. Yes, He will! You know when I first got religion way back
    yonder in Alabama, I never will forget the day, seems like the trees
    were praising the Lord that day, seems like the sun was shining just
    for me. I don't know how it happened to happen so fast, but when I
    came to myself, I was seven and a half miles down the road. I don't
    know how I got there, but I was full of the spirit. The hand of God
    had touched me. I meant to keep my happiness to myself, but I
    couldn't.
        (SONG: "SAID I WASN'T GONNA TELL NOBODY")
SINGERS: I SAID I WASN'T GONNA TELL NOBODY—
    BUT I JUST COULDN'T KEEP IT TO MYSELF,
    WHAT THE LORD HAS DONE FOR ME.
    YOU OUGHT TO HAVE BEEN THERE
    WHEN HE SAVED MY SOUL . . .
    THAT SUNDAY MORNING
    WHEN HE PUT MY NAME ON THE ROLL,
    AND I STARTED WALKING,
    AND I STARTED TALKING,
    AND I STARTED SINGING,
    AND I STARTED SHOUTING
    ABOUT WHAT THE LORD HAS DONE FOR ME.
ELDER: I SAID I WASN'T GONNA TESTIFY—
    BUT I COULDN'T KEEP IT TO MYSELF
    WHAT THE LORD HAS DONE FOR ME.
WOMAN: I SAID I WASN'T GONNA SHOUT FOR JOY
    BUT I COULDN'T KEEP IT TO MYSELF
    WHAT THE LORD HAS DONE FOR ME.
SINGERS: I SAID I WASN'T GONNA SING MY SONG—
    BUT I COULDN'T KEEP IT TO MYSELF
    WHAT THE LORD HAS DONE FOR ME.
        (General shouting.)
VOICES: Bless God! Hallelujah! Amen! Yes!
SINGERS: IF IT WASN'T FOR JESUS
    MY SOUL, YOUR SOUL WOULD BE LOST . . .

WOMAN: Is everybody happy? Praise the Lord! I want to tell you tonight that God is real in my life. And I'm thanking Him this evening for keeping me. For one of these days, we all will come to the end of our journey. And when we come to the end of our journey, we must come down to the chilly banks of Jordan. And when I get there I don't want nobody to stop me. I want to be able to cross over to see my Lord.

(SONG: "GET AWAY, JORDAN")

SINGERS: GET AWAY! GET AWAY, JORDAN!
GET AWAY! GET AWAY, CHILLY JORDAN!
GET BACK, GET WAY BACK, JORDAN.
I WANT TO CROSS OVER TO SEE MY LORD.

WOMAN: ONE DAY I WAS WALKING ALONE.
I HEARD A VOICE BUT I SAW NO ONE.
THE VOICE I HEARD SOUNDED SO SWEET,
IT RAN FROM MY HEAD TO THE SOLE OF MY FEET.
IF YOU DON'T BELIEVE I'VE BEEN REDEEMED,
JUST FOLLOW ME DOWN TO JORDAN STREAM.
JORDAN WATER IS CHILLY AND COLD,
MAY CHILL THE BODY BUT NOT MY SOUL!
GET AWAY! GET AWAY, JORDAN!
I WANT TO CROSS OVER TO SEE MY LORD!

WOMAN: I know there's nothing for Christians to be afraid of when we come to Jordan and cross over into the Promised Land. That's why I'm packing up—getting ready to go, ahead of time—because I'm ready, and I have no fear.

(SONG: "PACKING UP")

SINGERS: I'M ON MY WAY TO NEW JERUSALEM
WHERE THE SUN NEVER GOES DOWN.
EVERY DAY IN PREPARATION—
PACKING UP GETTING READY TO GO.
I'M PACKING, PACKING, GETTING READY TO GO.
I GOT MY SWORD, I GOT MY SHIELD . . .
GOT MY TICKET, SIGNED AND SEALED,
SO I'M PACKING UP, GETTING READY,
PACKING UP, GETTING READY TO GO.

ELDER: And it all began with that first Star in Bethlehem almost two thousand years ago—the Star that brought us to the Manger to kneel at the feet of Christ.

(SONG: "GOD BE WITH YOU")
SINGERS: GOD BE WITH YOU, GOD BE WITH YOU,
    GOD BE WITH YOU UNTIL WE MEET AGAIN.
    IF WE NEVER MEET HERE AGAIN,
    WE SHALL MEET IN THE END.
    GOD BE WITH YOU UNTIL WE MEET AGAIN.
    GOOD-NIGHT!
THE END

The Gospel Glow [WRITTEN IN PEN]
A Passion Play

or

The Gospel Glory
The Cradle to the Cross
A Passion Play on the Negro Spirituals

1962

AUTHOR'S NOTES: In terms of the Negro spirituals, this is a narrative of the life of Christ from His birth at Bethlehem to the evening of the Last Supper, His Passion on the Cross, the Resurrection and His Ascension, as might be related by an Elder of the church and sung by Brothers and Sisters of the choir.

SETTING: Simply a church rostrum. Or if done in a theatre, there may be platforms of varying heights, against a cyclorama. There need be no sets or props, unless pews for the SINGERS and a simple pulpit stand for the ELDER are desired.

Characters

AN ELDER
A SISTER
A BROTHER
A DEACON
SHEPHERDS
THREE WISE MEN

Mimes

MARY
JOSEPH

BLIND MAN
WOMAN
JUDAS
SIMON
MARTHA
OLD WOMAN
SHOUTERS
PANTOMIMISTS: Three dancers or mimes, perhaps four may be used
    in the GOSPEL GLORY to visualize certain sequences against the
    songs: the NATIVITY IN THE MANGER with MARY and
    JOSEPH; the BLIND MAN and the WOMAN BY THE WAYSIDE;
    the DANCE OF JUDAS, with his scattering of the gold pieces,
    his remorse and suicide; BLACK SIMON carrying the cross; THE
    MOURNING OF MARY AND MARTHA to the songs of the Cru-
    cifixion; and I CAN'T SET DOWN—an OLD SISTER too happy to
    sit down in Heaven; ending in general shouting and gospel dancing
    on the part of all the SINGERS just before the finale.

Scenes

Prologue: The Gospel Glory
    1. The Nativity
    2. The Deliverance
    3. Among the Elders
    4. The Baptism
    5. Sermon on the Mount
    6. Spreading the Word
    7. Great Tribulations
    8. End of Time
    9. The Miracles
    10. Rock of God
    11. Shadow of the Cross
    12. Gethsemane
    13. Betrayal
    14. Condemnation
    15. Golgatha
    16. Crucifixion
    17. Resurrection
    18. Ascension

19. Jubilation
Finale: The Gospel Glory

Songs

Prologue: The Gospel Glory
1. Mary Had A Baby
2. Didn't My Lord Deliver Daniel
3. Little Boy, How Old Are You
4. He Is King Of Kings
5. Preaching The Word of God
6. Go Where I Send Thee
7. My Lord, What A Morning
8. Where Shall I Be
9. Savior, Don't Pass Me By
10. Dry Bones
11. Get A Home In That Rock
12. A Pity And A Shame
13. Watch With Me One Hour
14. Lonesome Valley
15. Take My Mother Home
16. He Never Said A Word
17. Were You There
18. No Grave Can Hold His Body Down
19. Oh, Mary, Don't You Weep
20. Angel Rolled The Stone Away
21. He Rose From The Grave
22. Ride On King Jesus
23. Yes, There's One
24. Plenty Good Room
25. Set Down
Finale: The Gospel Glory

OPENING: *As the lights dim, in the darkness there is a burst of music—*
organ and piano. A spotlight centers on the ELDER alone, who speaks.
ELDER: Listen to the Gospel Glory! Wonder of our Savior's Story.
    (As the song begins, the light spreads to reveal the SINGERS in
    their robes.)
SINGERS: MY SOUL IS FILLED WITH THE GOSPEL GLORY!

GOSPEL GLORY! GOSPEL GLORY!
MY SOUL IS FILLED WITH THE GOSPEL GLORY!
GLORY TO HIS NAME!
IF YOU ASK ME HOW I GOT IT,
I WILL TELL MY STORY—
I GOT IT FROM THE LORD,
GOT IT FROM THE LORD ABOVE..... etc.....
BROTHER: THE DEVIL HAD A STAKE IN ME.
HE WOULD NOT LET ME GO.
BUT JESUS CAME INTO MY LIFE,
OH, NOW WHAT JOY I KNOW!
SINGERS: MY SOUL IS FILLED WITH THE GOSPEL GLORY.......
SISTER: I WAS A SINNER LOST IN SIN.
I DID NOT KNOW THE WAY.
WHEN JESUS CAME INTO MY LIFE,
THE DARKNESS TURNED TO DAY.
SINGERS: MY SOUL IS FILLED WITH THE GOSPEL GLORY.......
BROTHER: HOSANNA TO MY PRECIOUS LORD!
OH, LET HIS PRAISES RING!
SINCE JESUS CAME INTO MY LIFE,
I OWN HIM AS MY KING.
SINGERS: MY SOUL IS FILLED WITH THE GOSPEL GLORY.......
ELDER: From whence cometh the Gospel Glory?
SINGERS: The Bible?
ELDER: Do you know your Bible?
SINGERS: Well, I think I do.
SISTER: I *know* I do.
ELDER: I ask you again, do you know your Bible?
SINGERS: I think I do.
ELDER: If you know your Bible like you think you do—then tell me
about Christ.
SINGERS: Jesus Christ! Amen! Lord, my Christ!
ELDER: What did he do?
BROTHER: He healed the sick and He raised the dead.
ELDER: What else did He do?
SISTER: He made the lame to walk and the blind to see.
ELDER: Yes, He did! What else? What else?
DEACON: He came into this world to save poor me.
BROTHER: He did! Yes, He did. Hallello! That's why—
MY SOUL IS FILLED WITH THE GOSPEL GLORY!

WOMEN: GOSPEL GLORY!

MEN: GOSPEL GLORY!

SINGERS: MY SOUL IS FILLED WITH THE GOSPEL GLORY!
GLORY! GLORY! GOSPEL GLORY!
ASK ME HOW I GOT IT,
I WILL TELL MY STORY—
GOT IT FROM THE LORD,
GOT IT FROM THE LORD,
GOT IT FROM THE LORD ABOVE.

ELDER: The Lord, our Lord, Christ, who was once on earth, preaching and teaching in the Land of Galilee. My Lord, maker of miracles. Christ Jesus who cast out devils, restored the withered hand, and with five loaves of bread and two fishes—

SISTER: Two little fishes!

ELDER: He fed five thousand.

BROTHER: Yes, He did!

ELDER: Great God A-Mighty! Christ! My Christ! Tell me, who was Christ?

VOICES: He was born of the Virgin Mary.

MAN: He was born in a manger.

WOMAN: In Bethlehem of Judea.

ELDER: Parents turned away from the inn—no place to lay their heads that night, that Christmas night almost two thousand years ago.

> *(The lights dim as a spotlight circles MARY—the Madonna and Child—seated at center. Above the Mother and Child a WOMAN sings. Then, as the WOMAN withdraws to join the other SINGERS circled at either side and the light widens to cover the whole scene, SHEPHERDS and the THREE WISE MEN enter bearing gifts and bow down before the MOTHER and CHILD as a joyous song rises.)*

SINGERS: OH, LORD, SHOUT FOR JOY!
MARY HAD A BABY! SHOUT FOR JOY!
BORN IN A STABLE! SHOUT FOR JOY!
THEY LAID HIM IN A MANGER! SHOUT FOR JOY!
THEY NAMED HIM KING JESUS! SHOUT FOR JOY!
HE WAS THE PRINCE OF PEACE!
A MIGHTY COUNSELOR, THE KING OF KINGS!
THAT CHRISTMAS IN THE MORNING
ANGELS SANG HIS PRAISES. SHOUT FOR JOY!
SHEPHERDS CAME TO SEE HIM. SHOUT FOR JOY!

WISE MEN BROUGHT HIM PRESENTS. SHOUT FOR JOY!
ALL THE WORLD ADORED HIM! SHOUT FOR JOY!
THAT CHRISTMAS IN THE MORNING. SHOUT FOR JOY!
> (*JOSEPH enters, worried and apprehensive and, as the WISE
> MEN withdraw, HE wraps his cloak about MARY and the
> CHILD, picks up a bundle on a stick, and THEY exit, bound for
> Egypt*)

KING HEROD TRIED TO FIND HIM. SHOUT FOR JOY!
JOSEPH GOT THE WARNING. SHOUT FOR JOY!
THEY WENT AWAY TO EGYPT. SHOUT FOR JOY!
THEY WENT ACROSS THE DESERT. SHOUT FOR JOY!
HE WAS THE PRINCE OF PEACE!
A MIGHTY COUNSELOR, THE KING OF KINGS!
THAT CHRISTMAS IN THE MORNING
MARY RODE A DONKEY. SHOUT FOR JOY!
JOSEPH WALKED BESIDE THEM. SHOUT FOR JOY!
ANGELS WATCHING OVER. SHOUT FOR JOY.
OH, LORD, SHOUT FOR JOY!
HE WAS THE PRINCE OF PEACE!
A MIGHTY COUNSELOR, THE KING OF KINGS!
SHOUT FOR JOY!
> (*ELDER comes forward from among the SINGERS*)

ELDER: Little Jesus, born into this mean old world! Mary and Joseph
barred out of the Inn.
WOMAN: Wasn't that a pity?
SINGERS: LITTLE BOY, HOW OLD ARE YOU?
LITTLE BOY, HOW OLD ARE YOU?
TENOR: I'M ONLY TWELVE YEARS OLD
MEN: LAWYERS AND DOCTORS STOOD AND WONDERED
AS THOUGH THEY HAD BEEN STRUCK BY THUNDER
THEN THEY DECIDED WHILE THEY WONDERED
THAT ALL MANKIND MUST COME UNDER
SINGERS: LITTLE BOY, HOW OLD ARE YOU?
LITTLE BOY, HOW OLD ARE YOU?
TENOR: WELL, I'M ONLY TWELVE YEARS OLD.
SINGERS: THIS LITTLE BOY HAD THE KEY
TO THE HIDDEN MYSTERY.
THE LAWYERS DECIDED, AS WISE AS HE,
THEY'D BETTER LET THAT LITTLE BOY BE.
MEN: LITTLE BOY, HOW OLD ARE YOU?
LITTLE BOY, HOW OLD ARE YOU?

TENOR: SAID, I'M ONLY TWELVE YEARS OLD
MEN: THE LAST TIME THAT LITTLE BOY WAS SEEN
　　HE WAS STANDING ON MOUNT OLIVET GREEN
　　WHEN HE DISPERSED OF THE CROWD
　　HE ENTERED INTO A CLOUD
SINGERS: LITTLE BOY, HOW OLD ARE YOU?
　　LITTLE BOY, HOW OLD ARE YOU?
　　LITTLE BOY, HOW OLD ARE YOU?
MEN: I'M ONLY TWELVE YEARS OLD
ELDER: "Wist ye not," Christ said, "that I must be about my Father's business?" And even then His Father's business surpasseth understanding—for it led him from Bethlehem of Judea to the Mountain of Golgatha. In those days, John the Baptist said, "Prepare ye the way of the Lord, for one mightier than I cometh, the latchet of whose shoes I am not worthy to unloose. He shall baptize you with the Holy Ghost and with fire." It was John himself who, when Christ was about thirty years old, baptised our Lord in the River Jordan. Then it was that a voice came from Heaven saying, "Thou art my beloved Son in whom I am well pleased." Oh, yes!
SINGERS: HE'S KING OF KINGS, LORD OF LORDS
　　JESUS CHRIST, FIRST AND LAST,
　　NO MAN WORKS LIKE HIM.
ELDER: HE BUILT A KINGDOM IN THE AIR.
SINGERS: NO MAN WORKS LIKE HIM.
ELDER: HE MEETS THE SAINTS FROM EVERYWHERE.
SINGERS: NO MAN WORKS LIKE HIM.
ELDER: HE BROKE THE ROMAN KINGDOM DOWN.
SINGERS: NO MAN WORKS LIKE HIM.
ELDER: I KNOW THAT MY REDEEMER LIVES.
SINGERS: NO MAN WORKS LIKE HIM.
ELDER: CHRIST BY HIS DEATH, SWEET BLESSING GIVES.
SINGERS: NO MAN WORKS LIKE HIM.
　　OH, KING OF KINGS! LORD OF LORDS!
　　JESUS CHRIST, FIRST AND LAST,
　　NO MAN WORKS LIKE HIM.
ELDER: Now, when Christ was here on earth, who worked with Him?
SINGERS: Twelve disciples.
ELDER: Twelve disciples? Who were they?
BROTHER: Matthew, Mark, James and John.
SISTER: Peter.

DEACON: Judas, too.

ELDER: Matthew, Mark, James, John, Judas, Peter—which makes six. Who else? There's six more.

BROTHER: That other James.

ELDER: James? Who else? Five more.

SISTER: Simon, Philip, Andrew and Thomas. If you-all want to know the Bible, just ask me.

ELDER: Simon, Philip, Andrew and Thomas. We've only got eleven, Sister. One's missing. Who else?

SISTER: Timothy! Ha-ha-ha! Ha-ha!

BROTHER: Amen. Right, sister, right.

DEACON: Halleloo! Timothy!

SISTER: That makes twelve!

ELDER: Timothy! The twelve disciples who followed Christ to preach and teach his glory! Many others followed Christ, too, and His fame spread abroad in the land. So the high and mighty heard of Christ, and wondered who this man might be that other men called king, and who went about preaching to the people, and inspiring others to preach. Yes, he did!

> *(Here the singing and the sermon on the Mount intertwine as the Elder speaks between musical phrases)*

SINGERS: I HEARD THE PREACHING OF THE ELDER, PREACHING THE WORD, PREACHING THE WORD.

ELDER: Jesus went about all Galilee spreading the gospel of the kingdom.

SINGERS: I HEARD THE PREACHING OF THE ELDER, PREACHING THE WORD OF GOD.

ELDER: And His fame went throughout Syria.

SINGERS: PREACHING THE WORD OF GOD.

ELDER: And seeing the multitudes, Jesus went up into a mountain, and opened His mouth.

SINGERS: I HEARD THE PREACHING OF THE ELDER. . . . .

ELDER: There on the mountain He spake and said, "Blessed are the poor in spirit, for theirs is the kingdom of Heaven."

SINGERS: PREACHING THE WORD OF GOD.

ELDER: "Blessed are they that mourn, for they shall be comforted."

SINGERS: I HEARD THE PREACHING OF THE ELDER. . . . .

ELDER: "Blessed are the meek, for they shall inherit the earth."

SINGERS: PREACHING THE WORD OF GOD.

ELDER: "Blessed are they which do hunger and thirst after righteousness, for they shall be filled."

SINGERS: I HEARD THE PREACHING OF THE ELDER. . . . . .

ELDER: "Blessed are the merciful, for they shall obtain mercy."

SINGERS: PREACHING THE WORD OF GOD.

ELDER: "Blessed are the pure in heart, for they shall see God."

SINGERS: I HEARD THE PREACHING OF THE ELDER. . . . . . .

ELDER: "Blessed are the peacemakers, for they shall be called the children of God."

SINGERS: PREACHING THE WORD OF GOD.

ELDER: "Blessed are they which are persecuted for righteousness sake, for theirs is the kingdom of Heaven."

SINGERS: PREACHING THE WORD OF GOD.

ELDER: "Blessed are ye when men shall revile you, and persecute you, and shall say all manner of evil against you falsely for my sake."

SINGERS: I HEARD THE PREACHING OF THE ELDER. . . . .

ELDER: "Rejoice and be exceedingly glad, for great is your reward in Heaven."

SINGERS: PREACHING THE WORD OF GOD.

ELDER: "Ye are the salt of the earth."

SINGERS: I HEARD THE PREACHING OF THE ELDER,
PREACHING THE WORD OF GOD!

BROTHER: He meant those words for me.

DEACON: Preaching on the mountain, those words for me!

ELDER: His love come trickling down to all mankind. And Christ was loved by His disciples and they followed Him, and did as He told them to do, "Go forth and preach the gospel in all the lands about Galilee. Go spread the Word to all the world." That's what He told them, didn't He, church? Yes, He did! He said—

SINGERS: CHILDREN, GO WHERE I SEND THEE.
HOW SHALL I SEND THEE?
I'M GONNA SEND THEE ONE BY ONE.
ONE IS FOR THE LITTLE BABY
BORN OF THE VIRGIN MARY,
WRAPPED IN SWADDLING CLOTHING,
LAID IN A LONELY MANGER,
BORN, BORN IN BETHLEHEM.
CHILDREN, GO WHERE I SEND THEE.
HOW SHALL I SEND THEE?

I'M GONNA SEND THEE TWO BY TWO. . . . . . etc. . . . . etc.

(As they sing, the SINGERS, one by one, then two by two, etc., pan-
tomime this cumulative song until all are marching and singing
together.)

BORN, BORN IN BETHLEHEM . . . etc

ELDER: Sitting on the Mount of Olives, Jesus said, "Many shall come
in my name saying, "I am Christ" and shall deceive many. And ye
shall hear of wars and rumors of wars, for nation shall rise against
nation and kingdom against kingdom, and there shall be famines,
and pestilences, and earthquakes in divers places. "My Lord, what a
morning!"

(The CHORUS begins to sing softly as the Elder speaks over their
song quoting from Matthew 24)

SINGERS: MY LORD, WHAT A MORNING
WHEN THE STARS BEGIN TO FALL!
YOU'LL HEAR THE TRUMPET SOUND
TO WAKE THE NATIONS UNDERGROUND,
LOOKING TO MY GOD'S RIGHT HAND
WHEN THE STARS BEGIN TO FALL.

ELDER: "Then shall they deliver you up to be afflicted and shall kill
you. And ye shall be hated of all nations for my sake. But he that
shall endure unto the end, the same shall be saved. Then let them
that shall be in Judea flee into the mountains for there shall be great
tribulations, such as was not since the beginning of world."

SINGERS: MY LORD, WHAT A MORNING
WHEN THE STARS BEGIN TO FALL!
YOU'LL HEARD THE SINNER MOAN
TO WAKE THE NATIONS UNDERGROUND
LOOKING TO MY GOD'S RIGHT HAND
WHEN THE STARS BEGIN TO FALL!
MY LORD, WHAT A MORNING
WHEN THE STARS BEGIN TO FALL.
YOU'LL HEAR THE CHRISTIANS SHOUT
TO WAKE THE NATIONS UNDERGROUND
LOOKING TO MY GOD'S RIGHT HAND
WHEN THE STARS BEGIN TO FALL!
MY LORD, WHAT A MORNING!
MY LORD, WHAT A MORNING!
WHEN THE STARS BEGIN TO FALL. . . . . . .

ELDER: My God! . . . . . My God! . . . . . My God! Where shall I be?
  (*AN OLD MAN comes forward*)
DEACON: WHERE SHALL I BE WHEN THE FIRST TRUMPET
  SOUNDS?
SINGERS: WHERE SHALL I BE WHEN IT SOUNDS SO LOUD?
  WHEN IT SOUNDS SO LOUD TILL IT WAKES UP THE
  DEAD.
  WHERE SHALL I BE WHEN IT SOUNDS?
DEACON: GOING TO TRY ON MY ROBE WHEN THE FIRST
  TRUMPET SOUNDS
  GOING TO TRY ON MY ROBE WHEN IT SOUNDS SO LOUD.
SINGERS: WHEN IT SOUNDS SO LOUD TILL IT WAKES UP
  THE DEAD
  WHERE SHALL I BE WHEN IT SOUNDS.
  OH, BRETHREN, WHERE SHALL I BE WHEN IT SOUNDS?
  WHEN IT SOUNDS SO LOUD THAT IT WAKES UP THE
  DEAD,
  WHERE SHALL I BE WHEN IT SOUNDS?
SISTER: GOING TO TRY ON MY WINGS WHEN THE FIRST
  TRUMPET SOUNDS,
  GOING TO TRY ON MY WINGS WHEN IT SOUNDS SO
  LOUD.
ELDER: GOING TO TRY ON MY CROWN WHEN THE FIRST
  TRUMPET SOUNDS,
  GOING TO TRY ON MY CROWN WHEN IT SOUNDS SO
  LOUD.
SINGERS: WHEN IT SOUNDS SO LOUD THAT IT WAKES UP
  THE DEAD,
  WHERE SHALL I BE WHEN IT SOUNDS?
DEACON: In the Kingdom—that's where I'll be on that great gittin'
  up morning.
ELDER: In the Kingdom! That's where the righteous will be! Matthew
  Chapter 24 declares, He shall send His angels with a great sound of
  trumpet. They shall gather together his elect from the four winds,
  from one end of Heaven to the other. Before Him shall be gathered
  all nations and He shall separate them one from another, as a shepherd divideth his sheep from the goats. He shall set the sheep on His
  right hand, and the goats on the left. Then shall the King say unto
  them on his right hand, "Come, ye blessed of my Father, inherit

the Kingdom." Did he not cause the lame to walk and the blind
to see? Feed five thousand with just two little fishes and five loaves?
Confound the woman at the well, and raise Lazarus from the dead?

VOICES: Yes, He did! He did!

ELDER: All you need to do is call His name. Call—as the blind man
called, as the woman by the wayside called.

(A BLIND MAN and a WOMAN seek Jesus in the crowd)

WOMAN: I'M CRYING OUT, SAVIOR, SAVIOR,
SAVIOR DON'T YOU PASS ME BY.
I'M CRYING OUT, SAVIOR, SAVIOR,
CRYING OUT, SAVIOR, DON'T YOU PASS ME BY.
THE BLIND MAN STOOD ON THE WAYSIDE.
HE WAS BLIND AND COULD NOT SEE.
WHEN HE HEARD THAT JESUS WAS PASSING BY
HE SAID, "I HAVE NEED OF THEE."
THEN HE CALLED TO ONE OF HIS DISCIPLES,
"PRAY TELL ME WHEN HE'S NIGH."
HE CRIED OUT, SAVIOR, DON'T YOU PASS ME BY.

SINGERS: SAVIOR, LOVING SAVIOR,
SAVIOR, DON'T YOU PASS ME BY.
I'M CRYING OUT, SAVIOR, LOVING SAVIOR,
OH, SAVIOR, DON'T YOU PASS ME BY.

(The CROWD parts and the BLIND MAN exits toward Jesus)

WOMAN: NOW, WHILE JESUS WAS PASSING BY
HE HEARD A POOR WOMAN CRY,
"IF I COULD BUT HIS GARMENTS TOUCH
I WOULD GO AND PROPHESY."
SHE CALLED TO PETER, JAMES AND JOHN,
"PRAY TELL ME WHEN HE'S NIGH."

(The WOMAN feels the presence of Christ as he passes)

SINGERS: SHE CRIED OUT, SAVIOR, SAVIOR,
LOVING SAVIOR, DON'T YOU PASS ME BY.
I'M CRYING OUT SAVIOR, SAVIOR,
LOVING SAVIOR, DON'T YOU PASS ME BY.
SAVIOR, BLESSED SAVIOR,
SAVIOR, DON'T YOU PASS ME BY.

(The CROWD parts and the WOMAN exits following Christ)

ELDER: When they cried to Him, Jesus didn't pass them by. That day
Jesus had compassion on not only one, but two blind men and

touched their eyes. Immediately their eyes received sight, and they followed Him, as did the woman who sought his aid. Oh, master of miracles!

WOMAN: He calmed the waters.

DEACON: He healed the sick.

ELDER: He cast out devils. He restored life.

BROTHER: He raised the dead.

ELDER: Just like he raised Lazarus, in that great getting-up morning, He will raise me!

DEACON: Raise me! Raise me!

WOMAN: Me, and you!

ELDER: Take my dry bones and put them all together!

DEACON: THEM BONES, THEM BONES, THEM DRY BONES! OH, HEAR THE WORD OF THE LORD!

SINGERS: CONNECT THEM DRY BONES! HEAR THE WORD OF THE LORD!

    (SINGERS hum as DEACON continues)

DEACON: YOUR TOE BONE CONNECTED TO YOUR FOOT BONE,

    FOOT BONE CONNECTED TO YOUR HEEL BONE,

    HEEL BONE CONNECTED TO YOUR ANKLE BONE

    ANKLE BONE CONNECTED TO YOUR LEG BONE

    LEG BONE CONNECTED TO YOUR KNEE BONE

    KNEE BONE CONNECTED TO YOUR THIGH BONE,

    THIGH BONE CONNECTED TO YOUR HIP BONE,

    HIP BONE CONNECTED TO YOUR BACK BONE,

    BACK BONE CONNECTED TO YOUR SHOULDER BONE,

    SHOULDER BONE CONNECTED TO YOUR NECK BONE,

    NECK BONE CONNECTED TO YOUR HEAD BONE,

    HEAD BONE CONNECTED TO YOUR SKULL BONE,

    SKULL BONE CONNECTED TO YOUR NOSE BONE,

    NOSE BONE CONNECTED TO YOUR MOUTH BONE,

    MOUTH BONE CONNECTED TO YOUR CHIN BONE,

    CHIN BONE CONNECTED TO YOUR THROAT BONE,

    THROAT BONE CONNECTED TO YOUR BREAST BONE,

    BREAST BONE CONNECTED TO YOUR ARM BONES,

    ARM BONES CONNECTED TO YOUR WRIST BONES,

    WRIST BONES CONNECTED TO YOUR HAND BONES,

    HAND BONES CONNECTED TO YOUR FINGER BONES,

YOUR FINGER BONES CONNECTED TO THE LOVE OF
     GOD—
OH, HEAR THE WORD OF THE LORD!
SINGERS: THEM BONES, THEM BONES, THEM DRY BONES!
THEM BONES GONNA WALK AROUND!
THEM BONES, THEM BONES, THEM DRY BONES!
THEM BONES GONNA RISE AND WALK ABOVE GROUND!
THEM BONES, THEM BONES, THEM DRY BONES—
OH HEAR THE WORD OF THE LORD!
ELDER: In that great gittin' up morning! Halleloo! When the saints of
     God shall gather at His throne! That is what Christ came into the
     world to bring mankind—assurance, blessed assurance that our souls
     shall rise again. He said, "Upon this rock I build my church, and the
     gates of hell shall not prevail against it. Oh, rock of God!
SINGERS: I GOT A HOME IN THAT ROCK, DON'T YOU SEE?
     BETWEEN THE EARTH AND SKY,
     THOUGHT I HEARD MY SAVIOR CRY,
     YOU GOT A HOME IN THAT ROCK, DON'T YOU SEE?
DEACON: POOR MAN, LAZARUS, POOR AS I, DON'T YOU SEE?
MEN: POOR MAN, LAZARUS, POOR AS I,
     WHEN HE DIED HE FOUND A HOME ON HIGH.
SINGERS: HE HAD A HOME IN THAT ROCK, DON'T YOU SEE?
DEACON: RICH MAN, DIVES, HE LIVED SO WELL, DON'T
     YOU SEE?
MEN: RICH MAN, DIVES, HE LIVED SO WELL
     WHEN HE DIED HE FOUND A HOME IN HELL.
SINGERS: HE HAD NO HOME IN THAT ROCK, DON'T YOU
     SEE?
WOMEN: GOD GAVE NOAH THE RAINBOW SIGN,
     NO MORE WATER, BUT FIRE NEXT TIME.
     BETTER GET A HOME IN THAT ROCK, DON'T YOU SEE?
ELDER: The Rock of Salvation is founded in the Word of God—the
     Word that Christ spread far and wide throughout the land, until
     millions knew His name. When Jesus entered into Jerusalem that
     Sunday before He was to die upon the Cross—Christ riding on
     a colt—the people spread palms before Him in the streets. They
     strew His way with flowers and cried "Hosanna in the highest!"
     They did not know this Sunday marked the beginning of the end of
     Christ's thirty-three years upon this earth. The shadow of the Cross
     lay before Him. Palm Sunday, crowning with light the miracle of His

life upon the earth! Crowning with light the road to Golgotha, death and resurrection! Crowning with light the end of His earthly story—the closing forever in the *flesh* of His gospel glory. . . . . . . Within a few days, Christ was to die. Already they were conspiring against Him—the High Priests and the Romans—that He must die. Why? Because Christ looked after you and me, that's why. He looked after *me*, nobody! He looked after the poor and the needy. That's why they conspired against my Lord. . . . . Jesus said, "I was a stranger and ye took me not in; naked and ye clothed me not; hungered and ye gave me no drink." Jesus was talking about me, hungry. He was pleading for me, poor. He was looking after *me*. That's why the high and mighty got mad—the Pharisees and the scribes and the priests got mad. Did not Jesus drive the money changers from the temple? He said, "My house shall be called a house of prayer, but you have made it a den of thieves." They got mad. So they took counsel together to put Jesus to death.

SISTER: WASN'T THAT A PITY AND A SHAME? LORD! LORD!
SINGERS: WASN'T THAT A PITY AND A SHAME?
IT WAS A POOR LITTLE JESUS
BORN ON CHRISTMAS, BORN ON SUNDAY.
WASN'T THAT A PITY AND A SHAME?
POOR LITTLE JESUS, SON OF MARY,
DIDN'T HAVE NO CRADLE.
WASN'T THAT A PITY? WASN'T THAT A SHAME?
POOR LITTLE JESUS, LAID HIM IN A MANGER,
COULDN'T FIND NO HOTEL,
WASN'T THAT A PITY? WASN'T THAT A SHAME?
POOR LITTLE JESUS, BORN ON CHRISTMAS,
CRUCIFIED ON FRIDAY! PITY! PITY! PITY!
PITY! PITY! PITY AND A SHAME!
(The humming continues under sermon)
ELDER: But Jesus said, "Verily, verily, I say unto you, I will see you again." That's what Jesus said before He went to the Cross. "I will see you again and your hearts shall rejoice." Oh, the Gospel Glory! Wonder of our Savior's story.
WOMAN: Wonder! . . . . . Wonder! . . . . . Wonder!
VOICES: Gospel Glory! . . . . . Glory! . . . . . Glory!
ELDER: Jesus knew what He was talking about. Oh, yes! Jesus without money, without power—in the sense of this world—without position, without titles, poor like me, but Jesus knew whereof he spoke.

"I will see you again! The first shall be last and the last shall be first. Jesus the Son of God come to save me.

VOICES: Save me! Save me! Save me!

ELDER: So they conspired against Him. On the day of the unleaven bread, the Feast of the Passover, He ate His last Supper—Jesus and His Twelve Apostles. He brake the bread and gave it to them. "This is my body." He poured the wine and said, "This is my blood." He prophesied and said, "Truly the Son of Man goeth as it was determined." When the setting sun fell behind the hills of Jerusalem, Jesus knew that ere the sun rose again, ere the cock crew, Judas would betray Him, Peter would deny him thrice. All alone by Himself, He would go to His death. So Jesus got up from the table and went into the garden, the Garden of Gethsemane, to pray. To His disciples, He said:

OH, WATCH WITH ME ONE HOUR
WHILE I GO YONDER AND PRAY. . . . .

SINGERS: JUST WATCH WITH ME ONE HOUR
WHILE I GO YONDER AND PRAY

ELDER: JESUS LEFT HIS DISCIPLES
AND WENT A PACE AWAY

SINGERS: WATCH WITH ME ONE HOUR
WHILE I GO YONDER AND PRAY

ELDER: Jesus said, "My soul is exceedingly sorrowful, even unto death. Tarry ye here and watch with me."

SINGERS: WATCH WITH ME ONE HOUR
WHILE I GO YONDER AND PRAY.

ELDER: THE SPIRIT OF MAN IS WILLING
BUT THE FLESH OF MAN IS WEAK.
GETHSEMANE'S GARDEN'S CHILLING
TEARS ON MY JESUS' CHEEK.

SINGERS: OH, WATCH WITH ME ONE HOUR
WHILE I GO YONDER AND PRAY

ELDER: WATCH WITH ME ONE HOUR—

SINGERS: WHILE I GO YONDER AND PRAY

(SINGERS hum as ELDER continues)

ELDER: Jesus went alone a little farther into the Garden and fell on His face and prayed, saying, "Oh, my Father! Oh, my Father, if it be possible let this cup pass from me. Nevertheless, not as I will, but as Thou wilt. Thy will be done." And while he prayed, Judas, one of the disciples, snuck away.

VOICES: Snuck away! He snuck away! He snuck away!

ELDER: He snuck away from Gethsemane—that garden where Jesus fell down on His Face and cried to the Father, "Let this bitter hour pass from me! Oh, God, let this hour pass!"—because he was a young man who did not want to die. When Jesus rose up and looked around, His friends was all asleep. While Jesus prayed, His friend done gone to sleep. Jesus said:

WAKE UP FRIENDS, AND SLEEP NO MORE.

FOR MY HOUR IS NOW AT HAND.

THE ONE WHO IS TO BETRAY ME

IS LEADING THE MURDEROUS BAND.

SINGERS: WATCH WITH ME ONE HOUR

WHILE I GO YONDER AND PRAY.

ELDER: One hour! . . . . . . One hour! . . . . One hour!

SINGERS: JUST WATCH WITH ME ONE HOUR

WHILE I GO YONDER AND PRAY. . . . . . .

ELDER: But they didn't watch! They didn't watch—and Jesus was alone. He said, "Sleep on, for the hour is at hand." Jesus was not angry with them because they were asleep. But Judas was not asleep, no he wasn't! he had snuck away to give the soldiers a sign, say, "Whomsoever I shall kiss, that same is He—hold Him fast!"

    Judas! . . . . . Judas!

    Great God A-Mighty, Judas!

    Mean old traitor, Judas!

    Snuck away to the garden, snuck away,

    Where my Lord he did betray.

    Judas! . . . . . Judas!

    Lord have mercy on Judas!

    He made a deal, old Judas,

    For thirty pieces of silver

    He made a deal

    That my Jesus he would reveal.

    Judas! . . . . . Judas! . . . . . Judas!

    They seized my Lord

    With sword and staves

    And they took my Lord away,

    And Judas screamed

    And he ran to the mountain

    And he hung himself that day.

    For thirty pieces of silver

My Lord he did betray!
Judas! Great God A-Mighty, Judas!
Mean old traitor, Judas!
Judas! . . . . . Judas! . . . . .
Judas! . . . . .
(The body of Judas is seen hanging high above the heads of the SINGERS)

ELDER: In the Garden of Gethsemane, when the disciples awoke, they saw the mob, the mob around my Jesus! But the disciples fled away, because they were afraid. And the mob carried Jesus off, a prisoner in chains. Peter followed Jesus from afar. He didn't walk with Him, just followed, followed Jesus in chains. When they came to the Palace of the High Priest, Peter went in to see the trial. He sat in the back of the hall, afraid to own his Jesus, afraid to claim his Lord. Peter listened to the lies they told about Christ—and didn't dispute them. He watched the High Priest spit in Christ's face—and made no move. He saw them smite Him with the palms of their hands— and Peter uttered not a word for his poor mistreated Jesus. Not a word! When the guards asked Peter if he knew Jesus, he denied it. When they asked him again, Peter cried with an oath, "I do not know the man." When a third time they said, "Surely thou art also one of His disciples," Peter began to curse and swear. "*I say, I do not know the man.*" Then the cock crew. And Peter remembered the words of Jesus. "Before the cock crows, thou shalt deny me thrice." So Peter went out into the courtyard and wept bitterly. And Jesus was alone with his enemies. Alone! Alone!
JESUS WALKED HIS LONESOME VALLEY.
HE HAD TO WALK IT FOR HIMSELF.
NOBODY ELSE COULD WALK IT FOR HIM
HE HAD TO WALK IT FOR HIMSELF.

SINGERS: I MUST WALK MY LONESOME VALLEY.
I GOT TO WALK IT FOR MYSELF.
NOBODY ELSE CAN WALK IT FOR ME.
I GOT TO WALK IT FOR MYSELF.
I MUST GO AND STAND MY TRIAL.
I GOT TO STAND IT FOR MYSELF
NOBODY ELSE CAN STAND IT FOR ME.
I GOT TO STAND IT FOR MYSELF.
I GOT TO STAND MY TEST IN JUDGEMENT.

I GOT TO STAND IT FOR MYSELF.
NOBODY ELSE CAN STAND IT FOR ME.
I GOT TO STAND IT FOR MYSELF.
JESUS WALKED HIS LONESOME VALLEY.
HE HAD TO WALK IT FOR HIMSELF.
NOBODY ELSE COULD WALK IT FOR HIM,
HE HAD TO WALK IT FOR HIMSELF.

ELDER: So Jesus stood before the priests and the scribes. They did spit in his face, and buffeted Him, and others smote Him with the palms of their hands. When the morning was come, they bound Him and led Him away, and delivered Him to Pontius Pilate, the governor, for trial. Jesus stood before Pilate. Pilate asked of His accusers, "Tell me, what evil hath He done?" But the people cried, "Crucify Him," because they did not care. So Pilate called for water and washed his hands of the judgement, and got up from his throne and went away. The guards made sport of Jesus where he stood in the Council Hall. They stripped Him naked, put a crown of thorns on His head, a red robe about His body, and a reed from the river in His hands. They said "Ha! Ha! Ha! Ha! So you're the King! Ha! Ha!" And they bowed down in mockery before Jesus. They made fun of Jesus. Some of the guards was drunk and called Him out of His name—and nobody said, "Stop! That's Jesus."

SINGERS: Jesus! . . . . . Jesus! . . . . . Jesus!

ELDER: Oh, Yes! Peter denied Him because he was afraid. Judas betrayed Him for thirty pieces of silver. Pilate said, "I wash my hands." And the crowd said, "Kill Him! Kill Him!"

SINGERS: Kill Him! Kill Him! Kill Him!

ELDER: And His friends had fled away.

SINGERS: Have mercy on Jesus!

ELDER: His friends done fled away.

SINGERS: His friends! Oh-oooo-ooo-oo-o! His friends!

ELDER: His friends done fled away! Then they made a cross. They made Jesus shoulder that cross, and they stoned Him up the hill toward Calvary.

SINGERS: Oh, Lord, my Jesus!

ELDER: With the mob at His heels, shouting and hooting.

SINGERS: Um-mmmm-mmm-mm-m! My Lord! Lord Jesus!

ELDER: But stop, stop, stop! What about Mary? Mary, mother of Christ, Holy Mother Mary! Let's talk now about Mary—whose Son was on the way to the cross. Mary! Like every mother in the world, Mary loved her Son. Like your mother, like my mother, she loved her Child. And while all this was happening, don't think Mary didn't know. She knew. Mary knew. With a mother's intuition, nobody had to tell her that day that the sun had turned to blood. She knew. . . . . When Jesus came out from His trial, and Pilate had done washed his hands, Mary stopped her scrubbing and her washing and left her house and came into the street. And when she heard the mob there shouting and screaming at Jesus, agony seized her heart, pain shook her body. Cold sweat stood on her brow, and she thought she could not stand. But for His sake, Mary did not faint nor fall. *For His sake!* Oh, my friends, like Jesus's mother, stand up and suffer the pain of the Cross, the testing of this world. The Cross! His Cross, that cross too heavy for even Jesus that day to bear. He stumbled and fell! The soldiers scourged Him in the street, but He could not bear His cross. . . . . Then it was that Simon, a black man named Simon, appeared from out the crowd—a man who did not know Jesus. But he picked up His cross. Simon picked up His cross, followed Jesus. And way back yonder in the crowd, a ball of agony in her throat, the ice of agony in her heart, Mary, His mother, followed Jesus. . . . . And Jesus went up the hill of Golgatha.

SINGERS: Golgatha! . . . . . Golgatha!

ELDER: Golgatha! Jesus standing alone on that high hill, the Hill of Golgatha. Alone in the broiling sun, whilst the Romans planted three crosses in the ground—for that day they also hung two thieves.

SINGERS: Two thieves! Thieves! Thieves! Two thieves!

ELDER: My God! . . . . . My God!

SINGERS: My God!

ELDER: Why hast Thou forsaken me? Jesus had no water to cool His throat. No tree to shade His aching head! Nobody to say a friendly word to Jesus. Um-mmm-mm-m! Alone in that crowd on the Hill of Golgatha, with two thieves bound and dying, and the murmur of the mob all around Him. Then I imagine Jesus, at that moment, Jesus looked afar off in the distance, away over the heads of the crowd, and He saw there poor helpless Mary, His mother. Mary! Mary! Mary! His mother, Mary. . . . And there was anguish in His heart, oh, what anguish when He looked and saw His mother. And I imagine I heard Him cry, "Please, oh, somebody, please, somebody take my mother home."

I THINK I HEARD HIM SAY
AS HE WAS LIFTED TO THE
   CROSS,
I THINK I HEARD HIM SAY,
TAKE MY MOTHER HOME,
THEN I'LL DIE EASY.

OH, TAKE MY MOTHER
   HOME.
I THINK I HEARD HIM SAY

WHEN THEY WAS RAFFLING
OFF HIS CLOTHES,
I THINK I HEARD HIM SAY,

TAKE MY MOTHER HOME
THEN I'LL DIE EASY

TAKE MY MOTHER HOME.

I THINK I HEARD HIM CRY

WHEN THEY WAS COUNTING
OUT THE NAILS

I THINK I HEARD HIM CRY,
TAKE MY MOTHER HOME.
I'LL DIE THIS DEATH ON
   CALVARY
AIN'T GONNA DIE NO MORE

I'LL DIE THIS DEATH ON
   CALVARY
AIN'T GONNA DIE NO MORE.
I THINK I HEARD HIM SAY
WHEN HE WAS GIVING UP
   THE GHOST
I THINK I HEARD HIM SAY
PLEASE TAKE MY MOTHER
   HOME
PLEASE TAKE MY MOTHER
   HOME.

And then the skies began to darken, and the earth to tremble, and
the soldiers brought nails, four long nails, and then—and then—they
nailed Him to the tree. . . . .

WOMAN: Oh-ooo-oo-o!

ELDER: Four long iron nails—and they put one in the palm of His
left hand. The hammer said. . . . BAM! They put one in the palm of
His right hand. The hammer said. . . . BAM! They put one through
His left foot. . . . Bam! And one through His right foot. . . . BAM!
They nailed my Jesus to the cross. Nails in His hands! Nails in His
foot! Sword in His side! Thorns circling His head! Mob cussing and
hooting my Jesus! Umm! The spit of the mob in His face! Umm! His
body hanging on the cross! Umm! "Gimme a piece of His garment
for a souvenir!" Umm! Casting lots for His garments! Umm! Blood
from His wounded side! Umm! Streaming down His naked legs!
Umm! Dropping in the dust, His blood—that's what they did to my
Jesus! They stoned Him, first they stoned Him! Called Him everything but a child of God . . . Then they lynched Him on the cross.

(A WOMAN screams. Silence. Then very softly voices rise like a lament)

SOLO: WERE YOU THERE WHEN THEY CRUCIFIED MY LORD?
OH, SOMETIMES IT CAUSES ME TO TREMBLE, TREMBLE,
WERE YOU THERE WHEN THEY CRUCIFIED MY LORD?
WERE YOU THERE WHEN THEY CRUCIFIED MY LORD?
WERE YOU THERE WHEN THEY NAILED HIM TO THE TREE?
OH, SOMETIMES IT CAUSES ME TO TREMBLE, TREMBLE.
WERE YOU THERE WHEN THEY NAILED HIM TO THE TREE?
WERE YOU THERE WHEN HE BOWED HIS HEAD AND DIED?
OH, SOMETIMES IT CAUSES ME TO TREMBLE, TREMBLE.
WERE YOU THERE WHEN HE BOWED HIS HEAD AND DIED?
(Humming as ELDER speaks)
Joseph of Arimathea came and took the body of Jesus and wrapped it in fine linen and laid Him in a sepulchre which was hewn out of rock, and rolled a stone unto the door.

SINGERS: WERE YOU THERE WHEN THEY LAID HIM IN THE TOMB
OH, SOMETIMES IT CAUSES ME TO TREMBLE, TREMBLE.
WERE YOU THERE WHEN THEY LAID HIM IN THE TOMB?
(Silence as the music dies)

ELDER: I wasn't there. No, I wasn't there, but I know what Jesus said.
SISTER: I know too.
ELDER: What did He say, Sister? What did He say?
SISTER: AIN'T NO GRAVE CAN HOLD MY BODY DOWN.
SINGERS: AIN'T NO GRAVE CAN HOLD MY BODY DOWN.
BEFORE THE FIRST TRUMPETS SOUND
I'LL BE GETTING UP WALKING ROUND.
AIN'T NO GRAVE CAN HOLD MY BODY DOWN.
WHEN JESUS WAS HANGING ON THE CROSS,
WELL, IT MADE POOR MARY MOAN.
WHEN HE LOOKED, ALL HIS DISCIPLES
HAD TAKEN HIS MOTHER HOME.
IT'S A PITY. IT'S A SHAME,
HOW THEY CRUCIFIED HIS NAME!

AIN'T NO GRAVE CAN HOLD HIS BODY DOWN.
BEFORE THE FIRST TRUMPETS SOUND
HE'LL BE GETTING UP WALKING ROUND
AIN'T NO GRAVE CAN HOLD HIS BODY DOWN.

ELDER: The Scripture says that Mary, mother of Jesus, came with Martha to the tomb. She stood without the sepulchre weeping. As she wept, she stooped down and looked into the tomb, and seeth two angels dressed in white sitting, one at the head and the other at the feet, where the body of Jesus had lain. The angels said unto her, "Woman, why weepest thou?"

SINGERS: OH, MARY, DON'T YOU WEEP,
MARTHA, DON'T YOU MOAN.
MARY, DON'T YOU WEEP.
TELL MARTHA NOT TO MOAN.
PHARAOH'S ARMY GOT DROWNED
IN THE SEA ONE DAY.
LISTEN, MARY, DON'T YOU WEEP,
TELL YOUR SISTER, MARTHA,
MARTHA, NOT TO MOAN
IF I COULD I SURELY WOULD
STAND ON THE ROCK TONIGHT,
STAND RIGHT WHERE MOSES STOOD,
AND TELL 'EM PHARAOH'S ARMY
GOT DROWNED IN THE SEA ONE DAY.
OH, MARY, DON'T YOU WEEP,
MARTHA, DON'T YOU MOAN,
MARY, DON'T YOU WEEP. . . . . .

(MARY and MARTHA go toward the tomb)

ELDER: Martha and Mary, the Mother of Jesus, wondered how it was that when they looked in the tomb, Jesus was not there. And the big stone that had been in front of the tomb, it was not there. And they marvelled, and wondered who it was rolled the stone away.

SINGERS: THE ANGEL ROLLED THE STONE AWAY.
THE ANGEL ROLLED THE STONE AWAY.
'TWAS ON A BRIGHT AND SUNNY MORN
WHEN THE TRUMPET BEGAN TO SOUND,
THE ANGEL ROLLED THE STONE AWAY.

ELDER: SISTER MARY CAME A-RUNNING
AT THE BREAK OF DAY,

BROUGHT THE NEWS FROM HEAVEN—
THE STONE DONE ROLLED AWAY.
SINGERS: THE ANGEL ROLLED THE STONE AWAY.
SISTER: I AM LOOKING FOR MY SAVIOR
TELL ME WHERE HE LAY.
HIGH UP ON THE MOUNTAIN,
THE STONE DONE ROLLED AWAY.
SINGERS: THE ANGEL ROLLED THE STONE AWAY.
ELDER: PILATE AND HIS WISE MEN
DIDN'T KNOW WHAT TO SAY.
THE MIRACLE WAS ON THEM—
THE STONE DONE ROLLED AWAY.
SINGERS: THE ANGEL ROLLED THE STONE AWAY
'TWAS ON A BRIGHT AND SUNNY MORN
WHEN THE TRUMPET BEGAN TO SOUND
THE ANGEL ROLLED THE STONE AWAY.
VOICES: Hallelujah! Yes, he did! He did! He did! Did!
ELDER: Mary and the women who had gathered with her at the tomb
were sore perplexed when they found not the body of Jesus. But,
behold! Two men stood near them in shining garments. The women
were afraid and bowed down their faces to the earth, as the men said,
"Why seek ye the living among the dead? He is not here. He is risen."
SINGERS: HE ROSE! HE ROSE!
HE ROSE FROM THE GRAVE!
HE ROSE! HE ROSE!
HE ROSE FROM THE GRAVE!
AND THE LORD SHALL BEAR MY SPIRIT HOME.
    (MARY and MARTHA whirl about in wonderment)
SISTER MARY WENT A-RUNNING
TO FIND HER PRECIOUS LORD
AND THE LORD SHALL BEAR MY SPIRIT HOME.
SINGERS: HE ROSE! HE ROSE!
HE ROSE FROM THE GRAVE!
AND THE LORD SHALL BEAR MY SPIRIT HOME.
MEN: TWO ANGELS CAME FROM HEAVEN
AND ROLLED THE STONE AWAY.
AND THE LORD SHALL BEAR MY SPIRIT HOME.
SINGERS: HE ROSE! HE ROSE!
HE ROSE FROM THE GRAVE!
AND THE LORD SHALL BEAR MY SPIRIT HOME.

MEN: THE COLD GRAVE COULD NOT HOLD HIM,
   NOR DEATH'S IRON HAND
   AND THE LORD SHALL BEAR MY SPIRIT HOME.
SINGERS: HE ROSE! HE ROSE!
   HE ROSE FROM THE GRAVE!
   AND THE LORD SHALL BEAR MY SPIRIT HOME.
ELDER: He rose. On the third day He ascended into Heaven. He sitteth
   at the right hand of the Father. He shall come again with glory to
   judge the living and the dead. Of his kingdom, there shall be no
   end. And many shall be His Apostles, praising His name, the risen
   Christ—Jesus, my King!
MEN: RIDE ON, KING JESUS!
   NO MAN CAN HINDER HIM.
   RIDE ON, KING JESUS!
   NO MAN CAN HINDER HIM.
BROTHER: KING JESUS RIDES ON A MILK WHITE HORSE.
MEN: NO MAN CAN HINDER HIM.
BROTHER: THE RIVER OF JORDAN HE DID CROSS.
MEN: NO MAN CAN HINDER HIM.
BROTHER: IF YOU WANT TO FIND YOUR WAY TO GOD—
MEN: NO MAN CAN HINDER HIM.
BROTHER: THE GOSPEL HIGHWAY MUST BE TROD.
MEN: NO MAN CAN HINDER HIM.
SINGERS: RIDE ON, KING JESUS!
   NO MAN CAN HINDER HIM.
   RIDE ON, KING JESUS!
   NO MAN CAN HINDER HIM.
ELDER: He said, "I go to prepare a place for you."
SISTER: Yes, He did! He went to prepare a place for me.
ELDER: A place in the Kingdom! But while you are yet on earth—where
   every soul must live until you die—who is it stands by you in every
   need?
SISTER: Jesus!
ELDER: Yes, it's Jesus! And who is it—if you accept Him—guards your
   every waking, sleeping, walking, talking, living, breathing moment?
SISTER: Jesus! Thank God for Jesus!
ELDER: Jesus, born in Bethlehem of Judea! Preaching the Sermon on
   the Mount! Feeding ten thousand with just a few little old small
   loaves! Riding into Jerusalem on Palm Sunday to the Hosannas of
   the crowd! Saying, at the Last Supper, "This is My body and this is

My blood." Whipped up the Hill of Golgatha! Crucified! From the
cradle to the cross, the manger to the Mountain where He died for
you and me.

SISTER: For me! For me! Yes, for me!

ELDER: Tell the world about it, sister! Testify in song! Speak! Sing!
Shout!

SISTER: IS THERE ANYONE CAN HELP YOU?
ONE WHO UNDERSTANDS YOUR GRIEF
WHEN THE STORM OF LIFE
PLAYS YOU UNTIL YOU BLEED—
ONE WHO SYMPATHIZES WITH YOU
AND HIS WONDROUS LOVE IMPARTS,
GIVES YOU THE VERY BLESSING
THAT YOU NEED:
YES, THERE'S ONE! ONE, ONLY ONE!
OH, THE BLESSED JESUS IS THE ONE.
WHEN AFFLICTIONS PRESS YOUR SOUL
AND THE WAVES OF TROUBLE ROLL,
IF YOU NEED A FRIEND TO,
IF YOU NEED A FRIEND TO,
IF YOU NEED A FRIEND TO HELP YOU,
HE'S THE ONE. . . . . etc. . . . . . .

ELDER: And He has gone ahead to prepare a place in the Kingdom for
you and for me—a place in the Land of Life Everlasting.

WOMAN: Yes, He did! That's why I know
THERE'S PLENTY GOOD ROOM
IN MY FATHER'S KINGDOM
PLENTY GOOD ROOM, PLENTY GOOD ROOM,
JUST CHOOSE YOUR SEAT AND SET DOWN.
HE SAID TO PETER, JAMES AND JOHN,
'TIS WRITTEN I MUST DIE
TO SHED MY BLOOD ON CALVARY.
GO THOU AND PROPHESY.

SINGERS: OH, THERE'S PLENTY GOOD ROOM,
GOOD ROOM IN MY FATHER'S KINGDOM
JUST CHOOSE YOUR SEAT AND SET DOWN.

BROTHER: HOSANNA TO THE PRINCE OF PEACE
WHO CLOTHED HIMSELF WITH CLAY
AND ENTERED THE IRON GATES OF DEATH
AND TOOK DEATH'S STING AWAY.

SINGERS: THERE'S PLENTY GOOD ROOM
   IN MY FATHER'S KINGDOM.
   CHOOSE YOUR SEAT AND SET DOWN.
SISTERS: SOME OF THESE MORNINGS, BRIGHT AND FAIR,
   I'M GONNA TAKE MY WINGS AND CLEAVE THE AIR.
   SOME OF THESE MORNINGS, BRIGHT AND SOON,
   GONNA FLY RIGHT PAST THE SUN AND MOON.
SINGERS: OH, THERE'S PLENTY GOOD ROOM,
   GOOD ROOM IN MY FATHER'S KINGDOM
   PLENTY GOOD ROOM, PLENTY GOOD ROOM—
   JUST CHOOSE YOUR SEAT AND SET DOWN.
     (An OLD WOMAN comes forward)
SISTER: Set down? Did you-all say set down? Who said, set down?
SINGERS: Yes, set down.
SISTER: I CAN'T SET DOWN
   I JUST GOT TO HEAVEN
   AND I CAN'T SET DOWN.
BROTHER: WHY DON'T YOU SET DOWN?
SISTER: I CAN'T SET DOWN.
DEACON: SET DOWN, I TOLD YOU!
SISTER: GO AWAY, DON'T BOTHER ME.
   I CAN'T SET DOWN—
   BECAUSE I JUST GOT TO HEAVEN
   AND I CAN'T SET DOWN.
ELDER: WHO'S THAT YONDER DRESSED IN WHITE?
SISTER: IT LOOKS LIKE THE CHILDREN OF THE ISRAELITE.
ELDER: WHO'S THAT YONDER DRESSED IN RED?
SISTER: IT LOOKS LIKE THE CHILDREN THAT MOSES LED.
SINGERS: WHY DON'T YOU SET DOWN?
SISTER: I CAN'T SET DOWN.
   NO! NO! . . . . NO! NO!
   I CAN'T SET DOWN
   I JUST GOT TO HEAVEN
   AND I CAN'T SET DOWN.
BROTHER: Why can't you set down?
ELDER: Tell them, sister, tell them!
     (The music of "THE GOSPEL GLORY" begins and continues
     under speech to finale.)
SISTER: My soul is filled with the Gospel Glory, that's why I can't set
   down.

I CAN'T SET DOWN!
NO, NO, NO, NO! NO, NO!
I CAN'T SET DOWN
I GOT THE GOSPEL GLORY
AND I CAN'T SET DOWN.

ELDER: The Gospel Glory! Thank God for Jesus. Thank Him for His
life, His crucifixion. His resurrection. Thank God for His salvation.
Thank God for sending His son into the world that we might be
saved. Thank God for His spirit alive today in all its glory. Glory!
Glory!

SINGERS: MY SOUL IS FILLED WITH THE GOSPEL GLORY!
GOSPEL GLORY! GOSPEL GLORY!
MY SOUL IS FILLED WITH THE GOSPEL GLORY!
GLORY! GLORY! GOSPEL GLORY!
ASK ME HOW I GOT IT,
I WILL TELL THE STORY—
GOT IT FROM THE LORD,
GOT IT FROM THE LORD,
GOT IT FROM THE LORD ABOVE.

ELDER: HOSANNA TO MY PRECIOUS LORD!
OH, LET HIS PRAISES RING!
SINCE JESUS DIED, WAS CRUCIFIED,
I OWN HIM AS MY KING.

SINGERS: MY SOUL IS FILLED WITH THE GOSPEL GLORY!
GOSPEL GLORY! GOSPEL GLORY!
MY SOUL IS FILLED WITH THE GOSPEL GLORY!
GLORY! GLORY! GOSPEL GLORY!
ASK ME HOW I GOT IT,
I WILL TELL MY STORY—
GOT IT FROM THE LORD,
GOT IT FROM THE LORD,
GOT IT FROM THE LORD ABOVE.
GLORY! GLORY! . . . . . GLORY! GLORY!
GLORY! . . . . AMEN! . . . . AMEN!

BLACKOUT
THE END[1]

Master of Miracles
A Gospel Song-Play Based on the
Bible and the Negro Spirituals

1962

NO SETS: There may be platforms of varying heights, benches for the
 SINGERS, and a simple stand for the ELDER, if desired, or this
 presentation may be given in the rostrum of a church.

COSTUMES: The SINGERS may wear simple choir robes, the ELDER
 a Sunday-go-to-meeting suit, and the PANTOMIMISTS the clothing of Biblical days.

CHARACTERS: AN ELDER   A DEACON
                     A WOMAN   SINGERS
                     A BROTHER   PANTOMIMISTS

PANTOMIMISTS: (if used) There should be three mimes—or more if
 desired—at least two male, one female, who portray at various times,
 JOSEPH, MARY, A SHEPHERD, JOHN THE BAPTIST, SIN-
 NERS AT THE JUDGEMENT, JERUSALEMITES ON PALM
 SUNDAY, and GOSPEL SHOUTERS in jubilation at certain
 points. The pantomimists, who should move in rhythm to the music visualizing certain songs, may be dancers or not. Without pantomimists, this presentation may be given in a concert version.

THIS STORY of the life of Christ from the flight into Egypt to the
 last entry into Jerusalem, as derived from the Bible and traditional
 American religious songs, may be presented by any group of singers
 to whose soloists the speaking parts—except that of the NARRA-
 TOR or ELDER—may be assigned.

LENGTH: This performance may be shortened, if desired, by omitting
 some songs; or it may be lengthened by including additional spirituals, hymns, or gospel numbers suitable to the mood of the story,
 if such songs are already in the repertoire of the singers.

*There is an ORGAN or PIANO PRELUDE as the lights dim. Then on
 stage an ELDER and his congregation of SINGERS are revealed. The
 ELDER speaks against the music.*

ELDER: I am here to tell you about the miracles of Christ. You are a miracle. I am a miracle. That we are here in this world is a miracle. But the greatest miracle of all is Jehovah, Lord God the Father who—long before He gave His only begotten Son—created the heavens and the earth, and on the seventh day rested. Then He created man. What did He do that for? Male and female created He then. Why? I ask you, why? To give Himself a headache? To be worried with us and our sinful ways? No! He created you and me that we might be tested, tried, saved from sin, and find salvation— salvation through the miracle of grace. He began with Adam and Eve in the Garden—Adam and Eve who ate of the apple of sin before God could bat an eye. Oh, sinful man whom Christ was sent to save.

WOMAN: EVE, WHERE IS ADAM?

DEACON: EVE, WHERE IS ADAM?

ELDER: ADAM'S IN THE GARDEN PICKING UP LEAVES.

WOMEN: ADAM'S IN THE GARDEN PICKING UP LEAVES.

ELDER: HE DIDN'T COME SOON IN THE MORNING,
NEITHER IN THE HEAT OF THE DAY.
HE'S COME IN THE COOL OF THE EVENING
TO WASH MY SINS AWAY.

SINGERS: EVE, WHERE IS ADAM?
EVE, WHERE IS ADAM?
ADAM'S IN THE GARDEN PICKING UP LEAVES.

ELDER: Adam and Eve, Cain and Abel! Poor mankind! Where would we be had not the Lord God Jehovah sent His Son by way of the Manger, by way of that Manger in Bethlehem, to save us all? And ever since, everywhere, we've been talking about Jesus. Yes!

WOMAN: EVERYWHERE I GO, EVERYWHERE I GO, MY LORD,

SINGERS: EVERYWHERE I GO, SOMEBODY'S TALKING ABOUT JESUS.

WOMAN: THEY TURNED AWAY MARY AND JOSEPH FROM THE INN.

SINGERS: SOMEBODY'S TALKING ABOUT JESUS.

DEACON: BABY BORN IN BETHLEHEM.

SINGERS: SOMEBODY'S TALKING ABOUT JESUS.

WOMAN: BORN, BORN OF THE VIRGIN MARY.

SINGERS: SOMEBODY'S TALKING ABOUT JESUS.

ELDER: BORN, BORN ON A CHRISTMAS MORNING.

SINGERS: SOMEBODY'S TALKING ABOUT JESUS.

MEN: GLORY BE TO THE NEW BORN BABY!

SINGERS: EVERYWHERE I GO, EVERYWHERE I GO, MY LORD, EVERYWHERE I GO, SOMEBODY'S TALKING ABOUT JESUS.

> *(Enter JOSEPH and MARY)*

ELDER: Little Jesus! Mary and Joseph barred out of the inn. Jesus, born into this mean old world. Little Jesus, parents forced to flee into Egypt, lest King Herod seek the young Child to destroy Him. Oh, the road is rocky, but it won't be rocky long.

WOMAN: Right!

ELDER: Didn't my Lord deliver Daniel?

SINGERS: Yes!

ELDER: Then why not every man?

> *(DANCE OF JOSEPH AND MARY, WITH THE BABE, IN JOY AT DELIVERANCE)*

SINGERS: DIDN'T MY LORD DELIVER DANIEL, DANIEL, DANIEL?

DIDN'T MY LORD DELIVER DANIEL?

THEN WHY NOT EVERY MAN?

HE DELIVERED JONAH FROM THE BELLY OF THE WHALE,

DANIEL FROM THE LION'S DEN,

THE HEBREW CHILDREN FROM THE FIERY FURNACE,

THEN WHY NOT EVERY MAN?

DIDN'T MY LORD DELIVER DANIEL, DANIEL, DANIEL,

THEN WHY NOT EVERY MAN?

> *(Exit JOSEPH and MARY)*

ELDER: He delivered my Lord—for an angel appeared in a dream to Joseph in Egypt saying, "Arise and take the young Child and His mother and come into the land of Israel." So Joseph came and dwelt in a city called Nazareth, and Jesus was called a Nazarene. When Jesus was yet a young boy, He traveled with His parents to Jerusalem, and He went to sit in the temple among the elders.

WOMAN: Yes, He did! Among the scribes!

SINGERS: FOUR AND TWENTY ELDERS ON THEIR KNEES,

FOUR AND TWENTY ELDERS ON THEIR KNEES—

AND THEY ALL FALL TOGETHER

AND FACE THE RISING SUN.

LORD, HAVE MERCY, IF YOU PLEASE!

LET US ALL WORK TOGETHER ON OUR KNEES.

LET US ALL WORK TOGETHER ON OUR KNEES.

AND AS ONE PEOPLE FACE THE RISING SUN,
LORD, HAVE MERCY, IF YOU PLEASE.
FOUR AND TWENTY ELDERS ON THEIR KNEES. . . . .
ELDER: Those old men praying there, old wise men, rose up and asked
    Jesus questions, and the young Child answered them and all that
    heard him—according to Luke 2:47—were astonished at his answers
    —so astonished that they cried out—just as I would have cried out
    had I been there, "Little Boy, how old are You? Tell me."
MEN: LITTLE BOY, HOW OLD ARE YOU?
    LITTLE BOY, HOW OLD ARE YOU?
TENOR: SIR, I'M ONLY TWELVE YEARS OLD.
MEN: THIS LITTLE BOY HAD THEM TO REMEMBER
    HE WAS BORN THE TWENTY-FIFTH OF DECEMBER.
    LAWYERS AND DOCTORS WERE AMAZED—
    THEY HAD TO GIVE THE LITTLE BOY PRAISE.
SINGERS: LITTLE BOY, HOW OLD ARE YOU?
    LITTLE BOY, HOW OLD ARE YOU?
TENOR: I'M ONLY TWELVE YEARS OLD.
MEN: LAWYERS AND DOCTORS STOOD AND WONDERED
    AS THOUGH THEY HAD BEEN STRUCK BY THUNDER.
    THEN THEY DECIDED WHILE THEY WONDERED
    THAT ALL MANKIND MUST COME UNDER.
SINGERS: LITTLE BOY, HOW OLD ARE YOU?
    LITTLE BOY, HOW OLD ARE YOU?
TENOR: WELL, I'M ONLY TWELVE YEARS OLD.
SINGERS: THIS LITTLE BOY HAD THE KEY
    TO THE HIDDEN MYSTERY.
    THE LAWYERS DECIDED, AS WISE AS HE,
    THEY'D BETTER LET THAT LITTLE BOY BE.
MEN: LITTLE BOY, HOW OLD ARE YOU?
    LITTLE BOY, HOW OLD ARE YOU?
TENOR: SAID, I'M ONLY TWELVE YEARS OLD.
MEN: THE LAST TIME THAT LITTLE BOY WAS SEEN,
    HE WAS STANDING ON MOUNT OLIVET GREEN.
    WHEN HE DISPERSED OF THE CROWD,
    HE ENTERED UP INTO A CLOUD.
SINGERS: LITTLE BOY, HOW OLD ARE YOU?
    LITTLE BOY, HOW OLD ARE YOU?
    LITTLE BOY, HOW OLD ARE YOU?
MEN: I'M ONLY TWELVE YEARS OLD.

ELDER: "Wist ye not," He said, "that I must be about my Father's business?" And His Father's business surpasseth understanding—and it leads Him to the Cross. That is what I have come here to tell you now—how Jesus travelled the road from the cradle to the cross, from Bethlehem of Judea to the Mountain of Golgotha. And how in those days, John the Baptist said, "Prepare ye the way of the Lord, for One mightier than I cometh, the latchet of whose shoes I am not worthy to unloose. He shall baptize you with the Holy Ghost and with fire."

(JOHN THE BAPTIST enters)

It was John himself who, when Christ was about thirty years old, baptized our Lord in the River Jordan. Then it was that a voice came from heaven saying, "Thou art my beloved Son in whom I am well pleased."

(JOHN'S DANCE OF EXULTATION IN THE WILDERNESS)

SINGERS: JOHN SAW THE HOLY NUMBER.
JOHN SAW, OH, JOHN SAW,
SETTING ON THE GOLDEN ALTAR.
WORTHY, WORTHY IS THE LAMB,
IS THE LAMB, IS THE LAMB,
SETTING ON THE GOLDEN ALTAR.
I WANT TO GO TO HEAVEN WHEN I DIE,
SETTING ON THE GOLDEN ALTAR.
SHOUT SALVATION AS I FLY,
SETTING ON THE GOLDEN ALTAR.
IT'S A LITTLE WHILE LONGER HERE BELOW,
SETTING ON THE GOLDEN ALTAR.
THEN HOME TO GLORY WE SHALL GO,
SETTING ON THE GOLDEN ALTAR.
JOHN SAW, OH, JOHN SAW,
JOHN SAW THE HOLY NUMBER
SETTING ON THE GOLDEN ALTAR.

(JOHN exits dancing)

ELDER: Then it was that Christ went out into the wilderness, and fasted and prayed for forty nights and forty days, for He knew that man shall not live by bread alone. And when He had fasted and prayed, He departed into Galilee and began to preach, saying, "Repent—for the kingdom of heaven is at hand."

(Song and the Sermon on the Mount intertwine as the ELDER speaks between musical phrases)

SINGERS: I HEARD THE PREACHING OF THE ELDER,
PREACHING THE WORD, PREACHING THE WORD.

ELDER: And Jesus went about all Galilee preaching the gospel of the kingdom.

SINGERS: I HEARD THE PREACHING OF THE ELDER
PREACHING THE WORD OF GOD.

ELDER: And His fame went throughout Syria.

SINGERS: PREACHING THE WORD OF GOD.

ELDER: There followed behind Him great multitudes of people from beyond the Jordan.

SINGERS: PREACHING THE WORD OF GOD.

ELDER: And seeing the multitudes, Jesus went up into a mountain, and opened His mouth.

SINGERS: I HEARD THE PREACHING OF THE ELDER. . . . .

ELDER: There on the mountain He spake and said, "Blessed are the poor in spirit, for theirs is the kingdom of heaven."

SINGERS: PREACHING THE WORD OF GOD

ELDER: "Blessed are they that mourn, for they shall be comforted."

SINGERS: I HEARD THE PREACHING OF THE ELDER. . . . .

ELDER: "Blessed are the meek, for they shall inherit the earth."

SINGERS: PREACHING THE WORD OF GOD.

ELDER: "Blessed are they which do hunger and thirst after righteousness, for they shall be filled."

SINGERS: I HEARD THE PREACHING OF THE ELDER. . . . .

ELDER: "Blessed are the merciful, for they shall obtain mercy."

SINGERS: PREACHING THE WORD OF GOD.

ELDER: "Blessed are the pure in heart, for they shall see God."

SINGERS: I HEARD THE PREACHING OF THE ELDER. . . . .

ELDER: "Blessed are the peacemakers, for they shall be called the children of God."

SINGERS: PREACHING THE WORD. . . . .

ELDER: "Blessed are they which are persecuted for righteousness sake, for theirs is the kingdom of heaven."

SINGERS: PREACHING THE WORD OF GOD.

ELDER: "Blessed are ye when men shall revile you, and persecute you, and shall say all manner of evil against you falsely for my sake."

SINGERS: I HEARD THE PREACHING OF THE ELDER. . . . .

ELDER: "Rejoice and be exceedingly glad, for great is your reward in heaven."

SINGERS: PREACHING THE WORD OF GOD.

ELDER: "Ye are the salt of the earth."

SINGERS: I HEARD THE PREACHING OF THE ELDER,
PREACHING THE WORD OF GOD!

BROTHER: He meant those words for me!

DEACON: Preaching on the mountain those words for me!

WOMAN: I sought and I found Him—found Him for me!

SINGERS: OH, SEEK, AND YE SHALL FIND.
KNOCK, AND THE DOOR SHALL BE OPENED.
ASK, AND IT SHALL BE GIVEN.
AND THE LOVE COME TRICKLING DOWN.

WOMAN: DEACON, THE LORD'S BEEN HERE.

SINGERS: AND THE LOVE COME A TRICKLING DOWN.

DEACON: SISTER, THE LORD'S BEEN HERE.

SINGERS: AND THE LOVE COME TRICKLING DOWN.

ELDER: BROTHER, THE LORD'S BEEN HERE
AND THE LOVE COME TRICKLING DOWN!

SINGERS: SEEK, AND YE SHALL FIND!
KNOCK, AND THE DOOR SHALL BE OPENED!
ASK, AND IT SHALL BE GIVEN!
OH, THE LOVE COME TRICKLING DOWN!

ELDER: His love come trickling down to all mankind. And Christ was
loved by His disciples, and they followed Him. Matthew, Mark, and
John, Philip, Peter, Andrew, and the two James, Thomas, Judas,
Simon and Bartholomew. Christ found Matthew at the customs
house and said, "Follow me." And Matthew rose and followed Him.
He found Peter fishing in the sea, and He said—
PETER, PETER, PETER ON THE SEA,
DROP YOUR NETS AND FOLLOW ME.
He said, "I will make you a fisher of men."

SINGERS: PETER, PETER, PETER ON THE SEA,
DROP YOUR NETS AND FOLLOW,
DROP YOUR NETS AND FOLLOW ME.

DEACON: WHO DID, WHO DID, WHO DID SWALLOW JONAH?

SINGERS: DROP YOUR NETS AND FOLLOW ME.

DEACON: WHALE DID, WHALE DID, WHALE DID SWALLOW
JONAH.

SINGERS: DROP YOUR NETS AND FOLLOW ME.
PETER, PETER, PETER ON THE SEA,
DROP YOUR NETS AND FOLLOW,
DROP YOUR NETS AND FOLLOW ME.

ELDER: The disciples followed Christ, and did as He told them to do, "Go forth and preach the gospel in all the lands about Galilee." That's what He told them, didn't he, Church?

VOICES: Yes, He did!

SINGERS: CHILDREN, GO WHERE I SEND THEE.
HOW SHALL I SEND THEE?
I'M GONNA SEND THEE ONE BY ONE.
ONE IS FOR THE LITTLE BABY
BORN OF THE VIRGIN MARY,
WRAPPED IN SWADDLING CLOTHING,
LAID IN A LONELY MANGER,
BORN, BORN IN BETHLEHEM.
CHILDREN, GO WHERE I SEND THEE.
HOW SHALL I SEND THEE?
I'M GONNA SEND THEE TWO BY TWO. . . . etc. . . .

(As they sing, the SINGERS, one by one, two by two, etc., pantomime this cumulative song until all are marching and singing together.)

BORN, BORN IN BETHLEHEM. . . . .

ELDER: Sitting on the Mount of Olives, Jesus said, "Many shall come in My name saying, 'I am Christ,' and shall deceive many. And ye shall hear of wars and rumors of wars, for nation shall rise against nation, and kingdom against kingdom, and there shall be famines, and pestilences, and earthquakes in diverse places.

(The CHORUS begins softly to sing, and the ELDER speaks over their song quoting from Matthew 24)

SINGERS: MY LORD, WHAT A MORNING
WHEN THE STARS BEGIN TO FALL!
YOU'LL HEAR THE TRUMPET SOUND
TO WAKE THE NATIONS UNDERGROUND,
LOOKING TO MY GOD'S RIGHT HAND
WHEN THE STARS BEGIN TO FALL.

ELDER: Then shall they deliver you up to be afflicted and shall kill you. And ye shall be hated of all nations for my name's sake. But he that shall endure unto the end, the same shall be saved. Then let them that shall be in Judea flee into the mountains for then shall be great tribulation, such as was not since the beginning of the world.

SINGERS: MY LORD, WHAT A MORNING
WHEN THE STARS BEGIN TO FALL!
YOU'LL HEAR THE SINNER MOAN

TO WAKE THE NATIONS UNDERGROUND
LOOKING TO MY GOD'S RIGHT HAND
WHEN THE STARS BEGIN TO FALL.
MY LORD, WHAT A MORNING
WHEN THE STARS BEGIN TO FALL.
YOU'LL HEAR THE CHRISTIANS SHOUT
TO WAKE THE NATIONS UNDERGROUND
LOOKING TO MY GOD'S RIGHT HAND
WHEN THE STARS BEGIN TO FALL!
MY LORD, WHAT A MORNING,
MY LORD, WHAT A MORNING,
MY LORD, WHAT A MORNING
WHEN THE STARS BEGIN TO FALL. . . . .

ELDER: My God! . . My God! . . . . . My God!

> *(As the song continues SINNERS portray the terror of the Last Judgement)*

My God! Mercy, Lord! My God!

DEACON: WHERE SHALL I BE WHEN THE FIRST TRUMPET SOUNDS?

SINGERS: WHERE SHALL I BE WHEN IT SOUNDS SO LOUD?
WHEN IT SOUNDS SO LOUD TILL IT WAKES UP THE DEAD.
WHERE SHALL I BE WHEN IT SOUNDS?

> *(Hope causes the SINNERS to rise)*

DEACON: GOING TO TRY ON MY ROBE WHEN THE FIRST TRUMPET SOUNDS.
GOING TO TRY ON MY ROBE WHEN IT SOUNDS SO LOUD.

SINGERS: WHEN IT SOUNDS SO LOUD TILL IT WAKES UP THE DEAD,
WHERE SHALL I BE WHEN IT SOUNDS.
OH, BRETHREN, WHERE SHALL I BE WHEN IT SOUNDS?
WHEN IT SOUNDS SO LOUD THAT IT WAKES UP THE DEAD,
WHERE SHALL I BE WHEN IT SOUNDS?

> *(The SINNERS, suppliant, exit)*

ELDER: Oh, Lord! Lord, have mercy on me! He will!

WOMAN: I know He will!

ELDER: Yes, he will! Matthew chapter 24 declares, "He shall send His angels with a great sound of a trumpet. They shall gather together His elect from the four winds, from one end of heaven to the other. Before Him shall be gathered all nations, and He shall separate them one from another, as a shepherd divideth his sheep from the goats. He shall set the sheep on His right hand, but the goats on the left. Then shall the King say unto them on His right hand, 'Come, ye blessed of my Father, inherit the kingdom prepared for you from the foundation of the world.' "

(General SHOUTERS enter to movement and jubilation)

SINGERS: GOOD NEWS, THE CHARIOT'S A-COMING!
GOOD NEWS, THE CHARIOT'S A-COMING!
I DON'T WANT IT TO LEAVE ME BEHIND.
THERE'S A LONG WHITE ROBE IN THE HEAVEN I KNOW,
AND I DON'T WANT IT TO LEAVE A ME BEHIND.
THERE'S A STARRY CROWN IN THE HEAVEN I KNOW,
AND I DON'T WANT IT TO LEAVE A ME BEHIND.
THERE'S A GOLDEN HARP IN THE HEAVEN I KNOW,
AND I DON'T WANT IT TO LEAVE A ME BEHIND.
THERE'S SILVER SLIPPERS IN THE HEAVEN I KNOW,
AND I DON'T WANT IT TO LEAVE A ME BEHIND.
GOOD NEWS, THE CHARIOT'S A COMING—
AND I DON'T WANT IT TO LEAVE ME BEHIND. . . . .

ELDER: Be ye Christians in your heart—and He will not leave you behind! Preach and teach the word of God—and He will not leave you behind! Did He not cause the lame to walk and the blind to see? Walk the waters and calm the sea? Feed five thousand with two fishes and five loaves? Confound the woman at the well, and raise Lazarus from the dead?

VOICES: He did! Yes, He did!

ELDER: Oh, the wonder of His miracles!

BROTHER: THE BLIND MAN STOOD ON THE WAYSIDE.
HE WAS BLIND AND COULD NOT SEE.
HE HEARD THAT JESUS WAS PASSING BY.
HE SAID, "I HAVE NEED OF THEE."
HE SAID TO ONE OF HIS DISCIPLES,
"PRAY TELL ME WHEN HE'S NIGH."
HE CRIED OUT, "SAVIOR, DON'T PASS ME BY."

SINGERS: SAVIOR, BLESSED SAVIOR,
SAVIOR, DON'T YOU PASS ME BY.
I'M CRYING OUT, SAVIOR, SAVIOR,
SAVIOR, DON'T YOU PASS ME BY.

WOMAN: WHILE JESUS WAS PASSING BY
HE HEARD A POOR WOMAN CRY,

"IF I COULD BUT HIS GARMENTS TOUCH,
I WOULD GO AND PROPHESY."
WOMEN: SHE CALLED TO PETER, JAMES AND JOHN,
"PRAY TELL ME WHEN HE'S NIGH."
SINGERS: SHE CRIED OUT, SAVIOR, SAVIOR,
SAVIOR, DON'T YOU PASS ME BY.
I'M CRYING, SAVIOR, SAVIOR,
LOVING SAVIOR, DON'T PASS ME BY.
SAVIOR, BLESSED SAVIOR,
SAVIOR, DON'T YOU PASS ME BY.
ELDER: Savior and Shepherd, He didn't pass them by. That day Jesus
had compassion on not only one, but *two* men who were blind, and
touched their eyes. Immediately their eyes received sight, and they
followed Him. Oh, master of miracles!
DEACON: Shepherd and Master!
WOMAN: Master of miracles!
BROTHER: Savior!
ELDER: Then He came across the woman at the well, the woman of
Samaria, and He told her things she thought He did not know.
DEACON: But Jesus knew!
SINGERS: JESUS MET THE WOMAN AT THE WELL
AND HE TOLD HER EVERYTHING SHE'D DONE.
HE SAID, "WOMAN, WHERE IS YOUR HUSBAND."
SHE SAID, "OH, LORD, LORD, I DON'T HAVE ONE."
HE SAID, "WOMAN, WOMAN, YOU'VE HAD FIVE HUS-
BANDS.
BUT THE ONE YOU HAVE NOW IS REALLY NOT YOURS."
SHE WENT RUNNING, CRYING, "HO! HO! HO! HO!
YOU MUST BE THE PROPHET!"
WENT RUNNING CRYING, "HO! HO! HO! HO!
LORD, YOU MUST BE THE PROPHET
BECAUSE YOU'VE TOLD ME EVERYTHING I'VE DONE!"
ELDER: The woman said, "I know Messiah commeth which is called
Christ." And Jesus said unto her, "I that speak unto thee, am *He*."
And she marvelled as likewise did all who came in contact with
Jesus and He went about the land, and miracles followed His train.
Miracles!
WOMAN: He calmed the waters.
DEACON: He healed the sick.
ELDER: He cast out devils.

BROTHER: He raised the dead.

SINGERS: HE RAISED POOR LAZARUS, RAISED HIM UP,
HE RAISED HIM FROM THE DEAD, I TOLD YE SO,
WHILE MANY WERE STANDING BY,
JESUS LOOSENED THE MAN FROM UNDER THE GROUND,
TOLD HIM, "GO PROPHESY!"
TOLD HIM, "GO PROPHESY!"
HE GIVE HEAL UNTO THE SICK, YES, HE DID!
HE GIVE SIGHT UNTO THE BLIND, I KNOW HE DID!
HE DONE ABLE THE CRIPPLE TO WALK,
OH, HE RAISE THE DEAD FROM UNDER GROUND
AND GIVE THEM PERMISSION TO TALK.
OH, MOAN ALONG, MOAN ALONG, YE MOANING SOULS,
HEAVEN IS MY HOME.
JESUS BEEN HERE ONE TIME, LORD,
AND HE'S COMING AGAIN—
GET READY AND LET'S GO HOME.

ELDER: Like He raised Lazarus, I know in that great getting up morning, He will raise me!

DEACON: Raise me! Raise me!

WOMAN: Me, and you!

BROTHER: He'll take my dry bones and put them all together.

DEACON: Yes, He will!
THEM BONES, THEM BONES, THEM DRY BONES!
OH, HEAR THE WORD OF THE LORD!

SINGERS: OH, YES, CONNECT THEM DRY BONES,
HEAR THE WORD OF THE LORD!
(SINGERS hum as DEACON continues)

DEACON: YOUR TOE BONE CONNECTED TO YOUR FOOT BONE,
FOOT BONE CONNECTED TO YOUR HEEL BONE,
HEEL BONE CONNECTED TO YOUR ANKLE BONE,
ANKLE BONE CONNECTED TO YOUR LEG BONE,
LEG BONE CONNECTED TO YOUR KNEE BONE,
KNEE BONE CONNECTED TO YOUR THIGH BONE,
THIGH BONE CONNECTED TO YOUR HIP BONE,
HIP BONE CONNECTED TO YOUR BACK BONE,
BACK BONE CONNECTED TO YOUR SHOULDER BONE,
SHOULDER BONE CONNECTED TO YOUR NECK BONE,
NECK BONE CONNECTED TO YOUR HEAD BONE,

HEAD BONE CONNECTED TO YOUR SKULL BONE,
SKULL BONE CONNECTED TO YOUR NOSE BONE,
NOSE BONE CONNECTED TO YOUR MOUTH BONE,
MOUTH BONE CONNECTED TO YOUR CHIN BONE,
CHIN BONE CONNECTED TO YOUR THROAT BONE,
THROAT BONE CONNECTED TO YOUR BREAST BONE,
BREAST BONE CONNECTED TO YOUR ARM BONES,
ARM BONES CONNECTED TO YOUR WRIST BONES,
WRIST BONES CONNECTED TO YOUR HAND BONES,
HAND BONES CONNECTED TO YOUR FINGER BONES,
YOUR FINGER BONES CONNECTED TO THE LOVE OF
  GOD—
OH, HEAR THE WORD OF THE LORD!
SINGERS: THEM BONES, THEM BONES, THEM DRY BONES!
THEM BONES GONNA WALK AROUND!
THEM BONES, THEM BONES, THEM DRY BONES!
THEM BONES GONNA RISE AND WALK ABOVE GROUND!
THEM BONES, THEM BONES, THEM DRY BONES—
OH, HEAR THE WORD OF THE LORD!
ELDER: In that great gittin' up morning! Halleloo! When the saints of God shall gather at His throne! That is what Christ came into the world to bring mankind—assurance, blessed assurance that our souls shall rise again. He said, "Upon this rock I build my church, and the gates of hell shall not prevail against it." Oh, rock of God!
SINGERS: I GOT A HOME IN THAT ROCK, DON'T YOU SEE?
BETWEEN THE EARTH AND SKY,
THOUGHT I HEARD MY SAVIOR CRY,
YOU GOT A HOME IN THAT ROCK, DON'T YOU SEE?
DEACON: POOR MAN, LAZARUS, POOR AS I, DON'T YOU SEE?
MEN: POOR MAN, LAZARUS, POOR AS I,
WHEN HE DIED HE FOUND A HOME ON HIGH.
SINGERS: HE HAD A HOME IN THAT ROCK, DON'T YOU SEE.
DEACON: RICH MAN, DIVES, HE LIVED SO WELL, DON'T YOU SEE?
MEN: RICH MAN, DIVES, HE LIVED SO WELL
WHEN HE DIED HE FOUND A HOME IN HELL.
SINGERS: HE HAD NO HOME IN THAT ROCK, DON'T YOU SEE?
WOMEN: GOD GAVE NOAH THE RAINBOW SIGN, DON'T YOU SEE?

MEN: GOD GAVE NOAH THE RAINBOW SIGN, DON'T YOU
SEE?
SINGERS: GOD GAVE NOAH THE RAINBOW SIGN,
NO MORE WATER, BUT FIRE NEXT TIME.
BETTER GET A HOME IN THAT ROCK, DON'T YOU SEE?
(JERUSALEMITES enter with palms marching and dancing)
ELDER: The Rock of Salvation founded in the Word of God—the
word that Christ spread far and wide, throughout the land, until
millions knew His name. When He entered into Jerusalem that
Sunday before He was to die upon the Cross for you and me—
Christ riding on a colt—the people spread palms before Him in the
streets of Jerusalem. They strew His way with flowers, and cries,
"Hosanna, blessed is He that cometh in the name of the Lord!
Hosanna! Hosanna in the highest!" But they did not know that
this Sunday marked the beginning of the end of Christ's thirty-three
years upon this earth, and that the shadow of the Cross lay before
Him. Palm Sunday, crowning with the light the miracle of His life
upon earth! Crowning with light the road to Golgotha, death, and
resurrection! Crowning with light the end of His earthly story—the
closing forever in the flesh of His gospel glory. That is why, that day
of the palms, honoring His earthly visitation and magnifying His
name for all time to come, men sang in the streets of Jerusalem as
we sing now—
SINGERS: RIDE ON, KING JESUS
NO MAN CAN HINDER YOU!
RIDE ON, KING JESUS,
NO MAN CAN HINDER YOU!
*(Palms and flowers are strewn about the stage as the SINGERS
hail the entry of CHRIST into Jerusalem. Joyous Finale)*
KING JESUS RIDES
ON A MILK WHITE HORSE.
NO MAN CAN HINDER YOU!
THE RIVER OF JORDAN
HE DID CROSS.
NO MAN CAN HINDER YOU!
HE BUILT HIS THRONE
UP IN THE AIR.
NO MAN CAN HINDER YOU!
HE CALLED HIS SAINTS
FROM EVERYWHERE.

NO MAN CAN HINDER YOU!
IF YOU WANT TO FIND
YOUR WAY TO GOD,
NO MAN CAN HINDER YOU!
THE GOSPEL HIGHWAY
MUST BE TROD.
NO MAN CAN HINDER YOU!
RIDE ON KING JESUS!
RIDE ON KING JESUS!
RIDE ON, KING JESUS!
NO MAN CAN HINDER YOU!
CURTAIN[1]

The Prodigal Son
A Song-Play with Traditional Spirituals, Gospel Hymns, and Songs Illuminating the Bible Story Retold

1965

Cast
(In order of appearance)

EXHORTER
PRODIGAL SON
SISTER LORD
FATHER
MOTHER
JEZEBEL
SISTER WADDY
BROTHER JOHN
BROTHER ALEX
BROTHER JACOB
BROTHER JOSEPH
BROTHER PAUL
SISTER FATIMA
SISTER MERCY
BROTHER CALLIUS

Songs

Wade In The Water	SISTER LORD
Take The Lord God	BRO. CALLIUS
Rock With Jezebel	JEZEBEL
I Look Down The Road	SISTER LORD
Look At The Prodigal Son	SISTER WADDY
Devil, Take Yourself Away	EXHORTER
How I'm Gonna Make It	SISTER LORD

I'm Waiting For My Child	BRO. CALLIUS
Son, Get Off This Road	TRIO
Oh, Lord, Come By Here	ENSEMBLE
I Just Rise To Tell You	BRO. CALLIUS
When I Touch His Garment	SISTER LORD
You Better Take Time to Pray	BRO. CALLIUS
In The Countryside With Me	JEZEBEL
Done Found My Lost Sheep	MOTHER
Come On In The House	ENSEMBLE

Overture

The EXHORTER stands in silhouette at his altar against a murky sky as the PRODIGAL SON is prostrate in the foreground. SISTER LORD is heard singing

EXHORTER: Repent, repent and be saved! Likewise, I say unto you, there is joy in the presence of the angels of God over one sinner that repenteth.

SISTER LORD: WADE IN THE WATER
WADE IN THE WATER, CHILDREN,
GOD'S GONNA TROUBLE THE WATER.
SEE THOSE CHILDREN ALL DRESSED IN RED,
LOOKS LIKE THE BAND THAT MOSES LED,
SEE THOSE CHILDREN ALL DRESSED IN WHITE,
LOOKS LIKE THE HOST OF THE ISRAELITE.
WADE IN THE WATER CHILDREN,
GOD'S GONNA TROUBLE THE WATER.

EXHORTER: What men of you, having a hundred sheep, if he lose one of them, doth not leave the ninety-and-nine in the wilderness, and go after that which is lost until he find it. This is the parable of the Prodigal Son, who said to his father, "Father, give me the portion of goods that falleth unto me." And he gave him his portion of goods so that the young man might go out into the world and find his way.

(The FATHER and MOTHER bless the SON as he stands before them)

MOTHER: Son, be wary, wherever you go. Be wary! Take this locket. Keep it close to you. Go well, my son, go well.

(The MOTHER, FATHER and SON dance their farewells)

CALLIUS: TAKE THE LORD GOD WITH YOU
    EVERYWHERE YOU GO.
    JUST TAKE HIM EVERYWHERE YOU GO.
    YOU'RE GONNA NEED HIM ON YOUR JOURNEY
    EVERYWHERE YOU GO—
    TAKE HIM EVERYWHERE YOU GO.
        (*The PARENTS leave their SON to dance joyously down the road.
        He encounters JEZEBEL who entices him with her charms*)
JEZEBEL: IF ANYBODY ASKS YOU WHAT'S MY NAME,
    TELL 'EM JEZEBEL.
    NOT THE KIND OF WOMAN MEN CAN TAME,
    NO, NOT JEZEBEL.
    BORN TO RIDE A SHOOTING STAR
    DOWN THE MILKY WAY,
    MIDNIGHT IS MY MEETING TIME
    AT THE DEVIL'S CABARET:
        (*She seduces the PRODIGAL to accompany her*)
    BALLING, BRAWLING, NIGHT IS FALLING,
    COME WITH JEZEBEL!
    SWINGING, SINGING, DING-DONG-DINGING,
    JUMP WITH JEZEBEL!
    WIGGLING, GIGGLING, SWEET FINAGLING,
    MY NAME'S JEZEBEL.
    JOKING, JIVING, SWEET CONNIVING,
    JUMPING JEZEBEL!
    IF YOU WANT A LITTLE FUN,
    BE PREPARED TO PAY.
    CAPITAL F-U-N—FUN IN A GREAT BIG WAY!
    SINGING, SWINGING, ALL BELLS RINGING,
    DING-DONG, JEZEBEL!
    JAZZ WITH, JIVE WITH, JUMP WITH JEZE,
    JUMP WITH JEZEBEL!
        (*The PRODIGAL and JEZEBEL run off together as SISTER
        LORD enters singing and the EXHORTER crosses in the back-
        ground*)
SISTER LORD: I LOOK DOWN THE ROAD AND I WONDER
    I WONDER, GOD KNOWS I WONDER,
    JUST TO SEE HOW FAR THAT I WAS FROM GOD.
    BUT I BUCKLED UP MY SHOES AND I STARTED,
    OH, I STARTED, YES, I STARTED,

FOR I SAW HOW FAR THAT I WAS FROM GOD.
ONCE I HAD FRIENDS AND PLAYMATES,
YES, FRIENDS AND PLAYMATES
WHO DID NOT CARE HOW FAR I WAS FROM GOD.
BUT I BUCKLED UP MY SHOES AND I STARTED,
YES, STARTED, OH, I STARTED,
WHEN I SAW HOW FAR I WAS FROM GOD.

EXHORTER: And the younger son took his journey into a far country
and there wasted his substance with riotous living.

 (The PRODIGAL and his companions dance happily)

ENSEMBLE: LOOK AT THE PRODIGAL SON
ON THIS DOWNWARD ROAD,
LOOK AT THE PRODIGAL SON
ON THIS DOWNWARD ROAD.
HE LEFT HIS MOTHER AND FATHER,
HE DID LEAVE HIS BROTHERS, TOO.
NOW HE'S HERE ALL BY HIMSELF,
AND KNOWS NOT WHAT TO DO.
THIS ROAD IS FILLED WITH GAMBLERS,
WITH THIEVES AND ROBBERS, TOO,
THIS ROAD IS FILLED WITH EVERYTHING
THAT WILL BRING HARM TO YOU.
SO RISE, SON, AND GET MOVING,
GET MOVING ON YOUR WAY,
REPENT AND GO TO YOUR FATHER'S HOUSE
AND TELL HIM YOU HAVE SINNED TODAY.
ARISE, ARISE, AND GO BACK
TO YOUR FATHER'S HOME.

 (JEZEBEL entices the SON in a dance of seduction and he joins
 her as the others leave them alone)

JEZEBEL: COME AND TREAD MY PRIMROSE PATH,
GOLD DUST PAVES THE WAY.
CUT YOUR MAMA'S APRON STRINGS
WITH JEZEBEL TODAY.
SWINGING, SWAYING, HEY-HEY-HEYING,
JAZZY JEZEBEL!
JUMPING, JUMPING, JUMPING JEZE!
ROCK WITH JEZEBEL!

 (Tipsy young men and luscious ladies of the evening burst into
 orgiastic dance. A riotous party develops in which JEZEBEL makes

*frantic love to the PRODIGAL. But at the height of the party,
the EXHORTER rushes in to point an accusing finger and the
dancing suddenly stops)*

EXHORTER: Listen, son! Listen! Sin will gangrene your body and
putrefy your soul. You can't be wishy-washy about sin. Look sin in
the face and stare it down. Look sin dead in the eye, son, from here
on in and say, "I dare you to conquer me!" Sin ain't nothing but
the devil in disguise. He's got collapsible horns like a TV antennae.
Sin ain't nothing but a woman with her lipstick on and all kinds of
wig hats to hide her dandruff. Sin ain't nothing but a pusher with
junk for sale. Don't say a roach can't be your burial coach on the
way to a heroin grave. I didn't say *hero's*. A puff leads to a draw and
a draw to a pill and a pill to a sniff and a sniff to a pop and a pop
to a shot, then, oh, son, you're gone! Gone! Gone! Stoned! You're
hooked! . . . Sin will lead you to the miseries, son. So stand up and
look sin in the face and conquer it, I say. Look sin in the eye, in his
painted eye and know what the devil looks like in drag. Recognize
him in all his guises and say, Devil—
DEVIL, DEVIL! TAKE YOURSELF AWAY!
YESTERDAY I PLAYED WITH YOU,
BUT I AIN'T GONNA PLAY TODAY.
I'VE CHANGED MY PLAYGROUND,
CHANGED MY WAYS,
I'VE CHANGED MY HABITS,
AND I'VE CHANGED MY DAYS.
MY FEET ARE ANCHORED
ON THE GOSPEL SHORE,
AND I AIN'T GONNA PLAY NO MORE.

> *(As the revellers mockingly repeat his song, the EXHORTER leaves
> and the party resumes in full swing. Finally, all dance off leaving
> the PRODIGAL alone as SISTER LORD enters singing mourn-
> fully)*

SISTER LORD: HOW'S HE GONNA MAKE IT BACK TO GOD?
HOW'S HE GONNA MAKE IT?
GOD, JEHOVAH TAKE HIS HAND.
HOW'S HE GONNA MAKE IT?
YES, LORD TAKE HIS HAND.
HOW'S HE GONNA MAKE IT?
OH, JEHOVAH TAKE HIS HAND.
HOW'S HE GONNA MAKE IT BACK TO GOD?

(*SISTER LORD departs as the FATHER enters and in dance implores his SON to come home as CALLIUS unseen sings*)

CALLIUS: I'M WAITING FOR MY CHILD TO COME,
 I'M WAITING FOR MY CHILD TO COME.
 IF YOU CAN'T COME HOME
 SEND ME A LETTER—
 A LETTER WOULD MEAN SO MUCH TO ME.
 OH, MY CHILD, I'M WAITING
 FOR YOU TO COME,
 FOR YOU TO COME HOME.
 IF YOU CAN'T COME HOME
 PLEASE SEND ME A LETTER.
 A LETTER WOULD MEAN SO MUCH TO ME.
  (*The MOTHER hovers over her as two other women accompany her singing*)

TRIO: SON, GET OFF THIS ROAD!
 SON, GET OFF THIS ROAD!
 SATAN'S MIGHTY BUSY.
 HE'S MOVING DOWN YOUR WAY.
 IF YOU LET HIM IN ON YOU,
 THERE'S TROUBLE HERE TODAY.
 THESE PEOPLE, SON, ARE WICKED,
 THEY'VE STRAYED AWAY FROM GOD,
 SO COME ON, SON, AND JOIN WITH US,
 AND WALK WHERE THE SAINTS HAVE TROD.
 SON, GET OFF THIS ROAD.
 OH, SON, GET OFF THIS ROAD.
 YOUR FATHER, SON, IS WAITING,
 YOUR MOTHER IS WAITING TOO.
 EVERYONE IN YOUR FATHER'S HOUSE,
 IS WAITING TO WELCOME YOU.
 SO STOP THIS RIOTOUS LIVING,
 DON'T MAKE AN EARLY GRAVE,
 GO HOME AND TELL YOUR PARENTS, SON,
 HALLELU! THANK GOD, I'M SAVED.
 SON, GET OFF THIS ROAD.
 OH, SON, GET OFF THIS ROAD.
  (*The WOMEN leave the PRODIGAL alone as the EXHORTER enters*)

EXHORTER: And when he had spent all, there arose a mighty famine in that land; and he began to be in want. And he went and joined himself to a citizen of that country; and he sent him into the fields to feed swine. And he would fain have filled his belly with the husks that the swine did eat; and no man gave unto him.

(The SON dances his degradation and loneliness)

CALLIUS: SO HE WENT OUT IN THE BIG FIELDS
OF TALL GRASS AND VINE.
HE WALKED UP TO THE WOODEN GATE
AND BEGAN TO FEED WITH THE SWINE.
THE PRODIGAL SHOUTED "I'M HUNGRY.
I LONG TO REST AND DINE."
BUT THE PRODIGAL SON WAS SO FAR FROM HOME—
HIS MEAL WAS THE HUSK OF SWINE.
OH, LOOK AT THE PRODIGAL SON,
ON THIS DOWNWARD ROAD,
LOOK AT THE PRODIGAL SON,
ON THIS DOWNWARD ROAD.

EXHORTER: And when he came to himself, he said, "I will arise and go to my father and will say unto him, "Father, I have sinned against heaven and before thee and am no longer worthy to be called thy son."

(Rhythmic hand clapping is heard afar leading into a revival gathering which BROTHER CALLIUS opens with song as WORSHIPPERS bring benches to the scene and seat themselves on either side singing lustily)

WORSHIPPERS: COME BY HERE, LORD,
COME BY HERE!
OH, LORD, COME BY HERE!
A SINNER NEEDS YOU, LORD!
OH, LORD, COME BY HERE!

(The cadence changes as BROTHER CALLIUS steps forward to testify in song)

CALLIUS: I JUST RISE TO TELL YOU
WHAT THE GOOD LORD'S DONE FOR ME.
AMAZING GRACE, HOW SWEET THE SOUND,
THAT SAVED A WRETCH LIKE ME.
I ONCE WAS LOST BUT NOW I'M FOUND,
WAS BLIND, BUT NOW I SEE.
I JUST RISE TO TELL YOU
WHAT THE GOOD LORD DID FOR ME!

I WENT DOWN IN THE VALLEY
ONE DAY TO PRAY.
MY SOUL GOT LOST
AND I STAYED ALL DAY.
I STEPPED IN THE WATER
AND THE WATER WAS COLD.
IT CHILLED MY BODY
BUT NOT MY SOUL.
I HEARD THE VOICE
OF JEHOVAH SAY,
Come unto me,
I'LL GIVE YOU REST.
I JUST RISE TO TELL YOU
WHAT THE GOOD LORD DID FOR ME.
    (Again the tempo changes as the WORSHIPPERS reprise Oh,
    Lord, Come By Here)
WORSHIPPERS: COME BY HERE, LORD,
    COME BY HERE!
    OH, LORD, COME BY HERE . . . . .
EXHORTER: Oh, yes! You must come in by the Lamb! My Lord is
so high, you can't get over Him. He's so low, you can't get under
Him. He's so wide, you can't get by Him. You must come in by the
Lamb. Friends, I bring here among us a sinner, a backslider, one who
was once mighty but now sunk low, once rich but now poor, raised
a child of God but now lost. Pray for this young man, eating the
husk of pigs, his portion squandered, his pockets empty, and his soul
tormented . . . Let us pray for him! Let us pray for him—because he
could be your son. He could be your son . . . . . And who's to say
that you don't have a Jezebel in your house? Oh, let us pray.
    (All bow their heads)
We come before thee, knee bent and body bowed. Help this sinner
in our midst! Help him to see the light of your face, oh, Lord God
Jehovah! Help him to look up and not down for his salvation. Help
him to see that in this world there is only death and destruction,
damnation and eternal hell fire to come. Help him to see that in each
rose there is a thorn, in each false kiss the sting of a serpent. Oh, help
him to know that only yonder, yonder, yonder in your kingdom is
eternal life. Help him, Lord God, help him . . . . . Amen!
    (The strong and powerful voice of a woman rises in song)
SISTER LORD: WHEN I GO TO FACE MY LORD,

I WILL FACE MY LORD ALONE.
WHEN I WALK THAT STARRY STREET
UP TO HIS CRYSTAL THRONE,
I WILL GO ALL BY MYSELF,
YES I WILL GO ALL ALONE—
BUT WHEN I TOUCH HIS GARMENT,
HE'LL CLAIM ME FOR HIS OWN.
WORSHIPPERS: OH, WHEN I TOUCH HIS GARMENT,
WHEN I TOUCH HIS GARMENT,
WHEN I TOUCH HIS GARMENT,
HE WILL CLAIM ME FOR HIS OWN.
I'VE GOT TO GO ALL BY MYSELF,
I'VE GOT TO GO ALL ALONE,
BUT WHEN I TOUCH HIS GARMENT,
HE WILL CLAIM ME FOR HIS OWN.
SISTER LORD: ALL THE TROUBLES OF THIS WORLD
SUCH AS WEIGH ME DOWN TODAY,
ALL MY HEARTACHES, ALL MY WOES
HE WILL TAKE AWAY.
ON THE ROAD UP TO HIS THRONE,
I'VE GOT TO GO ALONE,
BUT WHEN I TOUCH HIS GARMENT,
HE WILL CLAIM ME FOR HIS OWN.
WORSHIPPERS: THERE WILL BE A SHOWER OF STARS,
THERE WILL BE A BLAZE OF LIGHT,
ALL AROUND MY SAVIOUR'S HEAD,
A DIADEM SO BRIGHT.
I WILL SEE IT FROM AFAR,
AS I STAND THERE ALL ALONE—
FOR WHEN I TOUCH HIS GARMENT,
HE WILL CLAIM ME FOR HIS OWN.
*(Suddenly JEZEBEL appears but the WORSHIPPERS rebuff her in
song as she switches contemptuously)*
WORSHIPPERS: DEVIL, DEVIL, DEVIL,
TAKE YOURSELF AWAY,
YESTERDAY I PLAYED WITH YOU,
BUT I AIN'T GONNA PLAY TODAY.
I'VE CHANGED MY PLAYGROUND,
CHANGED MY WAYS,
I'VE CHANGED MY HABITS

AND I'VE CHANGED MY DAYS,
MY FEET ARE ANCHORED
ON THE GOSPEL SHORE
AND I AIN'T GONNA PLAY NO MORE.
SISTER WADDY: I TURN AND LOOK BEHIND ME
AND THIS IS WHAT I SEE,
A WORLD FULL OF SINNERS,
JUST LIKE I USED TO BE.
MY HEART IS FILLED WITH PITY, LORD,
AND I FEEL THE NEED TO CRY.
SON, PITCH YOUR TENT
ON THE GOSPEL SHORE
AND LET THE WORLD GO BY.
　(The TEMPTRESS replies in song)
JEZEBEL: THE DEVIL HAS A PLAYGROUND
IN MY HEART TO STAY.
HE SET UP HIS TENTS OF SIN
AND INVITED ME TO PLAY.
IT IS SO NICE, SO CALM AND COOL,
AND I PLAY JUST LIKE A FOOL.
I'LL NEVER LOSE MY SWINGING SOUL—
NOW, I GUESS, I'VE GOT YOU TOLD.
WORSHIPPERS: DEVIL, DEVIL, DEVIL,
TAKE YOURSELF AWAY . . . . . .
　(JEZEBEL switches off impudently and disappears)
EXHORTER: Son, if you link your hand with the devil's, whose fault is
it? Whose fault is it when God's kingdom could be yours?
　*(The WORSHIPPERS warn the PRODIGAL again, backing
　CALLIUS in his song)*
CALLIUS: SON, YOU BETTER TAKE TIME,
YOU BETTER TAKE TIME,
TAKE TIME TO LET GOD GUIDE YOUR WAY.
YOU BETTER TAKE TIME TO BEG,
BEG HIM YOUR SOUL TO FREE.
YOU BETTER TAKE TIME TO CRY,
HAVE MERCY, LORD ON ME!
YOU BETTER TAKE TIME TO SEEK,
HALLELUJAH, SEEK HIS HAND.
YOU BETTER TAKE TIME
TO LET GOD GUIDE YOU

THROUGH THIS LAND.
TELL GOD IT'S A ROCKY ROAD,
TELL HIM THE NIGHT IS DARK,
TELL HIM THAT YOUR CHARIOT
HAS GOT NO PLACE TO PARK.
TELL HIM YOU'RE TIRED OF SINNERS,
HALLELUJAH, OF SINNING, TOO,
YOU BETTER TAKE TIME TO LET
GOD TAKE CARE OF YOU.
YES, YOU BETTER TAKE TIME, TAKE TIME,
TO LET GOD GUIDE YOUR WAY.
MOTHER: What can he do, Lord? What can he do?
EXHORTER: Repent, repent and be saved!
    (A mighty chant arises)
WORSHIPPERS: WADE IN THE WATER,
WADE IN THE WATER, CHILDREN,
GOD'S GONNA TROUBLE THE WATER.
SISTER LORD: SEE THOSE CHILDREN ALL DRESSED IN RED,
LOOKS LIKE THE BAND THAT MOSES LED.
SEE THOSE CHILDREN ALL DRESSED IN WHITE,
LOOKS LIKE THE HOST OF THE ISRAELITE.
WORSHIPPERS: WADE IN THE WATER,
WADE IN THE WATER, CHILDREN,
GOD'S GONNA TROUBLE THE WATER.
    (All depart except the SON and two COMMUNICANTS who
    dance the rites of repentance. Then the SON is left alone as JEZE-
    BEL enters to entice him once again to come with her as she sings)
JEZEBEL: THE CHARMS I'VE GOT ARE WORTH A LOT—
AND AS A CHARMER, I'M NOT LAZY.
WOULDN'T YOU LIKE TO BE
FREE AS A SINGING TREE
IN THE BREEZE WITH ME?
HEY, COME ON, LET'S BE CRAZY!
    (She attempts to lead him away as he weakens)
COME TO THE COUNTRYSIDE WITH ME—
AND SEE HOW PEACEFUL IT WON'T BE.
THERE IN THE SHADE AND SOLITUDE.
WE CAN *ooo-ou* IN SOLITUDE,
SO COME TO THE COUNTRYSIDE WITH ME.
    (She cuddles up to him enticingly)

KID, YOU'LL LOVE THE COUNTRYSIDE WITH ME
OUT WHERE THE AIR IS FRESH AND FREE.
THERE WHEN GENTLE BREEZES BLOW,
KISSES ARE AIR-COOLED—AND SLOW—
SO COME TO THE COUNTRYSIDE WITH ME.
CITY LIFE, BABY, IS JUST RUSH AND HURRY.
CITY WAYS, BABY, ARE A NATURAL WORRY.
I WANT YOU ALL TO MYSELF—
THE BIRDS CAN HAVE WHATEVER'S LEFT.
SO COME TO THE COUNTRYSIDE WITH ME.
SEE HOW SWEET AND FINE 'TWILL BE!
YOU CAN *bill*—AND I WILL *coo*
IN THE COUNTRYSIDE WITH YOU!
OOOOO-OOOOOOO-O-OOOOO-O!
IN THE COUNTRYSIDE WITH YOU—AND ME!
> (*In dance the PRODIGAL struggles to resist temptation—and finally repulses her, whereupon JEZEBEL turns on him scornfully*)

RAGGED, BROKE, YOU NO GOOD BLOKE,
STAY AWAY FROM JEZEBEL,
I'M SINGING, SWINGING,
DING-DONG-DINGING.
YOU'LL MISS JEZEBEL!
> (*JEZEBEL leaves laughing wildly as the EXHORTER appears. The FATHER approaches in the distance*)

EXHORTER: And he arose and came to his father. But when he was yet a great way off his father saw him and had compassion, and ran and fell on his neck and kissed him.
> (*The FATHER and MOTHER enter as the SON embraces them*)

MOTHER: DONE FOUND MY LOST SHEEP,
DONE FOUND MY LOST SHEEP,
MY HEART IS GLAD NOW—
MY BOY HAS COME HOME,
HE'LL NEVER MORE ROAM.
HALLELUJAH! NEVER ROAM!
DONE FOUND MY LOST SHEEP.
> (*The MOTHER and FATHER gently welcome the SON back to the fold*)

EXHORTER: And the father said to his servants, "Bring forth the best robe and put it on him. Put a ring on his hand and shoes on his feet and bring hither the fatted calf. Kill it, and let us eat and be merry for

this, my son, was dead and is alive again. He was lost, and is found."
Likewise, I say unto you, there is joy in the presence of the angels of
God over one sinner that repenteth.

*(All the people gather about the family reunited to chant in rever-
ence)*

ALL: AMEN . . . . AMEN . . . . AMEN!

EXHORTER: Everything's all right! Everything's all right, in our father's house. Bless God!

(There is a great burst of happy song as the parable ends)

ALL: EVERYTHING'S ALL RIGHT,
    EVERYTHING'S ALL RIGHT,
    IN YOUR FATHER'S HOUSE.
    COME ON IN THE HOUSE,
    WE'RE GONNA HAVE A GOOD TIME!
    COME ON IN THE HOUSE OF THE LORD.
    THERE IS PEACE AND JOY,
    IN YOUR FATHER'S HOUSE.
    COME ON IN THE HOUSE OF THE LORD.
    THE TABLE IS SPREAD
    IN YOUR FATHER'S HOUSE,
    COME ON IN THE HOUSE OF THE LORD.
    YOUR MOTHER'S ARMS OUTSPREAD
    IN YOUR FATHER'S HOUSE,
    YES, MOTHER'S ARMS OUTSPREAD,
    IN YOUR FATHER'S HOUSE,
    COME ON IN THE HOUSE OF THE LORD!

CURTAIN FALLS[1]

Miscellaneous Plays

For This We Fight represents another aspect of Hughes's wartime writing. Prepared for a Negro Freedom Rally on June 7, 1943, in Madison Square Garden, New York City, it played to a sold-out crowd. Rampersad wrote: "Paul Robeson sang 'Joe Hill' and led a cast of two hundred persons, including Canada Lee, Robert Earl Jones . . . and the rising black concert singer Muriel Rahn; among the speakers were Rev. Adam Clayton Powell, Jr., Ferdinand C. Smith, the black secretary of the mainly white, progressive National Maritime Union, and the popular socialist politician Representative Vito Marcantonio."[1]

That Hughes would be invited to provide this uncompromising piece, which defines the African American war effort as a struggle for black freedom, suggests his prominence as a playwright.

In a similar vein, Hughes wrote *The Ballot and Me*, a "Cavalcade of Negro History," for a voter registration drive at Harlem's St. James Presbyterian Church; the previous year at the request of his friend Dorothy Maynor, wife of the pastor, he had written "St. James: Sixty Years Young" for the church's anniversary celebration.[2]

For This We Fight

1943

Prologue

CHAIRMAN: Ladies and gentlemen, you have listened to the speeches of many distinguished leaders tonight. Now, I want to present to you an ordinary citizen of Harlem, a plain American, one of those Common Men by whom, and for whom, this war is being fought. He lives on Seventh Avenue. His wife is working in the Sperry Gyroscope Company. His children go to Public School 113. A few months ago he was inducted into the army, recently he came home on furlough from Fort Bragg down in Carolina. His name is Pvt. Henry Jackson. Night before last I went by to see about having him on this program. When I left him at the door, he assured me that he would be here. . . .

SOLDIER: Get over, Junior, let daddy sit down.

JUNIOR: O.K.

WIFE: Henry, I've got to rub out some stockings for me and Martha. You put the kids to bed, will you? Since you've been in the army, you haven't forgotten how, have you?

SOLDIER: Sure not, honey! I'll put 'em to bed.

WIFE: And don't keep them up talking too long. Remember, school tomorrow, Martha and Junior.

JUNIOR: We won't stay up too long, mama.

WIFE: Very well, honey.

    (WIFE exits)

JUNIOR: Say, daddy, I didn't finish asking you the questions I wanted to. You promised to tell me what this big meeting we're going to in the Garden is about, too.

SOLDIER: To try and answer some of these very questions you've been asking me, Junior. Close your book and I'll tell you.

JUNIOR: I didn't get to the main question, daddy. I wanted to tell you about the boy who sits across the aisle in school.

SOLDIER: Yes?

JUNIOR: He's colored just like me, and yesterday he said that he didn't see no sense in colored folks fighting this war—cause his father told him we don't have anything now—and we won't have anything after the war either, but Jim Crow!

Is he right, daddy?

SOLDIER: Do you think he's right, Junior?

JUNIOR: I HOPE he's not right, daddy, cause you're in it, and I want *you* to get something out of it.

SOLDIER: Thanks, pal.

JUNIOR: But you said yourself you had to ride the Jim Crow car all the way up from the South—and you're a soldier.

SOLDIER: I did, Junior.

JUNIOR: Then how can I answer that boy?

MARTHA: How can he, daddy?

SOLDIER: Listen son! Listen, Martha—tell him that if we give up hope, and don't work and don't try, and don't fight—we *never* will have anything! Tell him that liberty and freedom and democracy and all the good things in American life are here for us, just like everybody else—but they are *seeds* not yet grown into big plants. We have to help them grow. You know how it is with a little seed, Junior?

JUNIOR: I've seen grandpa down in Virginia plant seeds in spring.

SOLDIER: That's right! Then he waters and hoes and tends them. And by and by they break through the ground and start coming up. But you have to keep the frost off the little plants, you have to keep the bugs off, and the crows out of the field, and you have to give them water if the sun's too hot. Well, it's the same way with the freedom seed, Junior. It's planted deep in the soil of American life. We have to make it grow, and keep fighting off the field rats who attack it.

JUNIOR: You and me?

SOLDIER: Yes, you and me. A long time ago, you know, this country used to be a colony. This whole country wasn't free at all. But the people here wanted to be free and when the people start moving—they're hard to stop. They refused to pay taxes and they had a tea party—remember in history—The Boston Tea Party—where they threw all the wrongly taxed tea overboard into Boston Harbor.

Well, the foreign rulers didn't like that so they kept armies here to keep the people down—white people and colored people—all of us—dominated by guns and bayonets. Their soldiers were Red Coats.

SOLDIER: But the seed of freedom had to be planted. One snowy night in March, 1770, on a street corner, a Negro longshoreman, Crispus Attucks, passed. He heard a group of his fellow townsmen talking— freedom-talk.

Scene 1
Boston—1770

CITIZENS: Taxation, I tell you, without representation is tyranny. No sense in us remaining a colony, citizens. We want to be free.

> We got a right to be free.
> No more King George telling us what to do.
> No more taxes without voting.

ATTUCKS: Hey, citizens! What's wrong? What's the matter?

1ST CITIZEN: What's going on here? There's Crispus Attucks. Tell him what happened.

2ND CITIZEN: One of those drunken soldiers kicked my son.

1ST CITIZEN: It's getting so a Bostonian can't walk on his own streets anymore for the Red Coats.

ATTUCKS: We *can* walk—and we *will* walk. *(Crowd approves)*

2ND CITIZEN: And we'll vote, too, by God!

ATTUCKS: No more taxes to a foreign power!

> Enough of those soldiers on our soil!
> No more tribute to King George!

RED COAT: Halt where you *are*!

1ST CITIZEN: By whose authority?

RED COAT: By order of the crown! Who here utters treason to the king? Answer me, who?

1ST CITIZEN: Taxation without representation *is* tyranny! *(Crowd approves)* You know that. We can't vote.

2ND CITIZEN: We pay tribute to a king we never saw.

3RD CITIZEN: We support your garrisons on our soil.

2ND CITIZEN: We suffer indignities at your hands.

1ST CITIZEN: We are getting tired!

CITIZENS: Tired!

> Tired!
> Tired!

RED COAT: Put up your hands! How dare you shake your fists at a soldier of the crown? How dare you defy—

ATTUCKS: We do dare, soldier! This is our land. Our sweat and toil are building it. *You* are the stranger here. What right have you to threaten us with your bayonet?

RED COAT: Who are you, black fellow?

ATTUCKS: Crispus Attucks!

RED COAT: Behind this bayonet is a bullet, Crispus.

1ST CITIZEN: You hear? The Red Coat threatens to fire on us.

2ND CITIZEN: This bullying is going too far!

3RD CITIZEN: We're tired of this garrison!

RED COAT: Enough! Be quiet! I'll arrest you all. Put up your hands. How dare you. . . .

ATTUCKS: We do dare, soldier! Citizens, the way to get rid of these Red Coats is to strike at the root. *(Crowd approves)* But to reach the root, we might as well start here.

CITIZENS: Down with the tyrants!
Out with them! Get them!
Disarm them! Down with 'em!
Clean 'em out! Get 'em!

ATTUCKS: I guess I'm done for—but keep up the fight, citizen. Keep up our fight. . . . for. . . . freedom. . . .

JUNIOR: Did he die, father?

SOLDIER: Yes, Junior, Crispus Attucks died. That was the Boston Massacre—the first blow struck for American freedom. A Negro's blood made the first red stripes in our flag, and the freedom seed was planted—
(BLACKOUT)
July 4, 1776, we drew up our Declaration of Independence. It said:
(Trumpets. Martial music:)
We hold these truths to be self evident! All men are created equal; endowed with certain unalienable rights; among these life, liberty and the pursuit of happiness. . . .
Thus our Republic was born and we framed our Constitution—to form a more perfect Union, establish Justice, secure the Blessings of Liberty to ourselves and our Posterity. . . . .
(Light fades on flag to BLACKOUT)

JUNIOR: But there were slaves then, weren't there, daddy?

SOLDIER: Yes, Junior, there were slaves then, even in Boston, but they heard that word—Liberty. Among them was a young girl whose mistress taught her to read and write. She wrote poetry—beautiful poetry about freedom, even before she had it herself. So well did she write that she won her freedom, and the people of Boston gathered to hear her read her poems. They introduced her as "The former slave girl, Phillis Wheatley."

PHILLIS: Lo! Freedom comes. She moves divinely fair.

Olives and laurel bind her golden hair.

Freedom comes, arrayed with charms divine.

And in her train commerce and plenty shine.

To every realm shall peace her charms display,

And heavenly Freedom spread her golden ray.

SOLDIER: But thousands of Phillis' own people were not free. On the slave blocks in gunny sacks and rags, brown young girls stood as the auctioneer's hammer fell.

(Sound of slave auction, clinking of gold, hammer falling, voices bidding.)

Scene 2
New Orleans—1800

AUCTIONEER: What am I bid, gentlemen? What am I bid? A fine piece of black female flesh, gentlemen! Best buy I've seen this season. Young! Strong, too! Look at them legs! Plenty muscle. Bend down here, girl! Open your mouth! See! Good teeth! Healthy, do plenty of work! Good for house or field, or—come on, gentlemen, lemme have your bids. What am I bid? What am I bid?

VOICES: Two hundred I bid!

Three hundred! Three hundred!

Four!

Five hundred!

Seven hundred and fifty!

Eight! Eight hundred!

Nine! Nine hundred!

One thousand dollars!

AUCTIONEER: One Thousand Dollars! Do I hear another! Do I hear another? One thousand! Going! . . . . . Going! . . . . . Gone for One Thousand Dollars! Sold to Mr. John Robbaire for One Thousand Dollars. Take her! Make her work, now! Get your money's worth out of her. Get along, gal! . . . . . Bring on the next one, slaver. . . . . ah, a buck!

CHORUS: When Israel was in Egypt's land—

Let my people go!

Oppressed so hard they could not stand—
Let my people go!

AUCTIONEER: Here's a pack-horse for you, gentlemen! A field hand!
A cotton picker! Get up on the auction block there, boy!

(The SLAVE is stubborn. The AUCTIONEER gives him a push.)

Get on that block, I say!

SLAVE: No!

CHORUS: Go down, Moses,
Way down in Egypt land
And tell old Pharaoh
To let my people go!

AUCTIONEER: What? . . . . No? . . . Who're you talking to?

SLAVE: You!

AUCTIONEER: You must've gone crazy, talking like that to me. Get
up on that block!

SLAVE: No! I want to be free, not sold like a slave!

CHORUS: Thus saith the Lord, bold Moses said—
Let my people go!

AUCTIONEER: Shut up! Shut up, I say!
Shut up, back there in the slave pen! Cut out that singing! This ain't
no camp meeting. Hush, I say!

CHORUS: If not, I'll smite your first born dead—
Let my people go!

AUCTIONEER: Shut up, you black dog! Shut up! Shut up, before I
lash the hell out of you! Shut up!

CHORUS: Go down Moses,
Way down in Egypt land.

SOLDIER: You see, son, America was growing green and rich with
the help of our strong arm in the cotton fields and on the farms.
Wherever we worked, the land prospered. But *we* weren't free to
have our rightful share.

CHORUS: No more shall they in bondage toil.
Let my people go!
Let them come out of Egypt's soil.
Let my people go!

PREACHER: If I hear you right, Lord, you tells me to pick up my bed
and walk. But your children here in Louisiana ain't got no bed, Lord.
All we got is our feet—and we intends to walk. We intends to walk
out of slavery into freedom. Down here in the deep woods, Lord,
in the dark of the night, hear us, Lord, and show us the way out of

bondage. Give us strength, Lord, and show us how! Amen! . . . . .
Brothers, did you bring your guns?

SISTER: I ain't no brother, but I shure brung my gun!

PREACHER: AMEN!

BROTHER: I got a pitch fork.

BOY: Here de cane knife!

> *(A BROTHER rises as if to shout)*

SHOUTER: We raise de wheat—dey give us de corn.
We bake de bread—dey give us de crust.
We sift de meal—dey give us de husk.
We peel de meat—dey give us de skin.
And dat's de way dey take us in!
My old Mistress, she promised me
When she died she'd set me free.
She done lived so long that her head's got bald—
And she give out de notion of dyin' a-tall!
That's why, brothers and sisters,
I's brought my own weapons this evening, and
I'm gonna carve my *own* way to freedom!

SLAVES: Hallelujah!
Yes, indeedy! We means to be free.

PREACHER: Amen! Amen! Amen! Then start digging! Start digging!
We'll bury these weapons here in the woods till Denmark Vesey gives
us the signal. Then we all gonna rise—and tell old Pharaoh

CHORUS: . . . . . To let my people go!
Go down, Moses.
Way down in Egypt's land
And tell old Pharaoh
To let my people go!

> *(BLACKOUT)*

Scene 3
Fight Against Slavery

> *(The SOLDIER speaks in the darkness.)*

JUNIOR: Did they get free, daddy? Did they get free?

SOLDIER: Not then, son, not many. Their leaders—Denmark Vesey,
Nat Turner—were hunted, shot hung.

JUNIOR: Was that the end of freedom, daddy?

SOLDIER: Freedom has no end, son! It's so deep in the hearts of the people nothing can stop it. The slaves kept right on. By 1793, under Toussaint L'Ouverture, the Haitians rebelled against the French and freed themselves. So frightened by then had *our* slave holders become that they passed Fugitive Slave Laws in the North and used whips and dogs and guns to keep the slaves from rebelling or running away in the South—but they did run away!

They had help, too. The kindly Quakers established stations of the underground railroad where slaves were hidden and spirited away to Canada. White men like Wendell Phillips and William Lloyd Garrison were making great speeches against slavery. Listen to Lloyd Garrison.

(Spot on GARRISON making a fiery speech.)

GARRISON: Keep in bondage but a single human being, and the liberty of the world is in peril! Cost what it may, every slave on American soil must be free. Nothing takes precedence over the question of slavery!

(BLACKOUT)

SOLDIER: Along about then, a shy little woman named Harriet Beecher Stowe wrote UNCLE TOM'S CABIN picturing the cruelties of slavery. And Oberlin College opened its portals to Negro students, some of them escaped slaves. While down in Illinois, a white man, Elijah Lovejoy, published with his own hands his anti-slavery weekly—

(LOVEJOY shown at press)

—until the mob rushed his doors, destroyed his press, and dragged him off to death—lynched for freedom!

(Roar of mob. Riot. Press smashed.)

RUFFIANS: So you have the idea that Negroes should be free! We're gonna put an end to that kind of talk.

Slave-lovers! Traitor!

Rogue! Jacobin!

No-good agitator!

Fool! Slave-lover! Dolt!

Agitator! Agitator! Agitator!

Kill him! Lynch him! Kill him!

Scene 4
Harriet Tubman—1850

SOLDIER: The people of our land kept on, white men and Negroes, *liberty for all* their goal—as the clouds of conflict gathered and the lightning of freedom began to flash across the WHOLE sky of America.

(*Howl of wind and sound of storm.*)

Then there arose out of slavery itself a heroic black woman who organized band after band of slaves for escape. Defying death and danger, through trackless swamp and tangled forest, she brought out hundreds of her people.

With neither map nor compass, travelling by the dark of night, courageous, unafraid, she came to be known as the Moses of her people.

HARRIET: Folks, we's stopping here to rest—but only for a minute. Womens, nurse your babies. Mens, go on and do whatever you-all got to do—and don't tarry! You, Jason, throw away that iron pot. It's too heavy. We got to travel light and make time on this trip. De slavers prob'ly got rewards out for us already. We has to get twenty miles from here 'fo daybreak. Is you-all 'bout got your wind back? Cause I's aiming to head on through de swamp.

WOMAN: Harriet, Sam here done broke down. He say he cain't go no fu'ther.

HARRIET: Sam say which?

SAM: I just cain't make it no mo', Gen'ral Tubman.

HARRIET: You done got weary so soon, Sam, and we ain't hardly started?

SAM: I just cain't go through that swamp, I tell you. They's quick-sands down there—and moccasins.

HARRIET: You's scared, Sam?

SAM: Yes! I's gwine stay here. I cain't travel no mo!

HARRIET: But you *is* gonna travel some mo'! I's a woman and I can travel. I's made twenty trips down here from de North and back. How come you cain't make one?

SAM: My feets hurt—and I can't go no mo', Harriet Tubman! I's weak and I's tired. You-all go on, I'll stay behind.

HARRIET: Naw, you don't brother! No coach gets uncoupled from de freedom train. You one Negro that's gonna be free in spite of you'sef—cause you comin' wid us.

SAM: General, I cain't.

HARRIET: Sam, I told you when you started out wid me dat de road was hard, de path were dark, and there warn't no turnin' back. De freedom train don't mean to be stopped, neither sidetracked.

SLAVES: That's right!

Sure ain't!

We goin' on!

Amen!

HARRIET: We goin' on! Do you think I'm gonna leave you loose here
for the slave catchers to grab—and beat you and torture you till you
tell who you run away wid, and which a way we went, and how many
of us dere is? Naw, I ain't! not Harriet Tubman! You sees these mens
here? They intends to be free! You sees these womens? Freedom's
chillun—every one, goin' North—swamp or no swamp, snakes or
no snakes, tired or no tired. You gonna be free, too. You see this
here pistol?

SAM: I sees it, Gen'ral Tubman.

HARRIET: It shoots! *(To the others)* Get yourselves together, chillun. . . .
I reckon Sam here ain't tired no mo'.

SAM: Naw, Gen'ral Tubman, I ain't tired. I's comin' wid you! Yes, sir,
I's comin'!

HARRIET: All right! Folks, we goin' now.

Jason, I told you to leave that pot.

Lucy, that your baby?

LUCY: Yes'm!

HARRIET: Here, give it a good dose of this here paregoric—so it can
sleep, and dream, and be quiet—till we gets over on de Freedom
Side. Cain't no babies cry now, till we gets out of slave catchers
terr'tory. Look! De clouds is breakin'! You-all see that star? That's
de North Star—and it leads to de Promised Land!

WOMAN: Oh! Freedom!

Freedom over me!

CHORUS: And before I'd be a slave

I'd be buried in my grave

And go home to my Lord

And be free!

> *(BLACKOUT. Song rises to mighty climax in the darkness. Thun-
> der.)*

Scene 5
The Civil War

(The SOLDIER speaks in the darkness)

SOLDIER: Ever thicker the storm-clouds gathered, ever closer the thunder rolled. Then, like a flash of avenging lightning, a man appeared,

a white man with his Bible in one hand and his musket in the other—John Brown.

JOHN BROWN: God never meant any man to be a slave. God never meant any Christian to submit to the blot of slavery. It is my mission to take up arms in God's name—and break the devilish chains of slavery in this land.

SOLDIER: Harper's Ferry—1859.

(BLACKOUT)

Lee attacks Fort Sumter—1861.

(Bugle call)

The people were moving, son. It was no longer a matter for one person here or another there. It was the concern of *all* Americans who loved liberty. And there was a test, by fire and blood, a mighty test of whether a nation could endure half slave and half free—the Civil War.

JUNIOR: I know about that, Daddy. We learned all about the Civil War in school. We won it!

SOLDIER: It wasn't as easy as all that! For a time it even looked as if we would lose. Even as the war was being fought, we had to keep on asking for our rightful place in the fight for liberty.

Down in the White House, there sat a man so burdened with the cares of state, he sometimes forgot to take off his tall hat.

(Song swells up—then out. Spot reveals PRESIDENT LINCOLN. A SECRETARY enters.)

SECRETARY: Pardon me, Mr. Lincoln. Mr. Frederick Douglass is here to see you.

LINCOLN: Frederick Douglass? Show him in.

(DOUGLASS enters. LINCOLN rises and extends his hand.)

LINCOLN: Mr. Douglass, although this is the first time I've seen you, I know you and your work. I have read about you and the Secretary of War has spoken of you. I remember your urgent call for the need for enlisting Negro troops into our Union Army, as well as whites. Let me see—the exact words——

DOUGLASS: You cannot fight with your white hand alone, while you keep your black hand chained, helpless behind you.

LINCOLN: Brave words and true, Mr. Douglass. And, when the ranks of the Army were opened to your people, you did excellent work in the recruiting of Negro troops.

DOUGLASS: I firmly believe, Mr. President, that they who would be free, *themselves* must strike the first blow.

LINCOLN: We have gone far, Mr. Douglass. Colonel Shaw, as you know, has formed a mighty regiment of colored troops—the 54th Massachusetts.

DOUGLASS: Yes, Mr. President, we have gone far—but not far enough. Negroes *have* been armed. At first for self-protection, and now as soldiers. But their pay is not equal to whites. They are not promoted to officerships. They are not protected against reprisals and violence. They are not equally exchanged as prisoners of war. I make no plea for special privilege, Mr. Lincoln. But I am deeply grieved at the inequalities put upon my race. Nevertheless, I have urged every colored man to enlist, get an eagle on his button, and a musket on his shoulder. They have heeded my urgings and have joined the Army in many thousands. But now, I feel that I owe it to my long-suffering and abused people—and especially those in the Army—to expose their wrongs and plead their cause, that they may share in freedom's fight with even greater heart.

LINCOLN: I most earnestly want to hear you and shall take note of what you say, Mr. Douglass.

DOUGLASS: Sir, I want you to do more than take note. The war for freedom must not be slowed, and its success threatened by a tardy vacillating policy. Even now, our cause is going badly. . . . .

LINCOLN: I know that only too well, Mr. Douglass. Lee is at the very gates of Washington.

DOUGLASS: Then our deeds must not be too little or too late, Mr. President. Release the full forces of those who would fight for freedom.

LINCOLN: But, Mr. Douglass, I must act to keep all of our forces together. The voice of the people is not united, public opinion is not yet ready!

DOUGLASS: Let us listen to the people then. Even in the halls of Congress—
    (Spotlight up on THADDEUS STEVENS. DOUGLASS and LINCOLN turn to watch.)

STEVENS: Mr. Speaker, Mr. Speaker.

VOICE: I recognize the gentleman from Pennsylvania, Thaddeus Stevens.

STEVENS: The time is long past for hesitation. We must take every step we can to strengthen the equipment and morale of our troops. And most important, we must take offensive action—to carry the fight to the enemy, to strike swiftly and decisively, to bring a certain and quick Victory for our arms. Delay will be disastrous.

(Spotlight blacks out as voices are heard.)

"He's right, he's right!"

DOUGLASS: The people echo what Mr. Stevens says, Mr. President.
(Spotlight on TWO WOMEN, at other side of stage. LINCOLN and DOUGLASS turn.)

1ST WOMAN: I've heard we lost a battle, in the heart of Pennsylvania. How long will the war go on? How great will our losses be? When will our husbands and sons return to us?

2ND WOMAN: The war cannot be over, until we've *won*! The quicker and the harder we fight, the sooner we'll win Victory!
(Spotlight on WOMEN BLACKOUT)

DOUGLASS: Your power extends even beyond the battle lines of the South, Mr. President, if you will only use that power!
(Spotlight up on another area. TWO SLAVES are seen. LINCOLN and DOUGLASS turn.)

1ST SLAVE: Yes, the war's going on up North. A war for freedom. And we here in the South have to grow the food to make the Army of our masters stronger. If we were free, if we were only free. . . . .

2ND SLAVE: If we were free and with a rifle in our hands, there's no question which way we'd turn that rifle. . . .
(Spotlight on SLAVES blacks out.)

DOUGLASS: The people call for action, Mr. President. The Negroes of the North fight with their full hearts, when given the chance and the goal of full liberty not only in theory, but in practice as well. The slaves of the South will fight for us until death, if given that liberty. The people are with you. The trade unions support you. The time to strike is now!

LINCOLN: Mr. Douglass, I might seem slow but it cannot be shown that when I have once taken a position, I have ever retreated from it. And when I hear the voice of the people, I go along with them! Our cause shall not be lost for any short-sightedness or shortcoming! All of America must—and shall be free!
(BLACKOUT. "John Brown's Body")

SOLDIER: Yes, Junior, when the peoples joined their voices, we fought with greater strength. The man in the tall hat signed the Emancipation Proclamation! The slaves were freed, our full strength united. We won. The Civil War was over. And the fighting men came home, with great dreams in their hearts.

SOLDIER: Mary!

Junior!

(He presses the BOY to him.)

Martha!

It's over, Mary! All our people everywhere in America are free! Now we can settle down and live like folks. Martha, you can go to college. Junior, you can be a doctor. I'm going to take off this uniform and go back to work now, and get ahead in the world.

1ST KLANSMAN: So you think you'll get ahead, heh?

2ND KLANSMAN: Settle down and live like folks, huh?

3RD KLANSMAN: Send your black kids to college, will you?

4TH KLANSMAN: Look who's going to be a doctor!

5TH KLANSMAN: You'll get back to work all right—with a whip across your back!

1ST KLANSMAN: So you fought for freedom, heh?

(Loud mocking laughter suddenly cut short.)

SOLDIER: Yes, I fought for freedom! And I'll keep on fighting! Klan or no Klan, I intend to defend it!

CHORUS: Glory! Glory! Hallelujah!

His truth goes marching on!

(BLACKOUT. SOLDIER speaks in darkness.)

SOLDIER: Freedom from slavery was ours then. But you see, son, our enemies were still strong. The copperheads struck Lincoln down. And Thaddeus Stevens, the Great Commoner who fought for the 13th and 14th Amendments, went to his grave. Andrew "Tennessee" Johnson sat in the saddle. And the Klan rode.

(Hooves of horses in the dark.)

Scene 7
Reconstruction

TEACHER: Close your geographies, children. Now, who can tell me, what states are bounded on one side by the Ohio River?

(Various CHILDREN hold up their hands.)

CHILDREN: Me, teacher! I know.

I can tell!

Me! Me! Me!

TEACHER: Roberta, you tell me.

ROBERTA: The Ohio River is bounded by Mississippi State.

TEACHER: No, Roberta, not at all. Harold, suppose you try.

HAROLD: Kentucky, Ohio and Illinois.

TEACHER: That's right. Now what state is just below Ohio? Think carefully, and don't—

KLANSMAN: That'll do, Yankee! Teaching these Negro brats to read. You carpetbaggers got no business down South no how. Get on back up North where you belong. There'll be no more school in this county for Negroes.

TEACHER: Negroes have a right to learn. This is an outrage!

KLANSMAN: Outrage, hell! Get out! Get out! You Yankees you! Get out!

BLACKSMITH: On my journey now,

MOUNT Zion,

On my journey now. . . .

(Another KLANSMAN enters)

2ND KLANSMAN: Who told *you* to set up business in this town?

BLACKSMITH: Nobody, sir! But I has to earn my living and this is my home. I does honest work, and I don't harm nobody.

KLANSMAN: Well, you getting too prosperous around here, and we don't want you in town. You see this rope? *It* does harm.

(Laughter of KLAN offstage.)

BLACKSMITH: I sees it, sir.

KLANSMAN: Well, it'll be wrapped around your neck if you don't make yourself scarce before nightfall. Don't let the Klan ride! You hear?

BLACKSMITH: Yes, I hear, but I'll be damned if I'm gonna let you drive me out of town!

KLANSMAN: Don't talk back to me.

BLACKSMITH: I will talk back to you! My people's done worked 200 years in this country for nothing. And we've got as much right here as you is. Don't make any mistake about it—I'm here to stay. America's our land.

CLERK: So. . . . you want to vote, heh, George?

VOTER: My name's not George, sir. My name's Henry Jackson.

CLERK: I don't care what your name is. The law says you have to know the Constitution forwards and backwards. Recite the Constitution to me backwards.

VOTER: But, sir—

CLERK: But-ing ain't gonna do you no good. I said the Constitution—

VOTER: I know it. It says: "We the people of the United States, in order to form a more perfect Union, establish justice"—

CLERK: I said, backwards!

VOTER: But, sir, I—

CLERK: So you don't know it, do you?

VOTER: Not back—

CLERK: And you want to vote? Well, you not gonna vote, not in Georgia! You hear me—you dirty low-down—

SOLDIER: So it went in the days of reconstruction. Trickery, terror, violence, the Klan. But we kept on protecting that freedom plant. Negroes *did* vote in spite of all. And they elected to the Senate of our United States such black men as Bruce, and Langston and Revells.

SENATOR: Cling to your rights, citizens of the Southland. I, as your Senator, urge you to cling to the vote. Without the ballot, you have no power. The ballot is democracy in action.

> *(BLACKOUT)*

SOLDIER: Negro teachers set up schools. Lucy Laney founded Haines Institute in Georgia.

> *(Light reveals a NEGRO WOMAN TEACHER.)*

LUCY LANEY: Educate! Educate! Study and learn. Education is a tool to build our freedom. Get ready children—your chance will come.

> *(BLACKOUT)*

SOLDIER: Booker T. Washington founded Tuskegee.

> *(Light reveals BOOKER T. WASHINGTON at Tuskegee)*

WASHINGTON: Train the hand, the heart and the head.

> *(BLACKOUT)*

SOLDIER: Out of the Negro people, writers and poets came to sing our hopes and aspirations. Paul Laurence Dunbar.

> *(Light reveals DUNBAR)*

DUNBAR: The night is not all dark,

> Nor the day all it seems.
> Each may bring me this relief—
> My dreams—my dreams. . . . .

> *(BLACKOUT)*

SOLDIER: Freedom and progress—these were the Negro dreams. Opportunity, culture, the right to work, to learn, to vote, to fight—the right to be Americans. In spite of hardships, in spite of race-haters and the Klan, Negro achievement and Negro culture marches on.

CHORUS: Oh, didn't it rain!

> Yes, didn't it rain!

Scene 8
Cultural Sequence

SOLDIER: Born out of the sorrow songs of slavery, Negro music took on new joy and new vigor and swept across America, from the minstrels to the great musicals of Williams and Walker, and Cole and Johnson, from the composer Will Marion Cook to William Grant Still, from Blind Boone to Duke Ellington, from Black Patti to—Paul Robeson.

PAUL ROBESON
  Water Boy
  Joe Hill
  For this We Fight
  (BLACKOUT)

SOLDIER: You see, Junior, what great singers we have?

JUNIOR: Robeson was a football player, too, wasn't he, daddy?

SOLDIER: All-American! That's also what he is as a man—ALL-AMERICAN! He uses his songs as a weapon for freedom. The dance is a weapon, too.
  (Music for a dance begins.)
  Today a young woman brings to Broadway dances that interpret not only the culture, but the protest of the Negro people.
  "Jim Crow Train"—as danced by—Pearl Primus.
  (Spotlight falls on dancer.)
  PEARL PRIMUS
  (BLACKOUT)

SOLDIER: When your father was a kid, Junior—in fact, just about the time I was born—a black man gave America—and the world—a new music, a new song that he put down on the back of an old envelope one night in Memphis. Listen! The man who wrote that song—W. C. Handy and the *ST. LOUIS BLUES.*
  THE GREAT W. C. HANDY, IN PERSON, PLAYS HIS IMMORTAL *ST. LOUIS BLUES.*
  W. C. HANDY
  (BLACKOUT)

SOLDIER: The blues—those great, sad, strong, determined songs of the Negro people, warm as the beat of the human heart—a real part of Negro culture.
  (A Teutonic voice speaks.)

BUNDIST: Negro culture—bah! Der ist no Negro culture.

SOLDIER: There was Benjamin Banneker, there was Matt Henson, there was Dr. Carver. There's Marian Anderson, Richard Wright, Dr. Hinton! There's Judge William Hastie, there's Captain Mulzac.

BUNDIST: I say, there ist no Negro culture—

Scene 9
Enemy Agents

BUNDIST: Mein Fuehrer says, "Vot ist a Negro but a half-ape?" Only the Aryan race know the meaning of culture. The Klan agrees with me on that. That is why today, members of the Bund, we gather to greet our friends and fellow Aryans of America, the Ku Klux Klan! United against the Negro, the Jew, the Catholic and all such filthy elements, Brothers of the Bund, the day will come soon when the Master Race will take command—and such scum will be put where they belong. Brothers, tomorrow the world! Klansmen, join with us! Kleagle of the Klan, I gift you my hand! Aryans, heil!

VOICES: Heil!

Heil!

Heil!

(BLACKOUT)

SOLDIER: That, Junior, was Camp Nordland in New Jersey, 1938. But even now, during the war, the Nazi agents kept on working. His name may be Hoffman or Dusseldorf or plain John Smith or Harry Jones. He may speak with an accent or speak good American English—but his real name and his real voice is HITLER.

WOMAN: Why, I haven't enjoyed losing so much in weeks!

ENEMY AGENT: Dick, you and Mary sure played a good game of bridge!

DICK: We set you 300 points on that rubber.

ENEMY AGENT: Yes, that's one thing you do well, Dick. But you don't look out for your neighbors very well, so they tell me.

DICK: What do you mean, Joe?

ENEMY AGENT: You're in the city council, aren't you? Then why don't you introduce a bill to stop those Negroes from moving into white neighborhoods like ours? That housing project the government is getting ready to turn over to Negroes is right here.

WOMAN: Why, it's practically next door to us.

ENEMY AGENT: Of course, we don't mind, but the neighbors are all saying they'll be damned if a lot of black folks are going to move in there.

DICK: But, Joe, Negro war workers have to live somewhere.

ENEMY AGENT: True, but remember all those headlines in the papers about muggings . . .

WOMAN: Frightful, isn't it?

ENEMY AGENT: And I know you want Mary to be able to walk on the street safely.

DICK: I guess there's something in what you're saying, Joe.

> *(BLACKOUT. Low laughter of the KLAN. The SOLDIER explains to his SON.)*

SOLDIER: You see, Junior, with such talk, Hitler's agents sabotage the war effort, keep black workers from finding homes, and cause ordinary plain Americans to commit treason against the government. Look at this Bundist on Main Street.

> *(Lights up to reveal TWO MEN passing)*

1ST MAN: Bill, did you see that colored couple buying tickets to that show there?

2ND MAN: Sure did. Our best movie in town, and we have to sit beside colored folks. Shame, ain't it!

1ST MAN: Well, I don't know. . . .

2ND MAN: I'm telling you. Next thing they'll be taking your job, then trying to crash your parties and dances. . . .

1ST MAN: Say, there's maybe something to what you say. . . .

> *(BLACKOUT)*

MAN: Bus driver, make that Negro get out of that seat. He's supposed to sit behind *white* folks.

WOMAN: Ladies of the DAR, we really can't afford to have a Negress singing in our magnificent Constitution Hall. Why, Negroes would want to attend the concert. . . .

CRACKER: As a member of the local council of the Red Cross here in our town, I say, scientific or not, I ain't gonna have no black blood put into this blood bank to be poured into the veins of no relative of mine on the battlefield. Why, one drop of black blood makes a man a Negro in this state. Come to think of it, maybe we ought to take up the question of Jewish blood, too. . . . .

SOLDIER: Divide and rule! Divide and rule! That's the method of the Hitler agents in this country. Spread hate, confusion, suspicion of the Jews, of Negroes, of Catholics, of Mexicans. Make 'em hate each other instead of hating the enemy. Help the mobsters and the Klan continue their dangerous oppression. Hitler knows Jim-crowism weakens the war effort.

Scene 10
Discrimination in Industry

FOREMAN: What do *you* do?

1ST WORKER: Laborer.

FOREMAN: Hired. Go get a blank for trade school and we'll teach you to run a machine. Next! What's your trade?

2ND WORKER: Publisher.

FOREMAN: Hired, go in. *(To next)* What do you do?

3RD WORKER: Machinist.

FOREMAN: Need you badly. We need plenty more machinists, fellow, so if you know any, send 'em around.

 (A NEGRO is next in line. The FOREMAN addresses him gruffly.) What can you do, boy?

UNION NEGRO: Machinist, too.

FOREMAN: Can't use you. Come back next week—might be a janitor's job open. . . . Next!

UNION NEGRO: But I'm a skilled worker—experienced machinist.

FOREMAN: I said we can't use you.

UNION NEGRO: But why? You need machinists. Why not?

FOREMAN: Look at yourself, boy, and see! Move on, now. . . . Next!

UNION NEGRO: Say, listen, I'm a citizen. I got two brothers fighting in New Guinea. How come I can't work?

FOREMAN: Move on there! You want me to call the cops?

 (A WHITE WORKER steps out of line.)

UNION MAN: Say, foreman, just a minute.

FOREMAN: Yes?

UNION MAN: This is a war plant, and you're short as hell on skilled labor.

FOREMAN: That's right, brother. You know where I can get some more laborers?

UNION MAN: Sure.

FOREMAN: Lead me to 'em, son.

UNION MAN: There's one right here.

 (Pointing out the NEGRO.)

FOREMAN: Are you kidding? . . . . Say, is this any business of yours?

UNION MAN: Yes, it's my business. I'm a union man—Local 642. This fellow's in my union.

FOREMAN: Is he? Well, now you know personally I don't mind, but plenty of fellows don't want to work with a—er—colored fellow, union or not.

UNION MAN: Have you asked 'em?

FOREMAN: No, I ain't asked 'em. . . . Why don't you?

UNION MAN: I will . . . Hey, fellows, come over here a minute.

> *(Various WORKERS gather around him.)*

Listen, do you guys object to working with Joe here?

WORKERS: Hell, No! Why should we?

> I've got no objections.
>
> Sure not—he's damn good machinist.
>
> Production's got to roll, ain't it?
>
> Sure, let him in!
>
> Give him a job—and let's get back to work.

UNION MAN: O.K. fellows! *(To FOREMAN)* Listen, Bud, we've got a war to win. We need production, get me? What we want is a Victory Line—not a Color Line! If you don't employ that man, I'll take it up with the union council.

FOREMAN: O.K.! O.K.! O.K.! *(To the NEGRO)* Hey, you! Check in.

UNION MAN: Come on, buddy, we'll check in together.

> *(BLACKOUT. The SOLDIER speaks in the darkness.)*

SOLDIER: That's what a progressive union can do, Junior. Unfortunately, not all unions are like that. Take Tom Ray out in Oregon. And there are plenty of others. But the union boys are learning, and they're going to fix those guys themselves. Labor's in this war for victory! . . . As for the army, Negroes and whites go through the same draft boards together, pass the same medical exams, get on the train together—then at the induction center. . . .

Scene 11
Segregation in Army

SERGEANT: Carl Mazarik, Order Number 3306.

1ST WHITE: Yes, sir.

SERGEANT: Start the line over there. . . . Fred Wallenberg, Order Number 7721.

2ND WHITE: Here, sir.

(Behind him is a NEGRO.)

SERGEANT: Over there next to Mazarik. . . . . Kenneth Harper, 1863.

1ST NEGRO: Yes, sir.

SERGEANT: New line over there, you!

(Directs the NEGRO to opposite side.)

Paul Vennuti, 542.

3RD WHITE: Right here.

SERGEANT: To your left. . . . . Arthur Williams, 156.

(Another NEGRO steps up.)

UNION NEGRO: Here.

SERGEANT: On the right there. . . . . Carl Andorn, 7432.

UNION MAN: Yes, sir.

SERGEANT: Line up, left.

UNION MAN: I came with Williams there, sir.

SERGEANT: What's that?

UNION MAN: My buddy and I came together.

SERGEANT: What do you mean, came together? He's colored, ain't he?

UNION MAN: We're from the same neighborhood in Brooklyn, went to school together, played on the same football team, and since the war been working in the same defense plant together, same department, same union. We want to fight together.

SERGEANT: Oh, no! Not in this army. Colored and white ain't together. Get over there where I told you.

UNION NEGRO: Suppose I get in that line, too, then, with Andorn.

SERGEANT: No fresh talk out of you, private. You're in the army now. Negroes and whites are separate here.

UNION NEGRO: Just the way the Red Cross separates blood! Heh? I guess you know, Hitler likes it that way, Sergeant.

SERGEANT: One more word out of you, and you'll head right straight to the guard house. . . . Andorn, I told you to step over there.

UNION MAN: Look here, Sergeant! Williams and I work together, we vote together—why in hell can't we fight together?

SERGEANT: You can't, that's why! Listen, both of you, in the army— orders is orders. This is the official policy of the War Department. Its been that way for a long time.

UNION NEGRO: Well, times have changed! Today that policy helps Adolf Hitler and Company! We're fighting to change that Over There. *And the quicker we change it over here, the quicker we'll win Over There.*

(BLACKOUT.)

Scene 12
Negro Demands

JUNIOR: What can we do about it, daddy?

WIFE: Yes, Henry, what can we do about it?

SOLDIER: It's up to all those people out there in this audience tonight
—to you—and you—and you! You can do something about it! And
it's up to millions of Americans who believe in liberty throughout
the nation and who know these things are wrong. And it's up to
our President—our great wartime Commander-in-Chief—who can
speak out for the bill abolishing the poll-tax, for the anti-lynching
bill, and for the end of Jim-crowism in the armed forces and in
industry. Tell America, Mr. Roosevelt, this nation can't fight with
all its strength with its black arm chained by the color bar. Tell
the world, Mr. Roosevelt, that when we say *democracy,* we mean
DEMOCRACY! As for us soldiers, we've got to carry on against
fascism Over There—to keep it from getting over here to strengthen
reaction on our own shores. At the same time, *you've* got to battle
at home against fascism in American life—against the Jim Crow car,
against discrimination in uniform and factory, and against those poll-
tax senators like Bilbo and Connelly who say:
   (An ILLITERATE VOICE is heard.)

POLL-TAXER: No Negro is good enough to work beside a white man,
Order 8802 or not to the contrary. Now, you take that FEPC Roosevelt set up for the Jews and the Negroes—

SOLDIER: Yes, take the Fair Employment Practices Committee that
went on the rocks over the Railroad Brotherhoods; we've got to re-
vive that, strengthen it, and let Roosevelt know that 14 million Negro
people back him up 100% on it! We've got to let the Klan-minded
and the Bund-minded and the anti-Negro, anti-labor forces know
that they are not America, AND THEY WON'T RUN AMERICA!
Ladies and gentlemen, we're America—you out there, me here!
From Crispus Attucks at the Boston Massacre right down to today, we have always been on the side of Freedom—for we helped to
plant the seed with our blood. We helped to guard it and make it
grow. Now we want to see it blossom into full fruit. Now the day has
come to put a TIME LIMIT on Freedom. We want it NOW! Not
fifty years from today—but NOW! Freedom is not just something
to talk about. Freedom is something you can see—feel—eat—live!
Freedom has to be real—as a man is real! Tonight American Negro

soldiers are stationed all over the world—Alaska, India, Australia, North Africa, the West Indies, fighting for the liberty of the whole world. They won't be cheated of the Victory.

(In each corner of the star a NEGRO SOLDIER appears with the flag.)

At home we're tired of being Jim Crowed! We're tired of being segregated. We want to win this war, we want to fight shoulder to shoulder with everybody else—but we also want to train together, vote together, work together, fight together till fascism is conquered and be Americans together! We want Hitler not only out of Europe, but out of the U.S.A.

(Quietly)

I have just come up from the South in a Jim Crow car, from a segregated regiment, in a segregated corner of a southern camp. I know how high the wall of prejudice is. But that wall is not too high to scale. Dorrie Miller scaled it when he came up on deck on that battleship in Pearl Harbor and started shooting. Right there, Jim Crow started its Last stand. Things can't be the same again—and WON'T be!

(He steps forward.)

To break the power of Hitlerism and Jim Crowism all over the earth, folks—for this we fight! To make a world—including America— where everybody's free—for this we fight. Freedom of worship, freedom of press, freedom from want, freedom from fear—for this we fight. Freedom to vote, freedom to work, freedom to speak, freedom to hear. ATTENTION, America! For this we fight!

America, our homeland,
Ever dear will be,
That's why we want America
For ALL men to be free!
Let's put an end to the color bar!
Let's put an end to the Jim Crow car!
For the right to be men
In this land we defend—
For this we fight!

Freedom of worship, freedom of press,
Freedom from want and freedom from fear—
For this we fight! For this we fight!
Freedom to vote and freedom to work,

Freedom to speak and freedom to hear—
For this we fight! For this we fight!
America, our homeland,
Ever dear will be,
That's why we want America
For ALL men to be free!
Let's put an end to the color bar!
Let's smash to hell the Jim Crow car!
For the right to be men
In this land we defend—
!!!!! FOR THIS WE FIGHT!!!!!

END

The Ballot and Me
The Negro's Part in Suffrage
An Historical Sequence

1956

Characters
(In order of appearance)

(Contemporary George Washington's period, 1797–1883)
NARRATOR
SAMUEL FRAUNCES**
SOJOURNER TRUTH**

(1817–1895)
FREDERICK DOUGLASS**

(Representatives in Congress during Reconstruction 1869–1889)
JEFFERSON P. LONG
JOSEPH H. RAINEY
ROBERT O. DeLARGE
ALONZO J. RAINER
ROBERT B. ELLIOTT
BENJAMIN S. TURNER
JOHN R. LYNCH
JAMES T. RAPIER
JOSIAH T. WALLS
RICHARD H. CAIN
CHARLES E. NASH
JOHN A. HYMAN
JENE HARALSON
ROBERT SMALLS

(Senators—1879–1881 period)
HIRAM R. REVELS
BLANCHE K. BRUCE

(Representatives 1883–1897)
JOHN M. LANGSTON**
THOMAS E. MILLER
GEORGE W. MURRAY
JAMES E. O'HARA
HENRY P. CHEATHAM
GEORGE H. WHITE

(At time of 1895 Atlanta speech)
BOOKER T. WASHINGTON**

NOTE: *Speaking parts are marked with asterisks**. All except Sojourner Truth may read speeches from rostrum, and even she may read her long speech, but should learn rest of dialogue. Fraunces has only one line. "And I voted."*
SETTING: *A rostrum*
TIME: *The present, with flashbacks*
ACTION: *A NARRATOR comes to the rostrum and shouts four words very loudly as if opening a Town Meeting.*
NARRATOR: Ballot!
Suffrage!
Franchise!
Vote!
   (NARRATOR bangs his gavel)
The dictionary says:
"*Ballot*—the method of secret voting; originally by means of small balls placed in an urn or box."
"*Suffrage*—a vote given by a member of a body, state, or society, in assent to a proposition or in favor of the election of a person."
"*Franchise*—the right of voting at public elections."
"*Vote*—an intimation that one approves or disapproves, accepts or rejects, a proposal, motion, candidate for office, or the like."
The right to cast a ballot, to exercise suffrage, to vote is one of the basic rights of citizens in democracy—a democracy, that form of government in which control is vested in the people as a whole. The ballot is basic.
Negro Americans—you, me—are very much a part of this democracy. We're 15 million—and our vote counts. From the national to the local level, *your* vote counts. It counts in more and better jobs—

diplomatic posts abroad to local political patronage. It counts in education, in housing, in civil rights, in cleaner streets, in better garbage collection. The vote has value. Don't neglect your right to vote. Don't waste it. Don't forget it.

Maybe all of us would value the right of suffrage more if we stopped to look back a moment at what the struggle for the vote has cost. Back in the Middle Ages few people had control over their own lives, let alone over the land or the country. Kings and barons and chiefs and over-lords ran everything and everybody. Then came the Magna Carta in 1215 in England, and almost 400 years later the Bill of Rights, many of whose provisions were incorporated into our own Constitution in 1787 and into the American Bill of Rights in 1791. Some of those rights, we, the Negro people of America, are still trying to secure in full.

We came to these shores first as explorers—with Cortez, with Balboa, with Columbus. But we did not migrate in large numbers. The majority of our ancestors were brought to the Americas by force as slaves, dating from 1619. Slaves, like serfs in Europe, could not vote. But very early in our history, after the colonies won their freedom from the British—Crispus Attucks of Boston, a Negro, being the first man killed when resistance to the British started—free Negroes in the New England colonies voted. Some Negroes in our country have always voted from the very beginning of our United States, and fought to keep the vote and extend it to others. But sometimes it was a hard battle. You who have the vote here in New York, keep it, use it, and help others to get it.

After the Revolutionary War, free Negroes could vote anywhere, but in 1789 the Southern slave-holding states sensed danger in letting free Negroes vote, and began to disfranchise them. By 1834 no Negroes could vote in the South, and some Northern states like Pennsylvania and Indiana denied them the ballot, too. But colored men in New York, could vote if they owned property and had lived here for three years. This man could vote.

(SAMUEL FRAUNCES enters in colonial knickers)
Samuel Fraunces. He was the owner of Fraunces Tavern at Broad and Pearl Streets in New York City. At his tavern George Washington often dined, and when Washington became President, he made Samuel Fraunces his chief steward.
FRAUNCES: And I could vote.

NARRATOR: Fraunces was a man of means, a solid citizen, interested in the affairs of the day. Free Negroes in New York then could vote.
> *(Suddenly the spotlight focuses on a bonneted woman sitting in the audience in the corner of a pew who quickly speaks up loudly. She is SOJOURNER TRUTH)*

SOJOURNER: Could I vote? I lived in New York.

NARRATOR: No, Sojourner Truth. You were a woman, and in those days only men could vote.

SOJOURNER: Which were wrong! I believed everybody should vote, black and white, men and women! And I said so.

NARRATOR: I know you said so. You went to the first women's suffrage meetings, and you joined with Abby Kelly and Lucretia Mott and Frances Gage, white women, in speaking not only for Negro freedom, but for the freedom of women. You were a runaway slave who made yourself free.

SOJOURNER: And I wanted to vote.

NARRATOR: When they wouldn't let you sit on the platform because you were a Negro at the National Woman's Suffrage Convention in Akron, Ohio, in 1852, you sat where you are sitting now in the audience.

SOJOURNER: I did—until the going got hot *(she rises)* and the men speakers started baiting the women, and talking about the women is weak, not strong as men nor smart as men, and they even have to be helped into carriages. *(She comes to the rostrum)* Then I just walked up on that platform, sir, and told them men: "Nobody ever helped me into carriages or over mud puddles, or give me any best place. Ain't I a woman? Look at me! Look at my arm! I have plowed and planted and gathered into barns, and no man could head me. And ain't I a woman? I could work as much and eat as much as a man— when I could get it—and bear the lash as well—and ain't I a woman? I has had five chillun and seen 'em most all sold off into slavery, and when I cried out with a mother's grief, none but Jesus heared—and ain't I a woman? They talks about this thing in the head—intellect. What's that got to do with women's rights? If my cup won't hold but a pint and yourn holds a quart, wouldn't ye men be mean not to let me have my little half-measure full? If the first woman God made was strong enough to turn the world upside down all alone, I guess all us women together ought to be able to turn it back and get it right side up again. And now that they is asking to do it, *the mens better let 'em*."

(She returns to her pew)

NARRATOR: But it was almost three-quarters of a century before the country got around to giving you the vote, Sojourner Truth, before the 19th Amendment granting women's suffrage was passed.

SOJOURNER: It were finally passed—and about time, too! I took my freedom, but I didn't live long enough to vote.

NARRATOR: Freedom! That was the first thing most Negroes had to get. Before the Civil War most of us were slaves. But some Negroes, even in the South, had never been slaves. Some were born free, some were given their freedom, and some ran away to freedom in the North. Among the great runaways was Frederick Douglass who escaped from a Maryland plantation in 1838, and devoted his life to fighting for freedom for all, and for full citizenship rights for all. In his middle age:

(DOUGLASS enters, white haired, white beard, dignified, imposing) After Emancipation, after the Civil War was over, he made many speeches concerning the franchise.

DOUGLASS: I see no chance of bettering the condition of the freedman until he shall cease to be merely a freedman and shall become a citizen. I insist that there is no safety for him or anybody else in America outside the American government; to guard, protect, and maintain his liberty the freedman should have the ballot; the liberties of the American people are dependent upon the ballot-box, the jury-box, and the cartridge-box.

NARRATOR: And it took the cartridge-box to protect the rights of the freed Negroes in the early days of the Reconstruction. In 1867 Congress divided the South into five military districts, proclaimed universal suffrage, and placed federal marshalls at the polls to protect the Negro's newly granted right to vote. This right was made permanent by the passage in 1870 of the 15th Amendment to the Constitution of the United States. 700,000 Negroes were added to the voting rolls of the South, and many city and state offices were filled by the freedmen. With Negroes in state legislatures, new state constitutions were drawn up with provisions for free public schools for all, civil rights for all, and no property qualifications for voting— the most progressive acts of laws the South had ever known, many of them remaining on the books until today.

During the Reconstruction the Southern states sent 14 Negro Representatives and 2 Senators of color to Washington. The first Representative was from Georgia, elected in 1869, Jefferson P. Long.

(LONG enters to stand beside NARRATOR. In turn, as each man's name is called, each enters, alternately at left or right, to form two lines on each side of the platform)

Then in 1871 South Carolina elected four Negro Congressmen, Joseph H. Rainey.

(Enter RAINEY)

Robert O. DeLarge.

(Enter DeLARGE)

Alonzo J. Rainer.

(Enter RAINER)

And Robert B. Elliott.

(Enter ELLIOTT)

That same year Alabama elected Benjamin S. Turner.

(Enter TURNER)

In 1873 Mississippi elected John R. Lynch.

(Enter LYNCH)

Alabama elected James T. Rapier.

(Enter RAPIER)

Florida elected Josiah T. Walls.

(Enter WALLS)

And South Carolina elected Richard H. Cain.

(Enter CAIN)

In 1875 Louisiana sent Charles E. Nash to Washington.

(Enter NASH)

That same year to the House of Representatives North Carolina elected John A. Hyman.

(Enter HYMAN)

Alabama elected Jene Haralson.

(Enter HARALSON)

And South Carolina elected Robert Smalls.

(Enter SMALLS)

The only Negro Senators in American history came at the very end of the Reconstruction period. The first, elected in 1870, was Hiram R. Revels.

(Enter REVELS)

And second in 1875 was Blanche K. Bruce.

(Enter BRUCE)

Most of these men were as well qualified and as well educated as white officials of the times, and some better. Some were graduates of Oberlin or other leading Northern colleges. Elliott had studied abroad. Of those who served in Congress, the Republican leader, James G. Blaine, said, "They were as a rule studious, earnest, ambitious men, whose public conduct would be honorable to any race." Typical of the Negroes who served in the House of Representatives at Washington was Richard H. Cain, A.M.E. minister of South Carolina. Cain made a stirring speech in Congress regarding Civil Rights.

(CAIN steps forwards and speaks)

CAIN: I do not ask any legislation for the colored people of this country that is not applied to white people. All that we ask is equal laws, equal legislation, and equal rights throughout the length and breadth of this land. We do not come here begging for our rights. We come here clothed in the garb of American citizenship. We come *demanding* our rights in the name of justice, equity, and law, in the name of our children, in the name of our country.

NARRATOR: During the Reconstruction and in lesser degrees thereafter, many Negroes were active in state governments. For example, between 1868 and 1896 Louisiana elected 32 state senators of color and 95 representatives. P. B. S. Pinchback was Lieutenant-Governor and, in 1873, after the removal of the white incumbent, Pinchback became Acting-Governor of Louisiana. In Florida, Jonathan Gibbs, a Dartmouth graduate, became Secretary of State. And in South Carolina, the London-educated Francis L. Cardozo was from 1872 to 1876 the State Treasurer.

But when federal troops were removed from the South in 1877 and Negro voters no longer had protection at the polls, reaction set in. The Ku Klux Klan began to ride. Voters were intimidated, tarred and feathered, whipped, shot down. Black Codes were passed denying civil rights, and some states originated Grandfather Clauses which said that unless you or your parents had voted before the Civil War, you could not vote now—which meant freedmen were not eligible. Negro political power faded in the South. For a brief period during the rise of the Populist Party of farmers and poor whites, both Democrats and Republicans again sought the Negro vote to keep the Populists from becoming powerful. Then, from 1883 to 1897, six Negroes were elected as Representatives to Washington. They were: from Virginia, John M. Langston

(Enter LANGSTON)

from South Carolina, Thomas E. Miller and George W. Murray

(Enter MILLER and MURRAY)

And from North Carolina, James E. O'Hara, Henry P. Cheatham
(Enter O'HARA and CHEATHAM)
And the last of the Southern Representatives, George H. White of
North Carolina, elected in 1897.
(Enter WHITE)
When White completed his term in 1901, it was 27 years before
another Negro went to Congress.
One of the outstanding colored politicians was John M. Langston,
Congressman from Virginia, founder of the Law School at Howard
University, and first president of Virginia State College for Negroes.
Widely known as a speaker, Langston, in an address at Saratoga, New
York, in 1876, concerning the use of the ballot, said some wise things.
(LANGSTON comes forward)
LANGSTON: Perhaps never in the history of our country was there
a time when the duty of the American voter to consider well and
wisely what vote to cast, what party to bring to power and support
in power, was so imperative. In discharging our duty in this regard,
while we are fearless, we should be impartial and just. Let us not
make haste to condemn unduly, nor to accept without wise discrimination the claim of any candidate or party. We are called upon as
intelligent and earnest, patriotic and devoted citizens, to determine,
each for himself, how votes given for the Democratic or Republican
party, will tend to sustain the dignity and power of the Government,
and conserve our free institutions under the Constitution. Each of
us is held responsible to his own conscience, posterity and God for
the wisdom, or folly displayed in exercising our suffrage—the most
sacred, as it is the most valuable right which we possess on American
soil.
NARRATOR: Disenfranchised in the South by state laws, trickery, or terror, no more Negro Congressmen came from Dixie after Langston
and White. But quietly behind the scenes, a practical-minded man
of enormous political power emerged, consulted by national leaders
North and South on all problems relating to the Negro. He was a
friend of Presidents. That man was the great founder of Tuskegee
Institute, Booker T. Washington.
(Enter WASHINGTON)
WASHINGTON: Friends, the individual or race that own the property,
pays the taxes, possesses the intelligence and substantial character,
is the one which is going to exercise the greatest control in government, whether he lives in the North or whether he lives in the South.

There is no defense or security for any of us except in the highest intelligence and development of all. Education must be digested and assimilated in order to make it significant. The science, the art, the literature that fails to reach down and bring the humblest up to the enjoyment of the fullest blessings of our government is weak, no matter how costly the buildings or apparatus used, or how modern the methods of instruction employed. The study of arithmetic that does not result in making men conscientious in receiving and counting the ballots of their fellow men is faulty.

NARRATOR: Unfortunately, the unreconstructed rebels of the South continued to deny the right to vote, or failed to count, the ballots of Negro citizens at the turn of the century. When Charles H. White left Congress in 1901, it was more than a quarter of a century before we had there another national representative. In 1928 Oscar DePriest was elected to Congress from the First Illinois District—being the first Northern Negro ever to sit in the national legislature. As the great migrations from the South increased after each war, and the black populations of our Northern industrial cities grew, so Negro political power grew. Municipal judges, city councilmen, county officials, and state legislators of color from New York to Los Angeles became not uncommon. From Illinois, Arthur W. Michell FOLLOWED De Priest to Congress, then came William L. Dawson serving now. From New York Adam Clayton Powell, Jr. was elected in 1945, and most recently Charles C. Diggs of Detroit became the 27th man of color to sit in Congress. There should be more—more Powells, Dawsons, and Diggses in Washington. More James Watsons and Bessie Buchanans in state governments as in New York. More Hulan Jacks in more American city halls, as in Manhattan, and more judges such as Rivers, Paige, Stevens, Dickens, and Jane Bolin on the benches of municipalities across the nation. And we all—you, me—must use our vote wisely and use it well to elect to all sorts of offices, particularly the national offices, men who will bring to bear our democratic forces on all public officials to not only open up—but to *protect*—the ballot boxes of the South—so that Negro citizens may vote in Mississippi and Georgia and Alabama and South Carolina again—and again send to Congress *from the South* black men—

(A WOMAN cries from the audience)

SOJOURNER: And black women!

(SOJOURNER TRUTH rises and joins the others on the platform)

NARRATOR: Yes, and black women—representatives of the strength and calibre of those who served so nobly and so well in the dark and dangerous days of Reconstruction. Fellow citizens, your ballot has great value. Use it! When election time comes, to paraphrase by extension a young Negro leader in the South today, the Reverend Martin Luther King of Alabama, "If you can't fly, run! If you can't run, walk! If you can't walk, crawl—to the polls and vote!"

(Various ones cry in turn the word "vote!")

FRAUNCES: Vote!

SOJOURNER: Vote!

DOUGLASS: Vote!

CAIN: Vote!

LANGSTON: Vote!

WASHINGTON: Vote!

NARRATOR: Vote!

(All the characters on the platform come forward, point their fingers at the audience, and cry in unison several times the word, "vote!")

ALL TOGETHER: Vote! . . . . . . Vote! . . . . . Vote! . . . . Vote! . . . . . Vote . . . VOTE!

(Blackout. . . . Lights up again for bows. Then all the characters leave the platform except the NARRATOR who continues with the contemporary part of the program, introducing guests from the various political parties present)

Radio Plays

Hughes was not fond of radio, complaining in 1945 that, at least in his experience, radio "insistently censored any real dramatic approach to the actual problems of the Negro people. In that regard it has been almost as bad as Hollywood." On April 7, 1940, the day the U.S. Post Office released a Booker T. Washington stamp (the first stamp to so honor an African American), CBS broadcast *Booker T. Washington in Atlanta*. The network had, however, rejected Hughes's recently performed *The Organizer*, demurring that it was "too controversial for us to give it an emotional treatment on an essentially dramatic show." In 1941, at the urging of the Office of Civilian Defense—"since you have always written truth, and that is what counts in all times"—Hughes sent *Brothers*. It, too, was rejected as too controversial.[1] Similarly, in 1943, following a riot in Harlem, both the mayor and the War Board pressed Hughes for "pacifying material." Hughes complied, sending *In the Service of My Country*, "inspired by a picture of black and whites working in harmony to build the Alaska-Canada highway," and another script, *Pvt. Jim Crow*.[2] The former was immediately broadcast; the latter, about the daily humiliation blacks faced in the Armed Forces, was also praised but not produced.[3] Of historical interest, these plays represent Hughes's contributions to the war effort. Within the bitter limits of censorship, Hughes continually decried the racism that infected all aspects of America's conduct of the war, while recognizing the importance of encouraging African American support for it.

The texts of *In the Service of My Country, Brothers,* and *Pvt. Jim Crow* are from typescripts in the Langston Hughes Papers. The cover of the latter notes it was written "especially for the WRITERS WAR BOARD" and, in Hughes's hand, is dated 12/16/43 and noted as "author's copy." Notes on the cover pages of *In the Service of My Country* and *Brothers* also indicate they were sent to the Writers War Board. *Booker T. Washington in Atlanta* is taken from *Radio Drama in Action: Twenty-five Plays of a Changing World*, edited by Erik Barnouw (New York: Rinehart & Co., 1945).

Booker T. Washington in Atlanta

1940

(Clop-clop of hoofs . . . Sound of carriage)

WIFE: Booker!

BOOKER: Yes?

WIFE: Why do you look so woebegone?

BOOKER: Margaret, to tell the truth, I feel like a man on the way to the gallows.

CHILD: Papa, they won't hang you for making another speech, will they?

BOOKER: Not hardly, Portia! But the wrong word said—and my usefulness in the South would be finished.

WIFE: You're always nervous before a speech, Booker, as often as you've made them. But tomorrow in Atlanta, I'm sure you'll give the best talk you've ever made. There's nothing to worry about.

BOY: Geeminy! It'll be wonderful to see Atlanta, won't it, mom?

GIRL: And the Cotton Exposition!

BOY: Papa, will there be a merry-go-round for colored children?

BOOKER: I reckon so, son. One of the biggest buildings on the grounds is the colored people's building.

GIRL: Will there be a Ferris wheel?

BOY: And firecrackers?

WIFE: Booker T. Junior, don't bother your father with firecrackers! He's tired—working all night on his speech. And besides, if he opens his mouth, clay dust'll get in his throat and he'll be hoarse.

BOOKER: Margaret, dust can't hurt a country boy like me. When I was Junior's age I was working in a coal mine twelve hours a day—and I've still got my voice.

WIFE: Well, save it for speaking and I'll take care of these children. Lucius, slow Jennie down a bit. There's plenty of time to make the train.

LUCIUS: Yes, ma'am, Mis' Washington.

BOY: Here comes Farmer Krenshaw in his old mule wagon, papa.

GIRL: He's one of the nicest white men around.

BOOKER: Lucius, you might stop a moment.

(Horse slowing down)

FARMER: Howdy, folks.

BOOKER: Howdy-do, Mr. Krenshaw. Nice sun for cotton, isn't it?

FARMER: Plenty! I hear you gonna make a speech tomorrow, Washington, the opening of the Exposition?

BOOKER: It looks like I am, sir.

FARMER: Well, you pretty good. You've spoke in front of northern white folks, and southern colored folks, and us farmers around here too. But in Atlanta tomorrow you gonna have city folks *and* country folks, Yankees *and* Southerners—and colored folks added to that. Now, how you gonna please all them different kind o' folks, Washington? I figger you got yourself in a kinder tight place.

BOOKER: *(Laughing).* I'm afraid I have! But when I come back, I'll tell you what I said.

FARMER: Well, good luck to you, Washington.

BOOKER: Thank you, Mr. Krenshaw.

> *(Horse speeds up, blending into)*
> *(Music: Hoofbeat transition)*
> *(Train pulling in)*
> *(Ad libs of "good-bye," "good luck," etc.)*

STATION PORTER: Get you-all's bags an bundles together! Here she comes. You children get back from the track. . . . Auburn, Opelika, West Point, La Grange, Hogansville, Trimble, Atlanta! . . . Stand back 'cause she's a-blowin'!

> *(Train comes to a stop)*

'Board! All 'board!

STUDENT: We with you, Dr. Washington.

SECOND STUDENT: God bless you, Mr. Washington.

THIRD STUDENT: Good luck to you-all. Happy journey!

> *(Bell of departing train)*

ALL: Good-bye! Good-bye!

> *(Train starting into)*
> *(Music: Special pullman car . . . Music cross-fading to)*
> *(Wheel sounds)*

BOOKER: The way my students believe in me Margaret, I can't let them down in Atlanta.

WIFE: You won't, Booker. They believe in you because you have never let them down. And they know you started out like they did, poor and ignorant, no book learning, nobody to help you—but you kept on.

BOOKER: Out of slavery, and the coal mine.

WIFE: And tomorrow you'll sit on the platform with the Governor of Georgia!

BOOKER: It's been a long haul, Margaret, from a slave plantation in Virginia where I didn't know my father's name—a one-room cabin and a bundle of rags on the floor.

GIRL: Papa, you promised to tell us about it again sometime.

BOY: And about the cat hole.

GIRL: But you're always too busy.

BOY: Why don't you tell us now?

GIRL: Tell us, please, papa.

WIFE: Children—

BOY: Tell us about the cat hole.

BOOKER: Well, Junior, you see my mother's cabin on the planta-tion didn't have any windows in it—but there were plenty of holes where the rain leaked through. And there was a rickety door, and a cat hole cut in the wall for the cat to pass in and out during the night.

BOY: Why, couldn't the cat go out the door?

BOOKER: Could've. There were plenty of cracks in it. But *everybody* had a cat hole—so we had one, too.

BOY: And did your mother feed the cat?

BOOKER: She hardly had time to feed *us*. She was a slave. Why, I can remember . . .

    (Train sounds fade out)

MOTHER: *(Fading on)* Get up, you-all chillun—if you wants to eat this corn pone. It mighty nigh daybreak. I got to go to my work.

CHILD: *(Drowsily)* Yes'm, we's comin'.

BOY: I's sleepy, ma.

MOTHER: Sleepy, nothin'! You got no time to be sleepy. *(Gently)* Here, eat this, son.

BOY: Yes'm.

MOTHER And get on down yonder to de fields—'cause I don't want my chillun to get no floggin' this mornin'.

    (Fade in train)

GIRL: I don't like to hear about floggings, papa.

BOY: Tell us about freedom.

GIRL: And the war.

BOOKER: I didn't see the war. But I heard the white folks talking about the war, as I fanned the flies away from them at dinnertime. And I

knew it meant freedom—if the Yankees won. In the slave cabins at
night . . .

(*Fade train out*)

SLAVE: Mars Lincoln, dey say he gonna set us free!

SECOND SLAVE: Mars Lincoln, he gonna sign a paper that say . . .

THIRD SLAVE: No mo' work in de fields.

SLAVE: No mo' chillun sold away.

SECOND SLAVE: No mo' floggin's.

THIRD SLAVE: First thing I gwine do is learn to read.

SLAVE: First thing I gwine do is *rest.*

SECOND SLAVE: Yes, indeedy! Uh-hum-mmmmm!

THIRD SLAVE: Won't it be fun to be free!

(*Train in*)

BOOKER: Yet none of us wanted harm to come to our master's family.

BOY: But when freedom came, you went away?

BOOKER: Yes, my mother took us children to West Virginia and I went
to work in the salt furnaces. I was a big boy, yet I couldn't read or
write. But the number on my salt barrel was . . .

(*Train out*)

FOREMAN: Eighteen. Take that barrel and fill it, boy.

BOOKER: Eigh-teen? Is that what those two numbers mean, boss?

FOREMAN: A one and a eight, that's eighteen.

BOOKER: A one and a eight . . . one and eight . . . eigh-teen.

(*Train in*)

So I learned to make those numbers and to read them. And I wanted to
learn more. I talked so much about learning till my mother finally
got me a battered blue-backed speller somewhere, and all alone I
studied the alphabet.

GIRL: Why didn't you get somebody to help you?

BOOKER: There wasn't a colored person in town who knew how to
read. They had all been slaves.

GIRL: Oh!

BOY: And there was no school?

BOOKER: No, son, there was no school. And when a school was finally
established, it was a *pay* school and I couldn't go because I had to
work. But at night I studied my blue-backed speller by the firelight.

BOY: Like Lincoln did.

BOOKER: And finally I got my chance to go to school—by rising at
daybreak and working until classtime, then going back to work after
school. There were many big boys in the first grade then, so being

large didn't embarrass me. But what did embarrass me was that first day when the teacher was making out the roll, because I noticed all the other children had at least two names, or even three—but I had just been called Booker all my life. I didn't know what I would say when he got to me. And he was coming down the line.

    (Train out)

TEACHER: Your name, son?

BOY: Aloysius Wilkrus Jones, suh.

TEACHER: And yours?

GIRL: Mary Mackabee Johnson.

TEACHER: Yours?

SECOND BOY: Franklin Wadson Hall.

TEACHER: Yours, please.

THIRD BOY: I'm Robert E. Lee Grant.

    (Train in)

BOOKER: And all the time he kept getting closer to me, and I didn't know what I was going to say. I was mighty puzzled. I felt like I wanted to cry. But suddenly a bright idea came to me and when he said

    (Train out)

TEACHER: And your name is . . . ?

BOOKER: Booker T. Washington.

    (Train in)

It popped out just like that—as if I'd known it all my life. And ever since, that's been my name.

GIRL: Then you christened yourself, didn't you, papa?

BOOKER: I christened myself!

    (Laughter)

BOY: But you didn't stay long in school, did you, papa?

BOOKER: No. I had to go to work again, this time in the coal mines, a mile down in the dark.

GIRL: Weren't you afraid?

BOOKER: Yes. There were often explosions, and falling slate, and gas. But one day down there I happened to hear two miners talking about a great school for colored people somewhere in Virginia, so I crept as close as I could to hear what they were saying.

    (Train out)

MINER: They calls it Hampton. And if a boy ain't got no money, he can just work for his education.

SECOND MINER: How about his board and keep?

MINER: They say he can work for that too.

SECOND MINER: Dog scat my eyes! Where's it at?

MINER: Somewhere 'way 'cross Virginny, I'm . . .

(Train in)

BOOKER: I didn't know how far Hampton was, nor how to get to it, but I made up my mind then and there to go.

BOY: And when you got there, they weren't sure they wanted to let you in, were they, papa?

BOOKER: No, son, because I got there in rags, with no money, and I'd slept the night before under a sidewalk in Richmond. The school was crowded. There were so many students some of us slept in tents. And sometimes at night the tents blew away in the dead of winter—but we wanted an education—and we got it!

GIRL: It's nicer at Tuskegee.

BOOKER: But it wasn't always. We began in a stable and a hen house. We made our own bricks. I pawned my watch for materials, and begged for money. Then a white man gave us *ten thousand dollars*.

WIFE: Our first big sum.

BOOKER: And once an old colored woman over seventy brought a gift. She hobbled in in rags—but clean—leaning on a cane. She held out her gift.

(Train out)

OLD WOMAN: Mr. Washington, I's spent de best days o' my life in slavery. And God knows I's ignorant and po'. But I knows what you's tryin' to do. You tryin' to make better men and women for de cullud race. I ain't got no money, but I wants you to take dese here six eggs what I been savin' up, and I wants you to put dese six eggs into de edication of dese boys and girls.

(Train in)

BOOKER: And so we struggled! But I'm glad we had to struggle. We built Tuskegee from the ground up. Now, when a new student is tempted to mar some building by carving his initials on it with a jackknife, I've often heard an old student say, "Don't do that. That's *our* building. I helped to put it up." In the beginning folks said we would fail. But I have no patience with the man who talks of failure, children. I believe only in the man who talks success.

WIFE: And that's what you should say in your speech tomorrow, Booker.

BOOKER: My speech is ready, Margaret. It's not what I'm going to say that worries me, but how they'll take it. Will the Southerners be displeased? Will the Negroes be worried? Will the northern whites think I've compromised? For they'll all be there—former slaves and former slaveowners, graduates from Tuskegee, and teachers from Hampton. And thousands of Georgians . . .

WIFE: And when Governor Bullock introduces you in Exposition Hall . . .

(Fade out train scene)

GOVERNOR: Ladies and Gentlemen, we have with us today a representative of Negro civilization in the South, Professor Booker T. Washington of Tuskegee.

(A flurry of applause . . . A few cheers . . . Then dead silence)

BOOKER: Mr. President, Gentlemen of the Board of Directors, Citizens: One-third of the population of the South is of the Negro race. No enterprise seeking the material, civil, or moral welfare of this section can disregard this element of our population and reach the highest success. Once a ship lost at sea for many days suddenly sighted a friendly vessel. From the mast of the unfortunate vessel was seen a signal, "Water, water; we die of thirst!" The answer from the friendly vessel came back, "Cast down your bucket where you are." A second time the signal, "Water, water; send us water!" ran up the distressed vessel, and was answered, "Cast down your bucket where you are." And a third and fourth signal for water was answered, "Cast down your bucket where you are." The captain of the distressed vessel, at last heeding the injunction, cast down his bucket, and it came up full of fresh, sparkling water from the mouth of the Amazon River. To those of my race who underestimate the importance of cultivating friendly relations with the southern white man, who is their next-door neighbor, I would say: "Cast down your bucket where you are." Cast it down in making friend in every manly way of the people of all races by whom we are surrounded. Cast it down in agriculture, mechanics, in commerce, in domestic service, and in the professions. No race can prosper till it learns there is as much dignity in tilling a field as in writing a poem.

To those of the white race, I would repeat what I say to my own race, "Cast down your bucket where you are." Cast it down among the eight millions of Negroes whose habits you know, whose fidelity you have tested. Cast down your bucket among these people who have tilled your fields, cleared your forests, and brought forth treasures from the bowels of the earth. Cast down your bucket among my people, help and encourage them to the education of head, hand, and heart. Then you will find that they will buy your surplus land, make blossom the waste places in your fields, and run your factories. But there is no defense or security for any of us except in the highest intelligence and development of all.

Gentlemen of the Exposition, I pledge that in your effort to work out the intricate problem which God has laid at the doors of the South, you shall have at all times the help of my race. Only let this be constantly in mind . . .

(Music in)

that far beyond material benefits will be that higher good which, let us pray God, will result in a blotting out of sectional differences and racial animosities and suspicions, in a determination to administer absolute justice, and in a willing obedience among all classes to the mandates of law.

(Music: Up to finish)

Brothers

1942

AUTHOR'S NOTE: This script is written in an attempt to face and re-
solve some of the problems troubling the minds of some American
Negro citizens today in regard to our war effort and their own un-
resolved problems of democracy at home. The seamen of the Merchant Marine, including Negro seamen, are among the outstanding
heroes of this war. Here we let a Negro seaman speak.

ANNOUNCER: (INSERT NAME OF ORGANIZATION) presents
"BROTHERS", a radio play by Langston Hughes.

(Sound: wind howling)

ANNOUNCER: A convoy on the North Atlantic on a stormy night in
winter. An American ship is returning to home port after a voyage
to one of our far-flung bases of democracy. In the fo's'cle a group of
sailors sit around the mess-table playing cards.

(Sound: wind continues in background through scene.)

SWEDE: I'm hitting, Chips.

NORWAY: Hit me with a ten spot, Swede—and take these toothpicks.

SWEDE: Every toothpick's a cent, remember.

NORWAY: I don't forget when we paid off tomorrow.

SWEDE: Here's your ten spot.

NORWAY: Busted!

SWEDE: What you want, Frenchie?

FRENCHIE: Pass me. I'm O.K.

SWEDE: Sitting pretty, heh? How about you, Dominic?

ITALIAN: I do all right, too. Get yourself twenty-one.

SWEDE: One card for me. And that's just what I done—sixteen and
five—twenty-one.

ITALIAN: Well, I'll be dog-goned!

NORWAY: You lucky son-of-a-gun, you! I bust out, and you win from
every body else anyhow.

FRENCHIE: You got all the luck since Cowboy quit the game. Where
he go, anyhow?

SWEDE: To relieve Charlie on the bridge. Time for the watch to change,
you know.

(Sound: ship's bell in the distance heard over wind.)

NORWAY: There's eight bells now.

SWEDE: How can you hear it through all this storm?

ITALIAN: Norway's got good ears. He say he heard that torpedo go past the bow the other day.

FRENCHIE: And he say he could tell by the sound if it was German, Japanese, or I-talian.

NORWAY: Aw, mates, I ain't that good.

SWEDE: Lay out your toothpicks. I'm dealing. What you want, Chips?

NORWAY: Count me out. I'm climbing in me bunk.

FRENCHIE: Let's break up this game. Swede's won all the pesos.

ITALIAN: We don't stop yet. Harlem'll be here in a minute. He always like to play.

SWEDE: Harlem Charlie! Darn swell guy.

NORWAY: Sure, Charlie's O.K.

FRENCHIE: They was some on this boat said they didn't want to work with a colored guy.

SWEDE: That's right, Frenchie. But the union put him on—and a finer seaman never went to sea—black or white.

ITALIAN: Charlie learned his navigating on four-masters—where plenty other sailors learned, too. These steam tubs don't mean a thing to him, see.

(Sound: door opens. Wind up.)

FRENCHIE: Here he comes now.

NORWAY: Hey, Harlem, shut that wind-breaker!

FRENCHIE: Charlie, leave them waves outside the door!

(Sound: door bangs shut—wind down.)

CHARLIE: *(Fading in)* Old Papa Neptune's sure having a ball! But what you guys yelling about? It's plenty warm down here in the fo's'cle. So let her roll—cause we're rolling home tomorrow. And boys, home is Harlem.

NORWAY: How you know we're docking in New York?

CHARLIE: I can smell that New York Air, way out here. Destination may be secret, but I know I'm heading home.

FRENCHIE: Me, I live Fourteenth Street, downtown.

NORWAY: Me, Seaman's Home.

SWEDE: Me and my old lady in Brooklyn. I been American twenty years.

ITALIAN: I got second papers.

CHARLIE: I was born American. But we're all signing on for the next voyage, ain't we?

SAILORS: Sure!

Mais, oui, alors!

Ya, bet your boots!

Yes, indeed!

CHARLIE: Cause this cargo's got to cross—so we can win this war.

NORWAY: You bet we got to win *this* war. Norway's got to be free again.

FRENCHIE: France got to be free.

CHARLIE: We all got to be free. Just like the President said in that speech of his about the Four Freedoms. We all got to be free. Lemme get some hot coffee.

SWEDE: Harlem, take off them dripping oil-skins, come on let's play a little cards.

CHARLIE: Uh-hum! No cards for me tonight, men. I got home on my mind. And some little presents to wrap up for my mother.

SWEDE: And who else?

CHARLIE: My kid brother.

SWEDE: And who else?

CHARLIE: My girl-friend, Jack, my girl-friend.

SWEDE: Now you're talking.

CHARLIE: She's going to be crazy about these bracelets from—that's right. Whoa! We ain't suppose to say where we've been.

SWEDE: Nor where we're sailing for.

CHARLIE: Destination unknown! But we're rolling! And this time we're rolling home to Harlem. So—

(Sings)

Yo-Ho! Blow the man down!

ALL: Gimme some time to blow the man down!

CHARLIE: As I was walking down Hicklby Street—

ALL: Yo-Ho! Blow the man down! etc . . .

(Sound: fade out on sailors singing lustily. Then fade in tramp of a woman's footsteps up rickety stairs of tenement in Harlem. Foot steps alone several seconds. Then:)

MAMA: Uh! These steps sure is a trial! I must be getting old. Lemme see can I find my keys. Vincent! Vincent! Lemme in, son.

VINCENT: *(Within)* Coming, Mama.

(Sound: door opens.)

VINCENT: Gimme your packages, Mama. What you got good for supper?

MAMA: Secret, child! Keep your eyes out of them bags. I'm liable to have layovers in 'em.

(Sound: door closes)

VINCENT: Layovers?

MAMA: To catch meddlers! Only thing is, I couldn't get no sugar. But what's not having a few pounds of sugar—if we beat the pants off Hitler?

VINCENT: We got a few Hitlers at home to lick, too.

MAMA: We'll take care of them in due time. They ain't wandering all over the globe like Adolf is. And they ain't using bombing planes.

VINCENT: They got lynch ropes, though, and Jim Crow cars for Negroes.

MAMA: But they ain't got no Ges-*tap*-o.

VINCENT: O.K., Mama, you win. Otherwise you'll just stand here arguing all night and won't fix supper. What you got in the box, a chocolate cake?

MAMA: Son, I told you to keep out of these supper things! Yes, I got a cake. You know why? Somehow, I been had a feeling all day your brother might be home tonight off that ship.

VINCENT: Charlie? We haven't heard from him, have we?

MAMA: You think he's sending radiograms like a passenger? He's a sailor.

(Sound: rattling of pans and kitchen utensils.)

MAMA: This can's near empty. But if I had enough sugar, I'd bake a real cake, though, cause I got a feeling he's coming home. I had that feeling all day—and my mind seldom fools me . . . Vincent, say, listen!

(Sound: footsteps on stairs.)

VINCENT: Somebody's coming sure enough.

MAMA: Ain't them his feet coming up the stairs? I know his footsteps. Listen!

VINCENT: That's him!

MAMA: That's him! That's my boy! Charlie! Charlie! Charlie! Charlie!
(Sound: mother and son rushing through house. Door flies open. Shouts of greeting.)

CHARLIE: Mama!

MAMA: My boy!

CHARLIE: Vincent! What you know, old kid?

VINCENT: How are yuh, Jack?

MAMA: Did you have a rough trip?

VINCENT: Did you see any submarines?

MAMA: Was you in a big convoy?

VINCENT: Did you go to Iceland?

MAMA: Don't ask him where he's been! Did you have warm clothes?

VINCENT: Are you full of hard tack?

MAMA: My boy! Charlie! I felt you was coming! My boy!

CHARLIE: Look at the presents, Mama! Look! *(Music in)* I brought you some presents. Open that bag, brother, while I undo this bundle. See, Mama! All these presents. . . .

> *(Music up in joyous melody. Transition.)*
> *(Sound: food cooking. Pots and pans.)*

CHARLIE: Um-hummm-mm-m! Mom, that sure smells good! What you frying back there in the kitchen?

MAMA: *(From the kitchen)* Chicken. And I'm making you some hot biscuits, too.

VINCENT: Mama, stop talking about victuals. Charlie's mouth's watering now.

CHARLIE: After all that galley-hash I been eating at sea, it's time to water.

MAMA: I'm gonna shut the door so this cooking won't scent up the house. You two boys just set right there in the front room and talk. Dinner'll be ready directly. I know Vincent wants to talk to his big brother anyhow.

> *(Sound: door closing.)*

VINCENT: Big brother, nothing! I'm twenty-one now, Charlie.

CHARLIE: Grown up, huh, Vince?

VINCENT: Three times seven and hip, Jack.

CHARLIE: How come you ain't enlisted?

VINCENT: Enlisted?

CHARLIE: We're in a war, you know.

VINCENT: I registered. My draft number's up . . .

CHARLIE: You don't feel no call to go sooner?

VINCENT: Not as long as old Jim Crow's a captain in the army.

CHARLIE: You must not have been listening to the President's speeches.

VINCENT: I heard him on the air—but what's that got to do with it?

CHARLIE: Did you hear what he said about the Four Freedoms?

VINCENT: I heard him.

CHARLIE: Then I reckon you know if Jim Crow's a captain. The President's the Commander in Chief—and *he* don't believe in Jim Crow.

VINCENT: I hope he don't.

CHARLIE: I know he don't. He sent his voice all over the world—I heard him a thousand miles out in the sea—people everywhere heard him talking through the air about those Four Freedoms—freedom to talk, to express yourself; freedom to worship the Lord; freedom from want; and freedom from fear. Everywhere in the world, he said. People everywhere in the world heard him. And that's the kind of freedom people mean to have!

VINCENT: Colored people, too?

CHARLIE: That's what *I* mean to have, and I'm colored.

VINCENT: How're you gonna get it?

CHARLIE: By joining up with the folks who are fighting for it. Why do you think I'm steering that boat through submarines and mines and taking chances on dive bombers? Just for fun? No! I'm shipping out again tomorrow 'cause I want to get food and machine tools and ammunition to the places where we need 'em to fight Hitler and build bases against him and everybody like him.

VINCENT: We don't have any Hitlers here in America, I suppose.

CHARLIE: Sure, we got some *little* Hitlers here. But there's no use letting big Hitler get across the ocean to help 'em. For every fifth-columnist we've got with a lynch rope and a Jim Crow car to back him up, Hitler's got a thousand with tanks and dive bombers trying to get over here to help make things worse.

VINCENT: I guess I hadn't thought about it that way.

CHARLIE: Why, Hitler'd make a double-barreled padlocked ghetto out of Harlem so quick you couldn't say Flat Foot Floogie. If he ever got over here, a colored man would have to have a pass to get down to Times Square. And that's why you better get in the army, boy, and start gunning for him.

VINCENT: Hitler's against all kinds of freedoms, ain't he?

CHARLIE: Could we be here talking like this if the Gestapo was around?

VINCENT: You might be here, but I wouldn't.

CHARLIE: Then you better stop taking it easy, brother. I know you've got some arguments on your side: America's not perfect—Jim Crow enough to tickle Hitler to death, the Red Cross segregating black blood, and half the defense industries not employing Negro workers. Sure, things are not perfect, not by a long shot, but listen, Vincent, if you let your hands drop, you're just helping all those people who believe in the same ugliness Hitler believes in—force, and race hatred, and segregation—that old iron heel he's got on the neck of the Poles and the Norwegians and the Danes and lots of other folks who ain't even colored. We're fourteen million people—we Negro Americans—we can give the Fascists a mighty blow. Or we can just take it easy and let 'em bring over the Gestapo to back up the Ku Klux Klan. Do you get me, old man?

VINCENT: I get you, Charlie. Do you want to go with me to enlist tomorrow?

CHARLIE: Sure, I'll go with you, man, on my way to the boat.

VINCENT: 'Cause I want to fan them Four Freedoms with my fist.

CHARLIE: Till they sweep like the Four Winds all over the world.

VINCENT: And I want to kick them Nazis so hard Hitler and all his local brothers'll feel it in the seat of their Jim Crow pants.

CHARLIE: You're talking now, brother. Say,—
    (Sound: door opens.)

MAMA: Vincent! Charlie! bring your chairs and come on to dinner.

CHARLIE: WHee-ee-ooo! Coming. Do them biscuits smell good. But-ter me a dozen.
    (Sound: scuffle of chairs and feet making for the table.)

CHARLIE: Just looky here what Mama's got—fried chicken and gravy! Good old corn pudding! Sweet potatoes! Okra! Tapioca! And chocolate cake! Um-hum-m-m!

MAMA: You know, I would've made you a home-made cake, son, but sugar's scarce.

CHARLIE: Who cares about sugar, Mom, when we're gonna be free?

VINCENT: Mama.

MAMA: Yes, Vincent?

VINCENT: Tomorrow, I'm joining the army. Charlie's straightened me out on a thing or two.

MAMA: I'm proud of you, son. I kinder thought Charlie could help you think things through. I tried, but I reckon I didn't explain it good enough. All I could say was I know we's Americans, and this here is our country—and we got to beat the pants off Hitler! That's why little as I got, I'm buying War Bonds, and old as I am, I done gone back to school to learn how to put out them incinderary bombs.

CHARLIE: Mom, you always was O.K. with me.

MAMA: Sons, bow your heads and let's we bless this table . . . You Char-lie, stop eyeing that chicken! I ain't gonna say no long blessing . . . Lord, I thank you for this food. And I thank you for bringing my boys together with me here tonight. And I thank you for a country, Lord, by name America, where me and my boys can turn our hands

to help make the *whole* world free. I don't ask you for no special blessings, Lord. I just ask you to help *us* to help *ourselves.* Amen.
  (Music: triumphant. Beethoven's Fifth)
ANNOUNCER: You have just heard "BROTHERS", a radio play by Langston Hughes. It was produced by (INSERT NAME OF OR-GANIZATION) with a cast including (INSERT CAST CREDITS) STATION IDENTIFICATION.

Pvt. Jim Crow
A Radio Script

1943

(Music. Low ominous chords)
(Silence. Then the distant cawing of a crow)
CROW: Caw! Caw! . . . . . Caw! Caw! . . . . . Caw! Caw!
NARRATOR: No, that is not a buzzard. That is a scavenger bird of another name, a more evil bird. A buzzard feeds on death. This bird feeds on life.
(Cawing of crow up strong)
CROW: CAW! CAW! . . . . . CAW! CAW! . . . . . CAW! CAW!
NARRATOR: Its name is—JIM CROW.
(Chord fading to low rumbling dissonance)
From San Diego to Maine, Mobile to Seattle, this bird flies. Great flocks of them hover over our Southland, sometimes almost blotting out the sun, hiding the moon.
(Fade in, fade out, cawing of birds, now loud, now soft, far, near)
Even over New York, greatest city of the New World, the Jim Crow bird flies, lighting now here, now there. . . . . A young colored man in Harlem picks up the morning paper, carefully looks through the help-wanted ads, sees an urgent war-factory appeal, MEN NEEDED, in Queens. It's a job he thinks he can do. He has had four years of technical training in an industrial high school, so the young man goes out to Long Island to apply for work.
(Hum of factory sounds)
HARLEMITE: I see in the papers where you advertised for men this morning. I've had four years training in—
EMPLOYER: Sorry, bud, we didn't advertise for colored.
HARLEMITE: But you say here it's for war production, and—
EMPLOYER: I said we don't hire Negroes! Understand?
(Cawing of crows up strong)
CROW: CAW! CAW! . . . . . CAW! CAW! . . . . . CAW! CAW!
NARRATOR: No work that day for Johnny from Harlem. . . . Yesterday a mother and daughter were shopping in the Broadway-34th Street area. They are polite, well-dressed colored women.

(Roar of downtown traffic)

MOTHER: Hazel, aren't you a little hungry? I've still got to match this curtain material, so it'll be an hour or more before we get home.

DAUGHTER: I could stand a salad, mother.

MOTHER: Shall we try the automat today?

DAUGHTER: We just passed one and it's terribly crowded. And we've got too many parcels to carry our own trays. Let's go where we can sit down and relax a half hour.

MOTHER: That seems to be an attractive tea-room here. What lovely cakes in the window. And a sign, BLUEBERRY PIE! I love blueberry pie—although I really ought to watch my weight.

DAUGHTER: Just a little slice won't hurt you. Let's go in there, mother.

(Sudden chatter of voices in restaurant)

MOTHER: Oh, there's a pleasant table over in the alcove.

DAUGHTER: Even flowers on it. How nice!

MOTHER: Here, Hazel, put your handbag there on the chair. Pretty menu, isn't it? And the prices are reasonable. What do you think you'll take? Now this salad combination looks. . . . .

(Voice of white waitress cuts in)

WAITRESS: I'm sorry but—

MOTHER: Although I simply can't have Russian dressing. I mustn't indulge all my—

WAITRESS: I—I—er—

DAUGHTER: Mother, the waitress seems to have something to tell us.

MOTHER: Yes, we'll be ready to order in a moment.

WAITRESS: No, it's not that, m'am. I'm sorry, but—I can't take your order. They won't permit us to serve colored people here.

(The distant cawing of crows)

MOTHER: I beg your pardon?

WAITRESS: Colored people are not served here.

MOTHER: But this is New York City—not Dixie. We're Americans. My son is in the Navy in the Pacific.

WAITRESS: I'm really sorry, madam, it's not my fault. I just work here. But the manager asked me to tell you it's against the policy of this restaurant to serve Negroes.

(Up strong cawing of birds)

CROW: CAW! CAW! . . . . . CAW! CAW! . . . . . CAW! CAW! . . . . . CAW! CAW!

NARRATOR: It's a long ways back to Harlem for a decent meal when two women are downtown shopping. But this can happen to a

Negro any day in New York. Not always, or everywhere, or perhaps
not so blatantly. Perhaps they will simply say *all* the tables are reserved. Or perhaps no waiter will come to wait on you. Fortunately,
in New York there are always other restaurants. A meal is not utterly
urgent. . . . . But illness may be serious. Hospitalization is another
matter. A few years ago the wife of one of America's greatest colored
composers. . . . .
   (Music of "St. Louis Blues" in softly)
became suddenly gravely ill.
GIRL: Papa, Papa! We must get mother to the hospital right away. I
   don't believe we can wait for the doctor to come. I can't stand to
   see her suffer so. Is the car here?
FATHER: We're lucky I parked it just in front tonight. Son, come, we'll
   carry your mother to the elevator.
SON: Yes, dad.
   (Faint moans of sick woman)
GIRL: In five minutes, mother, we'll have you at the hospital. Don't
   worry, you'll be all right.
FATHER: It's just a few blocks away, honey. Let me lift you up.
   (Music)
   (Car starting, gathering speed, then slowing down. Brakes)
NARRATOR: The nearest hospital was on the edge of Negro Harlem.
   The husband went into the desk. . . .
FATHER: Nurse, my wife is very ill outside in the car. Through which
   entrance shall I carry her in?
NURSE: Er-uh-er, is it a sudden illness, or will she need prolonged
   treatments?
FATHER: She'll hardly be able to go home tonight. I want a private
   room for her, of course.
NURSE: Er-reh, well-er, have you tried Harlem Hospital?
FATHER: I tell you she's very ill, so I came directly here to the nearest
   hospital. Please hurry—
NURSE: I'm sorry, but we really haven't any beds right now for—er-
   colored patients. I'd advise you to try Harlem Hos—
   (A door opens quickly)
GIRL: Father! Father! I'm afraid mother is—Oh, she can't stand the
   pain! Please, hurry!
NURSE: I'll call Harlem Hospital and tell them you're coming.
FATHER: But that's a mile away. You have no room here?
NURSE: At the moment only for white patients. I'm sure at Harlem
   Hos—

(The father groans. Raucous cawing of the Jim Crow bird)
FATHER: God, forgive them! This is America!
CROW: Caw! Caw! . . . . . Caw! Caw! . . . . . Caw! Caw!
   (Music. Dramatic chord)
NARRATOR: Mrs. W. C. Handy died that night before she could receive
   hospitalization. No beds for Negroes. The dark and ugly wings of
   the Jim Crow bird that feeds on life, not death, stretch over Harlem,
   too. Yet New York City is not Dixie. This year is not 1860.
   (Music, in softly then up strong, band gaily playing Dixie)
This is 1943, and World War II.
   (Bugle call)
Jim Crow has gone into the army!
   (Up strong on bugle as crow caws)
CROW: CAW! CAW! . . . . . CAW! CAW! . . . . . . CAW! CAW!
   (Fade out on bugle)
OFFICER: Private Ingram Jones?
SOLDIER: Yes, sir.
OFFICER: You understand that state laws as well as United States Army
   regulations must be obeyed?
SOLDIER: Yes, sir.
OFFICER: As long as you are at this training camp, you are in the
   South, not in Harlem. At this camp, the only Post Exchange open
   to Negro troops is the one next to your barracks in Zone 12. That's
   the colored PX.
SOLDIER: Yes, sir. But my duties kept me down at the other end of the
   camp all day, sir, four miles from my barracks. It was very hot, sir. I
   went into the nearest PX to get a cold drink, and—
   (Voices of soldiers talking)
CLERK: What you want there, colored boy?
SOLDIER: Got a coke?
CLERK: What? . . . . A coke?
SOLIDER: Yes.
CLERK: Yes? . . . . . Do you know where you're at? You learn to say,
   "Yes, *sir*," to a white man in Georgia, black boy. You hear me?
SOLDIER: You're a civilian, not an officer. Why should I say, "Yes, sir,"
   to you?
CLERK: Because you're black, that's why! And in the South! I'll teach
   you Harlem Negras to talk back to me!
   (A sudden blow. Scuffling. Door slamming as soldier is thrown out)
I guess you'll show more respect to a white man next time.
   (Footsteps returning to counter)

Some of you Yankees can go pick that impudent black soldier up off the ground out there, if you want to.

(Music. Dissonance)

SOLDIER: That's the way it was, lieutenant! I didn't do nothing but ask for a cold drink, sir, and they threw me out. Almost knocked out two teeth, too.

OFFICER: Private Jones, you are not to enter any PX on this Post other than the one in Zone 12. Do you understand? You were wrong. You men have got to observe the laws of the South.

CROW: Caw! Caw! . . . . . Caw! . . . . . Caw! . . . . . Caw! Caw!

(Low rumble of drums)

NARRATOR: That is not good for a Negro boy in uniform, training to perhaps give his life for liberty and freedom and democracy. . . . . Ever stop to think about those great words? Did you ever stop to think that colored people love those words, too? . . . . . It is early evening at the entrance gates of another training camp for American soldiers in the South. A hundred men are gathered about the gate, waiting for the buses to come that will take those who have passes to town for movies, dances, USO, a date maybe. Among the soldiers at the gate there are a dozen colored soldiers. They know that only the rear seat in the bus is allotted to Negroes. Only six boys can crowd onto that seat, and it is the local custom that—

(Sound of bus arriving hailed by shouts of happy soldiers)

colored men must wait on the ground until all the whites have entered the bus. Sometimes—

1ST NEGRO: Boy, looks like we ain't gonna get on this bus a-tall. This here's the third bus now that's passed me up.

2ND NEGRO: You reckon the driver'd get mad if I spoke up and told him we've been here longer than any of these white boys? We been off duty since five o'clock, here it is seven.

1ST NEGRO: Looky there! Them white boys done taken our back seat again!

2ND NEGRO: Sure is!

1ST NEGRO: Another hour to wait.

2ND NEGRO: Say, Mr. Bus Driver! Ain't we gonna get no chance a-tall to ride tonight? We got to be back in camp at twelve—and here we ain't even started yet.

DRIVER: You-all boys see all these white mens waiting to ride, don't you?

2ND NEGRO: Yes, sir, but that back seat is supposed to be for colored folks.

DRIVER: Supposed to be—but not if white folks want it. You-all colored boys go on back to your barracks. You-all don't need to go in town tonight.

(Lonesome cawing of the Jim Crow bird)

CROW: Caw. . . . . Caw. . . . . Caw. . . . . . .

NARRATOR: Often Negro soldiers with passes do not get to go to town at all. The white soldiers have first choice of seats. Negroes must wait. If the whites fill the bus up—

(As motor starts)

DRIVER: You-all colored boys go on back to your barracks. I don't want no back-talk out of you. You ain't in Harlem, you know!

2ND NEGRO: No, but if I was—

(Shouts of impatient white soldiers drown out his statement)

PASSENGERS: Aw, start the bus!

We want to get to town!

Too bad, colored boys, you can't go!

Shove off, driver!

(Bus chugs off. Murmur of angry Negro voices. Caw of crow)

NARRATOR: That's the way race riots start! . . . . . You see, the Jim Crow bird is a trouble-making bird. He feeds on ugliness and strife. What good is a pass for a colored soldier when town is thirty miles from camp, and the buses won't let him ride. . . . . But just suppose those colored boys had gotten to town that night, where would they go in a small Southern city? Can't go to the movies: NEGROES NOT ADMITTED. Can't go to the USO Club: FOR WHITE SOLDIERS ONLY. In this town, they haven't gotten around to building one for colored troops yet! Tell me, white hostess, why is that?

HOSTESS: Well, you see, there are 15,000 white soldiers in this area. There's only a thousand or so Negro troops. They don't need a club so badly. But there will be one for our Negroes as soon as the Chamber of Commerce grants us a site. It can't be in a white neighborhood, you know, and there's nothing but shacks in the Negro district.

CROW: Caw!

NARRATOR: Nothing but shacks! That's the Negro district of the town in which the colored troops must seek their recreation: no USO Club, no theatres—nothing but shacks. The small poverty stricken colored population tries as best it can to entertain its boys. They use the little church basement. But the bootlegger—often white—and the gambler, and the prostitute furnish the easiest entertainment— in a district where there is nothing but shacks, since the authorities

"haven't gotten around yet" to providing a USO for colored soldiers. . . . . That's where Jim Crow isn't fair. It's never equal, never
on time, never "gets around" to solving its problems. . . . . At some
camps there are Negro officers, well-trained intelligent lieutenants,
captains. Some of them are from cities like Boston, Chicago, or New
York where the Jim Crow bird doesn't spread his wings over *every*
phase of life, and where transportation in trains and buses is the same
for all. But when a Negro officer comes on furlough from a Southern
camp:

> (*Train whistle in distance. Voices of crowd at station*)

NEGROES: Um-hum-m-m! So many peoples to get on this train. Sure
is! More colored than white, looks like. And we only got one coach.
White folks got eight or ten. Look at that fine looking colored
officer! Captain, heh? I reckon he is! He sure looks fine!

> (*Train bell as engine pulls into station*)

CONDUCTOR: All aboard! Colored passengers way down front. Jim
Crow car's ahead. Pullmans and Parlor Cars in rear.

LIEUTENANT: Goodbye, Captain! Good trip! Too bad you couldn't
get a Parlor Car seat as far as Washington.

CAPTAIN: Too much to expect if you're colored. I'll try and find a seat
on the Jim Crow car.

CONDUCTOR: All aboard!

> (*Puffing of train pulling out*)

LIEUTENANT Give my regards to Broadway!

CAPTAIN: O.K., lieutenant!

LIEUTENANT: And to Harlem!

> (*Train getting underway drowns out voices. Crow caws softly in
> rhythm with the rails as the Jim Crow car rocks on*)

NEGRO: My goodness! Can't another soul squeeze in this here Jim
Crow car.

GRANNY: Got to squeeze in. I'se too old to stand out here in this
vestibule.

PAPPY: Well, grandma, there sure ain't no seat for you. Yonder comes
the conductor. Ax him what to do?

CONDUCTOR: You-all'll have to get inside the car, folks, can't stand
out here in the way.

GRANNY: There ain't another inch inside that car.

CONDUCTOR: Make room! Get out of my way, now, and inside!

CAPTAIN: Conductor, say? Couldn't some of these people go into the
other coach? It's half empty.

CONDUCTOR: That's a white coach, Captain.

CAPTAIN: Then why aren't there sufficient colored coaches?

CONDUCTOR: Don't ask me, I ain't the railroad company. All I know is, white and colored can't ride together on this train.

CAPTAIN: We're fighting together for a common cause. I don't see why we can't ride together.

CONDUCTOR: Because you're a Negra, that's why! Don't get impudent, now. You may be an officer, but you're still black. Them bars don't mean a thing to me.

CAPTAIN: They should mean something to you, conductor. They were given me by Uncle Sam. He's your Uncle, too.

CONDUCTOR: Well, you can't stand here in this vestibule, officer or no. All you-all colored folks get inside! Push on in there! You, too, soldier!

(Murmur of resentful voices)

CAPTAIN: Listen, conductor! We pay the same fare as the other passengers, and there are empty seats in the next coach. You see that colored woman with that baby in her arms, standing? You see this old grandmother here, eighty or more, standing? You see this very next coach half-empty? You see my soldiers, dozens of them going home on furloughs, standing, maybe all the way to Washington? They can't move about the train like white soldiers. They can't go into the diner, nor into the club car. Just have to stay crowded up here in this half-passenger, half-baggage Jim Crow coach. Do you think that's fair, Conductor? And we're fighting, too,—and dying— from Sicily to Guadalcanal!

CONDUCTOR: You're in the South! Another word out of you, officer, and I'll put you off this train!

CROW: Caw! . . . . . Caw! . . . . . Caw! . . . . . Caw!

(Rising murmur of Negro voices)

MAN: You ain't gonna put this Captain off no train.

GRANNY: This boy's our son! He gonna fight for you.

SOLDIER: You sure ain't gonna put him off no train.

NARRATOR: And that's the way riots start.

(Roar of train rushing on into the night like doom)

CROW: CAW! CAW! . . . . . CAW! CAW! . . . . . CAW! CAW!

NARRATOR: So the Jim Crow car goes on into the night. For night it is, and dark, under the ominous wings of the Jim Crow bird. Listen, America:

CROW: CAW! CAW! . . . . . CAW! CAW! . . . . . CAW! CAW!

NARRATOR: Listen, New York City! Think! This is your problem, too! Think what it does to *you*, to your decent democratic dreams, to America's 13 million colored citizens, to our dark allies around the world.

(Ominous roar of the train in the dark)

Think what this Jim Crow car means on American rails! Think how the Fifth Columnists love the spreading wings of this dangerous evil bird. Listen!

(Continual cawing up strong and under)

EMPLOYER: I said we don't hire Negroes! Understand?

WAITRESS: I'm sorry, but colored people are not served here.

NURSE: No hospital beds just now for colored patients.

CLERK: You say, "Yes, sir" to a white man down South, black boy!

CROW: CAW! . . . . . CAW! . . . . . CAW! . . . . . CAW! . . . . . CAW!

DRIVER: You colored soldiers go on back to your barracks now. No seats in the bus tonight.

HOSTESS: The Chamber of Commerce has no building for a Negro USO.

CONDUCTOR: All aboard! Colored passengers down front! Jim Crow car ahead!

(Train sounds. Cawing of crow)

NARRATOR: Jim Crow car ahead! It can't be ahead on the Freedom Train, can it, America? Not if we want to go forward—there can't be any Jim Crow car on the Freedom Train! Hear that Jim Crow bird?

CROW: Caw! . . . . . Caw! . . . . . Caw! . . . . . Caw!

NARRATOR: Let's finish him off, today, NOW. Let's clip his wings. For the sake of America, let's stop that infernal caw, caw, CAW, CAW! I say, let's stop it!

(Caw of bird up strong)

CROW: CAW! CAW! CAW! CAW! CAW! CAW! CAW! CAW!!!

(Music: My Country, 'Tis of Thee)

END

In the Service of My Country

1944

(*Music. . . . . Suggesting vastness, quiet, night*)

NARRATOR: Summer. . . . Night. . . . Pinewoods. . . . A lonely stretch of the Alcan Highway on the Alaskan border. A single Army convoy truck carrying iron grids for a new bridge has pulled to the side of the road for the night. The two Negro soldiers in charge of the truck have wrapped themselves in blankets and lain down on the pine needles to sleep.

(*Quiet. A light snore interrupted by a soft Mississippi drawl*)

PVT: Say, Robbie?

CPL: Huh? . . . . Yeah, man? . . . . Can't you let a guy sleep?

PVT: How can you sleep and it's almost bright as day, with them Northern lights all over the sky?

CPL: I've seen Northern lights before, Private.

PVT: Where at, Corporal? You ain't never been in Alaska before, have you?

CPL: No, but I've been up the Saginaw River on a camping trip with my dad, and some nights up there you can see the aurora borealis all over the sky.

PVT: They don't have them things in the United States, do they?

CPL: No, I guess not, but they have them in Canada.

PVT: And too much of 'em in Alaska! When it's night, I think it should *be* night—and not no lights out of nowhere flashing all over the sky.

CPL: Man, that's the interesting thing about geography. When you travel you learn something, see things you never saw before.

PVT: Sure does! Like on this Alcan Highway. But listen, what was you doing on a camping trip way up in Canada, anyhow? First camp I ever saw was here in the army. You-all must've been rich colored folks.

CPL: Not rich. My old man was a mail clerk, but he liked fishing and wild places, and he used to take me with him on vacations.

PVT: My pa was a sharecropper down in Mississippi, and the furtherest he ever took me was out to pick cotton in the Delta River Bottoms.

Talk about rattlesnakes! It must-a been nice to grow up like you did in Harlem?

CPL: I didn't grow up in Harlem. I was born right next to you, in Alabama.

PVT: No?

CPL: Yes, I was.

PVT: And look how far from there we is now—Way up here in the airory boryalix building this here road! Where's this road going, Corporal?

CPL: Right on up to the tip of Alaska, I guess—there where our territory mighty near touches the Soviet Union's, then down through Siberia and through Asia—right into Europe. We're building a road right on around the world.

PVT: You and me?

CPL: Yes, you and me and the rest of the fellows in the Engineers. When you stop to think about it, man, this is going to be a history-road, this Alcan Road, a new road through new places! Even if we never see a battle, Private, we can say we've done one good thing in the service of our country—building this road.

PVT: Us, building a road! Right around the world!

CPL: Sure, round the top of the world and down into Europe! Why after the war, you and me, we can get in a car in Chicago and drive to Paris!

PVT: You reckon there ain't gonna be no color-line on this road?

CPL: No! There's no color-line in the building of it, is there? White and colored soldiers building it, aren't there? This is tomorrow's road, buddy. There won't be any color-line.

PVT: I always do hear you say that, Robbie? What make you so sure? If you lived down in Mississippi, you wouldn't be sure.

CPL: I grew up in Alabama, don't forget. But I guess I got to tell you all about my life's history to show you what I mean.

PVT: You promised to tell me before you went off to Officers School.

CPL: Well, between you and these Northern Lights, a soldier can't get his rest anyhow. You know, my old man was a soldier in the last war, ten months in France, got the Croix de Guerre for bravery and brought it back with him to Alabama. He hadn't been back a year when I was born. My old man was religious, and I was born on Wednesday—prayer-meeting day. My mother says that night he went to church and prayed a special prayer for me.

> *(Chorus. . . . . of Negro voices, softly, then in strong)*
> By and by,
> When de morning come,

> Saints and sinners
> All are gathered home,
> We'll tell de story
> How we overcome—
> And we'll understand it better,
> By and by!

VOICES: Amen! Amen! Amen!

> Bless God! Amen!

> Testify, Brother Robinson!

FATHER: This morning, church, the Lord blessed me with a son, my first born, James Robinson, Junior! I want you-all to rejoice with me, and bear me up whilst I prays a prayer for my little new born baby that has come into this world.

VOICES: Bless this father, Lord!

> Bless that chile!

> *(Rhythmic undertow of song as the church "bears him up" during prayer)*

FATHER: Lord, I thank you for a son. And I thank you that the mother and child is doing well. And I ask you, Lord, to bless them both. He's my boy, Lord, and you know who I am. I am James Robinson, Lord, black, and poor, and a soldier just come home not long from the wars. I fought your war, Lord, so's this world could be safe for democracy. I know it ain't safe yet. I know I got to work hard and pray long and keep clean myself and change the hearts of many people before it will be safe, Lord, this world, for everybody in it, black or white. But through Your will and in Your good name, it will be. . . . . Let my son grow up to carry on where I leave off. Let him help to build America and make it strong and clean and free. Alabama, too. He's a colored child, Lord, but don't let him wear his color like a shroud. Let him be proud, proud, proud! A builder, Lord, in the service of this country, working to make an America where you, and him, and me, and every man is free to live like a man. . . . I was a soldier, Lord. United States Army, 1918. I know what it is to fight for what I own, to travel way across the waters to protect what I own. If my son ever should be a soldier, Lord, let him serve well in the service of his country. Teach him to have faith, to have hope, to know that through Your strength and Your will there's power to change the world for good. Let the hand of friendship and not the hand of hate be his. . . . Go with my boy, Lord, and guide him from now henceforward wheresoever he may be. I ask you this evening in Thy name. Amen.

(Congregation bursts into song)
Oh, Mary,
Don't you weep,
Don't you moan.
Pharaoh's army
Got drowned!
Oh, Mary,
Don't you moan.
(Fading into night music of opening)

CPL: My old man taught me that he was as good as any other man, and that the colored people were just as much a part of America as any other people, that we had put as much labor, as much sweat, and as many tears into the building of this country of ours as any other folks. But my father wasn't much for speech-making and things like that. He was for doing. He said:

FATHER: Son, a man is just what he is, not what he *says* he is. Color don't make no difference. Now, you study your lessons—and learn. When you get ready to go to high school, I'm going to move our family up North, where the schools ain't Jim Crowed and tumble-down, and where you can get a solid education. You going to college. What you want to be, Robbie?

CHILD: I want to be a builder, papa. I want to build houses and buildings.

FATHER: An architecter?

CHILD: Yes sir, an architecter.

(Music up strong)

CPL: So we moved North. That's when I first came to Harlem. I was fourteen. That was the first time I ever went to school with white people. The kids were all nationalities—Italian-Americans, Armenian-Americans, Irish-Americans, Jewish-Americans, and just plain American Americans. And the teachers were white and colored. We got along fine. I found out that it wasn't what color you was that mattered—but how hard you studied, how hard you played on the school team that rated you with the teachers and the students. Colored kids were on the honor roll, and colored boys starred on the football team. Don't think I'm boasting Private, but I was a basketball star myself.

PVT: On a team with white boys?

CPL: Yes, center, on a team with white boys. We played together fine. City champs, three years straight.

PVT: And they didn't Jim Crow you, nor make you feel colored?

CPL: No, they were swell guys! There're lots of swell white guys in the world. Only thing, summer times when I went to look for a job, they could always pick up work faster than I could even in a big city like New York. That's where the color-line hit me first, and hardest. They could work in Wall Street or anywhere, being white. A colored boy trying to get through school had to look hard for a summer job. But my dad kept on saying:

FATHER: Don't let it down you, Robbie. Booker T. Washington always said, "Study and learn and make ready—and your chance will come." So don't let color down you. The Italian-Americans and the Jewish-Americans, and sometimes the Catholics and the Mexicans, don't have too easy a time of it. Keep your chin up, and make something out of yourself, son, no matter who rebuffs you, and you'll be better able then to help change them things that aren't good in American life. The world *can* change, you know, son. So don't get discouraged. The gutter is down there. It's easy to give up and lay down in the gutter—and give color for an excuse.

CHILD: I'm not going to lie in the gutter, Dad.

FATHER: O.K., Robbie!

　　(*Music*)

CPL: Along about that time Mussolini took over Ethiopia, and Hitler started raving and ranting in Europe against the Jews. My old man said Hitler sounded just like an Alabama Ku Klux Klaner he heard one time railing against Negroes when the Birmingham miners— white and colored—wanted two cents an hour raise. The Klan tried to split the miners up—white against black. That's when my old man explained to me why the weakest groups are always made the scapegoats when some devil in power wants to take people's minds off of more pressing problems like food and decent working hours. My old man explained to me how the policy of *divide and rule* works to a dictator's advantage. That's what Hitler uses—that tactic— divide and rule.

PVT: You had a smart old man, Robbie.

CPL: Sure did! But when the first compulsory service act came along just after I got out of high school, and I tried to join the army, and they told me at the Recruiting Office that they weren't accepting colored men right then, that kind of worried my old man. He had won a Croix de Guerre, and he couldn't see why his son couldn't join up like anybody else. That worried a lot of colored citizens. Remember?

PVT: It didn't worry me—cause you can't join nothing down in Mississippi, if you ain't white.

CPL: My old man was kind of hoping they wouldn't have segregated
regiments this time either, but they did. And some colored boys in
Harlem refused to register and went to jail rather than serve in a Jim
Crow Army. I guess you read about them. They said they went to
school with white boys, and worked with them. They didn't see why
they couldn't fight with them. I was all for not going, too, but my
old man said:

FATHER: Jim Crow Army—or Jim Crow jail? You can't do much good
in jail—unless you're Gandhi. I'm too old to fight again, but Robbie, you go in there when your call comes, apply for Officers Training School, and show the world that we've got Negroes who can
lead men.

(Music)

CPL: So I became a soldier, inducted at Governor's Island.

*(Hum of voices at induction station. Fade in, then out OFFICER
reading list of names of inductees. This scene to be corrected to
conform with official procedure.)*

OFFICERS: CHARLES MILLER
ISIDORE MOSCOVITZ
PATRICK MAHONEY
MILO URDICK
TESSA ZARETELLI
JAMES ROBINSON
ALEX GOLGONOV
FRANK EBERHARDT. . . . .
Attention! Repeat after me the Oath of Induction into the United
States Army.

(A hundred men take the oath of induction as OFFICER reads it)

OATH OF INDUCTION

(Music)

CPL: That day at Governor's Island, all kinds of guys became soldiers—
Southern guys, and Northern guys, Irish, Polish, Italian, Filipino,
Porto Rican, Scandinavian-American—all kinds of New York guys
became soldiers. . . . . Of course, I was the only kind they sepa-
rated, me and my buddies from Harlem, and put together in an
all-colored company. Don't know why they did it, but that's still
the old-fashioned way things are in the Army. After our basic training, they sent us up here on the Alcan Road, and we started building
this long old wonderful highway.

(Sound of trucks, dredges, axes, saws, trees falling, up and under)
And just like those Northern lights up there in the sky, all kinds of colors got all mixed up, white and colored soldiers building this road, Latin-American and Italian-American, Canadian and Georgia boys all have put their strength into the building of this road—and this road don't know what color a guy is.

(Music)
Hear them axes ringing? In Catholic hands and Jewish hands! See that old dredge scooping up dirt? Irish private running it! See that steam-roller rolling the roadbed smooth. Negro boy from Tennessee driving it! See those two privates from San Francisco's Chinatown setting that demolition charge? Hear it blow those stumps to hell and gone! This Alcan Road ain't no one man's road! It's us—the U.S. Engineers—that made it!

PVT: Remember the day, Robbie, you and me and a couple more guys sawed that big tree down?

CPL: And it nearly fell on that white boy from Texas?
(Sawing)

1ST PVT: This here's the thickest tree to saw through I ever seed.

2ND PVT: We might nigh got it, coz. It's leaning.

3RD PVT: Leaning, nothing! Man, it's falling!

1ST PVT: Hey, tell that white boy to get out of the way.
(Shouts. Cries of alarm.)

2ND PVT: Hey, fellow! Watch out! Hey! You'll get killed!

3RD PVT: Dog-gone it! He can't hear us! I'll get him.

1ST PVT: Watch out, fool! You'll get killed yourself! Keep out the way!

3RD PVT: I got to get him!
(Roar of crash as tree falls)

VOICES: Oh-ooo-oo-o!
(Then sighs of relief)

1ST PVT: Saved by a hair!

2ND PVT: He just did snatch that white boy clear.

4TH PVT: Boy, that was a close call!
(Voices come in to mike)

1ST PVT: Fellow, you didn't miss it much.

2ND PVT: Man, warn't you scared?

TEXAN: Scared? Why, I'd been mashed flatter'n a Texas flea twixt a hound dog's teeth, if that tree had-a fell on me. I sure do thank you, colored boy—I mean, buddy, for snatching me clear. Thanks—brother.

3RD PVT: Aw, that's all right! Tain't nothing!

(Music. Road construction sounds back strong)

CPL: A colored soldier saved a white soldier's life. "Tain't nothing!" Maybe someday a white boy will save a colored soldier's life. It has been done already at the front. Danger makes men friends.

PVT: Sure do! Remember the day the two bulldozers met?

CPL: When the roadbed from the North was cleared right down to where the roadbed from the South was ready to meet it.

PVT: And the last stump was drug out.

CPL: And the two machines and the two men driving them met—nose to nose—and one was a white soldier and one was colored.

PVT: And they got out and shook hands.

CPL: White hand and black hand clasped there in the middle of a new road.

(Music up)

(Brakes on, sound of machinery stopping. Cheers)

NEGRO: Well, we done it.

WHITE: Yep, we did it!

NEGRO: I'm Pvt. Willie Johnson, 932 Engineers.

WHITE: I'm Pvt. Mike O'Halloran, 64th Engineers.

NEGRO: We done it together, didn't we, men?

WHITE: We did it together!

(Popping of flash light bulbs)

NEGRO: What's that? A pistol shot?

WHITE: They're taking our pictures.

(Cheers)

(Gay music)

CPL: We opened up the road together, white and colored Americans. And we're still working on it, Private.

PVT: But you're going off to Officers School next week. I'm gonna miss you, Corporal.

CPL: Aw, go to sleep, guy. We got to be up at dawn and get this truck rolling.

PVT: How you gonna get up at dawn and it ain't never been light in Alaska yet? If I was to tell folks down on the Delta that it's midnight right now and bright as day, they'd say I was a dog-gone lie.

CPL: If I was to tell some of my former pals down in Alabama that a *colored* guy from Harlem and a *white* guy from Texas shook hands when this road met that they both built, and said to each other, "We did it!" folks would say I was a dog-gone lie. But you see, Americans *can* get together, and *do* get together, and we're going to be more

together than ever after this war is over. But right now I'm going to
Infantry School. I'm tired of driving bulldozers and trucks. I want to
march some. Maybe I'll come marching right on back up this Alcan
Highway around the top of the world on the way to Tokio with that
old aurora borealis lighting up the midnight sky, and we'll be singing
that song the 372nd sang in Harlem.

    (Male chorus)
    I'm marching!
    Yes, I'm marching!
    I'm marching down Freedom Road!
    There's no Fascist going to stop me,
    There's no Nazi going to keep me
    From marching down Freedom Road.
    Britain by our side,
    Might China as our Friend,
    I'm going after freedom
    And a new world at the end—
    That's why I'm marching,
    Double-timing,
    I'm fighting down Freedom Road.
    (Stamp of marching feet. Music up)

END

Ballet Librettos

Two of the great figures of African American dance, Katherine Dunham and Alvin Ailey, both sought ballet librettos from Hughes. "Did I tell you I did a libretto of THE ST. LOUIS BLUES for Katherine Dunham, a danceable story woven around the song? Hope she uses it. But she rather thinks she ought to do Latin American things—Cuba, Brazil, etc. Easier to sell to concert managers and Hollywood," Hughes wrote his friend Carl Van Vechten.[1] *Carmelita and the Cockatoo* perhaps more fit the bill. In 1941, Dunham's secretary wrote requesting specific revisions to an early draft, asking that it be made more "lyric and fairy-tale" in tone. It is not clear whether the request was satisfied; the project petered out. "I've always wanted to do something of yours," Dunham wrote in 1943; she pursued his *Brothers / Dos Hermanos* more intently, paying Hughes for the libretto in 1953 ("The only time a libretto ever paid off—at-tall!" he wrote Arna Bontemps). In 1963 Dunham was still seeking a way to put on that work. *The Conga Ends* may also have been written with Dunham in mind.

"I am floored by your scenarios and I want to do them all," Alvin Ailey wrote Hughes in 1961. In the same letter, he envisions "a dance revue composed of all your material," mentioning specifically *The Amazon Queen* and a dance survey based on *Mister Jazz*. He also describes his idea of "dance—a theater piece really—about our lady Bessie Smith—the overall concept was one involving Bessie's descent to Hell after her death." Hughes notes on this letter that he had sent Ailey *Bessie Smith Descends* five days earlier. During the same month they discussed *Ask Your Mama*, Hughes suggesting that Ailey contact composer Randy Weston, who had just begun working on the music. Unfortunately, neither Dunham nor Ailey ever did manage to stage a Hughes libretto. Yet these works represent his imaginative engagement with yet another genre not usually connected with him: ballet.[2]

Most of the librettos reproduced here are likely versions retyped after they were written. A note on *Blues to Be-bop* indicates it was composed in 1951. *Two Brothers* was completed in 1953; *Ask Your Mama* is dated 1961; and *Bessie Smith Descends*, 1963. Correspondence indicates that *Carmelita and the Cockatoo* was composed around 1941, as was *The Saint Louis Blues* (a second less coherent typescript in the Langston Hughes Papers is dated). The Beinecke Library dates *The Amazon Queen* as 1941 and *The Conga Ends* may be from that period as well, but neither of the texts transcribed is dated.

The Amazon Queen
A Ballet Libretto

1941

Characters

Amazon Queen
Pygmy
Warrior Maidens

Sets

Sc. 1—The Throne Yard
Sc. 2—A Jungle

THE STORY: *As the Amazon Queen sits peevishly on her outdoor throne, she happens to notice that one of the human heads adorning the pickets of her royal gate is all shriveled and shrunk by the sun. Indeed, it is about to fall off. Angrily she orders the women of her court to remove it at once. Then commands the WARRIOR MAIDENS to make ready for a foray into Pygmy Land in search of another and fresher head. The women gather their weapons of war and take off, led by the QUEEN. In the depth of the forest they come across a PYGMY squatting before his boiling pot. The MAIDENS attack the PYGMY but without success, whereupon the QUEEN draws her royal sword and sets to, but the PYGMY is too much for her, as well. Finally, she bursts into helpless tears. The tough little man cannot bear to see her weep. His heart is smitten. He asks her for a dance and, to the rhythms of the dance, he woos—and conquers her. The he takes command. He orders her to pick up his pot and follow him. Led by their new PYGMY KING, the QUEEN and her WARRIOR MAIDENS march meekly (but gaily) off behind him—for the QUEEN has lost her heart to a PYGMY who kept his head.*

NOTE: *This ballet may be performed with—or without—the spoken continuity. In any case the mood is one of broad and humorous burlesque. The*

music and drum should be highly syncopated, the sets bright, the WAR-
RIOR MAIDENS beautiful, and the PYGMY squat and strong.
SCENE 1: *The Throne-Yard of the Amazon Queen's palace. Frowning, she*
sits on her royal dais fanned by two WARRIOR MAIDENS. A dozen
others hover near the throne. The Queen looks mad. Suddenly she points
to the royal gate. The action coincides with the poetic continuity.
VOICE: Down in the Amazon an Amazon Queen
    Sat on her throne and looked real mean
    For she was looking at her picket gate
    Where human head proclaimed her royal state—
    But one of the heads had shriveled and dried
    In the Amazon sun till it looked plumb fried.
    Said the Amazon Queen to her Amazon staff,
    Snatch that head down before folks start to laugh!
    Then gather your shields and gather your swords,
    We're going to make war on the Pygmy lords—
    For what I want, *and I want it bad,*
    To decorate my gate, is a Pygmy head.
      (Roll of War Drums)
    Girls, breast your shields! Hip your swords!
    We're going to make war on the Pygmy lords.
      MARCH OF THE AMAZON MAIDENS
    So, way down yonder on the Amazon,
    They tucked up their skirts and to war were gone.
    With shielded breasts and sunbaked backs
    Off to war marched the Amazon WAACS.
Scene 2: *The Jungle. In its shady heart sits a PYGMY man tending to an*
old iron pot. Stealthily from tree to tree, the WARRIOR MAIDENS
creep towards him.
VOICE: They went into Pygmy Land
    Looking for the head of a Pygmy man.
    They came across a specimen hot
    Cooking his dinner in an old iron pot.
    The Queen told her women, Surround that man!
    I'll take his head with my own hand.
      SUDDENLY THE WOMEN LEAP UPON THE
      PYGMY, BUT HE SWINGS TO A VINE AND
      TARZAN-LIKE COMES DOWN BEHIND THE
      ASTONISHED MAIDENS.
    But that Pygmy's thoughts were otherwise.

He said, Death to any woman here that tries!
The Queen said, Charge him! Run him through!
The women tried hard, but they "no could do,"
For that little man was monkey-spry,
He leaped and he swung and he jumped too high.
Then the Queen herself drew her jeweled sword—
But that Pygmy pulled a switchblade! Oh, my Lord.
 DUEL OF THE PYGMY AND THE QUEEN.
To slice that man she furiously tried—
But she couldn't make a touch, so she broke down and cried!
Now, to see a woman dissolve in sobs
Gives even a Pygmy the soft heart-throbs.
 REMORSE OF THE PYGMY.
So that savage said with an amorous glance,
Queen, dry your tears! Come on, let's dance!
So the two of them let their weapons fall
And they started to dance a free for all.
 LOVE DANCE OF THE QUEEN AND THE PYGMY
The Pygmy danced so good, when he got through
The Queen said, It ain't your head I want, *it's YOU!*
But the Pygmy cried, Since I am a MAN,
Queen, you got to come under my command.
Put out my fire, pick up my pot,
And come on home with your Hottentot.
 THE QUEEN GIVES HIM HER CROWN AND
 HUMBLY OBEYS HIS COMMANDS
So it came to pass that one little man
Is now the King of Amazon Land.
And if you thought that Pygmy would be dead—
It was the Queen who lost her head!
 REPRISE: MARCH OF THE AMAZON MAIDENS
 LED THIS TIME BY THE PYGMY BEHIND WHOM
 TRAILS THE QUEEN WITH THE POT AND HER
 MAIDENS, ALL OF WHOM ARE TRYING TO RE-
 DUCE THEMSELVES TO PYGMY SIZE.
 Yes, it was the Queen who lost her head!
END

The Saint Louis Blues
A Ballet Libretto Based on the Famous American Classic by W. C. Handy

1941

Characters

SUGAR LOU—The St. Louis Woman
LILLY MAE—Buddy's Used-To-Be
BIG EYED BUDDY—Sugar Lou's man
A BOUNCER
A BLIND BEGGAR
A PIANO PLAYER
PATRONS OF THE BAR

TIME: *The Gay Nineties*
SETS: *1. Furnished room*
      2. A St. Louis bar
MUSIC: The St. Louis Blues
      A folk blues
      A cake walk
STORY: *LILLY MAE has been deserted by BIG EYED BUDDY, who left
      her to go to St. Louis with SUGAR LOU, a sporting woman who wears
      diamonds. As LILLY MAE sits at sunset in her window in Memphis,
      the blues overcome her, and she makes up her mind to go after BUDDY.
      She makes it to St. Louis and finds him there in a fine bar making merry
      with SUGAR LOU. She calls to him but he will not come. He laughs.
      And SUGAR LOU defies her. She draws her pistol to shoot SUGAR
      LOU but BUDDY rushes between them and he is killed instead. The
      two women, simple LILLY MAE and flashy SUGAR LOU, are left to
      mourn the same man, BIG EYED BUDDY of the box-back coat, the
      gold piece on his watch chain, and the rubies in the toes of his shoes. Their
      hearts are flooded with the ST. LOUIS BLUES.*

SCENE 1: *Sunset. Memphis. LILLY MAE packs her trunk. She is plainly dressed, poor, and homely, but she is going to St. Louis to find her man.*

VOICE: Memphis ain't nothin' without Big Eyed Buddy!

>   Ay, Lawd!
>
>   *(Sings:)*
>
> I hate to see that evenin' sun go down,
> Hate to see that evenin' sun go down,
> Cause my baby, he done left this town.
>   *(She pauses at the open window in the setting sun. In her hand is BIG EYED BUDDY's picture. She paces the floor in despair, then begins to pack her trunk, taking down her meager clothing from the hall tree.)*
> Feelin' tomorrow like I feel today,
> Feel tomorrow like I feel today,
> I'll pack my trunk and make my get-away.
>   *(Sadly she looks out of the window.)*
> Mississippi River is so long, deep and wide.
> I got to find my sweet man, he's on the other side.
>   Get me back to St. Louis,
>   Get me back to St. Louis
> So I can lose them mean old blues.
>   *(She puts BUDDY's picture in the trunk, locks it, and begins to drag it off.)*
> St. Louis Woman with her diamond rings. . . .
>   *(As the song continues the scene fades in transition to:)*

SCENE 2: *Interior of a gorgeously decorated Negro bar of the nineties, the sporting era in St. Louis. The crowd is dancing slowly to the blues.*

VOICE: . . . . Pull that man round by her apron strings.

> 'Twarn't for powder and for store-bought hair
> That man I love would not have gone nowhere.
>   *(As the scene blazes in light a full orchestra now joins the singers in the blues. WAITERS serve champagne, SPORTS come in and out, a BLIND BEGGAR passes with his cup, a fight starts and is quickly quelled by an enormous BOUNCER.)*
> I got the St. Louis Blues, jest as blue as I can be
> My man's got a heart like a rock cast in the sea,
> Else he never would have gone so far from me.
> St. Louis woman with your diamond rings. . . . *(The voice stops as though strained. The music repeats the phrases, then the voice joins in like a cracked record:)*

. . . . with your diamond rings. . . . with your diamond rings. . . . diamond rings. . . . diamond rings. . . .

> *(The DANCERS cease, sit down. There is a sound of cheers outside. Some rise to look as the swinging doors center open and SUGAR LOU, the St. Louis woman, enters on the arm of BIG EYED BUDDY. Both are dressed in the elegantly flashy clothes of the period. SUGAR LOU has on spangles, a picture hat with plumes, diamonds, and a diamond garter which she takes the liberty of showing. BIG EYED BUDDY has a box-back coat, a rich roller stetson hat, a gold piece as a watch fob, and highly polished sharp-toed tan shoes with a gem in each toe. BUDDY is SUGAR LOU's man—and she pays the bills. They are out for a spree. They do not know that LILLY MAE of Memphis, BUDDY's used-to-be, is in town.)*

MALE VOICE: Make my way for the cake-walk! Here comes Sugar Lou with her brand new man, Mr. Big Eyed Buddy! Strike up the band! Hit it, perfesser!

> *(The crowd parts, focusing on doorway center. As the orchestra strikes up a gay cake walk, SUGAR LOU and BUDDY dance down the steps, glittering and gorgeous in the spot light. The crowd, in admiration, eggs them on as they cut the various fancy capers of the time. Then all begin to dance. But SUGAR LOU and her man occupy the center of the stage and SUGAR LOU plays up to BUDDY amorously, begging him to:)*

VOICE: Throw your arms around me like de circle round de sun.
Baby, throw your arms around me like de circle round de sun,
And tell your pretty mama how you want your loving done.
I can love so slow and easy, love like a cyclone cloud.
Love so slow and easy, love like a cyclone cloud.
Make you purr like a kitten, or I can make you holler out loud.

> *(The crowd hollers out loud as SUGAR LOU dances a demonstration of her love. Then all begin to dance as the music settles down to a slow and easy blues and the room rocks with rhythm. Suddenly an ominous note creeps into the dancing and the folks huddle closer together: LILLY MAE has appeared in the doorway, one hand on a large black purse in which the outline of a colt 32:20 is clearly seen.)*

I love that man like a school boy loves his pie,
Like an old Kentucky colonel loves his rock and rye. . . .

*(Here again like a broken record the music gets stuck and the voice
repeats over and over:)*

. . . . rock and rye. . . . rock and rye. . . . rock and rye. . . .

*(LILLY MAE walks toward SUGAR LOU and BUDDY who are
locked in a rhythmical embrace and do not know she is there. From
somewhere a voice, a deep voice of fate, calls:)*

VOICE: Buddy!

*(But he does not hear her call. LILLY MAE reaches out and snatches
BUDDY from SUGAR LOU's arms. A cymbal crashes. Now only
the piano is heard playing a blues that seems to plead for love. In
pathetic pantomime poor dowdy LILLY MAE pleads with BIG
EYED BUDDY to take her back. But BUDDY pushes her away
and goes to join the outraged SUGAR LOU. To protect her man,
SUGAR LOU lifts her spangled skirt and from her jeweled garter
draws a glittering dagger. The cornets now join the piano in a blues
of anguish and danger as the crowd draws away.)*

SINGER: St. Louis woman with MY diamond rings. . . .

VOICE: Buddy!

(BUDDY laughs)

SINGER: Got your man tied to MY apron strings. . . .

*(SUGAR LOU casts off her picture hat and prepares for battle as
LILLY MAE answers:)*

But if it warn't for your powder and your store-bought hair
Buddy of mine would not've gone nowhere.
I got the St. Louis blues, blue as I can be.
That man's got a heart like a rock cast in the sea,
Else he never would've gone so far from me.

*(LILLY MAE draws her pistol and the two women back off belliger-
ently, glare at each other, then look at BUDDY who smiles proudly
as they dance, each for him, their dance of love to please and entice
him.)*

SINGER: I love that man like a schoolboy loves his pie,
Like an old Kentucky colonel loves his rock and rye.
I'll love that man until the day I die.

*(Suddenly the music stops. The women become aware of each other
again. SUGAR LOU darts at LILLY MAE with uplifted dagger,
but LILLY MAE raises her gun. BUDDY rushes between them.
The gun blazes. BUDDY falls dead. Both women stand paralyzed.
The man they love is gone. SUGAR LOU drops her knife, LILLY*

MAE her gun. The piano alone without orchestra plays a teasing blues. SUGAR LOU sinks in a sob to the floor. LILLY MAE falls to her knees over the body and begins to pray. The singer, orchestra, and full chorus rise in a burst of song:)

I got the St. Louis Blues. . . . .

END

Blues to Be-bop Ballet

1951

    (A Street. Dusk. A YOUNG MAN on stoop)
BLUES BOY: WHAT A BLUE EVENING!
   AND THE LIGHTS AIN'T COME ON YET.
    (WOMAN in window answers)
WOMAN: YES, THEY HAVE!
   LOOKY YONDER!
   THEY COME ON NOW!
BLUES BOY: HARLEM IN THE EVENING,
   IN THE EARLY, EARLY BLUE.
   LISTEN AND YOU'LL HEAR
   WHAT HARLEM SAYS TO YOU.
WOMAN: HARLEM IN THE MORNING,
   IN THE EARLY, EARLY BRIGHT.
   SOME FOLKS SAY GOODMORNING,
   AND SOME FOLKS SAY GOODNIGHT.
BOTH: HARLEM! HARLEM! HARLEM! . . . . . TONIGHT. . . . .
    (Dance of the early evening passers-by, pantomime of dressers in windows, of a man playing records. A bit of Boogie. A VOICE chants against the music)
VOICE: DOWN IN THE BASS
   THAT STEADY BEAT
   WALKING WALKING WALKING
   LIKE MARCHING FEET.

   DOWN IN THE BASS
   THAT BABY ROLL
   ROLLING LIKE I LIKE IT
   IN MY SOUL.
    (Neon signs scrawl their pleasure names on the walls cock-eyed, crooked, rose-colored, gay, as the VOICE continues)
WONDER BAR
*
WISHING WELL

*

MONTEREY
*

MINTON'S—Altar of Thelonius
*

MANDALAY
*

Spots where the booted
And unbooted play
*

LENOX
*

CASBAH
*

POOR JOHN'S
*

mirror-go-round
where a broken glass
smears re-bop
Sound

> (*Blues and pseudo-Bop give the beat for both the booted and un-
> booted who mingle on the sidewalks. Two women discuss the num-
> bers*)

1ST LADY: 6-0-1,
SEVEN-NINETY-TWO
PUT IN A NUMBER
AND SEE WHAT YOU CAN DO.
2ND LADY: IF I EVER HIT FOR A DOLLAR
I'M GONNA SALT EVERY DIME AWAY
IN THE POST OFFICE FOR A RAINY DAY.
I AIN'T GONNA PLAY BACK A CENT.
1ST LADY: WELL, HONEY,
I MIGHT COMBINATE A LITTLE
WITH MY RENT.

> (*Enter a* COLLEGE BOY *in tux with flowers as a lovely brownskin*
> GIRL *in an evening gown comes down the steps*)

2ND LADY: WHERE ARE YOU GOING, LORRAINE?
GIRL: TO A FORMAL, MRS. JOHNSON
1ST LADY: NOW, AIN'T THAT NICE.
COLLEGE BOY: HELLO!

(Offering flowers)
FOR YOU.
GIRL: FOR ME! OH, HOW SWEET! . . . .
DID YOU GET YOUR THEME DONE?
COLLEGE BOY: I WROTE IT EARLY THIS EVENING, BABY.
GIRL: WHAT'S IT LIKE?
COLLEGE BOY: TODAY—
(As he sings the light dims to a spot on the BOY and GIRL who sit on the stoop)
THE INSTRUCTOR SAID,
GO HOME AND WRITE
A PAGE TONIGHT.
AND LET THAT PAGE COME OUT OF YOU—
THEN, IT WILL BE TRUE.

I WONDER IF IT'S THAT SIMPLE?

I AM TWENTY-TWO, COLORED, BORN IN WINSTON-SALEM.
I WENT TO SCHOOL THERE, THEN DURHAM, THEN HERE
TO THIS COLLEGE ON THE HILL ABOVE HARLEM.
I AM THE ONLY COLORED STUDENT IN MY CLASS.
THE STEPS FROM THE HILL LEAD DOWN INTO HARLEM,
THROUGH A PARK, THEN I CROSS ST. NICHOLAS,
EIGHTH AVENUE, SEVENTH, AND I COME TO THE Y,
THE HARLEM BRANCH Y, WHERE I TAKE THE ELEVATOR
UP TO MY ROOM, SIT DOWN, AND WRITE THIS PAGE:

IT'S NOT EASY TO KNOW WHAT IS TRUE FOR YOU OR ME
AT TWENTY-TWO, MY AGE. BUT I GUESS I'M WHAT
I FEEL AND SEE AND HEAR. HARLEM, I HEAR YOU:
HEAR YOU, HEAR ME—WE TWO—YOU, ME, TALK ON THIS PAGE.
(I HEAR NEW YORK, TOO.) ME—WHO?

WELL, I LIKE TO EAT, SLEEP, DRINK, AND BE IN LOVE.
I LIKE TO WORK, READ, LEARN, AND UNDERSTAND LIFE.
I LIKE A PIPE FOR A CHRISTMAS PRESENT,
ON RECORDS—BESSIE, BOP, OR BACH.
I GUESS BEING COLORED DOESN'T MAKE ME *NOT* LIKE
THE SAME THINGS OTHER FOLKS LIKE WHO ARE OTHER RACES.

SO WILL MY PAGE BE COLORED THAT I WRITE?
BEING ME, IT WILL NOT BE WHITE.
BUT IT WILL BE
A PART OF YOU, INSTRUCTOR.
YOU ARE WHITE—
YET A PART OF ME, AS I AM A PART OF YOU.
THAT'S AMERICAN.
SOMETIMES PERHAPS YOU DON'T WANT TO BE A PART
      OF ME.
NOR DO I OFTEN WANT TO BE A PART OF YOU.
BUT WE ARE, THAT'S TRUE!

AS I LEARN FROM YOU,
I GUESS YOU LEARN FROM ME—
ALTHOUGH YOU'RE OLDER—AND WHITE—
AND SOMEWHAT MORE FREE.

THIS IS MY PAGE FOR ENGLISH B.

BUT LET'S NOT TALK ABOUT SERIOUS THINGS.
IT'S TIME FOR THE DANCE—
AND YOU LOOK SO LOVELY! GEE!
      (*The lights dim into the formal as the BOY sings a duet with the*
      GIRL, followed by a dreamy waltz)
COLLEGE BOY: GOLDEN GIRL
   IN A GOLDEN GOWN
   IN A MELODY NIGHT
   IN HARLEM TOWN.
GIRL: LAD TALL AND BROWN,
   TALL AND WISE
   COLLEGE BOY SMART.
BOTH: EYES IN EYES,
   THE MUSIC WRAPS
   US BOTH AROUND
   IN MELLOW MAGIC
   OF DANCING SOUND—
   TILL WE'RE THE HEART
   OF THE WHOLE BIG TOWN,
   GOLD AND BROWN,
   GOLD AND BROWN.

*(They exit dancing. Street fills with PEOPLE again as a strain of
Bop heralds the entrance of a HEP CAT who dances by singing)*
HEP CAT: I PLAY IT COOL
    AND DIG ALL JIVE.
    THAT'S THE REASON
    I STAY ALIVE.

    MY MOTTO,
    AS I LIVE AND LEARN,
    IS:
    DIG AND BE DUG
    IN RETURN.
        (Chorus of BOYS IN BERETS)
BOYS: DO YOU DIG, JACK?
    DO YOU DIG?
    DO YOU DIG, JACK?
    DO YOU DIG?
    IGAROOTIES,
    DO YOU DIG THE PLAY?
    SAY, DO YOU DIG?
        *(The HEP CAT glances at a large women in a window, winks,
        smiles, then tells the other boys)*
    I LIKES A WOMAN
    SIX OR EIGHT AND TEN YEARS OLDER'N MYSELF.
    I DON'T FOOL WITH THESE YOUNG GIRLS.
    YOUNG GIRL'LL SAY,
    DADDY, I WANT SO-AND-SO.
    I NEEDS THIS, THAT, AND THE OTHER.
    BUT A OLD WOMAN'LL SAY,
    HONEY, WHAT DOES *YOU* NEED?
    I JUST DRAWED MY MONEY TONIGHT
    AND IT'S ALL YOUR'N.
    THAT'S WHY I LIKES A OLDER WOMAN
    WHO CAN APPRECIATE ME:
    WHEN SHE CONVERSATIONS YOU
    IT AIN'T FOREVER, GIMME!

    DO YOU DIG, BOYS?
BOYS: DO YOU DIG, JACK?
    DO YOU DIG?
    DO YOU DIG, JACK?

DO YOU DIG?
IGAROOTIES,
DO YOU DIG THE PLAY?
SAY, DO YOU DIG?
    (Large WOMAN in window calls out to BOYS on stoop)
WOMAN: I DON'T DIG
AND I DON'T PLAY—
MY KIND OF MUSIC
GOES THIS-A-WAY.
    (She hits into a blues as the BOYS exit leaving only the HEP CAT.
    Her blues excites a long tall FELLOW on the next stoop into action)
I'M CALLING YOU, JERRY,
CALLING YOU, HEY! HEY! HEY!
CALLING YOU, JERRY,
HEY! HEY! HEY!
MY NAME IS CARRIE
AND I'M CALLING YOU TODAY.
    (The FELLOW stands beneath her window)
BLUES BOY: I HEAR YOU CALLING
AND I'VE GOT MY EYE ON YOU.
I HEAR YOU CALLING
AND I'VE GOT MY EYE ON YOU.
    (WOMAN answers)
WOMAN: I'VE HAD MY EYE ON YOU, DADDY,
FOR A LONG, LONG, LONG TIME, TOO.
    (BE-BOP BOY interrupts)
HEP CAT: WHO ARE YOU, POPPA?
BLUES BOY: I'M MR. BLUES.
WHO ARE YOU?
HEP CAT: MR. BE-BOP!
MOP AND STOP!
    (Blues become Bop and a dance battle starts as LADY rushes out
    to the stoop yelling)
WOMAN: YOU BOYS STOP, OR I'LL CALL A COP!
BLUES BOY: COP, HUH!
HEP CAT: COP? WHO CARES ABOUT A COP? ANKLE OVER
HERE, DEAR.
BLUES BOY: COME HERE TO ME!
    (Blues and Be-Bop Battle over the DAME, pulling and hauling
    her each to the other as the music alternates between the folk style

*and the ultra-modern. Finally a COP arrives just as the WOMAN
is about to succumb to the BOPPER's chorus)*

COP: WHAT'S GOING ON HERE?

HEP CAT: LISTEN, MR. COP,
    WHICH HAD YOU RATHER HEAR?

BLUES BOY: BLUES?

HEP CAT: OR BOP?

COP: DON'T KNOW ONE FROM THE OTHER.
    SHOW! MAKE ME KNOW!

BLUES BOY: WHEN A WOMAN DON'T LOVE YOU,
    OFFICER, THAT IS THE BLUES.
    WHEN A WOMAN DON'T LOVE YOU,
    THAT IS REALLY, REALLY, REALLY THE BLUES—
    WHEN YOU DONE LOST THE LAST THING
    LAST THING THAT YOU GOT TO LOSE,
    YES, OFFICER, THAT IS THE BLUES.
    ALSO IT'S THE BLUES WHEN I BEEN ROLLING,
    ROLLING AND TOSSING ALL NIGHT LONG—
    I DON'T DARE START THINKING IN THE MORNING.
    I DON'T DARE START THINKING IN THE MORNING.
    IF I THOUGHT THOUGHTS IN BED,
    THEM THOUGHTS WOULD BUST MY HEAD—
    SO I DON'T DARE START THINKING IN THE MORNING.
    I DON'T DARE REMEMBER IN THE MORNING,
    DON'T DARE REMEMBER IN THE MORNING.
    IF I RECALL THE DAY BEFORE,
    I WON'T GET UP NO MORE—
    SO I DON'T DARE REMEMBER IN THE MORNING.
    OFFICER, THEM'S THE BLUES!

HEP CAT: OOL-YA-KOO!
    WHAT A BORE!
    PLAIN AS THE NOSE ON YOUR FACE
    WHICH IS ALWAYS IN PLACE
    AND A CONSTANT DISGRACE!
    DIG THIS, MISTER COP,
    AND SEE IF IT DON'T MAKE YOU
    HOLLER, *MOP!*
        *(BOP BOY wins over COP and WOMAN, leaving BLUES BOY
        sitting lonely on steps as signs come on again and BE BOP PAIR*

*start off to dig the gay places. BLUES BOY sings) repeating the
song of the neon signs in part. Then:)*[1]

BLUES BOY: WHAT A BLUE EVENING!
   LORDY, I AM BLUE!
   WHAT A BLUE EVENING!
   LORDY, I AM BLUE!
   YOU WOULD BE BLUE, TOO,
   IF YOUR BABY MISTREATED YOU.

     *(Picture fades into BOP COUPLE gyrating blissfully to the ultra-
     modern irregular rhythms of Bop as stage fills with BERET BOYS
     and pert GIRLS in a Bop Ballet)*

CURTAIN

Two Brothers
Dos Hermanos

1953
A Ballet by Katherine Dunham
With Lyrics by Langston Hughes

SETTING: *A Little Plaza on a Saturday Night.*
A balcony. A well. Shutters. Doors.

Characters

MANUEL DOMINGO DEL PRADO
TACOS VENDOR
THE GIRL
THE WIFE, JUANA
TWO COMRADES
TOY VENDOR
MAMBO DANCER
THE MOTHER
SINGER
GUITAR PLAYER
JOSE MARIA DEL PRADO ORACION
NEIGHBORS AND CROWD

I—SEQUENCE AS THINGS ARE ON THE SURFACE

ACTION: *The TACOS VENDOR squats at one side of the plaza. The WIFE is nearby. The GIRL is in a doorway. At the opposite side is MANUEL seated with his bongos between his knees. Suddenly he attacks his drums and declares in a loud voice that he will have vengeance—blood—for the death of his brother.*

I.   MANUEL: Yo, Manuel Domingo del Prado,
        Tendra la sangre de lo quien mató a mi hermano
        Sin motivo ninguno—motivo ninguno—

Quien se lo mató, paga a mi—
Manuel Domingo del Prado!
A mi! Lo digo a mi!
Manuel Domingo del Prado—su hermano!
VOICES: His brother!
MANUEL: Su hermano!
VOICES: His brother.
TACOS VENDOR: Dos hermanos mas unidos nunca he visto.
  Nunca, nunca, en ningun familia, nunca he visto.
VOICES: Two brothers closer in no family never have been.
TACOS VENDOR: Dos hermanos mas unidos nunca he visto.
VOICES: Two brothers closer never have been.
MEN: Manuel Domingo. . . . . . .
WOMEN: Jose Maria. . . . . . .
MEN: Brothers. . . . . . .
WOMEN: Del Prado. . . . . . .
ALL: Oracion.
TACOS VENDOR: Tacos! Tengo tacos! Tacos! Tacos!
MANUEL: La vengaza!
  En sangre se lo pago—
  El que le mató—
  Que mató a mi hermano!
  Seguro que me pago—a mi—
  A mi—Manuel Domingo del Prado!
  Manuel Domingo del Prado Oracion.
TACOS VENDOR: Tacos! Tengo tacos!
  *(The TWO COMRADES enter down stage left to right, then cross
  to upstage left listening intently to the memories of the TACOS
  VENDOR)*
  FROM MY HANDS THEY BOUGHT THESE TACOS,
  THESE TWO BROTHERS—
  JOSE MARIA, MANUEL DOMINGO—
  LOS HERMANOS ORACION.
  GROWING, GROWING,
  DANCING, GROWING,
  BOYS, THEN YOUNG MEN EYEING WOMEN,
  IN THIS PLAZA SATURDAY EVENING.
  IN THIS PLAZA, AY, THE WOMEN!
  *(The TOY VENDOR enters. A MAMBO DANCER dances as the
  TACOS VENDOR's song fades into the music of a night of fiesta)*

LAS MUJERES EN FIESTA. . . . . . .
IN THIS PLAZA IN FIESTA,
MEN AND WOMEN IN FIESTA.
> *(MAMBO DANCER attracts the TWO COMRADES. One joins her, then the other in her dance)*

TACOS! TACOS! VENDO TACOS!

6. MANUEL: Eso es como baile mi hermano.

TACOS VENDOR: Like that, his brother used to dance. . . . . . .

7. > *(COMRADES, MAMBO DANCER, pas de trois, Saturday night fiesta. The music warm and seductive. Alone in his fury at the side of the plaza, MANUEL rages)*

8. MANUEL: Asi baile mi hermano!

Y ahora esta muerto!
Murdered! Murdered!
Murdered! Murdered!
> *(As the music mounts in intensity, there creeps into it a quality like the snarling of cats)*

Y a mi se lo pagará,
Lo quien le mató.
A mi se lo paga—
A Manuel Domingo, su hermano!
A Manuel Domingo del Prado Oracion!
Por la familia Oracion, a mi se lo pago!

9. > *(The GIRL moves from the shuttered doorway upstage left in the first moments of her reminiscence)*

THE GIRL: I was passing through the canefields. . . . . . .
> *(She breaks off in grief and exits to reappear on the balcony. The TACOS VENDOR, a TENOR, and then a SOPRANO join in a song about Jose Maria)*

10. TACOS VENDOR: Two brothers!

TENOR: DOS HERMANOS!
TACOS VENDOR: One—tall and slender
TENOR: LIKE A STALK OF CANE.
TACOS VENDOR: One—Short and stocky
TENOR: LIKE A STRONG YOUNG TREE.
> *(A SOPRANO joins them)*

TENOR and SOPRANO: NEVER COULD TWO BROTHERS CLOSER BE.
TENOR: LIKE A STALK OF CANE,
SOPRANO: LIKE A STRONG YOUNG TREE!

TRIO: MANUEL DOMINGO LIKE A STRONG YOUNG TREE,
    JOSE MARIA DEL PRADO LIKE A STALK OF CANE,
    TWO BROTHERS CLOSER, CLOSER,
    YOU WILL NEVER SEE AGAIN.
TACOS VENDOR: They bought my tacos,
    These tacos from me—
    LONG AGO AS CHILDREN, MANUEL DOMINGO
    WITH JOSE MARIA BY THE HAND.
    MANUEL WAS A LITTLE OLDER,
    THE FIRST TO BE A MAN.
    JOSE MARIA LOVED HIM,
    FOLLOWED HIM WITH PRIDE.
    MANUEL DOMINGO—
    JOSE MARIA BY HIS SIDE—
    BROTHERS, BROTHERS, BROTHERS
    SIDE BY SIDE.
        (*The GUITAR PLAYER comes downstage left playing tenuously
        to sit opposite MANUEL. Slowly the GIRL begins to dance alone
        on the balcony*)
SOPRANO: BUT SOON THEY BOTH WERE MEN
    DANCING AT FIESTAS,
    DANCING WITH THE WOMEN,
    YOUNG MEN AT FIESTAS,
    MANUEL DOMINGO AND
    JOSE MARIA DEL PRADO ORACION.
    JOSE MET HIS SWEETHEARTS
    DANCING AT FIESTAS,
    DANCING WITH HIS BROTHER,
TENOR: TWO BROTHERS AT FIESTAS—
SOPRANO: SO WE ALWAYS SAW THEM,
TENOR: TWO BROTHERS OUT TOGETHER
BOTH: DANCING AT FIESTAS—
    YOUNG JOSE MARIA,
TRIO: HAPPY! OH, SO HAPPY!
    HAPPY! OH, SO HAPPY!
    HAPPY! OH, SO HAP—
        (*Suddenly the GIRL on the balcony utters a piercing cry—as the
        song changes to a flamenco*)
GIRL: AY—YYYY—YYY—YY—Y. . . . . . .
        (*The cry continues over the next six lines of the song*)

TRIO: THE YOUNG JOSE MARIA
    CUT DOWN IN THE CANE FIELD—
GIRL: . . . . AY—YYYY—YYY—YY—Y. . . . . . .
TRIO: LIKE CANE CUT DOWN FOR SUGAR—
    MURDERED IN THE CANE FIELD!
GIRL: . . . . AY—YYYY—YYY—YY—Y. . . . . . .
TRIO: YOUNG JOSE MARIA DEL PRADO ORACION
    MURDERED IN THE CANE FIELD—
    GONE! . . . . GONE! . . . . GONE! . . . .
MEN: OH, WHAT A BITTER HARVEST
    ONLY BLOOD CAN YIELD—
    JOSE MARIA DEL PRADO
    CUT DOWN IN THE FIELD!
        (Here angry voices interrupt the song)
    A BITTER, BITTER HARVEST. . . . . . .
SPOKEN: What kind of machete?
MEN: ONLY BLOOD CAN YIELD. . . . . . .
SPOKEN: Whose the ugly hand?
MEN: JOSE MARIA DEL PRADO. . . . . . .
SPOKEN: What kind of machete?
MEN: CUT DOWN IN THE FIELD!
SPOKEN: Cut down such a man?
MEN: Bitter, bitter harvest!
WOMEN: GONE! . . . . GONE! GONE!
GIRL: . . . . AY—YYYY—YYY—YY—Y. . . . . . .
WOMEN: GONE! . . . . GONE! . . . .
MEN: JOSE MARIA DEL PRADO,
ALL: DEL PRADO ORACION!
SPOKEN: Jose Maria del Prado Oracion!
        (Quiet. Spotlight centers downstage off into the orchestra)

II.   **II—SEQUENCE LIKE A DREAM**

        *(Out of the quiet rises the sudden sweetness of a guitar, lyric and
        soft as the breeze in a cane field. With his back to the audience,
        from the orchestra pit comes the young man, JOSE MARIA. The
        GUITARIST, on stage left, speaks for him as he progresses)*
GUITARIST: When I was a boy, I loved my brother best. . . . . . .
        *(JOSE MARIA dances, then continues toward the GIRL on the
        balcony)*
    Then I loved you—but not as much as I loved another. . . . . . .

(The GIRL descends form the balcony and dances with JOSE MARIA. Now and then the MAMBO DANCER joins them, also the TWO COMRADES. The GIRL returns to the balcony. JOSE MARIA turns to his WIFE, and they remember their first meeting at the well)

It is my wife that I love more than any—even now.

(At his emphasis on "even now" there is a slight rustle of anticipation and uneasiness among the spectators. The wife, JUANA, moves for the first time. Illumination of the two at the well. A dance of courtship and love, leading into the wedding)

III—SEQUENCE BORN OF LOVE AND JOY

(The setting becomes that of a gay country wedding as the well is covered and becomes a platform for dancing. The GUITAR PLAYER turns inward toward the wedding scene as the MOTHER, RELATIVES, and various GUESTS enter.

The MOTHER places a veil on the WIFE and gives out colored streamers.

The scene grows to country festivities, drinking, drum playing, peasant dancing.

MANUEL rises and moves into the scene, his eyes on his BROTHER'S WIFE. The GIRL on the balcony seems to be the only one who notices MANUEL's interest in JOSE'S WIFE.

MANUEL draws closer to JUANA. As JOSE MARIA dances with the TWO COMRADES and the MAMBO DANCER, MANUEL and JUANA dance together, chiefly on the confined area of the covered well. As the others dance in simple gaiety, their dance becomes a magnet of passion.

Suddenly the GIRL on the balcony breaks the festivities by a cry to JOSE MARIA asking him if for this he has returned)

GIRL: Es por esto tu has regresado de la muerte?

GUITARIST: No, I did not come back from the land of the gone for this. I came back to speak about this morning.

IV—SEQUENCE BORN OF PAIN AND DEATH

(To the accompaniment of a slow drum beat, the scene changes and becomes as it was before the wedding. Through the guitarist, JOSE MARIA makes his statement)

GUITARIST: I was coming through the canefields, in the morning, to my work, and the sun was very hot. . . . . . .

16.   *(The stage becomes a canefield as everyone joins in a combite,*
            singing a Haitian or Cuban work song, perhaps like this one:)
CANE CUTTERS: A TÈ
      FEMME-LA DIT,
      MOUCHÉ, PINGA
      OU TOUCHÉ MOUIN,
      PINGA-EH!
      A TÈ
      M'AP MANDÉ QUI MOUNE
      QUI EN DE DANS CAILLE LÀ
      COMPÈ RÉPOND:
      C'EST MOUIN AVEC COUSINE MOUIN
      ASSEZ-É!
      MOUIN EN DEDANS DÉJA
      EN L'AI-OH!
      NAN POINT TAUREAU
      PASSÉ TAUREAU
      EN L'AI-OH!

17.   *(As the others go back to their places, JOSE MARIA stands alone*
            wiping his brow. He speaks through the GUITAR PLAYER)
GUITARIST: I saw my brother coming toward me.
      And by the way he looked at me, I knew. . . . . . .
            (Stage right MANUEL rises with bongos. The wife, JUANA, shows
            her increasing anxiety. To the spectators, slowly the truth comes.
                The machete drops from JOSE's hand as he falls murdered on the
            ground.
                The MOTHER shrieks as she gropes toward the edge of the well.
            JUANA rushes toward MANUEL and throws herself at his feet.
                Leaning on the well, the MOTHER looks first at one son, then
            the other—JOSE MARIA, then MANUEL DOMINGO)

18.   MOTHER: MY SON! . . . .
      MY SON! . . . .
            (Her opening arms from a distance embrace them both)
      MY SONS!
            (She leans toward JOSE MARIA with tenderness)
      MY BOY!
            (And to MANUEL DOMINGO with pity)
      MY BOY!
            (To both she sings in anguish)
      I BORE YOU IN TEARS,

AND I RAISED YOU IN JOY,
EACH ONE, MY SON!
EACH ONE, MY BOY!
SORROW! . . . . SORROW!
SORROW ON MY HEAD!
MY FIRST BORN IS LIVING.
MY YOUNG ONE IS DEAD.
WHAT CAN I CALL THIS SORROW?
WHAT WORDS FOR MY CRY?
AT THE HANDS OF A BROTHER
HIS BROTHER MUST DIE!
SORROW! SORROW! SORROW!
SORROW ON MY HEAD!
DEATH COMES TO CRADLE
MY LITTLE ONE'S HEAD.
SUCH A BITTER HARVEST
IN THE FIELDS OF CANE!
WHAT CAN I CALL THIS SORROW?
WHAT NAME FOR MY PAIN?
WHAT NAME FOR—
    (Heartbroken she turns toward MANUEL)
MY SON?
    (JOSE MARIA descends again into the darkness, leaving the stage
    into the orchestra, his mission accomplished, as his MOTHER's eyes
    follow him)
MY SON. . . . . . .

V—SEQUENCE OF THINGS AS THEY ARE AT THE CORE

    (The GIRL leans from the balcony toward JOSE MARIA.
    The MAMBO DANCER crosses to exit.
    The two COMRADES, the TACOS VENDOR, and the
    SINGER leave. A pall of horror falls over the plaza. A distant
    cry:)
TACOS VENDOR: Tacos! Tengo tacos! . . . . Tacos. . . . . . .
    (There is a chord on the guitar—from the GUITARIST who has
    remained seated—like an echo of the spirit of the dead brother.
    The MOTHER moves to sit at the front of the well singing, in
    two simple words, her love, her grief, and her horror. The first is
    gentle as she looks toward the earth)

20.   MOTHER: MY SON. . . . . . .
       (Then sternly she turns towards MANUEL)
       MY SON!
       (And with mounting revulsion cries)
       MY SON!
       (Half curse, half prayer)
       MY SON!

21.   *(But MANUEL is not looking at his MOTHER. As if by a magnet his eyes are drawn toward JUANA. He repeats, like an incantation, his opening declaration of vengeance)*
       MANUEL: Tendra la sangre de quien mato a Jose Maria
       Sin motivo ninguno—motivo ninguno—
       Quien se lo mato pago a mi—
       A Manuel Domingo del Prado!
       Yo digo a mi! A mi!
       Su hermano—
       (JUANA echoes the word "brother")
       JUANA: Su hermano. . . . . . .
       (She stands very still—like the eternal symbol of the fascination of woman for man—as MANUEL DOMINGO begins to circle slowly around and around her, muttering his ever weaker lie of vengeance)
       MANUEL: Motivo ninguno. . . . . . .
       Quien se lo mato. . . . . . .
       Pago a mi—
       Manuel Domingo!
       A mi. . . . . . .

22.   *(Suddenly he breaks away—but only a few steps—to pick up his bongos. Wildly he looks towards the plaza as if searching for his brother. MANUEL beats upon his bongos—but they will not play. Furiously, he pounds them with his fingers, then his whole hands—but they will not play.*
       Perhaps the GIRL on the balcony echoes her flamenco cry:
       GIRL: AY—YYYY—YYY—YY—Y!
       (MANUEL and his bongos fall at JUANA's feet.
       The music rises)
       CURTAIN

Ask Your Mama
A Dance Sequence for a Man, a Woman, and Two Narrators

1961

MAN: IN THE QUARTER OF THE NEGROES—   A Man and
    WHERE THE DOORS ARE DOORS OF PAPER—
    DUST OF DINGY ATOMS BLOWS A   a Woman
    SCRATCHY SOUND.

WOMAN: AMORPHOUS JACK-O-LANTERNS   move against
    CAPER.

MAN: AND THE WIND WON'T WAIT FOR   the sky,
    MIDNIGHT
    FOR FUN TO BLOW DOORS DOWN.

WOMAN: BY THE RIVER AND THE   perhaps on
    RAILROAD,
    WITH FLUID FAR-OFF GOING,   a levee,
    BOUNDARIES BIND UNBINDING
    A WHIRL OF WHISTLES BLOWING.   as a river

MAN: NO TRAINS OR STEAMBOATS GOING   mist rises
    IN THE QUARTER OF THE NEGROES,
    BUT THE RAILROAD AND THE RIVER   like a
    HAVE DOORS THAT FACE EACH WAY,
    AND THE ENTRANCE TO THE MOVIE'S   ghostly
    UP AN ALLEY UP THE SIDE.

WOMAN: *TELL ME HOW LONG*   curtain of
    HAVE I GOT TO WAIT?
    CAN I GET IT NOW—   the past
    OR MUST I HESITATE?

    half veiling

*(The MAN joins HER in repeating
the Blues as both sing)*

half revealing
ancient

BOTH: *BABY, HOW LONG
HAVE I GOT TO WAIT?
CAN I GET IT NOW—
OR MUST I HESITATE?*

memories

recalling

MAN: IN THE SHADOW OF THE NEGROES—

ancient
longings

WOMAN: THE TOM DOGS OF THE CABIN.
THE COCOA AND THE CANE BRAKE.

as the

MAN: THE CHAIN GANG AND THE SLAVE
BLOCK.

drums begin

WOMAN: TARRED AND FEATHERED
NATIONS.

a low

MAN: SEAGRAMS AND FOUR ROSES.

rumble

WOMAN: FIVE DOLLAR BAGS A DECK, OR
ONE STICK
AT THE CORNER CANDY STORE.

that

MAN: FILIBUSTER VERSUS VETO,
LIKE A SNAPPING TURTLE,
WON'T LET GO UNTIL IT THUNDERS!

mounts into
a crash of
thunder,

WOMAN: WON'T LET GO UNTIL IT
THUNDERS!

rising to
an ear-
splitting

MAN: TEARS THE BODY FROM THE
SHADOW!

crescendo.

BOTH: WON'T LET GO UNTIL IT THUNDERS!

MAN: IN THE QUARTER OF THE NEGROES
THEY ASKED ME RIGHT AT CHRISTMAS
IF MY BLACKNESS, WOULD IT RUB OFF?

SILENCE

TACIT.

WOMAN: WHAT DID YOU SAY?

MAN: SAID, ASK YOUR MAMA!   Figurine.

- - - - **2** - - - -

WOMAN: HIP BOOTS DEEP IN THE BLUES—   Traditional
                                                 blues
MAN: AND I NEVER HAD A HIP BOOT ON!   in
                                                 gradually
WOMAN: HAIR BLOWING BACK IN THE   mounting
    WIND—   up-tempo
                                                 as
MAN: AND I NEVER HAD THAT MUCH   if laughing
    HAIR!   to
                                                 itself. . . .
WOMAN: DIAMONDS IN PAWN—

MAN: AND I NEVER HAD A DIAMOND
    IN MY NATURAL LIFE.

WOMAN: YOU IN THE WHITE HOUSE—

MAN: AND NEVER HAD A BLACK HOUSE!

WOMAN: DO, JESUS!
MAN: LORD!   Happy
                                                 humorous
BOTH: AMEN!   dance.

- - - - **3** - - - -

MAN: WHERE IS LOTTE LENYA?   No melody
    AND WHO IS MACK THE KNIFE? but each
                                                 sentence is
    (THEY face each other)   punctuated
                                                 by a
WOMAN: WAS PORGY EVER MARRIED   rim-shot
    BEFORE TAKING BESS TO WIFE? on the

MAN: WHY WOULD MAI (NOT MAY)   drums
    BECOME JEWISH THE HARD WAY?   and a
                           single
WOMAN: IN THE QUARTER OF THE   pluck of
    NEGROES   a bass string
    ANSWER QUESTIONS ANSWER   until a
    AND ANSWERS WITH A QUESTION.   lonely flute
                           begins its
MAN: AND THE TALMUD IS CORRECTED   Muslim wail
    BY A STUDENT IN A FEZ—   that melts into
                           the blues
TELL ME HOW LONG—   and dancers
HAVE I GOT TO WAIT.   again move
                           in rhythm. . . .
BOTH: *CAN WE GET IT NOW?*
    OR MUST WE HESITATE?   SILENCE.

- - - - **4** - - - -

(The WOMAN dons a shawl and a bonnet such as Harriet Tub-
man wore in days of slavery. SHE tells that story against the hum-
ming of "The Battle Hymn of the Republic")

WOMAN: IN THE QUARTER OF THE NEGROES   TACIT.
    WHEN NIAGARA FALLS IS FROZEN
    THERE'S A BAR WITH WINDOWS FROSTED
    FROM THE COLD THAT MAKES NIAGARA
    GHOSTLY MONUMENT OF WINTER   Here "The
    TO A BAND THAT ONCE PASSED OVER   Battle Hymn"
    WITH A WOMAN WITH TWO PISTOLS   softly
    ON A TRAIN THAT LOST NO PASSENGERS   brings
    ON THE LINE WHOSE ROUTE WAS FREEDOM back
    THROUGH THE JUNGLE OF WHITE DANGER   memories
    TO THE HAVEN OF WHITE QUAKERS   of the
    WHOSE HAYMOW WAS A MANGER MANGER   great days
    WHERE THE CHRIST CHILD ONCE HAD LAIN. of the
    NOW THE WHITENESS AND THE WATER   struggle
    MELT TO WATER ONCE AGAIN   for freedom
    AND THE ROAR OF NIAGARA   only to
    DROWNS THE RUMBLE OF THAT TRAIN   merge into
    DISTANT ALMOST NOW AS DISTANT   the sadness

AS FORGOTTEN PAIN IN THE QUARTER
QUARTER OF THE NEGROES
WITH A BAR WITH FROSTED WINDOWS.

MAN: NO CONDUCTOR AND NO TRAIN!

BOTH: BONGO-BONGO! CONGO!
BUFFALO AND BONGO!

WOMAN: NIAGARA OF THE INDIANS!

BOTH: NIAGARA OF THE CONGO!
    (*WOMAN flings away her hat and shawl*)

of the
blues
ending in
the sudden
shriek of
the flute
and the
beat of
angry
drums.

SILENCE

- - - - **5** - - - -

MAN: LIVING TWENTY YEARS IN TEN
    BETTER HURRY, BETTER HURRY
    BEFORE THE PRESENT BECOMES WHEN—
    AND YOU'RE FIFTY WHEN YOU'RE FORTY

WOMAN: FORTY WHEN YOU'RE THIRTY.

MAN: THIRTY WHEN YOU'RE TWENTY.

WOMAN: TWENTY WHEN YOU'RE TEN
    IN THE QUARTER OF THE NEGROES—

MAN: WHERE THE PENDULUM IS SWINGING
    TO THE SHADOW OF THE BLUES—

WOMAN: AND EVEN WHEN YOU'RE WINNING
    THERE'S NO WAY NOT TO LOSE. . . . .

MAN: DON'T WORRY, BABY!
    YOUR NUMBER'S COMING OUT!
    THEN BOUQUETS I'LL SEND YOU
    AND DREAMS I'LL SEND YOU
    AND HORSES SHOD WITH GOLD

Cool
but
frantic
modern
jazz
begins
and
continues
under
with a
blues
tinge
until
a happy
shout
heralds
good
luck
and
joyous
music
into
softly

ON WHICH TO RIDE IF MOTORS CARS | throbbing
WOULD BE TOO TAME— | African
TRIUMPHAL ENTRY SEND YOU— | drums
SHOUTS FROM THE EARTH ITSELF— | beating
BARE FEET TO BEAT THE GREAT DRUM BEAT | against
OF GLORY TO YOUR NAME | very
AND MINE—ONE AND THE SAME: | far-out
YOU BAREFOOT, TOO. | jazz
| which
WOMAN: WHAT? . . . . . WHAT? . . . . . WHAT? | eventually
| ends
MAN: IN THE QUARTER OF THE NEGROES | in
WHERE AN ANCIENT RIVER FLOWS | discords
PAST HUTS THAT HOUSE A MILLION BLACKS | that
AND THE WHITE GOD NEVER GOES | leave
FOR THE MOON WOULD WHITE HIS | in
 WHITENESS | lonely
BEYOND ITS MASK OF WHITENESS | isolation
AND THE NIGHT MIGHT BE ASTONISHED | only
AND SO LOSE ITS REPOSE. | the
| drums
WOMAN: IN A TOWN NAMED AFTER STANLEY | until
NIGHT EACH NIGHT COMES NIGHTLY | they
AND THE MUSIC OF OLD MUSIC'S | are
BORROWED FOR THE HORNS | joined
THAT DON'T KNOW HOW TO PLAY | by
ON LPs THAT WONDER | the
HOW THEY EVER GOT THAT WAY. | swish
| of
MAN: BONGO-BONGO! SHANGO! | maracas. . . . .

WOMAN: PAPA LEGBA! SHANGO! | "

MAN: DAMBALLA WEDO! SHANGO! | "

WOMAN: BEDWARD! DADDY GRACE! | "
KINGSTON! REGLA! PORT-AU-PRINCE!

- - - - **6** - - - -

MAN: IN THE QUARTER OF THE NEGROES
    WHERE THE PALMS AND COCONUTS
    CHA CHA LIKE CASTANETS
    IN THE WIND'S FRENETIC FISTS—

WOMAN: WHERE THE SAND-SEEDS AND THE
    SEA GOURDS MAKE MARACAS OUT OF ME,
    ERZULIE PLAYS A TUNE
    ON THE BONGO OF THE MOON.

MAN: THE PAPA DRUM OF SUN
    AND THE MOTHER DRUM OF EARTH
    LOVE TOURISTS ONLY FOR
    THE MONEY THAT THEY'RE WORTH,
    IN THE QUARTER OF THE NEGROES.

WOMAN: MAMA, MAMACITA, PAPA,
    PAPIEMENTO!

MAN: DAMBALLA WEDO, OGUN, AND THE
    HORSE
    THAT LUGGED THE FIRST WHITE
    FIRST WHITE TOURIST UP THE MOUNTAIN
    TO THE CITADELLE OF SHADOWS,
    SHADOWS,
    WHERE THE SHADOWS OF THE NEGROES
    ARE GHOSTS OF FORMER GLORY.

WOMAN: TOUSSAINT WITH A THREAD,
    THREAD STILL PULLS HIS
    PROW OF STONE, STONE . . . . .

MAN: I BOIL A FISH AND SALT IT
    (AND MY PLANTAINS)
    WITH HIS GLORY

WOMAN: AY, BAHIA! AY, BAHIA!

Marginal notations (right column):

Maracas
only. . . . .

"

"

"

"

"

"

"

"

A flute
cries
and as
if in a
great
distance
melodies
of the
Carib
sea are
heard. . . . .

"

"

"

"

MAN: SUNSETS STAINED WITH BLOOD!   "

WOMAN: CLEAR GREEN CRYSTAL WATER!   Up strong
                                          then down
MAN: THE CRY THAT TURNED TO MUSIC—   into the
    WHERE THE SEA-SAND AND THE   moan of a
        SEA-GOURDS   prayer
    MAKE CLAVES OF MY SORROWS.   punctuated
                                          by the
WOMAN: DAMBALLA WEDO!   cries of
                                          voodoo
MAN: SHANGO!   against
                                          the
WOMAN: LEGBA!   increasingly
                                          insistent
MAN: PAPA LEGBA!   rhythms of
                                          the
WOMAN: ERZULIE!   gospel. . . .

MAN: OGUN!   "

WOMAN: THE VIRGIN!   "

MAN: JOHN JASPER!   "

WOMAN: JESUS!   "

MAN: DADDY GRACE!   "

WOMAN: PAPA LEGBA!   "

- - - - 7 - - - -

MAN: I TRIED, LORD KNOWS I TRIED!   The Man
                                          prays
WOMAN: DAMBALLA!   as the
                                          Woman
MAN: I PRAYED, LORD KNOWS I PRAYED.   dances
                                          to softly

WOMAN: DADDY!

MAN: I CLIMBED UP THAT STEEP HILL. . . . .

WOMAN: THE VIRGIN!

MAN: WITH A CROSS,
    LORD KNOWS I CLIMBED!
    BUT WHEN I GOT. . . . .

WOMAN: JOHN JASPER JESUS!

MAN: WHEN I GOT TO CALVARY. . . . .

WOMAN: UP THERE ON THAT HILL
    ALREADY—

MAN: THERE WAS THREE—AND ONE. . . .

WOMAN: YES, ONE. . . .

MAN: WAS BLACK AS ME.

syncopated gospel rhythms. . . . .

"

"

"

"

"

"

"

"

Lonely flute.

- - - - **8** - - - -

(BOTH begin to HUM an indefinite spiritual, speaking between phrases)

WOMAN: I WAITED TWENTY HOURS
    FOR THE MILLWHEEL TO BE MILLWHEEL,

MAN: WAITED TWENTY DAYS
    FOR THE BISQUIT TO BE BREAD,

WOMAN: WAITED TWENTY YEARS
    FOR SADNESS TO BE SORROW,

MAN: WAITED TWENTY MORE
    TO CATCH UP WITH TOMORROW. . . . .

It is not clear what the spiritual is until the instruments take up the tune of DEEP RIVER

    (Humming DEEP RIVER, the MAN   "
    pretends to be a very old Negro.
    The WOMAN becomes a young girl   "
    inquiring of the past)

WOMAN: GRANDPA, WHERE DID YOU MEET   "
    MY GRANDMA?
    AT MOTHER BETHEL'S IN THE MORNING?
    I'M ASKING, GRANDPA, ASKING.   "
    WERE YOU MARRIED BY JOHN JASPER
    OF THE DO-MOVE COSMIC CONSCIENCE?   "
    GRANDPA, DID YOU HEAR THE
    HEAR THE OLD FOLKS SAY HOW   "
    HOW TALL HOW TALL THE CANE GREW
    SAY HOW WHITE THE COTTON COTTON   "
    SPEAK OF RICE DOWN IN THE MARSH
        LAND
    SPEAK OF FREDERICK DOUGLASS' BEARD   "
    AND JOHN BROWN'S WHITE AND LONGER
    LINCOLN LIKE A CLOTHES BRUSH   "
    AND OF HOW SOJOURNER HOW
        SOJOURNER
    BARED HER BOSOMS, BARED IN PUBIC   "
    TO PROVE SHE WAS A WOMAN?
    WHAT SHE SAID ABOUT HER CHILDREN   "
    ALL SOLD DOWN THE RIVER—
    I LOOK AT THE STARS   "
    AND THEY LOOK AT THE STARS
    AND THEY WONDER WHERE I BE   "
    AND I WONDER WHERE THEY BE

        "

MAN: STARS. . . . . STARS. . . . . STARS

        "

WOMAN: GRANDPA, DID YOU FIND HER IN
        THE TV SILENCE
    OF A MILLION MARTHA ROUNDTREES?
    IN THE QUARTER OF THE NEGROES   SILENCE.
    DID YOU EVER EVER FIND HER?

                                        TACIT.

- - - - **9** - - - -

MAN: PRESSURE OF THE BLOOD IS HIGHER   A flute
   IN THE QUARTER OF THE NEGROES   cry
   WHERE BLACK SHADOWS MOVE LIKE   rises
     SHADOWS   ever
   CUT FROM SHADOWS CUT FROM SHADE.   sharper
   IN THE QUARTER OF THE NEGROES   and more
   SUDDENLY CATCHING FIRE   shrill
   FROM THE WINGTIP OF A MATCHTIP   until
   ON THE BREATH OF ORNETTE COLEMAN.   joined
   THERE IN NEON TOMBS THE MUSIC   by the
   FROM JUKE BOX JOINTS IS LAID   most
   AND FREE-DELIVERY TV SETS   eerie
   ON GRAVESTONES DATES ARE PLAYED   and
   AND EXTRA LARGE THE KINGS AND   advanced
     QUEENS   jazz
   AT EITHER SIDE ARRAYED   of our
   HAVE DOORS THAT OPEN OUTWARD   hectic
   TO THE QUARTER OF THE NEGROES—   times. . . . .
   WHERE THE PRESSURE OF THE BLOOD
   IS SLIGHTLY HIGHER
   DUE TO SMOLDERING SHADOWS   "
   THAT SOMETIMES TURN TO FIRE.

   (The MAN suddenly screams)   "

HELP ME, YARDBIRD! HELP ME!   Flute cry.

- - - - **10** - - - -

WOMAN: IN THE QUARTER OF THE   Bongoes. . . . .
     NEGROES—
   THE MASK IS PLACED BY OTHERS.   "

MAN: IBM ELECTRIC BONGO DRUMS ARE
   COSTLY.

    Flute cry

WOMAN: STRIP TICKETS ARE ILLUSION.   into
                                                      modern
MAN: ALL THAT MUSIC, ALL THAT DANCING   jazz. . . . .
    CONCENTRATED TO THE ESSENCE
    OF THE SHADOW OF A DOLLAR
    PAID AT THE BOX OFFICE—   "

WOMAN: WHERE THE LIGHTER IS THE   "
    DARKER
                                                       "
MAN: AND THE DARKER IS THE LIGHTER.
                                                       "
WOMAN: AND THE QUESTION OF THE MAMA
    IS THE ANSWER TO THE CHILD.   "

MAN: THE *ONLY* ANSWER TO THE CHILD?   "

    (The WOMAN turns her back)   "

WOMAN: THE *ONLY* ANSWER TO THE CHILD.   "

    (The MAN speaks directly to the audience)   "

MAN: THEN ASK *YOUR* MAMA.   Bass alone.

WOMAN: ASK YOUR MAMA.   SILENCE

    (WOMAN exits as lights fade)

MAN: ASK YOUR MAMA.   Flute cry.

                                                       A swirl
                                                       of jazz.

                                                       The End.

Bessie Smith Descends

1961

(Draft to be further developed)

There is a great clattering at the gates of Hell. A lightning flash! Crash! Devils with pitchforks raised rushing toward the gates. In white sequins, mountainous, gorgeous, and black Miss Bessie Smith enters. She sings:

Opening:

GET BACK, DEVILS,	In
CAUSE MISS BESSIE SMITH IS HERE.	perturbation
BACK BACK, DEVILS!	the DEVILS
I SAY, BESSIE SMITH IS HERE.	retreat
I DONE HAD MY HEAVEN—	step by
SO HELL I DO NOT FEAR.	step
	as
RUN ALL YOU DEVILS	Bessie
AND HIDE YOUR HEAD IN SHAME.	advances
RUN, YOU DEVILS,	toward
HIDE YOUR HEADS IN SHAME.	the
I'M A BIG BLACK GAL AND	center
BESSIE IS MY NAME.	of hell,
	smiling
IF YOU DID NOT LIVE	her
ON EARTH WHEN YOU HAD YOUR	million
CHANCE,	dollar
IF YOU HELLIONS DID NOT LIVE	smile.
ON EARTH WHEN YOU HAD YOUR	She snaps
CHANCE,	her
DON'T BLAME ME, DEVILS—	mighty
BESSIE'S GONNA DO HER DANCE.	fingers.

HEY! HEY!

1. *BESSIE'S DANCE IN HELL.* Before she finishes the HEAD DEVIL enters, moustache curled, to watch.

HEAD MISTER DEVIL,   MISTER DEVI
STICK YOUR PITCHFORK IN ME.   prances about
HEAD MISTER DEVIL, TRY TO   with his
STICK YOUR PITCHFORK IN ME.   pitchfork
IF YOU CAN LIFT MY ASS   twirling.
YOU'RE STRONGER THAN I THOUGHT
   YOU'D BE.

COME HERE, DEVIL,   BESSIE flirts
LEMME TANTALIZE YOUR TIME.   coyly with
LEMME, LEMME, LEMME   the DEVIL.
TANTALIZE YOUR TIME.   He responds
YOU MIGHT'VE HAD PLENTY WOMENS   with a
   UP ON EARTH,   devilish
BUT YOU NEVER HAD A WOMAN LIKE I'M.   grin. . . . .
                                            The young
IS YOU GOT A QUEEN IN HELL?   DEVILS bring
IF YOU AIN'T, THEN HERE AM I.   BESSIE a
YOU GOT A QUEEN IN HELL—   crown
DADDY, HERE AM I!   as she snaps
IF YOU CAN'T HAVE NO FUN IN HELL,   her mighty
AIN'T NO DAMN USE TO DIE.   fingers. . . . .

HEY! HEY!

2. *DANCE DUET: THE DEVIL AND BESSIE,* teasing, tantalizing, never
  touching, they have fun, until BESSIE's breath runs out.

I'M TIRED NOW, MISTER DEVIL,   BESSIE sits
LEMME SET DOWN AND THINK AWHILE.   on a red-hot
BESSIE'S TIRED NOW, MISTER DEVIL,   stone and
LEMME SET DOWN AND THINK AWHILE.   remembers
THE TRUTH IS, MISTER DEVIL,   the past as
BESSIE AIN'T YOUR CHILE.   old MA RAINEY
                                            appears with
REMEMBER OLD MA RAINEY?   her cupid-bow
SHE TRIED TO GUIDE ME RIGHT   lips, dressed
YES, OLD MA RAINEY   like a gypsy,
TRIED TO GUIDE ME RIGHT.   gold pieces
BUT LOVE TAKEN OLD MA RAINEY   dangling from

AND TRIPPED HER UP EVERY NIGHT.

SHE LOVED HER YOUNG MEN,
AGE 18, 19, 20, the limit 22.
TALK ABOUT YOUR YOUNG MEN,
18, 19, 20,—limit 22.
OLD WOMAN GIVES 'EM MONEY—
WHAT CAN A YOUNG GAL DO?
YOUNG GAL LIKE BESSIE—
WHAT CAN A YOUNG GAL DO?
OH-OOO-OO-O! BESSIE!
LITTLE OLD BESSIE!
BESSIE IS IN LOVE WITH YOU.

her ears, neck-
laces, bracelets,
a bag of money
in her bosom.
A vigorous
YOUNG
 MAN-BOY
enters dancing.
And at first he
is attracted to
BESSIE. . . . .

3. *DANCE TRIO: BESSIE AND THE MAN-BOY IN LOVE* (her first young love). . . . . But the gaudy, rich and famous older woman, MA RAINEY, comes between them, pulls from her bosom her bag of money and begins to scatter gold pieces in front of the dazzled YOUNG MAN-BOY who follows her trail, picking up the gold pieces, as HE and MA dance off arm in arm, leaving BESSIE alone.

WOMAN OLD ENOUGH TO BE YOUR
 GRANDMA,
DADDY, THAT DO NOT MAKE SENSE.
OLD ENOUGH TO BE YOUR GRANDMA,
BABY, THAT DO NOT MAKE SENSE.
WHAT'S THAT YOU SAYING, BABY?
YOU AIN'T GOT NO CON—CI—ENCE!

A MAN AIN'T GOT NO CON—CI—ENCE!

BABY, LOVE WAS HEAVEN,
THEN, BABY, LOVE WAS HELL!
HEAVEN, HEAVEN, HEAVEN,
THEN, BABY, IT WAS HELL.
AIN'T NO USE IN LIVIN'—
BUT I GUESS I MIGHT AS WELL—
IN HELL. . . . .

Again she
sits on the
red-hot stone
as gleefully
MISTER
DEVIL
and all his
little DEVILS
return to
mock her
loss. . . . .

4. *DANCE OF THE MOCKING DEVILS:* as BESSIE sits forlornly on the red-hot stone. SHE prays, but in blues tempo.

LORD, OH, GOD IN HEAVEN,
RESURRECT MY SOUL.
OH-OOO-OO-OO-OOOOOOOO!
PLEASE, LORD GOD IN HEAVEN,
RESURRECT MY SOUL.
THIS BODY'S TOO MUCH FOR ME, LORDY,
RESURRECT MY SOUL!

RESURRECT MY SPIRIT, LORDY!
MY BODY'S TOO MUCH FOR MY SOUL.

5. THE FORWARD MARCH OF BESSIE SMITH who rises and walks regally as if she is approaching some celestial throne as the blues takes on a gospel beat.

MISS BESSIE SMITH'S ASCENDING,
SINGING NOTE BY NOTE,
RISING SONG BY SONG UNTIL
SHE GETS SAINT PETER'S VOTE,
WALKING UP A SINGING STAIRCASE
TILL SHE GETS SAINT PETER'S VOTE.

WATCH OUT THERE, OLD GABRIEL,
BESSIE SMITH IS COMING TODAY.
WATCH OUT, SWEET DADDY GABRIEL,
BESSIE IS COMING TODAY.
PREPARE THE MILK AND HONEY
WHEN I REACH THE MILKY WAY.

ANGEL HARPS START STRUMMING,
MISS BESSIE'S COMING—
HEY! . . . . . HEY! . . . . . HEY!

All the DEVILS scream, *Hell! Hell! Hell!* They dance mockingly as BESSIE prays. . . . .

A sudden light envelopes BESSIE, warm, rich, mellow, kind and caressing as she rises singing. . . . . All but MISTER DEVI himself retreat step by step in awe. The black background of hell is suddenly spangled with stars.

But MISTER DEVIL blocks BESSIE's way

HEY! . . . . . HEY! . . . . . HEY!-EEE-Eee-ee-e

and her song
dies in her
throat as he
forces her
to the hot
seat on
which she
sinks like
a heavy sack.
SILENCE.

6. *DUET SERIOSO: BESSIE AND MISTER DEVIL,*
   whose minions lock the Gates of
   Hell, forcing BESSIE to realize
   that there is no exit. One by one
   the stars go out in HER sky, as the
   stone on which she sits glows more
   fiery red than ever.

DEVIL: You can't get up off that rock.
BESSIE: I can't get up off this rock?
DEVIL: No, you can't get up off that rock.
BESSIE: Well, I could dream, couldn't I?
   And even in hell, remember. . . . .
   I DONE HAD MY HEAVEN, ANYHOW . . .

BESSIE sings.
And the air
is filled
with the most
beautiful
BLUES any band
could ever
play. . . . .

END: SLOW FADE to blackout as BESSIE lifts
   her mighty head and smiles.
CURTAIN

Carmelita and the Cockatoo
A Ballet Libretto

Date Unknown

Characters

Carmelita
A Cockatoo

SET: *A Mexican garden.*

MUSIC: *Humorous Arrangement of Mexican Folk Tunes, or an original score with folk quality.*

STORY: *In the garden of Carmelita's house in tropical Mexico there lived a handsome Cockatoo accustomed to sit in a banana tree and gaze at the beautiful Carmelita as she ground the family corn for tortillas. He sang to her his song of love, and one day the bird made so bold as to come down and ply his suit with the maiden herself. As he strutted about the yard and lifted his brilliant tail in pride, Carmelita noticed what beautiful feathers he had. She thought how nicely they would become her as a head-dress. She smiled at the old bird, and finally let him take a peck at her cheek, whereupon she grabbed him around the neck and pulled all his tail feathers out. One remained, on which she stamped her pretty foot as he fled, so she took that one, too. From the feathers she made a handsome headdress which she donned as she mockingly repeated his song. While the plucked and disconsolate Cockatoo sat nursing his wounded pride in the old banana tree, Carmelita pranced about the garden bedecked in* his *feathers.*

CURTAIN: *CARMELITA sits grinding corn on her petate in the doorway of her hut in a beautiful garden of lush Mexican greenery. In the opposite corner in an old banana tree there perches a brilliant COCKA-TOO gazing with amorous eyes on the lovely nut-brown CARMELITA. The action of the dance fellows the continuity of the poem as spoken or sung by an offstage VOICE:*

VOICE: Down in Mexico there was a Cockatoo
Who lived in a banana glade.

That Cockatoo with his brilliant plumes
Fell in love¹ with a Mexican maid,
And everyday from his banana tree
He caroled: Cock-A-Doodle Dee-Dee-Dee!
Cock-A-Doodle! Dee! Dee! Dee!

Carmelita sat and ground her corn.
She listened and she heard—
But she paid no mind to his cooing sound
For he was just a bird.
But nevertheless from his banana tree
He caroled: Cock-A-Doodle Dee-Dee-Dee!
Cock-A-Doodle! Dee! Dee! Dee!

Then that Cockatoo from his perch came down
Dragging his feathers on the ground,
He lifted his brilliant tail so high
His dazzling plumes caught Carmelita's eye—
As underneath that old banana tree
He flirted: Cock-A-Doodle Dee-Dee-Dee!
Cock-A-Doodle! Dee! Dee! Dee!

Carmelita smiled as she saw that bird,
Your feathers are not bad.
To tell the truth, Mr. Cockatoo,
I'd like to have some for my head—
As underneath that old banana tree
He cooed his: Cock-A-Doodle Dee-Dee-Dee!
Cock-A-Doodle! Dee! Dee! Dee!

When that Cockatoo saw Carmelita smile
He made a great mistake.
His vermillion breast just swelled with pride
For he though he'd get a break—
So he shook that old banana tree
With a mighty: Cock-A-Doodle Dee! Dee! Dee!

Like so many men with a human past
He thought that *No* really meant *Yes,*
So Carmelita led him a merry chase
As he pursued her all over the place—
Underneath that green banana tree

Panting: Cock-A-Doodle Dee-Dee-Dee!
Cock-A-Doodle! Dee! Dee! Dee!

At last Carmelita of his suit grew tired,
So she grabbed him round the neck.
He mistook her clutch for a loving hug
And gave her check a peck—
Underneath that banana tree.
Cock-A-Doodle-Doodle-Dee Dee-Dee!
Cock-A-Doodle-DeeEEEee-dee-dee-e-e!

Carmelita, with a merciless aim,
Humbled that helpless male.
With a fiendish clutch, one by one,
She pulled the feathers from his tail—
Underneath that old banana tree
Howling: Cock-A-Doodle-Dee-Dee-Deee-ee-e!
COCK! A-DOODLE! Dee! Dee-ee-e! Dee!

It serves you right, so fresh and bold!
And now I do not care
About you any more, old bird,
Because your back is bare!
Underneath this old banana tree
Laughing: Cock-A-Doodle—Hee-Hee-Hee!
Ha-HA-HA-Ha! Hee! Hee! Hee!

Poor Cockatoo! Alack! Alas!
Flew back to his banana tree,
Nursing his wounded past
As her song came mockingly:
Cock-A-Doodle! Hee! Hee! Hee!
Ha! Ha! . . . . . Ha! Ha! . . . . . Hee! Hee! Hee!

With a sudden cry, that poor bird said,
It's more than I can bear!
Of a broken heart he fell down dead
As she stood laughing there
Beneath that green banana tree!
Cock-A-Doodle! Dee-dee-dee!
Ha! Ha! . . . . . Ha! Ha! . . . . . Hee! Hee!

Carmelita, with a heart of stone,
Put the feathers in her hair,
And of the rest she made a fan
Like flame in the evening air:
Cock-A-Doodle! Dee-dee-dee!
(His bird-song strangled there)
Ha! Ha! . . . . . Ha! Ha! . . . . . Hee! Hee! Hee!
(Like flame in the evening air)
Cock-A-Doodle! Dee-dee-dee!
Underneath that old banana tree
Ha! Ha! . . . . . Ha! Ha! . . . . . Hee—Hee!

The Conga Ends
(La Conga Se Va)
A Ballet Libretto

Date Unknown

Characters

MARIA   A free Mulatto
LUCUMI   A slave
CORPORAL   Of the guard
A VENDOR
TOWNSPEOPLE
SOLDIERS
SLAVES

SETTING: *A Square in Havana.*
    Dawn.
    Dusk.
TIME: *A Hundred Years Ago.*
MUSIC: *Authentic Cuban folk-tunes, sones, rhumbas.*
THE STORY: *In Cuba during slavery times, the Negro slaves were allowed one day of freedom a year, from sunup to sundown. They came to Havana to take part in the Carnival, bringing with them their music and their dance, their drums and gourds, cow-bells and claves. On this day a giant slave, LUCUMI, in the mask of a bull, meets and falls in love with a free Creole, MARIA, the fiancée of a CORPORAL of the Guard. Under cover of the carnival, they dance and flirt together. Finally they disappear into a house. But the sunset takes its toll on their happiness. Just as the warning cannon booms—the sunset gun— letting the slaves know that their day of freedom has come to an end, the CORPORAL returns and discovers LUCUMI emerging from the house with MARIA. The CORPORAL curses MARIA then turns on LUCUMI with his whip. MARIA flees. LUCUMI is flogged until the soldier is breathless. The CORPORAL then spits upon MARIA's door, turns and leaves. In the distance the slave music is heard fainter and*

fainter. Slowly LUCUMI crawls away to join the musicians. MARIA appears on the balcony. LUCUMI sees her, and she throws him a rose. The slave straightens his wounded back—and walks off like a free man as MARIA follows him with her eyes. La Conga Se va—*the Conga ends.*

CURTAIN: *A square in Old Havana. A house with a balcony overhead. It is dawn. The square is empty save for an old VENDOR who is setting up his stand at one side for the sale of masks, costumes, and the streamers and confetti of Carnival. (The masks can be rented, too.) The sun is just coming up. Windows open, a goat cart passes delivering milk. A housewife brushes off her doorstep. The first REVELLERS come into the square. A distant drum beat is heard, softly syncopated, another, then another.*

VOICES: Drums, slaves. . . . . slaves, drums. . . . The slaves are coming to town, bringing their drums and their music. The slaves are coming to town. Havana! Carnival—the one day of freedom in all the year for the slaves—their one short day to play and dance from sunrise to sunset—for at sunset, the warning cannon booms—and they must go back to their slave huts in the cane fields. But now it is dawn—on this day of Carnival for free men and slaves alike. Dawn. The slaves are coming to town. . . . .

A BEAUTIFUL CREOLE GIRL, MARIA, ENTERS ON THE ARM OF A CORPORAL. THEY DANCE FOR A MOMENT IN THE SQUARE:

DANCE OF THE COUPLE IN LOVE

THEN AN OFFICER AND THREE OF A SQUAD OF SOL-DIERS PASS. THE OFFICER COMMANDS THE CORPORAL TO FALL IN. RELUCTANTLY HE BIDS GOOD-BYE TO MARIA AND MARCHES OFF. *EXIT SOLDIERS.* MARIA, ABOUT TO ENTER HOUSE, STOPS TO LISTEN TO THE AP-PROACHING DRUMS. COYLY SHE COMES TO THE VEN-DOR TO BUY A DOMINO MASK TO TIE ACROSS HER EYES. NEARER AND NEAR COMES THE MUSIC OF RATTLE AND DRUM, BELL AND CLAVE. THEN A BAND OF SLAVES BURSTS LIKE A WHIRLWIND INTO THE SQUARE: BEAU-TIFUL BLACK PEOPLE, MEN AND WOMEN, IN THE RAGS OF FIELD HANDS. THE TOWNSPEOPLE DRAW APART SCORNFULLY, ALL BUT MARIA WHO LINGERS WITH

INTEREST. THE SLAVES DANCE A WILD DANCE TO THE
RHYTHM OF THEIR CRUDE INSTRUMENTS.

DANCE OF THE SLAVES

AS THE DANCE CEASES, ONE SLAVE, LUCUMI, A MAN
BIGGER AND STRONGER THAN THE REST, GOES TOWARD
THE VENDOR'S STAND. THE SLAVES, IN HORROR, TRY
TO BECKON HIM AWAY.

VOICE: The Slaves are not permitted to mask. Even though it is Carnival, the slaves are not permitted to mask. Only free people—
(MARIA puts on her mask)
only free people are permitted to mask. But Lucumi is bold. He rents
a mask and puts it on, also a toreador's cape. Because he is bold, the
others take courage, too. They too put on masks—masks of bulls
and beasts of the fields, masks of wild brave animals—that make
the slaves wild and brave, as well. They, too, costume themselves.
Thus disguised, intoxicated by the music, they mingle with the lovely
maidens of the town, and with the white gentle folk—who are not
slaves, but free.

CARNIVAL MUSIC. SERPENTINES AND CONFETTI. WELL-
DRESSED TOWNSPEOPLE ENTER AND DANCE GAILY
WITH THE MASKED SLAVES:

DANCE OF THE ANIMALS AND THE GENTLEFOLK

DURING THE DANCE, MARIA AND THE SLAVE WITH THE
BULL'S HEAD, LUCUMI, MEET AND DANCE TOGETHER.
LUCUMI MAKES VIOLENT LOVE TO MARIA. THE CROWD
STOPS DANCING TO WATCH THEM:

LOVE DANCE OF MARIA AND THE SLAVE

AT THE END OF THE DANCE, HE TAKES HER HAND AND
THEY RUSH AWAY TOGETHER THROUGH THE CROWD
INTO THE DOOR OF MARIA'S HOUSE. THE CROWD
LAUGHS AND CHEERS THEM ON. *EXIT MARIA AND
LUCUMI*
BLACKOUT

Scene 2

AS THE LIGHTS COME ON AGAIN, IT IS SUNSET. DISTANT
MUSIC HEARD, BUT HERE IN THE SQUARE THE SLAVES,
ONE BY ONE, SNEAK BACK TO RETURN THE MASKS AND
ROSES OF CARNIVAL TO THE VENDOR. AGAIN IN THE
RAGS OF SERVITUDE, THEY SADLY AWAIT THE BOOMING
OF THE SUNSET GUN. TAPPING DISCONSOLATELY ON
THEIR DRUMS, GETTING UP COURAGE FOR ONE FINAL
DANCE OF HOPELESS ABANDON.

FINAL DANCE OF THE SLAVES

THE TOWNSPEOPLE WATCH THEM. SUDDENLY THE
WARNING CANNON ON THE DISTANT FORT BOOMS!
THE DANCERS FREEZE IN THE POSTURES OF THEIR
DANCE.

VOICE: Sunset! The slaves must return to their cabins. The day of
freedom is ended. The sunset cannon sounds. The carnival is done.
La Conga se va—the Conga ends.

SOLDIERS ENTER TO PATROL THE SQUARE. THEY SIGNAL
TO THE SLAVES TO GATHER UP THEIR DRUMS AND RAT-
TLES AND GO. *EXIT SOLDIERS,* ALL EXCEPT THE COR-
PORAL WHO LOOKS ABOUT SEARCHINGLY FOR MARIA.
SUDDENLY HER DOORWAY OPENS AND SHE EMERGES
WITH LUCUMI IN THE BULL'S HEAD! THE SOLDIER
WATCHES AS LUCUMI GOES TOWARD THE VENDOR AND
REMOVES HIS MASK AND RED TOREADOR'S CAPE. AT
THAT MOMENT, MARIA LOWERS HER DOMINO FROM
HER EYES AND SEES THE CORPORAL. SHE SCREAMS AND
EXITS INTO HOUSE. LUCUMI TURNS.

VOICE: A slave! A dirty slave!

THE CORPORAL TAKES FROM HIS BELT A WHIP. THE SLAVES
COWER IN TERROR, ALL BUT LUCUMI WHO STANDS HIS
GROUND. THE CORPORAL LIFTS HIS WHIP AND STRIKES
LUCUMI. THE SLAVES BEGIN TO PLAY THEIR RATTLES
AND DRUM, BELLS AND CLAVES, AND GRADUALLY
CREEP AWAY IN ANGUISH AT THEIR HELPLESSNESS. THE
MUSIC BEGINS TO ROAR AND WAIL OFF STAGE. LUCUMI

DOUBLES HIS FISTS TO STRIKE THE CORPORAL—THEN REALIZES HE IS BUT A SLAVE, AND HELPLESS, HE DANCES TO THE BLOWS OF THE WHIP.

WHIP DANCE OF THE CORPORAL AND THE SLAVE

LUCUMI DANCES UNTIL HE FALLS AT THE FEET OF THE CORPORAL WHO, EXHAUSTED, DROPS HIS WHIP AS A BUGLE SOUNDS IN THE DISTANCE CALLING THE SOLDIERS TO BARRACKS. THE CORPORAL KICKS THE SLAVE AS HE GOES TO MARIA'S DOOR, SPITS ON IT, AND EXITS. THE BUGLE CALL DIES AND THE SUNSET FALLS ACROSS THE SQUARE, EMPTY NOW SAVE FOR LUCUMI WHO RISES PAINFULLY TO HIS HANDS AND KNEES, CRAWLING TOWARD THE MUSIC FAINTER AND FAINTER IN THE DISTANCE. AT THE VENDOR'S STAND HE PULLS HIMSELF UP, TURNS, AND LOOKS BACK AT THE HOUSE OF HIS BELOVED. MARIA APPEARS ON THE BALCONY IN THE GLOW OF THE SETTING SUN. SHE THROWS HIM A ROSE. HE KISSES IT, FORGETS HIS PAIN, AND WALKS OFF LIKE A MAN. THE MUSIC RISES TO A CRESCENDO IN A GREAT BURST OF DRUMS, AS THE CONGA ENDS.

END

Lyrics from Musicals

Street Scene

1947
Music by Kurt Weill

Street Scene (music by Kurt Weill, book by Elmer Rice, lyrics by Langston Hughes), along with *Porgy and Bess,* anchors the development of American opera. Weill's innovative merger of European operatic forms with those of the Broadway musical (the opera's thoroughly eclectic music ranges from traditionally operatic, in the style of Puccini, to jitterbug, jazz, and blues), the compelling 1929 Pulitzer Prize–winning play by Elmer Rice on which the opera is based, and Langston Hughes's apt and poetic lyrics represent a signal achievement. The project also was the first in which two prominent white artists had invited an African American collaborator on a play about whites.

For *Street Scene,* Weill sought lyrics that "lift[ed] the everyday language of the people into a simple, unsophisticated poetry." Hughes knew why he was chosen: "They wanted someone who understood the problem of the common people. . . . Someone who wrote simply."[1] The collaborative process, lasting more than a year, was intense; Rice's coauthorship of several songs is but one indication of how the three worked in concert. Billed as a dramatic musical, to avoid the elitist connotations of the term *opera, Street Scene* tried out in Philadelphia to savage reviews. However, the New York opening, on January 9, 1947, met with general, if not unanimous, acclaim. Still, the opera only ran for a respectable, but disappointing, 148 performances, although later its reputation grew—as opera, rather than as Broadway musical. Even during Hughes's lifetime, it was revived several times, and even optioned for a film. It was, among other things, Hughes's only truly lucrative venture in theater.

Describing his intentions to a prospective director for *Street Scene,* Weill wrote: "We will do it in one set like the original play . . . to avoid the conventional musical comedy technique and to work it out as a kind of popular Broadway opera (the dialogue will be spoken, but underscored, so that the audience should never know where the dialogue ends and the song starts—and by 'song' I mean arias, duets, trios and all forms of musical ensembles, and some real songs too) . . . music and drama . . . completely integrated."[2]

For reasons of permissions and copyright, included here are only those lyrics for which Hughes is attributed sole authorship in the piano score, edited by William Tarrasch.[3] The lyrics themselves are reprinted from the libretto,[4] which is keyed to the published piano score. "Moon Faced, Starry Eyed" is unique among these lyrics in having been previously written: Hughes had composed it some years before, Weill set it overnight, and it made its way into *Street Scene* virtually unchanged; it was later considered the best Broadway lyric of the season.[5]

Blues
I Got a Marble and a Star

I got a marble and a star,
And the star is in my pocket too.
Got a marble and a star,
The star is in my pocket too.
If you'll be real good,
I'll show that star to you.

I got a halo and a hat,
But my halo I don't wear.
Got a halo and a hat,
My halo I don't wear.
I'm gonna save that halo until I get up there.

Aria
Somehow I Never Could Believe

Somehow I never could believe
that life was meant to be all dull and gray.
Somehow I always will believe There'll be a brighter day.
Folks should try to find a way to get along together,
A way to make the world a singing happy place,
Full of laughter and kind words, and friendliness on ev'rybody's face.
But somehow in the world that I grew up in
the streets were dark with mis'ry and distress.
The endless daily grind was too much for them.
It took away all hope of happiness.

When I was a girl, I remember,
I used to dream about a party dress to wear.
But I never had a party dress
And I guess my dreams got lost somewhere—nobody seemed to care.

But when I grew up I said, "I'll make it!"
For I believed there'd be a lucky star above me.
In the fairy tales I read, the maiden always said:
"I know I'll find a fairy prince to love me."

So I went wand'ring down the pavements of New York,
And through the subway's roaring tunnels underground,
Hoping I'd discover some wonderful lover.
Frank was the one that I found.
Oh, on the day that we were married,
I took a flower from my bouquet
And I pressed it in a book and put the book away.

Sometimes now I go and take a look,
the flower's dry, the perfume's gone,
the petals all turned gray.
Oh dream of love! Should love turn out that way?
Should love turn out that way?

But then the babies came.
Their little arms made a ring-a-round-a-rosy about me,
Yet as they grew older, they, too, seemed to grow away,
Until even Willie, my little boy Willie
seems he can get along without me.

I don't know—it looks like something awful happens
In the kitchens where women wash their dishes.
Days turn to months—months turn to years,
The greasy soap-suds drown our wishes.

There's got to be a little happiness somewhere,
some hand to touch that's warm and kind!
And there must be two smiling eyes somewhere
that will smile back into mine.

I never could believe
that life was meant to be all dull and gray.
I always will believe
there'll be a brighter day!

Aria
Let Things Be Like They Always Was

Let things be like they always was, That's good enough for me.
Let things again be safe and sound, The way they used to be.
What's going on? Why is it so bad?
If you ask me, the world is going mad!

Look at these new fangled ideas going round:
Free love, divorce, and birth control.
Young girls smoking cigarettes,
Their dresses up around their necks,
And men coming in, breaking up decent people's homes.
But it ain't gonna be that way around here, You hear? You hear?
If anyone in my house wants that kind of stuff, Oh no! Oh, no!
My kids are gonna be brought up right!
Not running the streets as if they're wild all night.
In the old days they didn't carry on that way,
And I'm telling you they ain't gonna do it today!
With me that stuff will never go!
In my house I run the show!

Let things be like they always was.
That's good enough for me!
That's good enough for me!

Arioso
Lonely House

At night when ev'rything is quiet,
This old house seems to breathe a sigh.
Sometimes I hear a neighbour snoring,
Sometimes I hear a baby cry.
Sometimes I hear a staircase creaking,
Sometimes a distant telephone.
Then the quiet settles down again . . .
The house and I are all alone.

Lonely house, lonely me!
Funny, with so many neighbors, How lonely it can be!

Oh, lonely street! Lonely town!
Funny you can be so lonely with all these folks around.

I guess there must be something I don't comprehend.
Sparrows have companions, Even stray dogs find a friend.
The night for me is not romantic.
Unhook the stars and take them down.
I'm lonely in this lonely house In this lonely town.

Cavatina
What Good Would the Moon Be?

I've looked in the windows at diamonds,
They're beautiful but they're cold.
I've seen Broadway stars in fur coats
That cost a fortune so I'm told.
I guess I'd look nice in diamonds, and sables might add to my charms,
But if someone I don't care for would buy them
I'd rather have two loving arms!
What good would the moon be Unless the right one shared its beams?
What good would dreams-come-true be If love wasn't in those dreams?
And a primrose path—What would be the fun
Of walking down a path like that without the right one?
What good would the night be Unless the right lips whisper low:
Kiss me, oh, darling, kiss me, While ev'ning stars still glow?
No, it won't be a primrose path for me,
No, it won't be diamonds or gold, But maybe there will be,
Someone who'll love me, Someone who'll love just me
To have and to hold!

Song
Moon-faced, Starry-eyed

Moon-faced, starry-eyed, Peaches and cream with nuts on the side.
I never knew there was anyone living like you.
Moon-faced, starry-eyed, I'm gonna bust my vest with pride.
I never lived, Baby, not at all, 'til I met you.

> At six o'clock I expect your call, At seven o'clock I am in the hall,
> At eight o'clock if you don't come by, By nine o'clock, Baby, I die!

Moon-faced, starry-eyed, Cooking with gas when I'm by your side.
I swear my heart's nowhere without you.

Moon-faced, starry-eyed, You're whiskey straight with beer on the
side.
Can it be true that I'm loved by a Tarzan like you?
Moon-faced, starry-eyed, You took my heart on a buggy ride.
I don't know how I ever got along without you.

At six o'clock I'm getting' up steam, At seven o'clock, I'm on the
beam,
At eight o'clock, if the knob don't turn, By nine o'clock, Baby, I
burn.
Moon-faced, starry-eyed, Floating on clouds when I'm by your side,
I swear my heart's nowhere without you.

Duet
Remember That I Care[6]

SAM: Pain! Nothing but pain! That's all there is to life!
  Before we're born, until we die . . . Nothing but pain! Brutality!
    Strife!
  Too high a price to pay for life! Not worth it, not worth it to live!
  The scream of birth, The moan of death . . . What else has life to
    give?
ROSE: I don't know, Sam, sometimes I feel discouraged, too.
  Last night I could hardly sleep and I woke up depressed and blue.
  I thought I'd walk to the office, So I cut through the park by the
    mall.
  Ev'rything looked so fresh and green. Life seemed not so bad after
    all!
  What do you think I saw, Sam? A lilac-bush flow'ring bright.
  It made me think of that poem you said, Remember?
  When we sat in the Park one night.
SAM: Yes, I remember.
ROSE: It was just like tonight, we were both feeling sort of low,
  And all of a sudden, you began that poem.
SAM: In the dooryard fronting an old farmhouse near the whitewash'd
    palings,

Stands the lilac bush tall growing with heart-shaped leaves of green,
With many pointed blossoms rising delicate,
  with the perfume strong I love, With ev'ry leaf a miracle.
ROSE: A sprig with its flower I break.
  Yes, that's what I thought in the Park today,
  When I saw that bush, fresh and green.
  I wanted to break off a flower
  But I was afraid I might be seen.
  Maybe a park policeman Might come and take me away.
  "Do not pick the flowers" The signs forever say.
SAM:Don't! Don't! They always say Stand back! Keep off the grass!
  Don't pick the flowers! Don't pick the flowers! Don't take!
ROSE: But in our dreams, Sam! . . .
SAM: Yes in our dreams, Rose! . . .
ROSE: Yes in our dreams, . . .
BOTH: A sprig with its flower we break, A sprig with its flower we break.
  And the lilac bush is ours, Nothing can take it away!
  The lilac bush is ours, Forever and a day.
  And when you see the lilac bush Bright in the morning air,
  Remember, always remember, remember that I care!
  Remember that I care!

Song
A Boy Like You

Somebody's going to be so handsome,
Somebody's going to make me proud.
Somebody's going to be so wonderful,
He'll stand out from the crowd.
Such a manly arm I'll have to lean on,
When I walk down the avenue.
Somebody will always be my standby. Who do you think it is?
Guess Who?

Somebody will never, No, not ever, forget to care and understand.
Yes, that is the grandest feeling, That any woman ever knew,
To know I have somebody wonderful, To know I have a boy like you.

Duet
We'll Go Away Together

ROSE: When birds get old enough, They spread their wings and fly.
    It's natural for a bird to want to try the sky.
SAM: When two people are in love their souls grow wings and say:
    The nest is too small now, Come away, love, come away, come away!
    We'll go away together, just we two, just you and I,
    we'll build a house to shelter us beneath a happier sky.
ROSE: We'll go away together out of the shadows into light.
    we'll leave behind our yesterdays and make tomorrow bright.
SAM: Life is a sky-tall mountain, Where clouds play hide and seek,
    But love will blaze a trail for us up to the highest peak.
    Maybe we'll find a rainbow, Maybe there's stormy weather,
    But you'll be in my arms, my love, . . .
BOTH: When we go away together.
SAM: When we go away together.
ROSE: I've heard that people are much nicer and friendlier, when you
    get away from New York. Oh, if we could do it, Sam!
SAM: We can, if we just make up our minds that we will.
ROSE: We wouldn't need much to live on . . . just the two of us.
    Home need not be a palace or a golden castle in Spain.
    I'd be content with just a roof to keep out snow and rain.
BOTH: Just so we find a shelter from cold and wind and weather.
SAM: I'll warm you in my arms, my love,
BOTH: When we go away together. When we go, we two, away!

Just around the Corner
A Musical Comedy

1950
Book by Abby Mann and Bernard Drew
Lyrics by Langston Hughes
Music by Joe Sherman

Opening at the Ogunquit Playhouse in Maine on July 29, 1950, *Just around the Corner* received lukewarm reviews, although *Variety* praised both Sherman's music and Hughes's "thoughtful lyrics." Invited to join the production because of the success of *Street Scene,* Hughes had to fit lyrics to an already completed score. Joe Sherman recalled to biographer Arnold Rampersad: "Once Langston Hughes came in, the whole enterprise became more serious, sensitive, meaningful, because we had a poet's mind at work now."[1] Set in Greenwich Village during the Depression, the play follows the adventures of three young men who arrive in New York by boxcar to seek their fortunes. The only typescript of the play in the Langston Hughes Papers seems complete, although the list of musical numbers mentions more songs than exist in the text. A selection of the play's lyrics is included here.

Where Can That Somewhere Be?

Maybe somewhere—somewhere in the distance
There's a place that's waiting just for me
Maybe there's a home
For a rollin' stone.
WHERE CAN THAT SOMEWHERE BE?

Maybe somewhere—just around the corner
I will find a welcome mat for me
Near the open door
I've been lookin' for.
WHERE CAN THAT SOMEWHERE BE?

I'll know it when I get there
And I'll know it well somehow—
I'll recognize that somewhere
Tho' there's no tellin', no tellin' now . . .

Maybe somewhere—someone will be waiting
Who will want to share her dreams with me.
Maybe 'round this bend
Lies my journey's end
But there's no tellin' where that can be
'Til I find that someone for me . . .

No Telling

There's NO TELLING what's across the bridge.
No, NO TELLING
What lies over yonder ridge.
There's NO TELLING
Where tomorrow may lead
Doesn't the oak
Start from an acorn seed?!

There's NO TELLING
What day can bring,
No, NO TELLING
When my lucky bluebird lifts his head to sing . . .

Bust my bank! Break my heart!
I'll pick up the pieces and I'll make a new start.
Back me back! Box me in!
But I'm a guy who's fighting with a will to win!

There's NO TELLING
When the shadow's gone . . .
What you'll find ahead if you keep going on—

Keep plugging—
Keep slugging—
Keep laughing—
Keep loving . . .
For there's NO TELLING what you'll find . . . at dawn!

Push Cart Man

PUSH CART MAN,
PUSH CART MAN,
The last stars out see a lonely
PUSH CART MAN.
At dawn of day
You see him . . . pushing shadows away!

PUSH CART MAN,
PUSH CART MAN,
A great big smile that the early sunshine steals
While happy birds in my heart
Give wings to the wheels of my cart

Straight from the ground—
Look! Springtime I've found . . .
I've got a garden all day.
Carrots and string-beans,
Cabbages-greens!
Broccoli's like a bouquet!

So PUSH CART MAN,
PUSH CAT MAN,
The last stars out see a lonely PUSH CART MAN.
At dawn of day you see him . . . pushing shadows away!

Falling for You

VERSE:
Thirty-three cents in my pocket.
Maybe thirty-four—
But the way I feel
Anyone would think I had a million more.

Thirty odd cents in my pocket
But I just met you
And you smiled at me—
So that smile must be—
Why I feel so well-to-do.
Why I feel the way I do.

CHORUS:
FALLING FOR YOU
For me could be
As easy as falling off a log,
As easy as finding Frisco fog . . .
For me to fall for you.

FALLING FOR YOU
For me could be
As easy as liking apple pie,
As easy as ho-hum-me-oh-my,
For me to fall for you.

I'm convinced that
It's a cinch that
If you give the go-sign—
We'll find us a gold mine
Of kisses to spare!

FALLING FOR YOU
For me could be
A Thrill that would suit me to a T.
The end of my problems, one, two, three . . .
And dreams might still come true—!
If falling for me could be . . . for you.

FALLING FOR YOU
For me could be
As warm as a smile from F.D.R.
As lucky as catching a shooting star
For me to fall for you.

FALLING FOR YOU
For me could be
As breezy as strolling round the square,
As easy as spotting . . . camembert
For me to fall for you—

I'm convinced that
it's a cinch that
We're headin' for heaven . . .
A Fabulous heaven—
So whaddays say?!

FALLING FOR YOU
For me could be . . .
As wonderful as a fall can be—
Exciting as finding you close to me—

It's me for you
And you for me—

Then maybe the census will jump two or three—!
If FALLING FOR ME could be for you.

Swing's Gonna Rock Your Bones

Do you hear folks shoutin' "Good news!"
Good news has come to town!
It's a brand new thing
With a hot zing.
You'll hear it all around.
Let's say so long to the Charleston.
Farewell waltz-time ways!
Tell flappers, kick off galoshes!
Here come sunny days!

CHORUS

Brassy bright notes,
Sassy light notes,
You can scat and sing it,
You can buck and wing it—
SWING'S GONNA ROCK YOUR BONES.

Piper-pied notes,
Southern fried notes,
Hot right off the band-stand,
Makes you do a hand-stand,
SWING'S GONNA ROCK YOUR BONES.

It's hot
Like a radiator.
It's wild.
Like an alligator.
Can't stop.
Cause the rhythm's snappy!

Aw, man,
Makes you so happy . . . !

You can play it,
Hey, hey, hey it!
Let it hypnotize you,
Tease and tantalize you—
SWING'S GONNA ROCK YOUR BONES!

It's mad—
As an Easter hatter.

It hits—
Like a big league batter!

It's hot—
As a red hot heater . . .
Aw, Babe, what could be sweeter?!

Shake and stomp it,
Rip and romp it—
You can lindy hop it—
Ain't no way to stop it—
SWING'S . . . GONNA . . . ROCK . . . YOUR . . . BONES!

When I Was Your Age Young Man

When John D., and J. P.,
John Jacob and me
Were young,
Jazz, swing, and jive
Weren't even alive—
Rumbas unsung.

I never dreamed of asking my father for a dime
A young man *EARNED* his living in my time.
Then, if you got nowhere in business,
You went West and staked out land—
WHEN I WAS YOUR AGE, your stake was your break, young man.

When Carrie Nation
Was smashing up the nation
Putting the demon rum on the run,

Knee high to a duck,
I was trying my luck
Selling the New York Sun;

I never dreamed of sleeping later than five A.M.
Never answered back my Father when he said, "Young Man—
Ah-Hem—
If you don't get A's in all your studies
I'll disown you, don't you understand?"
WHEN I WAS YOUR AGE, one expected to be disowned, young man.

When the Flora Dora sextette
And Lillian Russell yet
Were the rage
And Sarah Bernhardt, Ada Rehan,
And George M. Cohan
Decorated our stage;

I never dreamed of owning a Cadillac Eight,
A horse and a carriage were sufficient for my date.
And you never thought of being intimate with a lady,
Until you asked for her hand—
WHEN I WAS YOUR AGE, it was her *hand*, young man.

Mark Twain,
And at the worst, Tom Paine,
Were the authors folks talked about.
Thank God, no Hemingway,
Folks weren't bold that way—
When my sister—your beloved aunt—came out;

The Chorus girls then all wore tights
And high necked long white nighties of nights
Boston wasn't the only place in God's green universe
Where Immodesty faced a certain ban—
WHEN I WAS YOUR AGE, nudity *was* immodesty, young man.

Kids from Dead Ends
Were not my friends
In the days of my innocent youth.
I obeyed the Golden Rule
Went to Sunday school
And chose my companions for integrity and truth.

I associated with boys like Edison, Herbert Hoover, and Ford.
Youths of such calibre by nothing were floored.
We knew pennies made dollars
So we saved them to invest in American Can—
When I was your age, if you got canned
You still had your can, Young Man.

WHEN I WAS YOUR AGE,
WHEN I WAS YOUR AGE,
WHEN I WAS YOUR AGE, YOUNG MAN.

Wouldn't It Be Nice

WOULDN'T IT BE NICE,
So nice believing kisses can be real?
WOULDN'T IT BE NICE
And wonderful if this is love you feel?

My heart would be a feather dancing,
Dancing in some mad whirl
But haven't I tried the idle chancing?
How many times have I cried
Over lips that have lied?

WOULDN'T IT BE NICE
So nice believing every "I love you",
Haven't I the right to gather up a dream or two?

I know that somewhere someone must be waiting
Who'll never, never let me go.
Darling, if you were the one. . . . .
Gee—
WOULDN'T IT BE NICE?

Rise and Meet the Sun Half Way

RISE AND MEET THE SUN HALF WAY,
Luck is just around the corner—
You're gonna turn that corner, if you
MEET THE SUN HALF WAY.

What a day for flying high.
Spread your wings and keep your chin up,
And if you keep a grin up,
Things will come your way.

Look, Sir, you're in luck, Sir—
Here's a buck sir, buy the town!

Who cares for a dollar
When I can holler.
Try an' keep me down!

MEET THE SUN HALF WAY
Every day's a brand new day—say!
Then luck is sure to stop you . . .
Grab you . . .
And bop you!
It's gonna be a great day
When you RISE AND MEET THE SUN HALF WAY!

CHORUS:
RISE AND MEET THE SUN HALF WAY—
Maybe there'll be rain from heaven,
You'll hit your lucky seven—
This might be your day!

RISE AND MEET THE SUN HALF WAY
Just believe that you're the berries.
Life's just a bowl of cherries—
Clouds will roll away.

Wake up early birdie
When the roosters start to crow,
Give out to your neighbors
Like Colombo on the radio—So

RISE AND MEET THE SUN HALF WAY
Open your heart today! Say!

Maybe your love will find you . . .

Bind you . . .
Entwine you!

Leave Mister Blues behind you—
RISE AND MEET THE SUN HALF WAY!

Two of Us

VERSE
Life is full of trials and tribulations;
It's no vacation
If the truth be known.
But love can make the future seem much brighter,
The burden lighter—
If you're not alone . . .

Ever since time has begun—
Two hearts are better than one.

CHORUS
TWO OF US
Can find the way together
TWO OF US
Wont' be afraid together

We don't need four leaf clovers—
Who needs a lucky charm?
Where there's a will there's a way
Long as we stay—together.

TWO OF US
A melody that's blending, for
TWO OF US
It's love without an ending.
We've got each other—
Let's thank the stars up above that
TWO OF US found love.

It's Hard to Be a Lady All Night Long

IT'S HARD TO BE A LADY ALL NIGHT LONG,
It's just a little hop from right to wrong.
I get tired reading

'Bout the things I'm needing,
Who wants to keep on reading all night long.

IT'S HARD TO BE A LADY—Heaven knows
Even though I'm fifty and each wrinkle shows
I'm no Aphrodite
When I'm in a nightie—
But when lights are out who the devil knows?!

A-Razz-ma-tazzy and a zass-zoo-zazz!
A-razz-ma-tazzy and a zazz-zoo-zazz
Scat it high! Scat it low!
Baby I'm rarin' to go!
Yeooow!

IT'S HARD TO BE A LADY—so darn hard
When you've got a body, but no body-guard.
Any proposition
Ignites the ignition
When it's "As you like it"—just to quote the Bard.

IT'S HARD TO BE A LADY—Oh, my, yes!
Being otherwise is so darn effortless.
Not that I'm abnormal—
Just a bit informal—
And at night I seem to crave more tenderness.

Ho-de-ho-dee-hi!
Skee-daddle-de-yeah!
Fill em up again and let's get high!
Skee-skaddle-dee-do-do!

IT'S HARD TO BE A LADY ALL NIGHT constantly.
All day long is rather long enough for me.
When the moon starts rising
I need fraternizing
That's when I go in for living recklessly.

IT'S HARD TO BE A LADY—no can do!
I'm fed up to here with playing "ingenue"
Though it isn't cricket
I'm for being wicked,
And I'll pay the Piper when the night is through!

Walk Me Around through the Village

Somehow we know spring has come again
To Washington Square.

Hearts beat in spring to love's old refrain
In Washington Square.

Time for a sweet rendezvous—
What could be better than dreamy romancing with you?

CHORUS
Walk me around through the village
Then lead me the longest way home.

I've got a room in the village
But hate to walk home alone.

Let's take a stroll through Christopher Street—
Stop at the Jumble Shop and eat.

We'll kiss on each street in the village
And maybe I'll never go home.
Walk me around through the village
Let's linger along the way home.

My room looks over the village,
But I view the view alone.

Let's take the air in Washington Square

Find us a bench with no one there.

We'll kiss on each street in the village,
And maybe I'll never go home.

Funny how empty a bench can be
When there's only me.
Big lonesome town—
Lost what I found—
Wish I were dancing, I wish I were dancing—

Waltz me around through the Village
The round-about way to go home.
You'd love my room in the Village,
I hate to climb up alone.

Let's lean on the fence in Sheridan Square,
Gaze in your eyes by lamp light there.
We'll kiss on each street in the Village
And maybe I'll never go home

Maybe we'll never go home. . . . ..

I'm Learning to Live All Alone

I'M LEARNING TO LIVE ALL ALONE
To be my own keeper,
My own cook and sweeper,
I'M LEARNING TO LIVE ALL ALONE

I'M LEARNING TO stand on my own,
I'm cutting my niche in
One room and a kitchen
Complete with a book and a phone.

There's no one who's tied me to his hemisphere
And no one's beside me when twilight is near . . .

I'M LEARNING TO LIVE ALL ALONE,
There's no use pretending,
It looks like I'm spending
The rest of my life all alone—!
Since day-dreams are all you can own. . . .
I'M LEARNING TO LIVE ALL ALONE.

Not Today

You're only worth a nickel in any man's land,
Worth slightly more than four cents—
I'm also worth a nickel in any man's land—
Somehow it just doesn't make sense!
And even you, Mr. Nickel, the last pal I've got
Will slip through my fingers as likely as not
For you'll find a home in some welcoming slot
But me . . .

I pound the pavement—lookin' for a job—
An unemployed someone a guy in the mob.

I'm not mad at the world
I'm an easy-going-guy—

And up till today
I kept the sun in my eye.
But now I feel scared
Though I can't tell you why.

Not too long ago I was a kid on the Coast
Like any of the Kids you see around
I had a mother and brothers—a little better than most
And a Dad—the best darned druggist in town.

Well, down in the cellar I had a work bench
Completely equipped from pliers to wrench
Gee, Dad was so proud of how handy I was—
He told everybody the things his kid does,
Yeah, but that was yesterday. . . .

Not today.
Today. . . .

I'm lookin' for a job, any kind of work
There ain't nothin' too hard, there's nothing I'll shirk
I've got muscles real hard
And a will made of steel.
All that I want's to be a cog in the wheel—
Some way to get by—
Just a fair and square deal.

CHORUS
Not today—come back tomorrow,
Not today—come back tomorrow,
Not today—come back tomorrow,
Not today—come back tomorrow,
Not today! Not today! Not today!

I've wheeled at a pick—and a shovel I've used
I've helped carry bricks till my hands were all bruised,
I've slung hash in the diners to earn me a bite
I've been a night watchman and stayed up through the night,
I've cut people's lawns for a lunch and a wave—
Then once on the road I even slept in a cave.
I've been rolled in a box-car by some guys I didn't know

But Cripes, I'm not kickin', that's part of the show
But I got a kick comin' cause I'm getting no place.
The same as a comet that's shooting through space
We're both looking somewhere to find a home base.
Not today.

Not today, come back tomorrow!
Not today, come back tomorrow . . .

It's hard to keep hoping,
Just hoping along,
When the cards are against you and everything's wrong
When a fellow's got nothing to keep his hope strong—
And what about love—?

Come back tomorrow!

People Like Us

People like us
Have to live from day to day.
For people like us
There has been no easy way
Though long ago we learned to know
Life may push you to and fro,
We carry dreams from day to day.

People like us
Wait for cabins in the sky.
For people like us
There's no pie until we die.
Though you and I have learned to see
What a see saw fate can be,
We carry dreams from day to day.

Life should flow
Like a dreamy river tide
Hearts should glow
With the love that burns inside.

But people like us,
We find rainbows hard to hold
And people like us

Never find a pot of gold.
We buy our rings installment-planned,
Still we're walking hand-in-hand—
We carry dreams from day to day.

Devil Is Responsible

VERSE
Why must we quarrel?
You think I'm immoral
'Cause I keep shadowing you.
I don't want to do it,
But I'm driven to it—
There is nothing I can do.
What earthy "Isery"
Could brew such hellish misery?

CHORUS
THE DEVIL IS RESPONSIBLE
For my loving you—
Something down inside of me
Makes me do the things I do.

THE DEVIL IS RESPONSIBLE
He's led me astray—
Got Heebie-Jeebies all day long,
At night there's hell to pay.

If the Devil would release me,
From this trance I'm in,
Maybe there wouldn't be
This urge to . . . roll in sin!

THE DEVIL IS RESPONSIBLE
FOR MY LOVING YOU,
In a tizzy,
Dumb and dizzy!
I'll give the devil his due. . . .
Cause Baby. . . . the devil is you!

THE DEVIL IS RESPONSIBLE
For this sudden heat.

He's put a midnight hex on me
And he's made me indiscreet.

THE DEVIL IS RESPONSIBLE
Now I'm hypnotized
Hallucinations all the time
These dreams I dream ain't wise!

If the devil would just let me,
I'd forget your charms. . . . .
But he keeps on pushing, pushing me. . . .
Right into your arms!

THE DEVIL IS RESPONSIBLE
For my heart's defeat.
Love's a Mickey—
Finn that's tricky—
A sweet but a devilish brew
When Baby . . . the Devil is you!

Cantatas

Many composers sought lyrics and librettos from Hughes, attracted to his simple, yet elegant, lyricism. He complied when he could. The African American composer Margaret Bonds was an old friend: she and Hughes had collaborated on *Tropics after Dark,* Bonds often shared her work and plans with him, and they had contemplated an opera, "Job."[1] Hughes first sent Bonds *Ballad of the Brown King* in 1954; this text, dated October 28, 1960, notes it is the version set by Bonds.

Jan Meyerowitz began collaborating with Hughes in the late 1940s; their first major project was *The Barrier.* Two more operas and several cantatas followed. Regarding *Five Foolish Virgins,* Meyerowitz recalled to biographer Arnold Rampersad Hughes's fondness for the story in Matthew 25:1–13: "He assumed that those five foolish virgins just had to be Negro . . . because they weren't ever on time." When the work was presented on February 11, 1954, at Town Hall in New York by a choir conducted by Margaret Hillis, its music was panned. There was no comment about the libretto. However, Meyerowitz's and Hughes's next work, *The Glory around His Head,* was a triumph. Following the performance on April 14, 1955, in Carnegie Hall by the New York Phil-harmonic Orchestra, conducted by Dimitri Mitropoulos and sung by the Westminster Choir led by Margaret Hillis, one reviewer applauded: "An arresting score, packed with tell-tale flashes of originality and a driv-ing attraction for the folk-like incantations of Langston Hughes's poetry text." Meyerowitz thought it the most important thing they had done together.[2] Finally, at the composer's request, Hughes wrote *Godly Is the House of God* in June 1955.[3]

Let Us Remember, alternately titled "Requiem for Martyrs," was com-missioned in 1964 by the Union of American Hebrew Congregations for its biennial meeting. Composer David Amram recalls an early meeting with a rabbi who feared Hughes might not "understand this particu-lar Jewish feeling we're after." Amram continues: "Hughes replied very casually, 'I understand, Rabbi, and I think I know the kind of feeling because it's something that's part of me. You see, my grandfather was Jewish.' "[4] Of the collaboration, Amram records: "Because Langston was such a consummate lyric artist and had written so much for voice, he was familiar with the problems that composers have. He presented me with many beautiful poems and allowed me to use whichever parts of them I wished."[5] Performed on November 15, 1965, at the San Fran-cisco Opera House by the Oakland Orchestra and a 150-voice chorus, the work garnered superlatives: "A stunning world premier of David Amram's all-embracing choral memoriam for all men that have died to preserve freedom," wrote one critic. "Amram's neoromantic six-part work spoke an eloquent language from the very poetic pen of Langston Hughes. The universal message set to music from the traditional 'Yiskor' is a work of moving profundity, of nobility, of compassion and of sincerity." "A frank and simple sermon in six long sections, in which hope answers horror in the final stanza"; "Let not the song be a dirge—a new world's in the making," wrote another.

With the exception of *Let Us Remember*, the texts are taken from typescripts in the Langston Hughes Papers. David Amram graciously supplied a copy of *Let Us Remember* as he received it from Hughes.

The Five Foolish Virgins

1953
Music by Jan Meyerowitz

Derived from St. Matthew, 25:1–13

I
THE KINGDOM OF HEAVEN
IS LIKENED TO TEN VIRGINS
WHO TOOK THEIR LAMPS
AND WENT TO MEET THE BRIDEGROOM—
TEN VIRGINS WITH THEIR LAMPS
WHO WENT TO MEET THE BRIDEGROOM—
AND NO MAN KNEW WHEN HE WOULD COME.

FIVE OF THOSE VIRGINS
HAD LAMPS THAT WERE QUITE EMPTY,
FOR THEIR OIL THEY HAD FORGOTTEN—
AND HAD HEADS THAT WERE QUITE EMPTY,
AND HAD HEARTS THAT WERE QUITE EMPTY
AND NO THOUGHT OF THE BRIDEGROOM
NOR WHEN HE WOULD BE COMING—
FOR NO MAN KNEW WHEN HE WOULD COME.

BUT THE FIVE OTHER VIRGINS
HAD THEIR LAMPS FILLED WITH OIL,
ALL FILLED WITH OIL FOR BURNING—
ALL READY FOR THE BRIDEGROOM—
FOR NO MAN KNEW WHEN HE WOULD COME.

THE KINGDOM OF HEAVEN
IS LIKENED TO TEN VIRGINS
WHO TOOK THEIR LAMPS
AND WENT TO MEET THE BRIDEGROOM—
TEN VIRGINS WITH THEIR LAMPS
WHO WENT TO MEET THE BRIDEGROOM—
AND NO MAN KNEW WHEN HE WOULD COME.

II
SAID THE FIVE FOOLISH VIRGINS,
OH, GIVE US OF YOUR OIL,
BEHOLD THE BRIDEGROOM COMETH,
AND OUR LAMPS, THEY ARE NOT BURNING!
OH, GIVE US OF YOUR OIL,
BEHOLD THE BRIDEGROOM COMETH!
THE BRIDEGROOM COMETH!

SAID THE FIVE WISE VIRGINS,
GO SEEK YE THEM THAT SELL,
AND BUY OIL FROM THE SELLERS
FOR YOUR LAMPS THAT ARE NOT BURNING—
FOR BEHOLD THE BRIDEGROOM COMETH
AND OUR LAMPS ARE TRIMMED AND BURNING
OUR LAMPS ARE TRIMMED AND LIGHTED
AND WE HAVE NO OIL FOR YOU.

III
AND THE BRIDEGROOM COMETH,
AND THEY WENT INTO THE MARRIAGE.
HE WAS TALL AS A PINE TREE
AND HIS EYES WERE STARS OF MORNING.
AND HIS SMILE WAS LIKE THE SUNRISE
AND HIS FACE WAS LIKE THE DAWNING.
AND THE FIVE WISE VIRGINS
IN ADORATION TURNING
WENT INTO THE MARRIAGE
WITH THEIR LAMPS TRIMMED AND BURNING,
WITH THEIR LAMPS TRIMMED AND BURNING.

LONG DID YOU WAIT, MY CHILDREN,
IN THE NIGHT
WITH YOUR LAMPS
AT THE DOOR.

LONG DID WE WAIT, BUT PATIENT,
LAMPS A-LIGHT
IN THE NIGHT
TO ADORE.

IV
BUT THE FIVE FOOLISH VIRGINS,
FOOLISH, FOOLISH VIRGINS,
WERE LATE IN RETURNING,
DELAYED IN RETURNING
FROM THEIR TRIP TO THE MARKET,
DELAYED IN RETURNING
SO THE DOORS WERE CLOSED AND BOLTED.

OPEN! OPEN! OPEN!
CRIED THE FIVE FOOLISH VIRGINS.
WE PRAY THEE, PRAY THEE, OPEN!
CRIED THE FIVE FOOLISH VIRGINS.
BUT THE DOOR DID NOT OPEN.
NO, THE DOOR DID NOT OPEN,
AND THE FIVE FOOLISH VIRGINS
HEARD THE BRIDEGROOM SAYING:

YOU KNOW NOT THE DAY
AND YOU KNOW NOT THE HOUR
WHEN THE SON OF A MAN IS COMING—
FOR NO MAN KNOWS WHEN HE WILL COME.
AND YOU WHO ARE NOT READY
FIND THE DOOR CLOSED AND BOLTED.
AND THE EARTH WILL SPLIT ASUNDER
AND SWALLOW UP THE TARDY!

V
THE KINGDOM OF HEAVEN
IS LIKENED TO TEN VIRGINS
WHO TOOK THEIR LAMPS
AND WENT TO MEET THE BRIDEGROOM—
AND NO MAN KNEW WHEN HE WOULD COME.
BUT FIVE WERE READY,
WITH THEIR LAMPS BRIGHT AND BURNING.
AND THEY WENT IN WITH THE BRIDEGROOM.
BUT FIVE WERE FOOLISH
AND THEIR LAMPS, THEY WERE NOT BURNING,
AT THE BRIDEGROOM'S COMING.

BE YOU THEREFORE READY!
READY! READY! READY!
LIGHTS BRIGHT AND BURNING,
WHEN THE BRIDEGROOM COMETH—
READY WHEN THE BRIDEGROOM COMETH!

Godly Is the House of God
A Song for the Dedication and Daily Rededication of a Church

1955
Music by Jan Meyerowitz

Upon this rock of faith is built
This church of God's eternal light,
And from this church of faith will glow
The love of God's eternal right.
    A nest of swallows He has made,
    And in my soul a nest of love
    Where I may light the candles of
    My faith from His eternal love.
This church a rock of faith shall be,
A godly house eternally,
And in this house of faith will shine
The holy light of God divine.
    How godly, yes, how godly is,
    How godly is the house of God!
    How godly, godly, godly is,
    How godly is the house of God!
This rock of faith, this church of God,
Eternal light, eternal right,
Where I may light the candles of
My faith from His eternal love!
    How godly, yes, how godly, oh!
    How godly is the house of God!
    The house, the house, the house of God!
    How godly is the house of God!
Of God! My god! Of God, my God! . . . .
    Extra verses:[1]
Make a joyful noise unto the Lord,
Filling His house with praise.
Enter His gates with thanksgiving,
Paeans of glory raise!

His power is everlasting,
Clothed in Majesty,
Mightier than the waters
Of the mighty sea.

Ringed are His walls with glory,
Filled are His halls with song,
Blest by the grace of His story,
Blest by the grace of His son.

Delighting in His statues,
Rejoicing in His word,
Filling the air with His praises
Till all the world has heard.

Rock of my faith! Church of my God,
Unto eternity! . . . .
Power everlasting! . . . .
God of majesty! God of majesty!
How godly, oh how godly. . . . etc. . . .

The Glory around His Head
A Cantata of the Resurrection

1957
Music by Jan Meyerowitz

I. Musical Prelude

II. *MY LORD NOT WANTED*

All his life by some folks not wanted,
At the Inn not wanted.
No, you can't be born in here!
Jesus Christ not wanted.
With the babe they fled to Egypt.
Pharaoh don't want you here!
In the temple not wanted!

Jesus Christ not wanted—
All His life not wanted
By the men who hate,
By the men who cheat,
By the men who live by the sword,
By the kings and princes,
And the robbers and killers—
None of them wanted my Lord!

My Lord, not wanted!
No, not wanted—
Except to throw to the mob,
Except to lead to the Cross,
Except to crucify,
Except to watch Him die—

Then He was wanted!
Wanted! . . . . . Wanted!
With two thieves He was wanted!

To carry His Cross—wanted!
To die—wanted!
Crucify Him!
Crucify Him!
Wanted!

THY WILL BE DONE

Jesus prayed in the garden in the evening.
Jesus prayed in the garden all alone.
Those who came to watch with Him were sleeping.
As He prayed in the garden all alone.

Jesus knew that one there would betray Him,
Another would deny Him before dawn.
With swords and staves they'd come to take Him,
And He would be their prisoner at dawn.

Oh, let this bitter cup pass from me!
But if it by Thy will, Thy will be done.
Alone was Jesus in the garden,
Alone—alone—was Mary's son.

IV. THE ROAD TO CALVARY

So the soldiers came and led Jesus away.
Pilate washed his hands of it all,
And Jesus was sentenced to die.
Jesus bearing His cross
Into a place called Golgotha
Where they crucified Him.

MY BODY AND MY BLOOD

When Jesus died at Calvary
For what the world believes,
On either side upon a Cross
They hung two thieves—

Two members of a lowly mob
Who stole to get their bread

Were tied upon a Cross that day
To taste of death instead.

One thief looked at Christ and said,
If you're so great
As your followers swear—
Save me! Save yourself!
Save my brother thief there!

But he did not speak for his brother,
High on the gallows tree,
For the other thief cried only,
Lord, remember me!

Christ had thorns upon His head
And in His mouth was gall.
From His palms the blood ran red
And on the ground did fall.

For the sins of man I suffer.
For the sins of man I die—
My body and my blood
Are the answer to your cry.

In the garden one betrayed me.
And Peter denied me thrice.
But you who cry, Remember me!
Go with me to Paradise.

VI. *THE CRUCIFIXION AND THE GLORY*

The soldiers took a spear
And pierced Him in the side,
And he died.

Don't you see
The Glory around His head?
Don't you see
The Glory around His head?
People thought that He was dead:
But don't you see the Glory,
The Glory around His head?

It was on a hill
That they nailed Him to the Cross.
It was on a hill so high.
It was on a hill
That they crucified my Lord—
But my Lord did not die!

Down they took His body.
They laid it in a tomb.
They sealed it with a stone.
But when they came to seek Him
The stone had rolled away:
And empty was the tomb!

He is not here,
For He is risen!
Not here! For He is risen!

Jesus lives!
He has not died!
Life eternal
Glorified!

On this Easter morning,
Brighter than the dawning,
Praise the Glory round his head,
Praise the blood that flowed from His side!
Praise the precious bread of life!
On this Easter morning
Brighter than the dawning
Praise the Glory round His head!
Don't you see the Glory round His head!
Glory!

Ballad of the Brown King
A Christmas Carol

1960
Music by Margaret Bonds

I
OF THE THREE WISE MEN WHO CAME TO THE KING,
ONE WAS A BROWN MAN, SO THEY SING.
OF THE THREE WISE MEN WHO FOLLOWED THE STAR,
ONE WAS A BROWN KING FROM AFAR.

II
THEY BROUGHT FINE GIFTS OF SPICES AND GOLD
IN JEWELED BOXED OF BEAUTY UNTOLD.
UNTO HIS HUMBLE MANGER THEY CAME
AND BOWED THEIR HEADS IN JESUS' NAME.

III
SING HALLELUJAH! HALLELUJAH!
HALLELUJAH! CHRIST, THE KING!

IV
MARY HAD A LITTLE BABY,
JESUS, THAT WAS HIS NAME.
ALL THE WORLD BECAME MUCH BRIGHTER
WHEN JESUS, LITTLE JESUS, CHRIST CHILD, CAME.
THAT WAS IN A LOWLY MANGER,
OUTSIDE THE NIGHT WAS COLD,
BUT WITHIN THAT LOWLY MANGER
BEHOLD HOW WARM HIS LOVE IS, OH, BEHOLD!
I, SO LOST, SO LOST AND LONELY,
NEVER MORE SHALL HE BE ALONE.
MARY HAD A LITTLE BABY,
JESUS, THAT WAS HIS NAME.
ALL THE WORLD BECAME MUCH BRIGHTER
WHEN JESUS, LITTLE JESUS, CAME.

V

NOW WHEN JESUS WAS BORN IN BETHLEHEM
IN THE DAYS OF HEROD, THE KING,
BEHOLD, THERE CAME WISE MEN FROM THE EAST
SAYING, WHERE IS HE? WHERE IS HE?
WHERE IS HE THAT IS BORN?
FOR WE HAVE SEEN HIS STAR,
HIS STAR IN THE EAST,
WE HAVE SEEN HIS STAR IN THE EAST!
WE HAVE SEEN HIS STAR!
OH, WE HAVE SEEN,
WE HAVE SEEN
HIS STAR!
HIS STAR!
STAR!
STAR!

VI

COULD ONE KING HAVE BEEN AN ETHIOPE
FROM AN ETHIOPIAN LAND?
I DO NOT KNOW JUST WHO HE WAS,
BUT HE WAS A KINGLY MAN.
COULD ONE HAVE BEEN AN EGYPTIAN KING
FROM THE LAND WHERE THE SUN SHINES BRIGHT?
I DO NOT KNOW JUST WHO HE WAS—
BUT HE FOLLOWED A STAR THAT NIGHT.
OH, COULD ONE HAVE BEEN A TALL DARK KING,
MAYBE ARABIAN?
I DO NOT KNOW JUST WHO HE WAS,
BUT HE WAS A WISE, WISE MAN.
OH, AMONG THE KINGS WHO CAME TO CALL,
ONE WAS DARK LIKE ME!
OH, I'M SO GLAD THAT HE WAS THERE,
OUR LITTLE CHRIST TO SEE.
    SING HALLELUJAH TO OUR KING!
    HALLELUJAH THEY DID SING!

VII

OH, SING OF THE KING WHO WAS TALL AND BROWN
CROSSING THE DESERT FROM A DISTANT TOWN,

CROSSING THE DESERT IN A CARAVAN
HIS GIFTS TO BRING FROM A DISTANT LAND,
HIS GIFTS TO BRING FROM A PALM-TREE LAND
ACROSS THE SAND BY CARAVAN,
WITH A SINGLE STAR TO GUIDE HIS WAY
TO BETHLEHEM WHERE THE CHRIST CHILD LAY.
OH, SING OF A KING WHO WAS TALL AND BROWN
AND THE OTHER KINGS THAT THIS KING FOUND
WHO CAME TO PUT THEIR PRESENTS DOWN
IN A LOWLY MANGER IN BETHLEHEM TOWN
WHERE THE KING OF KINGS, A BABE, WAS FOUND!
WHERE THE KING OF KINGS,
A BABE, WAS FOUND!
THREE KINGS—WHO CAME TO THE KING OF KINGS!
AND ONE WAS TALL AND BROWN.
OH, SING OF THE KING WHO WAS TALL AND BROWN!

VIII

THAT WAS A CHRISTMAS LONG AGO
WHEN THE THREE WISE MEN THERE BOWED SO LOW—
THE THREE WISE MEN WHO FOLLOWED THE STAR—
AND ONE WAS A BROWN MAN FROM AFAR.
THE THREE WISE MEN WHO CAME TO THE KING—
OH, ONE WAS A BROWN MAN SO THEY SING!

IX

ALLELUJAH, CHRIST THE KING!
ALLELUJAH, THEY DID SING!
ALLELUJAH, CHRIST THE KING!
ALLELUJAH! ALLELUJAH!
CHRIST. . . . . THE KING!

Let Us Remember

1965
Music by David Amram

I. LET THE SONG BE NOT A DIRGE

Let the song be not a dirge
no sack-cloth words and crying
but rather let the song be strong
with the greatness of your dying

Let the song take wings and rise
from the fire like a Phoenix flying
flying straight unto the sun
with the glory of your dying

Oh, mighty martyrs of ages past
oh, martyrs of today
the hatreds that beset your paths
faith will wipe away.

When the springtime sunrise comes
and glorious dawn is breaking
from the memories of your martyrdom
a new world's in the making.

II. HONORED DEAD

A little speech
for the speechless
a little prayer
for those who have forgotten how to pray.
A song for all singers without a song—
made from the roots of memory,
and the bark on the freedom tree,

and the leaves that have fallen from its crest,
that fall each time when winter comes—
winter that has to be
the winter that kills the highest leaves
at the top of the tree—
but *not* the roots
nor the bark
nor the trunk of the freedom tree,
not the roots of the song,
nor the memories from which the song is made
nor the prayers once prayed
nor the speeches once said
by the myriad millions
of the martyred dead.

Requiem for martyrs!
Music
for the words are said
music
to honor the honored dead.

Should names be named—
or none—
in honor of each nameless one?
The martyred names,
yesterday dying, alive today—
The Roman raids, the Avignon, the Crusades,
the inquisition, auto-da-fé—
victims in tapestries, mosaics on floor,
safe relief at history's door.
Hannah and her seven sons, Rabbi Akiba,
Gershon of Mainz, Trempledor!
Ah, Kiddush Hashem! Ah, Kiddush Hashem!
    Ah, Kiddush Hashem!
To sanctify the name of God—
echoed! echoed! echoed! echoed!
For the martyred names in the history's sod
our tears flow in the heart of God.
Our grief, transmitted everywhere,
tel-starred in the cosmic air—
Ah, Kiddush Hashem! Ah, Kiddush Hashem!
    Ah, Kiddush Hashem!

Our tears flow in the heart of God.
Echoed! Echoed! Echoed! Echoed!
Should these names stand for all who
perished that the freedom tree
might grow tall?
The freedom tree—
ever taller—
through each dark winter its green leaves fall—
lest the tree forget that summer is not all,
the freedom tree ever taller,
in time of trial its green leaves fall

Requiem for martyrs!
music a song
after the words are said.
Music a song
to honor the honored dead.

III. LET US REMEMBER

Remembering Egypt,
let not the oppressed become oppressors.
Remembering Ahasuerus,
let not the oppressed become oppressors.
Remembering Genghis,
let not the oppressed become oppressors.
Remembering Nicolas and all the Tzars,
let not the oppressed become oppressors.
Remembering the Cossacks of the Don
    let not the oppressed become oppressors,
      remembering all the land and all the times between—
let not the oppressed become oppressors.
Poland, Spain, Bavaria, Turkmenistan,
let not the oppressed become oppressors.
Auschwitz, Dachau, Buchenwald
let not the oppressed become oppressors.
Remember! Remember! Remember!
let not the oppressed become oppressors
Oh, remember—
Montgomery, Selma, and Savannah,
let not the oppressed become oppressors.

The hurricane lash and the fiery wind
that destroys only to begin again—
When faith like a Phoenix from the earth takes off
to spread its wings aloft, aloft—
but ever its eye on this earth of ours
where man must live, and man must forgive,
and forgiving begin again remembering,
lest the circle repeat, repeat, repeat
let not the oppressed become the oppressors.
Remembering always lest—
let not the oppressed become the oppressors.
let us remember
let not the oppressed become the oppressors
Oh, let us remember—
let not the oppressed become the oppressors.

IV. THE DREAM

Whose is the dream of freedom?
and in what soil may it take root?
only God's rain and the dew of God
can nourish its earthy shoot.
Only through the greatness of God can the sprout spring
from the root,
the root becomes tree,
and the dream becomes me.

Dust, wind-blown, to earth returns
to lift from the spirit eternal
lifted from the grace of God.
From the broken stem springs the new twig now,
from the broken trunk another bough,
from the sundered tree where lightning has struck,
a new world rises from the muck
becoming a thousand roots, buds,
a billion leaves, a flowering tree
whose each new seed
is the dream in me,
blossoming into the freedom tree.
From the broken stem springs the new twig now
from the broken trunk another bough,

dust, windblown, to earth returns
to lift from the sod—

Whose is the dream of freedom?
and in what soil may it take root?
Only God's rain and the dew of God
can nourish its earthy shoot.

V. HOPE

Blessed hope of mankind
speaking for the right,
seeking, seeking, seeking,
seeking through the night.
Blessed be the living!
Blessed by the light!
Blessed in forgiving—
sunrise after night.
Blessed hope of mankind,
seeking for the right.

Beaten by the wind, man's hope,
battered and beaten,
bending like a tree in the wind,
broken, even broken, yes? Broken—
Broken only to grow again!
Only to rise from its roots—
Man's hope! Man's dream! Man's song!
This song I sing—
Blessed be the living!
Blessed by the light!
Blessed in forgiving—
Sunrise after night.
Man's hope, man's hope in forgiving—the light.

VI. FINALE

Let the song be not a dirge,
no sackcloth words and crying,
but rather let the song be strong
with the greatness of your dying.

Let the song take wings and rise
from the fire like a Phoenix flying,
flying straight unto the sun
with the glory of your dying.

Oh, mighty martyrs of ages past,
Oh, martyrs of today,
the hatred that beset your paths,
faith will wipe away.

When the springtime sunrise comes
and the glorious dawn is breaking,
from the memories of your martyrdom
a new world's in the making.

The ancient darkness lasted long,
the centuries moved slowly,
but always, when the sun broke through,
the ark was still there holy.

Oftimes oppressors' will prevailed
in vile and deathly manner
but when gentler breezes blew
our faith was still a banner.

When the springtime sunrise comes
and glorious dawn is breaking
from the memories of your martyrdom
a new world's in the making.

O, martyrs of our yesterdays
in shrouds of honor sleeping,
we build your shining temples now
for joy, not for weeping.

You died that life be not a dirge
of sackcloth words and crying,
but that tomorrow's songs be strong
with the glory of your dying.

The greatness and the glory,
The greatness and the glory,
The greatness and the glory,
The glory of your dying.

Lyrics

Langston Hughes wrote hundreds of songs over his career: blues, gospel, art songs, and popular ballads in a variety of moods, once defending his attention to this activity by saying, "I've always wanted to be a songwriter . . . words to music reach so many more people than mere poetry on a printed page." As Arnold Rampersad observes, it is an odd comment for a poet. Hughes's outpouring, in fact, typically had a more practical goal. "The Lord has blessed me with ASCAP," he wrote his agent Max Lieber. And to his friend Arna Bontemps: "[M]y *determination* is to keep on! Just like dice, you have to pass *sometime*—if your bankroll will just hold out till 'sometime' comes!"[1]

Hughes most delighted in his talent for writing blues and gospel; for some of his gospel songs he even composed music, although by many accounts, he had absolutely no musical knowledge and could not carry a tune. Rampersad records that others would "listen intently to his moaning, then pick out a tune on the piano," questioning him until what they played matched the tune in his head. Yet, after working with him on *Street Scene,* Kurt Weill commented that for someone musically untrained, Hughes had "the most musical sense of anybody I have ever known."[2]

Given Hughes's immense output, the selection below is, of necessity, arbitrary. It includes some of the lyrics Hughes wrote to be set to music that never found a place in his own musicals and gospel plays, or in the work of others for which he was lyricist. The selection suggests the range of composers with whom he worked but is representative only. The most extensive information about Hughes's songs and musical settings of his poetry is Kenneth P. Neilson, *The World of Langston Hughes Music*.[3] Unless otherwise noted, the lyrics here are reproduced from typescripts held in the Langston Hughes Papers. Sometimes a note on the typescript will indicate that it reflects the lyric as set to the music, but the material is not consistent in this regard.

The Thirties

Ethiopia Marches On

1935
Music by Thelma Brown
Arrangement by Nora Holt

A note by Hughes on the typescript records that the song was "sung at NAACP, etc. during the war in Abyssinia"; another copy of the song says, "Written for performance by the Brown Sisters during the Ethiopian War."

Ethiopia, stretch forth your mighty hand.
Let the King of Kings lead his ebony band
Till the Conquering Lion of Judah's roar
Says, enemy, GO! And come no more.
Abyssinia, let the war drums roll!
Ethiopia, homeland of my soul!
I'm gonna stand by you till every foe is gone.
Abyssinia, march on and on!

Bow your head in prayer.
Lift your soul in song.
Let the war be short
And the freedom long.
Abyssinia! Abyssinia!
Abyssinia! March on and on!

I have been a slave.
I've been beaten down.
But you cannot keep me,
Keep me on the ground.

Ethiopian warriors
With your spears of gold.
Don't let Mussolini
Get into your fold.

Ethiopian women
Offer up their lives
On the field of battle
As a sacrifice.

Where the mighty Nile's
Great headwaters rise
And the black man's flag
In bright freedom flies.

All you colored peoples,
No matter where you be,
Take for your slogan:
AFRICA BE FREE!

All you colored peoples,
Be a man at last.
Say to Mussolini,
No! You shall not pass!

Nobody knows
The trouble I've seen—
But when I rise
I'm gonna rise mean!
Abyssinia! Abyssinia!
Abyssinia! March on and on!

Carnera thought that
He would have his way—
But the big Brown Bomber
Said Hey! . . . Hey! . . . Hey!

Mussolini's men
They may swing their capes—
But when Harlem starts
She's a cage of apes!

I would have this world
To be fine and free,
But when I say free
That means you and ME.

Get together, women!
Get together, men!
Let us tell the world
That this war must end.

Mussolini wants
To have his peace of mind,

But the peace we want
Is for all mankind.

And the peace we want
Means *every* man is free.
Listen, Mussolini,
Don't you mess with me!

Abyssinia, let the war drums roll!
Ethiopia, homeland of my soul!
I'm gonna stand by you till every foe is gone.
Abyssinia, march on and on!

The Forties

Mad Scene from Woolworth's

Music by Elliott Carpenter

Used in *Jump for Joy,* the 1941 socially oriented revue for which Duke
Ellington provided the music. Notes in LHP indicate that Charles Leonard composed a sketch version of the song for the revue, but the music
is by Elliott Carpenter. A letter from Carpenter to Hughes, February 25,
1941, mentions this piece and "How Can I Fall in Love" as the only two
songs used by Ellington in the revue of the several they submitted. In
a letter dated February 7, 1941, Carpenter tells Hughes he is rewriting
"Mad with a Dime."[4] This probably is the rewritten version.

I went down on the Avenue
With only ten cents to my name,
But when I passed the Ten Cent Store
I thought I'd go in just the same.
I walked up and down between the counters
Where so many pretty things are piled,
And what to buy with that one thin dime
Almost drove me wild.

Now I'm standing in the Ten Cent Store
Going mad with a dime.
If I only had a dollar
I could have such a good time.

I could buy some peanut brittle
And a jigsaw puzzle, too.
But I've got only a dime
So I don't know what to do.

Over there I see some lipsticks,
And here I see some lace
And on Counter Number Three
A hat-frame to fit my face.

Back in the hardware section
I see a sifter I've been needing,
Down here is some fish food
For my goldfish that needs feeding,
And over yonder is a rhyming book
On how to make songs rhyme—
So I'm standing in the Ten Cent Store
Going mad with a dime!

Shall I get a frame for the picture—
Or a picture for the frame?
Shall I spend my dime for hairpins—
Or get a bingo game?
Shall I buy a curtain pole—
Or shall I buy a curtain?
A plaster for my aching back—
Or one for my corn that's hurtin'?
Shall I eat my dime up
In cakes and soda pop—
Or go across the aisle
And get a sofa pillow top?
The struggle is terrific!
Oh! I can't make up my mind!
So I'm standing in the Ten Cent Store
Gong mad with a dime.

Shall I buy a box for pencils—
Or a pencil for the box?
Shall I buy some sox for baby—
Or a baby for the sox?
Shall I buy some eggs to beat—
Or a beater for the eggs?

Shall I buy myself some long drawers
'Cause these short ones freeze my legs?
Shall I buy a powder puff?
Or a ten-cent box of powder?
Shall I buy *two* nickel whistles
Or a dime one that blows louder?
Shall I buy a porcelain sauce pan
Or a sauce pan made of tin?
Or shall I buy a piggy bank
To put my one dime in?
Shall I buy a glass for the toothbrush—
Or a toothbrush for the glass?
Some paper for the shelves—
Or some paper for my Spanish class?
If I had a quarter
I'd buy both things at a time—
But I'm standing in the Woolworth Store
Going mad with a dime.

Shall I get some toilet soap for toilets?
Some Lux for lingerie?
Olderone for my sister—
Or some Life Buoy for me?
A strainer for the coffee?
Or some catnip for the cat?
A jabot for my mama?
Or a rat trap for the rat?
A tie rack? Or a towel rack?
Or a fancy bonbon plate?
Or one of them ten cent carpet slippers—
And TO HELL WITH THE TEN CENT MATE!!!
Should I get a turtle named Sid—
Or one who's name is Hyme?
Aw-ow-ooo-oo-o! I'm standing in the Five and Ten
Going mad with a dime!
            (RAVES)
Miss, gimme a malted milk!
No, make it a cherry coke!
No, wait! Gimme a banana split with hardware sauce—
Wrong! I mean lemon pie with whipped hammers!

Change it! I want a peanut butter bracelet!
No, a rat trap on rye!
I made a mistake, please—
Gimme a Listerine with lime!
Aw-oh! I'm standing in the Ten Cent Store
Going nuts with a dime!
      (YELLS MADLY, TOSSING DIME AWAY)
Yeoh-ooo-oo-o!

Madam, How Can I Fall In Love?

A Comedy Character Song to be sung by a Woman dressed as a Maid-of-All-Work, perhaps while bending over an ironing board as the phone keeps ringing, kids run in and out, dogs bark to be fed, etc.

Music by Elliott Carpenter

One day my madame said to me,
"How come you ain't got no boy-friend, Marie?"
I was serving, she was eating,
But what I said will bear repeating:

(Chorus)
When I work all day with no time to play,
Madame, how can I fall I love?
When I've fried your fish and I've washed every dish,
Madame, how can I fall in love?
When my hands are grimy from scrubbing the floor,
How can a maid find the key to love's door?
With a sleep-in job and no vacation,
How can I help breed the nation?
I work hard to get what I'm paid.
Madame, how can I fall in love?
My budget won't stand no beauty aid.
Madame, how can I fall in love?
You try everything from vitamins to cocoa butter—
No wonder someone else loves you
Besides your dear old mother!

With no stake to get a break,
Madame, when and how can I fall in love?

Patter:
"Serve your youth", the advertisements say.
But how can I—busting suds all day?
They guarantee a "skin you love to touch".
But not for me—'cause I slave too much.

(Repeat chorus)

With a sleep in job and no vacation,
How can I help breed the nation?
I cannot afford no vitamins nor cocoa butter.
Nobody seems to care for me
Except my dear old mother.
With no dough to get a beau,
Madame, when and where can I fall in love?

America's Young Black Joe[5]

1940
Music by Elliott Carpenter

One tenth of the population
Of this mighty nation
Was sun-tanned by nature long ago.
We're Americans by birth and training,
So our country will be gaining
When every citizen learns to know:

I'm America's Young Black Joe!
Manly, good-natured, smiling and gay,
My sky is sometimes cloudy
But it won't stay that way.
I'm comin', I'm comin'—
But my head AIN'T bending low!
I'm walking proud! I'm speaking out loud!
I'm America's Young Black Joe!
This is my own, my native land,
And I'm mighty glad that's true:
Land where my fathers worked

The same as yours worked too.
So from every mountain side
Let freedom's bright torch glow.
Standing hand in hand with democracy,
I'm America's Young Black Joe!

SPOKEN PATTER: [taped to music]

Now, you-all get your note books out
And take down some names I know.
I don't want you to think
Joe Louis is the only one—
Even if he is "the" Joe:
There's Henry Armstrong, three titles were his fame,
He beat everybody in the fighting game,
For in sports it's blow to blow
With American's Young Black Joe.
In the stadium Kenny Washington in a football suit—
Run, pass, kick, tackle, and block to boot.
On the gridiron I've got plenty to show,
Has American's Young Black Joe.
And don't forget track men like Ellerbee
Who piled up points for Tuskegee.
Nor Jessie Owens with his laurel wreath
Who made old Hitler grit his teeth.
Man! Look at those dark boys streaking by,
Feet just flying and head held high!
Looky yonder at Metcalf! Edwards!
Johnson! Toland! Down the field they go,
Swift and proud before the crowd—
America's Young Black Joe!
And don't think that athletes
Are my only claim to fame.
Here are a few others, name by name:
George Washington Carver, Richard Wright,
Marion Anderson, A. Philip Randolph,
Duke Ellington, Aaron Douglas, Paul Robeson,
Mary Bethune, Canada Lee, Katherine Dunham,
And a whole lot more, you know—
For we're:

BACK TO CHORUS:
America's Young Black Joe! Etc. . . . . .

Freedom Road

1942
Music by Emerson Harper

This version is taken from undated carbon and mimeograph sheet music in LHP, but extrinsic evidence suggests 1942. Other versions contain many additional verses, and one notes that Kenneth Spencer sang a version of this song at the Uptown Café Society midnight show. The script of a radio broadcast on WEAF, July 30, 1942, has Westbrook Van Voorhis speaking for the editors of *Time* magazine: "Tonight the American Negro soldier has a song of his own written by one of his own race . . . a song they could take into battle." In Hughes's comments, he insists that the "general American public fights this war to *save* liberty," while for the Negro "this is a war to gain *new freedom*."

Hand me my gun
Let the bugles blow loud
I'm on my way
With my head up proud
One objective
I've got in view
Keep a hold of freedom
For me and you

That's why I'm marching
Yes, I'm marching
I'm marching down FREEDOM ROAD

There's nothing goin' to stop me,
There's nobody goin' to keep me
From marching down FREEDOM ROAD

Hitler he may rant
Mussolini he may rave
I'm going after freedom
If it leads me to my grave

That's why I'm marching
Yes, I'm marching
I'm marching down FREEDOM ROAD

Ought to be plain
As the nose on your face
Room in this world
For ev'ry race
Some folks think
That Freedom just ain't right
They're the very folks
That I want to fight.

That's why I'm marching,
Folks, I'm marching
I'm marching down FREEDOM ROAD

There's no Fascist goin' to stop me
There's no Nazi goin' to keep me
From marching down FREEDOM ROAD

Britain by our side
Mighty Russia as our friend
I'm going after freedom
And a new world at the end
That's why I'm marching
Double timing
I'm fighting down FREEDOM ROAD

Go-and-Get-the-Enemy Blues

1942
Music by W. C. Handy

I
My gal wrote me a letter, said, "Baby, I love you true."
I wrote her a letter, "Sugar, I love you, too."
That's why I'm fighting this war—to keep them fascists away from you.

I drempt about my baby this morning long 'bout three.
Drempt about my baby this morning long 'bout three.

I thought my baby said, "BRING HITLER BACK TO ME."
Sweet Miss Susie Johnson ain't got no apple tree.
Miss Susie Johnson's yard ain't got no apple tree—
But if she had a tree every apple would belong to me.

I looked, Babe, at your picture and you looked like a movie star.
Your picture is here, Lawd, but you are so far!
I'm gonna win this war—and march back where you are:
      Cause I got those so bad,
      Evil and most mad,
      GO-AND-GET-THE-ENEMY BLUES!

II
We're fighting this war and fighting this war to win.
We're fighting a war and fighting a war to win—
If we don't win now, we'll have to start all over again.

Our enemies are so big, bad, brutal, and strong.
Our enemies are big, bad, brutal, and strong—
But what they're fighting for, everybody knows is wrong.

I ain't the kind of guy that likes to disagree.
I ain't the kind of guy that likes to disagree—
But I can dish it out, if you disagree with me.

It's just a lot of jive if you think I'm foolin' round.
It might look like I'm grinning but you will see me frown.
I'm windin' up to slap old Hitler down:
      Cause I got those so bad,
      Evil and most mad,
      GO-AND-GET-THE-ENEMY BLUES!

III
It don't take much to really get me fighting mad.
Says it don't take much to get me fighting mad.
When my dander's up, Jack, it certainly is too bad.

How long do you think this war is due to last?
Folks, how long you think this war is due to last?
I want to clean out the buzzards, kill that snake in the grass.

Americans ain't fighting just to fight for fun.
Americans ain't fighting just to fight for fun—
We're fighting to finish what somebody else begun.

I don't need no wireless for to telegraph the news.
I'm going cross the ocean, hip boots laced like shoes.
Gonna win this war—AND I DON'T MEAN TO LOSE.
But if I had my gal here, I could fight double-well,
But I got her in heart—so I'm gonna fight like hell.
When I get back home, she will hear me tell
      How I got those so bad,
      Evil and most mad,
      FINISH with the enemy,
      I mean SLAY the enemy,
      I mean SCALP the enemy,
      STORM AND BOMB the enemy,
      ANNIHILATE the enemy—
      GO-AND-GET-THE-ENEMY BLUES!

Alabam' Barbecue[6]

1942
Music by James P. Johnson

VERSE: It's a good old Southern custom to have a barbecue.
  If you never have seen one, let me show it to you:

CHORUS:
    Come along, Sue! Come along, Mae!
    Ev'rybody's happy!
    Come along, you! Come along, hey—
    Mammy, bring your pappy!
    Soda-pop, Sue! Barbecue, Mae!
    Mighty coalation! True!
    Plenty to eat! 'Lasses and meat—
    ALABAM' BARBECUE!
    Sashay to your baby!
    Grand change to your lady! Oh!
    Hoe-down to the boogie!

Eagle-rock! Roll it slow!
Ju-ba! Step on over!
Great prancin' and dancin' around.
Ju-ba! We're in clover!
Country folks goin' to town.
Music is sweet, so is the meat,
Everything is groovy.
Dancin' is fine, baby is mine—
Better'n a ten-cent movie!
Get along, Mae! Cuddle up, Sue!
Start to pair off two by two.
By and by, moon will rise—
ALABAM' BARBECUE!

Can't You Hear Those Drums?

1942
Music by James P. Johnson

The typescripts of the three lyrics with music by James P. Johnson all have notations indicating they were sent to Irving Mills, with whom, according to Arnold Rampersad, Hughes worked briefly on a "Negro film" with music by William Grant Still and Nathaniel Dett.[7] Perhaps Johnson was also involved.

VERSE:
Africa! Africa!
Magic land of music and of song.
Africa! Africa!
Gay with dancing when night comes along.

CHORUS
In my heart beats the jungle drums.
To their rhythm the jungle hums.
By the moonlight in the sweet night,
Can't you hear those drums?
Through the forest their throbbing comes.
'Neath the spell of the jungle drums
My heart's yearning, my blood's burning—
When I hear those drums.

Dusky dancers 'neath tall palm trees dancing.
Dreamy eyes that glow with love-light glancing.
Break my heart with the jungle drums!
Torn apart with the jungle drums!
By the moonlight in the sweet night,
Can't you hear those drums?

2nd verse:
Africa! Africa!
Where the palm trees sway so straight and tall.
Africa! Africa!
Through the dark your dusky drummers call:

2nd CHO:
In the darkness the jungle jumps
To the beat of the jungle drums.
Can't you hear them, dancing near them?
Rhythm of those drums!
Round the fire the drummer comes
Pounding on his old jungle drums.
Stars are hazy, folks go crazy,
Rhythm of those drums!
When the night is like a June night, baby,
And the sky is lit by moonlight. Hey! Hey!
We will dance to the jungle drums
Through the night till the morning comes.
Music fills me, rhythm thrills me—
Can't you hear those drums?

3rd CHORUS (For voodoo sequence)
Spirit of the old ju-ju king,
Tell me what will tomorrow bring?
When the stars go at the cock's crow,
Will my poor heart sing?
Can you take your old black cat's bone,
Make that rhythm let me alone?
Ask my loved one what have I done—
Must my poor heart moan?
Dusky throbbing of those drums that haunt me,
Softly sobbing full of love they taunt me.
How can I ever stand their beat?

Shakes me from my head to my feet!
By the moonlight in the sweet night,
Magic jungle drums!

CHANT: I (interlude)
Voodoo god, please, hold back the day.
Take the sweet night never away.
Night's for lovers, they know its charm.
Shelt'ring forest safe from all harm.
God of dancers, hold back the day.

CHANT II
Oh-goun! Ba-taam! Gods of great might!
Magic powers, protect our night.
We will worship before your shrine.
Voodoo idol, watch over mine.
Oh-goun! Bataam! Guard happiness!

(BACK TO CHORUS)

We'll Hammer It Out Together

1943
Music by Earl Robinson

A note on the typescript indicates the song was sung by Kenneth Spencer at the CIO Labor Victory Program, Sunday, June 18, 1944. According to Hughes's notes, * designates the portion of the song deleted by NBC; ** designates the new lines substituted on the program.

We'll hammer it out together,
White folks and black folks side by side,
We'll turn our strength into tanks and planes
To take the facists for a ride.
We'll hammer it out together.
That old assembly line will hum.
When all Americans unite as one,
The sooner will victory come

**Now down in Beaumont, Texas,
And over in Detroit
There's a fifth column band a-working
To divide up black and white.***

But we'll hammer it out together—
White folks and black folks hand in hand.
We'll work together and fight together
For Freedom and our land.

I know that we've got problems.
Some go back in history.
But we'll work them out together
And we'll come through, you and me—**

Let My People Go—Now

1944/1955
Music by Chappie Willet

Hughes wrote this song for Adam Clayton Powell Jr.'s 1944 campaign
for Congress; this version is dated 1955.

CHORUS:
Let my people go—now!
Let my people go—now!
Let my people go—now!
For you and me, it's liberty.

VERSES:
1.
Teachers, barbers, and railroad men
Want to see old Jim Crow end.
Brotherhood will know no skin
When Jim Crow's gone with the wind.
Doctors, lawyers, preachers and maids,
Farmers, welders, and nurses' aides,
They all have the very same need—
That is freedom! Yes, indeed!

2.
Go for a job, can't be employed,
Go for a meal, man looks annoyed.
Go to the polls to cast my vote,
Poll tax tries to get my goat.
Go to the show, it's go upstairs.
Get on the bus, it's way back there.

I've been put in the back too long—
Now I've got a brand new song:

3.
All we have is one desire—
Not to set the world on fire—
Just to try and end today
Jim Crow in the U.S.A.
Uncle Tom—he should be dead—
Still wears hanky on his head.
Got to teach old Tom the score,
So Tom can't hurt us no more.

4.
Work and pray and educate,
Still some folks say, "Wait, just wait."
We keep trying to find out how,
But they say the time ain't now!
World War II they told us to wait,
Just be patient and hesitate.
That's been fifteen years or more—
We don't want that stuff no more.

5.
North or South or anywhere
Let me go where I pay my fare.
Time to drop this color bar
Do away with the Jim Crow Car.
Democracy cannot survive
If prejudice is kept alive.
House divided cannot stand.
Get together! Change this land!

6.
Adam Powell will be the one
Who'll plead our case in Washington.
When in Congress he'll strut his stuff,
Call those old Poll-Taxers' bluff.
Adam Powell's the People's Voice,
Cause he is the People's Choice.
If you want democracy,
Cast your vote for Adam C.

7.
Frederick Douglass, leader brave,
Freed himself—a runaway slave.
Gave a message to our land—
Every Negro, be a *man*!
Adam Powell is long and tall—
Words boom out like a cannon ball.
When he speaks, he speaks for us.
In him we will put our trust.

The Heart of Harlem

1945
Music by Duke Ellington

A note on the typescript says, "Written for and copyrighted by the City-Wide Citizen's Committee on Harlem as a donation to their work by the author and composer." Hughes had long wanted to write a song with Ellington, and this is the only one they completed.

SPOKEN VERSE:

The buildings in Harlem
Are brick and stone—
But Harlem's much more
Than buildings alone:

CHORUS
It's a song
With a minor refrain.
It's a dream
You keep dreaming again.
It's a tear
You turn into a smile.
It's the sunrise
You know is coming after awhile—
THAT'S THE HEART OF HARLEM.
It's the shoes
That you get half-soled twice.
It's the kid
You hope will grow up nice.

It's the hand
Working hard all day long.
It's the prayer
You pray that keeps you going along—
THAT'S THE HEART OF HARLEM.

SPOKEN PATTER:
It's Joe Louis and Dr. W. E. B.
It's a stevedore, and a porter,
Marian Anderson, and me.
It's Father Divine's,
And the music of Earl Hines,
Adam Powell in Congress,
Our drivers on bus lines.
It's Dorothy Maynor,
And it's Billie Holiday.
It's the lectures at the Schomburg.
It's the Apollo down the way.
It's Father Shelton Bishop,
And it's shouting Mother Horne.
It's the Rennie and the Savoy
Where new dances are born.
It's a letter from that sailor
You've been waiting for.
Or the footsteps of that soldier
Furloughed from some foreign shore.
It's Canada Lee's pent house
At Five-Fifty-Five.
It's Small's Paradise,
And it's Jimmy's little dive.
It's 409 Edgecombe,
Or a cold-water walk-up flat,
But it's where I live
And it's where my love is at—

INTO 2ND CHORUS:

2nd CHORUS
It's the pride
All Americans know.

It's the faith
God gave us long ago.
It's the strength
To make your dreams come true.
It's a feeling
Warm and friendly given to you—
THAT'S THE HEART OF HARLEM.
It's the girl
With the rhythmical walk.
It's the boy
With the jive in his talk.
It's the man
With the muscles of steel.
It's the freedom
That a people never will yield—
THAT'S THE HEART OF HARLEM.

EXTRA CHORUS
It's a song. . . . . . .
. . . .
It's a dream. . . . . .
. . . .
A tear. . . . .
A smile. . . . .
Sunrise. . . . .
Coming after awhile—
IN THE HEART OF HARLEM.
It's shoes. . . . .
Dancing shoes. . . . .
It's the blues. . . .
Sometimes the blues—
The memory
And forgiveness of our wrong.
It's our freedom
We'll guard for the kids who come along—
THAT'S THE HEART OF HARLEM!

Checkin' on the Freedom Train

1947/1949
Music by Sammy Heyward

A note identifies this as "Singing Version from the poem as published in OUR WORLD, October, 1947." A typescript of Hughes's notes for *The Negro Handbook 1949*, edited by Florence Murray, records that Irving Berlin wrote the official inaugural song for the freedom train, but that Hughes "wrote an unofficial ballad, which gained wider popularity especially among Negroes and white left-wing groups."[8] Many southern cities insisted on segregated visitation of the train, which traveled through the country bearing such symbols of American democracy as the Declaration of Independence and was meant to inspire meditation on the meaning of U.S. citizenship. The Hughes/Heyward song was published by W. C. Handy.

> I read in the papers about the
>   Freedom Train.
> I heard on the radio about the
>   Freedom Train.
> I seen folks talkin' about the
>   Freedom Train.
> Lord, I been a-waitin' for the
>   Freedom Train!
>
> > WASH-ING-TON!
> > RICH-MOND!
> > DUR-HAM!
> > CHAT-TA-NOO-GA!
> > AT-LAN-TA!
> > WAY-CROSS, GEORGIA!

Lord, way down in Dixie only trains I see
Got Jim Crow coaches set aside for me.
I hope there's no Jim Crow on the Freedom Train,
No back door entrance to the Freedom Train,
No signs FOR COLORED on the Freedom Train,
No WHITE FOLKS ONLY on the Freedom Train.

> I'm gonna check up,
> I'm gonna check up,

I'm gonna check up,
On this Freedom Train!

Who's the engineer on the Freedom Train?
Can a coal black man drive the Freedom Train?
Or am I still a porter on the Freedom Train?
Is there ballot boxes on the Freedom Train?
Do colored folks vote on the Freedom Train?
When it stops in Mississippi will it be made plain
Everybody's got a right to board the Freedom Train?
Everybody's got a right to board the Freedom Train?

I'm gonna check up,
I'm gonna check up,
I'm gonna check up,
On this Freedom Train!

The Birmingham station's marked COLORED and WHITE.
White folks left, the colored right—
They even got a segregated lane.
Is that the way to get aboard the Freedom Train?

I'm gonna check up,
I'm gonna check up,
I'm gonna check up,
On this Freedom Train!

If my children ask, *Daddy, please explain*
Why a Jim Crow station for the Freedom Train,
What shall I tell my children? . . . . . You tell me—
'Cause freedom ain't freedom when a man ain't free.

I'm gonna check up,
I'm gonna check up,
I'm gonna check up,
On this Freedom Train!

When that old train she stops down in South Caroline,
Will them Greensville lynchers pay it any mind?
Or will that jury that turned 'em loose
Just cuss and spit tobacco juice?

I'm gonna check up,
I'm gonna check up,

> I'm gonna check up,
> On this Freedom Train!

When mother, who is eighty-three and black,
Takes her place in the Freedom line,
Will some old white man down there yell, *Get back!*
A Negra's got no place on this Freedom Track!

> I'm gonna check up,
> I'm gonna check up,
> I'm gonna check up,
> On this Freedom Train!

My brother named Jimmy died at Anzio.
He died for real and it wasn't no show.
Is this here freedom on the Freedom Train
Really freedom—or a show again?

> I'm gonna check up,
> I'm gonna check up,
> I'm gonna check up,
> On this Freedom Train!

Let the Freedom Train come zoomin' down the track
Gleamin' in the sunlight for white and black,
Not stoppin' at no stations marked COLORED and WHITE,
Just stoppin' in the fields in the broad daylight,
Stoppin' in the country in the wide open air
Where there never was a Jim Crow sign nowhere,
And no lily-white committees' politicians of note,
Nor poll-tax mayors for which colored can't vote,
And there won't be no kind o' color line—
The Freedom Train will be yours and mine!

Then maybe from their graves in Anzio
Black men and white'll say, *We want it so!*
Black men and white'll say, *Ain't it fine?*
At home they got a Freedom Train—
Freedom Train—that's yours and mine!

> Then I'll shout, GLORY FOR THE
>   FREEDOM TRAIN

I'll holler, BLOW YOUR WHISTLE,
    FREEDOM TRAIN
THANK GOD-A-MIGHT! HERE'S THE
    FREEDOM TRAIN!
    FREEDOM TRAIN!
    FREEDOM TRAIN!
GET ON BOARD OUR FREEDOM TRAIN!

Wonderful Window

1947
Music by Jan Meyerowitz

VERSE:
Every day I went to work
The same way.
But one day I chanced to stray
Off my way.
That was my lucky day:

CHORUS:
I saw a WONDERFUL WINDOW
With curtains of lace.
There like a vision
I saw your face.
It was a WONDERFUL WINDOW
Up a coupl'a floors.
Happy with sunshine
My eyes met yours.
    Lonely,
Down a little side street,
    Lucky,
Our eyes chanced to meet—
Then that WONDERFUL WINDOW
Became a wonderful door
From my heart to yours
Forevermore.

My Sunday with You

1947
Music by Jan Meyerowitz

Verse:
All the week's a workday,
But I count the days through—
One, two, three, four, five, six
Till my Sunday with you:

Chorus:
Monday, Tuesday, Wednesday,
I never feel blue
Because I'm always thinking of
My Sunday with you.
Thursday, Friday, Saturday,
The sun is shining through
I look forward to
My Sunday with you.

In the morning let's go to offer up praise,
But we will think of love while the organ plays
We'll take in a movie but forget about the screen,
Just hug and kiss me, babe, and learn how to lean.

Afterwards let's give the parlor a chance,
Put a record on the vic and let's dance!
Or just turn on that old radio
And while the music's playing let the hours go,
Or let's go to the beach with a sandwich or two
And take a little dip on my Sunday with you.
And when the day is darkening
The night will find us two,
Happy together on my Sunday with you.

Love Is Like Whiskey

1949
By Langston Hughes and Roger Segure

Love is like whiskey.
Love is like sherry wine.

Love is like whiskey.
Love is like sherry wine.
It can make you feel good all the time.

But when love leaves you,
It leaves you all beat down.
When love leaves you,
It leaves you all beat down.
You try to keep your head up,
But your heart is on the ground.

Some folks treats your heart
Just like an old pair of shoes,
Some folks treats your heart
Just like an old pair of shoes.
They kick it around
And does it like they choose.

Love, love, love,
Makes you walk on air.
Love, love, love,
Makes you walk on air.
Somebody touch you on the shoulder
You turn around ain't nobody there.

Early Blue Evening

1949
Music by Albert Hague

Verse:
Funny how you never miss the water
Until the well runs dry.
Reckon that's the reason
I sit here now and cry:

Chorus:
Early blue evening,
Early, early blue.
Sitting on my doorstep
Thinking of you.

Early blue evening,
Early, early blue,
Lonesome in my heart, babe,
Lonesome for you.

Up and down the street
I let my eyesight roam—
Wishing you would come back home.
Somewhere in this world
I wonder where you are.
Wherever you've gone, you've gone too far.

Early blue evening,
Early, early blue.
Lonesome in my heart, babe,
Longing just for you.

Five O'Clock Blues

1949[9]
Music by David Martin

I'm gonna take the five o'clock
And run down to K.C.
Gonna take the five o'clock
And run down to K.C.
I want to find out what's the reason
Why my gal left me.

They tell me that the five o'clock
Leaves 'bout half-past five.
They tell me that the five o'clock
Leaves 'bout half-past five.
I'm gonna catch the five o'clock
If I'm still alive.

I'm gonna pass by the pawn shop,
See what that man has got.
If he's got an owl-head pistol
I'll buy it on the spot.
I really love my gal

Lyrics 645

But sometimes my gal ain't nice.
I don't want to kill her—
Just sting her once or twice.

I'm gonna take that five o'clock
OOO-aw! Ah-ah! Eee-ee!
I'm gonna take that five o'clock
OOO-aw! Ah-ah! Eee-ee!

Why did my baby leave me?
Ba-ba! BOO-boo! BA-ba-boo-deh!
Why did my baby leave me?
Ba-ba! BOO-boo! BA-ba-boo-deh!
Why did my baby leave me?
Ba-ba! BOO-boo! BA-ba-boo-deh!

When I see my baby
Tippin', tippin' down the street,
When I see my baby
Tippin', tippin' down the street,
I'll look mean and evil—
But my heart will skip a beat.

I'm gonna take the five o'clock
And run down to K.C.
Gonna take the five o'clock,
And run down to K.C.
Because my Kansas City baby
Has put a charm on me.

Good Advice Blues

1949[10]
Music by David Martin

Gather round me, girlies,
Gather round me, please.
Gather round me, girlies,
Gather round me, please.
I got something to tell you
And I want to tell you at my ease.

I have found out that
A man, he ain't no good.
I have found out that
A man, he ain't no good.
A man would tell you that he loves you
Then leave you if he could.

I'm talking to you women—
Let me tell you what happened to me,
I'm talking to you women—
Let me tell you what happened to me,
I was sweet sixteen
When I lost my pedigree.

I have travelled from Boston
All the way out to L.A.
Yes, I have travelled from Boston
All the way out to L.A.
From coast to coast
Mens act the self-same way.

Gather round me, girlies,
Got some good advice for you.
Gather round me, girlies,
Got some good advice for you.
Take you men—love and leave 'em—
Cause that's the way they do!

Learn to love 'em and leave 'em—
That's the way men do!

That Eagle[11]

Music by Emerson Harper

Have you heard about that bird,
That mighty bird,—
Spreads his wings o'er
    Land and sea?
He's a U.S. bird,
I mean a U.S.A. bird
U.S. spells you and me: That

Chorus:
Eagle! That eagle!
That eagle's got his wings over me.
That eagle that eagle of the free!

Patter:
Uncle Sam is that eagle's name.
That eagle's not weak, neither is he tame,
That eagle is big,
That eagle is strong.
He can fly so high and stay so long,
And when he looks out of his eagle eye,—
All of our foes better rise and fly:

2.
I saw that eagle
Late at night,
Eagle was flying
With no tail-light.
I saw that eagle
In the early dawn,
Looked like a general
With his gold stars on.
I saw that eagle
Get in Hitler's hair.
Hitler said, Lawdy-mercy!
Lemme out of here!

3.
That eagle's wings
When he starts to soar,
Sounds just like the
Thunder's roar.
That eagle's claws
Make a might gash.
Eyes just like the
Lightning's flash.
Woe to the foes
That dare defy him—
That eagle will tear them
Limb from limb.

4.
That eagle ain't rich
That eagle ain't poor.
He watches over
Everybody's door.
That eagle ain't black,
That eagle ain't white.
His name's Uncle Sam
And he's full of might.
That eagle ain't Irish
That eagle ain't Jew—
That eagle is
Just me and you:

5.
I spied that eagle
On the wing.
I said, Listen, eagle,
To what I sing—
I don't want to fight
For no status quo
Cause that ain't nothing
But old Jim Crow.
That eagle said,
What you say is right—
For a brand new status
We're gonna fight.

6.
That eagle said
If we want to be free,
We've got to gain
The victory,
So if you cannot
Go to fight,
Buy WAR BONDS
For what is right.
While our boys are
Fighting and dying,
It's up to us to
Keep 'em flying:

7.
That eagle's head
Is tall and proud
When he speaks
He speaks out loud.
That eagle's beak
Is sharp and long,
Tears the veil
From the face of wrong.
That eagle's flying
Every day
To clear the path
For freedom's way:

That eagle! That Eagle!
That eagle's got his wings over me.
That eagle! That eagle! That eagle of the free.

The Fifties

Love Can Hurt You

1950[12]
Music by Juanita Hall

I hope my child
Will never love a man.
Oh, I hope my child
Will never love a man.
'Cause true love can hurt you
More than anything can.

I'm goin' down to the river
Ain't goin' there to swim.
Goin' down to the river
Ain't goin' there to swim.
My man left me—
I'm goin' there to think about him.

Love is like whiskey
Love is like red wine.

Love is like whiskey
It's like red red wine.
If you want to be happy
You've got to love all the time.

I'm goin' up in a tower
High as a treetop is tall.
Way up in a tower
Tall as a treetop is tall
I'm gonna think about my man
And let my fool self fall.

I hope my child
Will never love a man
Oh, I hope my child
Will never love a man
'Cause true love can hurt you
More than anything can.

Baby, What's Your Alibi?

1950
Music by David Martin

> Funny thing—how a little spat
> Can make you up and act like that.
> But if you want my affection, you better talk fast,
> And explain to me how it came to pass:

1st Chorus:
Baby, what's your alibi?
You weren't home when I came by.
The phone don't answer when I call.
I can't connect with you at all.

Baby, what's your alibi?
You've got your sugar wondering why
You have decided suddenly
To hold out on me.

You know—I know, too,
When we get together, me and you,

We melt in each other's arms—
We've got reciprocal charms!

Baby, what's your alibi?
Oh, won't you tell your honey why?
Now, come clean—stop being mean!
Just what *is* your alibi?

2nd Chorus:
Baby, what's your alibi?
You never let me catch your eye.
Nobody answers when I knock.
You must be upstairs taking stock.

Baby, what's your alibi?
Don't look at me and tell a lie.
If you've made up to disagree
Break your news to me.

You know—I know, too,
When we get to quarrelling, me and you,
We can always change around
And lay our tommyhawks down.

Baby, what's your alibi?
Oh, please don't look at me so sly!
Don't be small—tell baby all!
Just what *is* your alibi?

PATTER: Are you mad? Or just sad?
    Feelin' bad? I'll make you glad.
    Come on, let's dance! Gimme a chance!
    Baby, what's your alibi?

Song Lyrics[13]

1951

You ask me to explain
What goes through my brain
When I'm where you're at.
    Why?

Ask me something I can answer.
I can't answer that.

You ask me why it is
I don't mind my biz
When you're where I'm at.
    Why?
Ask me something I can answer.
I can't answer that.

In my very wildest dreams
I never knew, it seems,
How my heart could misbehave.
I did not realize
That I'd act most unwise
Begging you to let me be your slave.

I know it's strange indeed—
It's an inner need
To be where you're at.
    Why?
Ask me something I can answer.
I can't answer that.

When You Brought Me a Flower

1952
Words and music by Langston Hughes

WHEN YOU BROUGHT ME A FLOWER
On my breakfast tray
And you kissed me with the coffee,
I never knew such a wonderful you!
I ever tasted such coffee!

WHEN YOU BROUGHT ME A FLOWER
On my breakfast tray
And you hugged me with the toast,
Starting that way, what a wonderful day!
I never tasted such toast.

Sometimes a little thing
That is neither wise nor clever

Is the *very* little thing
The heart remembers forever.

WHEN YOU BROUGHT ME A FLOWER
On my breakfast tray
And you kissed me in the morning,
The birds all sang and a million bells rang—
For that was my love's dawning.

My Fire on Fire Island

1952

I built a fire on Fire Island,
Now there're only ashes there—
For you put out my fire on Fire Island
And left my hearthstone so bare.

I built a fire on Fire Island
And its flame was warm and bright.
You put out my fire on Fire Island
And sent me home through the night.

I thought you wanted
My affection,
Until you severed
That last connection.

Wonderful fire on Fire Island!
A rip tide pulled us apart.
Now all that's left of my fire on Fire Island
Are the embers of love in my heart.

My fire—on Fire—Island!

New World of Tomorrow

1952
Music by Sammy Heyward

Hughes notes that this was written as a new finale for *Don't You Want to Be Free?*[14]

I'd like to sing a new song,
But the words I cannot find.
I'd like to sing a new song.
I can hear it in my mind.
I'd like to sing a new song
Of a world that's fine and free—
For the new world of tomorrow
Must belong to you and me!

I'd like to sing a new song,
Yes, a song of black and white.
I'd like to sing a new song,
Everybody treated right.
I'd like to sing a new song
Of a world of liberty—
For the world of tomorrow
Will belong to you and me.

On a Pallet of Straw[15]

1954
Music by Jan Meyerowitz

They did not travel in an airplane.
They did not travel by car.
They did not travel on a streamline train.
They travelled on foot from afar.

They did not seek for a fine hotel.
They did not seek for an inn.
They did not seek for a bright motel.
They sought for a cattle bin.

Who were these travellers on the road?
Where were they going? And why?
They were Three Wise Men who came from the East,
And they followed a star in the sky.

What did they find when they got to the barn?
What did they find near the stall?
What did they find on a pallet of straw?
They found there the Lord of all!

The Sweet Flypaper of Life

1955
Music by David Martin

Some people say that life is hard,
That we're caught and can't get free.
Though it's true I may be caught,
Somehow I like to be:

In the sweet flypaper of life,
All tangled up in living!
Oh, what is life but love—
And what is love but giving?

In the sweet flypaper of life
I'm tangled up—and love it!
And what is life but love?
Don't want to rise above it.

Never learned much from books,
But what learning I've got
Taught me to give a little,
Take a little—*love* a lot!

In the sweet flypaper of life,
I won't get loose if I could
For what is life but love—
And love, oh, love is *so* good.

Carol of the Brown King[16]
(Perhaps Was His Steed a Camel?)

1956
Music by Roland Hayes

Of the three wise men who follow'd the Star
One was a black man from A-far (Africa)
They brought fine gifts of spices and gold
In jeweled hopes of beauty untold

Into His humble manger they came,
And bow'd their heads in Jesus's name.

Three wise men, one dark like me (was he)
Came to his Nativity.

Red Sun Blues[17]

1957
Music by Albert Hague

Little birds, little birds,
Ain't you gonna sing today
Little birds, little birds,
Ain't you gonna sing this morn?
I feel so lonesome,
My baby's gone away.

Red sun, red sun,
Ain't you gonna shine today?
Red sun, red sun,
Ain't you gonna shine today?
I can't sleep, can't eat,
My baby's gone away.

Gray skies, gray skies,
Won't you let the sun shine through?
Gray skies, gray skies,
Won't you let the sun shine through.
My baby's left me,
I don't know what to do.

It's a mighty blue morning
When your sugar leaves your bed.
If you got no sugar
You might as well be dead.

Regardless[18]

1959
Music by Leonard Feather

Verse:
Times may change,
Years come and go,

But no one will come
Between us, I know:

Chorus:
Regardless of what,
Regardless of who,
I'm gonna cling,
Sweet baby, to you.
Regardless of where,
Regardless of when,
We'll keep our love
Just like it began.

Maybe someone
Might like to cut in between—
But I'll still be your king
And you'll still be my queen.

Regardless of what
Tomorrow may bring—
I'll stick by you,
Regardless.

The Sixties

The Blues

Music by Sammy Price

Hughes wrote this song for *Mister Jazz*, which was originally intended as a curtain-opener for the Broadway production of Robert Glenn's one-act play from Hughes's poetry, *Shakespeare in Harlem*.

Tell me, Baby, where did
All this syncopation start?
It must have started, Baby,
In the human heart.
Adam's jazz! Eve's jazz.
Just Jazz!

Tell me, tell me, Daddy,
What's that note I hear?

Bessie Smith and Billie
Whispering in my ear,
Old Joe Turner who's
Done come and gone,
Ma Rainey, Mama Yancey—
How long? How long?

See-See Rider,
Skinny, tall, and black
Standing on the mountain
Trying to call his baby back.

When you laugh to keep from crying
'Cause there's a scream in your throat
And you can't break loose and holler—
It's a blue, blue note.
That's the Blues!
That's the Blues!
The Blues. . . . .

Who Is That Man

1963
Music by Margaret Bonds

Hughes identifies this lyric as being from "Simon Bore the Cross"
and as being broadcast on the Godino Opera Hour, WEVD, on April 9,
1963.

Who is that man who goes to help my son?
Who is he? Who is he?
I never saw him before.
Who is that man?
I never saw him around—
Now he's come to help my son
Bear the burden of his heavy cross.
Who is that man,
Who shares the suffering of my Jesus,
The glory of my precious son?
Who is that man?

Who is that man?
So dark, so beautiful his face!
Look at his face—
So strong and full of grace.
Who is he? Who is he?
Never in the market place
Have I beheld him
Could my prayers have sent him here?
God keep him strong
And bless his soul, the dark one—
Who is that man?

Requiem for Martyrs

Music by David Amram

Part of a six-section cantata Hughes wrote for composer David Amram, "Requiem for Martyrs" was performed to great acclaim on November 15, 1965, in San Francisco, with the Oakland Symphony Orchestra and a 150-voice chorus. Hughes's libretto was especially praised for its "simple, direct and yet evocative nature."[19]

A note in the file requesting the music suggests Hughes wished to use this lyric separately from the libretto.

Let the song be not a dirge,
No sackcloth words and crying,
But rather let the song be strong
With the greatness of your dying.

Let the song take wings and rise
From the fire like a phoenix flying,
Flying straight into the sun
With the glory of your dying.

Oh, freedom-martyrs of ages past,
Oh, martyrs of today,
The hatreds that beset your paths,
Faith will wipe away.

When the springtime sunrise comes
And glorious day is breaking,

From memories of your martyrdom
A new world's in the making.

You died that life be not a dirge
Of sackcloth words and crying,
But that tomorrow's songs be strong
With the glory of your dying—
The greatness and the glory,
The glory of your dying.

Undated lyrics

Love's Running Riot in My Bones

Music by Margaret Bonds

Verse:
Since I've met you, honey,
I've been feeling mighty funny,
And I really do believe you can prescribe
Some treatment for this feeling
That's nearly got me reeling.
It's a thing I can't describe:

Chorus:
Oh, my heart-beats are quite normal
And my conduct is most formal,
But love's always running riot in my bones.
Oh, these moans of passion internal
Have become so darn infernal,
For love's always running riot in my bones.
Now it all seems very stupid
To be wounded thus by Cupid,
And to let you set my tender heart on fire.
But my illness is so serious,
That I'm very near delirious
And I must admit I'm burning with desire.
Honey, listen to my moaning.

Please don't leave me here a-groaning.
Cause love's always running riot in my bones.

Down and Out

Music by Herbert Kingsley

Baby, if you love me
Help me when I'm down and out.
If you love me baby,
Help me when I'm down and out,
Cause I'm a po' gal
Nobody gives a damn about.

De credit man's done took ma clothes
And rent time's most nigh here.
Credit man's done took ma clothes.
Rent time's nearly here.
I'd like to buy a straightenin' comb,
An' I needs a dime fo' beer.

Oh, talk about yo' friendly friends
Bein' kind to you—
Yes, talk about yo' friendly friends
Bein' kind to you—
Just let yo'self git down and out
And then see what they'll do.

A Train Won't Wait

Music by Albert Hague

A train won't wait, but a woman will.
When her man's away she'll wait until
He makes a back-track to the old shack again.

A woman waits but an old train won't.
A man may forget but a woman don't.
She'll hold the sack, Jack, till he gets back again.

A train must go,
A woman will stay
To look after things
While her man's away.

The whistle's blowin'—and it's time to go.
You better get goin'! I'm feeling low!
A train won't wait but a woman will!

2nd release

Put out the cat,
Give chickens their feed.
The night's comin' on—
And it's you I need.

The engine's stokin' and it's time to go.
My throat is chokin', I'm feeling low!
A train won't wait but you know a woman will!

Ballad of Adam and Eve

Music by Elie Siegmeister

One day a leaf fell from a tree
And fluttered to the ground
And a girl named Eve picked up that leaf
And made herself a gown.

There was a young man passing by.
The sun was bright above.
And his name was Adam and he said,
Why don't you be my love?

A slith'ring snake lived in a tree.
That snake was filled with jealousy
Because he could not bear to see
Pretty lovers living happily.

He offered them an apple bright.
The sun was blazing red.
Of that apple bright a single bite

Turned love to pain instead—

Turned love to pain instead!

Pounding Futu
(Song of the Mothers)

The old and young, the ancient and new—
Through all the years of Africa,
Mothers pound futu.
    Sweet to eat, my sweet,
    Futu, futu, my baby for you.
Pounding the grain, the life giving grain,
Her babe on her back, she pounds the grain,
Bend and sway, up-down, up-down, pestle in bowl,
Baby up—baby down—rhythm in soul.
    Sweet to eat, my sweet,
    Futu, futu, my baby for you.
The rhythm of work from the pounding of grain
To the rhythm of love, giving love again
In the form of grain for the futu meal—
    Sweet to eat, my sweet,
    Futu, futu, my baby for you.
Babe on the back of the mother
Who bends, who rises, who bends again
To the rhythms of love and of life
In the pounding of grain—
    Sweet to eat, my sweet,
    Futu, futu, my baby for you.
    Futu, futu, for you,
    Futu, my baby, for you.

Newport Blues[20]

By Langston Hughes and Sammy Price

Friday night at Newport,
Friday night it rained.

Friday night at Newport,
Friday night it rained—
But Dizzy, Jerry, and Louis
Come on just the same.

I was settin' out there
In the rain and wet.
I was settin' out there
In the rain and wet.
I could have got pneumonia—
But I ain't got pneumonia yet.

Oh, the Newport blues is
Catchin' as catch can.
Yes, the Newport blues is
Catchin' as catch can.
You might sleep in the Viking
Or the beach—or in the can.

I was so miserable
Settin' out there in the rain.
So happy and miserable
Settin' out there in the rain.
But with all that goood jazz,
I sure would do it again.

I got the Newport blues.

Suicide

Hughes noted on the typescript that the song is for Vernon Duke.

Up a dismal staircase runs the path of doom.
Down a dusky hallway to a lonely room.
In a broken mirror, look and see your face.
Look and see the weary scars of hunger and disgrace:

But a knife is sharp and a rope pulls tight
And a poison acid burns—
And they all bring rest and they all bring peace
For which the tired heart yearns.

They all bring rest in a deep dark sleep—
From where no soul returns.

Look in the broken mirror! How many dreams are there?
Not a single dream at all! Nothing but despair!
Look in the empty pocketbook! Look at the tired hands!
Look at the faces in the street where nobody understands:

    Oh, a knife is sharp and a rope pulls tight
    And a poison acid burns—
    But they all bring rest and they all bring peace
    For which the tired heart yearns.
    They all bring rest in a deep dark sleep
    From where no soul returns.

Look! In the broken mirror, face that is broken by time.
Look! In the broken mirror, hands all dirty with grime.
Look! In the broken mirror, lips that are bitter as gall!
Look! In the broken mirror NOW!—Nothing! Nothing at all!

    Oh, a knife is sharp! A rope pulls tight!
    A poison acid burns!
    But they all bring rest and they all bring peace
    For which the tired heart yearns.
    They all bring rest in an endless sleep—
    From where no soul returns.

    From where no soul returns!

Notes

Troubled Island

1. William Grant Still to Hughes, July 10, 1948, LHP.
2. Tammy L. Kernoldle, "Arias, Communists, and Conspiracies: The History of Still's *Troubled Island,*" *Musical Quarterly* 83.1 (1999): 491, 497. This article contains a rich account of the opera's history and reception.
3. Ibid., 488; *Troubled Island: An Opera in Three Acts,* by William Grant Still, libretto by Langston Hughes (New York: Leeds Music Corporation, 1949).

The Organizer

1. Hughes to James P. Johnson, January 24, 1937, LHP.
2. Hughes did draw up an agreement with Johnson about rights in relation to the project, given Theodore Browne's claims to the text. See "A Collaboration of Jazz, Poetry, and Blues: *De Organizer,*" in Susan Duffy, *The Political Plays of Langston Hughes, with Introductions and Analysis* (Carbondale and Edwardsville: Southern Illinois University Press, 2000), 164. Many sources assume that *De Organizer* is the verse version of *Natural Man,* but there is no similarity between Browne's play and this libretto.
3. In most of the other typescripts, in LHP and in the Langston Hughes manuscripts at the Schomburg Center for Research in Black Culture, the line reads: "That man is like little David."
4. "Glad to See You Again," the song that begins with this line, is an insert in the version found among the James P. Johnson Papers by James Dapogny. The second rendition, as a duet, is assigned in Johnson's hand to a typescript of the song also among the Johnson papers.
5. Note on typescript in Hughes's hand, "Like 'Mama don't 'low no piano playin' here.'"

The Barrier

1. Typescript, LHP. According to Arnold Rampersad, *The Life of Langston Hughes, Volume 2, 1941–1967: I Dream a World* (New York: Oxford University Press, 1988), 450, it was published in the *New York Times,* January 15, 1950.
2. For more than a decade, from 1941 to 1954, Columbia University's Opera Workshop nurtured the development of American opera. So prestigious had it become by 1950 that *The Barrier* "was covered in nine publications besides the *Times,* including *Commonweal*—two articles in the *New Yorker,* and articles in *Newsweek* and *Time*" (Harlie Sponaugle, "Columbia University, the Columbia Opera Workshop and the Efflorescence of American Opera in the

1940s and 1950s," *USOperaweb* (autumn 2002). The quotation is in part II: http://www.usoperaweb.com/2002/september/columbia2.htm.

Esther

1. Hughes to Carl Van Vechten, March 17, 1957, LHP.
2. Personal communication, July 25, 2002.
3. Reviews quoted in Rampersad, *Life*, 2:267.
4. Ibid., 2:250.
5. Ibid., 2:267.
6. "Will" handwritten on the original, not by Hughes.

Port Town

1. Both letters quoted in Rampersad, *Life*, 2:321.

Tropics after Dark

1. Hughes to Margaret Bonds, July 14, 1940, LHP.
2. Hughes detailed the music in *Tropics after Dark* as follows:

Musical Outline:
Overture: Rhumba Medley

1. MARKET DAY IN MARTINIQUE	Chorus	Production
2. COWBOY FROM SOUTH PARKWAY	Comedian	Comedy solo
3. LONELY LITTLE MAIDEN BY THE SEA	Ingenue	Strip tease solo
4. I'LL MAKE YOU SAVVY SOMEHOW	Comedian	Comedy solo
5. PRETTY FLOWER OF THE TROPICS	Juvenile	Sentimental solo
6. THE WAY WE DANCE IN CHICAGO	Comedian	Jitterbug chorus
7. CHOCOLATE CARMENCITA	Juvenile	Hot number–cho

ACT II
Entre'act: Carnival Medley

8. DANCE OF THE MASKS (Cucaracha)	Company	Production
9. VOODOO MAN	Comedian	Solo & Devil Da
10. SWEET NOTHINGS IN SPANISH	Duet	Waltz Chorus
11. I'LL MAKE YOU SAVVY SOMEHOW (Repeat)	Comedian	Comedy
12. ORELIA & PETE	Cuban	Specialties
13. SUN GOES DOWN IN RHUMBA LAND	Finale	Entire Company

Costumes: Principals:

ACT I:	Juvenile	sport clothes
	Comedian	white sailor suit very tight
	Ingenue	slacks, bathing cape for 3; a flowery white dress for 5
ACT II:	Juvenile	Mess jacket formal
	Comedian	Carnival bull fighter's suit

Ingenue	Gown of Spanish lace for 10;
	Cuban Rhumba dress for 12

Chorus:
1. MARTINIQUE style full skirts and bandanas
5. FLOWER costumes, each girl a different flower
6. MOTHER HUBARDS, Jamaica peasant style
7. Nude Spanish with Cordova hats
8. Fantasia and masks
10. Gowns of black Spanish lace, mantillas, fans
13. Rhumba costumes, ruffles, red sashes & shoes

Overture: Rhumba Medley

MARKET DAY IN MARTINIQUE
(Production Number)
by
Bonds
Hughes
Bontemps

We are the market ladies
Down in Martinique.
We have lots of things to sell
Just tell us what you seek:

    Mangoes! Mangoes!
    Don't you want to buy some mangoes?
    I got mangoes taste like wine.
    Finest mangoes you can find.
    Mangoes! Mangoes!
    Don't you want to buy some mangoes?

    Magnolias! Magnolias!
    Don't you want to buy some magnolias?
    They're white as the foam of the sea.
    Perfumed with tropic mystery.
    Magnolias! Magnolias!
    Don't you want to buy some magnolias?

    Bananas! Bananas!
    Don't you want to buy some bananas?
    I got 'em red! I got 'em sweet!
    I got 'em yellow with sugar meat!
    Bananas! Bananas!
    Don't you want to buy some bananas?

Yams! Yams!
Don't you want to buy some yams?
I got yams taste like hams,
Great big good old juicy yams.
Yams! Yams!
Don't you want to buy some yams?

Sea-food! Sea-food!
Don't you want to buy some sea-food?
I got sea-food fresh and sweet.
Best old sea-food you want to eat.
Sea-food! Sea-food!
Don't you want to buy some sea-food?

Coconuts! Coconuts!
Don't you want to buy some coconuts?
My coconuts are full of juice.
Just the thing to make your joints get loose.
Coconuts! Coconuts!
Don't you want to buy some coconuts?

Dancin'! Dancin'!
Don't you want to buy some dancin'?
You all do the work while I play.
If you want to dance, throw your fruit away.
Dancin'! Dancin'!
Don't you want to buy some dancin'?

Repeat verse.

COWBOY FROM SOUTH PARKWAY
(Comedy Song)
by
Randolph
Bontemps
Hughes

I.

I'm a boulevard cowboy, a jitney man—
That's my pedigree.
And I live in the Carrie, 47th and Prairie.
Everybody in Chicago knows me.
You can dig me at Ernie's old Chicken Shack—
Pickin' bones, you know,
Take my gal to the Regal when *I'm* holding plenty jack
Make her stay home when *her* funds are low.

2.
Now, I wear a drape model, the latest style,
    ON CREDIT, MAN:
Striped red and gray.
And I put all my numbers in the Black Gold every day
But they come out in some book I don't play.
    SIDES AND FLAT.
Once at Kelley's big Keno I won the pot—
    KENOED IN TWELVE, BOY!
Mean Jack pot and all.
And the next day I lost back every single dime and dollar,
Left me muggin' way behind the 8 ball.
        3.
But I'm a boulevard cowboy, a jitney man—bad luck can't down me.
Cause I got a sweet baby, Jack, I really don't mean maybe,
And she gives me more than her sympathy.
When I tell my chick, "Honey, I'm down and out,"
Here is what she'll say—
"Jitney man, don't you worry, don't you scuffle, neither scurry—
You're my lovin' cowboy from South Parkway."

I'm just a cowboy from Oatmeal Boulevard!

LONELY LITTLE MAIDEN BY THE SEA
(Solo Strip Tease)
by
Bonds
Hughes
Bontemps

I've got two weeks vacation—
But please broadcast to the nation
That I'm not having any fun.
All the other girls seem happy
With boy friends that are snappy—
But I haven't got a one:

        I'm just a lonely little maiden by the sea.
        I haven't found a living soul to play with me.
            All this pretty sand
            And not a man to hold my hand.
        I'm bored stiff all the time! Poor me!
        Oh, if this lonely little maiden were to send
        A lonely letter to some all alone boy friend,
        Would he pack his bag and hurry

Here to keep me company—
I'm just a lonely little maiden by the sea.

I'LL MAKE YOU SAVVY SOMEHOW
(Comedy Number)
by
Randolph
Bontemps
Hughes

All this jive about "me no understand"
Gets on my nerves down here in a foreign land.
So from now on I'm gonna be rough:

> Now, if you no savvy, I'll make you savvy somehow.
> When I want something I always want it right now.
> I am meek and mild up to a point—
> When that point is reached I'll wreck the joint—
> Cause if you no savvy I'll make you savvy somehow.

PATTER:
You know I am a sailor who gets around the world,
And I got a way of meeting every situation, girl.
If I get to Cuba and I want to eat,
I just pinch the waitress and holler, "Meat."

If I get to Haiti and I need myself a drink
I just grab an empty glass and point and wink.
If I get to Martinique and desire a bed
I merely yawn and nod my sleepy head.

And if I get to the Virgin Islands and want a gal—
My Chicago jive will solve that, pal!
Cause when I want something I always want it right now—
So if you no savvy, I'll make you savvy somehow.

Don't understand your language and I don't know your style,
But just gimme service, baby, and you'll always see my smile
But should you get stubborn and can't see your way clear
To gimme what I want, I'll raise a ruckus here,

Cause I told you that I loved you, but you didn't understand.
You gave me your foot when I reached for your hand.
You started to holler when I grabbed you tight.
You acted like I was a varmint last night.

Now, when I say, Baby Doll, come here—
You pretend just like you can't even hear.
Now, I ain't the type of cat to start no row
But I don't care nothing about what no law don't allow:

Cause if you no savvy I'll make you savvy somehow.
When I want something I always want it right now.
I am meek and mild up to a point—
When that point is reached I'll wreck the joint—
Cause if you no savvy I'll make you savvy somehow.

PRETTY FLOWER OF THE TROPICS
by
Bonds
Hughes
Bontemps

How did I know when I took that cruise
That I'd lose my heart in Trinidad?
In a tropic bower, I found a flower
And this is what I said:
> Pretty flower of the tropics,
> I love you.
> Golden hour in the tropics
> When I found you—
> Your eyes are like the sunrise.
> Your lips are soft as dew.
> Your arms are warm and tender,
> Filled with tropic splendor.
> Just to see you means surrender.
> Pretty flower of the tropics,
> Hold my hand.
> You're the topic in the tropics
> That makes me feel so grand.
> There is something so sweet about you
> That no one in this world could doubt you.
> Dear, I can't do without you,
> Pretty flower of the tropics.

THAT'S THE WAY WE DANCE (IN CHICAGO)
(Jitterbug Number)
by
Randolph
Bontemps
Hughes

Ain't you heard about that music, Chicago style?
The kind of music that drives you wild?
Ain't you heard about the way we dance it out?
Then lemme tell you what it's all about:

First you grab your gal like a hep cat, Jack,
And jitterbug her lightly then you throw her back.
Let your hips swing loose when you're moving—
Swing most any way long's you groovin'.
You take it slow while she gets way down.
You're feelin' acrobatic, then you throw her round.
Then you separate, take a solo—
That's the way we dance in Chicago.
　　　Jump back and boogie!
　　　Aw! Boogie woogie!
　　　Peck a little! Truck a little!
Now if anyone here is still in doubt
As to what this jitterbuggin' is all about,
I'll expostulate all that I know
'Bout the way we dance in Chicago.

CHOCOLATE CARMENCITA
(First Act Finale)
by
Bonds
Hughes
Bontemps

Listen, dusky charmer, draw a little near.
There's something I want to whisper in your ear.
If you don't like flirting, I'm sorry as can be.
I have to do it 'cause my heart is hurting me:
　　　Dusky Rio Rita!
　　　Chocolate Carmencita!
　　　How I'd like to meet ya,
　　　You cute little baby!
　　　Where the maracas are shaking
　　　How I would like to be taking
　　　Time out for a little love making.
　　　It's for you I'm craving.
Got me misbehaving, Cuban Rio Rita.
Got me at your feet, yet I'm up a tree.
I'm up a tree till you belong to me,
My Chocolate Carmencita.

VOODOO MAN
(Comedy Song with Devil Dance)
by
Bonds
Hughes
Bontemps

I wish I was a Johnny Barrymore
Then maybe I could hold my paramour.
But she has gone away,
So far away from me.
Please listen to my plea:
    Voodoo man! Voodoo man!
    Make me a toby if you can.
    A toby that will bring my sweet gal back to me.
    Voodoo man! Voodoo man!
    Please make your hoodoo understand
    I want to hold my sugar close again to me.
    If your hoodoo spell don't bring my baby back,
    John De Conq'or Root, I'll have a heart attack!
    Go get a black cat's bone and sprinkle goofer dust
    Cause I've got to have my baby! Good Lawd, I must!
    Voodoo man! Voodoo man!
    Say you can help me! I know you can—
    Cause love has got me worried, Mister Voodoo Man!

DEVIL DANCE

SWEET NOTHINGS IN SPANISH
(Waltz Production Number)
by
Bonds
Hughes
Bontemps

Down in Rhumba land
It's hard to understand
If you don't know the lingo.
But when you talk to me
I'm lucky as can be—
I always seem to comprendo.
This game must never end tho:

My heart is burning
And we've let the moon vanish
While I've been learning
Your sweet nothings in Spanish.
Don't know what the words mean,
But I know how my heart hums.
It's beating in a way that's so very Americanish
While I listen to your sweet little nothings in Spanish.
You say, "Yo te Amo"
And tho I don't know Spanish
Your lips tell me, "I love you so"
And all my fears vanish.
When you say "Si, Si," and when you look at me.
The way you do,
Then I know I could listen forever
To your sweet nothings in Spanish
To your sweet nothings in Spanish.

ORELIA & PETE

I'LL MAKE YOU SAVVY SOMEHOW
(Reprise with Gambling)

BEFORE GAME:
    You shake your head and say you don't speak my lingo.
    You don't play poker and you no savvy bingo.
    You act like you don't even recognize Georgia skin—
    So let's see what you'll do when a dice game begin.

    I'm gonna get your money out of your pocket today.
    So you might as well give it to me some kind o' way.
    You know I don't care nothin' 'bout what no law don't allow——
    If you no savvy, Jack, I'll make you savvy somehow.

    (GAME AND DIALOGUE)

AFTER GAME:
    If you no savvy I'll make you savvy somehow.
    I'm mighty tired o' you no savvying now.
    To tell you the truth if you don't gimme back
    Every last red cent of my hard-earned jack
    I'll make you savvy so fast your head will crack.

    I got Indian blood so don't let me start no pow-wow
    If you no savvy, man, you sure better learn how.
    You may be deaf, you may be Spanish and dumb—
    But I'm gonna start you to talking some.

Now I ain't the type of guy to start no row.
But I don't care nothing 'bout what no law don't allow
Hep cat or not, Jim, you sure better meow———
    (DRAWS SWITCHBLADE)
Cause if you no savvy, I'll make you savvy NOW.

WHEN THE SUN GOES DOWN IN RHUMBA LAND
by
Bonds
Hughes
Bontemps

Come a little closer,
Let me whisper in your ear
A message from a sunny tropic clime.
We work hard all day
But when the night draws near
Everybody knows
That's dancing time!
    When the sun goes down in rhumba land,
    And the one you love has you by the hand
    That is something only angels understand
    When the sun goes down in rhumba land.
    When the moon come up in rhumba land
    By the beaches where the white waves kiss the sand
    And the maidens all are fair
    With sweet flowers in their hair—
    Well, a man ain't nothing there if he ain't a man.
    So you find your partner and you say,
    Don't you hear that music's lovin' call
    By that tropic water-fall
    When the sun goes down in rhumba land?

Simply Heavenly

1. Rampersad, *Life*, 2:270–71. A similar concern about *Tambourines to Glory* accounts for Hughes's notes on the nature of simplicity that preface that play.
2. Hughes to Owen Dodson, November 18, 1958; Randolph Edmonds to Hughes, July 4, 1963, LHP.
3. Hughes to William L. Patterson, June 8, 1957, quoted in Rampersad, *Life*, 2:272.
4. Hughes to Webster Smalley, November 23, 1961, LHP; slight variations in some lyrics at the request of Bourne Music Co.

5. Hughes to Dodson, November 18, 1958; Dodson to Hughes, November 21, 1958, LHP.

Jericho–Jim Crow

1. Rampersad, *Life*, 2:372.
2. Hughes used this phrase in a cover note he always inserted in requested copies of *Don't You Want to Be Free?* Langston Hughes Papers.
3. Quoted in Rampersad, *Life*, 2:371.

Tambourines to Glory

1. Langston Hughes to Arna Bontemps, July 26, 1956; "*Tambourines to Glory* Is Fulfillment of 10 Year Dream for Noted Author," clipping, no source. Both in LHP.
2. Rampersad, *Life*, 2:255.
3. Hughes to Webster Smalley, November 23, 1963, LHP.
4. Hughes detailed the music in *Tambourines to Glory* as follows:

Prologue: TAMBOURINES TO GLORY Buddy and Ensemble
    Copyright © 1958 by Langston Hughes and Jobe Huntley
Act I
Scene 1: LORD ABOVE Essie and Laura
    Copyright © 1959 by Langston Hughes and Jobe Huntley
    UPON THIS ROCK Essie and Laura
    Copyright © 1959 by Langston Hughes and Jobe Huntley
Scene 2: WHEN THE SAINTS GO MARCHING IN * Birdie Lee
Scene 3: SCAT CAT! Gloriettas
    Copyright © 1959 by Langston Hughes and Jobe Huntley
    HAND ME DOWN MY WALKING CANE * Gloria and Gloriettas
    NEW YORK BLUES Pianist
    Copyright © 1959 by Langston Hughes and Jobe Huntley
Scene 4: LOVE IS ON THE WAY Laura
    Copyright © 1960 by Langston Hughes and Jobe Huntley
Scene 5: UPON THIS ROCK (Reprise) Brother Bud
Scene 6: NEW YORK BLUES Buddy
Scene 7: AS I GO Deaconess Hobbs
    Copyright © 1960 by Langston Hughes and Jobe Huntley
    A FLOWER IN GOD'S GARDEN Marietta
    Copyright © 1960 by Langston Hughes and Jobe Huntley
    BACK TO THE FOLD Crow-For-Day
    Copyright © 1950 by Langston Hughes and Jobe Huntley
    I'M GONNA TESTIFY Birdie Lee
    Copyright © 1960 by Langston Hughes and Jobe Huntley
    THE NINETY-AND-NINE * Laura
    DEVIL TAKE YOURSELF AWAY Buddy
    Copyright © 1960 by Langston Hughes and Jobe Huntley

Act II

Scene 1: LITTLE BOY, LITTLE BOY * Marietta and C.J.

MOON OUTSIDE MY WINDOW C.J.

Copyright © 1959 by Langston Hughes and Jobe Huntley

Scene 2: WHAT HE'S DONE FOR ME* Choir

WHEN I TOUCH HIS GARMENT Choir

Copyright © 1950 by Langston Hughes and Jobe Huntley

Scene 3: HOME TO GOD Essie

Copyright © 1949 by Langston Hughes and Jobe Huntley

WHO'LL BE A WITNESS? * Laura and Birdie

I'M GONNA TESTIFY (Reprise) Birdie Lee

CHILDREN, WE SHALL ALL BE FREE * Laura

LEANING ON THE EVERLASTING ARMS* Crow-For-Day

Scene 5 [sic]: THANK GOD, I'VE GOT THE BIBLE Essie

Copyright © 1960 by Langston Hughes and Jobe Huntley

Scene 6: GOD'S GOT A WAY Crow-For-Day

Copyright © 1959 by Langston Hughes and Jobe Huntley

LET THE CHURCH SAY AMEN Birdie Lee

Copyright © 1949 by Langston Hughes and Jobe Huntley

I HAVE SINNED Laura

Copyright © 1963 by Langston Hughes

TAMBOURINES TO GLORY Ensemble

* Traditionals or hymns.

Gospel Plays

1. "Gospel Singers: New Asset to American Theatre," *The Collected Works of Langston Hughes, Volume 9, Essays on Art, Race, Politics, and World Affairs,* ed. Christopher C. De Santis (Columbia: University of Missouri Press, 2002), 300.

2. Rampersad, *Life,* 2:347, 346.

3. Hughes to Arna Bontemps, November 7, 1962.

4. Hughes to Vinette Carroll, September 12, 1963; "Memo for Langston Hughes to the Producers of 'Black Nativity' re: U.S.A. tour," March 4, 1963, LHP.

5. Rampersad, *Life,* 2:345.

6. Press release by Alfred Duckett Associates, "New Langston Hughes Gospel Play to Have Brooklyn Premiere," n.d., LHP. The press release calls the play "Gospel Glow"; Rampersad, *Life,* ibid., 393.

7. After the final song in the *Players Magazine* rendition, the text in LHP continues:

(*BROTHER CALLIUS steps forward*)

CALLIUS: OH, LORD I WANT TWO WINGS TO FLY AWAY!

OH, LORD I WANT TWO WINGS TO FLY AWAY!

I WANT TO BE AT REST WITH THE LORD.

WELL, I WANT TWO WINGS TO VEIL MY FACE!

HALLELUJAH, TWO AND TWO MAKES FOUR I KNOW,

BUT TO FLY I FIND I NEED TWO MORE.
I WANT TO BE, I WANT TO BE,
I WANT TO BE AT REST WITH THE LORD.
*(All march jubilantly off through the auditorium except JEZEBEL who
has taken center stage as the EXHORTER pushes the PRODIGAL away
from her. But the PRODIGAL breaks away to run smiling off with
JEZEBEL. Then all return to form a tableaux and sing farewell)*
GOOD NIGHT, GOOD NIGHT,
KEEP LIFTING JEHOVAH'S NAME.
GOD'S ANGELS WILL WATCH YOUR SLEEPING,
AND WIPE THE TEARS WHEN YOU'RE WEEPING,
MAY YOU REST WITH GOD'S BLESSINGS,
EVER REJOICING, ALWAYS CONFESSING,
GOOD NIGHT, GOOD NIGHT,
KEEP LIFTING JEHOVAH'S NAME.
THE END

Black Nativity

The Gospel Glow

1. Hughes detailed the music in *The Gospel Glow* as follows:

Sources of songs

Songs <u>underlined</u> may be pantomimed

1. THE GOSPEL GLORY	ORIGINAL
2. <u>MARY HAD A BABY</u>	AM. FOLK SONGS FOR XMAS, 47; ODETTA: XMAS SPIRITUALS
3. <u>DIDN'T MY LORD DELIVER DANIEL</u>	HAMPTON: FOLK SONGS, 65 ROBESON, OTHELLO L-301
4. LITTLE BOY, HOW OLD ARE YOU?	ART OF ROLAND HAYES, Vol. 1 Vanguard Record VRS 448
5. HE IS KING OF KINGS	HAMPTON: FOLK SONGS, 146 BAYARD RUSTIN, 12 SPIRITUALS
6. PREACHING THE WORD OF GOD	HAMPTON FOLK SONGS, 62 JOHNSON: SPIRITUALS Vol 2, 90
7. <u>GO WHERE I SEND THEE</u>	AM. FOLK SONGS FOR XMAS, 70 ODETTA: XMAS SPIRITUALS
8. MY LORD, WHAT A MORNING	JOHNSON: SPIRITUALS, Vol 1, 162 BELAFONTE: RCA Victor LPM 2022
9. WHERE SHALL I BE?	HAMPTON FOLK SONGS, 173 JOHNSON: SPIRITUALS Vol 1, 136
10. <u>SAVIOR, DON'T PASS ME BY</u>	ERNESTINE WASHINGTON, MANOR SP 1144, NIGHTINGALES PEACOCK PLP-101
11. DRY BONES	DELTA RHYTHM BOYS, DECCA 68502 BOOK OF NEGRO FOLKLORE, 253
12. <u>GOT A HOME IN THAT ROCK</u>	JOHNSON: SPIRITUAL, Vol 1, 96 THE WEAVERS, Vanguard VRS 9010
13. A PITY AND A SHAME	AM. FOLK SONGS FOR XMAS, 52 ODETTA: XMAS SPIRITUALS
14. WATCH WITH ME ONE HOUR	OLD HYMN
15. LONESOME VALLEY	WORK: AMERICAN NEGRO SONGS, 108 CLARA WARD, VANGUARD, VRS 9101
16. <u>TAKE MY MOTHER HOME</u>	BELAFONTE, RCA Victor LPM 1150
17. WERE YOU THERE?	HAMPTON: FOLK SONGS, 106 ROLAND HAYES, Vanguard VRS 448
18. NO GRAVE CAN HOLD HIS BODY DOWN	ODETTA: CARNEGIE HALL, VRS 9076

19. OH, MARY DON'T YOU WEEP	WORK: AMERICAN NEGRO SONGS, 176
	ROLAND HAYES, VRS-448
20. ANGEL ROLLED THE STONE AWAY	JOHNSON: SPIRITUALS, Vol 2, 118
21. HE ROSE FROM THE GRAVE	HAMPTON: FOLK SONGS, 213–215
	SISTER THARPE, Decca 75261
22. RIDE ON KING JESUS	WORK: NEGRO SONGS, 49
	ROBERTA MARTIN SINGERS
	SAVOY 45 RPM 4100
23. PLENTY GOOD ROOM	ROLAND HAYES, VRS 448
24. SET DOWN	SISTER THARPE, Decca 45–68816
END THE GOSPEL GLORY	Reprise: ORIGINAL

Visualization

Sequences to be pantomimed or dance

1. (Song 3)   THE VIRGIN MARY seated; SHEPHERDS enter; THREE WISE MEN come bearing gifts; general jubilation until JOSEPH and MARY begin their FLIGHT INTO EGYPT which merges into a DANCE OF DELIVERANCE. (AWAY IN A MANGER).

2. (Song 4)   DIDN'T MY LORD DELIVER DANIEL? The DANCE OF DELIVERANCE as JOSEPH and MARY find shelter in Israel.

3. (Song 8)   CHILDREN, GO WHERE I SEND THEE. The entire group of SINGERS marching two by two, three by three, etc., as the song indicates—spreading the Gospel to the world.

4. (Song 11)   SAVIOR, DON'T YOU PASS ME BY. THE BLIND MAN and the WOMAN BY THE WAYSIDE seek Christ and find Him in ecstasy.

5. (Song 13)   GOT A HOME IN THAT ROCK. Shouting and general jubilation in which all the dancers take part.

6. (Song 16)   JUDAS! JUDAS! In which JUDAS dances his agony and death by hanging himself on a hilltop.

7. (Song 18)   HE NEVER SAID A MUMBLIN' WORD. MARY, the Mother of Christ enters and sinks prostrate during the Crucifixion.

8. (Song 21)   OH, MARY DON'T YOU WEEP. MARY and MARTHA comfort each other, taking heart as the dawn breaks on Resurrection Morn.

9. (Song 22)   THE ANGEL ROLLED THE STONE AWAY. Wonderment on the part of MARY and MARTHA.

10. (Song 23) HE ROSE FROM THE GRAVE. General jubilation.

11. (Song 25) SET DOWN, I CAN'T SET DOWN. An OLD WOMAN dances the theme of the song, too happy in Heaven to sit down.

12. (Song 25) General shouting and jubilation until finale.

In addition to these specific visualizations, SINGERS and OTHERS should be walked in rhythm, and changed in position from song to song to create interesting and varied stage pictures; and the ELDER should be permitted the full range of the platform during his sermon. Behind the group of SINGERS chosen for movement, there may be a permanent CHOIR in the CHOIR LOFT for background for the action below. Or the CHOIR may be used like an orchestra in the pit. But there should be a mobile group of at least eight to ten or twelve SINGERS, some having lines, and engaging in pantomime during the telling of the story. They may also at times screen with their bodies Christ, who is never seen but whose presence may be indicated by a light moving on stage.

Master of Miracles

1. Hughes gave the sources of the music in *Master of Miracles* as follows:

1. *ADAM'S IN THE GARDEN*	SOUL, SOUL SEARCHING Katie Bell Nubin Verve Records MG V-3004 (Willis James Collection)
2. *SOMEBODY'S TALKING ABOUT JESUS*	ODETTA: Christmas Spirituals Vanguard VRS-9079
3. *DIDN'T MY LORD DELIVER DANIEL?*	ROBESON: Let Freedom Sing! Othello Records L-301 AMERICAN NEGRO SPIRITUALS Johnson, Vol 1, p. 148 RELIGIOUS FOLK SONGS, Hampton p. 65
4. *FOUR AND TWENTY ELDERS*	ART OF ROLAND HAYES (As One People) Vol 2 Vanguard VRS-449
5. *LITTLE BOY, HOW OLD ARE YOU?*	ART OF ROLAND HAYES (Lit'l Boy) Vol 1 Vanguard VRS-448
6. *JOHN SAW THE HOLY NUMBER*	RELIGIOUS FOLK SONGS Hampton, p. 63
7. *I HEARD THE PREACHING*	RELIGIOUS FOLK SONGS Hampton, p. 62 AMERICAN NEGRO SPIRITUALS Johnson, Vol II, p. 90
8. *SEEK AND YE SHALL FIND*	RELIGIOUS FOLK SONGS Hampton, p. 20
9. *PETER ON THE SEA*	RELIGIOUS FOLK SONGS Hampton, p. 68
10. *CHILDREN, GO WHERE I SEND THEE*	ODETTA: Christmas Spirituals Vanguard VRS-9079 THE WEAVERS AT CARNEGIE Vanguard VRS-9010 MY PRAYER: Lillian Hayman Simpson Records

11. *MY LORD, WHAT A MORNING*	MY LORD WHAT A MORNIN' Harry Belafonte RCA Victor LPM-2022 MARIAN ANDERSON SINGS SPIRITUALS RCA Victor Red Seal Mo-1238 AMERICAN NEGRO SPIRITUALS Johnson, Vol 1, p. 162
12. *WHERE SHALL I BE?*	RELIGIOUS FOLK SONGS Hampton, p. 173 AMERICAN NEGRO SPIRITUALS Johnson, Vol 1, p. 136
13. *GOOD NEWS, CHARIOT'S COMING*	ART OF ROLAND HAYES Vol 2, Vanguard VRS-449 RELIGIOUS FOLK SONGS Hampton, p. 90
14. *SAVIOR, DO NOT PASS ME BY*	SONGS OF PRAISE The Nightingales Peacock Records, PLP-101 SAVIOR, DON'T PASS ME BY Ernestine B. Washington Manor. S-1144-S
15. *THE WOMAN AT THE WELL*	MAHALIA JACKSON Columbia LP CL 644 LOOK UP, Pilgrim Travellers Andex LP A-5001 MARTIN*MORRIS PUB. Co. HILL AND RANGE SONGS, Inc.
16. *HE RAISED POOR LAZARUS*	RELIGIOUS FOLK SONGS Hampton, p. 66
17. *DRY BONES*	DRY BONES Delta Rhythm Boys Decca 78-68502 BOOK OF NEGRO FOLKLORE, Hughes-Bontemps (Doubleday) p. 253
18. *I GOT A HOME IN THAT ROCK*	THE WEAVERS AT CARNEGIE Vanguard VRS 9010 AMERICAN NEGRO SPIRITUALS Johnson, Vol 1, p. 96 AMERICAN NEGRO SONGS Work, p. 169
19. *RIDE ON, KING JESUS*	MARIAN ANDERSON SINGS RCA Victor 78, Red Seal MO-1238, RIDE ON KING JESUS Roberta Martin Singers Savoy 45 RPM 45-4100 AMERICAN NEGRO SONGS Work, p. 49

The Prodigal Son

1. For Hughes's original conclusion to *The Prodigal Son*, see above, 679–80.

Miscellaneous plays

1. Rampersad, *Life*, 2:71.
2. Hughes wrote several such works, including "Jubilee: A Cavalcade of Negro Theatre," which he wrote for the 1940 Negro Exposition in Chicago.

Radio Plays

1. Rampersad, *Life*, 2:75, 1:384, 2:39.
2. Another short radio play, *John Henry Hammers It Out*, starring Paul Robeson, was broadcast on June 25, 1943, on WEAF in New York. Hughes's songs for this play are in LHP, but there is no script for the play itself.
3. Rampersad, *Life*, 2:77.

Ballet Librettos

1. Hughes to Carl Van Vechten, November 8, 1941, LHP.
2. Eleanora Deren for Katherine Dunham to Hughes, October 23, 1941; Katherine Dunham to Hughes, November 28, 1943; Hughes to Arna Bontemps, September 22, 1953; Alvin Ailey to Hughes, July 17, 1961; Hughes to Alvin Ailey, July 30, 1961. All in LHP.

Blues to Be-Bop Ballet

1. "Repeating the song of the neon signs in part. Then:)" is added in pen.

Ask Your Mama

1. "A" handwritten on the original, not by Hughes.

Carmelita and the Cockatoo

1. "Love" in pencil, correcting poor carbon, not by Hughes.

Street Scene

1. Quoted in Rampersad, *Life*, 2:109.
2. Quoted in Foster Hirsch, *Kurt Weill on Stage: From Berlin to Broadway* (New York: Alfred A. Knopf, 2002), 259.
3. *Street Scene: An American Opera* (based on Elmer Rice's play, music by Kurt Weill, book by Elmer Rice, lyrics by Langston Hughes [New York: Chappell Music Company, n.d.]) An ensemble piece, "The Woman Who Lived Up

There" is also credited solely to Hughes, but its multi-voiced and narrative quality makes it difficult to reproduce.

4. *Street Scene: An American Opera,* music by Kurt Weill, book by Elmer Rice, lyrics by Langston Hughes (n.p.: Chappell & Co. and TRO-Hampshire House Publishing Corp., n.d.).

5. Rampersad, *Life,* 2:423.

6. The quoted poem is from Walt Whitman, "When Lilacs Last in the Dooryard Bloom'd."

Just around the Corner

1. Quoted in Rampersad, *Life,* 2:157.

Cantatas

1. As early as 1955, Bonds wrote to Hughes: "Last night . . . I analyzed what I must accomplish in 1956 . . . third, 'Job'. It wasn't liquor talking when I said 'That's for the "Twentieth".' It must be the most mature, profound writing I've ever done—and it must live up to its libretto which I've never felt about your other two operas—and not out of any childish jealousy, but cold analisis [*sic*]. 'Job' must not be shown to the public until it is RIGHT in every way" (Margaret Bonds to Hughes, December 27, 1955, LHP). Drafts of "Job" in the LHP are dated 1966–1967.

2. Rampersad, *Life,* 2:229, 233, 247.

3. The music for the cantatas Hughes wrote with Meyerowitz, *On a Pallet of Straw* (included in the Lyrics section of this volume), *The Glory around His Head,* and *Godly Is the House of God* are available from Broude Brothers. The latter is entitled *How Godly is the House of God.*

4. Actually it was one of his great-grandfathers (Rampersad, *Life,* 2:382).

5. David Amram, *Vibrations: The Adventures and Musical Times of David Amram* (New York: Viking, 1968), 443. Amram also recollects his connection with Hughes in *Offbeat: Collaborating with Kerouac* (New York: Thunder's Mouth Press, 2002). His web site contains reviews of the 1965 performance of *Let Us Remember* (http://www.fmp.com/amram/reviews_conversations.html).

Godly Is the House of God

1. These are dated a week later than the first text; a note on the typescript reads: "Derived from PSALMS 98 to 122."

Lyrics

1. Quoted in Rampersad, *Life,* 2:49.

2. Ibid., 372, 123.

3. Kenneth P. Neilson, *The World of Langston Hughes Music: A Bibliography of Musical Settings of Langston Hughes' Work with Recordings and Other Listings* (Hollis, N.Y.: All Seasons Art, 1982).

4. Letters in LHP.

5. A note on the typescript calls this the "original version," and a note in the file says, "Inspired by Joe Louis and dedicated to American Negro Youth." This version includes patter taken from a music sheet version, also in LHP. A version of the patter is printed as part of the poem in *The Collected Poems of Langston Hughes*, ed. Arnold Rampersad (New York: Vintage, 1995): 565–66.

6. An alternate version, "Caroline Barbecue," is dated 1943.

7. Rampersad, *Life*, 2:53.

8. Various notes in LHP.

9. Although this version is undated, other versions in LHP are dated 1949.

10. Although this version is undated, others in LHP are dated 1949–1950.

11. Taken from a mimeograph in LHP; no date, but likely composed during the war years.

12. Rampersad dates this composition as 1950 (*Life*, 2:177). The typescript is undated.

13. No title; note on cover sheet says, "Revised and sent to: Mary Lou Williams at her request, Nov 14, 1951."

14. See *The Collected Works of Langston Hughes, Volume 5, The Plays to 1942: "Mulatto" to "The Sun Do Move."*

15. This appears in the *Collected Poems of Langston Hughes* in a slightly different form.

16. There is a slightly different version of this lyric in *The Collected Poems of Langston Hughes.*

17. These are Hughes's original lyrics; the song sheet, also in LHP, contains somewhat different lyrics.

18. These are Hughes's lyrics; the file in LHP also contains the lyrics as set by Leonard Feather, dated 1960. They are somewhat different.

19. Rampersad, *Life*, 2:394–95.

20. Although the typescript in LHP credits Sammy Price with the music and calls the song "Newport Blues," in fact the music was composed by Otis Spann, and the song is known as "Goodbye, Newport Blues."

Permissions